I0762010

Maqāmāt Abī Zayd al-Sarūjī

Letter from the General Editor

The Library of Arabic Literature makes available Arabic editions and English translations of significant works of Arabic literature, with an emphasis on the seventh to nineteenth centuries. The Library of Arabic Literature thus includes texts from the pre-Islamic era to the cusp of the modern period, and encompasses a wide range of genres, including poetry, poetics, fiction, religion, philosophy, law, science, travel writing, history, and historiography.

Books in the series are edited and translated by internationally recognized scholars. They are published as hardcovers in parallel-text format with Arabic and English on facing pages, as English-only paperbacks, and as downloadable Arabic editions. For some texts, the series also publishes separate scholarly editions with full critical apparatus.

The Library encourages scholars to produce authoritative Arabic editions, accompanied by modern, lucid English translations, with the ultimate goal of introducing Arabic's rich literary heritage to a general audience of readers as well as to scholars and students.

The Library of Arabic Literature is supported by a grant from the New York University Abu Dhabi Institute and is published by NYU Press.

Philip F. Kennedy
General Editor, Library of Arabic Literature

About This Scholarly Edition

This book is part of a subseries within the Library of Arabic Literature that showcases edited Arabic texts with full critical apparatus, in keeping with the Library's commitment to promoting scholarship on the Arabic literary heritage. These books are intended primarily for scholars and complement our bilingual publications.

Maqāmāt Abī Zayd al-Sarūjī

AL-ḤARĪRĪ

Edited by
MICHAEL COOPERSON

Foreword by
ABDELFATTAH KILITO

Volume Editor
DEVIN J. STEWART

NEW YORK UNIVERSITY PRESS
New York

NEW YORK UNIVERSITY PRESS
New York

Library of Congress Cataloging-in-Publication Data

Names: Ḥarīrī, 1054-1122, author. | Cooperson, Michael, 1965- editor.
Title: Maqāmāt Abī Zayd al-Sarūjī / al-Ḥarīrī ; edited by Michael Cooperson.
Other titles: Maqāmāt
Description: New York : New York University Press, 2020. | Includes bibliographical references. | Summary: "Maqāmāt Abī Zayd al-Sarūjī is a scholarly, Arabic-only edition of the celebrated work by al-Ḥarīrī, which is also available in English translation from the Library of Arabic Literature as Impostures. This work consists of fifty stories about the adventures of the itinerant con man and master of persuasion Abū Zayd al-Sarūjī, as told by the equally itinerant and often clueless narrator al-Ḥārith ibn Hāmmam"-- Provided by publisher.
Identifiers: LCCN 2019056333 (print) | LCCN 2019056334 (ebook) | ISBN 9781479800896 (hardcover) | ISBN 9781479800926 (ebook) | ISBN 9781479800919 (ebook)
Classification: LCC PJ7755.H3 M3 2020 (print) | LCC PJ7755.H3 (ebook) | DDC 892.7/83407--dc23
LC record available at https://lccn.loc.gov/2019056333
LC ebook record available at https://lccn.loc.gov/2019056334

New York University Press books are printed on acid-free paper, and their binding materials are chosen for strength and durability.

Typeset in Tasmeem, using DecoType Emiri.

Series design, typesetting, and digitization by Stuart Brown.

Manufactured in the United States of America
c10 9 8 7 6 5 4 3 2 1

Table of Contents

توطئة: مديح الانتحال

بفضل الهمذانيّ، نموذج الحريريّ، انبثق فجأة في الأدب العربيّ نمط بشريّ، المكدي البليغ. إحدى خصائص المقامات أن تكون الشخصيّة الرئيسيّة رجلاً أديبًا، لكنّه أيضًا شحّاذ صفيق وعيّار يمارس الكُدية دون حساب من ضمير. المكر لديه مبدأ حيويّ، وطبع ثانٍ.

يقتفي الحريريّ خطى سلف شهير يمتدحه في مقدّمة مقاماته. غير أنّ موقفه ملتبس إذ يجعل بطله أبا زيد السروجيّ يقول إنّه يفوق بطل الهمذانيّ، أبا الفتح الإسكندريّ. وعلى مدى سبعة قرون أمّن القرّاء على هذه الدعوى وجهروا بأفضلية الحريريّ. إنّ مناخًا صراعيًا يسود مجموع مؤلَّفه، فهو إن جاز القول قد غصب مجد مؤسّس نوع المقامة، الهمذانيّ، الذي كاد يطويه النسيان إذ لم يستردّ الاعتبار إلّا حوالي أواخر القرن التاسع عشر. وهكذا المقلّد قد كسف المُبدعَ، لتكون مقامات الحريريّ دليلاً، إذا ما كانت الحاجة إلى دليل، أنّ نسخة يمكن أن تتفوّق على الأصل.

غير أنّ نجاح المقلّد لا يُغتفر دائمًا. يُبحث عن ثغرات في مُصنَّفه، وتُرصد فيه أو يُخال الكشف فيه عن انتحالات، وقد يبلغ الأمر إلى اتّهامه بغصبه عمدًا. ذلك على الأقلّ ما حصل للحريريّ إذ زعموا أنّه ليس مؤلّف مقاماته. هو الذي كرّسها لاحتيالات ودجل أبي زيد قد وُصِم بالاحتيال والدجل. فقد سرت ببغداد فورًا بعد صدورها شائعة، أوردها ياقوت في معجم الأدباء، بها مقوّمات موضوع رواية جيّد: أثناء هجومهم على قافلة قد يكون عربٌ بَدْوٌ أخذوا من بين المنهوبات جرابًا لبعض المغاربة، وعرضوه للبيع بالبصرة، ويكون الحريريّ قد اشتراه فوجد فيه مخطوطًا فادّعاه، وهو بالذات مخطوط المقامات المنسوبة إليه. . .

خمدت هذه الشائعة بعد بعض الوقت، لكنّ إحدى حجج «الحسّاد» الذين أشاعوها تظلّ مزعجة: يؤكّدون أنّهم لم يتعرّفوا، في المقامات التي يدّعيها، على طريقة وأسلوب كتاباته السالفة. ويستخلصون من ذلك أنّها بقلم رحّالة، قد يكون، ولم لا، من غرب العالم الإسلاميّ (انظر عبد الفتّاح كيليطو، بحبر خفيّ، الدار البيضاء، دار توبقال، ٢٠١٨، ص. ٧٣–٩٢). لكن هل المؤلّف محكوم بأن يكون تحت قبضة أسلوب وحيد وأن ليس بقدرته الكتابة بطريقة مختلفة؟ أهو رهينة طريقته، قَدَره المتعذّر تجاوزه؟

وأيًّا كان، يلزم التسليم بأنّ أسلوب الحريريّ، المتميّز سلفًا عن أسلوب الهمذانيّ، يختلف، حسب الحسّاد، عن أسلوب كتاباته السالفة. فقد يُقال إنّ الحريريّ، منفصلاً عن ذاته، كان متعدّدًا. يستشهد بورخيس في أحد أحاديثه بقول ويتمان: «أناقض نفسي، في داخلي كثرة (I contradict myself, I contain multitudes)». قد تنطبق العبارة على الحريريّ، لكن أيضًا، وبشكل أفضل، على أبي زيد السروجيّ، الشخصيّة الرئيسيّة في حكاياته حيث ليس الكائن سوى سلسلة لا تنقطع من المظاهر والانعكاسات. فالبرقشة خصيصة أبي زيد، وعالمه، وكذا صيغة تأليف الكتاب.

أبو زيد، مطرودًا من الصليبيّين عن مسقط رأسه مدينة سَروج، يحيا حياة تطواف ويجوب الدنيا طولاً وعرضًا. يعتاش، أثناء تسكّعه، بالتحايل وأساسًا بالصدقات الممنوحة له اعترافًا بموهبته الخطابيّة وإنجازاته الأدبيّة. ليست الشفقة هي الباعث على مساعدته، وإنّما أساسًا تأثيرُ حذقه للأدب وقوّة خطابه. إنّه شاعر مُكدٍّ (هوميروس، وفق أسطورة عتيقة، كان واحدًا منهم). الكُدية، في المقامات، فنٌّ، نوع، أي سلوك وطريقة للكينونة والتفكير، بل امتياز، أناقة. وقد نضيف، خلطٌ للأنواع، إذ فنّ الأدب يزاوج فنّ الخداع. ومن ثمّ فالأدب يعرض نفسه مكرًا في هذا العالم من الترقيش وتنافر الألوان. وأوّل ضحايا أبي زيد هم بالضبط أهل الأدب. يتسلّل إلى قربهم، فينجح دومًا في إغرائهم واحتياز

هِبَاتهم. في البدء ينبذونه لسحنته البذّة وهيأته الرثّة، لكن ما أن يفتح فاه حتّى يسحرهم فتَحُول النفرةُ إعجابًا.

أبو زيد لا يعرض نفسه أبدًا بنفس المظهر. مغيّرًا مظهره على هواه وعارضًا في كل مناسبة وجهًا جديدًا، فهوممثّل يلعب أدوارًا مختلفة، تارة متعاميًا، وتارة مُتعارجًا، وأخرى شيخًا هرمًا، وطورًا فقيهًا، وطورًا متفالجًا، وآخر صاحب دعوى ماكرًا، وحينًا واعظًا، وحينًا بائع تعاويذ . . . رصيده يتبدّل من مقامة لأخرى، وبالضرورة أيضًا موضوع خطابه. وفي الأغلب يبلغ من إتقانه لدوره أن لا يتعرّف عليه لأوّل وهلة الحارث بن همّام الراوي الذي يصادفه في كلّ مقامة ويتبعه كظلّه. أبو زيد، متعدّدًا، لا يمكن أن يكون إلّا متنكّرًا لذاته: في كلّ عرض له يحمل قناعًا جديدًا؛ هويته المؤقّتة والعابرة، هي في كلّ لحظة استعارة وانتحال. لكن من هو في الحقيقة؟ بمعنى ما، لنكرّر ذلك، ما هو إلّا تتالي مظاهره العديدة. وهكذا لن نعجب إذا ما شُبّه بالقمر. غير أنّ كوكب الليل ينتهي بأن يترك المكان لنجم النهار، لكن أهناك شمسٌ في مقامات الحريريّ؟

لنورد، في البدء، ما يتعلّل به أبو زيد لتبرير حالاته المختلفة. إذا ما صدّقناه، فالذنب ذنب الزمان، والليالي والأيّام، وبكلمة، ذنب الدهر، المسؤول الرئيسيّ عن تقلّبات الحياة، وعواثر الحظّ. الدهر يُدبّر مجموع الأحداث التي تصيب وجود الإنسان. يحدث أحيانًا أن يكون رحيمًا: في بعض المقامات، يكون أبوزيد موضع عناية الولاة، يختال سيّدًا عظيمًا، مكنوفًا بالخدم وشارات الثراء. لكنّ الأغلب أن يكون الدهر مرادفًا للعداوة والمعاكسة، فلا اطمئنان إليه، فهو بالضرورة خادع، قُلّبٌ، يقلب الأحوال، يَعِد ولا يفي بما وعد، كالبرق الخُلَّب. فإذا كان الدهر هو مثالَ المكر، فلا عجب أن يكون أبو زيد على صورته، كما لاحظ الشريشيّ، أحد شُرّاح الحريريّ؛ فقد كتب أنّ له صفاته، وهو استعارة عنه وتجسيد.

الالتباس يتشرّب خطاباته التي، لمرّات عديدة، ليست على ما تبدو عليه. ذلك راجعٌ إلى استخدامه المتكرّر لصورة بلاغيّة، التورية، قائمة على المعنى

المزدوج لنصّ: المعنى الظاهر يُخفي معنى آخر. فضلاً عن أنّ الملفوظ قد تكون له وجهتان مزدوجتان، وعندئذ يتلقّاه نمطان من المتلقّين بطريقة مختلفة. علاوة على هذا، شكل المعكوس يروق الحريريّ. مثال ذلك رسالة تُقرأ من أوّلها إلى آخرها أو من آخرها إلى أوّلها: تُقرأ معكوسة فتحفظ ملفوظها هو هو. والإنجاز الأرفع يكون أنّ رسالة مقروءة على وجهها تعرض نصًّا، ومقروءة معكوسة تكشف نصها مغايرًا تمامًا. اضطرابٌ على نحو ما نجميّ وكونيّ، تطلع فيه الشمس ذات الآن من المشرق والمغرب. إحدى الرسائل، يعرضها أبو زيد في حبور أمام صاغين مشدوهين، «تجلّت في لونين. . . إن بزغت من مشرقها فناهيك برونقها، وإن طلعت من مغربها فيا لعجبها» (مقامات الحريري، القاهرة، المطبعة الحسينية، ١٩٢٩، ص. ١٦٢).

وبالمِثْل، ففوضى الدهر على نحو ما تتصادى مع مؤلَّف الحريريّ نفسه حيث لا استرسال البتّة بين الخمسين حكاية المكوّنة له. ومن باديء النظر، تركيبها المُشتَّت والاعتباطي يمثّل بطريقة ما تقلّبات وانقلابات الدهر. لا انتقال ولا معبر من واحدة لأخرى، وإذا ما كان هناك استرسال سرديّ، فهو واهٍ ومُصطنَع (المقامة الثّنية والثلاثون تبدو امتدادًا سرديًا للواحدة والثلاثين).

لكن ليس الأمر بهذه البساطة. إذا كانت كلّ مقامة مستقلّة، فيربطها مع ذلك بمُجاوِراتها عودةُ ظهور الشخصيّة الرئيسيّة والراوي. وانطباع التفكّك يبدو أكثر، بالتأكيد، لدى الهمذانيّ حيث نظام تتالي المقامات لا يبدو خاضعًا لتصميم دقيق. وأكثر من ذلك، فشخصيّته الرئيسية، أبو الفتح الإسكندريّ، لا تظهر في جميع المقامات، فيما لدى الحريريّ، أبو زيد حاضر من البدء حتّى الختام، ومن ثمّ، فالمظهر المبنيّ لكتابه غير قابل للجدل. لا شكّ أنّه رتّب فصوله وفق نظام محدّد، ويتكوّن انطباع قويّ أوضعيف بأنْ لا تنبغي قراءتها وفق ترتيب مخالف لما قدّره مؤلّفها. القارئ، بالطبع، حرٌّ في اختيار صيغة قراءته، ويمكنه أن يسمح لنفسه (ولن يغفل ذلك) بأن يجول فيها على هواه، لكنّه لن يفعل ذلك، كما أعتقد،

دون نوع من التردّد، لأنّ لديه إحساساً بأنّ كلّ مقامة هي في موضعها الصحيح. ومؤشّرات مختلفة تدعم لديه هذا الرأي. فكما تشير إلى ذلك منذ البدء عددٌ من الطبعات، يُلمَح أساسٌ موضوعاتي وبلاغي في مجموع المؤلَّف، المتكوّن من خمس سلاسل من عشر مقامات: نقرأ فيه أن المقامة الأولى في كلّ سلسلة زهديّةٌ، والسادسة أدبيّةً، والخامسة والعاشرة هزليتان. وعلى أيّ حال، فمن المستحيل إطلاقًا تغيير موضع المقامة الأولى التي تصف لقاء البدء بين الشريكين، كما تغيير موضع الأخيرة التي تورد افتراقهما النهائيّ. يلتقيان في كلّ فصل ليفترقا بعد ذلك، لكنّنا نعلم أنّهما سيلتقيان من جديد، ونلفي أنفسنا معهما. نعلم أنّ وراء القناع يستخفي أبو زيد وأنّ هويته ستنكشف عاجلاً أو آجلاً. فالاتّساق السرديّ مضمون بدوام الاسم، اسمه واسم راويه، الحارث بن همّام.

هذا الأخير قرينٌ للبطل، وبمعنى ما، من العسير عدم التفكير، فيما يخصّهما، في الدكتور جيكل والمستر هايد. الحارث دائمًا هنا ليتابع أفعال وحركات أبي زيد، ومعاينة مشاهده ونقل خطاباته. إنّه، هو أيضًا، بالتالي، في ترحال مستمرّ. كثير من الحكايات يكون الانطلاق فيها بحثًا عن كنز، أو جزيرة، أو امرأة. أمّا الحارث فهو في بحث مستمرّ عن أبي زيد، أو إذا شئنا، عن الأدب، الكلمة السحريّة التي تعني، من بين ما تعني، فنونَ الأدب. لا وجود لأميّ في المقامات، الجميع في سعي نحو الأدب، في الطرقات والساحات العامّة، في المساجد، والخانات ودور الكتب، ووسط المآدب ومجالس الشراب. فيها يُتذوّق الخطاب البليغ، والكلمة السائرة، والجناس المتقن، وتُترصّدُ أسرار فنّ القراءة وفنّ الكتابة. إنّه مهرجان لغة الأدب الخاصّة، التي يعرفها الجميع ويمارسها، والمتُداوَلة في كلّ مكان. الأدب هو الموضوع الرّئيسي، والشّخصية الرئيسيّة الحقّة لكتاب الحريريّ حيث يُستحضَر فيه كلّ ما يتّصل بفنون الأدب، شعرها ونثرها، ومراسيم الكتابة، والأغراض، والموضوعات الشعريّة والوعظيّة، والشخوص النموذجيّة، والحيوانات النمطيّة المتوّجة بالألقاب.

في المقامة الخمسين، الأخيرة، أبوزيد يتوب. عن ماذا بالضبط؟ صحيح أنّه قد ارتكب شناعات، كذب، وسرق، وابتزّ. والحال أنّه، في هذه المقامة الأخيرة، يحصل أمرٌ غير متوقّع: يقصد، وفق عادته، أن يستغفل، فيعترف بأفاعيله أمام جمهور المؤمنين في جامع البصرة (مدينة الراوي، وأيضًا مدينة الحريريّ)، ويلتمس منهم أن يدعوا لله ليغفر له. الحارث، لمعرفته الجيّدة به، تخالجه الشكوك حول صدقه ويرى أنّ ذلك احتيال جديد منه. لكنّه يعلم بعدئذ أنّ دعاء أهل البصرة قد استُجيب وأنّ أبا زيد قد وقع في فخّ لعبته. فقد وضع حدًّا لتطوافاته، ولحياة المُكدّي، ولكلّ شكل من المغامرة، وهو يحيا منذئذ حياة زاهدة. يقصد الحارث سروج ليراه، المدينة التي في ذات الوقت، وهو أمر جدير بالملاحظة، كان قد أخلاها الصليبيّون، وليتأكّد من حقيقة توبة أبي زيد وزهده التامّ في خيرات الدنيا.

تنبغي ملاحظة أنّ توبة الشخصيّة الرئيسيّة متلوة عن قريب بعودته إلى سروج، المدينة التي كان كثير الحنين إليها. وجد أخيرًا مرسى، فلا يغادر بيته إلّا للصلاة في المسجد. بعد الامتداد، الانكماش. يعيش وحيدًا، وهو الذي يحبّ لذيذ الطعام لا يقتات إلّا بالخبز المغموس في الزيت. أمر جدير بالملاحظة، ما عاد يتكلّم، إلّا بقصد الصلاة. لا يحمل أيّ قناع، إلّا باعتبار الزهد قناعه الأعلى، ذاك الذي ليس بمقدوره الخلاص منه.

توبته ليس فحسب دينيّة، أدبيّة هي أيضًا. يتخلّى عن فنون الأدب، ويتوب من الأدب، ومنطويات ذلك اللفظ، واللغة، وقواعد العيش، ونوادي اللقاء، والمساجلات الكلاميّة، والمشاهدين . . . ومن بين كلّ أنواع الأدب، يكرس نفسه لواحد هو الوعظ. المخاطَب هذه المرّة هو لله، الذي يتوجّه إليه بخطابات التقوى شعرًا ونثرًا مسجوعًا. ومن ثمّ لم يعد بمقدور الحارث أن يلعب دور الراوي. ماذا سيروي يا ترى مستقبَلاً، فيما أبو زيد قد اعتزل في الصمت؟ هذا الأخير، مودّعًا إيّاه، يوجّه له نصيحته الأخيرة، وصيّته الروحيّة:

«اجعل الموت نصب عينيك» وتنتهي المقامة الخمسون بهذه الكلمات: «فودّعته وعبراتي يتحدّرن من المآقي وزفراتي يتصعّدن من التراقي وكانت هذه خاتمة التلاقي».

ما يلفت النظر هنا، هو موقف الحارث: يبكي لأنّه يفقد صديقًا، أستاذًا رائعًا علّمه الأدب. وهولا ينتقد قراره بالعيش زاهدًا، ولا يستحسنه. إنّه يحترم اختياره، لكنّه ليس منجذبًا بتاتًا بمثاله. ليس هو الذي سيجعل الموت على الدوام نصب عينيه، وليس هو الذي سيهجر الأدب. الحريريّ كذلك، بالتّكيد، وإلّا ما كان ليكتب مقاماته الشهيرة. أمّا القارئ . . .

عبد الفتّاح كيليطو
رباط

ترجمة: عبد الكبير الشرقاوي

Acknowledgments

This edition is the work of many hands. I am first and foremost indebted to Matthew Keegan, who shared his digital copies of two early manuscripts of the *Maqāmāt*, including Cairo Adab 105, which was to serve as my base text. Prof. Keegan also reviewed the first draft of my Arabic text, improving many readings and correcting many errors. I am very grateful for his expertise in the textual history of the *Maqāmāt*, and his generosity in sharing it.

The first draft was also reviewed by the volume editor, Devin Stewart, one of the world's leading experts on the *maqāmah* genre, and a prodigy of lexical and grammatical knowledge. Two anonymous reviewers also provided helpful notes on an early sample of the text and translation, the latter being published separately by the Library of Arabic Literature as *Impostures*.

The initial collation and transcription of *maqāmāt* 5, 7, 8, 34, 40, 44–47, 49, and 50 are the work of Rory MacDonald.

Shortly before I was due to submit the edition, incoming LAL board member Bilal Orfali—an authority on Arabic palaeography among many other things—generously offered to give it a final check. His notes helped me to improve a number of readings, and to purge errors introduced by my clumsiness at the keyboard.

The Library of Arabic Literature is fortunate to have at its disposal the talents of Stuart Brown, whose skills as a digital production manager are paired with a relentless dedication to getting everything right. This is the first LAL volume to be published with a fully vocalized prose text. The amount of close work involved in making it as readable and as error-free as possible has been prodigious, and the bulk of that has fallen on Stuart. I can only hope that the Arabic of this edition is as good as he has made it look.

Any errors I have managed to sneak past so many able collaborators are entirely my responsibility.

For providing access to digital copies of al-Wasiti's illustrated manuscript and of de Sacy's edition, I thank gallica.bnf.fr and archive.org respectively. I am grateful to Luke Yarbrough for bringing to my attention an additional manuscript, UCLA A286, which proved useful in interpreting a problematic passage.

I also thank Justin Stearns for giving me a copy of the 1873 Beirut edition of the *Maqāmāt*. I am indebted to Abdelfattah Kilito for generously agreeing to write the Foreword, and to Abdelkebir Cherkaoui for translating it into Arabic.

As always, I am grateful to the members of the Executive and Editorial Boards of Library of Arabic Literature, especially to Philip Kennedy, James Montgomery, and Shawkat M. Toorawa, and to our editorial director, Chip Rossetti, who kept the project on track and answered queries both reasonable and unreasonable at all hours of the day and night. I thank the Library for offering the two-year fellowship during which most of the editing was done, and for making it possible for Rory MacDonald to assist with the edition. It is a pleasure to thank New York University Abu Dhabi as well as the Emirate of Abu Dhabi for providing such a congenial working environment, and for supporting the project in matters large and small.

I am indebted to my wife, Mahsa Maleki, for agreeing to drop everything and relocate to the Emirates for two years; to our families in Iran and the United States for their help and support; and to Rustin and Rylan for not seeming to mind how busy the *maga mett*, as they called them, kept their father.

Introduction

In 382/992, in the city of Nishapur in the northeast corner of what is now Iran, a young visitor named al-Hamadhānī astounded the city's elite by defeating a local celebrity in a prose-and-poetry slam.[1] At various points during the contest, al-Hamadhānī offered to produce pieces of language subject to odd constraints: an essay without the word "the" in it, for example, or one containing verses embedded in it diagonally. Dismissing such games as "verbal jugglery," his opponent demanded that he improvise a bureaucratic letter on a topic suggested by the audience. Al-Hamadhānī accepted this conventional challenge but added a twist that let him show off his talent: he improvised his letter starting from the last word and working backward.

Al-Hamadhānī, called "The Wonder of the Age," died young. His greatest work, at least in retrospect,[2] is a collection of unusual stories called *maqāmāt*, a term I translate (following a suggestion by Shawkat Toorawa) as "impostures."[3] Although al-Hamadhānī's fifty-odd Impostures differ

1. Or so he later claimed. Rowson ("Religion and Politics") seems to believe him, while Hämeen-Anttila is more skeptical (*Maqama*, 24–27). For an illuminating study of the "vizier culture" that promoted literary rivalries of this kind, see England, *Medieval Empires.*

2. Hämeen-Anttila has pointed out that al-Hamadhānī "was not seen primarily as a *maqama* writer by his contemporaries" and suggests that his reputation as the master of the genre may have arisen because of al-Ḥarīrī's later efforts to outdo him (Hämeen-Anttila, *Maqama*, 117–25).

3. Etymologically, *maqāmah* indicates any occasion when one stands, and by extension a speech made before an audience. As used by al-Ḥarīrī and al-Hamadhānī, its obvious sense is that of a verbal performance delivered to strangers while standing in a mosque, market, or street, as opposed to one delivered while seated in comfort among friends, as would be the case in a *majlis.* Even so, the term's wide application as a designation for literary works has generated much discussion. My position is that of Katia Zakharia, who argues that no single definition is adequate to the variety of documented uses (Zakharia, *Abū Zayd*, 93–101). I would add that even if the connection between "standing" and a particular kind of speech was at some point clear, it was evidently lost over time—just as, for example, no one today is quite sure what the word "tragedy" originally meant. In practice, a *maqāmah* is simply the genre, or any single example of it, known by that name. Throughout this book, I will use the capitalized word (Imposture, Impostures) to refer to the genre or to individual *maqāmāt.* I will use *Impostures* in italics only when referring to al-Ḥarīrī's text.

widely in content, certain characters and themes recur.[1] Every Imposture has a narrator who travels from one city or region to another. Everywhere he goes, he encounters an enigmatic figure endowed with stunning eloquence. In some cases, this figure shows off his wit at a gathering of scholars. In others he is found begging in a market or a mosque. Some Impostures contain little more than speeches and verses, but others go on to tell a story that exposes the eloquent preacher as a sinner and a fraud.[2]

Although the so-called picaresque Impostures (that is, the ones with stories) have attracted the most attention in modern times, pre-modern Arabic readers were more interested in the verbal performances. Indeed, the Imposture's most striking feature is its form. Whether spoken by the narrator, the eloquent stranger, or one of the occasional characters, the frame story and the speeches are almost all in rhymed prose. The speeches are punctuated by verse, which unlike the prose has a single rhyme and a consistent number of feet per line. Strikingly, none of al-Hamadhānī's Impostures are palindromic, lipogrammatic, or otherwise constrained, even though al-Hamadhānī claimed he could produce texts that were.[3] But even without those flourishes, his work was regarded as the freakish production of a boy genius unlikely to be imitated, let alone outdone.

So matters stood until 495/1101–2,[4] when an unlikely prospect named al-Ḥarīrī[5] decided to challenge the Wonder of the Age.[6] Al-Ḥarīrī (who was

1. Al-Hamadhānī's Impostures were collected, copied, and published at different times, but apparently never by the author himself, making it impossible to know whether we have them all or whether all the ones attributed to him are genuine. See Pomerantz and Orfali, "Three Maqāmāt." Whether he was the first to write Impostures is a question much debated in the secondary literature. For an incisive summary see Malti-Douglas, "Maqāmāt," 247–51, and Hämeen-Anttila, *Maqama*, 64–73.

2. For a more detailed overview see Hämeen-Anttila, *Maqama*, 38–61.

3. Prendergast, *Maqamat*, 21.

4. On the date see MacKay, "Certificates," 8–9.

5. More fully Abū Muḥammad al-Qāsim ibn ʿAlī al-Ḥarīrī al-Baṣrī al-Ḥarāmī, "al-Qāsim, the father of Muḥammad, the son of ʿAlī the silk trader, from the quarter of the Ḥarām tribe in Basra." One biographer calls him Ibn al-Ḥarīrī (Yāqūt, *Muʿjam*, 5:2202), implying that the silk trader in question was an ancestor.

6. Most critics no longer believe that he was inspired by meeting with a real mountebank named Abū Zayd: see Zakharia, "Norme." But one version of the story seems plausible enough: see the note to Imposture 48. Al-Ḥarīri's preface speaks vaguely of a patron; see further the notes to §0.3.

born in 446/1054 and died in 516/1122)[1] was a proud citizen of the southern Iraqi town of Basra. During his lifetime, the town was governed by a motley parade of Abbasid caliphs, Seljuk sultans, Arab chieftains, and Turkish emirs.[2] One source reports that al-Ḥarīrī was a wealthy landowner while another claims he was employed by the Abbasid administration in Baghdad to report on local affairs. Though "extremely clever and articulate," he was also "short, ugly, stingy, and filthy in his person"[3]—all liabilities in a world where knowledge was transmitted face to face and being an author often meant performing one's works in public. Most damningly, al-Ḥarīrī was unable to compose on the spot. While thinking, he would pull at his beard, which he did so often that he plucked the hairs out.[4] After he presented his first Imposture he was asked to write another, but even after weeks of solitary effort, "blackening page after page," he "found himself unable to put two words together."[5] Later, after he had managed to produce forty episodes, he was asked, while calling on a high official in Baghdad, to improvise one more. "Taking pen case and paper, he went off to a corner of the audience room and remained there for a good long while, but no inspiration came and he left the room, mortified."[6] So unlikely a superstar did he seem that he was widely accused of plagiarizing his stories from a visiting North African.

But al-Ḥarīrī had the last laugh. When the *Impostures* were finished, he took his scribbled manuscript to Baghdad. There he read the work aloud to one al-Mubārak al-Anṣārī, who made a fair copy. In Rajab 504/January 1111, al-Ḥarīrī invited a group of prominent literary and legal scholars to hear the first five Impostures read aloud. The attendees must have liked what they heard, as many of them returned for session after session to hear the whole work through. Just over a month later, on Shaʿban 7, 504/February

1. The major pre-modern biographies are Yāqūt, *Muʿjam*, 5:2202–16, and Ibn Khallikān, *Wafayāt*, 4:63–68. The essential modern studies are de Sacy, *Séances*, 2:1–50, and Zakharia, *Abū Zayd*, 23–51.

2. On the complex political history see de Sacy, *Séances*, 2 (introduction, by M. Reynaud and M. Derenbourg): 5–14, 21–27, 28–31, 42, 50.

3. Yāqūt, *Muʿjam*, 5:2206.

4. This is a real condition known as trichotillomania. One of my college roommates dealt with stress by yanking on his hair, a habit that eventually produced a distinct bald spot on the top of his head.

5. Yāqūt, *Muʿjam*, 5:2204.

6. Ibn Khallikān, *Wafayāt*, 4:65.

18, 1111, the first public reading of the Impostures came to an end, with at least thirty-eight senior men of letters in attendance. The auditors' names and the precise date of the last session are carefully noted on al-Mubārak's fair copy, which by some miracle has survived into modern times.

After the first reading of the Impostures was finished, the fair copy was used to teach the Impostures another twenty-nine times. The last of these teach-ins took place in Damascus in Rabiʿ al-Awwal 683/June 1284.[1] As impressive as its diffusion is, this manuscript is only one of the seven hundred copies reportedly approved by al-Ḥarīrī himself. This number means that he was approached seven hundred times by people who wanted him to confirm that they had studied an authentic copy of his work.[2] After his death, the Impostures continued to grow in popularity. As one of his biographers puts it:

> The Impostures have enjoyed a reception unlike anything else in literary history. The work is of such a high standard, so marvelous in expression, and so copious in vocabulary, as to carry all before it. The author's choice of words, and his careful arrangement of them, are such that one might well despair of imitating him, much less of matching his achievement. The work is justly celebrated by critics as well as admirers, and has received more than its due of accolades.[3]

Unlike al-Hamadhānī's, al-Ḥarīrī's Impostures are clearly intended to fit together as a collection. In the first Imposture, the narrator, al-Ḥārith, meets the eloquent rogue, Abū Zayd, for the first time; in the last Imposture, Abū Zayd supposedly reforms. There is also more consistency across the stories. With a few notable exceptions, all of them feature Abū Zayd as "a clever and unscrupulous protagonist, disguised differently in each episode," who "succeeds, through a display of eloquence, in swindling money out of the gullible narrator"—namely, al-Ḥārith, "who only realizes

1. This account is based on MacKay, "Certificates."
2. Yāqūt, *Muʿjam*, 2205. As Asma Sayeed and Bilal Abdelhady have pointed out to me, al-Ḥarīrī might well have authorized dozens of copies at a time by reading aloud to large groups of people. Thus the number seven hundred, though doubtless an approximation, need not be dismissed as a mere figure of speech.
3. Yāqūt, *Muʿjam*, 2205. It should be noted that not all readers have agreed (as Yāqūt implies) that al-Ḥarīrī outdid his predecessor. For example, Margoliouth and Pellat flatly describe his Impostures as "no more than a pale reflection of those of al-Hamadhānī" ("al-Ḥarīrī").

[Abū Zayd's] identity . . . when it is too late."[1] In effect, al-Ḥarīrī has taken one of al-Hamadhānī's plots and standardized it. He is also more consistent than his predecessor in matters of form. Al-Hamadhānī may have one poem in an Imposture, or several, or none, while al-Ḥarīrī often has just two. Similarly, al-Hamadhānī frequently drops out of rhyme in transitional passages, while al-Ḥarīrī almost never drops out of rhyme unless he is quoting a Qur'anic verse or pious formula.

Most famously, al-Ḥarīrī made a point of including examples of the kinds of trick writing that his predecessor had claimed to be able to produce. In Imposture 28, the roguish Abū Zayd delivers a sermon in which every word consists entirely of undotted letters (excluding, that is, half the letters in the Arabic alphabet). In Imposture 6, he dictates a letter in which every second word contains only dotted letters and the remaining words only undotted ones. In Impostures 8, 35, 43, and 44, he composes a story or poem that seems to be about one thing but contains so many words with double meanings that it can be read as telling an equally coherent story about something else. In Imposture 16, he extemporizes several palindromes (sentences that read the same backward as forward). In Imposture 17, he delivers a sermon that can be read word by word from the end to produce a different but equally plausible speech. In 32, he produces ninety legal riddles, each based on a pun. And in 46, he trains schoolchildren to perform feats such as taking all the words that contain the rare letter *ẓā'* and putting them into a poem. To some critics, manipulations like these have seemed an embarrassing waste of time, and evidence of the decadence of "Oriental taste."[2] To my mind, however, they lie at the heart of al-Ḥarīrī's enterprise.

1. Stewart, "Maqāmah," 145.

2. Reinaud and Derenbourg attribute al-Ḥarīrī's "decadence" to Persian and Hellenistic influences (quoted in de Sacy, *Séances*, 2:54). Rückert felt the need to apologize for what he calls "der falscher Orientalischer Geschmack," but suggests that it is redeemed by humor (Rückert, *Verwandlungen*, VI and XII). Ernest Renan was more severe, commenting that the Impostures, "appréciée d'après nos idées européennes, dépasse tout ce qu'il est permis d'imaginer en fait de mauvais goût." For him, al-Ḥarīrī is primarily of interest as an exemplar of "Arab decadence." See Renan, "Les Séances de Hariri," 288 and 300; I thank Maurice Pomerantz for this reference. For a deconstruction of Renan's views see Kilito, *Séances*, 202–8. Also noteworthy here is Devin Stewart's observation that in pronouncing these harsh judgments, European scholars were not necessarily expressing "Orientalist disdain for Arabic literary sensibilities" but rather "parroting views prominent in Arabic literary studies in the Islamic world" (Stewart, "Classical Arabic *Maqāmāt*").

As Matthew Keegan has recently argued, the Impostures are about learning.[1] Here it is useful to recall that twelfth-century Arabic was not simply a means of communication in the ordinary sense. For one thing, native speakers had long been in the minority in the territories captured by Islam, and in many places still were. Thus it was by no means guaranteed that any given Muslim, much less anyone living under Muslim rule, could speak the language. Moreover, Arabic was the language in which God had revealed the Qur'an to the Prophet Muḥammad. For non-native speakers, learning it meant fully inhabiting one's identity as a Muslim—and not coincidentally making oneself eligible for opportunities denied to one's monolingual Persian-, Coptic-, Berber-, or Aramaic-speaking cousins. This aspirational quality of Arabic is evident from the eagerness with which al-Ḥarīrī's characters debate fine points of grammar, semantics, and etymology. It also explains their palpable fear of making mistakes, as well as their chagrin when Abū Zayd outdoes them in punning, rhyming, riddling, or whatever the challenge might be.

Yet Abū Zayd does more than take cocky neophytes down a peg. He does things with language that are practically impossible—at least, if one imagines him doing them on the spot. In imagining a character with such extraordinary powers, al-Ḥarīrī seems to be grappling with the problem of divine and human language. When God conveyed his final revelation to humankind, he did so in Arabic. With the end of revelation, Arabic becomes a merely human language once again. As such, it can be used to inform, guide, or illuminate, but it can also be used to lie, cheat, defraud, swindle, and deceive. Yet even when it is being used dishonestly, it retains its numinous character: that is, its memory of having once been the voice of the Eternal.[2] Like Milton's Satan, it retains, even after its fall, some of its original God-given beauty:

> . . . his form had not yet lost
> All her Original brightness, nor appear'd
> Less than Arch Angel ruind, and th' excess
> Of Glory obscur'd . . . [3]

1. Keegan, "Commentarial Acts," 81–117.

2. On the language of the Qur'an as "the Discourse of the Eternal" see, e.g., Lumbard, "The Quran in Translation."

3. *Paradise Lost*, 1:589–94.

It is this numinous character of Arabic that makes verbal miracles possible. It allows Abū Zayd to compose sermons without dots, or verses full of *ẓāʾ*-words, or speeches that can be read both backward and forward. These are not idle tricks: as Katia Zakharia has argued, games played with a sacred language are never just games.[1] Rather, Abū Zayd's performances convey what Stephen Greenblatt has called "a pervasive sense . . . that there is something uncanny about language, something that is not quite human."[2]

If we take this tack, a number of things make sense. The narrator, al-Ḥārith ibn Hammām, begins many of the routines by telling us that he went to one town or another in search of some inspiring oratory. This quest appears insufficiently motivated unless we read it as a thwarted reflex of a spiritual search. In late antique Egypt, Christians would journey into the desert in search of holy men, and when they found them, would say, "Give me a word," meaning a memorable summation of some spiritual precept.[3] This is the sort of word al-Ḥārith is looking for, even if he calls it *adab* (an Arabic word meaning "disciplined self-presentation" as well as "literary and linguistic training").[4] Naturally enough, he is drawn to the shabby, hermit-like figure he sees haranguing crowds all over the world. And indeed, Abū Zayd is always up to the task of saying whatever needs to be said as eloquently as possible. Otherwise, there is nothing definite or stable about him: he varies so much in appearance and demeanor that al-Ḥārith almost always fails to recognize him. Abū Zayd may be what Abdelfattah Kilito says he is: a sorcerer's apprentice who loses control of the forces he has set in motion.[5] But the most economical explanation for his vaporous indeterminacy is that he is Arabic itself. To paraphrase Sheldon Pollock's

1. Zakharia, *Abū Zayd*, 45.

2. [Shakespeare], *Norton Shakespeare*, 68.

3. "In his early days, Abba Euprepius went to see an old man and said to him, Abba, give me a word so that I may be saved": [Proclus], *Procli Archiepiscopi Constantinopolitani Opera omnia*, Euprepius 7, col. 172, translated in Ward, *Sayings*, 62. For more examples see Theodore 20, col. 192 (*Sayings*, 76); Hierax 1, col. 232 (*Sayings*, 104).

4. Angelika Neuwirth has argued that the *adab* that al-Ḥārith is looking for is a kind of antinomian practice manifested in *ʿajāʾib* or marvels of rhetoric (Neuwirth, "Adab Standing Trial," 211). To me, those marvels are cognate with the wonder (*thauma*) inspired by the piety and eloquence of the church fathers. For examples of wonder see, e.g., [Proclus], *Procli Archiepiscopi Constantinopolitani Opera omnia*, Achilles 6, col. 124–25 (Ward, *Sayings*, 30); Benjamin 2, col. 144 (Ward, *Sayings*, 43); John the Dwarf 7, col. 205 (Ward, *Sayings*, 87).

5. Kilito, *Séances*, 226.

description of Sanskrit, he is the language of God in the world of men.[1] And that language is so powerfully in excess of material reality that it overwhelms the agreed-upon relationship of word and object. This unmooring of meaning creates what Daniel Beaumont, one of al-Ḥarīrī's most perceptive readers, calls the work's "dreamy, haunting mood."[2] It also makes Abū Zayd's manifestations of piety seem forced and unconvincing. By this I do not mean that the real Abū Zayd is a sinner or a hypocrite. As Beaumont reminds us, there is no real Abū Zayd, only "the materialization of a function."[3] Rather, I mean that when language becomes unmoored from reality, it becomes unmoored from the sacred as well. Al-Ḥarīrī's language is saturated with the Qur'an, the Hadith (reports of the Prophet's words and actions), the rhythms of ritual, and the vocabulary of the religious sciences. But that language is left to fend for itself in a world that seems largely hostile to its purposes, where "the truth is incessantly discovered to be a pack of lies."[4] Of course, Abū Zayd prays to God to deliver him from poverty and exile, and see him safely to Sarūj, his lost hometown. But the entity that actually defines his life is chance, which is usually malign.

The result of Abū Zayd's predicament is a desperate search for a passage through or around language. At least, this is one way to make sense of his trajectory. For his part, al-Ḥārith so craves spiritual experience that he is willing to scour the earth "from Ghana to Fergana" (§9.1) in search of words to help him find it. Strangely, though, none of Abū Zayd's sermons move him to tears of penitence. What al-Ḥārith fails to understand is that the word is not God. His teacher's speeches are about themselves; the divine must be approached by other means, if it is approachable at all. This is why, despite their humor and occasional raunchiness, the *Impostures* are suffused with a desperate sadness.[5] Language remains marvelous, but even as we marvel, we know we are seeing an imposture.

1. Pollock, *Language of the Gods*.
2. Beaumont, "Trickster," 13.
3. Beaumont, "Mighty," 148–49.
4. Kennedy, *Recognition*, 306.
5. Zakharia describes al-Ḥarīrī's project as "an attempt to reconcile his certainties about language with the reality of the world he inhabits," an effort she describes as "tragic" (*Abū Zayd*, 48).

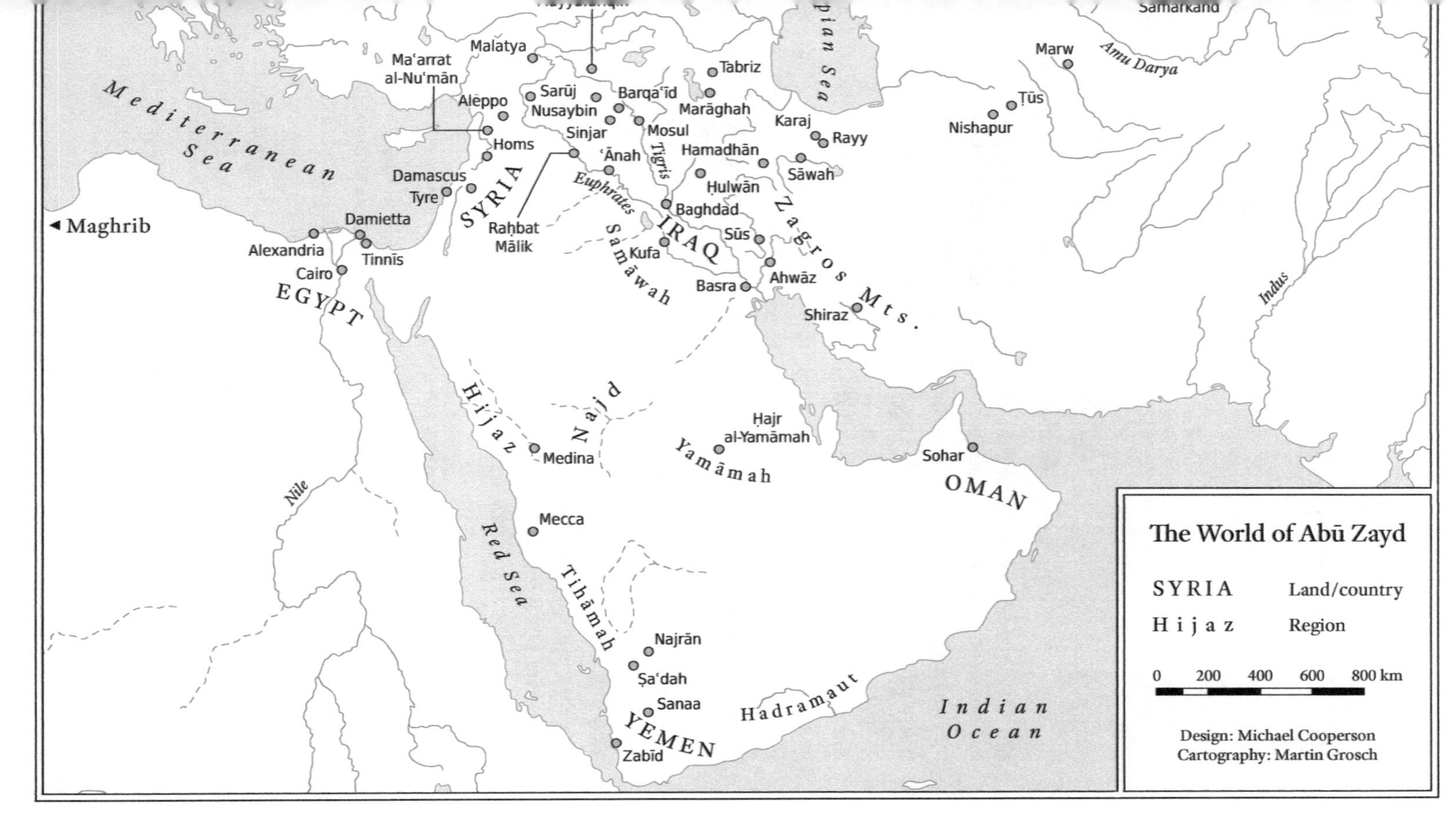

Malatya
Ma'arrat al-Nu'mān
Aleppo
Sarūj
Nusaybin
Barqa'īd
Tabriz
Marāghah
Mediterranean Sea
Homs
Sinjar
Mosul
Karaj
Rayy
Marw
Amu Darya
Ṭūs
Nishapur
Damascus
Tyre
SYRIA
'Ānah
Tigris
Hamadhān
Sāwah
Euphrates
Ḥulwān
Baghdad
Maghrib
Damietta
Alexandria
Tinnīs
Raḥbat Mālik
Samāwah
IRAQ
Kufa
Sūs
Zagros Mts.
Cairo
EGYPT
Basra
Ahwāz
Shiraz
Indus
Hijaz
Najd
Ḥajr al-Yamāmah
Yamāmah
Medina
Sohar
OMAN
Nile
Mecca
Red Sea
Tihāmah
Najrān
Ṣa'dah
Sanaa
YEMEN
Zabīd
Hadramaut
Indian Ocean
The World of Abū Zayd
SYRIA Land/country
Hijaz Region
0 200 400 600 800 km
Design: Michael Cooperson
Cartography: Martin Grosch

Note on the Edition

Although al-Ḥarīrī's *Maqāmāt Abī Zayd al-Sarūjī* is reckoned a difficult work to read, the textual tradition is remarkably stable. We have a fair copy made directly from the author's draft, and many other early attestations of the text. This edition aims primarily to present a text as close to the fair copy as possible, with full account taken in the notes of significant variations attested in a sample of other recensions.

The base text is Cairo Adab 105, copied by Abū l-Muʿammar al-Mubārak al-Anṣārī from al-Ḥarīrī's now-lost autograph in 504/1111, the year the *Maqāmāt* were completed, and read back to and corrected by the author himself. It consists of 146 folios, with 19 or 20 lines per page. It is complete, and the text itself is copiously vocalized and almost entirely legible. Besides its close association with the author, Cairo 105 is valuable because it was used repeatedly as a teaching text, with the result that some errors in the fair copy have been corrected, whether by the author or by later readers. (For a very detailed account of this manuscript and its history, see Pierre MacKay, "Certificates.") Strikingly, it gives only numbers, not titles, for each *maqāmah*, except for 26 (*al-Raqṭāʾ*). The present edition overrides Cairo 105 only when it contains a crux against which the other manuscripts and de Sacy's edition agree. Siglum: ق.

I have collated Cairo 105 with two other manuscripts. The first is Istanbul University A 4566, which lacks a colophon but contains a note dated early Muḥarram 514/April 1120, allegedly in al-Ḥarīrī's hand, claiming to have heard and corrected a reading of the text. MacKay believes the note to be a forgery (MacKay, "Certificates," 28–29) but Matthew Keegan, following Helmut Ritter ("Autographs," 69), disagrees. Keegan goes on to suggest, based on a comparison with Cairo 105, that the entire Istanbul manuscript may be an autograph. While I cannot resolve that question, I agree with him that "at the very least, the Istanbul MS represents an early 6th/12th century copy" (Keegan, "Commentarial Acts," 154–55). It consists of 185 folios with 13–15 lines per page. It lacks certificates of transmission, which suggest that it was a collector's item rather than a teaching text. Even so, it was read as least once, as the borders contain intrusive gilt decoration clearly intended to cover up marginal notes (though one gloss, on folio 112, is left intact and labeled as being "in the hand of al-Ḥarīrī"). Where it agrees with Cairo 105, which is nearly all of the time, Istanbul 4566 is useful for confirming the vocalization of words. A noteworthy feature is the episode titles, which are added in a different hand and do not always agree with the conventional modern ones. Siglum: ش.

The second manuscript is France's Bibliothèque Nationale MS Arabe 5847. This is the famous illustrated copy completed by al-Wāsiṭī in 634/1236–37. It consists of 167 folios of almost fully voweled text (15 lines per page), though there are several gaps, evidently because pages containing illustrations have been removed. Because this manuscript is well known and readily available, and has not, as far as I know, been used as a source of any of the extant editions, it seemed worthwhile to keep track of its differences with respect to Cairo 105, which turned out to be few. Also, the illustrations tell us how one reader imagined what is happening in certain scenes. Although it is relatively late, this manuscript identifies episodes by number only, not title. Siglum: و.

For one problematic passage in §43.12, I also consulted UCLA Minassian A286, completed by Yaḥyā ibn Muḥammad ibn ʿAlī ibn al-Mubārak al-Jalālī in 15 Jumādā I 587/10 June 1198. This MS is unfortunately incomplete and heavily damaged.

The present text has also been systematically collated with the following printed editions:

Les séances, edited by Silvestre de Sacy (1822). This fully voweled and copiously annotated edition is based on ten manuscripts, unfortunately undated (see vol. 1, pp. vi–vii), but none the same as Cairo 105. Its reputation as an excellent edition is confirmed by its close correspondence to Cairo 105. Siglum: د.

Al-Sharīshī, *Sharḥ Maqāmāt al-Ḥārīrī*, edited by Muḥammad Abū l-Faḍl Ibrāhīm (1992). It is based on five Cairo MSS: Adab 105; Adab Ṭalʿat 4479, which also claims to have been certified by the author; Adab 259, dated 663/1264–65; Adab 1529, dated 729/1328–29; and an unnumbered MSS dated 1165/1751–52. Abū l-Faḍl Ibrāhīm appears to have accepted accretions from the later MSS that do not appear in Cairo 105. (These accretions also appear in the 1873 Beirut edition, which I did not collate systematically since it does not cite its manuscript sources.) This edition also contains many typographical errors. It is useful mostly because it contains the indispensable commentary by al-Sharīshī. But since it is the most readily available modern print and PDF edition it seemed worthwhile to keep track of its deviations from Cairo 105. Siglum: ف.

Because the *Maqāmāt* contains many rare words, and deals frequently with matters of morphology and inflection, this edition uses full voweling throughout. For the sake of consistency and readability, the spelling has been modernized. Cairo 105 does not, for example, indicate *hamzah* on *kursī wāw*, but this edition does. I have added no punctuation except for a period at the end of each unit of rhymed prose. Within the constraints of the printed page, the verses have been laid out roughly as they are in Cairo 105.

The received text of the *Maqāmāt* contains two kinds of commentary by the author. These take the form of (1) glosses of single words, placed directly after the passage in which they appear; or (2) discussions of idioms, points of grammar, and the like, placed directly after the end of the *maqāmah* to which they refer. In Cairo 105, these appended remarks are introduced by a title (تفسير ما أودع هذه المقامة من . . .) or brief attribution (قال القاسم بن عليّ . . .). This edition presents the auto-commentaries in the same format as they appear in Cairo 105. Readers of the English-only volume should note that the interlinear commentaries, which are, so to speak, baked into the original, have been translated. The appended ones, however, have not, since they are glosses of Arabic words for which my English offers a idiomatic rather than a lexical translation. Even so, much of their content is paraphrased in the English-language Notes.

Although this work is usually referred to as "the *Maqāmāt* of al-Ḥarīrī," this Arabic edition is titled *Maqāmāt Abī Zayd al-Sarūjī* following the title given in the manuscripts.

Readers are advised to hear the whole work read aloud (from what seems to be the Beirut edition or a descendant of it) by Yaḥyā Fatḥī on YouTube. Those who like to read aloud for themselves should recall that the vowel endings of final rhyme-words in prose should not be pronounced, a fact often forgotten by modern students of classical Arabic literature.

List of Sigla

ق	Cairo Adab 105
س	Istanbul University A 4566
و	Bibliothèque Nationale MS Arabe 5847
د	De Sacy, *Les séances*
ف	Al-Sharīshī, *Sharḥ Maqāmāt al-Ḥārīrī*

مَقَامَاتُ أَبِي زَيْدٍ السَّرُوجِيِّ

بِسْمِ اللَّهِ الرَّحْمَٰنِ الرَّحِيمِ[1]

١٫٠ رَبِّ أَنْعَمْتَ فَزِدْ.[2] اَللّٰهُمَّ إِنَّا نَحْمَدُكَ عَلَى مَا عَلَّمْتَ مِنَ الْبَيَانِ. وَأَلْهَمْتَ مِنَ التِّبْيَانِ. كَمَا نَحْمَدُكَ عَلَى مَا أَسْبَغْتَ مِنَ الْعَطَاءِ. وَأَسْبَلْتَ مِنَ الْغِطَاءِ. وَنَعُوذُ بِكَ مِنْ شِرَّةِ اللَّسَنِ وَفُضُولِ الْهَذَرِ. كَمَا نَعُوذُ بِكَ مِنْ مَعَرَّةِ اللَّكَنِ وَفُضُوحِ الْحَصَرِ. وَنَسْتَكْفِي بِكَ الِافْتِتَانَ[3] بِإِطْرَاءِ الْمَادِحِ. وَإِغْضَاءِ الْمُسَامِحِ. كَمَا نَسْتَكْفِي بِكَ الِانْتِصَابَ لِإِزْرَاءِ الْقَادِحِ. وَهَتْكِ الْفَاضِحِ. وَنَسْتَغْفِرُكَ مِنْ سَوْقِ الشَّهَوَاتِ إِلَى سُوقِ الشُّبُهَاتِ. كَمَا نَسْتَغْفِرُكَ مِنْ نَقْلِ الْخُطُوَاتِ. إِلَى خِطَطِ الْخَطِيَّاتِ. وَنَسْتَوْهِبُ مِنْكَ تَوْفِيقًا قَائِدًا إِلَى الرُّشْدِ. وَقَلْبًا مُتَقَلِّبًا مَعَ الْحَقِّ. وَلِسَانًا مُتَحَلِّيًا بِالصِّدْقِ. وَنُطْقًا مُؤَيَّدًا بِالْحُجَّةِ. وَإِصَابَةً ذَائِدَةً عَنِ الزَّيْغِ. وَعَزِيمَةً قَاهِرَةً هَوَى النَّفْسِ. وَبَصِيرَةً نُدْرِكُ بِهَا عِرْفَانَ الْقَدْرِ. وَأَنْ تُسْعِدَنَا بِالْهِدَايَةِ إِلَى الدِّرَايَةِ. وَتَعْضُدَنَا بِالْإِعَانَةِ عَلَى الْإِبَانَةِ. وَتَعْصِمَنَا مِنَ الْغَوَايَةِ. فِي الرِّوَايَةِ. وَتَصْرِفَنَا عَنِ السَّفَاهَةِ. فِي الْفُكَاهَةِ. حَتَّى نَأْمَنَ حَصَائِدَ الْأَلْسِنَةِ. وَنُكْفَى غَوَائِلَ الزَّخْرَفَةِ.[4] فَلَا نَرِدَ مَوْرِدَ مَأْثَمَةٍ. وَلَا نَقِفَ مَوْقِفَ مَنْدَمَةٍ. وَلَا نُرْهَقَ بِتَبِعَةٍ وَلَا مَعْتَبَةٍ. وَلَا نُلْجَأَ إِلَى مَعْذِرَةٍ عَنْ بَادِرَةٍ.

٢٫٠ اَللّٰهُمَّ فَحَقِّقْ لَنَا هٰذِهِ الْمُنْيَةَ. وَأَنِلْنَا هٰذِهِ الْبُغْيَةَ. وَلَا تُضْحِنَا عَنْ ظِلِّكَ السَّابِغِ. وَلَا تَجْعَلْنَا مُضْغَةً لِلْمَاضِغِ. فَقَدْ مَدَدْنَا إِلَيْكَ يَدَ الْمَسْأَلَةِ. وَبَخَعْنَا بِالِاسْتِكَانَةِ لَكَ وَالْمَسْكَنَةِ. وَٱسْتَنْزَلْنَا كَرَمَكَ الْجَمَّ. وَمَنَّكَ[5] الَّذِي عَمَّ. بِضَرَاعَةِ الطَّلَبِ وَبِضَاعَةِ الْأَمَلِ. ثُمَّ بِالتَّوَسُّلِ بِمُحَمَّدٍ سَيِّدِ الْبَشَرِ. وَالشَّفِيعِ الْمُشَفَّعِ فِي الْمَحْشَرِ. الَّذِي خَتَمْتَ بِهِ النَّبِيِّينَ. وَأَعْلَيْتَ دَرَجَتَهُ فِي عِلِّيِّينَ. وَوَصَفْتَهُ فِي كِتَابِكَ الْمُبِينِ.

---

١ بعدها في د: قال الشيخ الأجلّ الأوحد أبو محمد القاسم بن علي بن محمد بن عثمان الحريري البصري برّد الله مضجعه. ٢ رب أنعمت فزد: ليس في د، س. ٣ ف: الافتتان. ٤ و: الزُّخْرُفة. ٥ ف: فضلك.

فَقُلْتَ وَأَنْتَ أَصْدَقُ الْقَائِلِينَ. ﴿إِنَّهُ لَقَوْلُ رَسُولٍ كَرِيمٍ ذِي قُوَّةٍ عِنْدَ ذِي الْعَرْشِ مَكِينٍ. مُطَاعٍ ثَمَّ أَمِينٍ﴾.[1] اَللّٰهُمَّ صَلِّ عَلَيْهِ وَعَلَى[2] آلِهِ الْهَادِينَ. وَأَصْحَابِهِ الَّذِينَ شَادُوا الدِّينَ. وَٱجْعَلْنَا لِهَدْيِهِ وَهَدْيِهِمْ مُتَّبِعِينَ. وَٱنْفَعْنَا بِمَحَبَّتِهِ وَمَحَبَّتِهِمْ أَجْمَعِينَ. إِنَّكَ عَلَى كُلِّ شَيْءٍ قَدِيرٌ. وَبِٱلْإِجَابَةِ جَدِيرٌ.

وَبَعْدُ فَإِنَّهُ[3] جَرَى بِبَعْضِ أَنْدِيَةِ الْأَدَبِ الَّذِي رَكَدَتْ فِي هٰذَا الْعَصْرِ رِيحُهُ. وَخَبَتْ مَصَابِيحُهُ. ذِكْرُ الْمَقَامَاتِ الَّتِي ٱبْتَدَعَهَا بَدِيعُ الزَّمَانِ. وَعَلَّامَةُ[4] هَمَذَانَ. رَحِمَهُ اللّٰهُ وَعَزَا إِلَى أَبِي الْفَتْحِ الْإِسْكَنْدَرِيِّ نَشْأَتَهَا. وَإِلَى عِيسَى بْنِ هِشَامٍ رِوَايَتَهَا. وَكِلَاهُمَا مَجْهُولٌ لَا يُعْرَفُ. وَنَكِرَةٌ لَا تَتَعَرَّفُ. فَأَشَارَ مَنْ إِشَارَتُهُ حُكْمٌ. وَطَاعَتُهُ غُنْمٌ. إِلَيَّ أَنْ أُنْشِئَ مَقَامَاتٍ أَتْلُو فِيهَا تِلْوَ الْبَدِيعِ. وَإِنْ لَمْ يُدْرِكِ الظَّالِعُ شَأْوَ الضَّلِيعِ. فَذَاكَرْتُهُ بِمَا قِيلَ فِيمَنْ أَلَّفَ بَيْنَ كَلِمَتَيْنِ. وَنَظَمَ بَيْتًا أَوْ بَيْتَيْنِ. وَٱسْتَقَلْتُ مِنْ هٰذَا الْمَقَامِ الَّذِي فِيهِ يَحَارُ الْفَهْمُ. وَيَفْرُطُ الْوَهْمُ. وَيُسْبَرُ غَوْرُ الْعَقْلِ. وَتَبِينُ[5] قِيمَةُ الْمَرْءِ. وَيُضْطَرُّ صَاحِبُهُ إِلَى أَنْ يَكُونَ كَحَاطِبِ لَيْلٍ. أَوْ جَالِبِ رَجْلٍ وَخَيْلٍ. وَقَلَّمَا سَلِمَ مِكْثَارٌ. أَوْ أُقِيلَ لَهُ عِثَارٌ.

فَلَمَّا لَمْ يُسْعِفْ بِٱلْإِقَالَةِ. وَلَا أَعْفَى مِنَ الْمَقَالَةِ. لَبَّيْتُ دَعْوَتَهُ تَلْبِيَةَ الْمُطِيعِ. وَبَذَلْتُ فِي مُطَاوَعَتِهِ جُهْدَ الْمُسْتَطِيعِ. وَأَنْشَأْتُ عَلَى مَا أُعَانِيهِ مِنْ قَرِيحَةٍ جَامِدَةٍ. وَفِطْنَةٍ خَامِدَةٍ. وَرَوِيَّةٍ نَاضِبَةٍ. وَهُمُومٍ نَاصِبَةٍ. خَمْسِينَ مَقَامَةً تَحْتَوِي عَلَى جِدِّ الْقَوْلِ وَهَزْلِهِ. وَرَقِيقِ اللَّفْظِ وَجَزْلِهِ. وَغُرَرِ الْبَيَانِ وَدُرَرِهِ. وَمُلَحِ الْأَدَبِ وَنَوَادِرِهِ. إِلَى مَا وَشَّحْتُهَا بِهِ مِنَ الْآيَاتِ. وَمَحَاسِنِ الْكِنَايَاتِ. وَرَصَّعْتُهُ فِيهَا مِنَ الْأَمْثَالِ الْعَرَبِيَّةِ. وَاللَّطَائِفِ الْأَدَبِيَّةِ. وَالْأَحَاجِيِّ النَّحْوِيَّةِ. وَالْفَتَاوَى اللُّغَوِيَّةِ.

---

١ في و استُبدلت الآية بأخرى وهي ﴿وَمَا أَرْسَلْنَاكَ إِلَّا رَحْمَةً لِّلْعَالَمِينَ﴾. ٢ بعدها في و سقطت بقية المقدمة ومطلع المقامة الأولى إلى كلمة «قريب» في القسم ١.٣ من هذه الطبعة. ٣ بعدها في د: قد. ٤ د: عَلَامَةَ.
٥ د: تَتَبَيَّنُ.

وَالرَّسَائِلِ الْمُبْتَكَرَةِ. وَالْخُطَبِ الْمُحَبَّرَةِ. وَالْمَوَاعِظِ الْمُبْكِيَةِ. وَالْأَضَاحِيكِ الْمُلْهِيَةِ. مِمَّا أَمْلَيْتُ جَمِيعَهُ عَنْ[1] لِسَانِ أَبِي زَيْدٍ السَّرُوجِيِّ. وَأَسْنَدْتُ رِوَايَتَهُ إِلَى الْحَارِثِ بْنِ هَمَّامٍ الْبَصْرِيِّ. وَمَا قَصَدْتُ بِالْإِحْمَاضِ فِيهِ. إِلَّا تَنْشِيطَ قَارِئِيهِ. وَتَكْثِيرَ سَوَادِ طَالِبِيهِ. وَلَمْ أُودِعْهُ مِنَ الْأَشْعَارِ الْأَجْنَبِيَّةِ. إِلَّا بَيْتَيْنِ فَذَّيْنِ أَسَّسْتُ عَلَيْهِمَا بِنْيَةَ الْمَقَامَةِ الْحُلْوَانِيَّةِ. وَآخَرَيْنِ تَوْأَمَيْنِ ضَمَّنْتُهُمَا الْمَقَامَةَ الْكَرَجِيَّةَ. وَمَا عَدَا ذٰلِكَ فَخَاطِرِي أَبُو عُذْرِهِ. وَمُقْتَضِبُ حُلْوِهِ وَمُرِّهِ.

٥،٠ هٰذَا مَعَ اعْتِرَافِي بِأَنَّ الْبَدِيعَ رَحِمَهُ اللهُ سَبَّاقُ غَايَاتٍ. وَصَاحِبُ آيَاتٍ. وَأَنَّ الْمُتَصَدِّيَ بَعْدَهُ لِإِنْشَاءِ مَقَامَةٍ. وَلَوْ أُوتِيَ بَلَاغَةَ قُدَامَةَ. لَا يَغْتَرِفُ إِلَّا مِنْ فُضَالَتِهِ. وَلَا يَسْرِي ذٰلِكَ الْمَسْرَى إِلَّا بِدَلَالَتِهِ. وَلِلّٰهِ[2] الْقَائِلُ

فَلَوْ قَبْلَ مَبْكَاهَا بَكَيْتُ صَبَابَةً   لِسُعْدَى[3] شَفَيْتُ النَّفْسَ قَبْلَ التَّنَدُّمِ
وَلٰكِنْ بَكَتْ قَبْلِي فَهَيَّجَ لِي الْبُكَا   بُكَاهَا فَقُلْتُ الْفَضْلُ لِلْمُتَقَدِّمِ

٦،٠ وَأَرْجُو أَنْ لَا أَكُونَ فِي الْهَذَرِ الَّذِي أَوْرَدْتُهُ. وَالْمَوْرِدِ الَّذِي تَوَرَّدْتُهُ. كَالْبَاحِثِ عَنْ حَتْفِهِ بِظِلْفِهِ. وَالْجَادِعِ مَارِنَ أَنْفِهِ بِكَفِّهِ. فَأُلْحَقَ ﴿بِالْأَخْسَرِينَ أَعْمَالًا الَّذِينَ ضَلَّ سَعْيُهُمْ فِي الْحَيَاةِ الدُّنْيَا وَهُمْ يَحْسَبُونَ أَنَّهُمْ يُحْسِنُونَ صُنْعًا﴾. عَلَى أَنِّي وَإِنْ أَغْمَضَ لِي الْفَطِنُ الْمُتَغَابِي. وَنَضَحَ عَنِّي الْمُحِبُّ الْمُحَابِي. لَا أَكَادُ أَخْلُصُ مِنْ غُمْرٍ جَاهِلٍ. أَوْ ذِي غِمْرٍ مُتَجَاهِلٍ. يَضَعُ مِنِّي لِهٰذَا الْوَضْعِ. وَيُنَدِّدُ بِأَنَّهُ مِنْ مَنَاهِي الشَّرْعِ. وَمَنْ نَقَدَ الْأَشْيَاءَ بِعَيْنِ الْمَعْقُولِ. وَأَنْعَمَ النَّظَرَ فِي مَبَانِي الْأُصُولِ. نَظَمَ هٰذِهِ الْمَقَامَاتِ. فِي سِلْكِ الْإِفَادَاتِ. وَسَلَكَهَا مَسْلَكَ الْمَوْضُوعَاتِ. عَنِ الْعَجْمَوَاتِ وَالْجَمَادَاتِ. وَلَمْ يُسْمَعْ بِمَنْ نَبَا سَمْعُهُ عَنْ تِلْكَ الْحِكَايَاتِ.

---

١ د: على. ٢ بعدها في ف: دَرُّ. ٣ د: بِسُعْدَى.

أَوْ أَثَّمَ رُوَاتَهَا فِي وَقْتٍ مِنَ الْأَوْقَاتِ. ثُمَّ إِذَا كَانَتِ الْأَعْمَالُ بِالنِّيَّاتِ. وَبِهَا ٱنْعِقَادُ الْعُقُودِ الدِّينِيَّاتِ. فَأَيُّ حَرَجٍ عَلَى مَنْ أَنْشَأَ مُلَحًا لِلتَّنْبِيهِ لَا لِلتَّمْوِيهِ. وَنَحَا بِهَا مَنْحَى التَّهْذِيبِ. لَا الْأَكَاذِيبِ. وَهَلْ هُوَ فِي ذٰلِكَ إِلَّا بِمَنْزِلَةِ مَنِ ٱنْتَدَبَ لِتَعْلِيمٍ. أَوْ هَدَى إِلَى صِرَاطٍ مُسْتَقِيمٍ.

عَلَى أَنَّنِي رَاضٍ بِأَنْ أَحْمِلَ الْهَوَى وَأَخْلُصَ مِنْهُ لَا عَلَيَّ وَلَا لِيَا

وَبِاللّٰهِ أَعْتَضِدُ فِيمَا أَعْتَمِدُ. وَأَعْتَصِمُ مِمَّا يَصِمُ. وَأَسْتَرْشِدُ. إِلَى مَا يُرْشِدُ. فَمَا الْمَفْزَعُ إِلَّا إِلَيْهِ. وَلَا الاِسْتِعَانَةُ إِلَّا بِهِ. وَلَا التَّوْفِيقُ إِلَّا مِنْهُ. وَلَا الْمَوْئِلُ إِلَّا هُوَ. عَلَيْهِ تَوَكَّلْتُ. وَإِلَيْهِ أُنِيبُ.[١]

١ بعدها في ف: وبه نَستعين وهوَ نِعمَ المُعين.

الْمَقَامَةُ الْأُولَى[١]

١٫١ حَدَّثَ الْحَارِثُ بْنُ هَمَّامٍ قَالَ. لَمَّا ٱقْتَعَدْتُ غَارِبَ الاِغْتِرَابِ وَأَنْأَتْنِي الْمَتْرَبَةُ عَنِ الْأَتْرَابِ. طَوَّحَتْ بِي طَوَائِحُ الزَّمَنِ. إِلَى صَنْعَاءِ الْيَمَنِ. فَدَخَلْتُهَا خَاوِيَ الْوِفَاضِ. بَادِيَ الْإِنْفَاضِ. لَا أَمْلِكُ بُلْغَةً. وَلَا أَجِدُ فِي جِرَابِي مُضْغَةً. فَطَفِقْتُ أَجُوبُ طُرُقَاتِهَا مِثْلَ الْهَائِمِ. وَأَجُولُ فِي حَوْمَاتِهَا جَوَلَانَ الْحَائِمِ. وَأَرُودُ فِي مَسَارِحِ لَمَحَاتِي. وَمَسَايِحِ غَدَوَاتِي وَرَوْحَاتِي. كَرِيمًا أُخْلِقُ لَهُ دِيبَاجَتِي. وَأَبُوحُ إِلَيْهِ بِحَاجَتِي. أَوْ أَدِيبًا تُفَرِّجُ رُؤْيَتُهُ غُمَّتِي. وَتُرْوِي رِوَايَتُهُ غُلَّتِي. حَتَّى أَدَّتْنِي خَاتِمَةُ الْمَطَافِ. وَهَدَتْنِي فَاتِحَةُ الْأَلْطَافِ.[٢] إِلَى نَادٍ رَحِيبٍ. مُحْتَوٍ عَلَى زِحَامٍ وَنَحِيبٍ.

٢٫١ فَوَلَجْتُ غَابَةَ الْجَمْعِ. لِأَسْبُرَ مَجْلَبَةَ الدَّمْعِ. فَرَأَيْتُ فِي بُهْرَةِ الْحَلْقَةِ. شَخْصًا شَخْتَ الْخِلْقَةِ. عَلَيْهِ أُهْبَةُ السِّيَاحَةِ. وَلَهُ رَنَّةُ النِّيَاحَةِ. وَهُوَ يَطْبَعُ الْأَسْجَاعَ بِجَوَاهِرِ لَفْظِهِ. وَيَقْرَعُ الْأَسْمَاعَ بِزَوَاجِرِ وَعْظِهِ. وَقَدْ أَحَاطَتْ بِهِ أَخْلَاطُ الزُّمَرِ. إِحَاطَةَ الْهَالَةِ بِالْقَمَرِ. وَالْأَكْمَامِ بِالثَّمَرِ. فَدَلَفْتُ إِلَيْهِ لِأَقْتَبِسَ مِنْ فَوَائِدِهِ. وَأَلْتَقِطَ بَعْضَ فَرَائِدِهِ. فَسَمِعْتُهُ يَقُولُ حِينَ خَبَّ فِي مَجَالِهِ. وَهَدَرَتْ شَقَاشِقُ ٱرْتِجَالِهِ

٣٫١ أَيُّهَا السَّادِرُ فِي غُلَوَائِهِ. السَّادِلُ ثَوْبَ خُيَلَائِهِ.[٣] الْجَامِحُ فِي جَهَالَاتِهِ. الْجَانِحُ إِلَى خُزَعْبِلَاتِهِ. إِلَامَ تَسْتَمِرُّ عَلَى غَيِّكَ. وَتَسْتَمْرِئُ مَرْعَى بَغْيِكَ. وَحَتَّامَ تَتَنَاهَى فِي زَهْوِكَ. وَلَا تَنْتَهِي عَنْ لَهْوِكَ. تُبَارِزُ بِمَعْصِيَتِكَ. مَالِكَ نَاصِيَتِكَ. وَتَجْتَرِئُ بِقُبْحِ سِيرَتِكَ. عَلَى عَالِمِ سَرِيرَتِكَ. وَتَتَوَارَى عَنْ[٤] قَرِيبِكَ. وَأَنْتَ بِمَرْأَى رَقِيبِكَ.

---

١ في هامش ق: وتُعْرَف بالصَّنْعانِيَّة، وفي هامش س: وهي تعرف باليمنية ، وفي د، ف: الصنعانية. ٢ د، ف: الإلْطاف. ٣ د، ف: جهلاته. ٤ إلى ههنا ساقط من و.

وَتَسْتَخْفِي مِنْ مَمْلُوكِكَ. وَمَا تَخْفَى خَافِيَةٌ عَلَى مَلِيكِكَ. أَتَظُنُّ أَنْ سَتَنْفَعُكَ حَالُكَ. إِذَا آنَ ٱرْتِحَالُكَ. أَوْ يُنْقِذُكَ مَالُكَ. حِينَ تُوبِقُكَ أَعْمَالُكَ. أَوْ يُغْنِي عَنْكَ نَدَمُكَ. إِذَا زَلَّتْ قَدَمُكَ. أَوْ يَعْطِفُ عَلَيْكَ مَعْشَرُكَ. يَوْمَ يَضُمُّكَ مَحْشَرُكَ.

٤،١ هَلَّا ٱنْتَهَجْتَ مَحَجَّةَ ٱهْتِدَائِكَ. وَعَجَّلْتَ مُعَالَجَةَ دَائِكَ. وَفَلَلْتَ شَبَاةَ ٱعْتِدَائِكَ. وَقَدَعْتَ نَفْسَكَ فَهِيَ أَكْبَرُ أَعْدَائِكَ. أَمَا ٱلْحِمَامُ مِيعَادُكَ. فَمَا إِعْدَادُكَ. وَبِٱلْمَشِيبِ إِنْذَارُكَ. فَمَا إِعْذَارُكَ.[1] وَفِي ٱللَّحْدِ مَقِيلُكَ. فَمَا قِيلُكَ. وَإِلَى ٱللهِ مَصِيرُكَ. فَمَنْ نَصِيرُكَ. طَالَمَا أَيْقَظَكَ ٱلدَّهْرُ فَتَنَاعَسْتَ. وَجَذَبَكَ ٱلْوَعْظُ فَتَقَاعَسْتَ. وَتَجَلَّتْ لَكَ ٱلْعِبَرُ فَتَعَامَيْتَ. وَحَصْحَصَ لَكَ ٱلْحَقُّ فَمَارَيْتَ.[2] وَأَذْكَرَكَ ٱلْمَوْتُ فَتَنَاسَيْتَ. وَأَمْكَنَكَ أَنْ تُؤَاسِيَ فَمَا آسَيْتَ.

٥،١ تُؤْثِرُ فَلْسًا تُوعِيهِ. عَلَى ذِكْرٍ تَعِيهِ. وَتَخْتَارُ قَصْرًا تُعْلِيهِ. عَلَى بِرٍّ تُولِيهِ. وَتَرْغَبُ عَنْ هَادٍ تَسْتَهْدِيهِ. إِلَى زَادٍ تَسْتَهْدِيهِ. وَتُغَلِّبُ حُبَّ ثَوْبٍ تَشْتَهِيهِ. عَلَى ثَوَابٍ تَشْتَرِيهِ. يَوَاقِيتُ ٱلصِّلَاتِ. أَعْلَقُ بِقَلْبِكَ مِنْ مَوَاقِيتِ ٱلصَّلَاةِ. وَمُغَالَاةُ ٱلصَّدُقَاتِ. آثَرُ عِنْدَكَ مِنْ مُوَالَاةِ ٱلصَّدَقَاتِ. وَصِحَافُ ٱلْأَلْوَانِ. أَشْهَى إِلَيْكَ مِنْ صَحَائِفِ ٱلْأَدْيَانِ. وَدُعَابَةُ ٱلْأَقْرَانِ. آنَسُ لَكَ مِنْ تِلَاوَةِ ٱلْقُرْآنِ. تَأْمُرُ بِٱلْعُرْفِ وَتَنْتَهِكُ حِمَاهُ. وَتَحْمِي عَنِ ٱلنُّكْرِ وَلَا تَتَحَامَاهُ. وَتُزَحْزِحُ عَنِ ٱلظُّلْمِ ثُمَّ تَغْشَاهُ. وَتَخْشَى ٱلنَّاسَ وَٱللهُ أَحَقُّ أَنْ تَخْشَاهُ. ثُمَّ أَنْشَدَ

تَبًّا لِطَالِبِ دُنْيَا ثَنَى[3] إِلَيْهَا ٱنْصِبَابَهْ
مَا يَسْتَفِيقُ غَرَامًا بِهَا وَفَرْطَ صَبَابَهْ
وَلَوْ دَرَى لَكَفَاهُ مِمَّا يَرُومُ صُبَابَهْ

١ س: اعتذارك. ٢ ف: تماريت. ٣ د: ثَنَّى.

٦،١ ثُمَّ إِنَّهُ لَبَّدَ عَجَاجَتَهُ. وَغَيَّضَ مُجَاجَتَهُ. وَٱعْتَضَدَ شَكْوَتَهُ. وَتَأَبَّطَ هِرَاوَتَهُ. فَلَمَّا رَنَتِ ٱلْجَمَاعَةُ إِلَى تَحَفُّزِهِ.[١] وَرَأَتْ تَأَهُّبَهُ لِمُزَايَلَةِ مَرْكَزِهِ. أَدْخَلَ كُلٌّ مِنْهُمْ يَدَهُ فِي جَيْبِهِ. فَأَفْعَمَ لَهُ سَجْلًا مِنْ سَيْبِهِ. وَقَالَ ٱصْرِفْ هٰذَا فِي نَفَقَتِكَ. أَوْ فَرِّقْهُ عَلَى رُفْقَتِكَ. فَقَبِلَهُ مِنْهُمْ مُغْضِيًا. وَٱنْثَنَى عَنْهُمْ مُثْنِيًا. وَجَعَلَ يُوَدِّعُ مَنْ يُشَيِّعُهُ. لِيَخْفَى عَلَيْهِ مَهْيَعُهُ. وَيُسَرِّبُ مَنْ يَتْبَعُهُ. لِكَيْ يُجْهَلَ مَرْبَعُهُ.

٧،١ قَالَ ٱلْحَارِثُ بْنُ هَمَّامٍ. فَٱتَّبَعْتُهُ مُوَارِيًا عَنْهُ عِيَانِي. وَقَفَوْتُ أَثَرَهُ[٢] مِنْ حَيْثُ لَا يَرَانِي. حَتَّى ٱنْتَهَى إِلَى مَغَارَةٍ. فَٱنْسَابَ فِيهَا عَلَى غَرَارَةٍ. فَأَمْهَلْتُهُ رَيْثَمَا خَلَعَ نَعْلَيْهِ. وَغَسَلَ رِجْلَيْهِ. ثُمَّ هَجَمْتُ عَلَيْهِ. فَوَجَدْتُهُ مُحَاذِيًا لِتِلْمِيذٍ. عَلَى خُبْزٍ سَمِيذٍ. وَجَدْيٍ حَنِيذٍ. وَقُبَالَتَهُمَا خَابِيَةُ نَبِيذٍ. فَقُلْتُ لَهُ يَا هٰذَا أَيَكُونُ ذَاكَ خَبَرَكَ.[٣] وَهٰذَا مَخْبَرَكَ.[٤]

٨،١ فَزَفَرَ زَفْرَةَ ٱلْقَيْظِ. وَكَادَ يَتَمَيَّزُ مِنَ ٱلْغَيْظِ. وَلَمْ يَزَلْ يُحَمْلِقُ إِلَيَّ. حَتَّى خِفْتُ أَنْ يَسْطُوَ عَلَيَّ. فَلَمَّا أَنْ خَبَتْ نَارُهُ. وَتَوَارَى أُوَارُهُ. أَنْشَدَ

لَبِسْتُ ٱلْخَمِيصَةَ أَبْغِي ٱلْخَبِيصَهْ   وَأَنْشَبْتُ شِصِّيَ فِي كُلِّ شِيصَهْ
وَصَيَّرْتُ وَعْظِيَ أُحْبُولَةً   أُرِيغُ ٱلْقَنِيصَ بِهِ[٥] وَٱلْقَنِيصَهْ
وَأَلْجَأَنِي ٱلدَّهْرُ حَتَّى وَلَجْتُ   بِلُطْفِ ٱحْتِيَالِي عَلَى ٱللَّيْثِ عِيصَهْ
عَلَى أَنَّنِي لَمْ أَهَبْ صَرْفَهُ   وَلَا نَبَضَتْ لِي مِنْهُ فَرِيصَهْ
وَلَا شَرَعَتْ بِي[٦] عَلَى مَوْرِدٍ   يُدَنِّسُ عِرْضِيَ نَفْسٌ حَرِيصَهْ
وَلَوْ أَنْصَفَ ٱلدَّهْرُ فِي حُكْمِهِ   لَمَا مَلَّكَ ٱلْحُكْمَ أَهْلَ ٱلنَّقِيصَهْ

---

١ س، و: تحفُّزه. ٢ د: إِثْرَهُ. ٣ س، و: خَبَرُكَ. ٤ س، و: مَخْبَرُكَ. ٥ د، ف: بها. ٦ و: لي.

٩،١ ثُمَّ قَالَ لِي[١] اُدْنُ فَكُلْ. وَإِنْ شِئْتَ فَقُمْ وَقُلْ. فَٱلتَفَتُّ إِلَى تِلْمِيذِهِ وَقُلْتُ عَزَمْتُ
عَلَيْكَ بِمَنْ تَسْتَدْفِعُ[٢] بِهِ الْأَذَى. لَتُخْبِرَنِّي[٣] مَنْ ذَا. فَقَالَ هٰذَا أَبُو زَيْدٍ السَّرُوجِيُّ
سِرَاجُ الْغُرَبَاءِ. وَتَاجُ الْأُدَبَاءِ. فَٱنْصَرَفْتُ مِنْ حَيْثُ أَتَيْتُ. وَقَضَيْتُ الْعَجَبَ
مِمَّا رَأَيْتُ.

---

١ ليس في ق. ٢ د: يُسْتَدْفَعُ. ٣ و: لتخبرَني، د: لَتُخْبِرَني.

الْمَقَامَةُ الثَّانِيَةُ[١]

١،٢ حَكَى الْحَارِثُ بْنُ هَمَّامٍ قَالَ. كَلِفْتُ مُذْ مِيطَتْ عَنِّي التَّمَائِمُ. وَنِيطَتْ بِي الْعَمَائِمُ. بِأَنْ أَغْشَى مَعَانَ الْأَدَبِ. وَأُنْضِيَ إِلَيْهِ رِكَابَ الطَّلَبِ. لِأَعْلَقَ مِنْهُ بِمَا يَكُونُ لِي زِينَةً بَيْنَ الْأَنَامِ. وَمُزْنَةً عِنْدَ الْأُوَامِ. وَكُنْتُ لِفَرْطِ اللَّهَجِ بِاقْتِبَاسِهِ. وَالطَّمَعِ فِي تَقَمُّصِ لِبَاسِهِ. أُبَاحِثُ كُلَّ مَنْ جَلَّ وَقَلَّ. وَأَسْتَسْقِي الْوَبْلَ وَالطَّلَّ. وَأَتَعَلَّلُ بِعَسَى وَلَعَلَّ.

٢،٢ فَلَمَّا حَلَلْتُ حُلْوَانَ. وَقَدْ بَلَوْتُ الْإِخْوَانَ. وَسَبَرْتُ الْأَوْزَانَ. وَخَبَرْتُ مَا شَانَ وَزَانَ. أَلْفَيْتُ بِهَا أَبَا زَيْدٍ السَّرُوجِيَّ يَتَقَلَّبُ فِي قَوَالِيبِ[٢] الِانْتِسَابِ. وَيَخْبِطُ فِي أَسَالِيبِ الِاكْتِسَابِ. فَيَدَّعِي تَارَةً أَنَّهُ مِنْ آلِ سَاسَانَ. وَيَعْتَزِي مَرَّةً إِلَى أَقْيَالِ غَسَّانَ. وَيَبْرُزُ طَوْرًا فِي شِعَارِ الشُّعَرَاءِ. وَيَلْبَسُ حِينًا كِبْرَ الْكُبَرَاءِ. بَيْدَ أَنَّهُ مَعَ تَلَوُّنِ حَالِهِ. وَتَبَيُّنِ مُحَالِهِ. يَتَحَلَّى بِرُوَاءٍ وَرِوَايَةٍ. وَمُدَارَاةٍ وَدِرَايَةٍ. وَبَلَاغَةٍ رَائِعَةٍ. وَبَدِيهَةٍ مُطَاوِعَةٍ. وَآدَابٍ بَارِعَةٍ. وَقَدَمٍ لِأَعْلَامِ الْعُلُومِ فَارِعَةٍ. فَكَانَ لِمَحَاسِنِ آلَاتِهِ. يُلْبَسُ عَلَى عِلَّاتِهِ. وَلِسَعَةِ رِوَايَتِهِ. يُصْبَى إِلَى رُؤْيَتِهِ. وَلِخَلَابَةِ عَارِضَتِهِ. يُرْغَبُ عَنْ مُعَارَضَتِهِ. وَلِعُذُوبَةِ إِيرَادِهِ. يُسْعَفُ بِمُرَادِهِ. فَتَعَلَّقْتُ بِأَهْدَابِهِ. لِخَصَائِصِ آدَابِهِ. وَنَافَسْتُ فِي مُصَافَاتِهِ. لِنَفَائِسِ صِفَاتِهِ.

فَكُنْتُ بِهِ أَجْلُو هُمُومِي وَأَجْتَلِي زَمَانِيَ طَلْقَ الْوَجْهِ مُلْتَمِعَ الضِّيَا
أَرَى قُرْبَهُ قُرْبَى وَمَغْنَاهُ غُنْيَةً وَرُؤْيَتَهُ رِيًّا وَمَحْيَاهُ لِي حَيَا

١ في هامش ق: وتُعرف بِالْحُلْوانية؛ وَفي هامش س: تعرف، تليها كلمة مطموسة، وفي د: الحلوانية. ٢ ف: قوالب.

٣،٢ وَلَبِثْنَا عَلَى ذٰلِكَ بُرْهَةً. يُنْشِئُ لِي كُلَّ يَوْمٍ نُزْهَةً. وَيَدْرَأُ عَنْ قَلْبِي شُبْهَةً. إِلَى أَنْ جَدَحَتْ لَهُ يَدُ ٱلْإِمْلَاقِ. كَأْسَ ٱلْفِرَاقِ. وَأَغْرَاهُ عَدَمُ ٱلْعُرَاقِ. بِتَطْلِيقِ ٱلْعِرَاقِ. وَلَفَظَتْهُ مَعَاوِزُ ٱلْإِرْفَاقِ. إِلَى مَفَاوِزِ ٱلْآفَاقِ. وَنَظَمَهُ فِي سِلْكِ ٱلرِّفَاقِ. خُفُوقُ رَايَةِ ٱلْإِخْفَاقِ. فَشَحَذَ لِلرِّحْلَةِ غِرَارَ عَزْمَتِهِ. وَظَعَنَ يَقْتَادُ ٱلْقَلْبَ بِأَزِمَّتِهِ.

فَمَا رَاقَنِي مَنْ لَاقَنِي بَعْدَ بُعْدِهِ   وَلَا شَاقَنِي مَنْ سَاقَنِي لِوِصَالِهِ
وَلَا لَاحَ لِي مُذْ نَدَّ نِدٌّ لِفَضْلِهِ   وَلَا ذُو خِلَالٍ حَازَ مِثْلَ خِلَالِهِ

٤،٢ وَٱسْتَسَرَّ عَنِّي حِينًا. لَا أَعْرِفُ لَهُ عَرِينًا. وَلَا أَجِدُ عَنْهُ مُبِينًا. فَلَمَّا أُبْتُ مِنْ غُرْبَتِي. إِلَى مَنْبِتِ شُعْبَتِي. حَضَرْتُ دَارَ كُتُبِهَا ٱلَّتِي هِيَ مُنْتَدَى ٱلْمُتَأَدِّبِينَ. وَمُلْتَقَى ٱلْقَاطِنِينَ مِنْهُمْ وَٱلْمُتَغَرِّبِينَ. فَدَخَلَ ذُو لِحْيَةٍ كَثَّةٍ. وَهَيْئَةٍ رَثَّةٍ. فَسَلَّمَ عَلَى ٱلْجُلَّاسِ. وَجَلَسَ فِي أُخْرَيَاتِ ٱلنَّاسِ. ثُمَّ أَخَذَ يُبْدِي مَا فِي وِطَابِهِ. وَيُعْجِبُ ٱلْحَاضِرِينَ بِفَصْلِ خِطَابِهِ. فَقَالَ لِمَنْ يَلِيهِ. مَا ٱلْكِتَابُ ٱلَّذِي تَنْظُرُ فِيهِ. فَقَالَ دِيوَانُ أَبِي عُبَادَةَ. ٱلْمَشْهُودِ لَهُ بِٱلْإِجَادَةِ. فَقَالَ هَلْ عَثَرْتَ لَهُ فِيمَا لَمَحْتَهُ. عَلَى بَدِيعٍ ٱسْتَمْلَحْتَهُ. قَالَ نَعَمْ قَوْلُهُ

كَأَنَّمَا يَبْسِمُ[1] عَنْ لُؤْلُؤٍ   مُنَضَّدٍ أَوْ بَرَدٍ أَوْ أَقَاحْ

فَإِنَّهُ أَبْدَعَ فِي ٱلتَّشْبِيهِ ٱلْمُودَعِ فِيهِ.

٥،٢ فَقَالَ لَهُ يَا لَلْعَجَبِ.[2] وَلَضَيْعَةِ ٱلْأَدَبِ. لَقَدِ ٱسْتَسْمَنْتَ يَا هٰذَا ذَا وَرَمٍ. وَنَفَخْتَ فِي غَيْرِ ضَرَمٍ. أَيْنَ أَنْتَ مِنَ ٱلْبَيْتِ ٱلنَّدْرِ. ٱلْجَامِعِ مُشَبَّهَاتِ[3] ٱلثَّغْرِ. وَأَنْشَدَ

---

١ و، د: تبسم. ٢ د: لِلْعَجَبِ. ٣ س: مشبّهات.

نَفْسِي ٱلْفِدَاءُ لِثَغْرٍ رَاقَ مَبْسِمُهُ[١] وَزَانَهُ شَنَبٌ نَاهِيكَ مِنْ شَنَبِ
يَفْتَرُّ عَنْ لُؤْلُؤٍ رَطْبٍ وَعَنْ بَرَدٍ وَعَنْ أَقَاحٍ وَعَنْ طَلْعٍ وَعَنْ حَبَبِ

٦،٢ فَٱسْتَجَادَهُ مَنْ حَضَرَ وَٱسْتَحْلَاهُ. وَٱسْتَعَادَهُ مِنْهُ وَٱسْتَمْلَاهُ. وَسُئِلَ لِمَنْ هٰذَا ٱلْبَيْتُ. وَهَلْ حَيٌّ قَائِلُهُ أَمْ مَيْتٌ. فَقَالَ أَيْمُ ٱللهِ لَلْحَقُّ أَحَقُّ أَنْ يُتَّبَعَ. وَلَلصِّدْقُ حَقِيقٌ بِأَنْ يُسْتَمَعَ. إِنَّهُ يَا قَوْمِ. لَنَجِيُّكُمْ[٢] مُذُ ٱلْيَوْمِ. قَالَ فَكَأَنَّ ٱلْجَمَاعَةَ ٱرْتَابَتْ بِعُزْوَتِهِ.[٣] وَأَبَتْ تَصْدِيقَ دِعْوَتِهِ.[٤] فَتَوَجَّسَ مَا هَجَسَ فِي أَفْكَارِهِمْ. وَفَطِنَ لِمَا بَطَنَ مِنِ ٱسْتِنْكَارِهِمْ. وَحَاذَرَ أَنْ يَفْرُطَ إِلَيْهِ ذَمٌّ.[٥] فَقَرَأَ ﴿إِنَّ بَعْضَ ٱلظَّنِّ إِثْمٌ﴾.

٧،٢ ثُمَّ قَالَ يَا رُوَاةَ ٱلْقَرِيضِ. وَأُسَاةَ ٱلْقَوْلِ ٱلْمَرِيضِ. إِنَّ خُلَاصَةَ ٱلْجَوْهَرِ تَظْهَرُ بِٱلسَّبْكِ. وَيَدَ[٦] ٱلْحَقِّ تَصْدَعُ رِدَاءَ ٱلشَّكِّ. وَقَدْ قِيلَ فِيمَا غَبَرَ مِنَ ٱلزَّمَانِ. عِنْدَ ٱلِامْتِحَانِ. يُكْرَمُ ٱلرَّجُلُ أَوْ يُهَانُ. وَهَا أَنَا قَدْ عَرَّضْتُ خَبِيئَتِي لِلِاخْتِبَارِ. وَعَرَضْتُ حَقِيبَتِي عَلَى ٱلِاعْتِبَارِ. فَٱبْتَدَرَ أَحَدُ مَنْ حَضَرَ. وَقَالَ أَعْرِفُ بَيْتًا لَمْ يُنْسَجْ عَلَى مِنْوَالِهِ. وَلَا سَمَحَتْ[٧] قَرِيحَةٌ بِمِثَالِهِ. فَإِنْ آثَرْتَ ٱخْتِلَابَ ٱلْقُلُوبِ. فَٱنْظِمْ عَلَى هٰذَا ٱلْأُسْلُوبِ. وَأَنْشَدَ

فَأَمْطَرَتْ لُؤْلُؤًا مِنْ نَرْجِسٍ فَسَقَتْ وَرْدًا وَعَضَّتْ عَلَى ٱلْعُنَّابِ بِٱلْبَرَدِ

فَلَمْ يَكُنْ إِلَّا كَلَمْحِ ٱلْبَصَرِ أَوْ أَقْرَبَ. حَتَّى أَنْشَدَ فَأَغْرَبَ.

سَأَلْتُهَا حِينَ زَارَتْ نَضْوَ بُرْقُعِهَا ٱلْـقَانِي وَإِيدَاعَ سَمْعِي أَطْيَبَ ٱلْخَبَرِ
فَزَحْزَحَتْ شَفَقًا غَشَّى سَنَا قَمَرٍ وَسَاقَطَتْ لُؤْلُؤًا مِنْ خَاتَمٍ عَطِرِ

١ و، ف: مَبْسِم. ٢ س: لَنَجِيُّكم. ٣ هكذا في ق، س، و؛ وفي د: بعَزْوَته، ف: بِعِزْوته. ٤ هكذا في ق، س، و.
٥ يعدها في د: أو يلحقه وصم، وفي ف: أو يلحقه وهم. ٦ د: ويَدُ. ٧ د: سَمُحَتْ.

فَحَارَ ٱلْحَاضِرُونَ لِبَدَاهَتِهِ. وَٱعْتَرَفُوا بِنَزَاهَتِهِ. فَلَمَّا آنَسَ ٱسْتِئْنَاسَهُمْ بِكَلَامِهِ. ٨،٢
وَٱنْصِبَابَهُمْ إِلَى شِعْبِ إِكْرَامِهِ. أَطْرَقَ كَطَرْفَةِ ٱلْعَيْنِ. ثُمَّ قَالَ وَدُونَكُمْ بَيْتَيْنِ آخَرَيْنِ. وَأَنْشَدَ

وَأَقْبَلَتْ يَوْمَ جَدَّ ٱلْبَيْنُ فِي حُلَلٍ   سُودٍ تَعَضُّ بَنَانَ ٱلنَّادِمِ ٱلْحَصِرِ
فَلَاحَ لَيْلٌ عَلَى صُبْحٍ أَقَلَّهُمَا   غُصْنٌ وَضَرَّسَتِ ٱلْبِلَّوْرَ[١] بِٱلدُّرَرِ

فَحِينَئِذٍ ٱسْتَسْنَى ٱلْقَوْمُ قِيمَتَهُ. وَٱسْتَغْزَرُوا دِيمَتَهُ. وَأَجْمَلُوا عِشْرَتَهُ. وَجَمَّلُوا قِشْرَتَهُ.

٩،٢ قَالَ ٱلْمُخْبِرُ بِهٰذِهِ ٱلْحِكَايَةِ فَلَمَّا رَأَيْتُ تَلَهُّبَ جَذْوَتِهِ. وَتَأَلُّقَ جَلْوَتِهِ. أَمْعَنْتُ ٱلنَّظَرَ فِي تَوَسُّمِهِ. وَسَرَّحْتُ ٱلطَّرْفَ فِي مِيسَمِهِ. فَإِذَا هُوَ شَيْخُنَا ٱلسَّرُوجِيُّ. وَقَدْ أَقْمَرَ لَيْلُهُ ٱلدَّجُوجِيُّ. فَهَنَّأْتُ نَفْسِي بِمَوْرِدِهِ. وَٱبْتَدَرْتُ ٱسْتِلَامَ يَدِهِ. وَقُلْتُ لَهُ مَا ٱلَّذِي أَحَالَ صِفَتَكَ. حَتَّى جَهِلْتُ مَعْرِفَتَكَ. وَأَيُّ شَيْءٍ شَيَّبَ لِحْيَتَكَ. حَتَّى أَنْكَرْتُ حِلْيَتَكَ. فَأَنْشَأَ يَقُولُ

وَقْعُ ٱلشَّوَائِبِ شَيَّبْ   وَٱلدَّهْرُ بِٱلنَّاسِ قُلَّبْ
إِنْ دَانَ يَوْمًا لِشَخْصٍ   فَفِي غَدٍ يَتَغَلَّبْ
فَلَا تَثِقْ بِوَمِيضٍ   مِنْ بَرْقِهِ فَهْوَ خُلَّبْ
وَٱصْبِرْ إِذَا هُوَ أَضْرَى   بِكَ ٱلْخُطُوبَ وَأَلَّبْ
فَمَا عَلَى ٱلتِّبْرِ عَارٌ   فِي ٱلنَّارِ حِينَ يُقَلَّبْ

ثُمَّ نَهَضَ مُفَارِقًا مَوْضِعَهُ. وَمُسْتَصْحِبًا ٱلْقُلُوبَ مَعَهُ.

١ س: البَلّور.

المَقامةُ الثّانيةُ[١]

١٫٢ رَوَى الحارِثُ بْنُ هَمّامٍ قالَ. نَظَمَني وَأَخْدانًا لي نادٍ. لَمْ يَخِبْ فيهِ مُنادٍ. وَلا كَبا قَدْحُ زِنادٍ. وَلا ذَكَتْ نارُ عِنادٍ. فَبَيْنَا نَحْنُ نَتَجاذَبُ أَطْرافَ الأَناشيدِ. وَنَتَوارَدُ طُرَفَ الأَسانيدِ. وَقَفَ[٢] بِنا[٣] شَخْصٌ عَلَيْهِ سَمَلٌ. وَفي مَشْيِهِ[٤] قَزَلٌ. فَقالَ يا أَخايِرَ الذَّخائِرِ. وَبَشائِرَ العَشائِرِ. عِموا صَباحًا. وَٱنْعَموا[٥] ٱصْطِباحًا. وَٱنْظُروا إِلَى مَنْ كانَ ذا نَدِيٍّ وَنَدًى. وَجِدَةٍ وَجَدًى. وَعَقارٍ وَقُرًى. وَمَقارٍ وَقِرًى. فَما زالَ بِهِ قُطوبُ الخُطوبِ. وَحُروبُ الكُروبِ. وَشَرَرُ شَرِّ الحَسودِ. وَٱنْتِيابُ النُّوَبِ السّودِ. حَتّى صَفِرَتِ الرّاحَةُ. وَقَرِعَتِ[٦] السّاحَةُ. وَغارَ المَنْبَعُ. وَنَبا المَرْبَعُ. وَأَقْوَى المَجْمَعُ. وَأَقَضَّ المَضْجَعُ. وَٱسْتَحالَتِ الحالُ. وَأَعْوَلَ العِيالُ. وَخَلَتِ المَرابِطُ. وَرَحِمَ الغابِطُ. وَأَوْدَى النّاطِقُ وَالصّامِتُ. وَرَثَى لَنا الحاسِدُ وَالشّامِتُ.

٢٫٢ وَأُلْنا لِلدَّهْرِ[٧] المُوقِعِ. وَالفَقْرِ المُدْقِعِ. إِلَى أَنِ ٱحْتَذَيْنا الوَجَى. وَٱغْتَذَيْنا الشَّجَى. وَٱسْتَبْطَنّا الجَوَى. وَطَوَيْنا الأَحْشاءَ عَلَى الطَّوَى. وَٱكْتَحَلْنا السُّهادَ. وَٱسْتَوْطَنّا الوِهادَ. وَٱسْتَوْطَأْنا القَتادَ. وَتَناسَيْنا الأَقْتادَ. وَٱسْتَطَبْنا الحَيْنَ المُجْتاحَ. وَٱسْتَبْطَأْنا اليَوْمَ المُتاحَ. فَهَلْ مِنْ حُرٍّ آسٍ. أَوْ سَمْحٍ مُؤاسٍ. فَوَالَّذي ٱسْتَخْرَجَني مِنْ قَيْلَةٍ. لَقَدْ أَمْسَيْتُ أَخا عَيْلَةٍ. لا أَمْلِكُ بَيْتَ لَيْلَةٍ.

---

١ في هامش ق: وتُعرف بِالحُلْوانية؛ وَفي هامش س: تعرف، تليها كلمة مطموسة، وفي د: الحلوانية. ٢ ف: قوالب.

٣،٣ قَالَ ٱلْحَارِثُ بْنُ هَمَّامٍ. فَأَوَيْتُ لِمَفَاقِرِهِ. وَلَوَيْتُ إِلَى ٱسْتِنْبَاطِ فِقَرِهِ. فَأَبْرَزْتُ دِينَارًا. وَقُلْتُ لَهُ ٱخْتِبَارًا. إِنْ مَدَحْتَهُ نَظْمًا. فَهُوَ لَكَ حَتْمًا. فَٱنْبَرَى يُنْشِدُ فِي ٱلْحَالِ. مِنْ غَيْرِ ٱنْتِحَالٍ.

أَكْرِمْ بِهِ أَصْفَرَ رَاقَتْ صُفْرَتُهْ   جَوَّابَ آفَاقٍ تَرَامَتْ سَفْرَتُهْ
مَأْثُورَةً سُمْعَتُهُ وَشُهْرَتُهْ   قَدْ أُودِعَتْ سِرَّ ٱلْغِنَى أَسِرَّتُهْ
وَقَارَنَتْ نُجْحَ ٱلْمَسَاعِي خَطْرَتُهْ   وَحُبِّبَتْ إِلَى ٱلْأَنَامِ غُرَّتُهْ
كَأَنَّمَا مِنَ ٱلْقُلُوبِ نُقْرَتُهْ   بِهِ يَصُولُ مَنْ حَوَتْهُ صُرَّتُهْ
وَإِنْ تَفَانَتْ أَوْ تَوَانَتْ عِتْرَتُهْ   يَا حَبَّذَا نُضَارُهُ وَنَضْرَتُهْ[1]
وَحَبَّذَا مَغْنَاتُهُ وَنُصْرَتُهْ   كَمْ آمِرٍ بِهِ ٱسْتَتَبَّتْ إِمْرَتُهْ
وَمُتْرَفٍ لَوْلَاهُ دَامَتْ حَسْرَتُهْ   وَجَيْشِ هَمٍّ هَزَمَتْهُ كَرَّتُهْ
وَبَدْرِ تِمٍّ أَنْزَلَتْهُ بَدْرَتُهْ   وَمُسْتَشِيطٍ تَتَلَظَّى جَمْرَتُهْ
أَسَرَّ نَجْوَاهُ فَلَانَتْ شِرَّتُهْ   وَكَمْ أَسِيرٍ أَسْلَمَتْهُ أُسْرَتُهْ
أَنْقَذَهُ حَتَّى صَفَتْ مَسَرَّتُهْ   وَحَقِّ مَوْلًى أَبْدَعَتْهُ فِطْرَتُهْ
لَوْلَا ٱلتُّقَى لَقُلْتُ جَلَّتْ قُدْرَتُهْ

٤،٣ ثُمَّ بَسَطَ يَدَهُ. بَعْدَ مَا أَنْشَدَهُ. وَقَالَ أَنْجَزَ حُرٌّ مَا وَعَدَ. وَسَحَّ خَالٌ إِذْ رَعَدَ. فَنَبَذْتُ ٱلدِّينَارَ إِلَيْهِ. وَقُلْتُ خُذْهُ غَيْرَ مَأْسُوفٍ عَلَيْهِ. فَوَضَعَهُ فِي فِيهِ. وَقَالَ بَارِكِ ٱللّٰهُمَّ فِيهِ. ثُمَّ شَمَّرَ لِلِٱنْثِنَاءِ. بَعْدَ تَوْفِيَةِ ٱلثَّنَاءِ. فَنَشَأَتْ لِي مِنْ فُكَاهَتِهِ نَشْوَةُ غَرَامٍ. سَهَّلَتْ عَلَيَّ ٱئْتِنَافَ ٱغْتِرَامٍ. فَجَرَّدْتُ دِينَارًا آخَرَ وَقُلْتُ لَهُ هَلْ لَكَ فِي أَنْ تَذُمَّهُ. ثُمَّ تَضُمَّهُ. فَأَنْشَدَ مُرْتَجِلًا. وَشَدَا عَجِلًا.

١ ف: نُقْرَتُهُ.

تَبًّا لَهُ مِنْ خَادِعٍ مُمَاذِقِ أَصْفَرَ ذِي وَجْهَيْنِ كَالْمُنَافِقِ
يَبْدُو بِوَصْفَيْنِ لِعَيْنِ الرَّامِقِ زِينَةِ مَعْشُوقٍ وَلَوْنِ عَاشِقِ
وَحُبُّهُ عِنْدَ ذَوِي الْحَقَائِقِ يَدْعُو إِلَى ٱرْتِكَابِ سُخْطِ الْخَالِقِ
لَوْلَاهُ لَمْ تُقْطَعْ يَمِينُ سَارِقِ وَلَا بَدَتْ مَظْلِمَةٌ[1] مِنْ فَاسِقِ
وَلَا ٱشْمَأَزَّ بَاخِلٌ مِنْ طَارِقِ وَلَا شَكَا الْمَمْطُولُ مَطْلَ الْعَائِقِ
وَلَا ٱسْتُعِيذَ مِنْ حَسُودٍ رَاشِقِ وَشَرُّ مَا فِيهِ مِنَ الْخَلَائِقِ
أَنْ لَيْسَ يُغْنِي عَنْكَ فِي الْمَضَايِقِ إِلَّا إِذَا فَرَّ فِرَارَ الآبِقِ
وَاهًا لِمَنْ يَقْذِفُهُ مِنْ حَالِقِ وَمَنْ إِذَا نَاجَاهُ نَجْوَى الْوَامِقِ
قَالَ لَهُ قَوْلَ الْمُحِقِّ الصَّادِقِ لَا رَأْيَ فِي وَصْلِكَ لِي فَفَارِقِ

فَقُلْتُ لَهُ مَا أَغْزَرَ وَبْلَكَ. فَقَالَ وَالشَّرْطُ أَمْلَكُ. فَنَفَحْتُهُ بِالدِّينَارِ الثَّانِي. وَقُلْتُ لَهُ عَوِّذْهُمَا بِالْمَثَانِي. فَأَلْقَاهُ فِي فَمِهِ. وَقَرَنَهُ بِتَوْأَمِهِ. وَٱنْكَفَأَ يَحْمَدُ مَغْدَاهُ. وَيَمْدَحُ النَّادِيَ وَنَدَاهُ.

قَالَ الْحَارِثُ بْنُ هَمَّامٍ فَنَاجَانِي قَلْبِي بِأَنَّهُ أَبُو زَيْدٍ. وَأَنَّ تَعَارُجَهُ لِكَيْدٍ. ٥،٣
فَٱسْتَعَدْتُهُ وَقُلْتُ لَهُ قَدْ عُرِفْتَ بِوَشْيِكَ. فَٱسْتَقِمْ فِي مَشْيِكَ. فَقَالَ إِنْ كُنْتَ ٱبْنَ هَمَّامٍ. فَحُيِّيتَ بِإِكْرَامٍ. وَحَيِيتَ بَيْنَ كِرَامٍ. فَقُلْتُ أَنَا الْحَارِثُ.[2] فَكَيْفَ حَالُكَ وَالْحَوَادِثُ. فَقَالَ أَتَقَلَّبُ فِي الْحَالَيْنِ بُؤْسٍ وَرَخَاءٍ. وَأَنْقَلِبُ مَعَ الرِّيحَيْنِ زَعْزَعٍ وَرُخَاءٍ. فَقُلْتُ كَيْفَ ٱدَّعَيْتَ الْقَزَلَ. وَمَا مِثْلُكَ مَنْ هَزَلَ. فَٱسْتَسَرَّ بِشْرُهُ الَّذِي كَانَ تَجَلَّى. ثُمَّ أَنْشَدَ حِينَ وَلَّى.

١ د: مَظْلَمَة. ٢ هكذا بعد التصحيح في س، وفي د: والحوادث.

تَعَارَجْتُ لَا رَغْبَةً فِي الْعَرَجْ وَلٰكِنْ لِأَقْرَعَ بَابَ الْفَرَجْ
وَأُلْقِيَ حَبْلِي عَلَى غَارِبِي وَأَسْلُكَ مَسْلَكَ مَنْ قَدْ مَرَجْ
فَإِنْ لَامَنِي الْقَوْمُ قُلْتُ ٱعْذِرُوا فَلَيْسَ عَلَى أَعْرَجَ مِنْ حَرَجْ

الْمَقَامَةُ الرَّابِعَةُ[1]

٤،١ أَخْبَرَ الْحَارِثُ بْنُ هَمَّامٍ قَالَ. ظَعَنْتُ إِلَى دِمْيَاطَ. عَامَ هِيَاطٍ وَمِيَاطٍ. وَأَنَا يَوْمَئِذٍ مَرْمُوقُ الرَّخَاءِ. مَوْمُوقُ الْإِخَاءِ. أَسْحَبُ مَطَارِفَ الثَّرَاءِ. وَأَجْتَلِي مَعَارِفَ السَّرَّاءِ. فَرَافَقْتُ صَحْبًا قَدْ شَقُّوا عَصَا الشِّقَاقِ. وَارْتَضَعُوا أَفَاوِيقَ الْوِفَاقِ. حَتَّى لَاحُوا كَأَسْنَانِ الْمُشْطِ فِي الِاسْتِوَاءِ. وَكَالنَّفْسِ الْوَاحِدَةِ فِي الْتِئَامِ الْأَهْوَاءِ. وَكُنَّا مَعَ ذٰلِكَ نَسِيرُ النَّجَاءَ. وَلَا نَرْحَلُ إِلَّا كُلَّ هَوْجَاءَ. وَإِذَا نَزَلْنَا مَنْزِلًا. أَوْ وَرَدْنَا مَنْهَلًا. اِخْتَلَسْنَا اللُّبْثَ. وَلَمْ نُطِلِ الْمُكْثَ.

٤،٢ فَعَنَّ لَنَا إِعْمَالُ الرِّكَابِ. فِي لَيْلَةٍ فَتِيَّةِ الشَّبَابِ. غُدَافِيَّةِ الْإِهَابِ. فَأَسْرَيْنَا إِلَى أَنْ نَضَا اللَّيْلُ شَبَابَهُ. وَسَلَتَ الصُّبْحُ خِضَابَهُ. فَحِينَ مَلِلْنَا السُّرَى. وَمِلْنَا إِلَى الْكَرَى. صَادَفْنَا أَرْضًا مُخْضَلَّةَ الرُّبَا. مُعْتَلَّةَ الصَّبَا. فَتَخَيَّرْنَاهَا مُنَاخًا لِلْعِيسِ. وَمَحَطًّا لِلتَّعْرِيسِ. فَلَمَّا حَلَّهَا الْخَلِيطُ. وَهَدَأَ بِهَا الْأَطِيطُ وَالْغَطِيطُ. سَمِعْتُ صَيِّتًا مِنَ الرِّجَالِ. يَقُولُ لِسَمِيرِهِ فِي الرِّحَالِ كَيْفَ حُكْمُ سِيرَتِكَ. مَعَ جِيلِكَ وَجِيرَتِكَ.

٤،٣ فَقَالَ أَرْعَى الْجَارَ. وَلَوْ جَارَ. وَأَبْذُلُ الْوِصَالَ. لِمَنْ صَالَ. وَأَحْتَمِلُ الْخَلِيطَ. وَلَوْ أَبْدَى التَّخْلِيطَ. وَأَوَدُّ الْحَمِيمَ. وَلَوْ جَرَّعَنِي الْحَمِيمَ. وَأُفَضِّلُ الشَّفِيقَ. عَلَى الشَّقِيقِ. وَأَفِي لِلْعَشِيرِ. وَإِنْ لَمْ يُكَافِئْ بِالْعَشِيرِ. وَأَسْتَقِلُّ الْجَزِيلَ. لِلنَّزِيلِ. وَأَغْمُرُ الزَّمِيلَ. بِالْجَمِيلِ. وَأُنَزِّلُ[2] سَمِيرِي. مَنْزِلَةَ أَمِيرِي. وَأُحِلُّ أَنِيسِي. مَحَلَّ رَئِيسِي. وَأُودِعُ مَعَارِفِي. عَوَارِفِي. وَأُولِي مُرَافِقِي. مَرَافِقِي. وَأُلِينُ مَقَالِي. لِلْقَالِي. وَأُدِيمُ

---

١ في هامش ق: الدميابلوطية (هكذا)، وفي س، د، ف: الدِمّياطية. ٢ د: أُنْزِلُ.

تَسَآلِي. عَنِ السَّالِي. وَأَرْضَى مِنَ الْوَفَاءِ. بِاللَّفَاءِ. وَأَقْنَعُ مِنَ الْجَزَاءِ. بِأَقَلِّ الْأَجْزَاءِ. وَلَا أَتَظَلَّمُ. حِينَ أُظْلَمُ. وَلَا أَنْقَمُ. وَلَوْ لَدَغَنِي الْأَرْقَمُ.

٤،٤ فَقَالَ لَهُ صَاحِبُهُ وَيْكَ يَا بُنَيَّ إِنَّمَا يُضَنُّ بِالضَّنِينِ. وَيُنَافَسُ فِي الثَّمِينِ. لٰكِنْ أَنَا لَا آتِي. غَيْرَ الْمُؤَاتِي. وَلَا أَسِمُ الْعَاتِي. بِمُرَاعَاتِي. وَلَا أُصَافِي. مَنْ يَأْبَى إِنْصَافِي. وَلَا أُوَاخِي. مَنْ يُلْغِي الْأَوَاخِي. وَلَا أُمَالِي. مَنْ يُخَيِّبُ آمَالِي. وَلَا أُبَالِي بِمَنْ صَرَمَ حِبَالِي. وَلَا أُدَارِي. مَنْ جَهِلَ مِقْدَارِي. وَلَا أُعْطِي زِمَامِي. مَنْ يُخْفِرُ ذِمَامِي. وَلَا أَبْذُلُ وِدَادِي. لِأَضْدَادِي. وَلَا أَدَعُ إِيعَادِي. لِلْمُعَادِي. وَلَا أَغْرِسُ الْأَيَادِي. فِي أَرْضِ الْأَعَادِي. وَلَا أَسْمَحُ بِمُوَاسَاتِي. لِمَنْ يَفْرَحُ بِمَسَآتِي. وَلَا أَرَى الْتِفَاتِي. إِلَى مَنْ يَشْمَتُ بِوَفَاتِي. وَلَا أَخُصُّ بِحِبَائِي. إِلَّا أَحِبَّائِي. وَلَا أَسْتَطِبُّ لِدَائِي. غَيْرَ أَوِدَّائِي. وَلَا أُمَلِّكُ خُلَّتِي. مَنْ لَا يَسُدُّ خَلَّتِي. وَلَا أُصْفِي نِيَّتِي. لِمَنْ يَتَمَنَّى مَنِيَّتِي. وَلَا أُخْلِصُ دُعَائِي. لِمَنْ لَا يُفْعِمُ وِعَائِي. وَلَا أُفْرِغُ ثَنَائِي. عَلَى مَنْ يُفَرِّغُ إِنَائِي.

٥،٤ وَمَنْ حَكَمَ بِأَنْ أَبْذُلَ وَتَخْزُنَ. وَأَلِينَ وَتَخْشُنَ. وَأَذُوبَ وَتَجْمُدَ. وَأَذْكُو وَتَخْمُدَ، لَا وَاللهِ بَلْ نَتَوَازَنُ فِي الْمَقَالِ. وَزْنَ الْمِثْقَالِ. وَنَتَحَاذَى فِي الْفِعَالِ. حَذْوَ النِّعَالِ. حَتَّى نَأْمَنَ التَّغَابُنَ. وَنُكْفَى التَّضَاغُنَ. وَإِلَّا فَلِمَ أُعِلُّكَ وَتُعِلُّنِي. وَأُقِلُّكَ وَتَسْتَقِلُّنِي. وَأَجْتَرِحُ لَكَ وَتَجْرَحُنِي. وَأَسْرَحُ إِلَيْكَ وَتُسَرِّحُنِي، وَكَيْفَ يُجْتَلَبُ إِنْصَافٌ بِضَيْمٍ. وَأَنَّى تُشْرِقُ[١] شَمْسٌ[٢] مَعَ غَيْمٍ. وَمَتَى أُصْحَبَ وُدٌّ[٣] بِعَسْفٍ. وَأَيُّ حُرٍّ رَضِيَ بِخُطَّةِ خَسْفٍ، وَلِلهِ أَبُوكَ حَيْثُ يَقُولُ

---

١ د: تَشْرُقُ. ٢ ف: نفس. ٣ س: أَصْحَبَ وُدًّا (هكذا، مع إضافة ألف بحبر غير حبر الناسخ)، ف: أُصْحِبَ وُدٌّ.

٦،٤ جَـزَيْتُ مَنْ أَعْـلَقَ بِي وُدَّهُ ... جَـزَاءَ مَنْ يَبْـنِي عَلَى أُسِّـهِ
وَكِـلْتُ لِلْخِلِّ كَمَا كَالَ لِي ... عَلَى وَفَـاءِ الْكَيْـلِ أَوْ بَخْسِـهِ
وَلَمْ أُخَـسِّـرْهُ وَشَـرُّ الْوَرَى ... مَنْ يَوْمُـهُ أَخْـسَرُ مِنْ أَمْسِـهِ
وَكُلُّ مَنْ يَطْلُبُ عِنْدِي جَنًى ... فَـمَا لَهُ إِلَّا جَـنَى غَـرْسِـهِ
لَا أَبْتَـغِي الْغَـبْنَ وَلَا أَنْثَـنِي ... بِصَفْقَـةِ الْمَغْبُونِ فِي حِسِّـهِ
وَلَسْـتُ بِـالْمُوجِبِ حَـقًّا لِمَنْ ... لَا يُوجِـبُ الْحَقَّ عَلَى نَفْسِـهِ
وَرُبَّ مَـذَّاقِ[1] الْهَوَى خَـالَنِي ... أَصْـدُقُـهُ الْوُدَّ عَـلَى لَبْسِـهِ
وَمَــا دَرَى مِنْ جَـهْـلِهِ أَنَّنِي ... أَقْضِي غَرِيمِي الدَّيْنَ مِنْ جِنْسِهِ
فَاهْجُرْ مَنِ ٱسْتَغْبَاكَ هَجْرَ الْقِلَى ... وَهَبْـهُ كَالْمَلْحُودِ فِي رَمْسِـهِ
وَٱلْبَسْ لِمَنْ فِي وَصْلِهِ لُبْسَةٌ ... لِبَاسَ مَنْ يَـرْغَبُ عَنْ أُنْسِـهِ
وَلَا تُـرَجِّ الْوُدَّ مِـمَّنْ يَـرَى ... أَنَّكَ مُحْتَـاجٌ إِلَى فَـلْسِـهِ

٧،٤ قَالَ الْحَارِثُ بْنُ هَمَّامٍ. فَلَمَّا وَعَيْتُ مَا دَارَ بَيْنَهُمَا. تُقْتُ إِلَى أَنْ أَعْرِفَ عَيْنَهُمَا. فَلَمَّا لَاحَ ٱبْنُ ذُكَاءَ. وَأَلْحَفَ الْجَوَّ الضِّيَاءَ. غَدَوْتُ قَبْلَ ٱسْتِقْلَالِ الرِّكَابِ. وَلَا ٱغْتِدَاءَ الْغُرَابِ. وَجَعَلْتُ أَسْتَقْرِي صَوْبَ الصَّوْتِ اللَّيْلِيِّ. وَأَتَوَسَّمُ الْوُجُوهَ بِالنَّظَرِ الْجَلِيِّ. إِلَى أَنْ لَمَحْتُ أَبَا زَيْدٍ وَٱبْنَهُ يَتَحَادَثَانِ. وَعَلَيْهِمَا بُرْدَانِ رَثَّانِ. فَعَلِمْتُ أَنَّهُمَا نَجِيَّا لَيْلَتِي. وَمُسْنَدَا[2] رِوَايَتِي. فَقَصَدْتُهُمَا قَصْدَ كَلِفٍ بِدَمَاثَتِهِمَا. رَاثٍ لِرَثَاثَتِهِمَا. وَأَبْحْتُهُمَا التَّحَوُّلَ إِلَى رَحْلِي. وَالتَّحَكُّمَ فِي كُثْرِي وَقُلِّي. وَطَفِقْتُ أُسَيِّرُ بَيْنَ السَّيَّارَةِ فَضْلَهُمَا. وَأَهُزُّ الْأَعْوَادَ الْمُثْمِرَةَ لَهُمَا. حَتَّى[3] غُمِرَا بِالنُّحْلَانِ. وَٱتُّخِذَا[4] مِنَ الْخُلَّانِ. وَكُنَّا بِمُعَرَّسٍ نَتَبَيَّنُ مِنْهُ بُنْيَانَ الْقُرَى. وَنَتَنَوَّرُ نِيرَانَ الْقِرَى.

١ في هاشية د: مُذَّلق. ٢ هكذا في هامش ق، ومتنَيْ س، و؛ وفي متنَيْ ق، ف: صاحِبَا؛ وفي هامش س: مُعْتَزَى.
٣ هكذا في هامش ق، وفي س، د؛ وفي و، ف: إلى أن. ٤ و: اتُّخِذَ.

فَلَمَّا رَأَى أَبُو زَيْدٍ ٱمْتِلَاءَ كِيسِهِ. وَٱنْجِلَاءَ بُؤْسِهِ. قَالَ لِي إِنَّ بَدَنِي قَدِ ٱتَّسَخَ. وَدَرَنِي قَدْ رَسَخَ. أَفَتَأْذَنُ لِي فِي قَصْدِ قَرْيَةٍ لِأَسْتَحِمَّ. وَأَقْضِيَ هٰذَا ٱلْمُهِمَّ.

فَقُلْتُ إِذَا شِئْتَ فَالسُّرْعَةَ السُّرْعَةَ. وَالرَّجْعَةَ الرَّجْعَةَ. فَقَالَ سَتَجِدُ مَطْلَعِي ٨،٤
عَلَيْكَ. أَسْرَعَ مِنِ ٱرْتِدَادِ طَرْفِكَ إِلَيْكَ. ثُمَّ ٱسْتَنَّ ٱسْتِنَانَ ٱلْجَوَادِ فِي ٱلْمِضْمَارِ. وَقَالَ لِٱبْنِهِ بَدَارِ بَدَارِ. وَلَمْ نَخَلْ أَنَّهُ غَرَّ. وَطَلَبَ ٱلْمَفَرَّ. فَلَبِثْنَا نَرْقُبُهُ رِقْبَةَ[1] ٱلْأَعْيَادِ. وَنَسْتَطْلِعُهُ بِالطَّلَائِعِ وَالرُّوَّادِ. إِلَى أَنْ هَرِمَ النَّهَارُ. وَكَادَ جُرْفُ[2] ٱلْيَوْمِ يَنْهَارُ. فَلَمَّا طَالَ أَمَدُ الِانْتِظَارِ. وَلَاحَتِ الشَّمْسُ فِي ٱلْأَطْمَارِ. قُلْتُ لِأَصْحَابِي قَدْ تَنَاهَيْنَا فِي ٱلْمُهْلَةِ. وَتَمَادَيْنَا فِي الرِّحْلَةِ. إِلَى أَنْ أَضَعْنَا الزَّمَانَ. وَبَانَ أَنَّ الرَّجُلَ مَانَ.[3] فَتَأَهَّبُوا لِلظَّعْنِ. وَلَا تَلْوُوا عَلَى خَضْرَاءِ الدِّمَنِ.

وَنَهَضْتُ لِأَحْدِجَ رَاحِلَتِي. وَأَتَحَمَّلَ لِرِحْلَتِي. فَوَجَدْتُ أَبَا زَيْدٍ قَدْ كَتَبَ. ٩،٤
عَلَى ٱلْقَتَبِ.

يَا مَنْ غَدَا لِي سَاعِدًا وَمُسَاعِدًا دُونَ ٱلْبَشَرْ
لَا تَحْسَبَنْ أَنِّي نَأَيْتُكَ عَنْ مَلَالٍ أَوْ أَشَرْ
لٰكِنَّنِي مُذْ لَمْ أَزَلْ مِمَّنْ إِذَا طَعِمَ ٱنْتَشَرْ

قَالَ فَأَقْرَأْتُ ٱلْجَمَاعَةَ ٱلْقَتَبَ. لِيَعْذِرَهُ مَنْ كَانَ عَتَبَ. فَأُعْجِبُوا بِخُرَافَتِهِ. وَتَعَوَّذُوا مِنْ آفَتِهِ. ثُمَّ إِنَّا ظَعَنَّا. وَلَمْ نَدْرِ مَنِ ٱعْتَاضَ عَنَّا.

١ بعدها في د: أَهِلَّة. ٢ د، ف: جُرُف. ٣ ف: قد مان.

المَقَامَةُ الخَامِسَةُ[1]

١،٥ حَكَى الحَارِثُ بْنُ هَمَّامٍ قَالَ سَمَرْتُ بِالْكُوفَةِ فِي لَيْلَةٍ أَدِيمُهَا ذُو لَوْنَيْنِ. وَقَمَرُهَا كَتَعْوِيذٍ مِنْ لُجَيْنٍ.[2] مَعَ رُفْقَةٍ غُذُوا بِلِبَانِ الْبَيَانِ. وَسَحَبُوا عَلَى سَحْبَانَ ذَيْلَ النِّسْيَانِ. مَا فِيهِمْ إِلَّا مَنْ يُحْفَظُ عَنْهُ وَلَا يُتَحَفَّظُ مِنْهُ. وَيَمِيلُ الرَّفِيقُ إِلَيْهِ وَلَا يَمِيلُ عَنْهُ. فَاسْتَهْوَانَا السَّمَرُ. إِلَى أَنْ غَرَبَ الْقَمَرُ. وَغَلَبَ السَّهَرُ. فَلَمَّا رَوَّقَ اللَّيْلُ الْبَهِيمُ. وَلَمْ يَبْقَ إِلَّا التَّهْوِيمُ. سَمِعْنَا مِنَ الْبَابِ نَبْأَةَ مُسْتَنْبِحٍ. ثُمَّ تَلَتْهَا صَكَّةُ مُسْتَفْتِحٍ. فَقُلْنَا مَنِ الْمُلِمُّ فِي اللَّيْلِ الْمُدْلَهِمِّ.

٢،٥ فَقَالَ

يَا أَهْلَ ذَا ٱلْمَغْنَى وُقِيتُمْ شَرَّا   وَلَا لَقِيتُمْ مَا بَقِيتُمْ ضُرَّا
قَدْ دَفَعَ اللَّيْلُ ٱلَّذِي ٱكْفَهَرَّا   إِلَى ذَرَاكُمْ شَعِثًا مُغْبَرَّا
أَخَا سِفَارٍ طَالَ وَٱسْبَطَرَّا   حَتَّى ٱنْثَنَى مُحْقَوْقِفًا مُصْفَرَّا
مِثْلَ هِلَالِ ٱلْأُفْقِ حِينَ ٱفْتَرَّا   وَقَدْ عَرَا فِنَاءَكُمْ مُعْتَرَّا
وَأَمَّكُمْ دُونَ ٱلْأَنَامِ طُرَّا   يَبْغِي قِرًى وَمِنْكُمُ مُسْتَقَرَّا
فَدُونَكُمْ ضَيْفًا قَنُوعًا حُرَّا   يَرْضَى بِمَا أَحْلَوْلَى وَمَا أَمَرَّا
وَيَنْثَنِي عَنْكُمْ يَنُثُّ الْبِرَّا

٣،٥ قَالَ الحَارِثُ بْنُ هَمَّامٍ فَلَمَّا خَلَبَنَا[3] بِعُذُوبَةِ نُطْقِهِ. وَعَلِمْنَا مَا وَرَاءَ بَرْقِهِ. ابْتَدَرْنَا فَتْحَ الْبَابِ. وَتَلَقَّيْنَاهُ بِالتَّرْحَابِ. وَقُلْنَا لِلْغُلَامِ هَيَّا هَيَّا. وَهَلُمَّ مَا تَهَيَّا. فَقَالَ الضَّيْفُ

---

١ في هامش ق وهامش س: تُعْرَفُ بِالكُوفِيَّةِ، في ف: وَهْيَ الكُوفِيَّةُ، وفي د: الكُوفِيَّةُ. ٢ في ف: لُجَيْنٍ. ٣ د: خُبِلْنَا.

وَالَّذِي أَحَلَّنِي ذَرَاكُمْ.[١] لَا تَلَمَّظْتُ بِقِرَاكُمْ.[٢] أَوْ تَضْمَنُوا لِي أَنْ لَا تَتَّخِذُونِي كَلًّا. وَلَا تَجَشَّمُوا لِأَجْلِي أَكْلًا.[٣] فَرُبَّ أَكْلَةٍ هَاضَتِ ٱلْآكِلَ. وَحَرَمَتْهُ مَآكِلَ. وَشَرُّ ٱلْأَضْيَافِ مَنْ سَامَ ٱلتَّكْلِيفَ. وَآذَى ٱلْمُضِيفَ. وَخُصُوصًا أَذًى يَعْتَلِقُ بِٱلْأَجْسَامِ. وَيُفْضِي إِلَى ٱلْأَسْقَامِ. وَمَا قِيلَ فِي ٱلْمَثَلِ ٱلَّذِي سَارَ سَائِرُهُ. خَيْرُ ٱلْعَشَاءِ سَوَافِرُهُ. إِلَّا لِيُعَجَّلَ التَّعَشِّي. وَيُجْتَنَبَ أَكْلُ اللَّيْلِ ٱلَّذِي يُعْشِي.[٤] اللّٰهُمَّ إِلَّا أَنْ تَقِدَ نَارُ الْجُوعِ. وَتَحُولَ دُونَ ٱلْهُجُوعِ.

٤،٥ قَالَ فَكَأَنَّهُ أُطْلِعَ[٥] عَلَى إِرَادَتِنَا فَرَمَى عَنْ قَوْسِ عَقِيدَتِنَا. لَا جَرَمَ أَنَّا[٦] آنَسْنَاهُ بِٱلْتِزَامِ الشَّرْطِ. وَأَثْنَيْنَا[٧] عَلَى خُلُقِهِ[٨] السَّبْطِ. وَلَمَّا[٩] أَحْضَرَ ٱلْغُلَامُ مَا رَاجَ. وَأُذْكِيَ بَيْنَنَا السِّرَاجَ. تَأَمَّلْتُهُ فَإِذَا هُوَ أَبُو زَيْدٍ. فَقُلْتُ لِصَحْبِي لِيَهْنِكُمُ[١٠] الضَّيْفُ ٱلْوَارِدُ بَلِ ٱلْمَغْنَمُ ٱلْبَارِدُ. فَإِنْ يَكُنْ أَفَلَ قَمَرُ الشِّعْرَى فَقَدْ طَلَعَ قَمَرُ الشِّعْرِ. أَوِ ٱسْتَسَرَّ بَدْرُ النَّثْرَةِ فَقَدْ تَبَلَّجَ بَدْرُ النَّثْرِ. فَسَرَتْ حُمَيَّا ٱلْمَسَرَّةِ فِيهِمْ. وَطَارَتِ السِّنَةُ عَنْ مَآقِيهِمْ. وَرَفَضُوا الدَّعَةَ ٱلَّتِي كَانُوا نَوَوْهَا. وَثَابُوا إِلَى نَشْرِ ٱلْفُكَاهَةِ بَعْدَ مَا طَوَوْهَا. وَأَبُو زَيْدٍ مُكِبٌّ عَلَى إِعْمَالِ يَدَيْهِ. حَتَّى إِذَا ٱسْتَرْفَعَ مَا لَدَيْهِ. قُلْتُ لَهُ أَطْرِفْنَا بِغَرِيبَةٍ مِنْ غَرَائِبِ أَسْمَارِكَ. أَوْ عَجِيبَةٍ مِنْ عَجَائِبِ أَسْفَارِكَ. فَقَالَ لَقَدْ بَلَوْتُ مِنَ ٱلْعَجَائِبِ مَا لَمْ يَرَهُ الرَّاؤُونَ. وَلَا رَوَاهُ الرَّاوُونَ. وَإِنَّ مِنْ أَعْجَبِهَا مَا عَايَنْتُهُ اللَّيْلَةَ قُبَيْلَ ٱنْتِيَابِكُمْ. وَمَصِيرِي إِلَى بَابِكُمْ. فَٱسْتَخْبَرْنَاهُ عَنْ طُرْفَةِ مَرْآهُ. فِي مَسْرَحِ مَسْرَاهُ.

٥،٥ فَقَالَ إِنَّ مَرَامِيَ ٱلْغُرْبَةِ. لَفَظَتْنِي إِلَى هٰذِهِ التُّرْبَةِ. وَأَنَا ذُو مَجَاعَةٍ وَبُوسَى. وَجِرَابٍ كَفُؤَادِ أُمِّ مُوسَى. فَنَهَضْتُ حِينَ سَجَى الدُّجَى. عَلَى مَا بِي مِنَ ٱلْوَجَى. لِأَرْتَادَ

---

١ د: ذَرَيْكُمْ؛ ف: ذَارَكُمْ. ٢ د: بِقِرَيْكُمْ. ٣ د: أُكْلًا. ٤ د: يعشّي. ٥ ف، و: آطَّلَعَ. ٦ د: إِنَّا. ٧ د: أَثْنَيْنَاهُ.
٨ د: خُلْقه. ٩ د: فَلَمَّا. ١٠ هكذا في ق، س، د، وفي د: يهنئك، وهي مطموسة في و.

مُضِيفًا. أَوْ أَقْتَادَ رَغِيفًا. فَسَاقَنِي حَادِي السَّغَبِ. وَالْقَضَاءُ الْمُكَنَّى أَبَا الْعَجَبِ. إِلَى أَنْ وَقَفْتُ عَلَى بَابِ دَارٍ. فَقُلْتُ عَلَى بِدَارٍ.

٦،٥ حُيِّيتُمُ يَا أَهْلَ هٰذَا الْمَنْزِلِ   وَعِشْتُمُ فِي خَفْضِ عَيْشٍ خَضِلِ
مَا عِنْدَكُمْ لِابْنِ سَبِيلٍ مُرْمِلِ   نِضْوِ سُرًى خَابِطِ لَيْلٍ أَلْيَلِ
جَوِي الْحَشَى عَلَى الطَّوَى مُشْتَمِلِ   مَا ذَاقَ مُذْ يَوْمَانِ طَعْمَ مَأْكَلِ
وَلَا لَهُ فِي أَرْضِكُمْ مِنْ مَوْئِلِ   وَقَدْ دَجَى جُنْحُ الظَّلَامِ الْمُسْبَلِ
وَهْوَ مِنَ الْحَيْرَةِ فِي تَمَلْمُلِ   فَهَلْ بِهٰذَا الرَّبْعِ عَذْبُ الْمَنْهَلِ
يَقُولُ لِي أَلْقِ عَصَاكَ وَٱدْخُلِ   وَٱبْشِرْ[١] بِبِشْرٍ وَقِرًى مُعَجَّلِ

٧،٥ قَالَ فَبَرَزَ إِلَيَّ جُوذَرٌ. عَلَيْهِ شَوْذَرٌ. وَقَالَ

وَحُرْمَةِ الشَّيْخِ ٱلَّذِي سَنَّ الْقِرَى   وَأَسَّسَ الْمَحْجُوجَ فِي أُمِّ الْقُرَى
مَا عِنْدَنَا لِطَارِقٍ إِذَا عَرَا   سِوَى الْحَدِيثِ وَالْمُنَاخِ فِي الذَّرَى
وَكَيْفَ يَقْرِي مَنْ نَفَى عَنْهُ الْكَرَى   طَوًى بَرَى أَعْظُمَهُ لَمَّا ٱنْبَرَى[٢]
فَمَا تَرَى فِيمَا ذَكَرْتُ مَا تَرَى

٨،٥ فَقُلْتُ مَا أَصْنَعُ بِمَنْزِلٍ قَفْرٍ. وَمُنْزِلٍ[٣] حِلْفِ فَقْرٍ. وَلٰكِنْ يَا فَتَى مَا ٱسْمُكَ. فَقَدْ فَتَنَنِي فَهْمُكَ. فَقَالَ ٱسْمِي زَيْدٌ. وَمَنْشَأِي[٤] فَيْدٌ. وَوَرَدْتُ هٰذِهِ الْمَدَرَةَ أَمْسِ. مَعَ أَخْوَالِي مِنْ بَنِي عَبْسٍ. فَقُلْتُ لَهُ زِدْنِي إِيضَاحًا عِشْتَ وَنُعِشْتَ. فَقَالَ أَخْبَرَتْنِي أُمِّي بَرَّةُ. وَهِيَ كَٱسْمِهَا بَرَّةٌ. أَنَّهَا نَكَحَتْ عَامَ الْغَارَةِ بِمَاوَانَ. رَجُلًا مِنْ سَرَاةِ سَرُوجَ وَغَسَّانَ. فَلَمَّا آنَسَ مِنْهَا الْإِثْقَالَ. وَكَانَ بَاقِعَةً عَلَى مَا يُقَالُ. ظَعَنَ

---

١ د: أَبْشِرْ. ٢ «وكيف... انبرى» ساقط من ف. ٣ ف: مَنْزِلٍ. ٤ بهذا الرسم في ق، س، و؛ وفي ف: مَنْشِئِ.

عَنْهَا سِرًّا. وَهَلُمَّ جَرًّا. فَمَا يُعْرَفُ أَحَيٌّ هُوَ فَيُتَوَقَّعَ. أَمْ أُودِعَ اللَّحْدَ الْبَلْقَعَ. قَالَ أَبُو زَيْدٍ فَعَلِمْتُ بِصِحَّةِ الْعَلَامَاتِ أَنَّهُ وَلَدِي. وَصَدَفَنِي عَنِ التَّعَرُّفِ إِلَيْهِ صِفْرُ يَدِي. فَفَصَلْتُ عَنْهُ بِكَبِدٍ مَرْضُوضَةٍ. وَدُمُوعٍ مَفْضُوضَةٍ. فَهَلْ سَمِعْتُمْ يَا أُولِي الْأَلْبَابِ. بِأَعْجَبَ مِنْ هٰذَا الْعُجَابِ. فَقُلْنَا[1] لَا وَمَنْ عِنْدَهُ عِلْمُ الْكِتَابِ. فَقَالَ أَثْبِتُوهَا فِي عَجَائِبِ الِاتِّفَاقِ. وَخَلِّدُوهَا بُطُونَ الْأَوْرَاقِ. فَمَا سُيِّرَ مِثْلُهَا فِي الْآفَاقِ. فَأَحْضَرْنَا الدَّوَاةَ وَأَسَاوِدَهَا. وَرَقَشْنَا الْحِكَايَةَ عَلَى مَا سَرَدَهَا. ثُمَّ ٱسْتَنْبَطْنَاهُ[2] عَنْ مُرْتَاهُ. فِي ٱسْتِضْمَامِ فَتَاهُ. فَقَالَ إِذَا ثَقُلَ رُدْنِي. خَفَّ عَلَيَّ أَنْ أَكْفُلَ ٱبْنِي. فَقُلْنَا إِنْ كَانَ يَكْفِيكَ نِصَابٌ مِنَ الْمَالِ. أَلَّفْنَاهُ لَكَ فِي الْحَالِ. فَقَالَ وَكَيْفَ لَا يُقْنِعُنِي نِصَابٌ. وَهَلْ يَحْتَقِرُ قَدْرَهُ إِلَّا مُصَابٌ.

٩٫٥ قَالَ الرَّاوِي فَٱلْتَزَمَ مِنْهُ كُلٌّ مِنَّا قِسْطًا. وَكَتَبَ لَهُ بِهِ قِطًّا. فَشَكَرَ عِنْدَ ذٰلِكَ الصُّنْعَ. وَٱسْتَنْفَدَ فِي الثَّنَاءِ الْوُسْعَ. حَتَّى أَنَّنَا ٱسْتَطَلْنَا الْقَوْلَ. وَٱسْتَقْلَلْنَا الطَّوْلَ. ثُمَّ إِنَّهُ نَشَرَ مِنْ وَشْيِ السَّمَرِ. مَا أَزْرَى بِالْحِبَرِ. إِلَى أَنْ أَظَلَّ التَّنْوِيرُ. وَجَشَرَ الصُّبْحُ الْمُنِيرُ. فَقَضَّيْنَاهَا لَيْلَةً غَابَتْ شَوَائِبُهَا إِلَى أَنْ شَابَتْ ذَوَائِبُهَا. وَكَمُلَ سُعُودُهَا إِلَى أَنِ ٱنْفَطَرَ عُودُهَا. وَلَمَّا ذَرَّ قَرْنُ الْغَزَالَةِ. طَمَرَ طُمُورَ الْغَزَالَةِ. وَقَالَ ٱنْهَضْ بِنَا لِنَقْبِضَ الصِّلَاتَ. وَنَسْتَنِضَّ الْإِحَالَاتِ. فَقَدِ ٱسْتَطَارَتْ صُدُوعُ كَبِدِي. مِنَ الْحَنِينِ إِلَى وَلَدِي. فَوَصَلْتُ جَنَاحَهُ. حَتَّى سَنَّيْتُ نَجَاحَهُ. فَحِينَ أَحْرَزَ الْعَيْنَ فِي صُرَّتِهِ. بَرَقَتْ أَسَارِيرُ مَسَرَّتِهِ. وَقَالَ لِي جُزِيتَ خَيْرًا عَنْ خُطَا قَدَمَيْكَ. وَاللهُ خَلِيفَتِي عَلَيْكَ. فَقُلْتُ أُرِيدُ أَنْ أَتَّبِعَكَ لِأُشَاهِدَ وَلَدَكَ النَّجِيبَ. وَأُنَافِثَهُ لِكَيْمَا[3] يُجِيبَ. فَنَظَرَ إِلَيَّ نَظْرَةَ الْخَادِعِ إِلَى الْمَخْدُوعِ. وَضَحِكَ حَتَّى تَغَرْغَرَتْ مُقْلَتَاهُ بِالدُّمُوعِ. ثُمَّ أَنْشَدَ

١ د: قلنا. ٢ ف: اسْتَبْطَنَّاه. ٢ س، و: لكي.

يَا مَنْ تَظَنَّى السَّرَابَ مَاءً   لَمَّا رَوَيْتُ ٱلَّذِي رَوَيْتُ ١٠٫٥
مَا خِلْتُ أَنْ يَسْتَسِرَّ مَكْرِي   وَأَنْ يُخِيلَ ٱلَّذِي عَنَيْتُ
وَاللهِ مَا بَرَّةٌ بِعِرْسِي   وَلَا لِيَ ٱبْنٌ بِهِ ٱكْتَنَيْتُ
وَإِنَّمَا لِي فُنُونُ سِحْرٍ   أَبْدَعْتُ فِيهَا وَمَا ٱقْتَدَيْتُ
لَمْ يَحْكِهَا الْأَصْمَعِيُّ فِيمَا   حَكَى وَلَا حَاكَهَا الْكُمَيْتُ
تَخِذْتُهَا وُصْلَةً إِلَى مَا   تَجْنِيهِ كَفِّي مَتَى اشْتَهَيْتُ
وَلَوْ تَعَافَيْتُهَا لَحَالَتْ   حَالِي وَلَمْ أَحْوِ مَا حَوَيْتُ
فَمَهِّدِ الْعُذْرَ أَوْ فَسَامِحْ   إِنْ كُنْتُ أَجْرَمْتُ أَوْ جَنَيْتُ

ثُمَّ إِنَّهُ وَدَّعَنِي وَمَضَى. وَأَوْدَعَ قَلْبِي جَمْرَ الْغَضَا.

ٱلْمَقَامَةُ ٱلسَّادِسَةُ[١]

١،٦ رَوَى ٱلْحَارِثُ بْنُ هَمَّامٍ قَالَ حَضَرْتُ دِيوَانَ ٱلنَّظَرِ بِٱلْمَرَاغَةِ. وَقَدْ جَرَى بِهِ ذِكْرُ ٱلْبَلَاغَةِ. فَأَجْمَعَ مَنْ حَضَرَ مِنْ فُرْسَانِ ٱلْيَرَاعَةِ. وَأَرْبَابِ ٱلْبَرَاعَةِ. عَلَى أَنَّهُ لَمْ يَبْقَ مَنْ يُنَقِّحُ ٱلْإِنْشَاءَ. وَيَتَصَرَّفُ فِيهِ كَيْفَ شَاءَ. وَلَا خَلَفَ. بَعْدَ ٱلسَّلَفِ. مَنْ يَبْتَدِعُ طَرِيقَةً غَرَّاءَ. أَوْ يَفْتَرِعُ[٢] رِسَالَةً عَذْرَاءَ. وَأَنَّ ٱلْمُفْلِقَ مِنْ كُتَّابِ هٰذَا ٱلْأَوَانِ. ٱلْمُتَمَكِّنَ مِنْ أَزِمَّةِ ٱلْبَيَانِ. كَٱلْعِيَالِ عَلَى ٱلْأَوَائِلِ. وَلَوْ مَلَكَ فَصَاحَةَ سَحْبَانِ وَائِلٍ.

٢،٦ وَكَانَ بِٱلْمَجْلِسِ كَهْلٌ جَالِسٌ فِي ٱلْحَاشِيَةِ. عِنْدَ مَوَاقِفِ ٱلْحَاشِيَةِ. فَكَانَ كُلَّمَا شَطَّ ٱلْقَوْمُ فِي شَوْطِهِمْ. وَنَثَرُوا ٱلْعَجْوَةَ وَٱلنَّجْوَةَ مِنْ نَوْطِهِمْ. يُنْبِئُ تَخَازُرُ طَرْفِهِ. وَتَشَامُخُ أَنْفِهِ. أَنَّهُ مُخْرَنْبِقٌ لِيَنْبَاعَ. وَمُجْرَمِّزٌ سَيَمُدُّ ٱلْبَاعَ. وَنَابِضٌ يَبْرِي ٱلنِّبَالَ. وَرَابِضٌ يَبْغِي ٱلنِّضَالَ. فَلَمَّا نُثِلَتِ ٱلْكَنَائِنُ. وَفَاءَتِ ٱلسَّكَائِنُ. وَرَكَدَتِ ٱلزَّعَازِعُ. وَكَفَّ ٱلْمُنَازِعُ.[٣] أَقْبَلَ عَلَى ٱلْجَمَاعَةِ وَقَالَ.

٣،٦ لَقَدْ جِئْتُمْ شَيْئًا إِدًّا. وَجُرْتُمْ عَنِ ٱلْقَصْدِ جِدًّا. وَعَظَّمْتُمُ ٱلْعِظَامَ ٱلرُّفَاتَ. وَٱفْتَتُّمْ فِي ٱلْمَيْلِ إِلَى مَنْ فَاتَ. وَغَمَصْتُمْ جِيلَكُمُ ٱلَّذِينَ فِيهِمْ لَكُمُ ٱللِّدَاتُ. وَمَعَهُمُ ٱنْعَقَدَتِ ٱلْمَوَدَّاتُ. أَأُنْسِيتُمْ[٤] يَا جَهَابِذَةَ ٱلنَّقْدِ. وَمَوَابِذَةَ ٱلْحَلِّ وَٱلْعَقْدِ. مَا أَبْرَزَتْهُ طَوَارِفُ ٱلْقَرَائِحِ. وَبَرَّزَ فِيهِ ٱلْجَذَعُ عَلَى ٱلْقَارِحِ. مِنَ ٱلْعِبَارَاتِ ٱلْمُهَذَّبَةِ. وَٱلِٱسْتِعَارَاتِ ٱلْمُسْتَعْذَبَةِ. وَٱلرَّسَائِلِ ٱلْمُوَشَّحَةِ. وَٱلْأَسَاجِيعِ ٱلْمُسْتَمْلَحَةِ. وَهَلْ لِلْقُدَمَاءِ إِذَا أُنْعِمَ ٱلنَّظَرُ. مَنْ حَضَرَ. غَيْرُ ٱلْمَعَانِي ٱلْمَطْرُوقَةِ ٱلْمَوَارِدِ. ٱلْمَعْقُولَةِ ٱلشَّوَارِدِ.

---

١ في هامش ق، وهامش س: وتُعرف بالحَيْفاء، وفي د: الحيفاء، وفي ف: وهي الحيفاء. ٢ د: يقترع. ٣ بعدها في د: وسكنَتِ الزَّماجِرُ. وسكَتَ المزجورُ والزَّاجِرُ. ٤ د: أَنْسِيتُم.

الْمَأْثُورَةِ عَنْهُمْ لِتَقَادُمِ الْمَوَالِدِ. لَا لِتَقَدُّمِ الصَّادِرِ عَلَى الْوَارِدِ. وَإِنِّي لَأَعْرِفُ الْآنَ مَنْ إِذَا أَنْشَا.[1] وَشَّى. وَإِذَا عَبَّرَ. حَبَّرَ. وَإِنْ أَسْهَبَ. أَذْهَبَ. وَإِذَا أَوْجَزَ. أَعْجَزَ. وَإِنْ بَدَهَ. شَدَهَ. وَمَتَى ٱخْتَرَعَ. خَرَعَ.

٤،٦ فَقَالَ لَهُ نَاظُورَةُ الدِّيوَانِ. وَعَيْنُ أُولَٰئِكَ الْأَعْيَانِ. مَنْ قَارِعُ هَٰذِهِ الصَّفَاةِ. وَقَرِيعُ هَٰذِهِ الصِّفَاتِ. فَقَالَ إِنَّهُ قِرْنُ مَجَالِكَ. وَقَرِينُ جِدَالِكَ. وَإِذَا شِئْتَ فَرُضْ نَجِيبًا. وَٱدْعُ مُجِيبًا. لِتَرَى عَجِيبًا. فَقَالَ لَهُ يَا هَٰذَا إِنَّ الْبُغَاثَ[2] بِأَرْضِنَا لَا يَسْتَنْسِرُ. وَالتَّمْيِيزَ عِنْدَنَا بَيْنَ الْفِضَّةِ وَالْقِضَّةِ مُتَيَسِّرٌ. وَقَلَّ مَنِ ٱسْتَهْدَفَ لِلنِّضَالِ. فَخَلَصَ مِنَ الدَّاءِ الْعُضَالِ. أَوِ ٱسْتَثَارَ نَقْعَ الِامْتِحَانِ. فَلَمْ يُقْذَ بِالِامْتِهَانِ. فَلَا تُعَرِّضْ عِرْضَكَ لِلْمَفَاضِحِ. وَلَا تُعْرِضْ عَنْ نَصَاحَةِ النَّاصِحِ. فَقَالَ كُلُّ ٱمْرِئٍ أَعْرَفُ بِوَسْمِ قِدْحِهِ. وَسَيَتَفَرَّى اللَّيْلُ عَنْ صُبْحِهِ. فَتَنَاجَتِ الْجَمَاعَةُ فِيمَا يُسْبَرُ بِهِ قَلِيبُهُ. وَيُعْمَدُ فِيهِ تَقْلِيبُهُ.

٥،٦ فَقَالَ أَحَدُهُمْ ذَرُوهُ فِي حِصَّتِي. لِأَرْمِيَهُ بِحَجَرِ قِصَّتِي. فَإِنَّهَا عُضْلَةُ الْعُقَدِ. وَمِحَكُّ الْمُنْتَقِدِ. فَقَلَّدُوهُ فِي هَٰذَا الْأَمْرِ الزَّعَامَةَ. تَقْلِيدَ الْخَوَارِجِ أَبَا نَعَامَةَ. فَأَقْبَلَ عَلَى الْكَهْلِ وَقَالَ ٱعْلَمْ أَنِّي أُوَالِي. هَٰذَا الْوَالِي. وَأُرَفِّحُ حَالِي. بِالْبَيَانِ الْحَالِي. وَكُنْتُ أَسْتَعِينُ عَلَى تَقْوِيمِ أَوَدِي. فِي بَلَدِي. بِسَعَةِ ذَاتِ يَدِي. مَعَ قِلَّةِ عَدَدِي. فَلَمَّا ثَقُلَ حَاذِي. وَنَفِدَ رَذَاذِي. أَمَّمْتُهُ[3] مِنْ أَرْجَائِي. بِرَجَائِي. وَدَعَوْتُهُ لِإِعَادَةِ رُوَائِي وَإِرْوَائِي. فَهَشَّ لِلْوِفَادَةِ وَٱرْتَاحَ. وَغَدَا بِالْإِفَادَةِ وَرَاحَ. فَلَمَّا ٱسْتَأْذَنْتُهُ فِي الْمُرَاحِ. إِلَى الْمُرَاحِ. عَلَى كَاهِلِ الْمِرَاحِ. قَالَ قَدْ أَزْمَعْتُ أَنْ لَا أُزَوِّدَكَ بَتَاتًا. وَلَا أَجْمَعَ لَكَ شَتَاتًا. أَوْ تُنْشِئَ أَمَامَ ٱرْتِحَالِكَ. رِسَالَةً تُودِعُهَا شَرْحَ حَالِكَ. حُرُوفُ إِحْدَى كَلِمَتَيْهَا يَعُمُّهَا النَّقْطُ. وَحُرُوفُ الْأُخْرَى لَمْ يُعْجَمْنَ قَطُّ. وَقَدِ ٱسْتَأْنَيْتُ

---

١ ق، س، د: أنشأ. ٢ د: البِغاث؛ ف: البُغاث. ٣ د: أَمَمْتُه.

بَيَانِي حَوْلًا . فَمَا أَحَارَ قَوْلًا . وَنَبَّهْتُ فِكْرِي سَنَةً . فَمَا ٱزْدَادَ إِلَّا سِنَةً . وَٱسْتَعَنْتُ بِقَاطِبَةِ ٱلْكُتَّابِ . فَكُلٌّ مِنْهُمْ قَطَّبَ وَتَابَ . فَإِنْ كُنْتَ صَدَعْتَ عَنْ وَصْفِكَ بِٱلْيَقِينِ . ﴿فَأْتِ بِآيَةٍ إِنْ كُنْتَ مِنَ ٱلصَّادِقِينَ﴾ .

فَقَالَ لَهُ لَقَدِ ٱسْتَسْعَيْتَ يَعْبُوبًا . وَٱسْتَسْقَيْتَ أُسْكُوبًا . وَأَعْطَيْتَ ٱلْقَوْسَ بَارِيَهَا . ٦،٦
وَأَنْزَلْتَ ٱلدَّارَ بَانِيَهَا . ثُمَّ فَكَّرَ رَيْثَمَا ٱسْتَجَمَّ قَرِيحَتَهُ . وَٱسْتَدَرَّ لِقْحَتَهُ . وَقَالَ أَلْقِ دَوَاتَكَ . [1] وَخُذْ أَدَاتَكَ . وَٱكْتُبْ .

ٱلْكَرَمُ ثَبَّتَ ٱللهُ جَيْشَ سُعُودِكَ يَزِينُ . وَٱللُّؤْمُ غَضَّ ٱلدَّهْرُ جَفْنَ حَسُودِكَ يَشِينُ . وَٱلْأَرْوَعُ يُثِيبُ . وَٱلْمُعْوِرُ يُخِيبُ . وَٱلْحُلَاحِلُ يُضِيفُ . وَٱلْمَاحِلُ يُخِيفُ . وَٱلسَّمْحُ يُغْذِي . وَٱلْمَحِكُ [2] يُقْذِي . وَٱلْعَطَاءُ يُنْجِي . وَٱلْمِطَالُ يُشْجِي . وَٱلدُّعَاءُ يَقِي . وَٱلْمَدْحُ يُنَقِّي . وَٱلْحُرُّ يَجْزِي . وَٱلْإِلْطَاطُ يُخْزِي . وَٱطِّرَاحُ ذِي ٱلْحُرْمَةِ غَيٌّ . وَمَحْرَمَةُ بَنِي ٱلْآمَالِ بَغْيٌ . وَمَا ضَنَّ إِلَّا غَبِينٌ . وَلَا غَبِنَ إِلَّا ضَنِينٌ . وَلَا خَزَنَ إِلَّا شَقِيٌّ . وَلَا قَبَضَ رَاحَهُ تَقِيٌّ . وَمَا فَتِئَ وَعْدُكَ يَفِي . وَآرَاؤُكَ تَشْفِي . وَهِلَالُكَ يُضِي . وَحِلْمُكَ يُغْضِي . وَآلَاؤُكَ تُغْنِي . وَأَعْدَاؤُكَ تُثْنِي . وَحُسَامُكَ يُفْنِي . وَسُؤْدَدُكَ يُقْنِي . وَمُوَاصِلُكَ يَجْتَنِي . وَمَادِحُكَ يَقْتَنِي . وَسَمَاحُكَ يُغِيثُ . وَسَمَاؤُكَ تَغِيثُ . وَدَرُّكَ يَفِيضُ . وَرَدُّكَ يَغِيضُ . وَمُؤَمِّلُكَ شَيْخٌ حَكَاهُ فَيْءٌ . وَلَمْ يَبْقَ لَهُ شَيْءٌ . أَمَّكَ بِظَنٍّ حِرْصُهُ يَثِبُ . وَمَدَحَكَ بِنُخَبٍ . مُهُورُهَا تَجِبُ . وَمَرَامُهُ يَخِفُّ . وَأَوَاصِرُهُ تَشِفُّ . وَإِطْرَاؤُهُ يُجْتَذَبُ . وَمَلَامُهُ يُجْتَنَبُ . وَوَرَاءَهُ ضَفَفٌ . مَسَّهُمْ شَظَفٌ . وَحَصَّهُمْ جَنَفٌ . وَعَمَّهُمْ قَشَفٌ . وَهُوَ فِي دَمْعٍ يُجِيبُ . وَوَلَهٍ يُذِيبُ . وَهَمٍّ تَضَيَّفَ . وَكَمَدٍ نَيَّفَ . لِمَأْمُولٍ خَيَّبَ . وَإِهْمَالٍ شَيَّبَ . وَعَدُوٍّ نَيَّبَ . وَهُدُوٍّ تَغَيَّبَ . وَلَمْ يَزِغْ وُدُّهُ فَيُغْضَبَ . وَلَا خَبُثَ عُودُهُ فَيُقْضَبَ . وَلَا نَفَثَ صَدْرُهُ

١ بعدها في ف: وَاقْرُبْ. ٢ س، و: المَحْك.

فَيُنْفَضَ. وَلَا نَشْرَ وَصْلُهُ فَيُبْغَضَ. وَمَا يَقْتَضِي كَرَمُكَ نَبْذَ حُرَمِهِ. فَبَيِّضْ أَمَلَهُ بِتَخْفِيفِ أَلَمِهِ. يَبُثَّ[1] حَمْدَكَ بَيْنَ عَالَمِهِ. بَقِيتَ لِإِمَاطَةِ شَجَبٍ. وَإِعْطَاءِ نَشَبٍ. وَمُدَاوَاةِ شَجَنٍ. وَمُرَاعَاةِ يَفَنٍ. مَوْصُولاً بِخَفْضٍ. وَسُرُورٍ غَضٍّ. مَا غُشِيَ مَعْهَدُ غَنِيٍّ. أَوْ خُشِيَ وَهْمُ غَبِيٍّ. وَالسَّلَامُ.

٧،٦ فَلَمَّا فَرَغَ مِنْ إِمْلَاءِ رِسَالَتِهِ. وَجَلَّى فِي هَيْجَاءِ الْبَلَاغَةِ عَنْ بَسَالَتِهِ. أَرْضَتْهُ الْجَمَاعَةُ فِعْلاً وَقَوْلاً. وَأَوْسَعَتْهُ حَفَاوَةً وَطَوْلاً. ثُمَّ سُئِلَ مِنْ أَيِّ الشُّعُوبِ نِجَارُهُ. وَفِي أَيِّ الشِّعَابِ وِجَارُهُ. فَقَالَ

غَسَّانُ أُسْرَتِيَ الصَّمِيمَهْ   وَسَرُوجُ تُرْبَتِي الْقَدِيمَهْ
فَالبَيْتُ مِثْلُ الشَّمْسِ إِشْرَاقًا   وَمَنْزِلَةً جَسِيمَهْ
وَالرَّبْعُ كَالْفِرْدَوْسِ مَطْيَبَةً   وَمَنْزَهَةً وَقِيمَهْ
واهًا لِعَيْشٍ كَانَ لِي   فِيهَا وَلَذَّاتٍ عَمِيمَهْ
أَيَّامَ أَسْحَبُ مِطْرَفِي[2]   فِي رَوْضِهَا مَاضِي الْعَزِيمَهْ
أَخْتَالُ فِي بُرْدِ الشَّبَا   بِ وَأَجْتَلِي النِّعَمَ الْوَسِيمَهْ
لَا أَتَّقِي نُوَبَ الزَّمَا   نِ وَلَا حَوَادِثَهُ الْمُلِيمَهْ
فَلَوْ أَنَّ كَرْبًا مُتْلِفٌ   لَتَلِفْتُ مِنْ كُرَبِي الْمُقِيمَهْ
أَوْ يُفْتَدَى عَيْشٌ مَضَى   لَفَدَتْهُ مُهْجَتِيَ الْكَرِيمَهْ
فَالْمَوْتُ خَيْرٌ لِلْفَتَى   مِنْ عَيْشِهِ عَيْشَ الْبَهِيمَهْ
تَقْتَادُهُ بُرَةُ الصَّغَا   رِ إِلَى الْعَظِيمَةِ وَالْهَضِيمَهْ
وَيَرَى السِّبَاعَ تَنُوشُهَا   أَيْدِي الضِّبَاعِ الْمُسْتَضِيمَهْ

١ س، د، و، ف: يُنْثَ.   ٢ د، ف: مُطْرَفِي.

وَالذَّنْبُ لِلْأَيَّامِ لَوْ   لَا شُؤْمُهَا لَمْ تَنْبُ شِيمَهْ
وَلَوِ ٱسْتَقَامَتْ كَانَتِ الْـ   أَحْوَالُ فِيهَا مُسْتَقِيمَهْ

ثُمَّ إِنَّ خَبَرَهُ نَمَا إِلَى الْوَالِي. فَمَلَأَ فَاهُ بِاللَّآلِي. وَسَامَهُ أَنْ يَنْضَوِيَ إِلَى أَحْشَائِهِ. وَيَلِيَ دِيوَانَ إِنْشَائِهِ. فَأَحْسَبَهُ الْحِبَاءُ. وَظَلَفَهُ عَنِ الْوِلَايَةِ الْإِبَاءُ.

٨،٦ قَالَ الرَّاوِي وَكُنْتُ عَرَفْتُ عُودَ شَجَرَتِهِ. قَبْلَ إِينَاعِ ثَمَرَتِهِ. وَكِدْتُ أُنَبِّهُ عَلَى عُلُوِّ قَدْرِهِ. قَبْلَ ٱسْتِنَارَةِ بَدْرِهِ. فَأَوْحَى إِلَيَّ بِإِيمَاضِ جَفْنِهِ. أَنْ لَا أُجَرِّدَ عَضْبَهُ مِنْ جَفْنِهِ. فَلَمَّا خَرَجَ بَطِينَ الْخُرْجِ. وَفَصَلَ فَائِزًا بِالْفُلْجِ. شَيَّعْتُهُ قَاضِيًا حَقَّ الرِّعَايَةِ. وَلَاحِيًا لَهُ عَلَى رَفْضِ الْوِلَايَةِ. فَأَعْرَضَ مُتَبَسِّمًا. وَأَنْشَدَ مُتَرَنِّمًا.

لَجَوْبُ الْبِلَادِ مَعَ الْمَتْرَبَهْ   أَحَبُّ إِلَيَّ مِنَ الْمَرْتَبَهْ
لِأَنَّ الْوُلَاةَ لَهُمْ نَبْوَةٌ   وَمَعْتَبَةٌ يَا لَهَا مَعْتَبَهْ
وَمَا فِيهِمُ مَنْ يَرُبُّ الصَّنِيعَ   وَلَا مَنْ يُشَيِّدُ مَا رَتَّبَهْ
فَلَا يَخْدَعَنْكَ لُمُوعُ السَّرَابِ   وَلَا تَأْتِ أَمْرًا إِذَا مَا ٱشْتَبَهْ
فَكَمْ حَالِمٍ سَرَّهُ حُلْمُهُ   وَأَدْرَكَهُ الرَّوْعُ لَمَّا ٱنْتَبَهْ

الْمَقَامَةُ السَّابِعَةُ[١]

١،٧ حَكَى الْحَارِثُ بْنُ هَمَّامٍ قَالَ أَزْمَعْتُ الشُّخُوصَ مِنْ بَرْقَعِيدَ. وَقَدْ شِمْتُ بَرْقَ عِيدٍ. فَكَرِهْتُ الرِّحْلَةَ عَنْ تِلْكَ الْمَدِينَةِ. أَوْ أَشْهَدَ بِهَا يَوْمَ الزِّينَةِ. فَلَمَّا أَظَلَّ بِفَرْضِهِ وَنَفْلِهِ. وَأَجْلَبَ بِخَيْلِهِ وَرَجْلِهِ. اِتَّبَعْتُ السُّنَّةَ فِي لُبْسِ الْجَدِيدِ. وَبَرَزْتُ مَعَ مَنْ بَرَزَ لِلتَّعْيِيدِ. وَحِينَ ٱلْتَأَمَ جَمْعُ الْمُصَلَّى وَٱنْتَظَمَ. وَأَخَذَ الزِّحَامُ بِالْكَظَمِ. طَلَعَ شَيْخٌ فِي شَمْلَتَيْنِ. مَحْجُوبُ الْمُقْلَتَيْنِ. وَقَدِ ٱعْتَضَدَ شِبْهَ الْمِخْلَاةِ. وَٱسْتَقَادَ لِعَجُوزٍ كَالسِّعْلَاةِ. فَوَقَفَ وَقْفَةَ مُتَهَافِتٍ. وَحَيَّى تَحِيَّةَ خَافِتٍ. وَلَمَّا فَرَغَ مِنْ دُعَائِهِ. أَجَالَ خَمْسَهُ فِي وِعَائِهِ. فَأَبْرَزَ مِنْهُ رِقَاعًا قَدْ كُتِبْنَ بِأَلْوَانِ الْأَصْبَاغِ. فِي أَوَانِ الْفَرَاغِ. فَنَاوَلَهُنَّ عَجُوزَهُ الْحَيْزَبُونَ. وَأَمَرَهَا بِأَنْ تَتَوَسَّمَ الزَّبُونَ. فَمَنْ آنَسَتْ نَدَى يَدَيْهِ. أَلْقَتْ وَرَقَةً مِنْهُنَّ لَدَيْهِ.

٢،٧ قَالَ فَأَتَاحَ لِي الْقَدَرُ الْمَعْتُوبُ. رُقْعَةً فِيهَا مَكْتُوبٌ.

لَقَدْ أَصْبَحْتُ مَوْقُوذًا بِأَوْجَاعٍ وَأَوْجَالِ
وَمَمْنُوًّا بِمُخْتَالٍ وَمُحْتَالٍ وَمُغْتَالِ
وَخَوَّانٍ مِنَ الْإِخْوَا نِ قَالٍ لِي لِإِقْلَالِي
وَإِعْمَالٍ مِنَ الْعُمَّا لِ فِي تَضْلِيعِ أَعْمَالِي
فَكَمْ أَصْلَى بِأَذْحَالٍ وَإِمْحَالٍ وَتَرْحَالِ
وَكَمْ أَخْطِرُ فِي بَالٍ وَلَا أَخْطُرُ فِي بَالِ

١ في هامش ق وفوق العنوان في س: تُعرَف بالبَرقَعيديَّة، وفي د: البَرقَعيديَّة، وفي ف: وهي البَرقَعيديَّة.

فَلَيْتَ الدَّهْرَ لَمَّا جَا   رَ أَطْفَا لِيَ أَطْفَالِي
فَلَوْ لَا أَنَّ أَشْبَا   لِيَ أَغْلَالِي وَأَعْلَالِي
لَمَا جَهَّزْتُ آمَالِي   إِلَى آلِيَ[1] وَلَا وَالِ
وَلَا جَرَّرْتُ أَذْيَالِي   عَلَى مَسْحَبِ إِذْلَالِي
فَمِحْرَابِيَ أَحْرَى بِي   وَأَسْمَالِيَ أَسْمَى لِي
فَهَلْ حُرٌّ يَرَى تَخْفِيـفَ أَثْقَالِي بِمِثْقَالِ
وَيُطْفِي حَرَّ بَلْبَالِي   بِسِرْبَالٍ وَسِرْوَالِ

٣،٧ قَالَ الْحَارِثُ بْنُ هَمَّامٍ فَلَمَّا ٱسْتَعْرَضْتُ حُلَّةَ الْأَبْيَاتِ تُقْتُ إِلَى مَعْرِفَةِ مُلْحِمِهَا. وَرَاقِمِ عَلَمِهَا. فَنَاجَانِي الْفِكْرُ بِأَنَّ الْوُصْلَةَ إِلَيْهِ الْعَجُوزُ. وَأَفْتَانِي بِأَنَّ حُلْوَانَ الْمُعَرِّفِ يَجُوزُ. فَرَصَدْتُهَا وَهِيَ تَسْتَقْرِي الصُّفُوفَ صَفًّا صَفًّا. وَتَسْتَوْكِفُ الْأَكُفَّ كَفًّا فَكَفًّا.[2] وَمَا إِنْ يَنْجَحُ لَهَا عَنَاءٌ. وَلَا يَرْشَحُ عَلَى يَدِهَا إِنَاءٌ. فَلَمَّا أَكْدَى ٱسْتِعْطَافُهَا. وَكَدَّهَا مَطَافُهَا. عَاذَتْ بِالِاسْتِرْجَاعِ. وَمَالَتْ إِلَى إِرْجَاعِ الرِّقَاعِ. وَأَنْسَاهَا الشَّيْطَانُ ذِكْرَ رُقْعَتِي. فَلَمْ تَعُجْ إِلَى بُقْعَتِي. وَآبَتْ إِلَى الشَّيْخِ بَاكِيَةً لِلْحِرْمَانِ. شَاكِيَةً تَحَامُلَ الزَّمَانِ. فَقَالَ إِنَّا لِلّٰهِ. وَأُفَوِّضُ أَمْرِي إِلَى اللهِ. وَلَا حَوْلَ وَلَا قُوَّةَ إِلَّا بِاللهِ. ثُمَّ أَنْشَدَ

لَمْ يَبْقَ صَافٍ وَلَا مُصَافٍ   وَلَا مَعِينٌ وَلَا مُعِينُ
وَفِي الْمَسَاوِي بَدَا التَّسَاوِي   فَلَا أَمِينٌ وَلَا ثَمِينُ

---

١ د، ف: آلٍ. ٢ د، ف: كَفًّا.

٧،٤ ثُمَّ قَالَ لَهَا مَنِّي النَّفْسَ وَعِدِيهَا. وَٱجْمَعِي الرِّقَاعَ وَعُدِّيهَا. فَقَالَتْ لَقَدْ عَدَدْتُهَا. لَمَّا ٱسْتَعَدْتُهَا. فَوَجَدْتُ يَدَ الضِّيَاعِ. قَدْ غَالَتْ إِحْدَى الرِّقَاعِ. فَقَالَ تَعْسًا لَكِ يَا لَكَاعِ. أَنُحْرَمُ وَيْحَكِ الْقَنَصَ وَالْحِبَالَةَ. وَالْقَبَسَ وَالذُّبَالَةَ. إِنَّهَا لَضِغْثٌ عَلَى إِبَّالَةٍ. فَٱنْصَاعَتْ تَقْتَصُّ مَدْرَجَهَا. وَتَنْشُدُ مُدْرَجَهَا. فَلَمَّا دَانَتْنِي قَرَنْتُ بِالرُّقْعَةِ. دِرْهَمًا وَقِطْعَةً. وَقُلْتُ لَهَا إِنْ رَغِبْتِ فِي الْمَشُوفِ الْمُعْلَمِ. وَأَشَرْتُ إِلَى الدِّرْهَمِ. فَبُوحِي بِالسِّرِّ الْمُبْهَمِ. وَإِنْ أَبَيْتِ أَنْ تَشْرَحِي. فَخُذِي الْقِطْعَةَ وَٱسْرَحِي. فَمَالَتْ إِلَى ٱسْتِخْلَاصِ الْبَدْرِ التِّمِّ. وَالْأَبْلَجِ الْهِمِّ. وَقَالَتْ دَعْ جِدَالَكَ. وَسَلْ عَمَّا بَدَا لَكَ. فَٱسْتَطْلَعْتُهَا طِلْعَ الشَّيْخِ وَبَلْدَتِهِ.[1] وَالشِّعْرِ وَنَاسِجِ بُرْدَتِهِ. فَقَالَتْ إِنَّ الشَّيْخَ مِنْ أَهْلِ سَرُوجَ. وَهُوَ الَّذِي وَشَّى الشِّعْرَ الْمَنْسُوجَ. ثُمَّ خَطِفَتِ الدِّرْهَمَ خَطْفَةَ الْبَاشِقِ. وَمَرَقَتْ مُرُوقَ السَّهْمِ الرَّاشِقِ.

٧،٥ فَخَالَجَ قَلْبِي أَنَّ أَبَا زَيْدٍ هُوَ الْمُشَارُ إِلَيْهِ. وَتَأَجَّجَ كَرْبِي لِمُصَابِهِ بِنَاظِرَيْهِ. وَآثَرْتُ أَنْ أُفَاجِيَهُ[2] وَأُنَاجِيَهُ. لِأَعْجُمَ عُودَ فِرَاسَتِي فِيهِ. وَمَا كُنْتُ لِأَصِلَ إِلَيْهِ إِلَّا بِتَخَطِّي رِقَابِ الْجَمْعِ. الْمَنْهِيِّ عَنْهُ فِي الشَّرْعِ. وَعِفْتُ أَنْ يَتَأَذَّى بِي قَوْمٌ. أَوْ يَسْرِيَ إِلَيَّ لَوْمٌ. فَسَدِكْتُ[3] بِمَكَانِي. وَجَعَلْتُ شَخْصَهُ قَيْدَ عِيَانِي. إِلَى أَنِ ٱنْقَضَتِ الْخُطْبَةُ. وَحَقَّتِ الْوَثْبَةُ. فَخَفَفْتُ إِلَيْهِ. وَتَوَسَّمْتُهُ عَلَى ٱلتِّحَامِ جَفْنَيْهِ. فَإِذَا الْمَعِيُّ الْأَلْمَعِيَّةُ ٱبْنُ عَبَّاسٍ. وَفِرَاسَتِي فِرَاسَةُ إِيَاسٍ. فَعَرَّفْتُهُ حِينَئِذٍ شَخْصِي. وَآثَرْتُهُ بِأَحَدِ قُمُصِي. وَأَهَبْتُ بِهِ إِلَى قُرْصِي. فَهَشَّ لِعَارِفَتِي وَعِرْفَانِي. وَلَبَّى دَعْوَةَ رُغْفَانِي. وَٱنْطَلَقَ وَيَدِي زِمَامُهُ. وَظِلِّي إِمَامُهُ. وَالْعَجُوزُ ثَالِثَةُ الْأَثَافِي. وَالرَّقِيبُ ٱلَّذِي لَا يَخْفَى عَلَيْهِ خَافِي.

١ د: بُلْدَتِهِ. ٢ هكذا في ق، و، ف؛ وفي س: غير مشكّلة؛ وفي د: أفاجِيَه. ٣ ف: سكدت.

فَلَمَّا ٱسْتَحْلَسَ وُكْنَتِي. وَأَحْضَرْتُهُ عُجَالَةَ مُكْنَتِي. قَالَ يَا حَارِثُ. أَمَعَنَا ثَالِثٌ. ٦،٧
فَقُلْتُ لَيْسَ إِلَّا ٱلْعَجُوزُ. قَالَ مَا دُونَهَا سِرٌّ مَحْجُوزٌ. ثُمَّ فَتَحَ كَرِيمَتَيْهِ. وَرَأْرَأَ بِتَوْأَمَتَيْهِ. فَإِذَا سِرَاجَا وَجْهِهِ يَتَقِدَانِ. كَأَنَّهُمَا ٱلْفَرْقَدَانِ. فَٱبْتَهَجْتُ بِسَلَامَةِ بَصَرِهِ. وَعَجِبْتُ مِنْ غَرَائِبِ سِيَرِهِ. وَلَمْ يُلْقِنِي قَرَارٌ. وَلَا طَاوَعَنِي ٱصْطِبَارٌ. حَتَّى سَأَلْتُهُ مَا دَعَاكَ إِلَى ٱلتَّعَامِي. مَعَ سَيْرِكَ فِي ٱلْمَعَامِي. وَجَوْبِكَ ٱلْمَوَامِي. وَإِيغَالِكَ فِي ٱلْمَرَامِي. فَتَظَاهَرَ بِٱللُّكْنَةِ. وَتَشَاغَلَ بِٱللُّهْنَةِ. حَتَّى إِذَا قَضَى وَطَرَهُ. أَثَارَ إِلَيَّ نَظَرَهُ. وَأَنْشَدَ

وَلَمَّا تَعَامَى ٱلدَّهْرُ وَهُوَ أَبُو ٱلْوَرَى   عَنِ ٱلرُّشْدِ فِي أَنْحَائِهِ وَمَقَاصِدِهْ
تَعَامَيْتُ حَتَّى قِيلَ إِنِّي أَخُو عَمًى   وَلَا غَرْوَ أَنْ يَحْذُو ٱلْفَتَى حَذْوَ وَالِدِهْ

ثُمَّ قَالَ لِي ٱنْهَضْ إِلَى ٱلْمُخْدَعِ[1] فَأْتِنِي[2] بِغَسُولٍ يَرُوقُ ٱلطَّرْفَ. وَيُنَقِّي ٧،٧
ٱلْكَفَّ. وَيُنَعِّمُ ٱلْبَشَرَةَ. وَيُعَطِّرُ ٱلنَّكْهَةَ. وَيَشُدُّ ٱللِّثَةَ. وَيُقَوِّي ٱلْمَعِدَةَ. وَلْيَكُنْ نَظِيفَ ٱلظَّرْفِ. أَرِيجَ ٱلْعَرْفِ. فَتِيَّ ٱلدَّقِّ. نَاعِمَ ٱلسَّحْقِ. يَحْسَبُهُ ٱللَّامِسُ ذَرُورًا. وَيَخَالُهُ ٱلنَّاشِقُ كَافُورًا. وَٱقْرِنْ بِهِ خِلَالَةً نَقِيَّةَ ٱلْأَصْلِ. مَحْبُوبَةَ ٱلْوَصْلِ. أَنِيقَةَ ٱلشَّكْلِ. مَدْعَاةً إِلَى ٱلْأَكْلِ. لَهَا نَحَافَةُ ٱلصَّبِّ. وَصِقَالُ[3] ٱلْعَضْبِ. وَآلَةُ ٱلْحَرْبِ. وَلُدُونَةُ ٱلْغُصْنِ ٱلرَّطْبِ. قَالَ فَنَهَضْتُ فِيمَا أَمَرَ. لِأَدْرَأَ عَنْهُ ٱلْغَمَرَ. وَلَمْ أَهِمْ إِلَى[4] أَنَّهُ قَصَدَ أَنْ يَخْدَعَ. بِإِدْخَالِي ٱلْمُخْدَعَ.[5] وَلَا تَظَنَّيْتُ أَنَّهُ سَخِرَ مِنَ ٱلرَّسُولِ. فِي ٱسْتِدْعَاءِ ٱلْخِلَالَةِ وَٱلْغَسُولِ. فَلَمَّا عُدْتُ بِٱلْمُلْتَمَسِ. فِي أَقْرَبَ مِنْ رَجْعِ ٱلنَّفَسِ. وَجَدْتُ ٱلْجَوَّ قَدْ خَلَا. وَٱلشَّيْخَ وَٱلشَّيْخَةَ قَدْ أَجْفَلَا. فَٱسْتَشَطْتُ مِنْ مَكْرِهِ غَضَبًا. وَأَوْغَلْتُ فِي إِثْرِهِ طَلَبًا. فَكَانَ كَمَنْ قُمِسَ فِي ٱلْمَاءِ. أَوْ عُرِجَ بِهِ إِلَى عَنَانِ ٱلسَّمَاءِ.

---

١ د: ٱلمِخْدَع. ٢ و: فَإِتِنِي. ٣ ف: صقالة. ٤ ليس في د. ٥ د: ٱلمِخْدَعَ.

الْمَقَامَةُ الثَّامِنَةُ[1]

١،٨ أَخْبَرَ الْحَارِثُ بْنُ هَمَّامٍ قَالَ رَأَيْتُ مِنْ أَعَاجِيبِ الزَّمَانِ. أَنْ تَقَدَّمَ خَصْمَانِ. إِلَى قَاضِي مَعَرَّةِ النُّعْمَانِ. أَحَدُهُمَا قَدْ ذَهَبَ مِنْهُ الْأَطْيَبَانِ. وَالْآخَرُ كَأَنَّهُ قَضِيبُ الْبَانِ. فَقَالَ الشَّيْخُ أَيَّدَ اللهُ الْقَاضِيَ. كَمَا أَيَّدَ بِهِ الْمُتَقَاضِيَ. إِنَّهُ كَانَتْ لِي مَمْلُوكَةٌ رَشِيقَةُ الْقَدِّ. أَسِيلَةُ الْخَدِّ. صَبُورٌ عَلَى الْكَدِّ. تَخُبُّ أَحْيَانًا كَالنَّهْدِ. وَتَرْقُدُ أَطْوَارًا فِي الْمَهْدِ. وَتَجِدُ فِي تَمُّوزَ مَسَّ الْبَرْدِ. ذَاتُ عَقْلٍ وَعِنَانٍ. وَحَدٍّ وَسِنَانٍ. وَكَفٍّ بِبَنَانٍ. وَفَمٍ بِلَا أَسْنَانٍ. تَلْذَعُ[2] بِلِسَانٍ نَضْنَاضٍ. وَتَرْفُلُ فِي[3] ذَيْلٍ فَضْفَاضٍ. وَتُجْلَى فِي سَوَادٍ وَبَيَاضٍ. وَتُسْقَى وَلٰكِنْ مِنْ غَيْرِ حِيَاضٍ. نَاصِحَةٌ خُدَعَةٌ. خُبَأَةٌ طُلَعَةٌ. مَطْبُوعَةٌ عَلَى الْمَنْفَعَةِ. وَمِطْوَاعَةٌ فِي الضِّيقِ وَالسَّعَةِ. إِذَا قَطَعْتَ وَصَلَتْ. وَمَتَى فَصَلْتَهَا عَنْكَ انْفَصَلَتْ. وَطَالَمَا خَدَمَتْكَ فَجَمَّلَتْ. وَرُبَّمَا جَنَتْ عَلَيْكَ فَآلَمَتْ وَمَلْمَلَتْ. وَإِنَّ هٰذَا الْفَتَى اسْتَخْدَمَنِيهَا لِغَرَضٍ. فَأَخْدَمْتُهُ إِيَّاهَا بِلَا عِوَضٍ. عَلَى أَنْ يَجْتَنِيَ نَفْعَهَا. وَلَا يُكَلِّفَهَا إِلَّا وُسْعَهَا. فَأَوْلَجَ فِيهَا مَتَاعَهُ. وَأَطَالَ بِهَا اسْتِمْتَاعَهُ. ثُمَّ أَعَادَهَا[4] وَقَدْ أَفْضَاهَا. وَبَذَلَ عَنْهَا قِيمَةً لَا أَرْضَاهَا.

٢،٨ فَقَالَ الْحَدَثُ أَمَّا الشَّيْخُ فَأَصْدَقُ مِنَ الْقَطَا. وَأَمَّا الْإِفْضَاءُ فَفَرَطَ عَنْ خَطَا. وَقَدْ رَهَنْتُهُ. عَلَى[5] أَرْشِ مَا أَوْهَنْتُهُ. مَمْلُوكًا لِي مُتَنَاسِبَ الطَّرَفَيْنِ. مُنْتَسِبًا إِلَى الْقَيْنِ. نَقِيًّا مِنَ الدَّرَنِ وَالشَّيْنِ. يُقَارِنُ مَحَلُّهُ سَوَادَ الْعَيْنِ. يُفْشِي الْإِحْسَانَ.

---

١ في هامش ق: تُعْرَفُ بِالمَعَرِّيَّةِ، وفي هامش س: الإبرية، و في د: المَعَرِّيَّةُ، وفي ف: وَهْيَ المَعَرِّيَّةُ. ٢ مطموسة في س، وفي د، ف: تَلْدَغُ. ٣ بعدها في ق: ثَوْبٍ (مشطوبة). ٤ ف: بعدها إِلَيَّ. ٥ د، ف: عَنْ.

وَيُنْشِي[1] الاِسْتِحْسَانَ. وَيُغْذِي الْإِنْسَانَ. وَيَتَحَامَى اللِّسَانَ. إِنْ سُوِّدَ جَادَ. أَوْ وَسَمَ أَجَادَ. وَإِذَا زُوِّدَ وَهَبَ الزَّادَ. وَمَتَى ٱسْتُزِيدَ زَادَ. لَا يَسْتَقِرُّ بِمَغْنًى. وَقَلَّمَا يَنْكِحُ إِلَّا مَثْنًى.[2] يَسْخُو بِمَوْجُودِهِ. وَيَسْمُو عِنْدَ جُودِهِ. وَيَنْقَادُ مَعَ قَرِينَتِهِ. وَإِنْ لَمْ تَكُنْ مِنْ طِينَتِهِ. وَيُسْتَمْتَعُ بِزِينَتِهِ. وَإِنْ لَمْ يُطْمَعْ فِي لِينَتِهِ.

٣،٨ فَقَالَ لَهُمَا الْقَاضِي إِمَّا أَنْ تُبِينَا. وَإِلَّا فَبِينَا. فَٱبْتَدَرَ الْغُلَامُ وَقَالَ

أَعَارَنِي إِبْرَةً لِأَرْفُوَ أَطْمَا   رًا عَفَاهَا الْبِلَى وَسَوَّدَهَا
فَٱنْخَرَمَتْ فِي يَدِي عَلَى خَطَإٍ   مِنِّيَ لَمَّا جَذَبْتُ مِقْوَدَهَا
فَلَمْ يَرَ الشَّيْخُ أَنْ يُسَامِحَنِي   بِأَرْشِهَا إِذْ رَأَى تَأَوُّدَهَا
بَلْ قَالَ هَاتِ إِبْرَةً تُمَاثِلُهَا   أَوْ قِيمَةً بَعْدَ أَنْ تُجَوِّدَهَا
وَٱعْتَاقَ مِيلِي رَهْنًا لَدَيْهِ وَنَا   هِيكَ بِهَا سُبَّةً تَزَوَّدَهَا
فَالْعَيْنُ مَرْهَى لِرَهْنِهِ وَيَدِي   تَقْصُرُ عَنْ أَنْ تَفُكَّ مِرْوَدَهَا
فَٱسْبُرْ بِذَا الشَّرْحِ غَوْرَ مَسْكَنَتِي   وَٱرْثِ لِمَنْ لَمْ يَكُنْ تَعَوَّدَهَا

٤،٨ فَأَقْبَلَ الْقَاضِي عَلَى الشَّيْخِ وَقَالَ إِيهٍ. بِغَيْرِ تَمْوِيهٍ. فَقَالَ

أَقْسَمْتُ[3] بِالْمَشْعَرِ الْحَرَامِ وَمَنْ   ضَمَّ مِنَ النَّاسِكِينَ خَيْفُ مِنَى
لَوْ سَاعَفَتْنِي الْأَيَّامُ لَمْ يَرَنِي[4]   مُرْتَهِنًا مِيلَهُ الَّذِي رَهَنَا
وَلَا تَصَدَّيْتُ أَبْتَغِي بَدَلًا   مِنْ إِبْرَةٍ غَالَهَا وَلَا ثَمَنَا
لَكِنَّ قَوْسَ الْخُطُوبِ تَرْشُقُنِي   بِمُصْمِيَاتٍ مِنْ هَاهُنَا وَهُنَا
وَخُبْرُ حَالِي كَخُبْرِ حَالَتِهِ   ضُرًّا وَبُؤْسًا وَغُرْبَةً وَضَنَى

١ ق: ينشئ. ٢ ق: مَثْنَى. ٣ في د: أُقْسِمُ. ٤ في د: تَرَنِي.

قَدْ عَـدَلَ الدَّهْـرُ بَيْنَـنَا فَأَنَـا   نَظِـيرُهُ فِي الشَّقَـاءِ وَهْوَ أَنَـا
لَا هُوَ يَسْـطِيعُ فَكَّ مِـرْوَدِهِ   لَمَّا غَـدَا فِي يَـدَيَّ مُـرْتَهَنَـا
وَلَا مَجَالِي لِضِيقِ ذَاتِ يَـدِي   فِيهِ ٱتِّسَـاعٌ لِلْعَفْوِ حِينَ جَـنَى
فَـهٰـذِهِ قِـصَّـتِي وَقِـصَّـتُهُ   فَـٱنْظُـرْ إِلَيْـنَا وَبَيْنَنَـا وَلَنَـا

٨،٥ فَلَمَّا وَعَى الْقَاضِي قَصَصَهُمَا. وَتَبَيَّنَ خَصَاصَتَهُمَا وَتَخَصُّصَهُمَا. أَبْرَزَ لَهُمَا دِينَارًا مِنْ تَحْتِ مُصَلَّاهُ. وَقَالَ اقْطَعَا بِهِ الْخِصَامَ وَٱفْصِلَاهُ. فَتَلَقَّفَهُ الشَّيْخُ دُونَ الْحَدَثِ. وَٱسْتَخْلَصَهُ عَلَى وَجْهِ الْجِدِّ لَا الْعَبَثِ. وَقَالَ لِلْحَدَثِ نِصْفُهُ لِي بِسَهْمِ مَبَرَّتِي. وَسَهْمُكَ لِي عَنْ[١] أَرْشِ إِبْرَتِي. وَلَسْتُ عَنِ الْحَقِّ أَمِيلُ. فَقُمْ وَخُذِ الْمِيلَ. فَعَرَا الْحَدَثَ لِمَا حَدَثَ ٱكْتِئَابٌ[٢] وَجَمَ لَهُ[٣] الْقَاضِي. وَهَيَّجَ أَسَفَهُ عَنِ الدِّينَارِ الْمَاضِي. إِلَّا أَنَّهُ جَبَرَ بَالَ الْفَتَى وَبَلْبَالَهُ. بِدُرَيْهِمَاتٍ رَضَخَ بِهَا لَهُ. وَقَالَ لَهُمَا اجْتَنِبَا الْمُعَامَلَاتِ. وَٱدْرَآ الْمُخَاصَمَاتِ. وَلَا تَحْضُرَانِي فِي الْمُحَاكَمَاتِ. فَمَا عِنْدِي كِيسُ الْغَرَامَاتِ.

٨،٦ فَنَهَضَا مِنْ عِنْدِهِ. فَرِحَيْنِ بِرِفْدِهِ. مُفْصِحَيْنِ بِحَمْدِهِ. وَالْقَاضِي مَا يَخْبُو ضَجَرُهُ. مُذْ بَضَّ[٤] حَجَرُهُ.[٥] وَلَا يَنْصُلُ كَمَدُهُ. مُذْ رَشَحَ جَلْمَدُهُ.[٦] حَتَّى إِذَا أَفَاقَ مِنْ غَشْيَتِهِ. أَقْبَلَ عَلَى غَاشِيَتِهِ. وَقَالَ قَدْ أُشْرِبَ حِسِّي. وَنَبَّأَنِي حَدْسِي. أَنَّهُمَا صَاحِبَا دَهَاءٍ. لَا خَصْمَا ٱدِّعَاءٍ. فَكَيْفَ السَّبِيلُ إِلَى سَبْرِهِمَا. وَٱسْتِنْبَاطِ سِرِّهِمَا. فَقَالَ لَهُ نِحْرِيرُ زُمْرَتِهِ. وَشَرَارَةُ جَمْرَتِهِ. إِنَّهُ لَنْ يَتِمَّ ٱسْتِخْرَاجُ خَبْئِهِمَا. إِلَّا بِهِمَا. فَقَفَّاهُمَا عَوْنًا يُرْجِعُهُمَا إِلَيْهِ. فَلَمَّا مَثَلَا بَيْنَ يَدَيْهِ. قَالَ لَهُمَا ٱصْدُقَانِي سِنَّ بَكْرِكُمَا. وَلَكُمَا الْأَمَانُ مِنْ تَبِعَةِ مَكْرِكُمَا. فَأَحْجَمَ الْحَدَثُ وَٱسْتَقَالَ. وَأَقْدَمَ الشَّيْخُ وَقَالَ.

---

١ في متن ق: على، وفي هامش ق وفي سائر النسخ ما أثبتناه . ٢ وبعدها في ف: وَٱكْفَهَرَّ عَلَى سَمَائِهِ سَحَابٌ.
٣ بعدها في د: قلب. ٤ س: نَضَّ. ٥ ساقط من س. ٦ د: جَلْمَدُهُ.

٧،٨ أَنَا السَّرُوجِيُّ وَهٰذَا وَلَدِي وَالشِّبْلُ فِي الْمَخْبَرِ مِثْلُ الْأَسَدِ
وَمَا تَعَدَّتْ يَدُهُ وَلَا يَدِي فِي إِبْرَةٍ يَوْمًا وَلَا فِي مِرْوَدِ
وَإِنَّمَا الدَّهْرُ الْمُسِيءُ الْمُعْتَدِي مَالَ بِنَا حَتَّى غَدَوْنَا نَجْتَدِي
كُلَّ نَدِيِّ الرَّاحَةِ عَذْبِ الْمَوْرِدِ وَكُلَّ جَعْدِ الْكَفِّ مَغْلُولِ الْيَدِ
بِكُلِّ فَنٍّ وَبِكُلِّ مَقْصَدِ بِالْجِدِّ إِنْ أَجْدَى وَإِلَّا بِالدَّدِ
لِنَجْلُبَ الرَّشْحَ إِلَى الْحَظِّ الصَّدِي وَنُنْفِدَ الْعُمْرَ بِعَيْشٍ أَنْكَدِ
وَالْمَوْتُ مِنْ بَعْدُ لَنَا بِالْمَرْصَدِ إِنْ لَمْ يُفَاجِي[١] الْيَوْمَ فَاجَا فِي غَدِ

٨،٨ فَقَالَ لَهُ الْقَاضِي لِلّٰهِ دَرُّكَ فَمَا أَعْذَبَ نَفَثَاتِ فِيكَ. وَوَاهًا لَكَ لَوْلَا خِدَاعٌ فِيكَ. وَإِنِّي لَكَ لَمِنَ الْمُنْذِرِينَ. وَعَلَيْكَ مِنَ الْحَذِرِينَ. فَلَا تُمَاكِرْ بَعْدَهَا الْحَاكِمِينَ. وَاتَّقِ سَطْوَةَ الْمُتَحَكِّمِينَ. فَمَا كُلُّ مُسَيْطِرٍ يُقِيلُ. وَلَا كُلَّ أَوَانٍ يُسْمَعُ الْقِيلُ. فَعَاهَدَهُ الشَّيْخُ عَلَى اتِّبَاعِ مَشُورَتِهِ. وَالِارْتِدَاعِ عَنْ تَلْبِيسِ صُورَتِهِ. وَفَصَلَ عَنْ جِهَتِهِ. وَالْخَتْرُ يَلْمَعُ مِنْ جَبْهَتِهِ.

قَالَ الْحَارِثُ بْنُ هَمَّامٍ فَلَمْ أَرَ أَعْجَبَ مِنْهَا فِي تَصَارِيفِ الْأَسْفَارِ. وَلَا قَرَأْتُ مِثْلَهَا فِي تَصَانِيفِ الْأَسْفَارِ.

١ د، ف: يفاجِ.

الْمَقَامَةُ التَّاسِعَةُ[1]

١،٩ أَخْبَرَ[2] الْحَارِثُ بْنُ هَمَّامٍ طَحَا بِي مَرَحُ الشَّبَابِ. وَهَوَى الِاكْتِسَابِ. إِلَى أَنْ جُبْتُ مَا بَيْنَ فَرْغَانَةَ. وَغَانَةَ. أَخُوضُ الْغِمَارَ. لِأَجْنِيَ الثِّمَارَ. وَأَقْتَحِمُ[3] الْأَخْطَارَ. لِكَيْ أُدْرِكَ الْأَوْطَارَ. وَكُنْتُ لَقِفْتُ مِنْ أَفْوَاهِ الْعُلَمَاءِ. وَثَقِفْتُ مِنْ وَصَايَا الْحُكَمَاءِ. أَنَّهُ يَلْزَمُ الْأَرِيبَ.[4] إِذَا دَخَلَ الْبَلَدَ الْغَرِيبَ. أَنْ يَسْتَمِيلَ قَاضِيَهُ. وَيَسْتَخْلِصَ مَرَاضِيَهُ. لِيَشْتَدَّ ظَهْرُهُ عِنْدَ الْخِصَامِ. وَيَأْمَنَ فِي الْغُرْبَةِ جَوْرَ الْحُكَّامِ. فَاتَّخَذْتُ هٰذَا الْأَدَبَ إِمَامًا. وَجَعَلْتُهُ لِمَصَالِحِي زِمَامًا. فَمَا دَخَلْتُ مَدِينَةً. وَلَا وَلَجْتُ عَرِينَةً. إِلَّا وَٱمْتَزَجْتُ بِحَاكِمِهَا ٱمْتِزَاجَ ٱلْمَاءِ بِالرَّاحِ. وَتَقَوَّيْتُ بِعِنَايَتِهِ تَقَوِّيَ الْأَجْسَادِ بِالْأَرْوَاحِ.

٢،٩ فَبَيْنَمَا أَنَا عِنْدَ حَاكِمِ الْإِسْكَنْدَرِيَّةِ. فِي عَشِيَّةٍ عَرِيَّةٍ. وَقَدْ أَحْضَرَ مَالَ الصَّدَقَاتِ. لِيَفُضَّهُ عَلَى ذَوِي الْفَاقَاتِ. إِذْ دَخَلَ شَيْخٌ عِفْرِيَةٌ. تَعْتَلُهُ ٱمْرَأَةٌ مُصْبِيَةٌ. فَقَالَتْ أَيَّدَ اللهُ الْقَاضِيَ. وَأَدَامَ بِهِ التَّرَاضِيَ. إِنِّي ٱمْرَأَةٌ مِنْ أَكْرَمِ جُرْثُومَةٍ. وَأَطْهَرِ أُرُومَةٍ. وَأَشْرَفِ خُؤُولَةٍ وَعُمُومَةٍ. مِيسَمِي الصَّوْنُ. وَشِيمَتِي الْهَوْنُ. وَخُلُقِي نِعْمَ الْعَوْنُ. وَبَيْنِي وَبَيْنَ جَارَاتِي بَوْنٌ. وَكَانَ أَبِي إِذَا خَطَبَنِي بُنَاةُ الْمَجْدِ. وَأَرْبَابُ الْجَدِّ. سَكَّتَهُمْ وَبَكَّتَهُمْ. وَعَافَ وُصْلَتَهُمْ وَصِلَتَهُمْ. وَٱحْتَجَّ بِأَنَّهُ عَاهَدَ اللهَ تَعَالَى بِحَلْفَةٍ. أَلَّا[5] يُصَاهِرَ غَيْرَ ذِي حِرْفَةٍ. فَقَيَّضَ الْقَدَرُ لِنَصَبِي. وَوَصَبِي. أَنْ حَضَرَ هٰذَا الْخُدَعَةُ نَادِيَ أَبِي. فَأَقْسَمَ بَيْنَ رَهْطِهِ. أَنَّهُ وَفْقُ شَرْطِهِ. وَٱدَّعَى أَنَّهُ طَالَمَا

---

١ في هامش ق: وتعرف بالإسكندرية، وفي هامش س: تعرف بالفرغانية، وفي د: الإسكندرية، وفي ف: وهي الإسكندرانية. ٢ فوقها في ق: قال (مشطوبة)؛ وفي س، د، ف: قال. ٣ س: وأهجم. ٤ د، ف: الأديب الأريب. ٥ و: أن لا.

نَظَمَ دُرَّةً إِلَى دُرَّةٍ. فَبَاعَهُمَا بِبَدْرَةٍ. فَٱغْتَرَّ أَبِي بِزَخْرَفَةِ مُحَالِهِ. وَزَوَّجَنِيهِ قَبْلَ ٱخْتِبَارِ حَالِهِ. فَلَمَّا ٱسْتَخْرَجَنِي مِنْ كِنَاسِي. وَرَحَّلَنِي عَنْ أُنَاسِي. وَنَقَلَنِي إِلَى كِسْرِهِ. وَحَصَّلَنِي تَحْتَ أَسْرِهِ. وَجَدْتُهُ قُعَدَةً جُثَمَةً. وَأَلْفَيْتُهُ ضُجَعَةً نُوَمَةً. وَكُنْتُ صَحِبْتُهُ بِرِيَاشٍ وَزِيٍّ. وَأَثَاثٍ وَرِيٍّ. فَمَا بَرِحَ يَبِيعُهُ فِي سُوقِ ٱلْهَضْمِ. وَيُتْلِفُ ثَمَنَهُ فِي ٱلْخَضْمِ وَٱلْقَضْمِ. إِلَى أَنْ مَزَّقَ مَا لِي[1] بِأَسْرِهِ. وَأَنْفَقَ مَالِي فِي عُسْرِهِ. فَلَمَّا أَنْسَانِي طَعْمَ ٱلرَّاحَةِ. وَغَادَرَ بَيْتِي أَنْقَى مِنَ ٱلرَّاحَةِ. قُلْتُ لَهُ يَا هٰذَا إِنَّهُ لَا مَخْبَأَ بَعْدَ بُوسٍ. وَلَا عِطْرَ بَعْدَ عَرُوسٍ. فَٱنْهَضْ لِلِاكْتِسَابِ بِصِنَاعَتِكَ. وَٱجْنِنِي ثَمَرَةَ بَرَاعَتِكَ. فَزَعَمَ أَنَّ صِنَاعَتَهُ قَدْ رُمِيَتْ بِٱلْكَسَادِ. لِمَا ظَهَرَ فِي ٱلْأَرْضِ مِنَ ٱلْفَسَادِ. وَلِي مِنْهُ سُلَالَةٌ. كَأَنَّهُ خِلَالَةٌ. وَكِلَانَا مَا يَنَالُ مَعَهُ شُبْعَةً. وَلَا تَرْقَأُ لَهُ مِنَ ٱلطَّوَى دَمْعَةٌ. وَقَدْ قُدْتُهُ إِلَيْكَ. وَأَحْضَرْتُهُ لَدَيْكَ. لِتَعْجُمَ عُودَ دَعْوَاهُ. وَتَحْكُمَ بَيْنَنَا بِمَا أَرَاكَ ٱللهُ.

٣،٩ فَأَقْبَلَ ٱلْقَاضِي عَلَيْهِ وَقَالَ[2] قَدْ وَعَيْتَ قَصَصَ عِرْسِكَ. فَبَرْهِنْ[3] عَنْ نَفْسِكَ. وَإِلَّا كَشَفْتُ عَنْ لَبْسِكَ. وَأَمَرْتُ بِحَبْسِكَ. فَأَطْرَقَ إِطْرَاقَ ٱلْأُفْعُوَانِ. ثُمَّ شَمَّرَ لِلْحَرْبِ ٱلْعَوَانِ. وَقَالَ

ٱسْمَعْ حَدِيثِي فَإِنَّهُ عَجَبُ   يُضْحِكُ مِنْ شَرْحِهِ وَيُنْتَحَبُ
أَنَا ٱمْرُؤٌ لَيْسَ فِي خَصَائِصِهِ   عَيْبٌ وَلَا فِي فَخَارِهِ رِيَبُ
سَرُوجُ دَارِي ٱلَّتِي وُلِدْتُ بِهَا   وَٱلْأَصْلُ غَسَّانُ حِينَ أَنْتَسِبُ
وَشُغْلِيَ ٱلدَّرْسُ وَٱلتَّبَحُّرُ فِي ٱلْـ   ـعِلْمِ طِلَابِي وَحَبَّذَا ٱلطَّلَبُ
وَرَأْسُ مَالِي سِحْرُ ٱلْكَلَامِ ٱلَّذِي   مِنْهُ يُصَاغُ ٱلْقَرِيضُ وَٱلْخُطَبُ

١ ف: حالي. ٢ س، د، ف: قال له. ٣ د: فبرهن الآن.

أَغُوصُ فِي لُجَّةِ الْبَيَانِ فَأَخْتَارُ اللَّآلِي مِنْهَا وَأَنْتَخِبُ
وَأَجْتَنِي الْيَانِعَ الْجَنِيَّ مِنَ الْقَوْلِ وَغَيْرِي لِلْعُودِ مُحْتَطِبُ[١]
وَآخُذُ اللَّفْظَ فِضَّةً فَإِذَا مَا صُغْتُهُ قِيلَ إِنَّهُ ذَهَبُ
وَكُنْتُ مِنْ قَبْلُ أَمْتَرِي نَشَبًا بِالْأَدَبِ الْمُقْتَنَى[٢] وَأَحْتَلِبُ
وَيَمْتَطِي أَخْمَصِي لِحُرْمَتِهِ مَرَاتِبًا لَيْسَ فَوْقَهَا رُتَبُ
وَطَالَمَا زُفَّتِ الصِّلَاتُ إِلَى رَبْعِي فَلَمْ أَرْضَ كُلَّ مَنْ يَهَبُ
فَٱلْيَوْمَ مَنْ يَعْلَقُ الرَّجَاءُ بِهِ أَكْسَدُ شَيْءٍ فِي سُوقِهِ الْأَدَبُ
لَا عِرْضُ أَبْنَائِهِ يُصَانُ وَلَا يُرْقَبُ فِيهِمْ إِلٌّ وَلَا سَبَبُ
كَأَنَّهُمْ فِي عِرَاصِهِمْ جِيَفٌ يُبْعَدُ مِنْ نَتْنِهَا وَيُجْتَنَبُ
فَحَارَ لُبِّي لِمَا مُنِيتُ بِهِ مِنَ اللَّيَالِي وَصَرْفُهَا عَجَبُ
وَضَاقَ ذَرْعِي لِضِيقِ ذَاتِ يَدِي وَسَاوَرَتْنِي الْهُمُومُ وَالْكُرَبُ
وَقَادَنِي دَهْرِي الْمُلِيمُ إِلَى سُلُوكِ مَا يَسْتَشِينُهُ الْحَسَبُ
فَبِعْتُ حَتَّى لَمْ يَبْقَ لِي لَبَدٌ[٣] وَلَا بَتَاتٌ إِلَيْهِ أَنْقَلِبُ
وَٱدَّنْتُ حَتَّى أَثْقَلْتُ سَالِفَتِي بِحَمْلِ دَيْنٍ مِنْ دُونِهِ الْعَطَبُ
ثُمَّ طَوَيْتُ الْحَشَا عَلَى سَغَبٍ خَمْسًا فَلَمَّا أَمَضَّنِي السَّغَبُ
لَمْ أَرَ إِلَّا جِهَازَهَا عَرَضًا أَجُولُ فِي بَيْعِهِ وَأَضْطَرِبُ
فَجُلْتُ فِيهِ وَالنَّفْسُ كَارِهَةٌ وَالْعَيْنُ عَبْرَى وَالْقَلْبُ مُكْتَئِبُ
وَمَا تَجَاوَزْتُ إِذْ عَبَثْتُ بِهِ حَدَّ التَّرَاضِي فَيَحْدُثَ الْغَضَبُ[٤]
فَإِنْ يَكُنْ غَاظَهَا تَوَهُّمُهَا أَنَّ بَنَانِي بِالنَّظْمِ تَكْتَسِبُ
أَوْ أَنَّنِي إِذْ عَزَمْتُ خِطْبَتَهَا زَخْرَفْتُ قَوْلِي لِيُنْجَحَ[٥] الْأَرَبُ

١ ف: يحتطب. ٢ ف: المنتقى. ٣ ف: سَبَدٌ. ٤ س، و: الغَصَب. ٥ د، ف: يَنْجَحَ.

فَوَٱلَّذِي سَارَتِ ٱلرِّفَاقُ إِلَى كَعْبَتِهِ تَسْتَحِثُّهَا ٱلنُّجُبُ
مَا ٱلْمَكْرُ بِٱلْمُحْصَنَاتِ مِنْ شِيَمِي[1] وَلَا شِعَارِي ٱلتَّمْوِيهُ وَٱلْكَذِبُ
وَلَا يَدِي مُذْ نَشَأْتُ نِيطَ بِهَا إِلَّا مَوَاضِي ٱلْيَرَاعِ وَٱلْكُتُبُ
بَلْ فِكْرَتِي تَنْظِمُ ٱلْقَلَائِدَ لَا كَفِّي وَشِعْرِي ٱلْمَنْظُومُ لَا ٱلسُّخُبُ
وَهٰذِهِ[2] ٱلْحِرْفَةُ ٱلْمُشَارُ إِلَى مَا كُنْتُ أَحْوِي بِهَا وَأَجْتَلِبُ
فَأْذَنْ لِشَرْحِي كَمَا أَذِنْتَ لَهَا وَلَا تُرَاقِبْ وَٱحْكُمْ بِمَا يَجِبُ

٤،٩ قَالَ فَلَمَّا أَحْكَمَ مَا شَادَهُ. وَأَكْمَلَ إِنْشَادَهُ. عَطَفَ ٱلْقَاضِي إِلَى ٱلْفَتَاةِ. بَعْدَ أَنْ شُغِفَ بِٱلْأَبْيَاتِ. وَقَالَ أَمَا إِنَّهُ قَدْ ثَبَتَ عِنْدَ جَمِيعِ ٱلْحُكَّامِ. وَوُلَاةِ ٱلْأَحْكَامِ. ٱنْقِرَاضُ جِيلِ ٱلْكِرَامِ. وَمَيْلُ ٱلْأَيَّامِ إِلَى ٱللِّئَامِ. وَإِنِّي لَإِخَالُ بَعْلَكِ صَدُوقًا فِي ٱلْكَلَامِ. بَرِيًّا مِنَ ٱلْمَلَامِ. وَهَا هُوَ قَدِ ٱعْتَرَفَ لَكِ بِٱلْقَرْضِ. وَصَرَّحَ عَنِ ٱلْمَحْضِ. وَبَيَّنَ مِصْدَاقَ ٱلنَّظْمِ. وَتَبَيَّنَ أَنَّهُ مَعْرُوقُ ٱلْعَظْمِ. وَإِعْنَاتُ ٱلْمُعْذِرِ مَلْأَمَةٌ. وَحَبْسُ ٱلْمُعْسِرِ مَأْثَمَةٌ.[3] وَكِتْمَانُ ٱلْفَقْرِ زَهَادَةٌ. وَٱنْتِظَارُ ٱلْفَرَجِ بِٱلصَّبْرِ عِبَادَةٌ. فَٱرْجِعِي إِلَى خِدْرِكِ. وَٱعْذِرِي أَبَا عُذْرِكِ. وَنَهْنِهِي مِنْ غَرْبِكِ. وَسَلِّمِي لِقَضَاءِ رَبِّكِ. ثُمَّ إِنَّهُ فَرَضَ لَهُمَا فِي ٱلصَّدَقَاتِ حِصَّةً. وَنَاوَلَهُمَا مِنْ دَرَاهِمِهَا قَبْصَةً. وَقَالَ[4] تَعَلَّلَا بِهٰذِهِ ٱلْعُلَالَةِ. وَتَنَدَّيَا بِهٰذِهِ ٱلْبُلَالَةِ. وَٱصْبِرَا عَلَى كَيْدِ ٱلزَّمَانِ وَكَدِّهِ. فَعَسَى ٱللهُ أَنْ يَأْتِيَ بِٱلْفَتْحِ أَوْ أَمْرٍ مِنْ عِنْدِهِ. فَنَهَضَا وَلِلشَّيْخِ فَرْحَةُ ٱلْمُطْلَقِ مِنَ ٱلْإِسَارِ. وَٱلْمُوسِرِ[5] بَعْدَ ٱلْإِعْسَارِ.

٥،٩ قَالَ ٱلرَّاوِي وَكُنْتُ عَرَفْتُ أَنَّهُ أَبُو زَيْدٍ سَاعَةَ بَزَغَتْ شَمْسُهُ. وَنَزَغَتْ عِرْسُهُ. وَكِدْتُ أُفْصِحُ عَنِ ٱفْتِنَانِهِ. وَإِثْمَارِ أَفْنَانِهِ. ثُمَّ أَشْفَقْتُ مِنْ عُثُورِ ٱلْقَاضِي عَلَى

١ د، س، و: خُلُقِي. ٢ د، ف: فهذه. ٣ ف: مألمة. ٤ د، ف: قال لهما. ٥ د، ف: وهِزَّة الموسر.

بُهْتَانِهِ. وَتَزْوِيقِ لِسَانِهِ. فَلَا يَرَى عِنْدَ عِرْفَانِهِ. أَنْ يُرَشِّحَهُ لِإِحْسَانِهِ. فَأَحْجَمْتُ عَنِ الْقَوْلِ إِحْجَامَ الْمُرْتَابِ. وَطَوَيْتُ ذِكْرَهُ كَطَيِّ السِّجِلِّ لِلْكِتَابِ. إِلَّا أَنِّي قُلْتُ بَعْدَمَا فَصَلَ. وَوَصَلَ إِلَى مَا وَصَلَ. لَوْ أَنَّ لَنَا مَنْ يَنْطَلِقُ فِي أَثَرِهِ. لَأَتَانَا بِفَصِّ خَبَرِهِ. وَمَا[1] يَنْشُرُ[2] مِنْ حِبَرِهِ. فَأَتْبَعَهُ الْقَاضِي أَحَدَ أُمَنَائِهِ. وَأَمَرَهُ بِالتَّجَسُّسِ عَلَى[3] أَنْبَائِهِ. فَمَا لَبِثَ أَنْ رَجَعَ مُتَدَهْدِهًا. وَقَهْقَرَ مُقَهْقِهًا. فَقَالَ لَهُ الْقَاضِي مَهْيَمْ. يَا بَا مَرْيَمْ.[4] فَقَالَ لَقَدْ عَايَنْتُ عَجَبًا. وَسَمِعْتُ مَا أَنْشَأَ لِي طَرَبًا. فَقَالَ لَهُ مَاذَا رَأَيْتَ. وَمَا[5] الَّذِي وَعَيْتَ. قَالَ لَمْ[6] يَزَلِ الشَّيْخُ مُذْ خَرَجَ يُصَفِّقُ بِيَدَيْهِ. وَيُخَالِفُ بَيْنَ رِجْلَيْهِ. وَيُغَرِّدُ بِمِلْءِ شِدْقَيْهِ. وَيَقُولُ

كِدْتُ أَصْلَى بِبَلِيَّهْ   مِنْ وَقَاحٍ شَمَّرِيَّهْ
وَأَزُورُ السِّجْنَ لَوْلَا   حَاكِمُ الْإِسْكَنْدَرِيَّهْ

٦،٩ فَضَحِكَ الْقَاضِي حَتَّى هَوَتْ دَنِيَّتُهُ. وَذَوَتْ سَكِينَتُهُ. فَلَمَّا فَاءَ إِلَى الْوَقَارِ. وَعَقَّبَ الِاسْتِغْرَابَ بِالِاسْتِغْفَارِ. قَالَ اللّٰهُمَّ بِحُرْمَةِ عِبَادِكَ الْمُقَرَّبِينَ. حَرِّمْ حَبْسِي عَلَى الْمُتَأَدِّبِينَ. ثُمَّ قَالَ لِذٰلِكَ الْأَمِينِ عَلَيَّ بِهِ. فَانْطَلَقَ مُجِدًّا بِطَلَبِهِ. ثُمَّ عَادَ بَعْدَ لَأْيِهِ. مُخْبِرًا بِنَأْيِهِ. فَقَالَ الْقَاضِي أَمَا إِنَّهُ لَوْ حَضَرَ. لَكُفِيَ الْحَذَرَ. ثُمَّ لَأَوْلَيْتُهُ مَا هُوَ بِهِ أَوْلَى. وَلَأَرَيْتُهُ أَنَّ الْآخِرَةَ خَيْرٌ لَهُ مِنَ الْأُولَى. قَالَ الْحَارِثُ بْنُ هَمَّامٍ فَلَمَّا رَأَيْتُ صَغْوَ الْقَاضِي إِلَيْهِ. وَفَوْتَ ثَمَرَةِ التَّنْبِيهِ عَلَيْهِ. غَشِيَتْنِي نَدَامَةُ الْفَرَزْدَقِ حِينَ أَبَانَ النَّوَارَ. وَالْكُسَعِيِّ لَمَّا اسْتَبَانَ النَّهَارَ.

---

١ س، و، ف: وبما. ٢ و: سينشر، ف: يُنْشَر. ٣ د، ف: عن. ٤ د، ف: يا أبا مريم. ٥ «ما»: ليس في ف.
٦ ف: ولم.

ٱلْمَقَامَةُ ٱلْعَاشِرَةُ[١]

حَكَى ٱلْحَارِثُ بْنُ هَمَّامٍ قَالَ هَتَفَ بِي دَاعِي ٱلشَّوْقِ. إِلَى رَحْبَةِ مَالِكِ بْنِ ١٠،١
طَوْقٍ. فَلَبَّيْتُهُ مُمْتَطِيًا شِمِلَّةً. وَمُنْتَضِيًا عَزْمَةً مُشْمَعِلَّةً. فَلَمَّآ أَلْقَيْتُ بِهَا ٱلْمَرَاسِي.
وَشَدَدْتُ أَمْرَاسِي. وَبَرَزْتُ مِنَ ٱلْحَمَّامِ بَعْدَ سَبْتِ رَاسِي. رَأَيْتُ غُلَامًا أُفْرِغَ فِي
قَالَبِ ٱلْجَمَالِ. وَأُلْبِسَ مِنَ ٱلْحُسْنِ حُلَّةَ ٱلْكَمَالِ. وَقَدِ ٱعْتَلَقَ شَيْخٌ بِرُدْنِهِ. يَدَّعِي
أَنَّهُ فَتَكَ بِٱبْنِهِ.

وَٱلْغُلَامُ يُنْكِرُ عِرْفَتَهُ. وَيُكْبِرُ قِرْفَتَهُ. وَٱلْخِصَامُ بَيْنَهُمَا مُتَطَايِرُ ٱلشَّرَارِ. وَٱلزِّحَامُ ١٠،٢
عَلَيْهِمَا يَجْمَعُ بَيْنَ ٱلْأَخْيَارِ وَٱلْأَشْرَارِ. إِلَى أَنْ تَرَاضَيَا بَعْدَ ٱشْتِطَاطِ ٱللَّدَدِ.
بِٱلتَّنَافُرِ إِلَى وَالِي ٱلْبَلَدِ. وَكَانَ مِمَّنْ يُزَنُّ بِٱلْهَنَاتِ. وَيُغَلِّبُ حُبَّ ٱلْبَنِينَ عَلَى
ٱلْبَنَاتِ. فَأَسْرَعَا إِلَى نَدْوَتِهِ. كَٱلسُّلَيْكِ فِي عَدْوَتِهِ. فَلَمَّا حَضَرَاهُ. جَدَّدَ ٱلشَّيْخُ
دَعْوَاهُ. وَٱسْتَدْعَى عَدْوَاهُ. فَٱسْتَنْطَقَ ٱلْغُلَامَ وَقَدْ فَتَنَهُ بِمَحَاسِنِ غُرَّتِهِ. وَطَرَّ عَقْلَهُ
بِتَصْفِيفِ طُرَّتِهِ. فَقَالَ إِنَّهَا أَفِيكَةُ أَفَّاكٍ. عَلَى غَيْرِ سَفَّاكٍ. وَعَضِيهَةُ مُحْتَالٍ. عَلَى
مَنْ لَيْسَ بِمُغْتَالٍ.

فَقَالَ ٱلْوَالِي لِلشَّيْخِ إِنْ شَهِدَ لَكَ عَدْلَانِ مِنَ ٱلْمُسْلِمِينَ. وَإِلَّا فَٱسْتَوْفِ مِنْهُ ١٠،٣
ٱلْيَمِينَ. فَقَالَ ٱلشَّيْخُ إِنَّهُ جَدَّلَهُ خَاسِيًا. وَأَفَاحَ دَمَهُ خَالِيًا. فَأَنَّى لِي شَاهِدٌ.
وَلَمْ يَكُنْ ثَمَّ مُشَاهِدٌ. وَلَكِنْ وَلِّنِي تَلْقِينَهُ[٢] ٱلْيَمِينَ. لِيَبِينَ لَكَ أَيَصْدُقُ أَمْ يَمِينُ. فَقَالَ
لَهُ أَنْتَ ٱلْمَالِكُ لِذَلِكَ. مَعَ وَجْدِكَ ٱلْمُتَهَالِكِ. عَلَى ٱبْنِكَ ٱلْهَالِكِ.

---

١ في هامش ق: الرَّحْبية، وفي هامش س: تعرف بالرحبية، د: الرحبية، ف: وتعرف بالرحبية. ٢ د: تلقية.

٤،١٠ فَقَالَ الشَّيْخُ لِلْغُلَامِ قُلْ وَالَّذِي زَيَّنَ الْجِبَاهَ بِالطُّرَرِ. وَالْعُيُونَ بِالْحَوَرِ. وَالْحَوَاجِبَ بِالْبَلَجِ. وَالْمَبَاسِمَ بِالْفَلَجِ. وَالْجُفُونَ بِالسَّقَمِ. وَالْأُنُوفَ بِالشَّمَمِ. وَالْخُدُودَ بِاللَّهَبِ. وَالثُّغُورَ بِالشَّنَبِ. وَالْبَنَانَ بِالتَّرَفِ. وَالْخُصُورَ بِالْهَيَفِ. إِنَّنِي مَا قَتَلْتُ ٱبْنَكَ سَهْوًا وَلَا عَمْدًا. وَلَا جَعَلْتُ هَامَتَهُ لِسَيْفِي غِمْدًا. وَإِلَّا فَرَمَى اللّٰهُ جَفْنِي بِالْعَمَشِ. وَخَدِّي بِالنَّمَشِ. وَطُرَّتِي بِالْجَلَحِ. وَطَلْعِي بِالْبَلَحِ. وَوَرْدِي[1] بِالْبَهَارِ. وَمِسْكَتِي بِالْبُخَارِ. وَبَدْرِي بِالْمُحَاقِ. وَفِضَّتِي بِالِاحْتِرَاقِ. وَشُعَاعِي بِالْإِظْلَامِ. وَدَوَاتِي بِالْأَقْلَامِ.

٥،١٠ فَقَالَ الْغُلَامُ الِاصْطِلَاءَ بِالْبَلِيَّةِ. وَلَا الْإِيلَاءَ بِهٰذِهِ الْأَلِيَّةِ. وَالِانْقِيَادَ لِلْقَوَدِ. وَلَا الْحَلِفَ[2] بِمَا لَمْ يَحْلِفْ بِهِ أَحَدٌ. وَأَبَى الشَّيْخُ إِلَّا تَجْرِيعَهُ الْيَمِينَ الَّتِي ٱخْتَرَعَهَا. وَأَمْقَرَ لَهُ جُرَعَهَا. وَلَمْ يَزَلِ التَّلَاحِي بَيْنَهُمَا يَسْتَعِرُ. وَمَحَجَّةُ التَّرَاضِي تَعِرُ.

٦،١٠ وَالْغُلَامُ فِي ضِمْنِ تَأَبِّيهِ. يَخْلُبُ الْوَالِيَ[3] بِتَلَوِّيهِ. وَيُطْمِعُهُ فِي أَنْ يُلَبِّيهِ. إِلَى أَنْ رَانَ هَوَاهُ عَلَى قَلْبِهِ. وَأَلَبَّ بِلُبِّهِ. فَسَوَّلَ لَهُ الْوَجْدُ الَّذِي تَيَّمَهُ. وَالطَّمَعُ الَّذِي تَوَهَّمَهُ. أَنْ يُخَلِّصَ الْغُلَامَ وَيَسْتَخْلِصَهُ. وَأَنْ يُنْقِذَهُ مِنْ حِبَالَةِ الشَّيْخِ ثُمَّ يَقْتَنِصَهُ.

٧،١٠ فَقَالَ لِلشَّيْخِ هَلْ لَكَ فِيمَا هُوَ أَلْيَقُ بِالْأَقْوَى. وَأَقْرَبُ لِلتَّقْوَى. قَالَ إِلَامَ تُشِيرُ لِأَقْتَفِيهِ.[4] وَلَا أَقِفَ فِيهِ.[5] فَقَالَ أَرَى أَنْ تُقْصِرَ عَنِ الْقِيلِ وَالْقَالِ. وَتَقْتَصِرَ[6] عَلَى مِائَةِ مِثْقَالٍ. لِأَتَحَمَّلَ مِنْهَا بَعْضًا. وَأَجْتَبِيَ الْبَاقِيَ لَكَ عَرْضًا. فَقَالَ الشَّيْخُ مَا مِنِّي خِلَافٌ. فَلَا يَكُنْ لِوَعْدِكَ إِخْلَافٌ.

٨،١٠ فَنَقَدَهُ الْوَالِي عِشْرِينَ. وَوَزَّعَ عَلَى وَزَعَتِهِ تَكْمِلَةَ خَمْسِينَ. وَرَقَّ ثَوْبُ الْأَصِيلِ. وَٱنْقَطَعَ لِأَجْلِهِ صَوْبُ التَّحْصِيلِ. فَقَالَ لَهُ خُذْ مَا رَاجَ. وَدَعْ عَنْكَ اللَّجَاجَ.

---

١ ف: وردتي. ٢ د، و: الحلْف. ٣ في ف: قلب الوالي. ٤ في هامش س: ضرورة. ٥ و: ولا أَقِفُ فيه؛ ف: ولا أقفَ لك فيه. ٦ بعدها في ف: منه.

وَعَلَيَّ فِي غَدٍ أَنْ أَتَوَصَّلَ. إِلَى أَنْ يَنِضَّ لَكَ ٱلْبَاقِي وَيَتَحَصَّلَ. فَقَالَ ٱلشَّيْخُ أَفْعَلُ[١] عَلَى أَنْ أُلَازِمَهُ لَيْلَتِي. وَيَرْعَاهُ إِنْسَانُ مُقْلَتِي. حَتَّى إِذَا أَعْفَى بَعْدَ إِسْفَارِ ٱلصُّبْحِ. بِمَا بَقِيَ مِنْ مَالِ ٱلصُّلْحِ. تَخَلَّصَتْ قَائِبَةٌ مِنْ قُوبٍ. وَبَرِئَ بَرَاءَةَ ٱلذِّئْبِ مِنْ دَمِ ٱبْنِ يَعْقُوبَ. فَقَالَ لَهُ ٱلْوَالِي مَا أُرَاكَ سُمْتَ شَطَطًا. وَلَا رُمْتَ فَرَطًا.

٩،١٠ قَالَ ٱلْحَارِثُ بْنُ هَمَّامٍ فَلَمَّا رَأَيْتُ حُجَجَ ٱلشَّيْخِ كَٱلْحُجَجِ ٱلسُّرَيْجِيَّةِ. عَلِمْتُ أَنَّهُ عَلَمُ[٢] ٱلسَّرُوجِيَّةِ. فَلَبِثْتُ إِلَى أَنْ زَهَرَتْ نُجُومُ ٱلظَّلَامِ. وَٱنْتَثَرَتْ عُقُودُ ٱلزِّحَامِ. ثُمَّ قَصَدْتُ فِنَاءَ ٱلْوَالِي. فَإِذَا ٱلشَّيْخُ لِلْفَتَى كَالِي. فَنَشَدْتُهُ ٱللهَ أَهُوَ أَبُو زَيْدٍ. فَقَالَ إِي وَمُحِلِّ ٱلصَّيْدِ. قُلْتُ مَنْ هٰذَا ٱلْغُلَامُ. ٱلَّذِي هَفَتْ لَهُ ٱلْأَحْلَامُ. قَالَ هُوَ فِي ٱلنَّسَبِ فَرْخِي. وَفِي ٱلْمَكْسَبِ[٣] فَخِّي.[٤] قُلْتُ فَهَلَّا ٱكْتَفَيْتَ بِمَحَاسِنِ فِطْرَتِهِ. وَكَفَيْتَ ٱلْوَالِيَ ٱلِافْتِتَانَ بِطُرَّتِهِ. فَقَالَ لَوْ لَمْ تَبْرُزْ جَبْهَتُهُ ٱلسِّينَ. لَمَا قَنَفْشْتُ ٱلْخَمْسِينَ.

١٠،١٠ ثُمَّ قَالَ بِتِ ٱللَّيْلَةَ عِنْدِي لِنُطْفِئَ نَارَ ٱلْجَوَى. وَنُدِيلَ ٱلْهَوَى. مِنَ ٱلنَّوَى. فَقَدْ أَجْمَعْتُ عَلَى أَنْ أَنْسَلَّ بِسُحْرَةٍ. وَأُصْلِيَ قَلْبَ ٱلْوَالِي نَارَ حَسْرَةٍ. قَالَ فَقَضَيْتُ ٱللَّيْلَةَ مَعَهُ فِي سَمَرٍ. آنَقَ مِنْ حَدِيقَةِ زَهَرٍ. وَخَمِيلَةِ شَجَرٍ. حَتَّى إِذَا لَأْلَأَ ٱلْأُفُقُ ذَنَبُ ٱلسِّرْحَانِ. وَآنَ ٱنْبِلَاجُ ٱلْفَجْرِ وَحَانَ. رَكِبَ مَتْنَ ٱلطَّرِيقِ. وَأَذَاقَ ٱلْوَالِيَ عَذَابَ ٱلْحَرِيقِ. وَسَلَّمَ إِلَيَّ سَاعَةَ ٱلْفِرَاقِ. رُقْعَةً مُحْكَمَةَ ٱلْإِلْصَاقِ. وَقَالَ ٱدْفَعْهَا إِلَى ٱلْوَالِي إِذَا سُلِبَ ٱلْقَرَارَ. وَتَحَقَّقَ مِنَّا ٱلْفِرَارَ. فَفَضَضْتُهَا فِعْلَ ٱلْمُتَمَلِّسِ. مِنْ مِثْلِ صَحِيفَةِ ٱلْمُتَلَمِّسِ.

١١،١٠ فَإِذَا فِيهَا مَكْتُوبٌ

١ س: أَفْعَلُ ذاك؛ ف: أقبل منك. ٢ ق: من علم. ٣ ف: المكتسب. ٤ و، ف: فخي.

قُلْ لِوَالٍ غَادَرْتُهُ بَعْدَ بَيْنِي   سَادِمًا نَادِمًا يَعَضُّ الْيَدَيْنِ
سَلَبَ الشَّيْخُ مَالَهُ وَفَتَاهُ   لُبَّهُ فَاصْطَلَى لَظَى حَسْرَتَيْنِ
جَادَ بِالْعَيْنِ حِينَ أَعْمَى هَوَاهُ   عَيْنَهُ فَٱنْثَنَى بِلَا عَيْنَيْنِ
خَفِّضِ الْحُزْنَ يَا مُعَنَّى فَمَا يُجْدِي طِلَابُ الآثَارِ مِنْ بَعْدِ عَيْنِ
وَلَئِنْ جَلَّ مَا عَرَاكَ كَمَا جَلَّ لَدَى الْمُسْلِمِينَ رُزْءُ الْحُسَيْنِ
فَقَدِ ٱعْتَضْتَ مِنْهُ فَهْمًا وَحَزْمًا   وَاللَّبِيبُ الْأَرِيبُ يَبْغِي ذَيْنِ
فَاعْصِ مِنْ بَعْدِهَا الْمَطَامِعَ وَٱعْلَمْ   أَنَّ صَيْدَ الظِّبَاءِ لَيْسَ بِهَيْنِ
لَا وَلَا كُلُّ طَائِرٍ يَلِجُ الْفَخَّ   وَلَوْ كَانَ مُحْدَقًا بِاللُّجَيْنِ
وَلَكَمْ مَنْ سَعَى لِيَصْطَادَ فَٱصْطِيدَ   وَلَمْ يَلْقَ غَيْرَ خُفَّيْ حُنَيْنِ
فَتَبَصَّرْ وَلَا تَشِمْ كُلَّ بَرْقٍ   رُبَّ بَرْقٍ فِيهِ صَوَاعِقُ حَيْنِ
وَٱغْضُضِ الطَّرْفَ تَسْتَرِحْ مِنْ غَرَامٍ   تَكْتَسِي فِيهِ ثَوْبَ ذُلٍّ وَشَيْنِ
فَبَلَاءُ الْفَتَى ٱتِّبَاعُ هَوَى النَّفْسِ وَبِذْرُ الْهَوَى طُمُوحُ الْعَيْنِ

قَالَ الرَّاوِي فَمَزَّقْتُ رُقْعَتَهُ شِذَرَ مِذَرَ. وَلَمْ أُبَلْ أَعَذَلَ أَمْ عَذَرَ.

الْمَقَامَةُ الْحَادِيَةَ عَشْرَةَ[1]

حَدَّثَ الْحَارِثُ بْنُ هَمَّامٍ قَالَ آنَسْتُ مِنْ قَلْبِي الْقَسَاوَةَ. حِينَ حَلَلْتُ سَاوَةَ. ١،١١
فَأَخَذْتُ بِالْخَبَرِ الْمَأْثُورِ. فِي مُدَاوَاتِهَا بِزِيَارَةِ الْقُبُورِ. فَلَمَّا صِرْتُ إِلَى مَحَلَّةِ الْأَمْوَاتِ. وَكِفَاتِ الرُّفَاتِ. رَأَيْتُ جَمْعًا عَلَى قَبْرٍ يُحْفَرُ. وَمَجْنُوزٍ يُقْبَرُ. فَانْحَزْتُ إِلَيْهِمْ مُتَفَكِّرًا فِي الْمَآلِ. مُتَذَكِّرًا مَنْ دَرَجَ مِنَ الْآلِ.

فَلَمَّا أَلْحَدُوا الْمَيْتَ. وَفَاتَ قَوْلُ لَيْتَ. أَشْرَفَ شَيْخٌ مِنْ رِبَاوَةٍ.[2] مُتَخَصِّرًا ٢،١١
بِهِرَاوَةٍ. وَقَدْ لَفَّعَ وَجْهَهُ بِرِدَائِهِ. وَنَكَّرَ شَخْصَهُ لِدَهَائِهِ. فَقَالَ ﴿لِمِثْلِ هٰذَا فَلْيَعْمَلِ الْعَامِلُونَ﴾. فَادَّكِرُوا أَيُّهَا الْغَافِلُونَ. وَشَمِّرُوا أَيُّهَا الْمُقَصِّرُونَ. وَأَحْسِنُوا النَّظَرَ أَيُّهَا الْمُتَبَصِّرُونَ. مَا لَكُمْ لَا يَحْزُنُكُمْ دَفْنُ الْأَتْرَابِ. وَلَا يَهُولُكُمْ هَيْلُ التُّرَابِ. وَلَا تَعْبَأُونَ بِنَوَازِلِ الْأَحْدَاثِ. وَلَا تَسْتَعِدُّونَ لِنُزُولِ الْأَجْدَاثِ. وَلَا تَسْتَعْبِرُونَ لِعَيْنٍ تَدْمَعُ. وَلَا تَعْتَبِرُونَ بِنَعْيٍ يُسْمَعُ. وَلَا تَرْتَاعُونَ لِإِلْفٍ يُفْقَدُ. وَلَا تَلْتَاعُونَ لِمَنَاحَةٍ تُعْقَدُ. يُشَيِّعُ أَحَدُكُمْ نَعْشَ الْمَيْتِ. وَقَلْبُهُ تِلْقَاءَ الْبَيْتِ. وَيَشْهَدُ مُوَارَاةَ نَسِيبِهِ. وَفِكْرُهُ فِي ٱسْتِخْلَاصِ نَصِيبِهِ. وَيُخَلِّي بَيْنَ وَدُودِهِ وَدُودِهِ. ثُمَّ يَخْلُو بِمِزْمَارِهِ وَعُودِهِ. طَالَمَا أَسِيتُمْ عَلَى ٱنْثِلَامِ الْحَبَّةِ. وَتَنَاسَيْتُمُ ٱخْتِرَامَ الْأَحِبَّةِ. وَٱسْتَكَنْتُمْ لِاعْتِرَاضِ الْعُسْرَةِ. وَٱسْتَهَنْتُمْ بِٱنْقِرَاضِ الْأُسْرَةِ. وَضَحِكْتُمْ عِنْدَ الدَّفْنِ. وَلَا ضَحِكَكُمْ سَاعَةَ الزَّفْنِ. وَتَبَخْتَرْتُمْ خَلْفَ الْجَنَائِزِ. وَلَا تَبَخْتُرَكُمْ يَوْمَ قَبْضِ الْجَوَائِزِ. وَأَعْرَضْتُمْ عَنْ تَعْدِيدِ النَّوَادِبِ. إِلَى إِعْدَادِ الْمَآدِبِ. وَعَنْ تَحَرُّقِ الثَّوَاكِلِ. إِلَى التَّأَنُّقِ فِي الْمَآكِلِ. لَا تُبَالُونَ بِمَنْ هُوَ بَالٍ. وَلَا تُخْطِرُونَ ذِكْرَ الْمَوْتِ

١ في هامش س: تُعرَف بالساويَّة، وفي د: الساويَّة، وفي ف: الساوية. ٢ في هامش س: رَباوة، وفي د: رُباوة.

بِبَالٍ.[١] حَتَّى كَأَنَّكُمْ قَدْ عَلِقْتُمْ مِنَ الْحِمَامِ. بِذِمَامٍ. أَوْ حَصَلْتُمْ مِنَ الزَّمَانِ. عَلَى أَمَانٍ. أَوْ وَثِقْتُمْ بِسَلَامَةِ الذَّاتِ. أَوْ تَحَقَّقْتُمْ مُسَالَمَةَ هَادِمِ اللَّذَّاتِ. كَلَّا سَاءَ مَا تَتَوَهَّمُونَ. ﴿ثُمَّ كَلَّا سَوْفَ تَعْلَمُونَ﴾.

ثُمَّ أَنْشَدَ

٣،١١ أَيَا مَنْ يَدَّعِي الْفَهْمْ إِلَى كَمْ يَا أَخَا الْوَهْمْ تُعَبِّي الذَّنْبَ وَالذَّمَّ
وَتُخْطِي الْخَطَأَ الْجَمّْ

أَمَا بَانَ لَكَ الْعَيْبْ أَمَا أَنْذَرَكَ الشَّيْبْ وَمَا فِي نُصْحِهِ رَيْبْ
وَلَا سَمْعُكَ قَدْ صَمّْ

أَمَا نَادَى بِكَ الْمَوْتْ أَمَا أَسْمَعَكَ الصَّوْتْ أَمَا تَخْشَى مِنَ الْفَوْتْ
فَتَحْتَاطَ وَتَهْتَمّْ

فَكَمْ تَسْدَرُ[٢] فِي السَّهْوْ وَتَخْتَالُ مِنَ الزَّهْوْ وَتَنْصَبُّ إِلَى اللَّهْوْ
كَأَنَّ الْمَوْتَ مَا عَمّْ

وَحَتَّامَ تَجَافِيكْ وَإِبْطَاءُ تَلَافِيكْ طِبَاعًا جَمَعَتْ[٣] فِيكْ
عُيُوبًا شَمْلُهَا انْضَمّْ

إِذَا أَسْخَطْتَ مَوْلَاكْ فَمَا تَقْلَقُ مِنْ ذَاكْ وَإِنْ أَخْفَقَ مَسْعَاكْ
تَلَظَّيْتَ مِنَ الْهَمّْ

٤،١١ وَإِنْ لَاحَ لَكَ النَّقْشْ مِنَ الْأَصْفَرِ تَهْتَشّْ وَإِنْ مَرَّ بِكَ النَّعْشْ
تَغَامَمْتَ وَلَا غَمّْ

١ و: لكم ل (هكذا). ٢ د: تسدِر. ٣ د: جَمَّعَت، و: جُمِّعت فيك.

تُعَاصِي النَّاصِحَ الْبَرّْ   وَتَعْتَاصُ وَتَزْوَرّْ   وَتَنْقَادُ لِمَنْ غَرّْ
وَمَنْ مَانَ وَمَنْ نَمّْ

وَتَسْعَى فِي هَوَى النَّفْسْ   وَتَحْتَالُ عَلَى الْفَلْسْ   وَتَنْسَى ظُلْمَةَ الرَّمْسْ
وَلَا تَذْكُرُ مَا ثَمّْ

وَلَوْ لَاحَظَكَ الْحَظّْ   لَمَا طَاحَ بِكَ اللَّحْظْ   وَلَا كُنْتَ إِذَا الْوَعْظْ
جَلَا الْأَحْزَانَ تَغْتَمّْ

سَتُذْرِي الدَّمَ لَا الدَّمْعْ   إِذَا عَايَنْتَ لَا جَمْعْ   يَقِي فِي عَرْصَةِ الْجَمْعْ
وَلَا خَالَ وَلَا عَمّْ

كَأَنِّي بِكَ تَنْحَطّْ   إِلَى اللَّحْدِ وَتَنْغَطّْ   وَقَدْ أَسْلَمَكَ الرَّهْطْ
إِلَى أَضْيَقَ مِنْ سَمّْ

هُنَاكَ الْجِسْمُ مَمْدُودْ   لِيَسْتَأْكِلَهُ الدُّودْ   إِلَى أَنْ يَنْخَرَ الْعُودْ
وَيُمْسِي الْعَظْمُ قَدْ رَمّْ

وَمِنْ بَعْدُ فَلَا بُدّْ   مِنَ الْعَرْضِ إِذَا اعْتُدّْ   صِرَاطٌ جِسْرُهُ مُدّْ
عَلَى النَّارِ لِمَنْ أَمّْ

فَكَمْ[1] مِنْ مُرْشِدٍ ضَلّْ   وَمِنْ ذِي عِزَّةٍ ذَلّْ   وَكَمْ مِنْ عَالِمٍ زَلّْ
وَقَالَ الْخَطْبُ قَدْ طَمّْ

فَبَادِرْ أَيُّهَا الْغُمْرْ   لِمَا يَحْلُو بِهِ الْمُرّْ   فَقَدْ كَادَ يَهِي الْعُمْرْ   ٥،١١
وَمَا أَقْلَعْتَ عَنْ ذَمّْ

وَلَا تَرْكَنْ إِلَى الدَّهْرْ   وَإِنْ لَانَ وَإِنْ سَرّْ   فَتُلْفَى كَمَنِ اغْتَرّْ
بِأَفْعَى تَنْفُثُ السَّمّْ

---

١ س، د: وكم.

وَخَفِّضْ مِنْ تَرَاقِيكْ فَإِنَّ ٱلْمَوْتَ لَاقِيكْ وَسَارٍ فِي تَرَاقِيكْ
وَمَا يَنْكُلُ إِنْ هَمّْ

وَجَانِبْ صَعَرَ ٱلْخَدّْ إِذَا سَاعَدَكَ ٱلْجَدّْ وَزُمَّ ٱللَّفْظَ إِنْ نَدّْ
فَمَا أَسْعَدَ مَنْ زَمّْ

وَنَفِّسْ عَنْ أَخِي ٱلْبَثّْ وَصَدِّقْهُ إِذَا نَثّْ وَرُمَّ ٱلْعَمَلَ ٱلرَّثّْ
فَقَدْ أَفْلَحَ مَنْ رَمّْ

وَرِشْ مَنْ رِيشُهُ ٱنْحَصّْ بِمَا عَمَّ وَمَا خَصّْ وَلَا تَأْسَ عَلَى ٱلنَّقْصْ
وَلَا تَحْرِصْ عَلَى ٱللَّمّْ

٦،١١ وَعَادِ ٱلْخُلُقَ ٱلرَّذْلْ وَعَوِّدْ كَفَّكَ ٱلْبَذْلْ وَلَا تَسْتَمِعِ ٱلْعَذْلْ
وَنَزِّهْهَا[١] عَنِ ٱلضَّمّْ

وَزَوِّدْ نَفْسَكَ ٱلْخَيْرْ وَدَعْ مَا يُعْقِبُ ٱلضَّيْرْ وَهَيِّئْ مَرْكَبَ ٱلسَّيْرْ
وَخَفْ مِنْ لُجَّةِ ٱلْيَمّْ

بِذَا أُوصِيتُ[٢] يَا صَاحْ وَقَدْ بُحْتُ كَمَنْ بَاحْ فَطُوبَى لِفَتًى رَاحْ
بِآدَابِي يَأْتَمّْ

ثُمَّ حَسَرَ رُدْنَهُ عَنْ سَاعِدٍ شَدِيدِ ٱلْأَسْرِ. قَدْ شَدَّ عَلَيْهِ جَبَائِرَ ٱلْمَكْرِ لَا ٱلْكَسْرِ. مُتَعَرِّضًا لِلِاسْتِمَاحَةِ. فِي مَعْرِضِ ٱلْوَقَاحَةِ. فَٱحْتَلَبَ بِهِ أُولَئِكَ ٱلْمَلَأَ. حَتَّى أَتْرَعَ كُمَّهُ وَمَلَأَ. ثُمَّ ٱنْحَدَرَ مِنَ ٱلرَّبْوَةِ. جَذِلًا بِٱلْحَبْوَةِ.

٧،١١ قَالَ ٱلرَّاوِي فَجَاذَبْتُهُ مِنْ وَرَائِهِ. حَاشِيَةَ رِدَائِهِ. فَٱلْتَفَتَ إِلَيَّ مُسْتَسْلِمًا. وَوَاجَهَنِي مُسَلِّمًا. فَإِذَا هُوَ شَيْخُنَا أَبُو زَيْدٍ بِعَيْنِهِ. وَمَيْنِهِ. فَقُلْتُ لَهُ

---

١ هكذا في ق،د؛ وفي س: نَزِّهًا. ٢ و،د: أوصَيْت.

إِلَى كَمْ يَا أَبَا زَيْدْ أَفَانِينُكَ فِي الْكَيْدْ لِيَنْحَاشَ لَكَ الصَّيْدْ
وَلَا تَعْبَأْ بِمَنْ ذَمّْ

فَأَجَابَ مِنْ غَيْرِ ٱسْتِحْيَاءٍ. وَلَا ٱرْتِيَاءٍ. وَقَالَ

تَبَصَّرْ وَدَعِ اللَّوْمْ وَقُلْ لِي هَلْ تَرَى الْيَوْمْ فَتًى لَا يَقْمُرُ الْقَوْمْ
مَتَى مَا دَسْتُهُ تَمّْ

فَقُلْتُ لَهُ بُعْدًا لَكَ يَا شَيْخَ النَّارِ. وَزَامِلَةَ الْعَارِ. فَمَا مَثَلُكَ فِي طُلَاوَةِ عَلَانِيَتِكَ. وَخِبْثَةِ نِيَّتِكَ. إِلَّا مَثَلُ رَوْثٍ مُفَضَّضٍ. أَوْ كَنِيفٍ مُبَيَّضٍ. ثُمَّ تَفَرَّقْنَا فَٱنْطَلَقْتُ ذَاتَ الْيَمِينِ وَٱنْطَلَقَ ذَاتَ الشِّمَالِ. وَنَاوَحْتُ مَهَبَّ الْجَنُوبِ وَنَاوَحَ مَهَبَّ الشَّمَالِ.

الْمَقَامَةُ الثَّانِيَةَ عَشْرَةَ[١]

١٢.١ حَكَى الْحَارِثُ بْنُ هَمَّامٍ قَالَ شَخَصْتُ مِنَ الْعِرَاقِ إِلَى الْغُوطَةِ. وَأَنَا ذُو جُرْدٍ مَرْبُوطَةٍ. وَجِدَةٍ مَغْبُوطَةٍ. يُلْهِينِي خُلُوُّ[٢] الذَّرْعِ. وَيَزْدَهِينِي حُفُولُ الضَّرْعِ. فَلَمَّا بَلَغْتُهَا بَعْدَ شِقِّ النَّفْسِ. وَإِنْضَاءِ الْعَنْسِ. أَلْفَيْتُهَا كَمَا تَصِفُهَا الْأَلْسُنُ. وَفِيهَا مَا تَشْتَهِي الْأَنْفُسُ وَتَلَذُّ الْأَعْيُنُ. فَشَكَرْتُ يَدَ النَّوَى. وَجَرَيْتُ طَلَقًا مَعَ الْهَوَى. وَطَفِقْتُ أَفُضُّ بِهَا خُتُومَ الشَّهَوَاتِ. وَأَجْتَنِي قُطُوفَ اللَّذَّاتِ. إِلَى أَنْ شَرَعَ سَفْرٌ فِي الْإِعْرَاقِ. وَقَدِ ٱسْتَفَقْتُ[٣] مِنَ الْإِغْرَاقِ. فَعَادَنِي عِيدٌ مِنْ تَذْكَارِ الْوَطَنِ. وَالْحَنِينِ إِلَى الْعَطَنِ. فَقَوَّضْتُ خِيَامَ الْغَيْبَةِ. وَأَسْرَجْتُ جَوَادَ الْأَوْبَةِ.

١٢.٢ وَلَمَّا تَأَهَّبَتِ الرِّفَاقُ. وَٱسْتَتَبَّ الِاتِّفَاقُ. أَلْحَنَا مِنَ الْمَسِيرِ. دُونَ ٱسْتِصْحَابِ الْخَفِيرِ. فَرُدْنَاهُ مِنْ كُلِّ قَبِيلَةٍ. وَأَعْمَلْنَا فِي تَحْصِيلِهِ أَلْفَ حِيلَةٍ. فَأَعْوَزَ وِجْدَانُهُ فِي الْأَحْيَاءِ. حَتَّى خِلْنَا أَنَّهُ لَيْسَ مِنَ الْأَحْيَاءِ. فَحَارَتْ لِعَوَزِهِ عُزُومُ السَّيَّارَةِ. وَٱنْتَدَوْا بِبَابِ جَيْرُونَ لِلِاسْتِشَارَةِ.[٤] فَمَا زَالُوا بَيْنَ عَقْدٍ وَحَلٍّ. وَشَزْرٍ وَسَحْلٍ. إِلَى أَنْ نَفِدَ التَّنَاجِي. وَقَنِطَ الرَّاجِي. وَكَانَ حِذَتَهُمْ شَخْصٌ مِيسَمُهُ مِيسَمُ الشُّبَّانِ. وَلَبُوسُهُ لَبُوسُ[٥] الرُّهْبَانِ. وَبِيَدِهِ سُبْحَةُ النِّسْوَانِ. وَفِي عَيْنِهِ[٦] تَرْجَمَةُ النَّشْوَانِ. وَقَدْ قَيَّدَ لَحْظَهُ بِالْجَمْعِ. وَأَرْهَفَ أُذُنَهُ لِٱسْتِرَاقِ السَّمْعِ. فَلَمَّا أَنَى[٧] ٱنْكِفَاؤُهُمْ. وَقَدْ بَرِحَ لَهُ خَفَاؤُهُمْ. قَالَ لَهُمْ يَا قَوْمِ لِيُفْرِخْ كَرْبُكُمْ. وَلْيَأْمَنْ سِرْبُكُمْ. فَسَأَخْفُرُكُمْ[٨] بِمَا يَسْرُو رَوْعَكُمْ. وَيَبْدُو طَوْعَكُمْ.

١ س: تعرف بالدمشقية؛ وفي د: الدمشقية؛ وفي ف: وهي الدمشقية. ٢ ق: خُلُوُ (؟). ٣ ف: أشفقتُ. ٤ ف: للاستخارة. ٥ هكذا في ق، د، ف؛ وفي هامش ق: وشارتُه شارَةُ، وفي س: شارته شارة، وفي هامشها: لبوسه لبوس. ٦ د، ف: عينيه. ٧ د: آن. ٨ د: سأَخْفِرُكُم.

قَالَ الرَّاوِي فَٱسْتَطْلَعْنَا مِنْهُ طِلْعَ الْخِفَارَةِ. وَأَسْنَيْنَا الْجِعَالَةَ لَهُ[١] عَنِ السِّفَارَةِ. فَزَعَمَ أَنَّهَا كَلِمَاتٌ لُقِّنَهَا فِي الْمَنَامِ. لِيَحْتَرِسَ بِهَا مِنْ كَيْدِ الْأَنَامِ. فَجَعَلَ بَعْضُنَا يُومِضُ[٢] إِلَى بَعْضٍ. وَيُقَلِّبُ طَرْفَيْهِ بَيْنَ لَحْظٍ وَغَضٍّ. وَتَبَيَّنَ لَهُ أَنَّا ٱسْتَضْعَفْنَا الْخَبَرَ. وَٱسْتَشْعَرْنَا الْخَوَرَ. فَقَالَ مَا لَكُمْ[٣] ٱتَّخَذْتُمْ جِدِّي عَبَثًا. وَجَعَلْتُمْ تِبْرِي خَبَثًا. وَلَطَالَمَا وَاللهِ جُبْتُ مَخَاوِفَ الْأَقْطَارِ. وَوَلَجْتُ مَقَاحِمَ الْأَخْطَارِ. فَغَنِيتُ بِهَا عَنْ مُصَاحَبَةِ خَفِيرٍ. وَٱسْتِصْحَابِ جَفِيرٍ. ثُمَّ إِنِّي سَأُنْفِي مَا رَابَكُمْ. وَأَسْتَسِلُّ الْحَذَرَ الَّذِي نَابَكُمْ. بِأَنْ أُوَافِقَكُمْ فِي الْبَدَاوَةِ. وَأُرَافِقَكُمْ فِي السَّمَاوَةِ. فَإِنْ صَدَقَكُمْ وَعْدِي. فَأَجِدُّوا سَعْدِي. وَأَسْعِدُوا جَدِّي. وَإِنْ كَذَبَكُمْ فَمِي. فَمَزِّقُوا أَدِمِي. وَأَرِيقُوا دَمِي. ٣،١٢

قَالَ الْحَارِثُ بْنُ هَمَّامٍ فَأُلْهِمْنَا تَصْدِيقَ رُؤْيَاهُ. وَتَحْقِيقَ مَا رَوَاهُ. فَنَزَعْنَا عَنْ مُجَادَلَتِهِ. وَٱسْتَهَمْنَا عَلَى مُعَادَلَتِهِ. وَفَصَمْنَا بِقَوْلِهِ عُرَى الرَّبَائِثِ. وَأَلْغَيْنَا ٱتِّقَاءَ الْعَابِثِ وَالْعَائِثِ. وَلَمَّا عُكِمَتِ الرِّحَالُ. وَأَزِفَ التَّرْحَالُ. ٱسْتَنْزَلْنَا كَلِمَاتِهِ الرَّاقِيَةَ. لِنَجْعَلَهَا الْوَاقِيَةَ الْبَاقِيَةَ. فَقَالَ لِيَقْرَأْ كُلٌّ مِنْكُمْ أُمَّ الْقُرْآنِ. كُلَّمَا أَظَلَّ الْمَلَوَانِ. ثُمَّ لِيَقُلْ بِلِسَانٍ خَاضِعٍ. وَصَوْتٍ خَاشِعٍ. اللَّهُمَّ يَا مُحْيِيَ الرُّفَاتِ. وَيَا دَافِعَ الْآفَاتِ. وَيَا وَاقِيَ الْمَخَافَاتِ. وَيَا كَرِيمَ الْمُكَافَاةِ. وَيَا مَوْئِلَ الْعُفَاةِ. وَيَا وَلِيَّ الْعَفْوِ وَالْمُعَافَاةِ. صَلِّ عَلَى مُحَمَّدٍ خَاتَمِ أَنْبِيَائِكَ. وَمُبَلِّغِ أَنْبَائِكَ. وَعَلَى مَصَابِيحِ أُسْرَتِهِ. وَمَفَاتِيحِ نُصْرَتِهِ. وَأَعِذْنِي[٤] مِنْ نَزَغَاتِ الشَّيَاطِينِ. وَنَزَوَاتِ السَّلَاطِينِ. وَإِعْنَاتِ الْبَاغِينَ. وَمُعَانَاةِ الطَّاغِينَ. وَمُعَادَاةِ الْعَادِينَ. وَعُدْوَانِ الْمُعَادِينَ. وَغَلَبِ الْغَالِبِينَ. وَسَلَبِ السَّالِبِينَ. وَحِيَلِ الْمُحْتَالِينَ. وَغِيَلِ الْمُغْتَالِينَ. وَأَجِرْنِي ٤،١٢

---

١ د، ف: له الجعالة. ٢ ما قبلها ساقط من النسخة الرقمية من و. ٣ ف: بالكم. ٤ بعدها في د: اللهمّ.

اللّٰهُمَّ مِنْ جَوْرِ ٱلْمُجَاوِرِينَ. وَسَطْوَةِ ٱلْجَائِرِينَ.[١] وَكُفَّ عَنِّي أَكُفَّ ٱلضَّائِمِينَ. وَأَخْرِجْنِي مِنْ ظُلُمَاتِ ٱلظَّالِمِينَ. وَأَدْخِلْنِي بِرَحْمَتِكَ فِي عِبَادِكَ ٱلصَّالِحِينَ. اللّٰهُمَّ حُطْنِي فِي تُرْبَتِي وَغُرْبَتِي. وَغَيْبَتِي وَأَوْبَتِي. وَنُجْعَتِي وَرَجْعَتِي. وَتَصَرُّفِي وَمُنْصَرَفِي. وَتَقَلُّبِي وَمُنْقَلَبِي. وَٱحْفَظْنِي فِي نَفْسِي وَنَفَائِسِي. وَعِرْضِي وَعَرَضِي. وَعَدَدِي وَعُدَدِي. وَسَكَنِي وَمَسْكَنِي. وَحَوْلِي وَحَالِي وَمَآلِي. وَمَالِي.[٢] وَلَا تُلْحِقْ بِي تَغْيِيرًا. وَلَا تُسَلِّطْ عَلَيَّ مُغِيرًا. وَٱجْعَلْ لِي مِنْ لَدُنْكَ سُلْطَانًا نَصِيرًا. اللّٰهُمَّ ٱحْرُسْنِي بِعَيْنِكَ. وَعَوْنِكَ. وَٱخْصُصْنِي بِأَمْنِكَ. وَمَنِّكَ. وَتَوَلَّنِي بِٱخْتِيَارِكَ وَخَيْرِكَ. وَلَا تَكِلْنِي إِلَى كِلَاءَةِ غَيْرِكَ. وَهَبْ لِي عَافِيَةً غَيْرَ عَافِيَةٍ. وَٱرْزُقْنِي رَفَاهِيَةً غَيْرَ وَاهِيَةٍ. وَٱكْفِنِي مَخَاشِيَ ٱللَّأْوَاءِ. وَٱكْنُفْنِي بِغَوَاشِي ٱلْآلَاءِ. وَلَا تُظْفِرْ بِي أَظْفَارَ ٱلْأَعْدَاءِ. إِنَّكَ سَمِيعُ ٱلدُّعَاءِ. ثُمَّ أَطْرَقَ لَا يُدِيرُ لَحْظًا. وَلَا يُحِيرُ لَفْظًا. حَتَّى قُلْنَا قَدْ أَبْلَسَتْهُ خَشْيَةٌ. أَوْ أَخْرَسَتْهُ غَشْيَةٌ. ثُمَّ أَقْنَعَ رَاسَهُ. وَصَعَّدَ أَنْفَاسَهُ. وَقَالَ أُقْسِمُ بِٱلسَّمَاءِ ذَاتِ ٱلْأَبْرَاجِ. وَٱلْأَرْضِ ذَاتِ ٱلْفِجَاجِ. وَٱلْمَاءِ ٱلثَّجَّاجِ. وَٱلسِّرَاجِ ٱلْوَهَّاجِ. وَٱلْبَحْرِ ٱلْعَجَّاجِ.[٣] وَٱلْهَوَاءِ وَٱلْعَجَاجِ. إِنَّهَا لَمِنْ أَيْمَنِ ٱلْعُوَذِ. وَأَغْنَى عَنْكُمْ مِنْ لَابِسِي ٱلْخُوَذِ. مَنْ دَرَسَهَا عِنْدَ ٱبْتِسَامِ ٱلْفَلَقِ. لَمْ يُشْفِقْ مِنْ خَطْبٍ إِلَى ٱلشَّفَقِ. وَمَنْ نَاجَى بِهَا طَلِيعَةَ ٱلْغَسَقِ. أَمِنَ لَيْلَتَهُ مِنَ ٱلسَّرَقِ. قَالَ[٤] فَتَلَقَّنَّاهَا حَتَّى أَتْقَنَّاهَا. وَتَدَارَسْنَاهَا لِكَيْ لَا نَنْسَاهَا.

١٢.٥ ثُمَّ سِرْنَا نُزْجِي ٱلْحَمُولَاتِ. بِٱلدَّعَوَاتِ. لَا بِٱلْحُدَاةِ. وَنَحْمِي ٱلْحُمُولَاتِ. بِٱلْكَلِمَاتِ لَا بِٱلْكُمَاةِ. وَصَاحِبُنَا يَتَعَهَّدُنَا بِٱلْعَشِيِّ وَٱلْغَدَاةِ. وَلَا يَسْتَنْجِزُ مِنَّا ٱلْعِدَاتِ. حَتَّى إِذَا عَايَنَّا أَطْلَالَ عَانَةَ. قَالَ لَنَا ٱلْإِعَانَةَ ٱلْإِعَانَةَ. فَأَحْضَرْنَاهُ ٱلْمَعْلُومَ

١ «سطوة الجائرين»: د: مجاورة الجائرين، وفي و: سطوة الجبارين، وفي ف: مجاورة الجائرين وسطوة الجبّارين.
٢ د، ف: ومالي ومآلي. ٣ ف: الفجّاج. ٤ بعدها في د: الراوي.

وَالْمَكْتُومَ. وَأَرَيْنَاهُ الْمَعْكُومَ وَالْمَخْتُومَ. وَقُلْنَا لَهُ اِقْضِ مَا أَنْتَ قَاضٍ. فَمَا تَجِدُ فِينَا غَيْرَ رَاضٍ. فَمَا ٱسْتَخَفَّهُ سِوَى الْخِفِّ.[1] وَلَا حَلِيَ بِعَيْنِهِ غَيْرُ الْعَيْنِ.[2] فَٱحْتَمَلَ مِنْهُمَا[3] وِقْرَهُ. وَنَاءَ بِمَا يَسُدُّ فَقْرَهُ. ثُمَّ خَالَسَنَا مُخَالَسَةَ الطَّرَّارِ. وَٱنْصَلَتَ مِنَّا ٱنْصِلَاتَ الْفَرَّارِ. فَأَوْحَشَنَا فِرَاقُهُ. وَأَدْهَشَنَا ٱمِّرَاقُهُ.[4] وَلَمْ نَزَلْ نَنْشُدُهُ بِكُلِّ نَادٍ. وَنَسْتَخْبِرُ عَنْهُ كُلَّ مُغْوٍ وَهَادٍ. إِلَى أَنْ قِيلَ إِنَّهُ مُذْ دَخَلَ عَانَةَ. مَا زَايَلَ الْحَانَةَ. فَأَغْرَانِي خُبْثُ هٰذَا الْقَوْلِ بِسَبْكِهِ. وَالِانْسِلَاكِ فِيمَا لَسْتُ مِنْ سِلْكِهِ. فَٱدَّلَجْتُ إِلَى الدَّسْكَرَةِ. فِي هَيْئَةٍ مُنَكَّرَةٍ. فَإِذَا الشَّيْخُ فِي حُلَّةٍ مُمَصَّرَةٍ. بَيْنَ دِنَانٍ وَمِعْصَرَةٍ. وَحَوْلَهُ سُقَاةٌ تَبْهَرُ. وَشُمُوعٌ تَزْهَرُ. وَآسٌ وَعَبْهَرٌ. وَمِزْمَارٌ وَمِزْهَرٌ. وَهُوَ تَارَةً يَسْتَبْزِلُ[5] الدِّنَانَ. وَطَوْرًا يَسْتَنْطِقُ الْعِيدَانَ. وَدَفْعَةً يَسْتَنْشِقُ الرَّيْحَانَ. وَأُخْرَى يُغَازِلُ الْغِزْلَانَ. فَلَمَّا عَثَرْتُ عَلَى لَبْسِهِ. وَتَفَاوُتِ يَوْمِهِ مِنْ أَمْسِهِ. قُلْتُ لَهُ أَوْلَى لَكَ يَا مَلْعُونُ. أَأُنْسِيتَ يَوْمَ جَيْرُونَ. فَضَحِكَ مُسْتَغْرِبًا. ثُمَّ أَنْشَدَ مُطَرِّبًا.[6]

لَزِمْتُ السِّفَارَ وَجُبْتُ الْقِفَارَ وَعِفْتُ النِّفَارَ لِأَجْنِي الْفَرَحْ ٦،١٢
وَخُضْتُ السُّيولَ وَرُضْتُ الْخُيولَ لِجَرِّ ذُيولِ الصِّبَى وَالْمَرَحْ
وَمِطْتُ الْوَقَارَ وَبِعْتُ الْعَقَارَ لِحَسْوِ الْعُقَارِ وَرَشْفِ الْقَدَحْ
وَلَوْلَا الطِّمَاحُ إِلَى شُرْبِ رَاحٍ لَمَا كَانَ بَاحَ فَمِي بِالْمُلَحْ
وَلَا كَانَ سَاقَ دَهَائِي الرِّفَاقَ لِأَرْضِ الْعِرَاقِ بِحَمْلِ السُّبَحْ
فَلَا تَغْضَبَنَّ وَلَا تَصْخَبَنَّ وَلَا تَعْتِبَنَّ فَعُذْرِي وَضَحْ
وَلَا تَعْجَبَنَّ لِشَيْخٍ أَبَنَّ بِمَغْنًى أَغَنَّ وَدَنٍّ طَفَحْ
فَإِنَّ الْمُدَامَ تُقَوِّي الْعِظَامَ وَتَشْفِي السَّقَامَ وَتَنْفِي التَّرَحْ

١ الخِفّ: هكذا في ق، س، و؛ وفي د: الخِفِّ والزَّيْن، وفي ف: الخِفّ والهَيْن. ٢ ف: الحلي والعين. ٣ و: منها.
٤ ف: امتراقه. ٥ ف: يستبدل. ٦ هكذا في ق، س، و؛ وفي د، ف: مُطْرِبًا.

وَأَصْفَى السُّرُورِ إِذَا مَا الْوَقُورْ أَمَاطَ سُتُورَ الْحَيَا وَاطَّرَحْ
وَأَحْلَى الْغَرَامِ إِذَا الْمُسْتَهَامُ أَزَالَ اكْتِتَامَ الْهَوَى وَافْتَضَحْ
فَبُحْ بِهَوَاكَ وَبَرِّدْ حَشَاكَ فَزَنْدُ أَسَاكَ بِهِ قَدْ قَدَحْ
وَدَاوِ الْكُلُومَ وَسَلِّ الْهُمُومَ بِبِنْتِ الْكُرُومِ الَّتِي تُقْتَرَحْ
وَخُصَّ الْغَبُوقَ بِسَاقٍ يَسُوقُ بَلَاءَ الْمَشُوقِ إِذَا مَا طَمَحْ
وَشَادٍ يُشِيدُ بِصَوْتٍ تَمِيدُ جِبَالُ الْحَدِيدِ لَهُ إِنْ صَدَحْ
وَعَاصِ النَّصِيحَ الَّذِي لَا يُبِيحُ وِصَالَ الْمَلِيحِ إِذَا مَا سَمَحْ
وَجُلْ فِي الْمِحَالِ وَلَوْ بِالْمُحَالِ وَدَعْ مَا يُقَالُ وَخُذْ مَا صَلَحْ
وَفَارِقْ أَبَاكَ إِذَا مَا أَبَاكَ وَمُدَّ الشِّبَاكَ وَصِدْ مَنْ سَنَحْ
وَصَافِ الْخَلِيلَ وَنَافِ الْبَخِيلَ وَأَوْلِ الْجَمِيلَ وَوَالِ الْمِنَحْ
وَلُذْ بِالْمَتَابِ أَمَامَ الذَّهَابِ فَمَنْ دَقَّ بَابَ كَرِيمٍ فَتَحْ

٧،١٢ فَقُلْتُ لَهُ بَخٍ بَخٍ[1] لِرِوَايَتِكَ. وَأُفٍّ وَتُفٍّ لِغَوَايَتِكَ. فَبِاللهِ مِنْ أَيِّ الْأَعْيَاصِ عِيصُكَ. فَقَدْ أَعْضَلَنِي عَوِيصُكَ. فَقَالَ مَا أُحِبُّ أَنْ أُفْصِحَ عَنِّي. وَلٰكِنِّي سَأُكَنِّي.[2]

أَنَا أُطْرُوفَةُ الزَّمَا نِ وَأُعْجُوبَةُ الْأُمَمْ
وَأَنَا الْحُوَّلُ الَّذِي احْـ ـتَالَ فِي الْعُرْبِ وَالْعَجَمْ
غَيْرَ أَنِّي ابْنُ حَاجَةٍ هَاضَهُ الدَّهْرُ فَاهْتَضَمْ
وَأَبُو صِبْيَةٍ بَدَوْا مِثْلَ لَحْمٍ عَلَى وَضَمْ
وَأَخُو الْعَيْلَةِ الْمُعِيلُ إِذَا احْتَالَ لَمْ يُلَمْ

١ هكذا في ق، وفي س: بَخْ بَخْ، وفي و، ف: بَخٍ بَخٍ؛ وفي د: بَخٍّ بَخٍّ. ٢ ف: ولكن سأُكَنِّي.

٨،١٢ قَالَ الرَّاوِي فَعَرَفْتُ حِينَئِذٍ أَنَّهُ أَبُو زَيْدٍ ذُو الرِّيْبِ وَالْعَيْبِ. وَمُسَوِّدُ وَجْهِ الشَّيْبِ. وَسَاءَنِي عِظَمُ تَمَرُّدِهِ. وَقُبْحُ تَوَرُّدِهِ. فَقُلْتُ لَهُ بِلِسَانِ الْأَنَفَةِ. وَإِدْلَالِ الْمَعْرِفَةِ. أَلَمْ يَأْنِ لَكَ يَا شَيْخَنَا. أَنْ تُقْلِعَ عَنِ[1] الْخَنَا. فَتَضَجَّرَ وَزَمْجَرَ. وَتَنَكَّرَ وَفَكَّرَ. ثُمَّ قَالَ إِنَّهَا لَيْلَةُ مِرَاحٍ[2] لَا تَلَاحٍ. وَنُهْزَةُ شُرْبِ رَاحٍ لَا كِفَاحٍ. فَعَدِّ عَمَّا بَدَا. إِلَى أَنْ نَتَلَاقَى غَدًا. فَفَارَقْتُهُ فَرَقًا مِنْ عَرْبَدَتِهِ. لَا تَعَلُّقًا بِعِدَتِهِ. وَبِتُّ لَيْلَتِي لَابِسًا حِدَادَ النَّدَمِ. عَلَى نَقْلِي خُطَى الْقَدَمِ. إِلَى ٱبْنَةِ الْكَرْمِ لَا الْكَرَمِ. وَعَاهَدْتُ اللهَ سُبْحَانَهُ[3] أَنْ لَا أَحْضُرَ بَعْدَهَا حَانَةَ نَبَّاذٍ. وَلَوْ أُعْطِيتُ مُلْكَ بَغْدَاذٍ. وَأَنْ لَا أَشْهَدَ مِعْصَرَةَ[4] الشَّرَابِ. وَلَوْ رُدَّ عَلَيَّ عَصْرُ الشَّبَابِ. ثُمَّ إِنَّنَا رَحَّلْنَا الْعِيسَ. وَقْتَ التَّغْلِيسِ. وَخَلَّيْنَا بَيْنَ الشَّيْخَيْنِ أَبِي زَيْدٍ وَإِبْلِيسَ.

١ بعدها في ق: هذا (مشطوبة). ٢ س: مَراح. ٣ بعدها في ف: وتعالى. ٤ هكذا في ق، س؛ وفي و: مَعصرة؛ د، ف: مِعْصرة.

الْمَقَامَةُ الثَّالِثَةَ عَشْرَةَ[١]

١٫١٣ رَوَى الْحَارِثُ بْنُ هَمَّامٍ قَالَ نَدَوْتُ بِضَوَاحِي الزَّوْرَاءِ. مَعَ مَشْيَخَةٍ مِنَ الشُّعَرَاءِ. لَا يَعْلَقُ لَهُمْ مُبَارٍ بِغُبَارٍ. وَلَا يَجْرِي مَعَهُمْ مُمَارٍ فِي مِضْمَارٍ. فَأَفَضْنَا فِي حَدِيثٍ يَفْضَحُ الْأَزْهَارَ. إِلَى أَنْ نَصَفْنَا[٢] النَّهَارَ. فَلَمَّا غَاضَ دَرُّ الْأَفْكَارِ. وَصَبَتِ النُّفُوسُ إِلَى الْأَوْكَارِ. لَمَحْنَا عَجُوزًا تُقْبِلُ مِنَ الْبُعْدِ. وَتُحْضِرُ إِحْضَارَ الْجُرْدِ. وَقَدِ اسْتَتْلَتْ صِبْيَةً أَنْحَفَ مِنَ الْمَغَازِلِ. وَأَضْعَفَ مِنَ الْجَوَازِلِ.

٢٫١٣ فَمَا كَذَّبَتْ إِذْ رَأَتْنَا. أَنْ عَرَتْنَا. حَتَّى إِذَا مَا حَضَرَتْنَا. قَالَتْ حَيَّا اللهُ الْمَعَارِفَ. وَإِنْ لَمْ يَكُنَّ مَعَارِفَ. اِعْلَمُوا يَا مَآلَ الْآمِلِ. وَثِمَالَ الْأَرَامِلِ. أَنِّي مِنْ سَرَوَاتِ الْقَبَائِلِ. وَسَرِيَّاتِ الْعَقَائِلِ. لَمْ يَزَلْ أَهْلِي وَبَعْلِي يَحُلُّونَ الصَّدْرَ. وَيَسِيرُونَ الْقَلْبَ. وَيُمْطُونَ الظَّهْرَ. وَيُولُونَ الْيَدَ. فَلَمَّا أَرْدَى الدَّهْرُ الْأَعْضَادَ. وَفَجَعَ بِالْجَوَارِحِ.[٣] وَانْقَلَبَ ظَهْرًا لِبَطْنٍ. نَبَا النَّاظِرُ. وَجَفَا الْحَاجِبُ. وَذَهَبَتِ الْعَيْنُ. وَفُقِدَتِ الرَّاحَةُ. وَصَلَدَ الزَّنْدُ. وَوَهَتِ الْيَمِينُ.[٤] وَبَانَتِ الْمَرَافِقُ. وَلَمْ يَبْقَ لَنَا ثَنِيَّةٌ وَلَا نَابٌ. فَمُذِ اغْبَرَّ الْعَيْشُ الْأَخْضَرُ. وَازْوَرَّ الْمَحْبُوبُ الْأَصْفَرُ. اِسْوَدَّ يَوْمِي الْأَبْيَضُ. وَابْيَضَّ فَوْدِي الْأَسْوَدُ. حَتَّى رَثَى لِيَ الْعَدُوُّ الْأَزْرَقُ. فَحَبَّذَا الْمَوْتُ الْأَحْمَرُ. وَتِلْوِي مَنْ تَرَوْنَ عَيْنُهُ فُرَارُهُ. وَتَرْجُمَانُهُ اصْفِرَارُهُ. قُصْوَى بُغْيَةِ أَحَدِهِمْ ثُرْدَةٌ. وَقُصَارَى مُنْيَتِهِ[٥] بُرْدَةٌ. وَكُنْتُ آلَيْتُ أَلَّا أَبْذُلَ الْحُرَّ. إِلَّا لِلْحُرِّ. وَلَوْ أَنِّي مُتُّ مِنَ الضُّرِّ. وَقَدْ نَاجَتْنِي الْقَرُونَةُ. بِأَنْ تُوجَدَ عِنْدَكُمُ الْمَعُونَةُ. وَآذَنَتْنِي فِرَاسَةُ

---

١ بعدها في س: تُعْرَف بالمَوْصِلِيَّة، وفي د: البغدادية، وفي ف: وتعرف بالبغدادية. ٢ د: نصَّفنا. ٣ بعدها في د، ف: الأكبادَ. ٤ د، ف: ووَهَنَتْ؛ وبعدها في ف: وضاعَ اليَسارُ. ٥ ف: أُمْنِيَّتِهِ.

الْحَوْبَاءِ. بِأَنَّكُمْ يَنَابِيعُ الْحِبَاءِ. فَنَضَّرَ اللّٰهُ ٱمْرَأً أَبَرَّ قَسَمِي. وَصَدَّقَ تَوَسُّمِي. وَنَظَرَ إِلَيَّ بِعَيْنٍ يُقْذِيهَا الْجُمُودُ. وَيُقَذِّيهَا الْجُودُ.

٣.١٣ قَالَ الْحَارِثُ بْنُ هَمَّامٍ فَهِمْنَا لِبَرَاعَةِ عِبَارَتِهَا. وَمُلَحِ ٱسْتِعَارَتِهَا. وَقُلْنَا لَهَا قَدْ فَتَنَ كَلَامُكِ. فَكَيْفَ إِلْمَامُكِ. فَقَالَتْ أُفَجِّرُ الصَّخْرَ. وَلَا فَخْرَ. فَقُلْنَا إِنْ جَعَلْتِنَا مِنْ رُوَاتِكِ. لَمْ نَبْخَلْ بِمُوَاسَاتِكِ. فَقَالَتْ لَأُرِيَنَّكُمْ أَوَّلاً شِعَارِي. ثُمَّ لَأُرْوِيَنَّكُمْ أَشْعَارِي. فَأَبْرَزَتْ رُدْنَ دِرْعٍ دَرِيسٍ. وَبَرَزَتْ بِرْزَةَ عَجُوزٍ دَرْدَبِيسٍ. وَأَنْشَأَتْ تَقُولُ

أَشْكُو إِلَى اللّٰهِ ٱشْتِكَاءَ الْمَرِيضِ رَيْبَ الزَّمَانِ الْمُتَعَدِّي الْبَغِيضْ
يَا قَوْمِ إِنِّي مِنْ أُنَاسٍ غَنُوا دَهْرًا وَجَفْنُ الدَّهْرِ عَنْهُمْ غَضِيضْ
فَخَارُهُمْ لَيْسَ لَهُ دَافِعٌ وَصِيتُهُمْ بَيْنَ الْوَرَى مُسْتَفِيضْ
كَانُوا إِذَا مَا نُجْعَةٌ أَعْوَزَتْ فِي السَّنَةِ الشَّهْبَاءِ رَوْضًا أَرِيضْ
تُشَبُّ لِلسَّارِينَ نِيرَانُهُمْ وَيُطْعِمُونَ الضَّيْفَ لَحْمًا غَرِيضْ
مَا بَاتَ جَارٌ لَهُمُ سَاغِبًا وَلَا لِرَوْعٍ قَالَ حَالَ الْجَرِيضْ
فَغَيَّضَتْ مِنْهُمْ صُرُوفُ الرَّدَى بِحَارَ جُودٍ لَمْ أَخَلْهَا تَغِيضْ
وَأَوْدَعَتْ مِنْهُمْ بُطُونَ الثَّرَى[1] أُسْدَ التَّحَامِي وَأُسَاةَ الْمَرِيضْ
فَمَحْمِلِي بَعْدَ الْمَطَايَا الْمَطَا وَمَوْطِنِي بَعْدَ الْيَفَاعِ[2] الْحَضِيضْ
وَأَفْرُخِي مَا تَأْتَلِي تَشْتَكِي بُؤْسًا لَهُ فِي كُلِّ يَوْمٍ وَمِيضْ
إِذَا دَعَا الْقَانِتُ فِي لَيْلِهِ مَوْلَاهُ نَادَوْهُ بِدَمْعٍ يَفِيضْ
يَا رَازِقَ النَّعَّابِ فِي عُشِّهِ وَجَابِرَ الْعَظْمِ الْكَسِيرِ الْمَهِيضْ

١ ف: وأودِعَتْ منهم بطونُ الثرى. ٢ ف: البقاع.

أَتِحْ لَنَا اللّٰهُمَّ مَنْ عِرْضُهُ مِنْ دَنَسِ الذَّمِّ نَقِيٌّ رَحِيضْ
يُطْفِئُ نَارَ الْجُوعِ عَنَّا وَلَوْ بِمَذْقَةٍ مِنْ حَازِرٍ أَوْ مَخِيضْ
فَهَلْ فَتًى يَكْشِفُ مَا نَابَهُمْ وَيَغْنَمُ الشُّكْرَ الطَّوِيلَ الْعَرِيضْ
فَوَالَّذِي تَعْنُو النَّوَاصِي لَهُ يَوْمَ وُجُوهُ الْجَمْعِ سُودٌ وَبِيضْ
لَوْلَاهُمُ لَمْ تَبْدُ لِي صَفْحَةٌ وَلَا تَصَدَّيْتُ لِنَظْمِ الْقَرِيضْ

٤،١٣ قَالَ الرَّاوِي فَوَاللهِ لَقَدْ صَدَعَتْ بِأَبْيَاتِهَا أَعْشَارَ الْقُلُوبِ. وَٱسْتَخْرَجَتْ خَبَايَا الْجُيُوبِ. حَتَّى مَاحَهَا مَنْ دِينُهُ الِامْتِيَاحُ. وَٱرْتَاحَ لِرِفْدِهَا مَنْ لَمْ نَخَلْهُ يَرْتَاحُ. فَلَمَّا ٱفْعَوْعَمَ جَيْبُهَا تِبْرًا. وَأَوْلَاهَا كُلٌّ مِنَّا بِرًّا. تَوَلَّتْ يَتْلُوهَا الْأَصَاغِرُ. وَفُوهَا بِالشُّكْرِ فَاغِرٌ. فَٱشْرَأَبَّتِ الْجَمَاعَةُ بَعْدَ مَمَرِّهَا. إِلَى سَبْرِهَا. لِتَبْلُوَ مَوَاقِعَ بِرِّهَا. فَكَفَلْتُ لَهُمْ بِٱسْتِنْبَاطِ السِّرِّ الْمَرْمُوزِ. وَنَهَضْتُ أَقْفُو أَثَرَ الْعَجُوزِ. حَتَّى ٱنْتَهَتْ إِلَى سُوقٍ مُغْتَصَّةٍ بِالْأَنَامِ. مُخْتَصَّةٍ بِالزِّحَامِ. فَٱنْغَمَسَتْ فِي الْغُمَارِ. وَٱمَّلَسَتْ مِنَ الصِّبْيَةِ الْأَغْمَارِ. ثُمَّ عَاجَتْ بِخُلُوِّ بَالٍ. إِلَى مَسْجِدٍ خَالٍ. فَأَمَاطَتِ الْجِلْبَابَ. وَنَضَتِ النِّقَابَ. وَأَنَا أَلْمَحُهَا مِنْ خَصَاصِ الْبَابِ. وَأَرْقُبُ مَا سَتُبْدِي مِنَ الْعُجَابِ. فَلَمَّا ٱنْسَرَتْ أُهْبَةُ الْخَفَرِ. رَأَيْتُ مُحَيَّا أَبِي زَيْدٍ قَدْ سَفَرَ.

٥،١٣ فَهَمَمْتُ أَنْ أَهْجُمَ عَلَيْهِ. لِأُعَنِّفَهُ عَلَى مَا أَجْرَى إِلَيْهِ. فَٱسْلَنْقَى ٱسْلِنْقَاءَ الْمُتَمَرِّدِينَ. ثُمَّ رَفَعَ عَقِيرَةَ الْمُغَرِّدِينَ. وَٱنْدَفَعَ يُنْشِدُ

يَا لَيْتَ شِعْرِي أَدَهْرِي أَحَاطَ عِلْمًا بِقَدْرِي
وَهَلْ دَرَى كُنْهَ غَوْرِي فِي الْخَدْعِ أَمْ لَيْسَ يَدْرِي
كَمْ قَدْ قَمَرْتُ بَنِيهِ بِحِيلَتِي وَبِمَكْرِي
وَكَمْ بَرَزْتُ بِعُرْفٍ عَلَيْهِمِ وَبِنُكْرِ

أَصْطَادُ قَوْمًا بِوَعْظٍ وَآخَرِينَ بِشِعْرِ
وَأَسْتَفِزُّ بِخَلٍّ عَقْلًا وَعَقْلًا بِخَمْرِ
وَتَارَةً أَنَا صَخْرُ وَتَارَةً أُخْتُ صَخْرِ
وَلَوْ سَلَكْتُ سَبِيلًا مَأْلُوفَةً طُولَ عُمْرِي
لَخَابَ قِدْحِي وَقَدْحِي وَدَامَ عُسْرِي وَخُسْرِي
فَقُلْ لِمَنْ لَامَ هٰذَا عُذْرِي فَدُونَكَ عُذْرِي

قَالَ الْحَارِثُ بْنُ هَمَّامٍ فَلَمَّا ظَهَرْتُ عَلَى جَلِيَّةِ[١] أَمْرِهِ. وَبَدِيعَةِ إِمْرِهِ. وَمَا زَخْرَفَ فِي شِعْرِهِ مِنْ عُذْرِهِ. عَلِمْتُ أَنَّ شَيْطَانَهُ الْمَرِيدَ. لَا يَسْمَعُ التَّفْنِيدَ. وَلَا يَفْعَلُ إِلَّا مَا يُرِيدُ. فَثَنَيْتُ إِلَى أَصْحَابِي عِنَانِي. وَأَبْثَثْتُهُمْ مَا أَثْبَتَهُ عِيَانِي. فَوَجَمُوا لِضَيْعَةِ الْجَوَائِزِ. وَتَعَاهَدُوا عَلَى مَحْرَمَةِ الْعَجَائِزِ. ٦.١٣

١ د: «طهرت على جلية»: في د: ظَهَرْتُ عليَّ جَلِيَّةٌ.

المَقَامَةُ الرَّابِعَةَ عَشْرَةَ[١]

١٤.١ حَكَى الحَارِثُ بْنُ هَمَّامٍ قَالَ نَهَضْتُ مِنْ مَدِينَةِ السَّلَامِ. لِحَجَّةِ[٢] الإِسْلَامِ. فَلَمَّا قَضَيْتُ بِعَوْنِ[٣] اللهِ التَّفَثَ. وَٱسْتَبَحْتُ الطِّيبَ وَالرَّفَثَ. صَادَفَ مَوْسِمُ الخَيْفِ. مَعْمَعَانَ الصَّيْفِ. فَٱسْتَظْهَرْتُ لِلضَّرُورَةِ. بِمَا يَقِي حَرَّ الظَّهِيرَةِ. فَبَيْنَمَا أَنَا تَحْتَ طِرَافٍ. مَعَ رُفْقَةٍ ظِرَافٍ. وَقَدْ حَمِيَ وَطِيسُ الحَصْبَاءِ. وَأَعْشَى الهَجِيرُ عَيْنَ الحِرْبَاءِ. إِذْ هَجَمَ عَلَيْنَا شَيْخٌ مُتَسَعْسِعٌ. يَتْلُوهُ فَتًى مُتَرَعْرِعٌ. فَسَلَّمَ الشَّيْخُ تَسْلِيمَ أَدِيبٍ أَرِيبٍ. وَحَاوَرَ مُحَاوَرَةَ قَرِيبٍ لَا غَرِيبٍ. فَأَعْجَبَنَا بِمَا نَثَرَ مِنْ سِمْطِهِ. وَعَجِبْنَا مِنِ ٱنْبِسَاطِهِ قَبْلَ بَسْطِهِ.

١٤.٢ وَقُلْنَا لَهُ مَا أَنْتَ. وَكَيْفَ وَلَجْتَ وَمَا ٱسْتَأْذَنْتَ. فَقَالَ أَمَّا أَنَا فَعَافٍ. وَطَالِبُ إِسْعَافٍ. وَسِرُّ ضُرِّي غَيْرُ خَافٍ. وَالنَّظَرُ إِلَيَّ شَفِيعٌ لِي كَافٍ. وَأَمَّا الِانْسِيَابُ. الَّذِي عَلِقَ بِهِ الِارْتِيَابُ. فَمَا هُوَ بِعُجَابٍ. إِذْ مَا عَلَى الكُرَمَاءِ مِنْ حِجَابٍ. فَسَأَلْنَاهُ أَنَّى ٱهْتَدَى إِلَيْنَا. وَبِمَ ٱسْتَدَلَّ عَلَيْنَا. فَقَالَ إِنَّ لِلْكَرَمِ نَشْرًا تَنُمُّ بِهِ نَفَحَاتُهُ. وَتُرْشِدُ إِلَى رَوْضِهِ فَوَحَاتُهُ. فَٱسْتَدْلَلْتُ بِتَأَرُّجِ عَرْفِكُمْ. عَلَى تَبَلُّجِ عُرْفِكُمْ. وَبَشَّرَنِي تَضَوُّعُ رَنْدِكُمْ. بِحُسْنِ المُنْقَلَبِ مِنْ عِنْدِكُمْ. فَٱسْتَخْبَرْنَاهُ حِينَئِذٍ عَنْ لُبَانَتِهِ. لِنَكْفُلَ[٤] بِإِعَانَتِهِ. فَقَالَ إِنَّ لِي مَأْرَبًا. وَلِفَتَايَ مَطْلَبًا. فَقُلْنَا كِلَا المَرَامَيْنِ سَيُقْضَى. وَكِلَاكُمَا سَوْفَ يُرْضَى.[٥] وَلٰكِنِ الكُبْرَ الكُبْرَ.

١ في هامش س: البغدادية؛ وفي د: المَكِّيَّة؛ وفي ف: وهي المكية. ٢ هكذا في س، وهي غير مشكّلة في ق، و؛ وفي د، ف: لِحَجَّة. ٣ في هامش س: نسخة الأخرى (هكذا) بِحَمْدِ. ٤ ف: نتكفّل. ٥ و: يَرْضَى.

فَقَالَ أَجَلْ وَمَنْ دَحَا السَّبْعَ الْغُبْرَ. ثُمَّ وَثَبَ لِلْمَقَالِ. كَالْمُنْشَطِ مِنَ الْعِقَالِ. ٣،١٤
وَأَنْشَدَ

إِنِّي ٱمْرُؤٌ أُبْدِعَ بِي   بَعْدَ الْوَجَى وَالتَّعَبِ
وَشُقَّتِي شَاسِعَةٌ   يَقْصُرُ عَنْهَا خَبَبِي
وَمَا مَعِي خَرْدَلَةٌ   مَطْبُوعَةٌ مِنْ ذَهَبِ
فَحِيلَتِي مُنْسَدَّةٌ   وَحَيْرَتِي تَلْعَبُ بِي
إِنِ ٱرْتَحَلْتُ رَاجِلًا   خِفْتُ دَوَاعِي الْعَطَبِ
وَإِنْ تَخَلَّفْتُ عَنِ الرُّفْقَةِ ضَاقَ مَذْهَبِي
فَزَفْرَتِي فِي صُعُدٍ   وَعَبْرَتِي فِي صَبَبِ
وَأَنْتُمُ مُنْتَجَعُ الرَّا   جِي وَمَرْمَى الطَّلَبِ
لُهَاكُمُ مُنْهَلَّةٌ   وَلَا ٱنْهِلَالَ السُّحُبِ
وَجَارُكُمْ فِي حَرَمٍ   وَوَفْرُكُمْ فِي حَرَبِ
مَا لَاذَ مُرْتَاعٌ بِكُمْ   فَخَافَ نَابَ النُّوَبِ
وَلَا ٱسْتَدَرَّ آمِلٌ   حِبَاءَكُمْ فَمَا حُبِي
فَٱنْعَطِفُوا فِي قِصَّتِي   وَأَحْسِنُوا مُنْقَلَبِي
فَلَوْ بَلَوْتُمْ عِيشَتِي   فِي مَطْعَمِي وَمَشْرَبِي
لَسَاءَكُمْ ضُرِّيَ الَّذِي   أَسْلَمَنِي لِلْكُرَبِ
وَلَوْ خَبَرْتُمْ حَسَبِي   وَنَسَبِي وَمَذْهَبِي
وَمَا حَوَتْ مَعْرِفَتِي   مِنَ الْعُلُومِ النُّخَبِ
لَمَا ٱعْتَرَتْكُمْ شُبْهَةٌ   فِي أَنَّ دَائِي أَدَبِي

فَلَيْتَ أَنِّي لَمْ أَكُنْ أُرْضِعْتُ ثَدْيَ ٱلْأَدَبِ
فَقَدْ دَهَانِي شُؤْمُهُ وَعَقَّنِي فِيهِ أَبِي

٤،١٤ فَقُلْنَا لَهُ أَمَّا أَنْتَ فَقَدْ صَرَّحَتْ أَبْيَاتُكَ بِفَاقَتِكَ. وَعَطَبِ نَاقَتِكَ. وَسَنُمْطِيكَ مَا يُوصِلُكَ إِلَى بَلَدِكَ. فَمَا مَأْرَبَةُ وَلَدِكَ. فَقَالَ لَهُ قُمْ يَا بُنَيَّ كَمَا قَامَ أَبُوكَ. وَفُهْ بِمَا فِي نَفْسِكَ لَا فُضَّ فُوكَ. فَنَهَضَ نُهُوضَ ٱلْبَطَلِ لِلْبِرَازِ. وَأَصْلَتَ لِسَانًا كَٱلْعَضْبِ ٱلْجُرَازِ. وَأَنْشَأَ[١] يَقُولُ

يَا سَادَةً فِي ٱلْمَعَالِي لَهُمْ مَبَانٍ مَشِيدَهْ
وَمَنْ إِذَا نَابَ خَطْبٌ قَامُوا بِدَفْعِ ٱلْمَكِيدَهْ
وَمَنْ يَهُونُ عَلَيْهِمْ بَذْلُ ٱلْكُنُوزِ ٱلْعَتِيدَهْ
أُرِيدُ مِنْكُمْ شِوَاءً وَجَرْدَقًا وَعَصِيدَهْ
فَإِنْ غَلَا فَرُقَاقٌ بِهِ تُوَارَى ٱلشَّهِيدَهْ
أَوْ لَمْ يَكُنْ ذَا وَلَا ذَا فَشَبْعَةٌ مِنْ ثَرِيدَهْ
فَإِنْ تَعَذَّرْنَ طُرًّا فَعَجْوَةٌ وَنَهِيدَهْ
فَأَحْضِرُوا مَا تَسَنَّى وَلَوْ شَظًى مِنْ قَدِيدَهْ
وَرَوِّجُوهُ فَنَفْسِي لِمَا يَرُوجُ مُرِيدَهْ
وَٱلزَّادُ لَا بُدَّ مِنْهُ لِرِحْلَةٍ[٢] لِي بَعِيدَهْ
وَأَنْتُمُ خَيْرُ رَهْطٍ يُدْعَوْنَ عِنْدَ ٱلشَّدِيدَهْ
أَيْدِيكُمُ كُلَّ يَوْمٍ لَهَا أَيَادٍ جَدِيدَهْ
وَرَاحُكُمْ وَاصِلَاتٌ شَمْلَ ٱلصِّلَاتِ ٱلْمُفِيدَهْ

---

١ د: وأنشد. ٢ في ق: لِشُقَّةٍ، وفي هامشها: رحلة صح.

وَبُغْيَتِي فِي مَطَاوِي   مَا تَرْفِدُونَ زَهِيدَهْ
وَفِيَّ أَجْرٌ وَعُقْبَى   تَنْفِيسِ كَرْبِي حَمِيدَهْ
وَلِي نَتَائِجُ فِكْرٍ   يَفْضَحْنَ كُلَّ قَصِيدَهْ

٥،١٤ قَالَ الْحَارِثُ بْنُ هَمَّامٍ فَلَمَّا رَأَيْنَا الشِّبْلَ يُشْبِهُ الْأَسَدَ. أَرْحَلْنَا الْوَالِدَ وَزَوَّدْنَا الْوَلَدَ. فَقَابَلَا الصُّنْعَ بِشُكْرٍ نَشَرَا أَرْدِيَتَهُ. وَأَدَّيَا بِهِ دِيَتَهُ. وَلَمَّا عَزَمَا عَلَى الِانْطِلَاقِ. وَعَقَدَا لِلرِّحْلَةِ حُبُكَ النِّطَاقِ. قُلْتُ لِلشَّيْخِ هَلْ ضَاهَتْ عِدَتُنَا عِدَةَ عُرْقُوبٍ. أَوْ[١] بَقِيَتْ حَاجَةٌ فِي نَفْسِ يَعْقُوبَ. فَقَالَ حَاشَ لِلهِ وَكَلَّا. بَلْ جَلَّ مَعْرُوفُكُمْ وَجَلَّى. فَقُلْتُ لَهُ فَدِنَّا كَمَا دِنَّاكَ. وَأَفِدْنَا كَمَا أَفَدْنَاكَ. أَيْنَ الدُّوَيْرَةُ. فَقَدْ مَلَكَتْنَا فِيكَ الْحَيْرَةُ. فَتَنَفَّسَ تَنَفُّسَ مَنِ ادَّكَرَ أَوْطَانَهُ. وَأَنْشَدَ وَالشَّهِيقُ يُلَعْثِمُ لِسَانَهُ.

سَرُوجُ دَارِي وَلَكِنْ   كَيْفَ السَّبِيلُ إِلَيْهَا
وَقَدْ أَنَاخَ الْأَعَادِي   بِهَا وَأَخْنَوْا عَلَيْهَا
فَوَالَّتِي سِرْتُ أَبْغِي   حَطَّ الذُّنُوبِ لَدَيْهَا
مَا رَاقَ طَرْفِي شَيْءٌ   مُذْ غِبْتُ عَنْ طَرْفَيْهَا

ثُمَّ اغْرَوْرَقَتْ عَيْنَاهُ بِالدُّمُوعِ. وَآذَنَتْ مَدَامِعُهُ بِالْهُمُوعِ. فَكَرِهَ أَنْ يَسْتَوْكِفَهَا. وَلَمْ يَمْلِكْ أَنْ يُكَفْكِفَهَا. فَقَطَعَ إِنْشَادَهُ الْمُسْتَحْلَى. وَأَوْجَزَ فِي الْوَدَاعِ وَوَلَّى.

١ و: أو هل.

الْمَقَامَةُ الْخَامِسَةَ عَشْرَةَ[1]

١٥.١ أَخْبَرَ الْحَارِثُ بْنُ هَمَّامٍ قَالَ أَرِقْتُ ذَاتَ لَيْلَةٍ حَالِكَةِ الْجِلْبَابِ. هَامِيَةِ الرَّبَابِ. وَلَا أَرَقَ صَبٍّ طُرِدَ عَنِ الْبَابِ. وَمُنِيَ بِصَدِّ الْأَحْبَابِ. فَلَمْ تَزَلِ الْأَفْكَارُ يَهِجْنَ هَمِّي. وَيُجِلْنَ فِي الْوَسَاوِسِ وَهْمِي. حَتَّى تَمَنَّيْتُ. لِمَضَضِ مَا عَانَيْتُ. أَنْ أُرْزَقَ سَمِيرًا مِنَ الْفُضَلَاءِ. لِيَقْصُرَ[2] طُولَ[3] لَيْلَتِي اللَّيْلَاءِ. فَمَا انْقَضَتْ مُنْيَتِي. وَلَا أَغْمَضَتْ مُقْلَتِي. حَتَّى قَرَعَ الْبَابَ قَارِعٌ. لَهُ صَوْتٌ خَاشِعٌ. فَقُلْتُ فِي نَفْسِي لَعَلَّ غَرْسَ التَّمَنِّي قَدْ أَثْمَرَ. وَلَيْلَ الْحَظِّ قَدْ أَقْمَرَ. فَنَهَضْتُ إِلَيْهِ عَجْلَانَ. وَقُلْتُ مَنِ الطَّارِقُ الْآنَ. فَقَالَ غَرِيبٌ أَجَنَّهُ اللَّيْلُ. وَغَشِيَهُ السَّيْلُ. وَيَبْتَغِي الْإِيوَاءَ لَا غَيْرُ.[4] وَإِذَا أَسْحَرَ قَدَّمَ السَّيْرَ.

١٥.٢ قَالَ[5] فَلَمَّا دَلَّ شُعَاعُهُ عَلَى شَمْسِهِ. وَنَمَّ عُنْوَانُهُ بِسِرِّ طِرْسِهِ. عَلِمْتُ أَنَّ مُسَامَرَتَهُ غُنْمٌ. وَمُسَاهَرَتَهُ نُعْمٌ. فَفَتَحْتُ الْبَابَ بِابْتِسَامٍ. وَقُلْتُ ادْخُلُوهَا بِسَلَامٍ. فَدَخَلَ شَخْصٌ قَدْ حَنَى الدَّهْرُ صَعْدَتَهُ. وَبَلَّلَ الْقَطْرُ بُرْدَتَهُ. فَحَيَّا بِلِسَانٍ عَضْبٍ. وَبَيَانٍ عَذْبٍ. ثُمَّ شَكَرَ عَلَى تَلْبِيَةِ صَوْتِهِ. وَاعْتَذَرَ مِنَ الطُّرُوقِ فِي غَيْرِ وَقْتِهِ. فَدَانَيْتُهُ بِالْمِصْبَاحِ الْمُتَّقِدِ. وَتَأَمَّلْتُهُ تَأَمُّلَ الْمُنْتَقِدِ. فَأَلْفَيْتُهُ شَيْخَنَا أَبَا زَيْدٍ بِلَا رَيْبٍ. وَلَا رَجْمِ غَيْبٍ. فَأَحْلَلْتُهُ مَحَلَّ مَنْ أَظْفَرَنِي بِقُصْوَى الطَّلَبِ. وَنَقَلَنِي مِنْ وَقْدِ الْكُرَبِ. إِلَى رَوْحِ الطَّرَبِ. ثُمَّ أَخَذَ يَشْكُو الْأَيْنَ. وَأَخَذْتُ فِي كَيْفَ وَأَيْنَ. فَقَالَ أَبْلِعْنِي رِيقِي. فَقَدْ أَتْعَبَنِي طَرِيقِي. فَظَنَنْتُهُ مُسْتَبْطِنًا لِلسَّغَبِ. مُتَكَاسِلًا لِهَذَا

١ في هامش س: تعرف بالفَرْضِيَّة؛ وفي د: الفَرَضية؛ وفي ف: الفَرَضية. ٢ و: لَيَقْصُرُ، ف: لِيُقَصِّرَ. ٣ في ق: يطولُ، وضمتها مشطوبة بفتحة؛ وفي س، و: طولُ. ٤ س: غيرٌ؛ و، ف: غيرَ. ٥ ليس في ق.

السَّبَبِ. فَأَحْضَرْتُهُ مَا يَحْضُرُ لِلضَّيْفِ الْمُفَاجِي. فِي اللَّيْلِ الدَّاجِي. فَٱنْقَبَضَ ٱنْقِبَاضَ الْمُحْتَشِمِ. وَأَعْرَضَ إِعْرَاضَ الْبَشِمِ. فَسُؤْتُ ظَنًّا بِٱمْتِنَاعِهِ. وَأَحْفَظَنِي حُؤُولُ طِبَاعِهِ. حَتَّى كِدْتُ أُغْلِظُ لَهُ فِي الْكَلَامِ. وَأَلْسَعُهُ بِحُمَةِ الْمَلَامِ. فَتَبَيَّنَ مِنْ لَمَحَاتِ نَاظِرِي. مَا خَامَرَ خَاطِرِي. فَقَالَ يَا ضَعِيفَ الثِّقَةِ. بِأَهْلِ الْمِقَةِ. عَدِّ عَمَّا أَخْطَرْتَهُ بِبَالِكَ. وَٱسْتَمِعْ إِلَيَّ لَا أَبَا لَكَ. فَقُلْتُ هَاتِ. يَا أَخَا التُّرَّهَاتِ.

٣،١٥ فَقَالَ اِعْلَمْ أَنِّي بِتُّ الْبَارِحَةَ حَلِيفَ إِفْلَاسٍ. وَنَجِيَّ وَسْوَاسٍ. فَلَمَّا قَضَى اللَّيْلُ نَحْبَهُ. وَغَوَّرَ الصُّبْحُ شُهْبَهُ.[١] غَدَوْتُ وَقْتَ الْإِشْرَاقِ. إِلَى بَعْضِ الْأَسْوَاقِ. مُتَصَدِّيًا لِصَيْدٍ يَسْنَحُ. أَوْ حُرٍّ يَسْمَحُ. فَلَحَظْتُ بِهَا تَمْرًا قَدْ حُسِّنَ تَصْفِيفُهُ. وَأُحْسِنَ إِلَيْهِ مَصِيفُهُ. فَجَمَعَ عَلَى التَّحْقِيقِ. صَفَاءَ الرَّحِيقِ. وَقُنُوءَ الْعَقِيقِ. وَقُبَالَتَهُ لِبَأٌ قَدْ بَرَزَ كَالْإِبْرِيزِ الْأَصْفَرِ. وَٱنْجَلَى فِي اللَّوْنِ الْمُزَعْفَرِ. فَهُوَ يُثْنِي عَلَى طَاهِيهِ. بِلِسَانِ تَنَاهِيهِ. وَيُصَوِّبُ رَأْيَ مُشْتَرِيهِ. وَلَوْ نَقَدَ حَبَّةَ الْقَلْبِ فِيهِ. فَأَسَرَتْنِي الشَّهْوَةُ بِأَشْطَانِهَا. وَأَسْلَمَتْنِي الْعَيْمَةُ إِلَى سُلْطَانِهَا. فَبَقِيتُ أَحْيَرَ مِنْ ضَبٍّ. وَأَذْهَلَ مِنْ صَبٍّ. لَا وُجْدٌ[٢] يُوصِلُنِي إِلَى نَيْلِ الْمُرَادِ. وَلَذَّةِ الِازْدِرَادِ. وَلَا قَدَمٌ[٣] تُطَاوِعُنِي عَلَى الذَّهَابِ. مَعَ حُرْقَةِ الِالْتِهَابِ. لٰكِنْ حَدَانِي الْقَرَمُ وَسَوْرَتُهُ. وَالسَّغَبُ وَفَوْرَتُهُ. عَلَى أَنْ أَنْتَجِعَ كُلَّ أَرْضٍ. وَأَقْتَنِعَ مِنَ الْوِرْدِ بِبَرْضٍ. فَلَمْ أَزَلْ سَحَابَةَ ذٰلِكَ النَّهَارِ. أُدْلِي دَلْوِي إِلَى الْأَنْهَارِ. وَهْيَ لَا تَرْجِعُ بِبِلَّةٍ. وَلَا تَجْلُبُ نَقْعَ غُلَّةٍ. إِلَى أَنْ صَغَتِ الشَّمْسُ لِلْغُرُوبِ. وَضَعُفَتِ النَّفْسُ مِنَ اللُّغُوبِ. فَرُحْتُ بِكَبِدٍ حَرَّى. وَٱنْثَنَيْتُ أُقَدِّمُ رِجْلًا وَأُؤَخِّرُ أُخْرَى.

٤،١٥ وَبَيْنَمَا أَنَا أَسْعَى وَأَقْعُدُ. وَأَهُبُّ وَأَرْكُدُ. إِذْ قَابَلَنِي شَيْخٌ يَتَأَوَّهُ آهَةَ الثَّكْلَانِ. وَعَيْنَاهُ تَهْمُلَانِ. فَمَا شَغَلَنِي مَا أَنَا فِيهِ مِنْ دَاءِ الذِّيبِ. وَالْخَوَى الْمُذِيبِ. عَنِ

---

١ د: شُهُبَه. ٢ و، ف: وُجْد. ٣ و، ف: قَدَم.

تَعَاطِي مُدَاخَلَتِهِ. وَالطَّمَعَ فِي مُخَاتَلَتِهِ. فَقُلْتُ لَهُ يَا هٰذَا إِنَّ لِبُكَائِكَ سِرًّا.[١] وَوَرَاءَ تَحَرُّقِكَ لَشَرًّا. فَأَطْلِعْنِي عَلَى بُرَحَائِكَ. وَٱتَّخِذْنِي مِنْ نُصَحَائِكَ. فَإِنَّكَ سَتَجِدُ مِنِّي طَبًّا آسِيًا. أَوْ عَوْنًا مُوَاسِيًا. فَقَالَ وَاللهِ مَا تَأَوُّهِي لِعَيْشٍ[٢] فَاتَ. وَلَا مِنْ دَهْرٍ ٱفْتَاتَ بَلْ لِانْقِرَاضِ الْعِلْمِ وَدُرُوسِهِ. وَأُفُولِ أَقْمَارِهِ وَشُمُوسِهِ. فَقُلْتُ وَأَيُّ حَادِثَةٍ نَجَمَتْ. وَقَضِيَّةٍ ٱسْتَعْجَمَتْ. حَتَّى هَاجَتْ لَكَ الْأَسَفَ. عَلَى فَقْدِ مَنْ سَلَفَ. فَأَبْرَزَ رُقْعَةً مِنْ كُمِّهِ. وَأَقْسَمَ بِأَبِيهِ وَأُمِّهِ. لَقَدْ أَنْزَلَهَا بِأَعْلَامِ الْمَدَارِسِ. فَمَا ٱمْتَازُوا عَنِ الْأَعْلَامِ الدَّوَارِسِ. وَٱسْتَنْطَقَ لَهَا أَحْبَارَ الْمَحَابِرِ. فَخَرِسُوا خَرَسَ[٣] سُكَّانِ الْمَقَابِرِ. فَقُلْتُ أَرِنِيهَا. فَلَعَلِّي أُغْنِي فِيهَا. فَقَالَ مَا أَبْعَدْتَ فِي الْمَرَامِ. فَرُبَّ رَمْيَةٍ مِنْ غَيْرِ رَامٍ. ثُمَّ نَاوَلَنِيهَا. فَإِذَا الْمَكْتُوبُ فِيهَا.

أَيُّهَا الْعَالِمُ الْفَقِيهُ الَّذِي فَا   قَ ذَكَاءً فَمَا لَهُ مِنْ شَبِيهِ
أَفْتِنَا فِي قَضِيَّةٍ حَادَ عَنْهَا   كُلُّ قَاضٍ وَحَارَ كُلُّ فَقِيهِ
رَجُلٌ مَاتَ عَنْ أَخٍ مُسْلِمٍ حُرٍّ   تَقِيٍّ مِنْ أُمِّهِ وَأَبِيهِ
وَلَهُ زَوْجَةٌ لَهَا أَيُّهَا الْحَبْرُ   أَخٌ خَالِصٌ بِلَا تَمْوِيهِ
فَحَوَتْ فَرْضَهَا وَحَازَ أَخُوهَا   مَا تَبَقَّى بِالْإِرْثِ دُونَ أَخِيهِ
فَٱشْفِنَا بِالْجَوَابِ عَمَّا سَأَلْنَا   فَهْوَ نَصٌّ لَا خُلْفَ يُوجَدُ فِيهِ

١٥،٥ فَلَمَّا قَرَأْتُ شِعْرَهَا. وَلَمَحْتُ سِرَّهَا. قُلْتُ لَهُ عَلَى الْخَبِيرِ بِهَا سَقَطْتَ. وَعِنْدَ ٱبْنِ بَجْدَتِهَا حَطَطْتَ. إِلَّا أَنِّي مُضْطَرِمُ الْأَحْشَاءِ. مُضْطَرٌّ إِلَى الْعَشَاءِ. فَأَكْرِمْ مَثْوَايَ. ثُمَّ ٱسْتَمِعْ فَتْوَايَ. فَقَالَ لَقَدْ أَنْصَفْتَ فِي الِاشْتِرَاطِ. وَتَجَافَيْتَ عَنِ الِاشْتِطَاطِ. فَصِرْ مَعِي. إِلَى مَرْبَعِي. لِتَظْفَرَ بِمَا تَبْتَغِي. وَتَنْقَلِبَ كَمَا يَنْبَغِي. قَالَ فَصَاحَبْتُهُ

١ د: لَسِرّ. ٢ ف: من عيش. ٣ في هامش س وفي و،د،ف: ولا خَرَسَ.

إِلَى ذَرَاهُ. كَمَا حَكَمَ اللهُ. فَأَدْخَلَنِي بَيْتًا أَحْرَجَ مِنَ التَّابُوتِ. وَأَوْهَنَ مِنْ بَيْتِ الْعَنْكَبُوتِ. إِلَّا أَنَّهُ جَبَرَ ضِيقَ رَبْعِهِ. بِتَوْسِعَةِ ذَرْعِهِ. فَحَكَّمَنِي فِي الْقِرَى. وَمَطَايِبِ مَا يُشْتَرَى. فَقُلْتُ أُرِيدُ أَزْهَى رَاكِبٍ عَلَى أَشْهَى مَرْكُوبٍ. وَأَنْفَعَ صَاحِبٍ مَعَ أَضَرِّ مَصْحُوبٍ. فَأَفْكَرَ سَاعَةً طَوِيلَةً. ثُمَّ قَالَ لَعَلَّكَ تَعْنِي بِنْتَ نُخَيْلَةٍ. مَعَ لِبَإٍ سُخَيْلَةٍ. فَقُلْتُ إِيَّاهُمَا عَنَيْتُ. وَلِأَجْلِهِمَا تَعَنَّيْتُ.

٦،١٥ فَنَهَضَ نَشِيطًا. ثُمَّ رَبَضَ مُسْتَنْشِطًا. وَقَالَ اعْلَمْ أَصْلَحَكَ اللهُ أَنَّ الصِّدْقَ نَبَاهَةٌ. وَالْكَذِبَ عَاهَةٌ. فَلَا يَحْمِلَنَّكَ الْجُوعُ الَّذِي هُوَ شِعَارُ الْأَنْبِيَاءِ. وَحِلْيَةُ الْأَوْلِيَاءِ. عَلَى أَنْ تَلْحَقَ بِمَنْ مَانَ. وَتَخَلَّقَ بِالْخُلُقِ الَّذِي يُجَانِبُ الْإِيمَانَ. فَقَدْ تَجُوعُ الْحُرَّةُ وَلَا تَأْكُلُ بِثَدْيَيْهَا. وَتَأْبَى الدَّنِيَّةَ وَلَوِ اضْطُرَّتْ إِلَيْهَا. ثُمَّ إِنِّي لَسْتُ لَكَ بِزَبُونٍ. وَلَا أُغْضِي عَلَى صَفْقَةِ مَغْبُونٍ. وَهَا أَنَا قَدْ أَنْذَرْتُكَ قَبْلَ أَنْ يَنْهَتِكَ السِّتْرُ. وَيَنْعَقِدَ بَيْنَنَا[١] الْوِتْرُ. فَلَا تُلْغِ تَدَبُّرَ الْإِنْذَارِ. وَحَذَارِ مِنَ الْمُكَاذَبَةِ حَذَارِ. فَقُلْتُ لَهُ وَالَّذِي حَرَّمَ أَكْلَ الرِّبَا. وَأَحَلَّ أَكْلَ اللِّبَا. مَا فُهْتُ بِزُورٍ. وَلَا دَلَّيْتُكَ بِغُرُورٍ. وَسَتَخْبُرُ حَقِيقَةَ الْأَمْرِ. وَتَحْمَدُ بَذْلَ اللِّبَإِ وَالتَّمْرِ. فَهَشَّ هَشَاشَةَ الْمَصْدُوقِ. وَانْطَلَقَ مُغِذًّا إِلَى السُّوقِ. فَمَا كَانَ بِأَسْرَعَ مِنْ أَنْ أَقْبَلَ بِهِمَا يَدْلَحُ. وَوَجْهُهُ يَكْلَحُ. فَوَضَعَهُمَا لَدَيَّ. وَضْعَ الْمُمْتَنِّ عَلَيَّ. وَقَالَ اضْرِبِ الْجَيْشَ بِالْجَيْشِ. تَحْظَ بِلَذَّةِ الْعَيْشِ. فَحَسَرْتُ عَنْ سَاعِدِ النَّهِمِ. وَحَمَلْتُ حَمْلَةَ الْفِيلِ الْمُلْتَهِمِ. وَهُوَ يَلْحَظُنِي كَمَا يَلْحَظُ الْحَنِقُ. وَيَوَدُّ مِنَ الْغَيْظِ لَوْ أَخْتَنِقُ.

٧،١٥ حَتَّى إِذَا هَلْقَمْتُ النَّوْعَيْنِ. وَغَادَرْتُهُمَا أَثَرًا بَعْدَ عَيْنٍ. أَقْرَدَتْ حَيْرَةٌ فِي إِظْلَالِ الْبَيَاتِ. وَفِكْرَةٌ فِي جَوَابِ الْأَبْيَاتِ. فَمَا لَبِثَ أَنْ قَامَ. وَأَحْضَرَ الدَّوَاةَ وَالْأَقْلَامَ. وَقَالَ قَدْ مَلَأْتَ الْجِرَابَ. فَأَمْلِ الْجَوَابَ. وَإِلَّا فَتَهَيَّأْ إِنْ نَكَلْتَ.

---

١ ف: فيما بيننا.

لِاغْتِرَامِ مَا أَكَلْتَ. فَقُلْتُ لَهُ مَا عِنْدِي إِلَّا التَّحْقِيقُ. فَٱكْتُبِ ٱلْجَوَابَ وَبِٱللهِ التَّوْفِيقُ.

قُلْ لِمَنْ يُلْغِزُ ٱلْمَسَائِلَ إِنِّي   كَاشِفٌ سِرَّهَا ٱلَّذِي تُخْفِيهِ[1]
إِنَّ ذَا ٱلْمَيِّتَ ٱلَّذِي قَدَّمَ ٱلشَّرْ   عُ أَخَا عِرْسِهِ عَلَى ٱبْنِ أَبِيهِ
رَجُلٌ زَوَّجَ ٱبْنَهُ عَنْ رِضَاهُ   بِحَمَاةٍ لَهُ وَلَا غَرْوَ فِيهِ
ثُمَّ مَاتَ ٱبْنُهُ وَقَدْ عَلِقَتْ مِنْهُ   فَجَاءَتْ بِٱبْنٍ يَسُرُّ ذَوِيهِ[2]
فَهُوَ ٱبْنُ ٱبْنِهِ بِغَيْرِ مِرَاءٍ   وَأَخُو عِرْسِهِ بِلَا تَمْوِيهِ
وَٱبْنُ الِابْنِ الصَّرِيحُ أَدْنَى إِلَى ٱلْجَدِّ   وَأَوْلَى بِإِرْثِهِ مِنْ أَخِيهِ
فَلِذَا حِينَ مَاتَ أُوجِبَ لِلزَّوْ   جَةِ ثُمْنُ التُّرَاثِ تَسْتَوْفِيهِ
وَحَوَى ٱبْنُ ٱبْنِهِ ٱلَّذِي هُوَ فِي ٱلْأَصْلِ   أَخُوهَا مِنْ أُمِّهَا بَاقِيهِ
وَتَخَلَّى ٱلْأَخُ ٱلشَّقِيقُ مِنَ ٱلْإِرْ   ثِ وَقُلْنَا يَكْفِيكَ أَنْ تَبْكِيهِ
هَاكَ مِنِّي ٱلْفُتْيَا ٱلَّتِي يَحْتَذِيهَا   كُلُّ قَاضٍ يَقْضِي وَكُلُّ فَقِيهِ

٨،١٥ قَالَ فَلَمَّا أَثْبَتَ ٱلْجَوَابَ. وَٱسْتَثْبَتُّ مِنْهُ الصَّوَابَ. قَالَ لِي أَهْلَكَ وَاللَّيْلَ. فَشَمِّرِ الذَّيْلَ. وَبَادِرِ السَّيْلَ. فَقُلْتُ إِنِّي بِدَارِ غُرْبَةٍ. وَفِي إِيوَائِي أَفْضَلُ قُرْبَةٍ. لَا سِيَّمَا وَقَدْ أَغْدَفَ جِنْحُ الظَّلَامِ. وَسَبَّحَ الرَّعْدُ فِي الْغَمَامِ. فَقَالَ ٱغْرُبْ عَافَاكَ اللهُ إِلَى حَيْثُ شِيتَ. وَلَا تَطْمَعْ فِي أَنْ تَبِيتَ. فَقُلْتُ وَلِمَ ذَاكَ. مَعَ خُلُوِّ ذَرَاكَ. قَالَ لِأَنِّي أَنْعَمْتُ النَّظَرَ. فِي ٱلْتِقَامِكَ مَا حَضَرَ. حَتَّى لَمْ تُبْقِ وَلَمْ تَذَرْ. فَرَأَيْتُكَ لَا تَنْظُرُ فِي مَصْلَحَتِكَ. وَلَا تُرَاعِي حِفْظَ صِحَّتِكَ. وَمَنْ أَمْعَنَ فِيمَا أَمْعَنْتَ. وَتَبَطَّنَ مَا تَبَطَّنْتَ. لَمْ[3] يَخْلُصْ مِنْ كِظَّةٍ مُدْنِفَةٍ. أَوْ هَيْضَةٍ مُتْلِفَةٍ. فَدَعْنِي بِٱللهِ

١ د: يُخفيه. ٢ في هامش س وفي د: بابن له يحكيه. ٣ بعدها في ف: يكَدْ.

كَفَافًا. وَٱخْرُجْ عَنِّي مَا دُمْتَ مُعَافًى. فَوَٱلَّذِي يُحْيِي وَيُمِيتُ. مَا لَكَ عِنْدِي مَبِيتٌ.

٩.١٥ فَلَمَّا سَمِعْتُ أَلِيَّتَهُ. وَبَلَوْتُ بَلِيَّتَهُ. خَرَجْتُ مِنْ بَيْتِهِ بِٱلرَّغْمِ. وَتَزَوُّدِ ٱلْغَمِّ. تَجُودُنِي ٱلسَّمَاءُ. وَتَخْبِطُ بِيَ ٱلظَّلْمَاءُ. وَتَنْبَحُنِي ٱلْكِلَابُ. وَتَتَقَاذَفُ بِيَ ٱلْأَبْوَابُ. حَتَّى سَاقَنِي إِلَيْكَ لُطْفُ ٱلْقَضَاءِ. فَشُكْرًا لِيَدِهِ ٱلْبَيْضَاءِ. فَقُلْتُ لَهُ أَحْبِبْ بِلِقَائِكَ ٱلْمُتَاحِ. إِلَى قَلْبِيَ ٱلْمُرْتَاحِ. ثُمَّ أَخَذَ يَفْتَنُّ بِحِكَايَاتِهِ. وَيُشْمِطُ مُضْحِكَاتِهِ بِمُبْكِيَاتِهِ. إِلَى أَنْ عَطَسَ أَنْفُ ٱلصَّبَاحِ. وَهَتَفَ دَاعِي ٱلْفَلَاحِ. فَتَأَهَّبَ لِإِجَابَةِ ٱلدَّاعِي. ثُمَّ عَطَفَ إِلَى وَدَاعِي. فَعُقْتُهُ عَنِ ٱلِانْبِعَاثِ. وَقُلْتُ ٱلضِّيَافَةُ ثَلَاثٌ. فَنَاشَدَ وَحَرَّجَ. ثُمَّ أَمَّ ٱلْمَخْرَجَ. وَأَنْشَدَ إِذْ عَرَّجَ.

لَا تَزُرْ مَنْ تُحِبُّ فِي كُلِّ شَهْرٍ   غَيْرَ يَوْمٍ وَلَا تَزِدْهُ عَلَيْهِ
فَٱجْتِلَاءُ ٱلْهِلَالِ فِي ٱلشَّهْرِ يَوْمٌ   ثُمَّ لَا تَنْظُرُ ٱلْعُيُونُ إِلَيْهِ

قَالَ ٱلْحَارِثُ بْنُ هَمَّامٍ فَوَدَّعْتُهُ بِقَلْبٍ دَامِي ٱلْقَرْحِ. وَوَدِدْتُ لَوْ أَنَّ لَيْلَتِي بَطِيئَةُ ٱلصُّبْحِ.

الْمَقَامَةُ السَّادِسَةَ عَشْرَةَ[1]

١٦،١ حَكَى الْحَارِثُ بْنُ هَمَّامٍ قَالَ شَهِدْتُ صَلَاةَ الْمَغْرِبِ. فِي بَعْضِ مَسَاجِدِ الْمَغْرِبِ. فَلَمَّا أَدَّيْتُهَا بِفَضْلِهَا. وَشَفَعْتُهَا بِنَفْلِهَا. أَخَذَ طَرْفِي رُفْقَةً قَدِ ٱنْتَبَذُوا نَاحِيَةً. وَٱمْتَازُوا صَفْوَةً صَافِيَةً. وَهُمْ يَتَعَاطَوْنَ كَأْسَ الْمُنَافَثَةِ. وَيَقْتَدِحُونَ زِنَادَ الْمُبَاحَثَةِ. فَرَغِبْتُ فِي مُحَادَثَتِهِمْ لِكَلِمَةٍ تُسْتَفَادُ. أَوْ أَدَبٍ يُسْتَزَادُ. فَسَعَيْتُ إِلَيْهِمْ. سَعْيَ الْمُتَطَفِّلِ عَلَيْهِمْ. وَقُلْتُ لَهُمْ أَتَقْبَلُونَ نَزِيلاً يَطْلُبُ جَنَى الْأَسْمَارِ. لَا جَنِيَّ[2] الثِّمَارِ. وَيَبْغِي مُلَحَ الْحِوَارِ. لَا مَلْحَاءَ الْحُوَارِ. فَحَلُّوا لِيَ الْحُبَى. وَقَالُوا مَرْحَبًا مَرْحَبًا.

١٦،٢ فَلَمْ أَجْلِسْ إِلَّا لَمْحَةَ بَارِقٍ خَاطِفٍ. أَوْ نَغْبَةَ طَائِرٍ خَائِفٍ. حَتَّى غَشِيَنَا جَوَّابٌ. عَلَى عَاتِقِهِ جِرَابٌ. فَحَيَّانَا بِالْكَلِمَتَيْنِ. وَحَيَّا الْمَسْجِدَ بِالتَّسْلِيمَتَيْنِ. ثُمَّ قَالَ يَا أُولِي الْأَلْبَابِ. وَالْفَضْلِ اللُّبَابِ. أَمَا تَعْلَمُونَ أَنَّ أَنْفَسَ الْقُرُبَاتِ. تَنْفِيسُ الْكُرُبَاتِ. وَأَمْتَنَ أَسْبَابِ النَّجَاةِ. مُؤَاسَاةُ ذَوِي الْحَاجَاتِ. وَإِنِّي وَمَنْ أَحَلَّنِي سَاحَتَكُمْ. وَأَتَاحَ لِيَ ٱسْتِمَاحَتَكُمْ. لَشَرِيدُ مَحَلٍّ قَاصٍ. وَبَرِيدُ صِبْيَةٍ خِمَاصٍ. فَهَلْ فِي الْجَمَاعَةِ. مَنْ يَفْثَأُ عَنَّا حُمَيَّا الْمَجَاعَةِ. فَقَالُوا لَهُ يَا هٰذَا إِنَّكَ حَضَرْتَ بَعْدَ الْعِشَاءِ. وَلَمْ يَبْقَ إِلَّا فَضَلَاتُ[3] الْعَشَاءِ. فَإِنْ كُنْتَ بِهَا قَنُوعًا. فَمَا تَجِدُ فِينَا مَنُوعًا. فَقَالَ إِنَّ أَخَا الشَّدَائِدِ. لَيَقْنَعُ بِلُفَاظَاتِ الْمَوَائِدِ. وَنُفَاضَاتِ الْمَزَاوِدِ. فَأَمَرَ كُلٌّ مِنْهُمْ عَبْدَهُ. أَنْ يُزَوِّدَهُ مَا عِنْدَهُ. فَأَعْجَبَهُ الصُّنْعُ وَشَكَرَ عَلَيْهِ. وَجَلَسَ يَرْقُبُ مَا يُحْمَلُ إِلَيْهِ.

---

١ في هامش س: تعرف بالمَغْرِبِيَّة؛ وفي د: المغربية؛ وفي ف: وتعرف بالمغربية. ٢ و: جَنَى. ٣ د، ف: فُضَلات؛ و: فُضالات.

٣،١٦ وَثُبْنَا نَحْنُ إِلَى ٱسْتِثَارَةِ مُلَحِ ٱلْأَدَبِ وَعُيُونِهِ. وَٱسْتِنْبَاطِ مَعِينِهِ مِنْ عُيُونِهِ. إِلَى أَنْ جُلْنَا فِيمَا لَا يَسْتَحِيلُ بِالِانْعِكَاسِ. كَقَوْلِكَ سَاكِبُ كَاسٍ. فَتَدَاعَيْنَا إِلَى أَنْ نَسْتَنْتِجَ لَهُ ٱلْأَفْكَارَ. وَنَفْتَرِعَ مِنْهُ ٱلْأَبْكَارَ. عَلَى أَنْ يَنْظِمَ ٱلْبَادِئُ ثَلَاثَ جُمَانَاتٍ فِي عِقْدِهِ. ثُمَّ تَتَدَرَّجَ ٱلزِّيَادَاتُ مِنْ بَعْدِهِ. فَيُرَبِّعَ ذُو مَيْمَنَتِهِ فِي نَظْمِهِ. وَيُسَبِّعَ صَاحِبُ مَيْسَرَتِهِ عَلَى رَغْمِهِ.

قَالَ ٱلرَّاوِي وَكُنَّا قَدِ ٱنْتَظَمْنَا عِدَّةَ أَصَابِعِ ٱلْكَفِّ. وَتَأَلَّفْنَا أُلْفَةَ أَصْحَابِ ٱلْكَهْفِ. فَٱبْتَدَرَ لِعُظْمِ مِحْنَتِي. صَاحِبُ مَيْمَنَتِي. وَقَالَ لُمْ أَخَا مَلَّ. وَقَالَ مُيَامِنُهُ كَبِّرْ رَجَاءَ أَجْرِ رَبِّكَ. وَقَالَ ٱلَّذِي يَلِيهِ مَنْ يَرُبَّ إِذَا بَرَّ يَنْمُ. وَقَالَ ٱلْآخَرُ سَكِّتْ كُلَّ مَنْ نَمَّ لَكَ تَكِسْ. وَأُفْضِتِ ٱلنَّوْبَةُ إِلَيَّ. وَقَدْ تَعَيَّنَ نَظْمُ ٱلسِّمْطِ ٱلسُّبَاعِيِّ عَلَيَّ. فَلَمْ يَزَلْ فِكْرِي يَصُوغُ وَيَكْسِرُ. وَيُثْرِي وَيُعْسِرُ. وَفِي ضِمْنِ ذٰلِكَ أَسْتَطْعِمُ. فَلَا أَجِدُ مَنْ يُطْعِمُ. إِلَى أَنْ رَكَدَ ٱلنَّسِيمُ. وَحَصْحَصَ ٱلتَّسْلِيمُ.

٤،١٦ فَقُلْتُ لِأَصْحَابِي لَوْ حَضَرَ ٱلسَّرُوجِيُّ هٰذَا ٱلْمَقَامَ. لَشَفَى ٱلدَّاءَ ٱلْعُقَامَ. فَقَالُوا لَوْ أُنْزِلَتْ[1] هٰذِهِ بِإِيَاسٍ. لَأَمْسَكَ عَلَى يَاسٍ. وَجَعَلْنَا نُفِيضُ فِي ٱسْتِصْعَابِهَا. وَٱسْتِغْلَاقِ بَابِهَا. وَذٰلِكَ ٱلزَّوْرُ[2] ٱلْمُعْتَرِي. يَلْحَظُنَا لَحْظَ ٱلْمُزْدَرِي. وَيُؤَلِّفُ ٱلدُّرَرَ وَنَحْنُ لَا نَدْرِي. فَلَمَّا عَثَرَ عَلَى ٱفْتِضَاحِنَا. وَنُضُوبِ ضَحْضَاحِنَا. قَالَ يَا قَوْمِ إِنَّ مِنَ ٱلْعَنَاءِ ٱلْعَظِيمِ. ٱسْتِيلَادَ ٱلْعَقِيمِ. وَٱلِٱسْتِشْفَاءَ بِٱلسَّقِيمِ. ﴿وَفَوْقَ كُلِّ ذِي عِلْمٍ عَلِيمٌ﴾.

٥،١٦ ثُمَّ أَقْبَلَ عَلَيَّ وَقَالَ سَأَنُوبُ مَنَابَكَ. وَأَكْفِيكَ مَا نَابَكَ. فَإِنْ شِئْتَ أَنْ تَنْثُرَ. وَلَا تَعْثُرَ. فَقُلْ مُخَاطِبًا لِمَنْ ذَمَّ ٱلْبُخْلَ. وَأَكْثَرَ ٱلْعَذْلَ. لُذْ بِكُلِّ مُؤَمَّلٍ إِذَا لَمَّ وَمَلَكَ بَذَلَ. وَإِنْ أَحْبَبْتَ أَنْ تَنْظِمَ. فَقُلْ لِلَّذِي تُعَظِّمُ.[3]

١ د، ف: نُزِّلَتْ. ٢ في متن ق: الضَّيْف، وفي الهامش ما أثبتنا، وهو الموجود في سائر الأصول. ٣ د، ف: تُعْظِم.

أُسُ أَرْمَلاً إِذَا عَرَا   وَارْعَ إِذَا الْمَرْءُ أَسَا
أَسْنِدْ أَخَا نَبَاهَةٍ   أَبِنْ إِخَاءً دَنَسَا
أُسُلُ جَنَابَ غَاشِمٍ   مُشَاغِبٍ إِنْ جَلَسَا
أَسْرِ إِذَا هَبَّ مِرًا   وَٱرْمِ بِهِ إِذَا رَسَا
أُسْكُنْ تَقَوَّ فَعَسَى   يُسْعِفُ وَقْتٌ نَكَسَا[1]

٦،١٦ قَالَ فَلَمَّا سَحَرَنَا بِآيَاتِهِ.[2] وَحَسَرَنَا بِبُعْدِ غَايَاتِهِ. مَدَحْنَاهُ حَتَّى ٱسْتَعْفَى. وَمَنَحْنَاهُ إِلَى أَنِ ٱسْتَكْفَى. ثُمَّ شَمَّرَ ثِيَابَهُ. وَٱزْدَفَرَ جِرَابَهُ. وَنَهَضَ يُنْشِدُ

لِلّٰهِ دَرُّ عِصَابَةٍ   صُدُقٍ[3] ٱلْمَقَالِ مَقَاوِلَا
فَاقُوا الْأَنَامَ فَضَائِلاً   مَأْثُورَةً وَفَوَاضِلَا
حَاوَرْتُهُمْ فَوَجَدْتُ سَحْـ   ـبَانًا لَدَيْهِمْ بَاقِلَا
وَحَلَلْتُ فِيهِمْ سَائِلاً   فَلَقِيتُ جُودًا سَائِلَا
أَقْسَمْتُ لَوْ كَانَ الْكِرَا   مُ حَيًا لَكَانُوا وَابِلَا

٧،١٦ ثُمَّ خَطَا قِيدَ[4] رُمْحَيْنِ. وَعَادَ مُسْتَعِيذًا مِنَ الْحَيْنِ. وَقَالَ يَا عِزَّ مَنْ عَدِمَ الْآلَ. وَكَنْزَ مَنْ سُلِبَ الْمَالَ. إِنَّ الْغَاسِقَ قَدْ وَقَبَ. وَوَجْهَ الْمَحَجَّةِ قَدِ ٱنْتَقَبَ. وَبَيْنِي وَبَيْنَ كِنِّي لَيْلٌ دَامِسٌ. وَطَرِيقٌ طَامِسٌ. فَهَلْ مِنْ مِصْبَاحٍ يُؤْمِنُنِي الْعِثَارَ. وَيُبَيِّنُ لِيَ الْآثَارَ. قَالَ فَلَمَّا جِيءَ بِالْمُلْتَمَسِ. وَجَلَّى الْوُجُوهَ ضَوْءُ الْقَبَسِ. رَأَيْتُ صَاحِبَ صَيْدِنَا. هُوَ أَبُو زَيْدِنَا. فَقُلْتُ لِأَصْحَابِي. هٰذَا الَّذِي أَشَرْتُ إِلَى أَنَّهُ إِذَا نَطَقَ أَصَابَ. وَإِنِ ٱسْتُمْطِرَ صَابَ. فَأَتْلَعُوا نَحْوَهُ الْأَعْنَاقَ. وَأَحْدَقُوا بِهِ

١ د: نُكِسا. ٢ و، د: بأبياته. ٣ س، ف: صُدْقٍ. ٤ د: قَيْدَ.

الْأَحْدَاقَ. وَسَأَلُوهُ أَنْ يُسَامِرَهُمْ لَيْلَتَهُ. عَلَى أَنْ يَجْبُرُوا عَيْلَتَهُ. فَقَالَ حُبًّا لِمَا أَحْبَبْتُمْ. وَرُحْبًا بِكُمْ إِذَا رَحَّبْتُمْ. غَيْرَ أَنِّي قَصَدْتُكُمْ وَأَطْفَالِي يَتَضَوَّرُونَ مِنَ الْجُوعِ. وَيَدْعُونَ لِي بِوَشْكِ الرُّجُوعِ. وَإِنِ ٱسْتَرَاثُونِي خَامَرَهُمُ الطَّيْشُ. وَلَمْ يَصْفُ لِيَ[1] الْعَيْشُ. فَدَعُونِي لِأَذْهَبَ فَأَسُدَّ مَخْمَصَتَهُمْ. وَأُسِيغَ غُصَّتَهُمْ. ثُمَّ أَنْقَلِبَ[2] إِلَيْكُمْ عَلَى الْأَثَرِ. مُتَأَهِّبًا لِلسَّمَرِ. إِلَى السَّحَرِ. فَقُلْنَا لِأَحَدِ الْغِلْمَةِ ٱتْبَعْهُ إِلَى فِئَتِهِ. لِيَكُونَ أَسْرَعَ لِفَيْئَتِهِ. فَٱنْطَلَقَ مَعَهُ مُضْطَبِنًا جِرَابَهُ. وَمُحْتَثًّا إِيَابَهُ.

فَأَبْطَآ بُطْأً جَاوَزَ حَدَّهُ. ثُمَّ عَادَ الْغُلَامُ وَحْدَهُ. فَقُلْنَا لَهُ مَا عِنْدَكَ مِنَ الْحَدِيثِ. عَنِ الْخَبِيثِ. فَقَالَ أَخَذَ بِي فِي طُرُقٍ مُتْعِبَةٍ. وَسُبُلٍ مُتَشَعِّبَةٍ. حَتَّى أَفْضَيْنَا إِلَى دُوَيْرَةٍ خَرِبَةٍ. فَقَالَ هَاهُنَا مُنَاخِي. وَوَكْرُ أَفْرَاخِي. ثُمَّ ٱسْتَفْتَحَ بَابَهُ. وَٱخْتَلَجَ مِنِّي جِرَابَهُ. وَقَالَ لَعَمْرِي لَقَدْ خَفَّفْتَ عَنِّي. وَٱسْتَوْجَبْتَ الْحُسْنَى مِنِّي. فَهَاكَ نَصِيحَةً هِيَ مِنْ نَفَائِسِ النَّصَائِحِ. وَمَغَارِسِ الْمَصَالِحِ. وَأَنْشَدَ ٨،١٦

إِذَا مَا حَوَيْتَ جَنَى نَخْلَةٍ ... فَلَا تَقْرَبَنْهَا[3] إِلَى قَابِلِ
وَإِمَّا سَقَطْتَ عَلَى بَيْدَرٍ ... فَحُصِّلْ مِنَ السُّنْبُلِ الْحَاصِلِ
وَلَا تَلْبَثَنَّ إِذَا مَا لَقَطْتَ ... فَتَنْشَبَ فِي كَفَّةِ الْحَابِلِ
وَلَا تُوغِلَنَّ إِذَا مَا سَبَحْتَ ... فَإِنَّ السَّلَامَةَ فِي السَّاحِلِ
وَخَاطِبْ بِهَاتِ وَجَاوِبْ بِسَوْفَ ... وَبِعْ آجِلًا مِنْكَ بِالْعَاجِلِ
وَلَا تُكْثِرَنَّ عَلَى صَاحِبٍ ... فَمَا مُلَّ قَطُّ سِوَى الْوَاصِلِ

ثُمَّ قَالَ ٱخْزُنْهَا فِي تَأْمُورِكَ. وَٱقْتَدِ بِهِ فِي أُمُورِكَ. وَبَادِرْ إِلَى صَحْبِكَ. فِي كَلَاءَةِ رَبِّكَ. فَإِذَا بَلَغْتَهُمْ فَأَبْلِغْهُمْ تَحِيَّتِي. وَٱتْلُ عَلَيْهِمْ وَصِيَّتِي. وَقُلْ لَهُمْ عَنِّي. إِنَّ السَّهَرَ

١ س، ف: لهم. ٢ و، د: أَنْقَلِبُ. ٣ ق: تَقْرَبَنْهَا.

فِي الْخُرَافَاتِ. لَمِنْ أَعْظَمِ الآفَاتِ. وَلَسْتُ أُلْغِي ٱحْتِرَاسِي. وَلَا أَجْلُبُ الْهَوَسَ إِلَى رَاسِي.

٩،١٦ قَالَ الرَّاوِي فَلَمَّا وَقَفْنَا[١] فَحْوَى شِعْرِهِ. عَلَى[٢] نُكْرِهِ وَمَكْرِهِ. تَلَاوَمْنَا عَلَى تَرْكِهِ. وَالِاغْتِرَارِ بِإِفْكِهِ. ثُمَّ تَفَرَّقْنَا بِوُجُوهٍ بَاسِرَةٍ. وَصَفْقَةٍ خَاسِرَةٍ.

---

١ ف: وقفنا على. ٢ ف: واطَّلَعْنا على.

الْمَقَامَةُ السَّابِعَةَ عَشْرَةَ[1] وَتُعْرَفُ بِالْقَهْقَرِيَّةِ[2]

١٫١٧ حَدَّثَ الْحَارِثُ بْنُ هَمَّامٍ قَالَ لَحَظْتُ فِي بَعْضِ مَطَارِحِ الْبَيْنِ. وَمَطَامِحِ الْعَيْنِ. فِتْيَةً عَلَيْهِمْ سِيمَا الْحِجَى. وَطُلَاوَةُ نُجُومِ الدُّجَى. وَهُمْ فِي مُمَارَاةٍ مُشْتَدَّةِ الْهُبُوبِ. وَمُبَارَاةٍ مُشْتَطَّةِ الْأُلْهُوبِ. فَهَزَّنِي لِقَصْدِهِمْ هَوَى الْمُحَاضَرَةِ. وَٱسْتِحْلَاءُ جَنَى الْمُنَاظَرَةِ. فَلَمَّا ٱلْتَحَقْتُ بِرَهْطِهِمْ. وَٱنْتَظَمْتُ فِي سِمْطِهِمْ. قَالُوا أَأَنْتَ مِمَّنْ يُبْلِي[3] فِي الْهَيْجَاءِ. وَيُلْقِي دَلْوَهُ فِي الدِّلَاءِ. فَقُلْتُ بَلْ أَنَا مِنْ نَظَّارَةِ الْحَرْبِ. لَا مِنْ أَبْنَاءِ الطَّعْنِ وَالضَّرْبِ. فَأَضْرَبُوا عَنْ حِجَاجِي. وَأَفَاضُوا فِي التَّحَاجِي.

٢٫١٧ وَكَانَ فِي بُحْبُوحَةِ حَلْقَتِهِمْ. وَإِكْلِيلِ رُفْقَتِهِمْ. شَيْخٌ قَدْ بَرَتْهُ الْهُمُومُ. وَلَوَّحَتْهُ السَّمُومُ. حَتَّى عَادَ أَنْحَلَ مِنْ قَلَمٍ. وَأَقْحَلَ مِنْ جَلَمٍ. إِلَّا أَنَّهُ كَانَ يُبْدِي الْعُجَابَ. إِذَا أَجَابَ. وَيُنْسِي سَحْبَانَ. كُلَّمَا أَبَانَ. فَأُعْجِبْتُ بِمَا أُوتِيَ مِنَ الْإِصَابَةِ. وَالتَّبْرِيزِ عَلَى تِلْكَ الْعِصَابَةِ. وَمَا زَالَ يَفْضَحُ كُلَّ مُعَمًّى. وَيُصْمِي فِي كُلِّ مَرْمًى. إِلَى أَنْ خَلَتِ الْجِعَابُ. وَنَفِدَ السُّؤَالُ وَالْجَوَابُ. فَلَمَّا رَأَى إِنْفَاضَ الْقَوْمِ. وَٱضْطِرَارَهُمْ إِلَى الصَّوْمِ. عَرَّضَ بِالْمُطَارَحَةِ. وَٱسْتَأْذَنَ فِي الْمُفَاتَحَةِ. فَقَالُوا لَهُ حَبَّذَا. وَمَنْ لَنَا بِذَا. فَقَالَ أَتَعْرِفُونَ رِسَالَةً أَرْضُهَا سَمَاؤُهَا. وَصُبْحُهَا مَسَاؤُهَا. نُسِجَتْ عَلَى مِنْوَالَيْنِ. وَتَجَلَّتْ فِي لَوْنَيْنِ. وَصَلَّتْ إِلَى جِهَتَيْنِ. وَبَدَتْ ذَاتَ وَجْهَيْنِ. إِنْ بَزَغَتْ مِنْ مَشْرِقِهَا. فَنَاهِيكَ بِرَوْنَقِهَا. وَإِنْ طَلَعَتْ مِنْ مَغْرِبِهَا. فَيَا لَعَجَبِهَا.

---

١ و: عَشَر. ٢ هكذا في متنَيْ ق، س؛ وليس في و؛ وفي د، ف: القهقهرية. ٣ هكذا في جميع النسخ.

٣،١٧ قَالَ فَكَأَنَّ الْقَوْمَ رُمُوا بِالصُّمَاتِ. أَوْ[١] حَقَّتْ عَلَيْهِمْ كَلِمَةُ الْإِنْصَاتِ. فَمَا نَبَسَ مِنْهُمْ إِنْسَانٌ. وَلَا فَاهَ لِأَحَدِهِمْ[٢] لِسَانٌ. فَحِينَ رَآهُمْ بُكْمًا كَالْأَنْعَامِ. وَصُمُوتًا كَالْأَصْنَامِ. قَالَ لَهُمْ قَدْ أَجَّلْتُكُمْ أَجَلَ الْعِدَّةِ. وَأَرْخَيْتُ لَكُمْ طِوَلَ الْمُدَّةِ. ثُمَّ هَاهُنَا مَجْمَعُ الشَّمْلِ. وَمَوْقِفُ الْفَصْلِ. فَإِنْ سَمَحَتْ خَوَاطِرُكُمْ مَدَحْنَا. وَإِنْ صَلَدَتْ زِنَادُكُمْ قَدَحْنَا. فَقَالُوا لَهُ وَاللهِ مَا لَنَا فِي لُجَّةِ هٰذَا الْبَحْرِ مَسْبَحٌ. وَلَا فِي سَاحِلِهِ مَسْرَحٌ. فَأَرِحْ أَفْكَارَنَا مِنَ الْكَدِّ. وَهَنِّئِ الْعَطِيَّةَ بِالنَّقْدِ. وَٱتَّخِذْنَا إِخْوَانًا يَثْبُتُونَ إِذَا وَثَبْتَ. وَيُثِيبُونَ مَتَى ٱسْتَثَبْتَ. فَأَطْرَقَ سَاعَةً. ثُمَّ قَالَ سَمْعًا لَكُمْ وَطَاعَةً. فَٱسْتَمْلُوا مِنِّي. وَٱنْقُلُوا عَنِّي.

٤،١٧ الْإِنْسَانُ صَنِيعَةُ الْإِحْسَانِ. وَرَبُّ الْجَمِيلِ فِعْلُ النَّدْبِ. وَشِيمَةُ الْحُرِّ ذَخِيرَةُ الْحَمْدِ. وَكَسْبُ الشُّكْرِ اسْتِثْمَارُ السَّعَادَةِ. وَعُنْوَانُ الْكَرَمِ تَبَاشِيرُ الْبِشْرِ. وَٱسْتِعْمَالُ الْمُدَارَاةِ يُوجِبُ الْمُصَافَاةَ. وَعَقْدُ الْمَحَبَّةِ يَقْتَضِي النُّصْحَ. وَصِدْقُ الْحَدِيثِ حِلْيَةُ اللِّسَانِ. وَفَصَاحَةُ الْمَنْطِقِ سِحْرُ الْأَلْبَابِ. وَشَرَكُ الْهَوَى آفَةُ النُّفُوسِ. وَمَلَلُ الْخَلَائِقِ شَيْنُ الْخَلَائِقِ. وَسُوءُ الطَّمَعِ يُبَايِنُ الْوَرَعَ. وَٱلْتِزَامُ الْحَزَامَةِ زِمَامُ السَّلَامَةِ. وَتَطَلُّبُ الْمَثَالِبِ شَرُّ الْمَعَايِبِ. وَتَتَبُّعُ الْعَثَرَاتِ يُدْحِضُ الْمَوَدَّاتِ. وَخُلُوصُ النِّيَّةِ خُلَاصَةُ الْعَطِيَّةِ. وَتَهْنِئَةُ النَّوَالِ ثَمَنُ السُّؤَالِ. وَتَكَلُّفُ الْكُلَفِ يُسَهِّلُ الْخَلَفَ. وَتَيَقُّنُ الْمَعُونَةِ يُسَنِّي الْمُؤُونَةَ. وَفَضْلُ الصَّدْرِ سَعَةُ الصَّدْرِ. وَزِينَةُ الرُّعَاةِ مَقْتُ السُّعَاةِ. وَجَزَاءُ الْمَدَائِحِ بَثُّ الْمَنَائِحِ. وَمَهْرُ الْوَسَائِلِ تَشْفِيعُ الْمَسَائِلِ. وَمَجْلَبَةُ الْغَوَايَةِ اسْتِغْرَاقُ الْغَايَةِ. وَتَجَاوُزُ الْحَدِّ يُكِلُّ الْحَدَّ. وَتَعَدِّي الْأَدَبِ يُحْبِطُ الْقُرَبَ. وَتَنَاسِي الْحُقُوقِ يُنْشِئُ الْعُقُوقَ. وَتَحَاشِي الرِّيَبِ يَرْفَعُ الرُّتَبَ. وَٱرْتِفَاعُ الْأَخْطَارِ بِٱقْتِحَامِ الْأَخْطَارِ. وَتَنَوُّهُ الْأَقْدَارِ بِمُؤَاتَاةِ

---

١ ق: و. ٢ س، و: لهم.

ٱلْأَقْدَارِ. وَشَرَفُ ٱلْأَعْمَالِ فِي تَقْصِيرِ ٱلآمَالِ. وَإِطَالَةُ ٱلْفِكْرَةِ تَنْقِيحُ ٱلْحِكْمَةِ. وَرَأْسُ ٱلرِّيَاسَةِ تَهَذُّبُ ٱلسِّيَاسَةِ. وَمَعَ ٱللَّجَاجَةِ تُلْغَى ٱلْحَاجَةُ. وَعِنْدَ ٱلْأَوْجَالِ تَتَفَاضَلُ ٱلرِّجَالُ. وَبِتَفَاضُلِ ٱلْهِمَمِ تَتَفَاوَتُ ٱلْقِيَمُ. وَبِتَزَيُّدِ ٱلسَّفِيرِ يَهِنُ ٱلتَّدْبِيرُ. وَبِخَلَلِ ٱلْأَحْوَالِ تَتَبَيَّنُ ٱلْأَهْوَالُ. وَبِمُوجَبِ[1] ٱلصَّبْرِ ثَمَرَةُ ٱلنَّصْرِ. وَٱسْتِحْقَاقُ ٱلْإِحْمَادِ بِحَسَبِ[2] ٱلِاجْتِهَادِ. وَوُجُوبُ ٱلْمُلَاحَظَةِ كِفَاءُ ٱلْمُحَافَظَةِ. وَصَفَاءُ ٱلْمُوَالِي بِتَعَهُّدِ ٱلْمَوَالِي. وَتَحَلِّي ٱلْمُرُوءَاتِ بِحِفْظِ ٱلْأَمَانَاتِ. وَٱخْتِبَارُ ٱلْإِخْوَانِ بِتَخْفِيفِ ٱلْأَحْزَانِ. وَدَفْعُ ٱلْأَعْدَاءِ بِكَفِّ ٱلْأَوِدَّاءِ. وَٱمْتِحَانُ ٱلْعُقَلَاءِ بِمُقَارَنَةِ ٱلْجُهَلَاءِ. وَتَبَصُّرُ ٱلْعَوَاقِبِ يُؤْمِنُ ٱلْمَعَاطِبَ. وَٱتِّقَاءُ ٱلشُّنْعَةِ يَنْشُرُ ٱلسُّمْعَةَ. وَقُبْحُ ٱلْجَفَاءِ يُنَافِي ٱلْوَفَاءَ. وَجَوْهَرُ ٱلْأَحْرَارِ عِنْدَ ٱلْأَسْرَارِ.

٥،١٧ ثُمَّ قَالَ هٰذِهِ مِئَتَا لَفْظَةٍ. تَحْتَوِي عَلَى أَدَبٍ وَعِظَةٍ. فَمَنْ سَاقَهَا هٰذَا ٱلْمَسَاقَ. فَلَا مِرَاءَ وَلَا شِقَاقَ. وَمَنْ رَامَ عَكْسَ قَالَبِهَا. وَأَنْ يَرُدَّهَا عَلَى عَقِبِهَا. فَلْيَقُلْ ٱلْأَسْرَارُ عِنْدَ ٱلْأَحْرَارِ. وَجَوْهَرُ ٱلْوَفَاءِ يُنَافِي ٱلْجَفَاءَ. وَقُبْحُ ٱلسُّمْعَةِ يَنْشُرُ ٱلشُّنْعَةَ. ثُمَّ عَلَى هٰذَا ٱلْمَسْحَبِ فَلْيَسْحَبْهَا. وَلَا يَرْهَبْهَا. حَتَّى تَكُونَ خَاتِمَةُ فِقَرِهَا. وَآخِرَةُ دُرَرِهَا وَرَبُّ ٱلْإِحْسَانِ صَنِيعَةُ ٱلْإِنْسَانِ.

٦،١٧ قَالَ ٱلرَّاوِي فَلَمَّا صَدَعَ بِرِسَالَتِهِ ٱلْفَرِيدَةِ. وَأُمْلُوحَتِهِ ٱلْمُفِيدَةِ. عَلِمْنَا كَيْفَ يَتَفَاضَلُ ٱلْإِنْشَاءُ. وَأَنَّ ﴿ٱلْفَضْلَ بِيَدِ ٱللهِ يُؤْتِيهِ مَنْ يَشَاءُ﴾. ثُمَّ ٱعْتَلَقَ كُلٌّ مِنَّا بِذَيْلِهِ. وَفَلَذَ لَهُ فِلْذَةً مِنْ نَيْلِهِ. فَأَبَى قَبُولَ فِلْذَتِي. وَقَالَ لَسْتُ أَرْزَأُ تَلَامِذَتِي. فَقُلْتُ لَهُ كُنْ أَبَا زَيْدٍ عَلَى شُحُوبِ سَحْنَتِكَ. وَنُضُوبِ مَاءِ وَجْنَتِكَ. فَقَالَ أَنَا هُوَ عَلَى نُحُولِي وَنُحُولِي. وَقَشَفِ مُحُولِي.

١ ف: موجِب. ٢ و: بحَسْب.

١٧،٧ فَأَخَذْتُ فِي تَثْرِيبِهِ. عَلَى تَشْرِيقِهِ وَتَغْرِيبِهِ. فَحَوْلَقَ وَٱسْتَرْجَعَ. ثُمَّ أَنْشَدَ مِنْ قَلْبٍ مُوجَعٍ.

سَلَّ الزَّمَانُ عَلَيَّ عَضْبَهْ ۝ لِيَرُوعَنِي وَأَحَدَّ غَرْبَهْ
وَٱسْتَلَّ مِنْ جَفْنِي كَرَا ۝ هُ مُرَاغِمًا وَأَسَالَ غَرْبَهْ
وَأَجَالَنِي فِي ٱلْأُفْقِ أَطْوِي شَرْقَهُ وَأَجُوبُ غَرْبَهْ
فَبِكُلِّ جَوٍّ طَلْعَةٌ ۝ فِي كُلِّ يَوْمٍ لِي وَغَرْبَهْ
وَكَذَا ٱلْمُغَرِّبُ شَخْصُهُ ۝ مُتَغَرِّبٌ وَنَوَاهُ غَرْبَهْ

ثُمَّ وَلَّى يَجُرُّ عِطْفَيْهِ. وَيَخْطِرُ بِيَدَيْهِ. وَنَحْنُ بَيْنَ مُتَلَفِّتٍ إِلَيْهِ. وَمُتَهَافِتٍ عَلَيْهِ. ثُمَّ لَمْ نَلْبَثْ أَنْ حَلَلْنَا ٱلْحُبَى. وَتَفَرَّقْنَا أَيَادِيَ سَبَا.

المَقامَةُ الثّامِنَةَ عَشْرَةَ[1]

١٨،١ حَكَى الحارِثُ بْنُ هَمّامٍ قالَ قَفَلْتُ ذاتَ مَرَّةٍ مِنَ الشّامِ. أَنْحُو مَدِينَةَ السَّلامِ. فِي رَكْبٍ مِنْ بَنِي نُمَيْرٍ. وَرُفْقَةٍ أُولِي خَيْرٍ وَمَيْرٍ. وَمَعَنا أَبُو زَيْدٍ السَّرُوجِيُّ عُقْلَةُ العَجْلانِ. وَسَلْوَةُ الثَّكْلانِ. وَأُعْجُوبَةُ الزَّمانِ. وَالْمُشارُ إِلَيْهِ بِالْبَنانِ فِي الْبَيانِ. فَصادَفَ نُزُولُنا سِنْجارَ. أَنْ أَوْلَمَ بِها أَحَدُ التُّجّارِ. فَدَعا إِلَى مَأْدُبَتِهِ الجَفَلَى. مِنْ أَهْلِ الحَضارَةِ وَالفَلا. حَتَّى سَرَتْ دَعْوَتُهُ إِلَى القافِلَةِ. وَجَمَعَ فِيها بَيْنَ الفَرِيضَةِ وَالنّافِلَةِ.

١٨،٢ فَلَمّا أَجَبْنا مُنادِيَهُ. وَحَلَلْنا نادِيَهُ. أَحْضَرَ مِنْ أَطْعِمَةِ اليَدِ وَاليَدَيْنِ. ما حَلا فِي الفَمِ وَحَلِيَ بِالعَيْنِ. ثُمَّ قَدَّمَ جامًا كَأَنَّما جُمِّدَ مِنَ الهَواءِ. أَوْ جُمِعَ مِنَ الهَباءِ. أَوْ صِيغَ مِنْ نُورِ الفَضاءِ. أَوْ قُشِرَ مِنَ الدُّرَّةِ البَيْضاءِ. وَقَدْ أُودِعَ لَفائِفَ النَّعِيمِ. وَضُمِّخَ بِالطِّيبِ العَمِيمِ. وَسِيقَ إِلَيْهِ شِرْبٌ مِنْ تَسْنِيمٍ. وَسَفَرَ عَنْ مَرْأًى وَسِيمٍ. وَأَرَجٍ نَسِيمٍ. فَلَمّا اضْطَرَمَتْ بِمَحْضَرِهِ الشَّهَواتُ. وَقَرِمَتْ إِلَى مَخْبَرِهِ اللَّهَواتُ. وَشارَفَ أَنْ تُشَنَّ عَلَى سِرْبِهِ الغاراتُ. وَيُنادَى[2] عِنْدَ نَهْبِهِ يا لَلثّاراتِ.[3] نَشَزَ أَبُو زَيْدٍ كَالمَجْنُونِ. وَتَباعَدَ عَنْهُ تَباعُدَ الضَّبِّ مِنَ النُّونِ. فَراوَدْناهُ عَلَى أَنْ يَعُودَ. وَأَنْ لا يَكُونَ كَقُدارٍ فِي ثَمُودَ. فَقالَ وَالَّذِي يَنْشُرُ الأَمْواتَ مِنَ الرِّجامِ. لا عُدْتُ دُونَ رَفْعِ الجامِ. فَلَمْ نَجِدْ بُدًّا مِنْ تَأَلُّفِهِ. وَإِبْرارِ حَلِفِهِ. فَأَشَلْناهُ وَالعُقُولُ مَعَهُ شائِلَةٌ. وَالدُّمُوعُ عَلَيْهِ سائِلَةٌ. فَلَمّا فاءَ إِلَى مَجْثِمِهِ. وَخَلَصَ مِنْ مَأْثَمِهِ. سَأَلْناهُ لِمَ قامَ.

١ في هامش س: تُعرف بالسِّنجارية؛ وفي د: السنجارية؛ وفي ف: تُعرف بالسنجارية. ٢ د: يُنادِي. ٣ س: لِلثارات.

وَلِأَيِّ مَعْنًى ٱسْتَرْفَعَ ٱلْجَامَ. فَقَالَ إِنَّ ٱلزُّجَاجَ نَمَّامٌ. وَإِنِّي آلَيْتُ مُذْ أَعْوَامٌ.[١] أَنْ لَا يَضُمَّنِي وَنَمُومًا مَقَامٌ. فَقُلْنَا وَمَا سَبَبُ يَمِينِكَ ٱلصَّرَّى. وَأَلِيَّتِكَ ٱلْحَرَّى.

٣،١٨ فَقَالَ[٢] كَانَ لِي جَارٌ لِسَانُهُ يَتَقَرَّبُ. وَقَلْبُهُ عَقْرَبٌ. وَلَفْظُهُ شُهْدٌ يَنْقَعُ. وَخَبْؤُهُ سَمٌّ مُنْقَعٌ. فَمِلْتُ لِمُجَاوَرَتِهِ. إِلَى مُحَاوَرَتِهِ. وَٱغْتَرَرْتُ بِمُكَاشَرَتِهِ. فِي مُعَاشَرَتِهِ. وَٱسْتَهْوَتْنِي خُضْرَةُ دِمْنَتِهِ. لِمُنَادَمَتِهِ. وَأَغْرَتْنِي خُدْعَةُ سِمَتِهِ. بِمُنَاسَمَتِهِ. فَمَازَجْتُهُ وَعِنْدِي أَنَّهُ جَارٌ مُكَاسِرٌ. فَبَانَ أَنَّهُ عُقَابٌ كَاسِرٌ. وَآنَسْتُهُ عَلَى أَنَّهُ حِبٌّ مُؤَانِسٌ. فَوَضَحَ[٣] أَنَّهُ حُبَابٌ مُؤَالِسٌ. وَمَالَحْتُهُ وَلَا أَعْلَمُ أَنَّهُ عِنْدَ نَقْدِهِ. مِمَّنْ يُفْرَحُ بِفَقْدِهِ. وَعَاقَرْتُهُ وَلَمْ أَدْرِ أَنَّهُ بَعْدَ فَرِّهِ. مِمَّنْ يُطْرَبُ لِمَفَرِّهِ.

٤،١٨ وَكَانَتْ عِنْدِي جَارِيَةٌ. لَا يُوجَدُ لَهَا فِي ٱلْكَمَالِ مُجَارِيَةٌ. إِنْ سَفَرَتْ خَجِلَ ٱلنَّيِّرَانِ. وَصَلِيَتِ ٱلْقُلُوبُ بِٱلنِّيرَانِ. وَإِنْ بَسَمَتْ أَزْرَتْ بِٱلْجُمَانِ. وَبِيعَ ٱلْمَرْجَانُ. بِٱلْمَجَّانِ. وَإِنْ رَنَتْ هَيَّجَتِ ٱلْبَلَابِلَ. وَحَقَّقَتْ سِحْرَ بَابِلَ. وَإِنْ نَطَقَتْ عَقَلَتْ لُبَّ ٱلْعَاقِلِ. وَٱسْتَنْزَلَتِ ٱلْعُصْمَ مِنَ ٱلْمَعَاقِلِ. وَإِنْ قَرَأَتْ شَفَتِ ٱلْمَفْؤُودَ. وَأَحْيَتِ ٱلْمَوْؤُودَ. وَخِلْتَهَا أُوتِيَتْ مِنْ مَزَامِيرِ آلِ دَاوُدَ. وَإِنْ غَنَّتْ ظَلَّ مَعْبَدٌ لَهَا عَبْدًا. وَقِيلَ سُحْقًا لِإِسْحٰقَ وَبُعْدًا. وَإِنْ زَمَرَتْ أَضْحَى زُنَامٌ عِنْدَهَا زَنِيمًا. بَعْدَ أَنْ كَانَ لِجِيلِهِ زَعِيمًا. وَبِٱلْإِطْرَابِ زَعِيمًا. وَإِنْ رَقَصَتْ أَمَالَتِ ٱلْعَمَائِمَ عَنِ ٱلرُّؤُوسِ. وَأَنْسَتْكَ رَقْصَ ٱلْحَبَبِ فِي ٱلْكُؤُوسِ. فَكُنْتُ أَزْدَرِي مَعَهَا حُمْرَ ٱلنَّعَمِ. وَأُحَلِّي بِتَمَلِّيهَا جِيدَ ٱلنِّعَمِ. وَأَحْجُبُ مَرْآهَا عَنِ ٱلشَّمْسِ وَٱلْقَمَرِ. وَأَذُودُ ذِكْرَاهَا عَنْ شَرَائِعِ ٱلسَّمَرِ. وَأَنَا مَعَ ذٰلِكَ أَلِيحُ. مِنْ أَنْ تَسْرِيَ بِرَيَّاهَا رِيحٌ. أَوْ يَكْهُنَ بِهَا سَطِيحٌ. أَوْ يَنُمَّ عَلَيْهَا بَرْقٌ مُلِيحٌ.

---

١ هكذا في ق، وفي س بتنوين الضمة مكتوب بحبر مغاير اللون؛ وفي د: أعوامٍ. ٢ بعدها في و، ف: إنّه. ٣ ف: فظهر.

٥،١٨ فَٱتَّفَقَ لِوَشَلِ[1] ٱلْحَظِّ ٱلْمَبْخُوسِ. وَنَكَدِ ٱلطَّالِعِ ٱلْمَنْحُوسِ. أَنْ أَنْطَقَتْنِي بِوَصْفِهَا حُمَيَّا ٱلْمُدَامِ. عِنْدَ ٱلْجَارِ ٱلنَّمَّامِ. ثُمَّ ثَابَ ٱلْفَهْمُ. بَعْدَ أَنْ صَرِدَ ٱلسَّهْمُ. فَأَحْسَسْتُ ٱلْخَبَالَ وَٱلْوَبَالَ. وَضَيْعَةَ مَا أُودِعَ ذٰلِكَ ٱلْغِرْبَالُ. بَيْدَ أَنِّي عَاهَدْتُهُ عَلَى عَكْمِ مَا لَفَظْتُهُ. وَأَنْ يَحْفَظَ ٱلسِّرَّ وَلَوْ أَحْفَظْتُهُ. فَزَعَمَ أَنَّهُ يَخْزُنُ ٱلْأَسْرَارَ. كَمَا يَخْزُنُ ٱللَّئِيمُ ٱلدِّينَارَ. وَأَنَّهُ لَا يَهْتِكُ ٱلْأَسْتَارَ. وَلَوْ عُرِّضَ لِأَنْ يَلِجَ ٱلنَّارَ. فَمَا[2] غَبَرَ عَلَى ذٰلِكَ ٱلزَّمَانِ. إِلَّا يَوْمٌ أَوْ يَوْمَانِ. حَتَّى بَدَا لِأَمِيرِ[3] تِلْكَ ٱلْمَدَرَةِ. وَوَالِيهَا ذِي ٱلْمَقْدُرَةِ. أَنْ يَقْصِدَ بَابَ قَيْلِهِ. مُجَدِّدًا عَرْضَ خَيْلِهِ. وَمُسْتَمْطِرًا عَارِضَ نَيْلِهِ. وَٱرْتَادَ أَنْ تَصْحَبَهُ تُحْفَةٌ تُلَائِمُ هَوَاهُ. لِيُقَدِّمَهَا بَيْنَ يَدَيْ نَجْوَاهُ. وَجَعَلَ يَبْذُلُ ٱلْجَعَائِلَ لِرُوَّادِهِ. وَيُسَنِّي ٱلْمَرَاغِبَ لِمَنْ يُظْفِرُهُ بِمُرَادِهِ. فَأَسَفَّ ذٰلِكَ ٱلْجَارُ ٱلْخَتَّارُ إِلَى بُذُولِهِ. وَعَصَى فِي ٱدِّرَاعِ ٱلْعَارِ عَذْلَ عَذُولِهِ. فَأَتَى ٱلْوَالِيَ نَاشِرًا أُذُنَيْهِ. وَأَبَثَّهُ مَا كُنْتُ أَسْرَرْتُهُ إِلَيْهِ. فَمَا رَاعَنِي إِلَّا ٱنْسِيَابُ صَاغِيَتِهِ إِلَيَّ. وَٱنْثِيَالُ حَفَدَتِهِ عَلَيَّ. يَسُومُنِي إِيثَارَهُ بِٱلدُّرَّةِ ٱلْيَتِيمَةِ. عَلَى أَنْ أَتَحَكَّمَ عَلَيْهِ ٱلْقِيمَةِ. فَغَشِيَنِي مِنَ ٱلْهَمِّ[4] مَا غَشِيَ فِرْعَوْنَ وَجُنُودَهُ مِنَ ٱلْيَمِّ. وَلَمْ أَزَلْ أُدَافِعُ عَنْهَا وَلَا يُغْنِي ٱلدِّفَاعُ. وَأَسْتَشْفِعُ إِلَيْهِ وَلَا يُجْدِي ٱلِٱسْتِشْفَاعُ. وَكُلَّمَا رَأَى مِنِّي ٱزْدِيَادَ ٱلِٱعْتِيَاصِ. وَٱرْتِيَادَ ٱلْمَنَاصِ. تَجَرَّمَ وَتَضَرَّمَ. وَحَرَقَ[5] عَلَيَّ ٱلْأُرَّمَ. وَنَفْسِي مَعَ ذٰلِكَ لَا تَسْمَحُ بِمُفَارَقَةِ بَدْرِي. وَبِأَنْ أَنْزِعَ قَلْبِي مِنْ صَدْرِي. حَتَّى آلَ ٱلْوَعِيدُ إِيقَاعًا. وَٱلتَّقْرِيعُ قِرَاعًا. فَقَادَنِي ٱلْإِشْفَاقُ مِنَ ٱلْحَيْنِ. إِلَى أَنْ قِضْتُهُ سَوَادَ ٱلْعَيْنِ. بِصُفْرَةِ ٱلْعَيْنِ. وَلَمْ يَحْظَ ٱلْوَاشِي بِغَيْرِ ٱلْإِثْمِ وَٱلشَّيْنِ. فَعَاهَدْتُ ٱللّٰهَ تَعَالَى مُذْ ذٰلِكَ ٱلْعَهْدِ. أَنْ لَا أُحَاضِرَ نَمَّامًا مِنْ بَعْدُ. وَٱلزُّجَاجُ مَخْصُوصٌ بِهٰذِهِ ٱلطِّبَاعِ ٱلذَّمِيمَةِ. وَبِهِ يُضْرَبُ ٱلْمَثَلُ فِي ٱلنَّمِيمَةِ. فَقَدْ جَرَى عَلَيْهِ سَيْلُ يَمِينِي. وَلِذٰلِكُمُ ٱلسَّبَبِ لَمْ تَمْتَدَّ إِلَيْهِ يَمِينِي.

١ و، ف: لوشك. ٢ بعدها في ف: إن. ٣ ف: إلى أمير. ٤ د: الغم. ٥ و، د، ف: حرّق.

فَلَا تَعْذُلُونِي بَعْدَمَا قَدْ شَرَحْتُهُ   عَلَى أَنْ حُرِمْتُمْ بِي ٱقْتِطَافَ ٱلْقَطَائِفِ
فَقَدْ بَانَ عُذْرِي صَنِيعِي وَإِنَّنِي   سَأَرْتُقُ فَتْقِي مِنْ تَلِيدِي وَطَارِفِي
عَلَى أَنَّ مَا زَوَّدْتُكُمْ مِنْ فُكَاهَةٍ   أَلَذُّ مِنَ ٱلْحَلْوَى لَدَى كُلِّ عَارِفِ

٦.١٨ قَالَ ٱلْحَارِثُ بْنُ هَمَّامٍ فَقَبِلْنَا ٱعْتِذَارَهُ. وَقَبَّلْنَا عِذَارَهُ. وَقُلْنَا لَهُ قِدْمًا وَقَذَتِ ٱلنَّمِيمَةُ خَيْرَ ٱلْبَشَرِ. حَتَّى ٱنْتَشَرَ عَنْ حَمَّالَةِ ٱلْحَطَبِ مَا ٱنْتَشَرَ. ثُمَّ سَأَلْنَاهُ عَمَّا أَحْدَثَ جَارُهُ ٱلْقَتَّاتُ. وَدُخْلُلُهُ ٱلْمُفْتَاتُ. بَعْدَ أَنْ رَاشَ لَهُ نَبْلَ ٱلسِّعَايَةِ. وَجَذَمَ حَبْلَ ٱلرِّعَايَةِ. فَقَالَ أَخَذَ فِي ٱلِاسْتِخْذَاءِ وَٱلِاسْتِكَانَةِ. وَٱلِاسْتِشْفَاعِ إِلَيَّ بِذَوِي ٱلْمَكَانَةِ. وَكُنْتُ حَرَّجْتُ عَلَى نَفْسِي. أَنْ لَا يَسْتَرْجِعَهُ أُنْسِي. أَوْ يَرْجِعَ إِلَيَّ أَمْسِي. فَلَمْ يَكُنْ لَهُ مِنِّي سِوَى ٱلرَّدِّ. وَٱلْإِصْرَارِ عَلَى ٱلصَّدِّ. وَهُوَ لَا يَكْتَئِبُ مِنَ ٱلنَّجْهِ. وَلَا يَتَّئِبُ مِنْ وَقَاحَةِ ٱلْوَجْهِ. بَلْ يُلِظُّ بِٱلْوَسَائِلِ. وَيُلِحُّ فِي ٱلْمَسَائِلِ. فَمَا أَنْقَذَنِي مِنْ إِبْرَامِهِ. وَلَا أَبْعَدَ عَلَيْهِ نَيْلَ مَرَامِهِ. إِلَّا أَبْيَاتٌ[١] نَفَثَ بِهَا ٱلصَّدْرُ ٱلْمَوْتُورُ. وَٱلْخَاطِرُ ٱلْمَبْتُورُ. فَإِنَّهَا كَانَتْ مَدْحَرَةً لِشَيْطَانِهِ. وَمَسْجَنَةً لَهُ فِي أَوْطَانِهِ. وَعِنْدَ ٱنْتِشَارِهَا بَتَّ طَلَاقَ ٱلْحُبُورِ. وَدَعَا بِٱلْوَيْلِ وَٱلثُّبُورِ. وَأَيِسَ[٢] مِنْ نَشْرِ وَصْلِي ٱلْمَقْبُورِ. كَمَا يَئِسَ ٱلْكُفَّارُ مِنْ أَصْحَابِ ٱلْقُبُورِ. فَنَاشَدْنَاهُ أَنْ يُنْشِدَنَا إِيَّاهَا. وَيُنْشِقَنَا رَيَّاهَا. فَقَالَ أَجَلْ. خُلِقَ ٱلْإِنْسَانُ مِنْ عَجَلٍ. ثُمَّ أَنْشَدَ لَا يَزْوِيهِ خَجَلٌ. وَلَا يَثْنِيهِ[٣] وَجَلٌ.

٧.١٨ وَنَدِيمٍ مَحَضْتُهُ صِدْقَ وُدِّي   إِذْ تَوَهَّمْتُهُ صَدِيقًا حَمِيمَا
ثُمَّ أَوْلَيْتُهُ قَطِيعَةَ قَالٍ   حِينَ أَلْفَيْتُهُ صَدِيدًا حَمِيمَا
خِلْتُهُ قَبْلَ أَنْ يُجَرَّبَ إِلْفًا   ذَا ذِمَامٍ فَبَانَ جِلْفًا ذَمِيمَا

---

١ و: أبياتٌ. ٢ و، د: يئس. ٣ د: يُثْنيه.

وَتَخَــيَّرْتُــهُ كَلِيــمًا فَــأَمْــسَى مِنْهُ قَلْبِي بِمَا جَنَاهُ كَلِيمَا
وَتَظَــنَّيْتُــهُ مُــعِينًا رَحِــيمًا فَتَــبَيَّنْتُــهُ لَعِيــنًا رَجِــيمَا
وَتَــرَاءَيْتُــهُ مُــرِيــدًا فَجَلَّى عَنْهُ سَبْكِي لَهُ مَـرِيدًا لَئِيمَا
وَتَوَسَّمْتُ أَنْ يَهُبَّ نَسِيمًا فَأَبَى أَنْ يَهُبَّ إِلَّا سَمُومَا
بِتُّ مِنْ لَسْعِهِ الَّذِي أَعْجَزَ الرَّا قِي سَلِيمًا وَبَاتَ مِنِّي سَلِيمَا
وَغَدَا أَمْرُهُ[1] غَدَاةَ ٱفْتَرَقْنَا مُسْتَقِيمًا وَٱلْجِسْمُ مِنِّي سَقِيمَا
لَمْ يَكُنْ رَائِعًا خَصِيبًا وَلٰكِنْ كَانَ بِالشَّرِّ رَائِعًا لِي خَصِيمَا
قُلْتُ لَمَّا بَلَوْتُهُ لَيْتَهُ كَا نَ عَدِيمًا وَلَمْ يَكُنْ لِي نَدِيمَا
بَغَّضَ الصُّبْحَ حِينَ نَمَّ إِلَى قَلْـ ـبِي لِأَنَّ الصَّبَاحَ يُلْفَى نَمُومَا
وَدَعَانِي إِلَى هَوَى اللَّيْلِ إِذْ كَا نَ سَوَادُ الدُّجَى رَقِيبًا كَتُومَا
وَكَفَى مَنْ يَشِي وَلَوْ فَاهُ بِالصِّدْ قِ أَثَامًا فِيمَا أَتَاهُ وَلُومَا

٨،١٨ قَالَ فَلَمَّا سَمِعَ رَبُّ الْمَنْزِلِ[2] قَرِيضَهُ وَسَجْعَهُ. وَٱسْتَمْلَحَ تَقْرِيظَهُ وَسَبْعَهُ. بَوَّأَهُ مِهَادَ كَرَامَتِهِ. وَصَدَّرَهُ عَلَى تَكْرِمَتِهِ. ثُمَّ ٱسْتَحْضَرَ عَشْرَ صِحَافٍ مِنَ الْغَرَبِ. فِيهَا حَلْوَاءُ الْقَنْدِ وَالضَّرَبِ. وَقَالَ لَهُ ﴿لَا يَسْتَوِي أَصْحَابُ ٱلنَّارِ وَأَصْحَابُ ٱلْجَنَّةِ﴾. وَلَا يَسَعُ أَنْ يُجْعَلَ الْبَرِيءُ كَذِي الظِّنَّةِ. وَهٰذِهِ الآنِيَةُ تَتَنَزَّلُ مَنْزِلَةَ الْأَبْرَارِ. فِي صَوْنِ الْأَسْرَارِ. فَلَا تُولِهَا[3] الْإِبْعَادَ. وَلَا تُلْحِقْ هُودًا بِعَادَ. ثُمَّ أَمَرَ خَادِمَهُ بِنَقْلِهَا إِلَى مَثْوَاهُ. لِيَحْكُمَ فِيهَا بِمَا يَهْوَاهُ. فَأَقْبَلَ عَلَيْنَا أَبُو زَيْدٍ وَقَالَ اِقْرَأُوا سُورَةَ الْفَتْحِ. وَأَبْشِرُوا بِٱنْدِمَالِ الْقَرْحِ. فَقَدْ جَبَرَ اللهُ ثُكْلَكُمْ. وَسَنَّى أُكْلَكُمْ. وَجَمَعَ فِي ظِلِّ الْحَلْوَاءِ شَمْلَكُمْ. ﴿وَعَسَىٰ أَنْ تَكْرَهُوا شَيْئًا وَهُوَ خَيْرٌ لَكُمْ﴾.

١ «وغدا أمره»: ف: وهذا نهجه. ٢ ف: البيت. ٣ د: تُولّها.

٩.١٨ وَلَمَّا هَمَّ بِالِانْصِرَافِ. مَالَ إِلَى ٱسْتِهْدَاءِ الصِّحَافِ. فَقَالَ لِلْآدِبِ إِنَّ مِنْ دَلَائِلِ الظَّرْفِ. سَمَاحَةَ الْمُهْدِي بِالظَّرْفِ. فَقَالَ كِلَاهُمَا[١] وَالْغُلَامُ. فَٱحْذِفِ الْكَلَامَ. وَٱنْهَضْ بِسَلَامٍ. فَوَثَبَ فِي الْجَوَابِ. وَشَكَرَهُ شُكْرَ الرَّوْضِ لِلسَّحَابِ. ثُمَّ ٱقْتَادَنَا أَبُو زَيْدٍ إِلَى حِوَائِهِ. وَحَكَّمَنَا فِي حَلْوَائِهِ. وَجَعَلَ يُقَلِّبُ الْأَوَانِي بِيَدِهِ. وَيَفُضُّ عَدَدَهَا عَلَى عَدَدِهِ. ثُمَّ قَالَ لَسْتُ أَدْرِي أَأَشْكُو ذٰلِكَ النَّمَّامَ أَمْ أَشْكُرُ. وَأَتَنَاسَى فَعْلَتَهُ أَمْ أَذْكُرُ. فَإِنَّهُ وَإِنْ كَانَ أَسْلَفَ الْجَرِيمَةَ. وَنَمْنَمَ النَّمِيمَةَ. فَمِنْ غَيْمِهِ ٱنْهَلَّتْ هٰذِهِ الدِّيمَةُ. وَبِسَيْفِهِ ٱنْحَازَتْ[٢] هٰذِهِ الْغَنِيمَةُ. وَقَدْ خَطَرَ بِبَالِي. أَنْ أَرْجِعَ إِلَى أَشْبَالِي. وَأَقْنَعَ بِمَا تَسَنَّى لِي. وَأَنْ لَا أُتْعِبَ نَفْسِي وَلَا أَجْمَالِي. وَأَنَا أُوَدِّعُكُمْ وَدَاعَ مُحَافِظٍ. وَأَسْتَوْدِعُكُمْ خَيْرَ حَافِظٍ. ثُمَّ ٱسْتَوَى عَلَى رَاحِلَتِهِ. رَاجِعًا فِي حَافِرَتِهِ. وَلَاوِيًا إِلَى زَافِرَتِهِ. فَغَادَرَنَا بَعْدَ أَنْ وَخَدَتْ عَنْسُهُ. وَزَايَلَنَا أُنْسُهُ. كَدَسْتٍ غَابَ صَدْرُهُ. أَوْ لَيْلٍ أَفَلَ بَدْرُهُ.

---

١ بعدها في ف: لك. ٢ بعدها في و، د: لي.

الْمَقَامَةُ التَّاسِعَةَ عَشْرَةَ[١]

رَوَى الْحَارِثُ بْنُ هَمَّامٍ قَالَ أَمْحَلَ الْعِرَاقُ ذَاتَ الْعُوَيْمِ. لِإِخْلَافِ أَنْوَاءِ الْغَيْمِ. ١،١٩
وَتَحَدَّثَ الرُّكْبَانُ بِرِيفِ نَصِيبِينَ. وَبُلَهْنِيَةِ أَهْلِهَا الْمُخْصِبِينَ. فَٱقْتَعَدْتُ مَهْرِيًّا.
وَٱعْتَقَلْتُ سَمْهَرِيًّا. وَسِرْتُ تَلْفِظُنِي أَرْضٌ إِلَى أَرْضٍ. وَيَجْذِبُنِي رَفْعٌ مِنْ خَفْضٍ.
حَتَّى بَلَغْتُهَا نِقْضًا عَلَى نِقْضٍ.[٢] فَلَمَّا أَنَخْتُ بِمَغْنَاهَا الْخَصِيبِ. وَضَرَبْتُ فِي
مَرْعَاهَا بِنَصِيبٍ. نَوَيْتُ أَنْ أُلْقِيَ بِهَا جِرَانِي. وَأَتَّخِذَ أَهْلَهَا جِيرَانِي. إِلَى أَنْ تَحْيَى[٣]
السَّنَةُ الْجَمَادُ. وَيَتَعَهَّدَ أَرْضَ قَوْمِي الْعِهَادُ. فَوَاللهِ مَا تَمَضْمَضَتْ مُقْلَتِي بِنَوْمِهَا.
وَلَا تَمَخَّضَتْ لَيْلَتِي عَنْ يَوْمِهَا. أَوْ أَلْفَيْتُ[٤] أَبَا زَيْدٍ السَّرُوجِيَّ يَجُولُ فِي أَرْجَاءِ
نَصِيبِينَ. وَيَخْبِطُ بِهَا خَبْطَ الْمُصَابِينَ وَالْمُصِيبِينَ. وَهُوَ يَنْثُرُ مِنْ فِيهِ الدُّرَرَ.
وَيَحْتَلِبُ بِكَفَّيْهِ الدِّرَرَ. فَوَجَدْتُ جِهَادِي قَدْ حَازَ مَغْنَمًا. وَقِدْحِيَ الْفَذَّ قَدْ صَارَ
تَوْأَمًا.

وَلَمْ أَزَلْ أَتَّبِعُ[٥] ظِلَّهُ أَيْنَمَا ٱنْبَعَثَ. وَأَلْتَقِطُ لَفْظَهُ كُلَّمَا نَفَثَ. إِلَى أَنْ عَرَاهُ مَرَضٌ ٢،١٩
ٱمْتَدَّ مَدَاهُ. وَعَرَقَتْهُ مُدَاهُ. حَتَّى كَادَ يَسْلُبُهُ ثَوْبَ الْمَحْيَا.[٦] وَيُسَلِّمُهُ إِلَى أَبِي
يَحْيَى. فَوَجَدْتُ لِفَوْتِ مَلْقَاهُ.[٧] وَٱنْقِطَاعِ سُقْيَاهُ. مَا يَجِدُهُ الْمُبْعَدُ عَنْ مَرَامِهِ.
وَالْمُرْضَعُ عِنْدَ فِطَامِهِ. ثُمَّ أُرْجِفَ بِأَنَّ رَهْنَهُ قَدْ غَلِقَ. وَمِخْلَبَ الْحِمَامِ بِهِ قَدْ
عَلِقَ. فَقَلِقَ صَحْبُهُ لِإِرْجَافِ الْمُرْجِفِينَ. وَٱنْثَالُوا إِلَى عَقْوَتِهِ مُوجِفِينَ.

١ في هامش س: تعرف بالنَّصيبية؛ وفي د: النصيبية؛ وفي ف: النصيبية. ٢ و: نَقْضًا على نَقْضٍ. ٣ و، د، ف: تَحْيَى. ٤ س: أُلفيت بها، د: دون أن ألفيت. ٥ س، د: أَتْبَعُ. ٦ و: المُحَيّا. ٧ د: لقياه.

حَيَارَى يَمِيدُ بِهِمْ شَجْوُهُمْ كَأَنَّهُمُ ٱرْتَضَعُوا ٱلْخَنْدَرِيسَا
أَسَالُوا ٱلْغُرُوبَ وَعَطُّوا ٱلْجُيُوبَ وَصَكُّوا ٱلْخُدُودَ وَشَجُّوا ٱلرُّؤُوسَا
يَوَدُّونَ لَوْ سَالَمَتْهُ ٱلْمَنُونُ وَغَالَتْ نَفَائِسَهُمْ وَٱلنُّفُوسَا

٣،١٩ قَالَ ٱلرَّاوِي وَكُنْتُ فِيمَنِ ٱلْتَفَّ بِأَصْحَابِهِ. وَأَغَذَّ إِلَى بَابِهِ. فَلَمَّا ٱنْتَهَيْنَا إِلَى فِنَائِهِ. وَتَصَدَّيْنَا لِٱسْتِنْشَاءِ أَنْبَائِهِ. بَرَزَ إِلَيْنَا فَتَاهُ. مُفْتَرَّةً شَفَتَاهُ. فَٱسْتَطْلَعْنَاهُ طِلْعَ الشَّيْخِ فِي شَكَاتِهِ. وَكُنْهَ قُوَى حَرَكَاتِهِ. فَقَالَ قَدْ كَانَ فِي قَبْضَةِ ٱلْمَرْضَةِ. وَعَرْكَةِ ٱلْوَعْكَةِ. إِلَى أَنْ شَفَّهُ الدَّنَفُ. وَٱسْتَشَفَّهُ التَّلَفُ. ثُمَّ مَنَّ ٱللهُ تَعَالَى بِتَقْوِيَةِ ذَمَائِهِ. فَأَفَاقَ مِنْ إِغْمَائِهِ. فَٱرْجِعُوا أَدْرَاجَكُمْ. وَٱنْضُوا ٱنْزِعَاجَكُمْ. فَكَأَنْ قَدْ غَدَا وَرَاحَ. وَسَاقَاكُمُ الرَّاحَ. فَأَعْظَمْنَا بُشْرَاهُ. وَٱقْتَرَحْنَا أَنْ نَرَاهُ. فَدَخَلَ مُؤْذِنًا بِنَا. ثُمَّ خَرَجَ آذِنًا لَنَا. فَلَقِينَا مِنْهُ لَقًى. وَلِسَانًا طُلَقًا.[١] وَجَلَسْنَا مُحْدِقِينَ بِسَرِيرِهِ. مُحَدِّقِينَ إِلَى أَسَارِيرِهِ. فَقَلَّبَ طَرْفَهُ فِي ٱلْجَمَاعَةِ. ثُمَّ قَالَ ٱجْتَلُوهَا بِنْتَ السَّاعَةِ. وَأَنْشَدَ

عَافَانِيَ ٱللهُ وَشُكْرًا لَهُ مِنْ عِلَّةٍ كَادَتْ تُعَفِّينِي
وَمَنَّ بِٱلْبُرْءِ عَلَى أَنَّهُ لَا بُدَّ مِنْ حَتْفٍ سَيَبْرِينِي
مَا يَتَنَاسَانِي وَلٰكِنَّهُ إِلَى تَقَضِّي ٱلْأُكْلِ يُنْسِينِي
إِنْ حُمَّ لَمْ يُغْنِ حَمِيمٌ وَلَا حِمَى كُلَيْبٍ مِنْهُ يَحْمِينِي
وَمَا أُبَالِي أَدْنَا يَوْمُهُ أَمْ أُخِّرَ ٱلْحَيْنُ إِلَى حِينِ
فَأَيُّ فَخْرٍ فِي حَيَاةٍ أَرَى فِيهَا ٱلْبَلَايَا ثُمَّ تُبْلِينِي

١ د: طَلْقًا.

٤،١٩ قَالَ فَدَعَوْنَا لَهُ بِٱمْتِدَادِ ٱلْأَجَلِ. وَٱرْتِدَادِ ٱلْوَجَلِ. ثُمَّ تَدَاعَيْنَا إِلَى ٱلْقِيَامِ. لِاتِّقَاءِ ٱلْإِبْرَامِ. فَقَالَ كَلَّا بَلِ ٱلْبَثُوا بَيَاضَ يَوْمِكُمْ عِنْدِي. لِتَشْفُوا بِٱلْمُفَاكَهَةِ وَجْدِي. فَإِنَّ مُنَاجَاتَكُمْ قُوتُ نَفْسِي. وَمَغْنَاطِيسُ أُنْسِي. فَتَحَرَّيْنَا مَرْضَاتَهُ. وَتَحَامَيْنَا مُعَاصَاتَهُ. وَأَقْبَلْنَا عَلَى ٱلْحَدِيثِ نَمْخُضُ زُبْدَهُ. وَنُلْغِي زَبَدَهُ. إِلَى أَنْ حَانَ وَقْتُ ٱلْمَقِيلِ. وَكَلَّتِ ٱلْأَلْسُنُ مِنَ ٱلْقَالِ وَٱلْقِيلِ. وَكَانَ يَوْمًا حَامِيَ ٱلْوَدِيقَةِ. يَانِعَ ٱلْحَدِيقَةِ. فَقَالَ إِنَّ ٱلنُّعَاسَ قَدْ أَمَالَ[١] ٱلْأَعْنَاقَ. وَرَاوَدَ ٱلْآمَاقَ. وَهُوَ خَصْمٌ أَلَدُّ. وَخِطْبٌ[٢] لَا يُرَدُّ. فَصِلُوا حَبْلَهُ بِٱلْقَيْلُولَةِ. وَٱقْتَدُوا فِيهِ بِٱلْآثَارِ ٱلْمَنْقُولَةِ.

٥،١٩ قَالَ ٱلرَّاوِي فَٱتَّبَعْنَا مَا قَالَ. وَقِلْنَا وَقَالَ. فَضَرَبَ ٱللهُ عَلَى ٱلْآذَانِ. وَأَفْرَغَ ٱلسِّنَةَ فِي ٱلْأَجْفَانِ. حَتَّى خَرَجْنَا مِنْ حُكْمِ ٱلْوُجُودِ. وَصُرِفْنَا بِٱلْهُجُودِ عَنِ ٱلسُّجُودِ. فَمَا ٱسْتَيْقَظْنَا إِلَّا وَٱلْحَرُّ قَدْ بَاخَ. وَٱلْيَوْمُ قَدْ شَاخَ. فَتَكَرَّعْنَا لِصَلَاةِ ٱلْعَجْمَاوَيْنِ. وَأَدَّيْنَا مَا حَلَّ مِنَ ٱلدَّيْنِ. ثُمَّ تَحَثْحَثْنَا لِلِٱرْتِحَالِ. إِلَى مُلْقَى ٱلرِّحَالِ. فَٱلْتَفَتَ أَبُو زَيْدٍ إِلَى شِبْلِهِ. وَكَانَ عَلَى شَاكِلَتِهِ وَشَكْلِهِ. وَقَالَ إِنِّي لَإِخَالُ أَبَا عَمْرَةَ. قَدْ أَضْرَمَ فِي أَحْشَائِهِمُ ٱلْجَمْرَةَ. فَٱسْتَدْعِ أَبَا جَامِعٍ. فَإِنَّهُ بُشْرَى كُلِّ جَائِعٍ. وَأَرْدِفْهُ بِأَبِي نُعَيْمٍ. ٱلصَّابِرِ عَلَى كُلِّ ضَيْمٍ. ثُمَّ عَزِّزْ بِأَبِي حَبِيبٍ. ٱلْمُحَبَّبِ إِلَى كُلِّ لَبِيبٍ. ٱلْمُقَلَّبِ بَيْنَ إِحْرَاقٍ وَتَعْذِيبٍ. وَأَهِبْ بِأَبِي ثَقِيفٍ. فَحَبَّذَا هُوَ مِنْ أَلِيفٍ. وَهَلُمَّ بِأَبِي عَوْنٍ.[٣] فَمَا مِثْلُهُ مِنْ عَوْنٍ. وَلَوِ ٱسْتَحْضَرْتَ أَبَا جَمِيلٍ. لَجَمَّلَ أَيَّ تَجْمِيلٍ. وَحَيَّ هَلْ[٤] بِأُمِّ ٱلْقِرَى. ٱلْمُذَكِّرَةِ بِكِسْرَى. وَلَا تَتَنَاسَ أُمَّ جَابِرٍ. فَكَمْ لَهَا مِنْ ذَاكِرٍ. وَنَادِ أُمَّ ٱلْفَرَجِ. ثُمَّ ٱفْتِكْ بِهَا وَلَا حَرَجَ. وَٱخْتِمْ بِأَبِي رَزِينٍ. فَهُوَ مَسْلَاةُ كُلِّ حَزِينٍ. وَإِنْ تَقْرِنْ بِهِ أَبَا ٱلْعَلَاءِ. تَمَحُ ٱسْمَكَ مِنَ ٱلْبُخَلَاءِ. وَإِيَّاكَ وَٱسْتِدْنَاءَ ٱلْمُرْجِفِيْنِ. قَبْلَ

---

١ بعدها ورقتان ناقصتان من نسختي الرقمية من س. ٢ و: خَطْب. ٣ «وهلُمَّ بأبي عوْنٍ. فما مثلُهُ من عوْنٍ»: في هامش ق. ٤ و: وَحَيْ هَلاً.

ٱسْتِقْلَالِ حُمُولِ ٱلْبَيْنِ. وَإِذَا نَزَعَ ٱلْقَوْمُ عَنِ ٱلْمِرَاسِ. وَصَافَحُوا أَبَا إِيَاسٍ. فَأَطِفْ عَلَيْهِمْ أَبَا آذَنَتْ ٱلسَّرْوِ.[١] فَإِنَّهُ عُنْوَانُ ٱلسَّرْوِ.

٦،١٩ قَالَ فَفَقِهَ ٱبْنُهُ لَطَائِفَ رُمُوزِهِ. بِلَطَافَةِ تَمْيِيزِهِ. فَطَافَ عَلَيْنَا بِالطَّيِّبَاتِ وَالطِّيبِ. إِلَى أَنْ آذَنَتْ[٢] ٱلشَّمْسُ بِالْمَغِيبِ. فَلَمَّا أَجْمَعْنَا عَلَى ٱلتَّوْدِيعِ. قُلْنَا لَهُ أَلَمْ تَرَ إِلَى هٰذَا ٱلْيَوْمِ ٱلْبَدِيعِ. كَيْفَ بَدَا صُبْحُهُ قَمْطَرِيرًا. وَمُسْيُهُ مُسْتَنِيرًا. فَسَجَدَ حَتَّى أَطَالَ. ثُمَّ رَفَعَ رَأْسَهُ وَقَالَ.

لَا تَيْأَسَنْ عِنْدَ ٱلنُّوَبْ   مِنْ فَرْجَةٍ تَجْلُو ٱلْكُرَبْ
فَلَكَمْ سَمُومٍ هَبَّ ثُمَّ   جَرَى نَسِيمًا وَٱنْقَلَبْ
وَسَحَابِ مَكْرُوهٍ تَنَشَّأَ   فَٱضْمَحَلَّ وَمَا سَكَبْ
وَدُخَانِ خَطْبٍ خِيفَ مِنْهُ   فَمَا ٱسْتَبَانَ لَهُ لَهَبْ
وَلَطَالَمَا طَلَعَ ٱلْأَسَى   وَعَلَى تَفِيئَتِهِ غَرَبْ
فَٱصْبِرْ إِذَا مَا نَابَ رَوْ   عٌ فَٱلزَّمَانُ أَبُو ٱلْعَجَبْ
وَتَرَجَّ مِنْ رَوْحِ ٱلْإِلٰهِ   لَطَائِفًا لَا تُحْتَسَبْ

قَالَ فَٱسْتَمْلَيْنَا أَبْيَاتَهُ ٱلْغُرَّ. وَوَالَيْنَا لِلّٰهِ تَعَالَى ٱلشُّكْرَ. وَوَدَّعْنَاهُ مَسْرُورِينَ بِبُرْئِهِ. مَغْمُورِينَ بِبِرِّهِ.

١ و: بالبيرو. ٢ د: دَنَتْ.

تَفْسِيرُ مَا تَضَمَّنَ هٰذِهِ ٱلْمَقَامَةُ مِنَ أَلْفَاظٍ لُغَوِيَّةٍ وَكُنًى طُفَيْلِيَّةٍ وَكِنَايَاتٍ صُوفِيَّةٍ

٧،١٩ قَوْلُهُ ذَاتَ ٱلْعُوَيْمِ يَعْنِي بِهِ ٱلزَّمَانَ ٱلْمُتَقَادِمَ وَمِثْلُهُ ذَاتَ ٱلزُّمَيْنِ. وَٱلسَّمْهَرِيَّةُ ٱلرِّمَاحُ وَفِي تَسْمِيَتِهَا بِذٰلِكَ قَوْلَانِ أَحَدُهَا أَنَّهَا سُمِّيَتْ بِهِ لِصَلَابَتِهَا مِنْ قَوْلِهِمُ ٱسْمَهَرَّ ٱلشَّيْءُ إِذَا ٱشْتَدَّ وَقِيلَ إِنَّهَا مَنْسُوبَةٌ إِلَى سَمْهَرٍ زَوْجِ رُدَيْنَةَ وَكَانَا جَمِيعًا يُقَوِّمَانِ ٱلرِّمَاحَ فَنُسِبَتْ إِلَيْهِمَا.[1] وَقَوْلُهُ ضَرَبَ[2] ٱللهُ عَلَى ٱلآذَانِ أَيْ أَنَامَنَا وَمِنْهُ قَوْلُهُ عَزَّ وَجَلَّ ﴿فَضَرَبْنَا عَلَى آذَانِهِمْ فِي ٱلْكَهْفِ﴾[3] أَيْ أَنَمْنَاهُمْ وَقِيلَ فِي تَفْسِيرِهِ مَنَعْنَاهُمُ ٱلسَّمْعَ. وَقَوْلُهُ تَكَرَّعْنَا لِصَلٰوةِ ٱلْعَجْمَاوَيْنِ أَيْ غَسَلْنَا أَكَارِعَنَا وَهُوَ كِنَايَةٌ عَنِ ٱلْوُضُوءِ وَٱلْعَجْمَاوَانِ صَلَاتَا ٱلظُّهْرِ وَٱلْعَصْرِ سُمِّيَتَا بِذٰلِكَ لِإِسْرَارِ ٱلْقِرَاءَةِ فِيهِمَا وَمِنْهُ ٱلْحَدِيثُ صَلٰوةُ ٱلنَّهَارِ عَجْمَاءُ. وَقَوْلُهُ هَلُمَّ أَيْ قُلْ لَهُ هَلُمَّ وَهِيَ[4] بِمَعْنَى هَاتِ وَأَقْبِلْ وَٱلْأَفْصَحُ أَنْ يُوَحَّدَ لَفْظُهَا مَعَ ٱلْمُذَكَّرِ وَٱلْمُؤَنَّثِ وَٱلِٱثْنَيْنِ وَٱلْجَمْعِ وَبِهِ نَطَقَ ٱلْقُرْآنُ فِي قَوْلِهِ تَعَالَى ﴿وَٱلْقَائِلِينَ لِإِخْوَانِهِمْ هَلُمَّ إِلَيْنَا﴾ وَمِنَ ٱلْعَرَبِ مَنْ يَقُولُ لِلْمُذَكَّرِ ٱلْوَاحِدِ هَلُمَّ وَلِلِٱثْنَيْنِ هَلُمَّا وَلِلْجَمِيعِ[5] هَلُمُّوا وَلِلْمُؤَنَّثِ ٱلْوَاحِدَةِ هَلُمِّي وَلِلِٱثْنَتَيْنِ هَلُمَّا وَلِلْجَمِيعِ[6] هَلْمُمْنَ. وَقَوْلُهُ حَيَّ هَلْ أَيْ عَجِّلْ[7] يُقَالُ حَيَّ هَلْ بِفُلَانٍ بِتَسْكِينِ ٱللَّامِ وَفَتْحِهَا وَبِتَنْوِينِهَا وَبِإِثْبَاتِ ٱلنُّونِ مَعَهَا وَمِنْهُ قَوْلُ ٱبْنِ مَسْعُودٍ رَحِمَ ٱللهُ فِي عُمَرَ[8] رَضِيَ ٱللهُ عَنْهُ إِذَا ذُكِرَ ٱلصَّالِحُونَ فَحَيَّ هَلًا بِعُمَرَ وَفِي

---

١ بعدها في د، ف: وقوله نِقْضًا على نِقْضٍ أي مهزولا على مهزول. ٢ س، د، ف: فضرب. ٣ بعدها في د: سَنينَ عَدَدًا (هكذا)، والصحيح ﴿سِنينَ عَدَدًا﴾ . ٤ س: وتُستعمل؛ ف: وهي تأتي. ٥ د، ف: للجمع. ٦ د، ف: للجمع. ٧ بعدها في س: وأَسْرِعْ إِلَيْه، وفي ف: وأسرع. ٨ بعدها في د: بن الخطاب.

حَيَّ هَلْ لُغَاتٌ أُخَرُ أَضْرَبْنَا عَنْ ذِكْرِهَا إِذْ لَيْسَ هٰذَا مَوْضِعَ اسْتِيفَاءِ شَرْحِهَا.[١] فَهٰذَا تَفْسِيرُ الْأَلْفَاظِ اللُّغَوِيَّةِ.

٨،١٩ وَأَمَّا تَفْسِيرُ الْكُنَى الطُّفَيْلِيَّةِ وَالْكِنَايَاتِ الصُّوفِيَّةِ فَأَبُو يَحْيَى كُنْيَةُ[٢] الْمَوْتِ وَأَبُو عَمْرَةَ كُنْيَةُ الْجُوعِ وَيُكْنَى أَيْضًا أَبَا مٰلِكٍ وَأَبُو جَامِعٍ الْخِوَانُ وَأَبُو نُعَيْمٍ الْخُبْزُ الْحُوَّارَى وَأَبُو حَبِيبٍ الْجَدْيُ وَأَبُو ثَقِيفٍ الْخَلُّ وَأَبُو عَوْنٍ الْمِلْحُ وَأَبُو جَمِيلٍ الْبَقْلُ وَأُمُّ الْقِرَى السِّكْبَاجُ وَأُمُّ جَابِرٍ الْهَرِيسَةُ وَأُمُّ الْفَرَجِ الْجُوذَابَةُ وَأَبُو رَزِينٍ الْخَبِيصُ وَأَبُو الْعَلَاءِ الْفَالُوذُ وَأَبُو إِيَاسٍ الْغَسُولُ وَالْمُرْجِفَانِ الطَّسْتُ وَالْإِبْرِيقُ وَأَبُو السَّرْوِ الْبَخُورُ.

١ «أُخَرُ أَضْرَبْنَا عن ذِكْرِها إذْ ليسَ هٰذا مَوْضِعَ استيفاءِ شَرْحِها»: في س: كثيرة إلا أن سيبويه لم يذكر منها إلا ثلاث لغات وهي حي هلَا وحي هلاً وحي هُلَ وزاد غيره حي هَلْ بِعُمَر وحيَّهَلَ بعمر وحيَّهَلَنْ بعمر وحَيْهَلَنْ بعمر وحيَّ هلَ إلى عمر وحيَّ هلْ على عمر. ٢ بعدها في د: مَلَك.

ٱلْمَقَامَةُ ٱلْعِشْرُونَ[١]

١٫٢٠ حَكَى ٱلْحَارِثُ بْنُ هَمَّامٍ قَالَ يَمَّمْتُ مَيَّافَارِقِينَ. مَعَ رُفْقَةٍ مُوَافِقِينَ. لَا يُمَارُونَ فِي ٱلْمُنَاجَاةِ. وَلَا يَدْرُونَ مَا طَعْمُ ٱلْمُدَاجَاةِ. فَكُنْتُ بِهِمْ كَمَنْ لَمْ يَرِمْ عَنْ وَجَارِهِ. وَلَا ظَعَنَ عَنْ أَلِيفِهِ وَجَارِهِ. فَلَمَّا أَنَخْنَا بِهَا مَطَايَا ٱلتَّسْيَارِ. وَٱنْتَقَلْنَا عَنِ ٱلْأَكْوَارِ. إِلَى ٱلْأَوْكَارِ. تَوَاصَيْنَا بِتَذْكَارِ ٱلصُّحْبَةِ. وَتَنَاهَيْنَا عَنِ ٱلتَّقَاطُعِ فِي ٱلْغُرْبَةِ. وَٱتَّخَذْنَا نَادِيًا نَعْتَمِرُهُ طَرَفَيِ ٱلنَّهَارِ. وَنَتَهَادَى فِيهِ طُرَفَ ٱلْأَخْبَارِ.

٢٫٢٠ فَبَيْنَمَا نَحْنُ بِهِ فِي بَعْضِ ٱلْأَيَّامِ. وَقَدِ ٱنْتَظَمْنَا فِي سِلْكِ ٱلِٱلْتِئَامِ. وَقَفَ عَلَيْنَا ذُو مِقْوَلٍ جَرِيٍّ. وَجَرْسٍ جَهْوَرِيٍّ. فَحَيَّا تَحِيَّةَ نَفَّاثٍ فِي ٱلْعُقَدِ. قَنَّاصٍ لِلْأُسْدِ وَٱلنَّقَدِ. ثُمَّ قَالَ

عِنْدِيَ يَا قَوْمِ حَدِيثٌ عَجِيبْ   فِيهِ ٱعْتِبَارٌ لِلَّبِيبِ ٱلْأَرِيبْ
رَأَيْتُ فِي رَيْعَانِ عُمْرِي أَخَا   بَأْسٍ لَهُ حَدُّ ٱلْحُسَامِ ٱلْقَضِيبْ
يُقْدِمُ فِي ٱلْمَعْرَكِ إِقْدَامَ مَنْ   يُوقِنُ بِٱلْفَتْكِ وَلَا يَسْتَرِيبْ
فَيَفْرُجُ ٱلضِّيقَ بِكَرَّاتِهِ   حَتَّى يُرَى مَا كَانَ ضَنْكًا رَحِيبْ
مَا بَارَزَ ٱلْأَقْرَانَ إِلَّا ٱنْثَنَى   عَنْ مَوْقِفِ ٱلطَّعْنِ بِرُمْحٍ خَضِيبْ
وَلَا سَمَا يَفْتَحُ مُسْتَصْعِبًا   مُسْتَغْلِقَ ٱلْبَابِ مَنِيعًا مَهِيبْ
إِلَّا وَنُودِي حِينَ يَسْمُو لَهُ   نَصْرٌ مِنَ ٱللهِ وَفَتْحٌ قَرِيبْ
هٰذَا وَكَمْ مِنْ لَيْلَةٍ بَاتَهَا   يَمِيسُ فِي بُرْدِ ٱلشَّبَابِ ٱلْقَشِيبْ

١ في هامش س: تُعرف بالفارقية؛ د: الفارقية؛ ف: هي الفارقية.

يَـرْتَشِـفُ الْغِـيدَ وَيَـرْشُفْنَـهُ وَهْوَ لَدَى الْكُلِّ الْمُفَدَّى الْحَبِيبْ
فَـلَمْ يَـزَلْ يَبْتَـزُّهُ دَهْـرُهُ مَا فِيهِ مِنْ بَطْشٍ وَعُودٍ صَلِيبْ
حَـتَّى أَصَـارَتْـهُ اللَّيَـالِي لَقًى يَعَـافُـهُ مَنْ كَانَ مِـنْهُ قَـرِيبْ
قَـدْ أَعْجَـزَ الرَّاقِيَ تَحْـلِيـلُ مَـا بِـهِ مِنَ الدَّاءِ وَأَعْيَـا الطَّبِـيبْ
وَصَـارَمَ الْبِـيضَ وَصَـارَمْنَـهُ مِنْ بَعْدِ مَا كَانَ الْمُجَابَ الْمُجِيبْ
وَآضَ كَالْمَنْكُوسِ فِي خَلْقِـهِ وَمَنْ يَعِشْ يَلْقَ دَوَاهِي الْمَشِيبْ
وَهَـا هُوَ الْيَوْمَ مُـسَجًّى فَـمَنْ يَـرْغَبُ فِي تَكْفِـينِ مَيْتٍ غَـرِيبْ

٣،٢٠ ثُمَّ إِنَّهُ أَعْلَنَ بِالنَّحِيبِ. وَبَكَى بُكَاءَ الْمُحِبِّ عَلَى الْحَبِيبِ. وَلَمَّا رَقَأَتْ دَمْعَتُهُ. وَٱنْفَثَأَتْ لَوْعَتُهُ. قَالَ يَا نُجْعَةَ الرُّوَّادِ. وَقُدْوَةَ الْأَجْوَادِ. وَاللهِ مَا نَطَقْتُ بِبُهْتَانٍ. وَلَا أَخْبَرْتُكُمْ إِلَّا عَنْ عِيَانٍ. وَلَوْ كَانَ فِي عَصَايَ سَيْرٌ. وَلِغَيْمِي مُطَيْرٌ. لَاسْتَأْثَرْتُ بِمَا دَعَوْتُكُمْ إِلَيْهِ. وَلَمَا وَقَفْتُ مَوْقِفَ الدَّالِّ عَلَيْهِ. وَلٰكِنْ كَيْفَ الطَّيَرَانُ بِلَا جَنَاحٍ. وَهَلْ عَلَى مَنْ لَا يَجِدُ مِنْ جُنَاحٍ.

٤،٢٠ قَالَ الرَّاوِي فَطَفِقَ الْقَوْمُ يَأْتَمِرُونَ. فِيمَا يَأْمُرُونَ. وَيَتَخَافَتُونَ. فِيمَا يَأْتُونَ. فَتَوَهَّمَ أَنَّهُمْ[١] عَلَى صَرْفِهِ بِحِرْمَانٍ. أَوْ مُطَالَبَتِهِ بِبُرْهَانٍ. فَفَرَطَ مِنْهُ أَنْ قَالَ يَا يَلَامِعَ الْقَاعِ. وَيَرَامِعَ الْبِقَاعِ. مَا هٰذَا الِٱرْتِيَاءُ. الَّذِي يَأْبَاهُ الْحَيَاءُ. حَتَّى كَأَنَّكُمْ كُلِّفْتُمْ مَشَقَّةً. لَا شُقَّةً. أَوِ ٱسْتُوهِبْتُمْ بَلْدَةً. لَا بُرْدَةً. أَوْ هُزِزْتُمْ لِكِسْوَةِ الْبَيْتِ. لَا لِتَكْفِينِ الْمَيْتِ. أُفٍّ[٢] لِمَنْ لَا تَنْدَى صَفَاتُهُ. وَلَا تَرْشَحُ حَصَاتُهُ. فَلَمَّا بَصُرَتِ الْجَمَاعَةُ بِذَلَاقَتِهِ. وَمَرَارَةِ مَذَاقَتِهِ. رَفَأَهُ كُلٌّ مِنْهُمْ بِنَيْلِهِ. وَٱحْتَمَلَ طَلَّهُ خَوْفَ سَيْلِهِ.

---

١ بعدها في ف: يتمالئون. ٢ د، ف: أُفِّ.

٥،٢٠ قَالَ ٱلْحَارِثُ بْنُ هَمَّامٍ وَكَانَ هٰذَا ٱلسَّائِلُ وَاقِفًا خَلْفِي. وَمُحْتَجِبًا بِظَهْرِي عَنْ طَرْفِي. فَلَمَّا أَرْضَاهُ ٱلْقَوْمُ بِسَيْبِهِمْ. وَحَقَّ عَلَيَّ ٱلتَّأَسِّي بِهِمْ. خَلَعْتُ خَاتَمِي مِنْ خِنْصِرِي. وَلَفَتُّ إِلَيْهِ بَصَرِي. فَإِذَا هُوَ شَيْخُنَا ٱلسَّرُوجِيُّ بِلَا فِرْيَةٍ. وَلَا مِرْيَةٍ. فَأَيْقَنْتُ أَنَّهَا أُكْذُوبَةٌ تَكَذَّبَهَا. وَأُحْبُولَةٌ نَصَبَهَا. إِلَّا أَنِّي طَوَيْتُهُ عَلَى غَرِّهِ. وَصُنْتُ شَغَاهُ عَنْ فَرِّهِ. فَخَصَصْتُهُ بِٱلْخَاتَمِ. وَقُلْتُ أَرْصِدْهُ لِنَفَقَةِ ٱلْمَأْتَمِ. فَقَالَ وَاهًا لَكَ. فَمَا أَضْرَمَ شُعْلَتَكَ. وَأَكْرَمَ فَعْلَتَكَ. ثُمَّ ٱنْطَلَقَ يَسْعَى قُدُمًا. وَيُهَرْوِلُ هَرْوَلَتَهُ قِدْمًا. فَنَزَعْتُ إِلَى عِرْفَانِ مَيِّتِهِ. وَٱمْتِحَانِ دَعْوَى حَمِيَّتِهِ. فَقَرَعْتُ ظُنْبُوبِي. وَأَلْهَبْتُ أُلْهُوبِي. حَتَّى أَدْرَكْتُهُ عَلَى غَلْوَةٍ. وَٱجْتَلَيْتُهُ فِي خَلْوَةٍ. فَأَخَذْتُ بِجُمْعِ أَرْدَانِهِ. وَعُقْتُهُ عَنْ سَنَنِ مَيْدَانِهِ. وَقُلْتُ لَهُ وَٱللهِ مَا لَكَ مِنِّي مَلْجَأٌ وَلَا مَنْجًى. أَوْ تُرِيَنِي مَيِّتَكَ ٱلْمُسَجَّى. فَكَشَفَ عَنْ سَرَاوِيلِهِ. وَأَشَارَ إِلَى غُرْمُولِهِ. فَقُلْتُ لَهُ قَاتَلَكَ ٱللهُ فَمَا أَلْعَبَكَ بِٱلنُّهَى. وَأَحْيَلَكَ عَلَى ٱللُّهَى. ثُمَّ عُدْتُ إِلَى أَصْحَابِي عَوْدَ ٱلرَّائِدِ ٱلَّذِي لَا يَكْذِبُ أَهْلَهُ. وَلَا يُبَرْقِشُ قَوْلَهُ. فَأَخْبَرْتُهُمْ بِٱلَّذِي رَأَيْتُ. وَمَا وَرَّيْتُ وَلَا رَاءَيْتُ. فَقَهْقَهُوا مِنْ كَيْتَ وَكَيْتَ. وَلَعَنُوا ذٰلِكَ ٱلْمَيْتَ.

الْمَقَامَةُ الْحَادِيَةُ وَالْعِشْرُونَ[1]

١،٢١ حَدَّثَ[2] الْحَارِثُ بْنُ هَمَّامٍ قَالَ عُنِيتُ مُذْ أَحْكَمْتُ تَدْبِيرِي. وَعَرَفْتُ قَبِيلِي مِنْ دَبِيرِي. بِأَنْ أُصْغِيَ إِلَى الْعِظَاتِ. وَأُلْغِيَ الْكَلِمَ الْمُحْفِظَاتِ. لِأَتَحَلَّى بِمَحَاسِنِ الْأَخْلَاقِ. وَأَتَخَلَّى مِمَّا يَسِمُ بِالْإِخْلَاقِ. وَمَا زِلْتُ آخُذُ نَفْسِي بِهٰذَا الْأَدَبِ. وَأُخْمِدُ بِهِ جَمْرَةَ الْغَضَبِ. حَتَّى صَارَ التَّطَبُّعُ فِيهِ طِبَاعًا. وَالتَّكَلُّفُ لَهُ هَوًى مُطَاعًا.

٢،٢١ فَلَمَّا حَلَلْتُ بِالرَّيِّ. وَقَدْ حَلَلْتُ حِبَى الْغَيِّ. وَعَرَفْتُ الْحَيَّ مِنَ اللَّيِّ. رَأَيْتُ بِهَا ذَاتَ بُكْرَةٍ. زُمْرَةً إِثْرَ[3] زُمْرَةٍ. وَهُمْ مُنْتَشِرُونَ انْتِشَارَ الْجَرَادِ. وَمُسْتَنُّونَ اسْتِنَانَ الْجِيَادِ. وَمُتَوَاصِفُونَ وَاعِظًا يَقْصِدُونَهُ. وَيُحِلُّونَ ابْنَ سَمْعُونَ دُونَهُ. فَلَمْ يَتَكَاءَدْنِي لِاسْتِمَاعِ الْمَوَاعِظِ. وَاخْتِبَارِ الْوَاعِظِ. أَنْ أُقَاسِيَ اللَّاغِطَ. وَأَحْتَمِلَ الضَّاغِطَ. فَأَصْحَبْتُ إِصْحَابَ الْمِطْوَاعَةِ. وَانْخَرَطْتُ فِي سِلْكِ الْجَمَاعَةِ. حَتَّى أَفْضَيْنَا إِلَى نَادٍ جَمَعَ الْأَمِيرَ وَالْمَأْمُورَ وَحَشَدَ النَّبِيهَ وَالْمَغْمُورَ. وَفِي وَسَطِ هَالَتِهِ. وَوَسْطِ أَهِلَّتِهِ. شَيْخٌ قَدْ تَقَوَّسَ وَاقْعَنْسَسَ. وَتَقَلْنَسَ وَتَطَلَّسَ. وَهُوَ يَصْدَعُ بِوَعْظٍ يَشْفِي الصُّدُورَ. وَيُلَيِّنُ الصُّخُورَ. فَسَمِعْتُهُ يَقُولُ. وَقَدِ افْتَتَنَتْ بِهِ الْعُقُولُ.

٣،٢١ ابْنَ آدَمَ مَا أَغْرَاكَ بِمَا يَغُرُّكَ. وَأَضْرَاكَ بِمَا يَضُرُّكَ. وَأَلْهَجَكَ بِمَا يُطْغِيكَ. وَأَبْهَجَكَ بِمَنْ يُطْرِيكَ. تُعْنَى بِمَا يُعَنِّيكَ. وَتُهْمِلُ مَا يَعْنِيكَ. وَتَنْزِعُ فِي قَوْسِ تَعَدِّيكَ. وَتَرْتَدِي الْحِرْصَ الَّذِي يُرْدِيكَ. لَا بِالْكَفَافِ تَقْتَنِعُ. وَلَا مِنَ الْحَرَامِ تَمْتَنِعُ. وَلَا لِلْعِظَاتِ تَسْتَمِعُ. وَلَا بِالْوَعِيدِ تَرْتَدِعُ. دَأْبُكَ أَنْ تَتَقَلَّبَ مَعَ الْأَهْوَاءِ. وَتَخْبِطَ خَبْطَ الْعَشْوَاءِ. وَهَمُّكَ أَنْ تَدْأَبَ فِي الِاحْتِرَاثِ. وَتَجْمَعَ

١ في هامش س: تعرف بالرَّازِيَّة؛ وفي و: وهي الرازية؛ وفي د: الرازية. ٢ د: حكى. ٣ و: في إثر.

التُّرَاثَ لِلْوُرَّاثِ. يُعْجِبُكَ التَّكَاثُرُ بِمَا لَدَيْكَ. وَلَا تَذْكُرُ مَا بَيْنَ يَدَيْكَ. وَتَسْعَى أَبَدًا لِغَارِيْكَ. وَلَا تُبَالِي أَلَكَ أَمْ عَلَيْكَ. أَتَظُنُّ أَنْ سَتُتْرَكُ سُدًى. وَأَلَّا[1] تُحَاسَبَ غَدًا. أَمْ تَحْسَبُ أَنَّ الْمَوْتَ يَقْبَلُ الرُّشَى. أَوْ يُمَيِّزُ بَيْنَ الْأَسَدِ وَالرَّشَا. كَلَّا وَاللهِ لَنْ يَدْفَعَ الْمَنُونَ. مَالٌ وَلَا بَنُونَ. وَلَا يَنْفَعُ أَهْلَ الْقُبُورِ. سِوَى الْعَمَلِ الْمَبْرُورِ. فَطُوبَى لِمَنْ سَمِعَ وَوَعَى. وَحَقَّقَ مَا ٱدَّعَى. وَنَهَى النَّفْسَ عَنِ الْهَوَى. وَعَلِمَ أَنَّ الْفَائِزَ مَنِ ٱرْعَوَى. ﴿وَأَنَّ لَيْسَ لِلْإِنْسَانِ إِلَّا مَا سَعَى. وَأَنَّ سَعْيَهُ سَوْفَ يُرَى.﴾

ثُمَّ أَنْشَدَ إِنْشَادَ وَجِلٍ. بِصَوْتٍ زَجِلٍ. ٤،٢١

لَعَمْرُكَ مَا تُغْنِي الْمَغَانِي وَلَا الْغِنَى إِذَا سَكَنَ الْمُثْرِي الثَّرَى وَثَوَى بِهِ
فَجُدْ فِي مَرَاضِي اللهِ بِالْمَالِ رَاضِيًا بِمَا تَقْتَنِي مِنْ أَجْرِهِ وَثَوَابِهِ
وَبَادِرْ بِهِ صَرْفَ الزَّمَانِ فَإِنَّهُ بِمِخْلَبِهِ الْأَشْغَى يَغُولُ وَنَابِهِ
وَلَا تَأْمَنِ الدَّهْرَ الْخَؤُونَ وَمَكْرَهُ فَكَمْ خَامِلٍ أَخْنَى عَلَيْهِ وَنَابِهِ
وَعَاصِ هَوَى النَّفْسِ الَّذِي مَا أَطَاعَهُ أَخُو ضَلَّةٍ إِلَّا هَوَى مِنْ عِقَابِهِ[2]
وَحَافِظْ عَلَى تَقْوَى الْإِلٰهِ وَخَوْفِهِ لِتَنْجُوَ مِمَّا يُتَّقَى مِنْ عِقَابِهِ
وَلَا تَلْهَ[3] عَنْ تَذْكَارِ ذَنْبِكَ وَٱبْكِهِ بِدَمْعٍ يُضَاهِي الْوَبْلَ[4] حَالَ مَصَابِهِ
وَمَثِّلْ لِعَيْنَيْكَ الْحِمَامَ وَوَقْعَهُ وَرَوْعَةَ مَلْقَاهُ وَمَطْعَمَ صَابِهِ
وَإِنَّ قُصَارَى مَسْكَنِ[5] الْحَيِّ حُفْرَةٌ سَيَنْزِلُهَا مُسْتَنْزَلًا عَنْ قِبَابِهِ
فَوَاهًا لِعَبْدٍ سَاءَهُ سُوءُ فِعْلِهِ وَأَبْدَى التَّلَافِي قَبْلَ إِغْلَاقِ بَابِهِ

١ س،د،ف: أن لا. ٢ و،د: عُقابه. ٣ و،د: تَلْهُ. ٤ و،ف: الْمُزْنَ. ٥ ف: منزلِ.

٥،٢١ قَالَ فَظَلَّ الْقَوْمُ بَيْنَ عَبْرَةٍ يُذْرُونَهَا. وَتَوْبَةٍ يُظْهِرُونَهَا. حَتَّى كَادَتِ الشَّمْسُ تَزُولُ. وَالْفَرِيضَةُ تَعُولُ. فَلَمَّا خَشَعَتِ الْأَصْوَاتُ. وَٱلْتَأَمَ الْإِنْصَاتُ. وَٱسْتَكَنَّتِ الْعَبَرَاتُ. وَالْعِبَارَاتُ. اِسْتَصْرَخَ مُسْتَصْرِخٌ بِالْأَمِيرِ الْحَاضِرِ. وَجَعَلَ يَجْأَرُ إِلَيْهِ مِنْ عَامِلِهِ الْجَائِرِ. وَالْأَمِيرُ صَاغٍ إِلَى خَصْمِهِ. لَاهٍ عَنْ كَشْفِ ظُلْمِهِ. فَلَمَّا أَيِسَ[1] مِنْ رَوْحِهِ. اِسْتَنْهَضَ الْوَاعِظَ لِنُصْحِهِ. فَنَهَضَ نَهْضَةَ الشِّمِّيرِ. وَأَنْشَدَ مُعَرِّضًا بِالْأَمِيرِ.

عَجَبًا لِرَاجٍ أَنْ يَنَالَ وِلَايَةً   حَتَّى إِذَا مَا نَالَ بُغْيَتَهُ بَغَى
يُسْدِي وَيُلْحِمُ فِي الْمَظَالِمِ وَالْغًا   فِي وِرْدِهَا طَوْرًا وَطَوْرًا مُولِغَا
مَا إِنْ يُبَالِي حِينَ يَتَّبِعُ الْهَوَى   فِيهَا أَأَصْلَحَ دِينَهُ أَمْ أَوْتَغَا
يَا وَيْحَهُ لَوْ كَانَ يُوقِنُ أَنَّهُ   مَا حَالَةٌ إِلَّا تَحُولُ لَمَا طَغَا
أَوْ لَوْ تَبَيَّنَ مَا نَدَامَةُ مَنْ صَغَا   سَمْعًا إِلَى إِفْكِ الْوُشَاةِ لَمَا صَغَا
فَٱنْقَدْ لِمَنْ أَضْحَى الزِّمَامُ بِكَفِّهِ   وَتَغَاضَ إِنْ أَلْغَى الرِّعَايَةَ أَوْ لَغَا
وَٱرْعَ الْمُرَارَ إِذَا دَعَاكَ لِرَعْيِهِ   وَرِدِ الْأُجَاجَ إِذَا حَمَاكَ السَّيِّغَا
وَٱحْمِلْ أَذَاهُ وَلَوْ أَمَضَّكَ مَسُّهُ   وَأَسَالَ غَرْبَ الدَّمْعِ مِنْكَ وَأَفْرَغَا
فَلَيُضْحِكَنْكَ الدَّهْرُ مِنْهُ إِذَا نَبَا   عَنْهُ وَشَبَّ لِكَيْدِهِ نَارَ الْوَغَى
وَلَيُنْزِلَنَّ بِهِ الشَّمَاتَ إِذَا بَدَا   مُتَخَلِّيًا مِنْ شُغْلِهِ مُتَفَرِّغَا
وَلَتَأْوِيَنَّ لَهُ إِذَا مَا خَدُّهُ   أَضْحَى عَلَى تُرْبِ الْهَوَانِ مُمَرَّغَا[2]
هٰذَا لَهُ وَلَسَوْفَ يُوقَفُ مَوْقِفًا   فِيهِ يُرَى رَبُّ الْفَصَاحَةِ أَلْثَغَا
وَلَيُحْشَرَنَّ أَذَلَّ مِنْ فَقْعِ الْفَلَا   وَيُحَاسَبَنَّ عَلَى النَّقِيصَةِ وَالشَّغَا

١ س: يَئِسَ، و: تبيَّن. ٢ د، ف، و: ممرِّغًا.

وَيُؤَاخَذَنَّ مَا ٱجْتَنَى وَمَنِ اجْتَنَى   وَيُطَـالَبَنَّ بِمَا ٱحْتَسَى وَبِمَا ٱرْتَغَـا
وَيُنَـاقَشَنَّ عَلَى الدَّقَـائِقِ مِثْلِ مَا   قَدْ كَانَ يَفْعَلُ[1] بِالْوَرَى بَلْ أَبْلَغَـا
حَـتَّى يَعَـضَّ عَلَى الْوِلَايَـةِ كَفَّـهُ   وَيَوَدُّ لَوْ لَمْ يَبْـغِ مِنْـهَا مَـا بَغَـا

٦،٢١ ثُمَّ قَالَ أَيُّهَا الْمُتَوَشِّحُ بِالْوِلَايَةِ. الْمُتَرَشِّحُ لِلرِّعَايَةِ. دَعِ الْإِدْلَالَ بِدَوْلَتِكَ. وَالِاغْتِرَارَ بِصَوْلَتِكَ. فَإِنَّ الدَّوْلَةَ رِيحٌ قُلَّبٌ. وَالْقُدْرَةَ[2] بَرْقٌ خُلَّبٌ. وَإِنَّ أَسْعَدَ الرُّعَاةِ مَنْ سَعِدَتْ بِهِ رَعِيَّتُهُ. وَأَشْقَاهُمْ فِي الدَّارَيْنِ مَنْ سَاءَتْ رِعَايَتُهُ. فَلَا تَكُ مِمَّنْ يَذَرُ الْآخِرَةَ وَيُلْغِيهَا. وَيُحِبُّ الْعَاجِلَةَ وَيَبْتَغِيهَا. وَيَظْلِمُ الرَّعِيَّةَ وَيُؤْذِيهَا. ﴿وَإِذَا تَوَلَّىٰ سَعَىٰ فِي ٱلْأَرْضِ لِيُفْسِدَ فِيهَا﴾. فَوَاللهِ مَا يَغْفُلُ الدَّيَّانُ. وَلَا تُهْمَلُ يَا إِنْسَانُ. بَلْ سَيُوضَعُ لَكَ الْمِيزَانُ.[3] وَكَمَا تَدِينُ[4] تُدَانُ.

٧،٢١ قَالَ فَوَجَمَ الْوَالِي لِمَا سَمِعَ. وَٱمْتُقِعَ لَوْنُهُ وَٱنْتُقِعَ. وَجَعَلَ يَتَأَفَّفُ مِنَ الْإِمْرَةِ. وَيُرْدِفُ الزَّفْرَةَ بِالزَّفْرَةِ. ثُمَّ عَمَدَ إِلَى الشَّاكِي فَأَشْكَاهُ. وَإِلَى الْمَشْكُوِّ فَأَشْجَاهُ. وَأَلْطَفَ الْوَاعِظَ وَحَبَاهُ. وَعَزَمَ عَلَيْهِ[5] أَنْ يَغْشَاهُ. فَٱنْقَلَبَ عَنْهُ الْمَظْلُومُ مَنْصُورًا. وَالظَّالِمُ مَحْصُورًا. وَبَرَزَ الْوَاعِظُ يَتَهَادَى بَيْنَ رُفْقَتِهِ. وَيَتَبَاهَى بِفَوْزِ صَفْقَتِهِ. وَٱعْتَقَبْتُهُ أَخْطُو مُتَقَاصِرًا. وَأُرِيهِ لَمْحًا بَاصِرًا. فَلَمَّا ٱسْتَشَفَّ مَا أُخْفِيهِ. وَفَطِنَ لِتَقَلُّبِ وَجْهِي[6] فِيهِ. قَالَ خَيْرُ دَلِيلَيْكَ مَنْ أَرْشَدَ. ثُمَّ ٱقْتَرَبَ مِنِّي وَأَنْشَدَ.

٨،٢١ أَنَـا الَّذِي تَعْـرِفُـهُ يَـا حَـارِثُ   حِـدْثُ مُلُوكٍ فَكِهٌ مُنَـافِثُ
أُطْـرِبُ مَا لَا تُطْـرِبُ الْمَثَـالِثُ   طَوْرًا أَخُو جِـدٍّ وَطَوْرًا عَـابِثُ
مَـا غَــيَّرَتْنِي بَعْــدَكَ الْحَوَادِثُ   وَلَا ٱلْتَحَى عُودِي خَطْبٌ كَارِثُ

١ ف: يصنع. ٢ ف: الإمرة. ٣ بعدها في ف: ولا تُلغَى الإساءةُ ولا الإحسان. ٤ د: تُدين. ٥ ف: واستدعى منه. ٦ ف: طرفي.

وَلَا فَــرَى نَــابِي حَــدُّ[1] فَــارِثُ   بَلْ مِخْلَبِي بِكُلِّ صَيْدٍ ضَــابِثُ
وَكُلُّ سَــرْحٍ فِيهِ ذِئْبِي عَــائِثُ   حَتَّى كَأَنِّي لِلْأَنَــامِ وَارِثُ
سَــامُهُمُ وَحَــامُهُمُ وَيَــافِثُ

٩،٢١ قَالَ الْحَارِثُ بْنُ هَمَّامٍ فَقُلْتُ لَهُ تَاللهِ إِنَّكَ لَأَبُو زَيْدٍ. وَلَقَدْ قُمْتَ لِلهِ وَلَا عَمْرُو بْنَ عُبَيْدٍ. فَهَشَّ هَشَاشَةَ الْكَرِيمِ إِذَا أُمَّ. وَقَالَ اِسْمَعْ يَا ابْنَ أُمَّ.[2]

عَــلَيْكَ بِــالصِّــدْقِ وَلَوْ أَنَّــهُ   أَحْــرَقَكَ الصِّــدْقُ بِنَــارِ الْوَعِــيدْ
وَٱبْــغِ رِضَى اللهِ فَأَغْــبَى الْوَرَى   مَنْ أَسْخَطَ الْمَوْلَى وَأَرْضَى الْعَبِيدْ

ثُمَّ إِنَّهُ وَدَّعَ أَخْدَانَهُ. وَٱنْطَلَقَ يَسْحَبُ أَرْدَانَهُ. فَطَلَبْنَاهُ مِنْ بَعْدُ بِالرَّيِّ. وَٱسْتَنْشَرْنَا خَبَرَهُ مِنْ مَدَارِجِ الطَّيِّ. فَمَا فِينَا مَنْ عَرَفَ قَرَارَهُ. وَلَا دَرَى أَيُّ الْجَرَادِ عَارَهُ.

١ . ف: فرى حدّي نابُ. ٢ . بعدها في ف: ثمّ أنشأ يقول.

الْمَقَامَةُ الثَّانِيَةُ وَالْعِشْرُونَ[1]

١،٢٢ حَكَى الْحَارِثُ بْنُ هَمَّامٍ قَالَ أَوَيْتُ فِي بَعْضِ الْفَتَرَاتِ. إِلَى سِقْيِ الْفُرَاتِ. فَلَقِيتُ بِهَا كُتَّابًا أَبْرَعَ مِنْ بَنِي الْفُرَاتِ. وَأَعْذَبَ أَخْلَاقًا مِنَ الْمَاءِ الْفُرَاتِ. فَأَطَفْتُ بِهِمْ لِتَهَذُّبِهِمْ وَلَا لِذَهَبِهِمْ. وَكَاثَرْتُهُمْ لِأَدَبِهِمْ لَا لِمَآدِبِهِمْ. فَجَالَسْتُ مِنْهُمْ أَضْرَابَ الْقَعْقَاعِ[2] بْنِ شَوْرٍ. وَوَصَلْتُ بِهِمْ إِلَى الْكَوْرِ بَعْدَ الْحَوْرِ. حَتَّى إِنَّهُمْ أَشْرَكُونِي فِي الْمَرْتَعِ وَالْمَرْبَعِ. وَأَحَلُّونِي مَحَلَّ الْأُنْمُلَةِ مِنَ الْإِصْبَعِ. وَٱتَّخَذُونِي ٱبْنَ أُنْسِهِمْ عَهْدَ[3] الْوِلَايَةِ وَالْعَزْلِ. وَخَازِنَ سِرِّهِمْ فِي الْجِدِّ وَالْهَزْلِ.

٢،٢٢ فَٱتَّفَقَ أَنْ نُدِبُوا فِي بَعْضِ الْأَوْقَاتِ. لِاسْتِقْرَاءِ مَزَارِعِ الرُّزْدَاقَاتِ. فَٱخْتَارُوا مِنَ الْجَوَارِي الْمُنْشَآتِ. جَارِيَةً حَالِكَةَ الشِّيَاتِ. تَحْسَبُهَا جَامِدَةً وَهِيَ تَمُرُّ مَرَّ السَّحَابِ. وَتَنْسَابُ فِي الْحَبَابِ كَالْحُبَابِ. ثُمَّ دَعَوْنِي إِلَى الْمُوَافَقَةِ. وَٱسْتَدْعَوْنِي لِلْمُرَافَقَةِ.[4] فَلَمَّا تَوَرَّكْنَا عَلَى الْمَطِيَّةِ الدَّهْمَاءِ. وَتَبَطَّنَّا الْوَلِيَّةَ الْمَاشِيَةَ عَلَى الْمَاءِ. أَلْفَيْنَا بِهَا شَيْخًا عَلَيْهِ سَحْقُ سِرْبَالٍ. وَسِبُّ بَالٍ. فَعَافَتِ الْجَمَاعَةُ مَحْضَرَهُ. وَعَنَّفَتْ مَنْ أَحْضَرَهُ. وَهَمَّتْ بِإِبْرَازِهِ مِنَ السَّفِينَةِ. لَوْلَا مَا ثَابَ إِلَيْهَا مِنَ السَّكِينَةِ. فَلَمَّا لَمَحَ مِنَّا ٱسْتِثْقَالَ ظِلِّهِ. وَٱسْتِبْرَادَ طَلِّهِ. تَعَرَّضَ لِلْمُنَافَثَةِ فَصُمِّتَ. وَحَمْدَلَ بَعْدَ أَنْ عَطَسَ فَمَا شُمِّتَ. فَأَخْرَدَ يَنْظُرُ فِيمَا آلَتْ حَالُهُ إِلَيْهِ. وَيَنْتَظِرُ نُصْرَةَ الْمَبْغِيِّ عَلَيْهِ.

---

١ بعدها في س: تُعْرَف بالفُراتية؛ وفي د، ف: الفراتية. ٢ ف: قعقاع. ٣ ف، و: عند. ٤ «ثم دعوني إلى الموافقة واستدعوني للمرافقة»: في ف: ثم دعوني إلى المرافقة فلبيت بلسان الموافقة.

٣،٢٢ وَجُلْنَا نَحْنُ فِي شُجُونٍ. مِنْ جِدٍّ وَمُجُونٍ. إِلَى أَنِ ٱعْتَرَضَ ذِكْرُ ٱلْكِتَابَتَيْنِ وَفَضْلِهِمَا. وَتِبْيَانِ أَفْضَلِهِمَا. فَقَالَ قَائِلٌ إِنَّ كَتَبَةَ ٱلْإِنْشَاءِ أَنْبَلُ ٱلْكُتَّابِ. وَمَالَ مَائِلٌ إِلَى تَفْضِيلِ ٱلْحُسَّابِ. وَٱحْتَدَّ ٱلْحِجَاجُ. وَٱمْتَدَّ ٱللَّجَاجُ. حَتَّى إِذَا لَمْ يَبْقَ لِلْجِدَالِ مَطْرَحٌ. وَلَا لِلْمِرَاءِ مَسْرَحٌ. قَالَ ٱلشَّيْخُ لَقَدْ أَكْثَرْتُمْ يَا قَوْمُ ٱللَّغَطَ. وَأَثَرْتُمُ ٱلصَّوَابَ وَٱلْغَلَطَ. وَإِنَّ جَلِيَّةَ ٱلْحُكْمِ عِنْدِي. فَٱرْتَضُوا بِنَقْدِي. وَلَا تَسْتَفْتُوا أَحَدًا بَعْدِي.

٤،٢٢ اِعْلَمُوا أَنَّ صِنَاعَةَ ٱلْإِنْشَاءِ أَرْفَعُ. وَصِنَاعَةَ ٱلْحِسَابِ أَنْفَعُ. وَقَلَمَ ٱلْمُكَاتَبَةِ خَاطِبٌ. وَقَلَمَ ٱلْمُحَاسَبَةِ حَاطِبٌ. وَأَسَاطِيرُ[1] ٱلْبَلَاغَةِ تُنْسَخُ لِتُدْرَسَ. وَدَسَاتِيرُ[2] ٱلْحُسْبَانَاتِ تُنْسَخُ وَتُدْرَسُ. وَٱلْمُنْشِئُ جُهَيْنَةُ ٱلْأَخْبَارِ. وَحَقِيبَةُ ٱلْأَسْرَارِ. وَنَجِيُّ ٱلْعُظَمَاءِ. وَكَبِيرُ ٱلنُّدَمَاءِ. وَقَلَمُهُ لِسَانُ ٱلدَّوْلَةِ. وَفَارِسُ ٱلْجَوْلَةِ. وَلُقْمَانُ ٱلْحِكْمَةِ. وَتَرْجُمَانُ ٱلْهِمَّةِ. وَهُوَ ٱلْبَشِيرُ وَٱلنَّذِيرُ. وَٱلشَّفِيعُ وَٱلسَّفِيرُ. بِهِ تُسْتَخْلَصُ ٱلصَّيَاصِي. وَتُمْلَكُ ٱلنَّوَاصِي. وَيُقْتَادُ ٱلْعَاصِي. وَيُسْتَدْنَى ٱلْقَاصِي. وَصَاحِبُهُ بَرِيءٌ مِنَ ٱلتَّبِعَاتِ. آمِنٌ كَيْدَ ٱلسُّعَاةِ. مُقَرَّظٌ بَيْنَ ٱلْجَمَاعَاتِ. غَيْرُ مُعَرَّضٍ لِنَظْمِ ٱلْجَمَاعَاتِ.

٥،٢٢ فَلَمَّا ٱنْتَهَى فِي ٱلْفَصْلِ. إِلَى هٰذَا ٱلْفَصْلِ. لَحَظَ مِنْ لَمَحَاتِ ٱلْقَوْمِ أَنَّهُ ٱزْدَرَعَ حُبًّا وَبُغْضًا. وَأَرْضَى بَعْضًا وَأَحْفَظَ بَعْضًا. فَعَقَّبَ كَلَامَهُ بِأَنْ قَالَ إِلَّا أَنَّ صِنَاعَةَ ٱلْحِسَابِ مَوْضُوعَةٌ عَلَى ٱلتَّحْقِيقِ. وَصِنَاعَةَ ٱلْإِنْشَاءِ مَبْنِيَّةٌ عَلَى ٱلتَّلْفِيقِ. وَقَلَمَ ٱلْحَاسِبِ ضَابِطٌ. وَقَلَمَ ٱلْمُنْشِئِ خَابِطٌ. وَبَيْنَ إِتَاوَةِ تَوْظِيفِ ٱلْمُعَامَلَاتِ. وَتِلَاوَةِ طَوَامِيرِ ٱلسِّجِلَّاتِ. بَوْنٌ لَا يُدْرِكُهُ قِيَاسٌ. وَلَا يَعْتَوِرُهُ ٱلْتِبَاسٌ. إِذِ ٱلْإِتَاوَةُ تَمْلَأُ ٱلْأَكْيَاسَ. وَٱلتِّلَاوَةُ تُفَرِّغُ ٱلرَّاسَ. وَخَرَاجُ ٱلْأَوَارِجِ يُغْنِي ٱلنَّاظِرَ. وَٱسْتِخْرَاجُ

---

١ س، د، ف: وأساطيرَ. ٢ س، د، ف: ودساتيرَ.

الْمَدَارِجِ يُعَنِّي النَّاظِرَ. ثُمَّ إِنَّ الْحَسَبَةَ حَفَظَةُ الْأَمْوَالِ. وَحَمَلَةُ الْأَثْقَالِ. وَالنَّقَلَةُ الْأَثْبَاتُ. وَالسَّفَرَةُ الثِّقَاتُ. وَأَعْلَامُ الْإِنْصَافِ. وَالِانْتِصَافِ. وَالشُّهُودُ الْمَقَانِعُ فِي الْأَخْلَافِ.[1] وَمِنْهُمُ الْمُسْتَوْفِي الَّذِي هُوَ يَدُ السُّلْطَانِ. وَقُطْبُ الدِّيوَانِ. وَقِسْطَاسُ الْأَعْمَالِ. وَالْمُهَيْمِنُ عَلَى الْعُمَّالِ. وَإِلَيْهِ الْمَآبُ فِي السِّلْمِ وَالْهَرْجِ. وَعَلَيْهِ الْمَدَارُ فِي الدَّخْلِ وَالْخَرْجِ. وَبِهِ مَنَاطُ الضَّرِّ وَالنَّفْعِ. وَفِي يَدِهِ رِبَاطُ الْإِعْطَاءِ وَالْمَنْعِ. وَلَوْلَا قَلَمُ الْحُسَّابِ. لَأَوْدَتْ ثَمَرَةُ الِاكْتِسَابِ. وَلَاتَّصَلَ التَّغَابُنُ إِلَى يَوْمِ الْحِسَابِ. وَلَكَانَ نِظَامُ الْمُعَامَلَاتِ مَحْلُولًا. وَجُرْحُ الظُّلَامَاتِ مَطْلُولًا. وَجِيدُ التَّنَاصُفِ مَغْلُولًا. وَسَيْفُ التَّظَالُمِ مَسْلُولًا. عَلَى أَنَّ يَرَاعَ الْإِنْشَاءِ مُتَقَوِّلٌ. وَيَرَاعَ الْحِسَابِ مُتَأَوِّلٌ. وَالْمُحَاسِبُ مُنَاقِشٌ. وَالْمُنْشِئُ أَبُو بَرَاقِشَ. وَلِكِلَيْهِمَا حُمَةٌ حِينَ يَرْقَى. إِلَى أَنْ يُلْقَى وَيُرْقَى. وَإِعْنَاتٌ فِيمَا يُنْشَا. حَتَّى يُغْشَى وَيُرْشَى. ﴿إِلَّا ٱلَّذِينَ آمَنُوا وَعَمِلُوا ٱلصَّالِحَاتِ وَقَلِيلٌ مَا هُمْ﴾.

٦٫٢٢ قَالَ الْحَارِثُ بْنُ هَمَّامٍ فَلَمَّا أَمْتَعَ الْأَسْمَاعَ. بِمَا رَاقَ وَرَاعَ. ٱسْتَنْسَبْنَاهُ فَٱسْتَرَابَ. وَأَبَى الِانْتِسَابَ. وَلَوْ وَجَدَ مُنْسَابًا لَانْسَابَ. فَحَصَلْتُ مِنْ لَبْسِهِ عَلَى غُمَّةٍ. حَتَّى ٱدَّكَرْتُ بَعْدَ أُمَّةٍ. فَقُلْتُ وَالَّذِي سَخَّرَ الْفَلَكَ الدَّوَّارَ. وَالْفُلْكَ السَّيَّارَ. إِنِّي لَأَجِدُ رِيحَ أَبِي زَيْدٍ. وَإِنْ كُنْتُ أَعْهَدُهُ ذَا رُوَاءٍ وَأَيْدٍ. فَتَبَسَّمَ ضَاحِكًا مِنْ قَوْلِي. وَقَالَ أَنَا هُوَ عَلَى ٱسْتِحَالَةِ حَالِي وَحَوْلِي. فَقُلْتُ لِأَصْحَابِي هٰذَا الَّذِي لَا يُفْرَى فَرِيُّهُ. وَلَا يُبَارَى عَبْقَرِيُّهُ.

٧٫٢٢ فَخَطَبُوا مِنْهُ الْوُدَّ. وَبَذَلُوا لَهُ الْوُجْدَ. فَرَغِبَ عَنِ الْأُلْفَةِ. وَلَمْ يَرْغَبْ فِي التُّحْفَةِ. وَقَالَ أَمَّا بَعْدَ أَنْ سَحَقْتُمْ حَقِّي. لِأَجْلِ سَحْقِي. وَكَسَفْتُمْ بَالِي. لِإِخْلَاقِ سِرْبَالِي. فَمَا أَرَاكُمْ إِلَّا بِالْعَيْنِ السَّخِينَةِ. وَلَا لَكُمْ مِنِّي إِلَّا صُحْبَةُ السَّفِينَةِ. ثُمَّ أَنْشَدَ

---

١ و، ف: الإخلاف.

اِسْمَعْ أُخَيَّ وَصِيَّةً مِنْ نَاصِحٍ   مَا شَابَ مَحْضَ النُّصْحِ مِنْهُ بِغِشِّهِ
لَا تَعْجَلَنْ بِقَضِيَّةٍ مَبْتُوتَةٍ   فِي مَدْحِ مَنْ لَمْ تَبْلُهُ أَوْ خَدْشِهِ
وَقِفِ الْقَضِيَّةَ فِيهِ حَتَّى تَجْتَلِي   وَصْفَيْهِ فِي حَالَيْ رِضَاهُ وَبَطْشِهِ
وَيَبِينَ خُلَّبُ بَرْقِهِ مِنْ صِدْقِهِ   لِلشَّائِمِينَ وَوَبْلُهُ مِنْ طَشِّهِ
فَهُنَاكَ إِنْ تَرَ مَا يَشِينُ فَوَارِهِ   كَرَمًا وَإِنْ تَرَ مَا يَزِينُ فَأَفْشِهِ
وَمَنِ ٱسْتَحَقَّ الِارْتِقَاءَ فَرَقِّهِ   وَمَنِ ٱسْتَحَطَّ فَحُطَّهُ فِي حَشِّهِ
وَٱعْلَمْ بِأَنَّ التِّبْرَ فِي عِرْقِ الثَّرَى   خَافٍ إِلَى أَنْ يُسْتَثَارَ بِنَبْشِهِ
وَفَضِيلَةُ الدِّينَارِ يَظْهَرُ سِرُّهَا   مِنْ حَكِّهِ لَا مِنْ مَلَاحَةِ نَقْشِهِ
وَمِنَ الْغَبَاوَةِ أَنْ تُعَظِّمَ جَاهِلًا   لِصِقَالِ مَلْبَسِهِ وَرَوْنَقِ رَقْشِهِ
أَوْ أَنْ تُهِينَ مُهَذَّبًا فِي نَفْسِهِ   لِدُرُوسِ بِزَّتِهِ وَرَثَّةِ فُرْشِهِ[1]
وَلَكَمْ أَخِي طِمْرَيْنِ هِيبَ لِفَضْلِهِ   وَمُفَوَّفِ الْبُرْدَيْنِ عِيبَ لِفُحْشِهِ
وَإِذَا الْفَتَى لَمْ يَغْشَ عَارًا لَمْ تَكُنْ   أَسْمَالُهُ إِلَّا مَرَاقِيَ عَرْشِهِ
مَا إِنْ يَضُرُّ الْعَضْبَ كَوْنُ قِرَابِهِ   خَلَقًا وَلَا الْبَازِي حَقَارَةُ عُشِّهِ

ثُمَّ مَا عَتَّمَ أَنِ ٱسْتَوْقَفَ الْمَلَّاحَ. وَصَعِدَ مِنَ السَّفِينَةِ وَسَاحَ. فَنَدِمَ كُلٌّ مِنَّا عَلَى مَا فَرَّطَ فِي ذَاتِهِ. وَأَغْضَى جَفْنَهُ عَلَى قَذَاتِهِ. وَتَعَاهَدْنَا عَلَى أَلَّا نَحْتَقِرَ شَخْصًا لِرَثَاثَةِ بُرْدِهِ. وَأَلَّا نَزْدَرِيَ سَيْفًا مَخْبُوءًا فِي غِمْدِهِ.

١ س، د: فَرْشِهِ.

الْمَقَامَةُ الثَّالِثَةُ وَالْعِشْرُونَ[1]

١،٢٣ حَكَى الْحَارِثُ بْنُ هَمَّامٍ قَالَ نَبَا بِي مَأْلَفُ الْوَطَنِ. فِي شَرْخِ الزَّمَنِ. لِخَطْبٍ خُشِيَ. وَخَوْفٍ غَشِيَ. فَأَرَقْتُ كَأْسَ الْكَرَى. وَنَصَصْتُ رِكَابَ السُّرَى. وَجُبْتُ فِي سَيْرِي وُعُورًا لَمْ تُدَمِّثْهَا الْخُطَى. وَلَا ٱهْتَدَتْ إِلَيْهَا الْقَطَا. حَتَّى وَرَدْتُ حِمَى الْخِلَافَةِ. وَالْحَرَمَ الْعَاصِمَ مِنَ الْمَخَافَةِ. فَسَرَوْتُ إِيجَاسَ الرَّوْعِ وَٱسْتِشْعَارَهُ. وَتَسَرْبَلْتُ لِبَاسَ الْأَمْنِ وَشِعَارَهُ. وَقَصَرْتُ هَمِّي عَلَى لَذَّةٍ أَجْتَنِيهَا. وَمُلْحَةٍ أَجْتَلِيهَا.

٢،٢٣ فَبَرَزْتُ يَوْمًا إِلَى الْحَرِيمِ لِأَرُوضَ طِرْفِي. وَأُجِيلَ فِي طُرَفِهِ[2] طَرْفِي. فَإِذَا فُرْسَانٌ مُتَتَالُونَ. وَرِجَالٌ مُنْثَالُونَ. وَشَيْخٌ طَوِيلُ اللِّسَانِ. قَصِيرُ الطَّيْلَسَانِ. قَدْ لَبَّبَ فَتًى جَدِيدَ الشَّبَابِ. خَلَقَ[3] الْجِلْبَابِ. فَرَكَضْتُ إِثْرَ[4] النَّظَّارَةِ. حَتَّى وَافَيْنَا بَابَ الْإِمَارَةِ. وَهُنَاكَ صَاحِبُ الْمَعُونَةِ مُتَرَبِّعًا فِي دَسْتِهِ. وَمُرَوِّعًا بِسَمْتِهِ. فَقَالَ لَهُ الشَّيْخُ أَعَزَّ اللهُ الْوَالِيَ. وَجَعَلَ كَعْبَهُ الْعَالِيَ. إِنِّي كَفَلْتُ هٰذَا الْغُلَامَ فَطِيمًا. وَرَبَّيْتُهُ يَتِيمًا. ثُمَّ لَمْ آلُهُ تَعْلِيمًا. فَلَمَّا مَهَرَ وَبَهَرَ. جَرَّدَ سَيْفَ الْعُدْوَانِ وَشَهَرَ. وَلَمْ أَخَلْهُ يَلْتَوِي عَلَيَّ وَيَتَّقِحُ. حِينَ يَرْتَوِي مِنِّي وَيَلْتَقِحُ. فَقَالَ لَهُ الْفَتَى عَلَامَ عَثَرْتَ مِنِّي. حَتَّى تَنْشُرَ هٰذَا الْخِزْيَ عَنِّي. فَوَاللهِ مَا سَتَرْتُ وَجْهَ بِرِّكَ. وَلَا هَتَكْتُ حِجَابَ سِرِّكَ.[5] وَلَا شَقَقْتُ عَصَا أَمْرِكَ. وَلَا أَلْغَيْتُ تِلَاوَةَ شُكْرِكَ. فَقَالَ لَهُ الشَّيْخُ وَيْلَكَ وَأَيُّ رَيْبٍ أَخْزَى مِنْ رَيْبِكَ. وَهَلْ عَيْبٌ أَفْحَشُ مِنْ عَيْبِكَ. وَقَدِ ٱدَّعَيْتَ سِحْرِي

---

١ في هامش س: تُعرف بالخَليفيّة؛ وفي د: الحَريميّة؛ وفي ف: الشَّعْرية. ٢ ف: طُرُقه. ٣ و: خَلِق. ٤ ف: في إثرِ. ٥ ف: سترك.

وَٱسْتَلْحَقْتَهُ. وَٱنْتَحَلْتَ شِعْرِي وَٱسْتَرَقْتَهُ. وَٱسْتِرَاقُ ٱلشِّعْرِ عِنْدَ ٱلشُّعَرَاءِ. أَفْظَعُ مِنْ سَرِقَةِ ٱلْبَيْضَاءِ وَٱلصَّفْرَاءِ. وَغَيْرَتُهُمْ عَلَى بَنَاتِ ٱلْأَفْكَارِ. كَغَيْرَتِهِمْ عَلَى ٱلْبَنَاتِ ٱلْأَبْكَارِ. فَقَالَ ٱلْوَالِي لِلشَّيْخِ وَهَلْ حِينَ سَرَقَ سَلَخَ. أَمْ مَسَخَ أَمْ نَسَخَ. فَقَالَ وَٱلَّذِي جَعَلَ ٱلشِّعْرَ دِيوَانَ ٱلْعَرَبِ. وَتَرْجُمَانَ ٱلْأَدَبِ. مَا أَحْدَثَ سِوَى أَنْ بَتَرَ شَمْلَ شَرْحِهِ. وَأَغَارَ عَلَى ثُلُثَيْ سَرْحِهِ. فَقَالَ لَهُ أَنْشِدْ أَبْيَاتَكَ بِرُمَّتِهَا. لِيَضِحَ[١] مَا ٱحْتَازَهُ مِنْ جُمْلَتِهَا. فَأَنْشَدَ

٣،٢٣ يَا خَاطِبَ ٱلدُّنْيَا ٱلدَّنِيَّةِ إِنَّهَا شَرَكُ ٱلرَّدَى وَقَرَارَةُ ٱلْأَكْدَارِ[٢]
دَارٌ مَتَى مَا أَضْحَكَتْ فِي يَوْمِهَا أَبْكَتْ غَدًا بُعْدًا لَهَا مِنْ دَارِ
وَإِذَا أَظَلَّ سَحَابُهَا لَمْ يَنْتَقِعْ مِنْهُ صَدًى لِجَهَامِهِ ٱلْغَرَّارِ
غَارَاتُهَا مَا تَنْقَضِي وَأَسِيرُهَا لَا يُفْتَدَى بِجَلَائِلِ ٱلْأَخْطَارِ
كَمْ مُزْدَهًى بِغُرُورِهَا حَتَّى بَدَا مُتَمَرِّدًا مُتَجَاوِزَ ٱلْمِقْدَارِ
قَلَبَتْ لَهُ ظَهْرَ ٱلْمِجَنِّ وَأَوْلَغَتْ فِيهِ ٱلْمُدَى وَنَزَتْ لِأَخْذِ ٱلثَّارِ
فَٱرْبَأْ بِعُمْرِكَ أَنْ يَمُرَّ مُضَيَّعًا فِيهَا سُدًى مِنْ غَيْرِ مَا ٱسْتِظْهَارِ
وَٱقْطَعْ عَلَائِقَ حُبِّهَا وَطِلَابِهَا تَلْقَ ٱلْهُدَى وَرَفَاهَةَ ٱلْأَسْرَارِ
وَٱرْقُبْ إِذَا مَا سَالَمَتْ مِنْ كَيْدِهَا حَرْبَ ٱلْعِدَى وَتَوَثُّبَ ٱلْغَدَّارِ
وَٱعْلَمْ بِأَنَّ خُطُوبَهَا تَفْجَا وَلَوْ طَالَ ٱلْمَدَى وَوَنَتْ سُرَى ٱلْأَقْدَارِ

٤،٢٣ فَقَالَ لَهُ ٱلْوَالِي ثُمَّ مَاذَا. صَنَعَ هٰذَا. فَقَالَ أَقْدَمَ لِلُؤْمِهِ فِي ٱلْجِزَاءِ. عَلَى أَبْيَاتِي ٱلسُّدَاسِيَّةِ ٱلْأَجْزَاءِ. فَحَذَفَ مِنْهَا جُزْءَيْنِ. وَنَقَصَ مِنْ أَوْزَانِهَا وَزْنَيْنِ. حَتَّى صَارَ

١ ف: لِيَتَّضِحَ. ٢ تقسمت الأبيات كما يلي في س، و: يا خاطِبَ الدُّنيا الدَّنِيَّةِ إِنَّها شَرَكُ الرَّدَى / وقَرارَةُ الأكدارِ //.

الرُّزْءُ فِيهَا رُزْءَيْنِ. فَقَالَ لَهُ بَيِّنْ مَا أَخَذَ. وَمِنْ أَيْنَ فَلَذَ. فَقَالَ أَرْعِنِي سَمْعَكَ. وَأَخْلِ لِلتَّفَهُّمِ عَنِّي ذَرْعَكَ. حَتَّى تَتَبَيَّنَ كَيْفَ أَصْلَتَ عَلَيَّ. وَتَقْدُرَ[1] قَدْرَ ٱجْتِرَامِهِ إِلَيَّ. ثُمَّ أَنْشَدَ. وَأَنْفَاسُهُ تَتَصَعَّدُ

يَا خَاطِبَ الدُّنْيَا الدَّنِيَّةِ إِنَّهَا شَرَكُ الرَّدَى
دَارٌ مَتَى مَا أَضْحَكَتْ فِي يَوْمِهَا أَبْكَتْ غَدَا
وَإِذَا أَظَلَّ سَحَابُهَا لَمْ يَنْتَقِعْ مِنْهُ صَدَى
غَارَاتُهَا مَا تَنْقَضِي وَأَسِيرُهَا لَا يُفْتَدَى
كَمْ مُزْدَهًى بِغُرُورِهَا حَتَّى بَدَا مُتَمَرِّدَا
قَلَبَتْ لَهُ ظَهْرَ الْمِجَنِّ وَأَوْلَغَتْ فِيهِ الْمُدَى
فَٱرْبَأْ بِعُمْرِكَ أَنْ يَمُرَّ مُضَيَّعًا فِيهَا سُدَى
وَٱقْطَعْ عَلَائِقَ حُبِّهَا وَطِلَابِهَا تَلْقَ الْهُدَى
وَٱرْقُبْ إِذَا مَا سَالَمَتْ مِنْ كَيْدِهَا حَرْبَ الْعِدَى
وَٱعْلَمْ بِأَنَّ خُطُوبَهَا تَفْجَا وَلَوْ طَالَ الْمَدَى

٥،٢٣ فَٱلْتَفَتَ الْوَالِي إِلَى الْغُلَامِ وَقَالَ تَبًّا لَكَ مِنْ خِرِّيجٍ مَارِقٍ. وَتِلْمِيذٍ سَارِقٍ. فَقَالَ الْفَتَى بَرِئْتُ مِنَ الْأَدَبِ وَبَنِيهِ. وَلَحِقْتُ بِمَنْ يُنَاوِيهِ. وَيُقَوِّضُ مَبَانِيهِ. إِنْ كَانَتْ أَبْيَاتُهُ نَمَتْ إِلَى عِلْمِي. قَبْلَ أَنْ أَلَّفْتُ نَظْمِي. وَإِنَّمَا ٱتَّفَقَ تَوَارُدُ الْخَوَاطِرِ. كَمَا قَدْ يَقَعُ الْحَافِرُ عَلَى الْحَافِرِ. قَالَ فَكَأَنَّ الْوَالِيَ جَوَّزَ صِدْقَ زَعْمِهِ. فَنَدِمَ عَلَى بَادِرَةِ ذَمِّهِ. فَظَلَّ يُفَكِّرُ فِيمَا يَكْشِفُ لَهُ عَنِ الْحَقَائِقِ. وَيُمَيِّزُ بِهِ الْفَائِقَ. مِنَ الْمَائِقِ. فَلَمْ يَرَ إِلَّا أَخْذَهُمَا بِالْمُنَاضَلَةِ. وَلَزَّهُمَا فِي قَرَنِ الْمُسَاجَلَةِ. فَقَالَ لَهُمَا إِنْ

١ ف: تُقَدِّر.

أَرَدْتُمَا ٱفْتِضَاحَ ٱلْعَاطِلِ. وَٱتِّضَاحَ ٱلْحَقِّ مِنَ ٱلْبَاطِلِ. فَتَرَاسَلَا فِي ٱلنَّظْمِ وَتَبَارَيَا. وَتَجَاوَلَا فِي حَلْبَةِ ٱلْإِجَازَةِ وَتَجَارَيَا. ﴿لِيَهْلِكَ مَنْ هَلَكَ عَنْ بَيِّنَةٍ. وَيَحْيَىٰ مَنْ حَيَّ عَنْ بَيِّنَةٍ﴾. فَقَالَا بِلِسَانٍ وَاحِدٍ. وَجَوَابٍ مُتَوَارِدٍ. قَدْ رَضِينَا بِسَبْرِكَ. فَمُرْنَا بِأَمْرِكَ. فَقَالَ إِنِّي مُولَعٌ مِنْ أَنْوَاعِ ٱلْبَلَاغَةِ بِٱلتَّجْنِيسِ. وَأَرَاهُ لَهَا كَٱلرَّئِيسِ. فَٱنْظِمَا ٱلْآنَ عَشَرَةَ أَبْيَاتٍ تُلْحِمَانِهَا بِوَشْيِهِ. وَتُرَصِّعَانِهَا بِحَلْيِهِ. وَضَمِّنَاهَا شَرْحَ حَالِي. مَعَ إِلْفٍ[1] بَدِيعِ ٱلصِّفَةِ. أَلْمَى ٱلشَّفَةِ. مَلِيحِ ٱلتَّثَنِّي. كَثِيرِ ٱلتِّيهِ وَٱلتَّجَنِّي. مُغْرًى بِتَنَاسِي ٱلْعَهْدِ. وَإِطَالَةِ ٱلصَّدِّ. وَإِخْلَافِ ٱلْوَعْدِ. وَأَنَا لَهُ كَٱلْعَبْدِ. قَالَ فَبَرَزَ ٱلشَّيْخُ مُجَلِّيًا. وَتَلَاهُ ٱلْفَتَى مُصَلِّيًا. وَتَجَارَيَا بَيْتًا فَبَيْتًا عَلَى هٰذَا ٱلنَّسَقِ. إِلَى أَنْ كَمَلَ[2] نَظْمُ ٱلْأَبْيَاتِ وَٱتَّسَقَ. وَهِيَ

٦،٢٣ وَأَحْوَى حَوَى رِقِّي بِرِقَّةِ لَفْظِهِ[3]   وَغَادَرَنِي إِلْفَ ٱلسُّهَادِ بِغَدْرِهِ
تَصَدَّى لِقَتْلِي بِٱلصُّدُودِ وَإِنَّنِي   لَفِي أَسْرِهِ مُذْ حَازَ قَلْبِي بِأَسْرِهِ
أُصَدِّقُ مِنْهُ ٱلزُّورَ خَوْفَ ٱزْوِرَارِهِ   وَأَرْضَى ٱسْتِمَاعَ ٱلْهُجْرِ خَشْيَةَ هَجْرِهِ
وَأَسْتَعْذِبُ ٱلتَّعْذِيبَ مِنْهُ وَكُلَّمَا   أَجَدَّ عَذَابِي جَدَّ بِي حُبُّ بِرِّهِ
تَنَاسَى ذِمَامِي وَٱلتَّنَاسِي مَذَمَّةٌ   وَأَحْفَظُ قَلْبِي وَهْوَ حَافِظُ سِرِّهِ
وَأَعْجَبُ مَا فِيهِ ٱلتَّبَاهِي بِعُجْبِهِ   وَأُكْبِرُهُ عَنْ أَنْ أَفُوهَ بِكِبْرِهِ
لَهُ مِنِّيَ ٱلْمَدْحُ ٱلَّذِي طَابَ نَشْرُهُ   وَلِي مِنْهُ طَيُّ ٱلْوُدِّ مِنْ بَعْدِ نَشْرِهِ
وَلَوْ كَانَ عَدْلًا مَا تَجَنَّى وَقَدْ جَنَى   عَلَيَّ وَغَيْرِي يَجْتَنِي رَشْفَ ثَغْرِهِ
وَلَوْلَا تَثَنِّيهِ ثَنَيْتُ أَعِنَّتِي   بِدَارًا إِلَى مَنْ أَجْتَلِي نُورَ بَدْرِهِ
وَإِنِّي عَلَى تَصْرِيفِ أَمْرِي وَأَمْرِهِ   أَرَى ٱلْمُرَّ حُلْوًا فِي ٱنْقِيَادِي لِأَمْرِهِ

١ بعدها في د: لي. ٢ د: كَمُلَ. ٣ ف: ثَغْرِه.

٧،٢٣ فَلَمَّا أَنْشَدَاهَا الْوَالِي مُتَرَاسِلَيْنِ. بُهِتَ لِذَكَاءَيْهِمَا الْمُتَعَادِلَيْنِ. وَقَالَ أَشْهَدُ بِاللهِ أَنَّكُمَا فَرْقَدَا سَمَاءٍ. وَكَزَنْدَيْنِ فِي وِعَاءٍ. وَأَنَّ هٰذَا الْحَدَثَ لَيُنْفِقُ مِمَّا آتَاهُ اللهُ. وَيَسْتَغْنِي بِوُجْدِهِ عَمَّنْ سِوَاهُ. فَتُبْ أَيُّهَا الشَّيْخُ مِنِ اتِّهَامِهِ. وَثُبْ إِلَى إِكْرَامِهِ. فَقَالَ الشَّيْخُ هَيْهَاتَ أَنْ تُرَاجِعَهُ مِقَتِي. أَوْ تَعْلَقَ بِهِ ثِقَتِي. وَقَدْ بَلَوْتُ كُفْرَانَهُ لِلصَّنِيعِ. وَمُنِيتُ مِنْهُ بِالْعُقُوقِ الشَّنِيعِ. فَاعْتَرَضَهُ الْفَتَى وَقَالَ يَا هٰذَا إِنَّ اللَّجَاجَ شُؤْمٌ. وَالْحَنَقَ لُؤْمٌ. وَتَحْقِيقَ[1] الظِّنَّةِ إِثْمٌ. وَإِعْنَاتَ[2] الْبَرِيءِ ظُلْمٌ. وَهَبْنِي اقْتَرَفْتُ جَرِيرَةً. أَوِ اجْتَرَحْتُ كَبِيرَةً. أَمَا تَذْكُرُ إِذَا أَنْشَدْتَنِي لِنَفْسِكَ. فِي إِبَّانِ أُنْسِكَ.

٨،٢٣ سَامِحْ أَخَاكَ إِذَا خَلَطْ   مِنْهُ الْإِصَابَةَ بِالْغَلَطْ
وَتَجَافَ عَنْ تَعْنِيفِهِ   إِنْ زَاغَ يَوْمًا أَوْ قَسَطْ
وَاحْفَظْ صَنِيعَكَ عِنْدَهُ   شَكَرَ الصَّنِيعَةَ أَمْ غَمَطْ
وَأَطِعْهُ إِنْ عَاصَى وَهُنْ   إِنْ عَزَّ وَادْنُ إِذَا شَحَطْ
وَاقْنَ الْوَفَاءَ وَلَوْ أَخَلَّ   بِمَا اشْتَرَطْتَ وَمَا اشْتَرَطْ
وَاعْلَمْ بِأَنَّكَ إِنْ طَلَبْتَ   مُهَذَّبًا رُمْتَ الشَّطَطْ
مَنْ ذَا الَّذِي مَا سَاءَ قَطُّ   وَمَنْ لَهُ الْحُسْنَى فَقَطْ
أَوَمَا تَرَى الْمَحْبُوبَ وَالْـ   ـمَكْرُوهَ لُزًّا فِي نَمَطْ
كَالشَّوْكِ يَبْدُو فِي الْغُصُو   نِ مَعَ الْجَنِيِّ الْمُلْتَقَطْ
وَلَذَاذَةُ الْعُمْرِ الطَّوِيـ   ـلِ يَشُوبُهَا نَغَصُ الشَّمَطْ
وَلَوِ انْتَقَدْتَ بَنِي الزَّمَا   نِ وَجَدْتَ أَكْثَرَهُمْ سَقَطْ[3]

١ دد: وتحقيقُ. ٢ د: وإعناتُ. ٣ بعدها في ف: رُضْتُ البَلاغَةَ والبَرا / عَةَ والشَّجاعَةَ والخِطَطْ // فوجَدتُ أحسنَ ما يُرى / سَبْرَ العُلومِ معًا فَقَطْ // .

٩،٢٣ قَالَ فَجَعَلَ الشَّيْخُ يُنَضْنِضُ نَضْنَضَةَ الصِّلِّ. وَيُحَمْلِقُ حَمْلَقَةَ الْبَازِي الْمُطِلِّ. ثُمَّ قَالَ وَالَّذِي زَيَّنَ السَّمَاءَ بِالشُّهُبِ. وَأَنْزَلَ الْمَاءَ مِنَ السُّحُبِ. مَا رَوْغِي عَنِ الاِصْطِلَاحِ. إِلَّا لِتَوَقِّي الاِفْتِضَاحِ. فَإِنَّ هٰذَا الْفَتَى ٱعْتَادَ أَنْ أَمُونَهُ. وَأُرَاعِيَ شُؤُونَهُ. وَقَدْ كَانَ الدَّهْرُ يَسُحُّ. فَلَمْ أَكُنْ أَشُحُّ. فَأَمَّا الآنَ فَالْوَقْتُ عَبُوسٌ. وَحَشْوُ الْعَيْشِ بُوسٌ. حَتَّى إِنَّ بِزَّتِي هٰذِهِ عَارَةٌ. وَبَيْتِي لَا تَطُورُ بِهِ فَارَةٌ. قَالَ فَرَقَّ لِمَقَالِهِمَا قَلْبُ الْوَالِي. وَأَوَى لَهُمَا مِنْ غِيَرِ اللَّيَالِي. وَصَبَا إِلَى ٱخْتِصَاصِهِمَا بِالْإِسْعَافِ. وَأَمَرَ النَّظَّارَةَ بِالاِنْصِرَافِ.

١٠،٢٣ قَالَ الرَّاوِي وَكُنْتُ مُتَشَوِّفًا إِلَى مَرْأَى الشَّيْخِ لَعَلِّي أَعْلَمُ عِلْمَهُ. إِذَا عَايَنْتُ وَسْمَهُ. وَلَمْ يَكُنِ الزِّحَامُ يُسْفِرُ[١] عَنْهُ. وَلَا يُفْرِجُ لِي فَأَدْنُوَ مِنْهُ. فَلَمَّا تَقَوَّضَتِ الصُّفُوفُ. وَأَجْفَلَ الْوُقُوفُ. تَوَسَّمْتُهُ فَإِذَا هُوَ أَبُو زَيْدٍ وَالْفَتَى فَتَاهُ. فَعَرَفْتُ حِينَئِذٍ مَغْزَاهُ فِيمَا أَتَاهُ. وَكِدْتُ أَنْقَضُّ عَلَيْهِ. لِأَسْتَعْرِفَ إِلَيْهِ. فَزَجَرَنِي بِإِيمَاضِ طَرْفِهِ. وَٱسْتَوْقَفَنِي بِإِيمَاءِ كَفِّهِ. فَلَزِمْتُ مَوْقِفِي. وَأَخَّرْتُ مُنْصَرَفِي. فَقَالَ الْوَالِي مَا مَرَامُكَ. وَلِأَيِّمَا سَبَبٍ مَقَامُكَ. فَٱبْتَدَرَهُ الشَّيْخُ وَقَالَ إِنَّهُ أَنِيسِي. وَصَاحِبُ مَلْبُوسِي. فَتَسَمَّحَ عِنْدَ هٰذَا الْقَوْلِ بِتَأْنِيسِي. وَرَخَّصَ فِي جُلُوسِي. ثُمَّ أَفَاضَ عَلَيْهِمَا خِلْعَتَيْنِ. وَوَصَلَهُمَا بِنِصَابٍ مِنَ الْعَيْنِ. وَٱسْتَعْهَدَهُمَا أَنْ يَتَعَاشَرَا بِالْمَعْرُوفِ. إِلَى إِظْلَالِ الْيَوْمِ الْمَخُوفِ. فَنَهَضَا مِنْ نَادِيهِ. مُنْشِدَيْنِ بِشُكْرِ أَيَادِيهِ. وَتَبِعْتُهُمَا لِأَعْرِفَ مَثْوَاهُمَا. وَأَتَزَوَّدَ مِنْ نَجْوَاهُمَا. فَلَمَّا أَجَزْنَا حِمَى الْوَالِي. وَأَفْضَيْنَا إِلَى الْفَضَاءِ الْخَالِي. أَدْرَكَنِي أَحَدُ جَلَاوِزَتِهِ. مُهِيبًا بِي إِلَى حَوْزَتِهِ. فَقُلْتُ لِأَبِي زَيْدٍ مَا أَظُنُّهُ ٱسْتَحْضَرَنِي. إِلَّا لِيَسْتَخْبِرَنِي. فَمَاذَا أَقُولُ. وَفِي أَيِّ وَادٍ مَعَهُ أَجُولُ. فَقَالَ بَيِّنْ لَهُ غَبَاوَةَ قَلْبِهِ. وَتَلَعُّبِي بِلُبِّهِ. لِيَعْلَمَ أَنَّ رِيحَهُ لَاقَتْ إِعْصَارًا.

[١] هكذا في ق، وفي س: يَسْفِرُ؛ وهي غير مشكلة في و؛ وفي د: يَسْفِر؛ وفي ف: يُسْفِر.

وَجَدْوَلَهُ صَادَفَ تَيَّارًا. فَقُلْتُ أَخَافُ أَنْ يَتَّقِدَ غَضَبُهُ. فَيَلْفَحَكَ لَهَبُهُ. أَوْ يَسْتَشْرِيَ طَيْشُهُ. فَيَسْرِيَ إِلَيْكَ بَطْشُهُ. فَقَالَ إِنِّي أَرْحَلُ الآنَ إِلَى الرُّهَا. وَأَنَّى يَلْتَقِي سُهَيْلٌ وَالسُّهَى.

١١،٢٣ فَلَمَّا حَضَرْتُ الْوَالِيَ وَقَدْ خَلَا مَجْلِسُهُ. وَٱنْجَلَى تَعَبُّسُهُ. أَخَذَ يَصِفُ أَبَا زَيْدٍ وَفَضْلَهُ. وَيَذُمُّ الدَّهْرَ لَهُ. ثُمَّ قَالَ نَشَدْتُكَ اللهَ أَلَسْتَ الَّذِي أَعَارَهُ الدَّسْتَ. فَقُلْتُ لَا وَالَّذِي أَحَلَّكَ فِي هٰذَا الدَّسْتِ. مَا أَنَا بِصَاحِبِ ذٰلِكَ الدَّسْتِ. بَلْ أَنْتَ الَّذِي تَمَّ عَلَيْهِ الدَّسْتُ. فَٱزْوَرَّتْ مُقْلَتَاهُ. وَٱحْمَرَّتْ وَجْنَتَاهُ. وَقَالَ وَاللهِ مَا أَعْجَزَنِي قَطُّ فَضْحُ مُرِيبٍ. وَلَا تَكْشِيفُ مَعِيبٍ. وَلٰكِنْ مَا سَمِعْتُ بِأَنَّ شَيْخًا دَلَّسَ. بَعْدَمَا تَطَلَّسَ.[١] فَبِهٰذَا تَمَّ لَهُ أَنْ لَبَّسَ.[٢] أَفَتَدْرِي أَيْنَ سَكَعَ. ذٰلِكَ اللُّكَعُ. قُلْتُ أَشْفَقَ مِنْكَ لِتَعَدِّي طَوْرِهِ. فَظَعَنَ عَنْ بَغْدَاذَ مِنْ فَوْرِهِ. فَقَالَ لَا قَرَّبَ اللهُ لَهُ نَوًى. وَلَا كَلَأَهُ أَيْنَ ثَوَى. فَمَا زَاوَلْتُ أَشَدَّ مِنْ نُكْرِهِ. وَلَا ذُقْتُ أَمَرَّ مِنْ مَكْرِهِ. وَلَوْلَا حُرْمَةُ أَدَبِهِ. لَأَوْغَلْتُ فِي طَلَبِهِ. إِلَى أَنْ يَقَعَ[٣] فَأُوقِعَ بِهِ. وَإِنِّي لَأَكْرَهُ أَنْ تَشِيعَ فَعْلَتُهُ بِمَدِينَةِ السَّلَامِ. فَأَفْتَضِحَ بَيْنَ الْأَنَامِ. وَتَحْبَطَ مَكَانَتِي عِنْدَ الْإِمَامِ. وَأَصِيرَ ضُحْكَةً[٤] الْخَاصِّ وَالْعَامِّ. فَعَاهَدَنِي عَلَى أَلَّا[٥] تَفُوهَ[٦] بِمَا ٱعْتَمَدَ. مَا دُمْتُ حِلًّا بِهٰذَا الْبَلَدِ.

قَالَ الْحَارِثُ بْنُ هَمَّامٍ. فَعَاهَدْتُهُ مُعَاهَدَةَ مَنْ لَا يَتَأَوَّلُ. وَوَفَيْتُ لَهُ كَمَا وَفَى السَّمَوْءَلُ.

---

١ بعدها في ف: وتقلّس. ٢ بعدها في د: فما كُنية ذلك القُريد. فقلت أبو زيد. فقال إنه بأبي كيد. أليَقُ منه بأبي زيد. ٣ بعدها في ف: في يدها. ٤ ف: ضحكةً بين. ٥ و، د: أن لا. ٦ د: أتفوّه، وفي ف: أفُوهَ.

الْمَقَامَةُ الرَّابِعَةُ وَالْعِشْرُونَ[1]

١،٢٤ أَخْبَرَ[2] الْحَارِثُ بْنُ هَمَّامٍ قَالَ عَاشَرْتُ بِقَطِيعَةِ الرَّبِيعِ. فِي إِبَّانِ الرَّبِيعِ. فِتْيَةً وُجُوهُهُمْ أَبْلَجُ مِنْ أَنْوَارِهِ. وَأَخْلَاقُهُمْ أَبْهَجُ مِنْ أَزْهَارِهِ. وَأَلْفَاظُهُمْ أَرَقُّ مِنْ نَسِيمِ أَسْحَارِهِ. فَٱجْتَلَيْتُ مِنْهُمْ مَا يَزْرِي[3] عَلَى الرَّبِيعِ الزَّاهِرِ. وَيُغْنِي عَنْ رَنَّاتِ الْمَزَاهِرِ. وَكُنَّا تَقَاسَمْنَا عَلَى حِفْظِ الْوِدَادِ. وَحَظْرِ الِاسْتِبْدَادِ. وَأَلَّا[4] يَنْفَرِدَ[5] أَحَدُنَا بِٱلْتِذَاذٍ. وَلَا يَسْتَأْثِرَ وَلَوْ بِرَذَاذٍ.[6] فَأَجْمَعْنَا فِي يَوْمٍ سَمَا دَجْنُهُ. وَنَمَا حُسْنُهُ. وَحَكَمَ بِالِاصْطِبَاحِ مُزْنُهُ. عَلَى أَنْ نَلْتَهِيَ بِالْخُرُوجِ. إِلَى بَعْضِ الْمُرُوجِ. لِنَسْرَحَ النَّوَاظِرَ. فِي[7] النَّوَاضِرِ. وَنَصْقُلَ الْخَوَاطِرَ. بِشَيْمِ الْمَوَاطِرِ. فَبَرَزْنَا وَنَحْنُ كَالشُّهُورِ عِدَّةً. وَكَنَدْمَانَيْ جَذِيمَةَ مَوَدَّةً. إِلَى حَدِيقَةٍ أَخَذَتْ[8] زُخْرُفَهَا وَٱزَّيَّنَتْ. وَتَنَوَّعَتْ أَزَاهِيرُهَا وَتَلَوَّنَتْ. وَمَعَنَا الْكُمَيْتُ الشَّمُوسُ. وَالسُّقَاةُ الشُّمُوسُ. وَالشَّادِي الَّذِي يُطْرِبُ السَّامِعَ وَيُلْهِيهِ. وَيَقْرِي كُلَّ سَمْعٍ مَا يَشْتَهِيهِ.

٢،٢٤ فَلَمَّا ٱطْمَأَنَّ بِنَا الْجُلُوسُ. وَدَارَتْ عَلَيْنَا الْكُؤُوسُ. وَغَلَ عَلَيْنَا ذِمْرٌ. عَلَيْهِ طِمْرٌ. فَتَجَهَّمْنَاهُ تَجَهُّمَ الْغِيدِ الشَّيْبَ. وَوَجَدْنَا صَفْوَ يَوْمِنَا قَدْ شِيبَ. إِلَّا أَنَّهُ سَلَّمَ تَسْلِيمَ أُولِي الْفَهْمِ. وَجَلَسَ يَفُضُّ لَطَائِمَ[9] النَّثْرِ وَالنَّظْمِ. وَنَحْنُ نَنْزَوِي مِنِ ٱنْبِسَاطِهِ. وَنَنْبَرِي لِطَيِّ بِسَاطِهِ. إِلَى أَنْ غَنَّى شَادِينَا الْمُغْرِبُ. وَمُغَرِّدُنَا الْمُطْرِبُ.

---

١ في هامش س: تعرف بالربيعية؛ وفي د: القطيعية؛ وفي ف: النحوية؛ وهي مطموسة في و. ٢ س، و، د، ف: حكى. ٣ و، د، ف: يُزْري. ٤ و، د: أن لا. ٥ و، د: يتفرد. ٦ في هامش س، وفي و: بقطرة رذاذ. ٧ د، ف: في الرياض. ٨ س: قد أخذت. ٩ د: لطائف.

إِلَامَ سُعَادُ لَا تَصِلِينَ حَبْلِي وَلَا تَأْوِينَ لِي مِمَّا أُلَاقِي
صَبَرْتُ عَلَيْكِ حَتَّى عِيلَ صَبْرِي وَكَادَتْ تَبْلُغُ الرُّوحُ التَّرَاقِي
وَهَا أَنَا قَدْ عَزَمْتُ عَلَى ٱنْتِصَافٍ أُسَاقِي فِيهِ خِلِّي مَا يُسَاقِي
فَإِنْ وَصْلاً أَلَذُّ بِهِ فَوَصْلٌ وَإِنْ صُرْمًا فَصُرْمٌ كَالطَّلَاقِ

٣،٢٤ قَالَ فَٱسْتَفْهَمْنَا ٱلْعَابِثَ بِٱلْمَثَانِي. لِمَ نَصَبَ ٱلْوَصْلَ ٱلْأَوَّلَ وَرَفَعَ ٱلثَّانِي. فَأَقْسَمَ بِتُرْبَةِ أَبَوَيْهِ. لَقَدْ نَطَقَ بِمَا ٱخْتَارَهُ سِيبَوَيْهِ. فَتَشَعَّبَتْ حِينَئِذٍ آرَاءُ ٱلْجَمْعِ. فِي تَجْوِيزِ النَّصْبِ وَالرَّفْعِ. فَقَالَتْ فِرْقَةٌ رَفْعُهُمَا هُوَ الصَّوَابُ. وَقَالَتْ طَائِفَةٌ لَا يَجُوزُ فِيهِمَا إِلَّا الِانْتِصَابُ. وَٱسْتَبْهَمَ عَلَى آخَرِينَ الْجَوَابُ. وَٱسْتَعَرَ بَيْنَهُمُ الِاصْطِخَابُ. وَذٰلِكَ ٱلْوَاغِلُ يُبْدِي ٱبْتِسَامَ ذِي مَعْرِفَةٍ. وَإِنْ لَمْ يَفُهْ بِبِنْتِ شَفَةٍ. حَتَّى إِذَا سَكَنَتِ الزَّمَاجِرُ. وَصَمَتَ ٱلْمَزْجُورُ وَالزَّاجِرُ. قَالَ يَا قَوْمِ أَنَا أُنَبِّئُكُمْ بِتَأْوِيلِهِ. وَأُمَيِّزُ صَحِيحَ ٱلْقَوْلِ مِنْ عَلِيلِهِ. إِنَّهُ لَيَجُوزُ رَفْعُ ٱلْوَصْلَيْنِ وَنَصْبُهُمَا. وَٱلْمُغَايَرَةُ فِي ٱلْإِعْرَابِ بَيْنَهُمَا. وَذٰلِكُمْ بِحَسَبِ ٱخْتِلَافِ ٱلْإِضْمَارِ. وَتَقْدِيرِ ٱلْمَحْذُوفِ فِي هٰذَا ٱلْمِضْمَارِ.

٤،٢٤ قَالَ فَفَرَطَ مِنَ ٱلْجَمَاعَةِ إِفْرَاطٌ فِي مُمَارَاتِهِ. وَٱنْخِرَاطٌ إِلَى مُبَارَاتِهِ. فَقَالَ أَمَّا إِذْ[١] دَعَوْتُمْ نَزَالِ. وَتَلَبَّبْتُمْ لِلنِّضَالِ.

فَمَا كَلِمَةٌ هِيَ إِنْ شِئْتُمْ حَرْفٌ مَحْبُوبٌ. أَوِ ٱسْمٌ لِمَا فِيهِ حَرْفٌ حَلُوبٌ.
وَأَيُّ ٱسْمٍ يَتَرَدَّدُ بَيْنَ فَرْدٍ حَازِمٍ. وَجَمْعٍ مُلَازِمٍ.
وَأَيَّةُ هَاءٍ إِذَا ٱلْتَحَقَتْ أَمَاطَتِ الثِّقَلَ. وَأَطْلَقَتِ ٱلْمُعْتَقَلَ.
وَأَيْنَ تَدْخُلُ السِّينُ فَتَعْزِلُ ٱلْعَامِلَ. مِنْ غَيْرِ أَنْ تُجَامِلَ.

---

١ د: إذا.

وَمَا مَنْصُوبٌ أَبَدًا عَلَى الظَّرْفِ. لَا يَخْفِضُهُ سِوَى حَرْفٍ.
وَأَيُّ مُضَافٍ أَخَلَّ مِنْ عُرَى الْإِضَافَةِ بِعُرْوَةٍ. وَٱخْتَلَفَ حُكْمُهُ بَيْنَ مَسَاءٍ وَغُدْوَةٍ.
وَمَا الْعَامِلُ الَّذِي يَتَّصِلُ آخِرُهُ بِأَوَّلِهِ. وَيَعْمَلُ مَعْكُوسُهُ مِثْلَ عَمَلِهِ.
وَأَيُّ عَامِلٍ نَائِبُهُ أَرْحَبُ مِنْهُ وَكْرًا. وَأَعْظَمُ مَكْرًا. وَأَكْثَرُ لِلّٰهِ تَعَالَى ذِكْرًا.
وَفِي أَيِّ مَوْطِنٍ يَلْبَسُ الذُّكْرَانُ. بَرَاقِعَ النِّسْوَانِ. وَتَبْرُزُ رَبَّاتُ الْحِجَالِ. بِعَمَائِمِ الرِّجَالِ.
وَأَيْنَ يَجِبُ حِفْظُ الْمَرَاتِبِ. عَلَى الْمَضْرُوبِ وَالضَّارِبِ.
وَمَا ٱسْمٌ لَا يُفْهَمُ[١] إِلَّا بِٱسْتِضَافَةِ كَلِمَتَيْنِ. أَوِ الِاقْتِصَارِ مِنْهُ عَلَى حَرْفَيْنِ. وَفِي وَضْعِهِ الْأَوَّلِ ٱلْتِزَامٌ. وَفِي الثَّانِي إِلْزَامٌ.
وَمَا وَصْفٌ إِذَا رُدِفَ[٢] بِالنُّونِ. نَقَصَ صَاحِبُهُ فِي الْعُيُونِ. وَقُوِّمَ بِالدُّونِ. وَخَرَجَ مِنَ الزَّبُونِ. وَتَعَرَّضَ لِلْهُونِ.

فَهٰذِهِ ثِنْتَا عَشْرَةَ مَسْأَلَةً وَفْقَ عَدَدِكُمْ. وَزِنَةَ لَدَدِكُمْ. وَلَوْ زِدْتُمْ زِدْنَا. وَإِنْ عُدْتُمْ عُدْنَا.

٥،٢٤ قَالَ الْمُخْبِرُ بِهٰذِهِ الْحِكَايَةِ فَوَرَدَ عَلَيْنَا مِنْ أَحَاجِيِّهِ[٣] اللَّاتِي هَالَتْ. لَمَّا ٱنْهَالَتْ. مَا حَارَتْ لَهُ الْأَفْكَارُ وَحَالَتْ. فَلَمَّا أَعْجَزَنَا الْعَوْمُ فِي بَحْرِهِ. وَٱسْتَسْلَمَتْ تَمَائِمُنَا لِسِحْرِهِ. عَدَلْنَا مِنِ ٱسْتِثْقَالِ الرُّؤْيَةِ لَهُ إِلَى ٱسْتِنْزَالِ الرِّوَايَةِ عَنْهُ. وَمِنْ بَغْيِ التَّبَرُّمِ بِهِ إِلَى ٱبْتِغَاءِ التَّعَلُّمِ مِنْهُ. فَقَالَ وَالَّذِي نَزَّلَ النَّحْوَ فِي الْكَلَامِ. مَنْزِلَةَ الْمِلْحِ فِي الطَّعَامِ.[٤] لَا أَنَلْتُكُمْ مَرَامًا. وَلَا شَفَيْتُ لَكُمْ غَرَامًا. أَوْ تُخَوِّلُنِي كُلُّ يَدٍ.

١ ف: يُعْرَف. ٢ ف: أُرْدِفَ. ٣ و، د: أحاجِيهِ. ٤ بعدها في د، و: وحَجَبَ مَطالِعَه عَنْ بَصائِرِ الطَّغامِ؛ وبعدها في د: وحَجَبَهُ عَنْ بَصائِرِ الطَّغامِ.

وَيَخْتَصَّنِي كُلٌّ مِنْكُمْ بِيَدٍ. فَلَمْ يَبْقَ فِي الْجَمَاعَةِ إِلَّا مَنْ أَذْعَنَ لِحُكْمِهِ.[١] وَنَبَذَ إِلَيْهِ خُبْأَةَ كُمِّهِ. فَكَشَفَ حِينَئِذٍ عَنْ أَسْرَارِ أَلْغَازِهِ. وَبَدَائِعِ إِعْجَازِهِ. مَا جَلَا بِهِ صَدَأَ الْأَذْهَانِ. وَجَلَّى مَطْلَعَهُ بِنُورِ الْبُرْهَانِ.

٦،٢٤ قَالَ الرَّاوِي فَهِمْنَا. حِينَ فَهِمْنَا. وَعَجِبْنَا. إِذْ أُجِبْنَا. وَنَدِمْنَا. عَلَى مَا نَدَّ مِنَّا. وَأَخَذْنَا نَعْتَذِرُ إِلَيْهِ ٱعْتِذَارَ الْأَكْيَاسِ. وَنَعْرِضُ عَلَيْهِ ٱرْتِضَاعَ الْكَاسِ. فَقَالَ مَأْرَبٌ لَا حَفَاوَةٌ. وَمَشْرَبٌ لَمْ يَبْقَ لَهُ عِنْدِي حَلَاوَةٌ.[٢] ثُمَّ شَمَخَ[٣] بِأَنْفِهِ صَلَفًا. وَنَأَى بِجَانِبِهِ أَنَفًا. وَأَنْشَدَ

نَهَانِيَ الشَّيْبُ[٤] عَمَّا فِيهِ أَفْرَاحِي   فَكَيْفَ أَجْمَعُ بَيْنَ الرَّاحِ وَالرَّاحِ
وَهَلْ يَجُوزُ ٱصْطِبَاحِي مِنْ مُعَتَّقَةٍ   وَقَدْ أَنَارَ مَشِيبُ الرَّأْسِ إِصْبَاحِي
آلَيْتُ لَا خَامَرَتْنِي الْخَمْرُ مَا عَلِقَتْ   رُوحِي بِجِسْمِي وَأَلْفَاظِي بِإِفْصَاحِي[٥]
وَلَا ٱكْتَسَتْ لِي بِكَاسَاتِ السُّلَافِ يَدٌ   وَلَا أَجَلْتُ قِدَاحِي بَيْنَ أَقْدَاحِ
وَلَا صَرَفْتُ إِلَى صِرْفٍ مُشَعْشَعَةٍ   هَمِّي وَلَا رُحْتُ مُرْتَاحًا إِلَى رَاحِ
وَلَا نَظَمْتُ عَلَى مَشْمُولَةٍ أَبَدًا   شَمْلِي وَلَا ٱخْتَرْتُ نَدْمَانًا سِوَى الصَّاحِي
مَحَا الْمَشِيبُ مِرَاحِي حِينَ خَطَّ عَلَى   رَأْسِي فَأَبْغِضْ بِهِ مِنْ كَاتِبٍ مَاحِ
وَلَاحَ يَلْحَى عَلَى جَرْيِ الْعِنَانِ إِلَى   مَلْهًى فَسُحْقًا لَهُ مِنْ لَائِحٍ لَاحِ
وَلَوْ لَهَوْتُ وَفَوْدِي شَائِبٌ لَخَبَا   بَيْنَ الْمَصَابِيحِ مِنْ غَسَّانَ مِصْبَاحِي
قَوْمٌ سَجَايَاهُمُ تَوْقِيرُ ضَيْفِهِمُ   وَالشَّيْبُ ضَيْفٌ لَهُ التَّوْقِيرُ يَا صَاحِ

١ في و: فلما حَصَلَتْ تحتَ وِكائِهِ. أضرَمَ شُعلةَ ذكائِهِ؛ وفي د: فلمّا حصّلَه تحتَ وِكائِهِ. أضرَمَ شُعلةَ ذكائِهِ. ٢ بعدها في ف: فأَطَلْنا مُراوَدَتَهُ. وَوالَيْنا مُعاوَدَتَهُ. ٣ ف: فشمخ. ٤ س: الشَّيب. ٥ ق: بإفصاحِ؛ وفي الهامش: حي معا (أي يمكن قراءة الكلمة بالمدّ أو بلا مدّ).

ثُمَّ إِنَّهُ ٱنْسَابَ ٱنْسِيَابَ ٱلْأَيْمِ. وَأَجْفَلَ إِجْفَالَ الْغَيْمِ. فَعَلِمْتُ أَنَّهُ سِرَاجُ سَرُوجَ. وَبَدْرُ ٱلْأَدَبِ ٱلَّذِي يَجْتَابُ ٱلْبُرُوجَ. وَكَانَ قُصَارَانَا التَّحَرُّقَ لِبُعْدِهِ. وَالتَّفَرُّقَ مِنْ بَعْدِهِ.

تَفْسِيرُ مَا أُودِعَ هٰذِهِ ٱلْمَقَامَةَ مِنْ نُكَتِ[1] ٱلْعَرَبِيَّةِ وَٱلْأَحَاجِيِّ ٱلنَّحْوِيَّةِ

٧،٢٤ أَمَّا صَدْرُ ٱلْبَيْتِ ٱلْأَخِيرِ مِنَ ٱلْأُغْنِيَةِ ٱلَّذِي هُوَ فَإِنْ وَصْلاً[2] أَلَذُّ بِهِ فَوَصْلٌ[3] نَظِيرُ قَوْلِهِمُ ٱلْمَرْءُ مَجْزِيٌّ بِعَمَلِهِ إِنْ خَيْرًا فَخَيْرٌ وَإِنْ شَرًّا فَشَرٌّ وَهٰذِهِ ٱلْمَسْأَلَةُ أَوْدَعَهَا سِيبَوَيْهِ كِتَابَهُ وَجَوَّزَ فِي إِعْرَابِهَا أَرْبَعَةَ أَوْجُهٍ أَحَدُهَا وَهُوَ أَجْوَدُهَا أَنْ تَنْصِبَ خَيْرًا ٱلْأَوَّلَ وَتَرْفَعَ ٱلثَّانِي وَتَنْصِبَ شَرًّا ٱلْأَوَّلَ وَتَرْفَعَ الثَّانِي وَيَكُونُ تَقْدِيرُهُ إِنْ كَانَ عَمَلُهُ خَيْرًا فَجَزَاؤُهُ خَيْرٌ وَإِنْ كَانَ عَمَلُهُ شَرًّا فَجَزَاؤُهُ شَرٌّ فَيَنْتَصِبُ[4] ٱلْأَوَّلُ عَلَى أَنَّهُ خَبَرُ كَانَ وَيَرْتَفِعُ[5] ٱلثَّانِي عَلَى أَنَّهُ خَبَرُ مُبْتَدَإٍ مَحْذُوفٍ وَقَدْ حَذَفْتَ فِي هٰذَا ٱلْوَجْهِ كَانَ وَٱسْمَهَا لِدَلَالَةِ حَرْفِ ٱلشَّرْطِ ٱلَّذِي هُوَ إِنْ عَلَى تَقْدِيرِهَا وَحَذَفْتَ أَيْضًا ٱلْمُبْتَدَأَ لِدَلَالَةِ ٱلْفَاءِ ٱلَّتِي هِيَ جَوَابُ ٱلشَّرْطِ عَلَيْهِ لِأَنَّهُ كَثِيرًا مَا يَقَعُ بَعْدَهَا. وَالْوَجْهُ الثَّانِي أَنْ تَنْصِبَهَا جَمِيعًا وَيَكُونُ تَقْدِيرُ ٱلْكَلَامِ إِنْ كَانَ عَمَلُهُ خَيْرًا فَهُوَ يُجْزَى خَيْرًا وَإِنْ كَانَ شَرًّا عَمَلُهُ فَهُوَ يُجْزَى شَرًّا فَيَنْتَصِبُ ٱلْأَوَّلُ عَلَى أَنَّهُ خَبَرُ كَانَ وَيَنْتَصِبُ ٱلثَّانِي ٱنْتِصَابَ ٱلْمَفْعُولِ بِهِ. وَالْوَجْهُ الثَّالِثُ أَنْ تَرْفَعَهُمَا جَمِيعًا وَيَكُونُ تَقْدِيرُ ٱلْكَلَامِ إِنْ كَانَ فِي عَمَلِهِ خَيْرٌ فَجَزَاؤُهُ خَيْرٌ فَيَرْتَفِعُ خَيْرٌ ٱلْأَوَّلُ عَلَى أَنَّهُ ٱسْمُ كَانَ وَيَرْتَفِعُ خَيْرٌ ٱلثَّانِي عَلَى مَا بُيِّنَ فِي شَرْحِ ٱلْوَجْهِ ٱلْأَوَّلِ. وَقَدْ يَجُوزُ أَنْ يَرْتَفِعَ

---

١ س، و، د، ف: النكت. ٢ ق: وَصَلا. ٣ ق: وَصَل. ٤ ف: فتنصب. ٥ ف: وترفع.

خَيْرٌ الْأَوَّلُ عَلَى أَنَّهُ فَاعِلُ كَانَ وَيُجْعَلُ كَانَ الْمُقَدَّرَةُ هَاهُنَا هِيَ التَّامَّةُ الَّتِي تَأْتِي بِمَعْنَى حَدَثَ وَوَقَعَ فَلَا تَحْتَاجُ إِلَى خَبَرٍ كَقَوْلِهِ تَعَالَى ﴿وَإِنْ كَانَ ذُو عُسْرَةٍ﴾ وَيَكُونُ التَّقْدِيرُ فِي الْمَسْأَلَةِ إِنْ كَانَ خَيْرٌ فَجَزَاؤُهُ خَيْرٌ أَيْ إِنْ حَدَثَ خَيْرٌ فَجَزَاؤُهُ خَيْرٌ. وَالْوَجْهُ الرَّابِعُ هُوَ أَضْعَفُهَا أَنْ تَرْفَعَ الْأَوَّلَ عَلَى مَا تَقَدَّمَ شَرْحُهُ فِي الْوَجْهِ الثَّالِثِ وَتَنْصِبَ عَلَى مَا بُيِّنَ ذِكْرُهُ فِي الْوَجْهِ الثَّانِي وَيَكُونُ التَّقْدِيرُ إِنْ كَانَ فِي عَمَلِهِ خَيْرٌ فَهُوَ يُجْزَى خَيْرًا وَعَلَى حَسَبِ هٰذَا التَّفْسِيرِ وَالْمُقَدَّرَاتِ الْمَحْذُوفَاتِ فِيهِ يَجْرِي إِعْرَابُ الْبَيْتِ الَّذِي عُنِيَ بِهِ وَمِمَّا يَنْتَظِمُ فِي هٰذَا السِّلْكِ قَوْلُهُمُ الْمَرْءُ مَقْتُولٌ بِمَا قَتَلَ بِهِ إِنْ سَيْفًا فَسَيْفٌ وَإِنْ خَنْجَرًا فَخَنْجَرٌ.

٨،٢٤ أَمَّا الْكَلِمَةُ الَّتِي هِيَ حَرْفٌ مَحْبُوبٌ أَوِ ٱسْمٌ لِمَا فِيهِ حَرْفٌ حَلُوبٌ فَهِيَ نَعَمْ إِنْ أَرَدْتَ بِهَا تَصْدِيقَ الْأَخْبَارِ أَوِ الْعِدَةَ عِنْدَ السُّؤَالِ فَهِيَ حَرْفٌ وَإِنْ عَنَيْتَ بِهَا الْإِبِلَ فَهِيَ ٱسْمٌ وَالنَّعَمُ يُذَكَّرُ وَيُؤَنَّثُ وَيَنْطَلِقُ عَلَى الْإِبِلِ وَعَلَى كُلِّ مَاشِيَةٍ فِيهَا إِبِلٌ وَفِي الْإِبِلِ الْحَرْفُ وَهِيَ النَّاقَةُ الضَّامِرُ سُمِّيَتْ حَرْفًا تَشْبِيهًا لَهَا بِحَرْفِ السَّيْفِ وَقِيلَ إِنَّهَا الضَّخْمَةُ تَشْبِيهًا لَهَا بِحَرْفِ الْجَبَلِ. وَأَمَّا الِاسْمُ الْمُرَدَّدُ بَيْنَ فَرْدٍ حَازِمٍ وَجَمْعٍ مُلَازِمٍ فَهِيَ سَرَاوِيلُ قَالَ بَعْضُهُمْ هُوَ وَاحِدٌ وَجَمْعُهُ سَرَاوِيلَاتٌ فَعَلَى هٰذَا الْقَوْلِ هُوَ فَرْدٌ وَكَنَى عَنْ ضَمِّهِ الْخَصْرَ بِأَنَّهُ حَازِمٌ. وَقَالَ آخَرُونَ هُوَ جَمْعٌ وَاحِدُهُ سِرْوَالٌ مِثْلُ شِمْلَالٍ وَشَمَالِيلَ[1] فَهُوَ عَلَى هٰذَا الْقَوْلِ جَمْعٌ. وَمَعْنَى قَوْلِنَا[2] مُلَازِمٌ أَيْ لَا يَنْصَرِفُ وَإِنَّمَا لَمْ يَنْصَرِفْ هٰذَا النَّوْعُ مِنَ الْجَمْعِ وَهُوَ كُلُّ جَمْعٍ ثَالِثُهُ أَلِفٌ وَبَعْدَهَا حَرْفٌ مُشَدَّدٌ أَوْ حَرْفَانِ أَوْ ثَلَاثَةٌ[3] لِثِقَلِهِ وَتَفَرُّدِهِ دُونَ غَيْرِهِ مِنَ الْجُمُوعِ بِأَنْ لَا نَظِيرَ لَهُ فِي الْأَسْمَاءِ الْآحَادِ.[4]

---

١ بعدها في ف: وسربال وسرابيل. ٢ س، و، د، ف: قوله. ٣ بعدها في د، ف: أوسطها ساكن. ٤ بعدها في د، ف: وقد كنى في هذه الأحجية عما لا ينصرف بالملازم كما كنى في التي قبلها عما ينصرف باللازم.

٩،٢٤ وَأَمَّا الْهَاءُ الَّتِي إِذَا الْتَحَقَتْ أَمَاطَتِ الثِّقَلَ وَأَطْلَقَتِ الْمُعْتَقَلَ فَهِيَ الْهَاءُ اللَّاحِقَةُ بِالْجَمْعِ الْمُقَدَّمِ ذِكْرُهُ كَقَوْلِكَ[١] صَيَارِفَةٌ وَصَيَاقِلَةٌ فَيَنْصَرِفُ هٰذَا الْجَمْعُ عِنْدَ الْتِحَاقِ الْهَاءِ بِهِ لِأَنَّهَا قَدْ أَصَارَتْهُ إِلَى أَمْثَالِ الْآحَادِ نَحْوَ رَفَاهِيَةٍ وَكَرَاهِيَةٍ فَخَفَّ بِهٰذَا السَّبَبِ وَصُرِّفَ لِهٰذِهِ الْعِلَّةِ. وَقَدْ كَنَى فِي هٰذِهِ الْأُحْجِيَّةِ عَمَّا لَا يُصْرَفُ بِالْمُعْتَقَلِ كَمَا كَنَى فِي الَّتِي قَبْلَهَا عَمَّا لَا يَنْصَرِفُ بِالْمُلَازِمِ. وَأَمَّا السِّينُ الَّتِي تَعْزِلُ الْعَامِلَ مِنْ غَيْرِ أَنْ تُجَامِلَ فَهِيَ إِذَا دَخَلَتْ[٢] عَلَى الْفِعْلِ الْمُسْتَقْبَلِ وَتَفْصِلُ بَيْنَهُ وَبَيْنَ أَنْ الَّتِي كَانَتْ قَبْلَ دُخُولِهَا مِنْ أَدَوَاتِ النَّصْبِ فَيَرْتَفِعُ حِينَئِذٍ الْفِعْلُ وَتَنْقُلُ أَنْ عَنْ كَوْنِهَا النَّاصِبَةَ لِلْفِعْلِ إِلَى أَنْ تَصِيرَ الْمُخَفَّفَةَ مِنَ الثَّقِيلَةِ وَذٰلِكَ كَقَوْلِهِ سُبْحَانَهُ ﴿عَلِمَ أَنْ سَيَكُونُ مِنكُم مَّرْضَىٰ﴾ وَتَقْدِيرُهُ عَلِمَ أَنَّهُ سَيَكُونُ.

١٠،٢٤ وَأَمَّا الْمَنْصُوبُ عَلَى الظَّرْفِ الَّذِي لَا يَخْفِضُهُ سِوَى حَرْفٍ فَهُوَ عِنْدَ وَلَا[٣] يَجُرُّهُ غَيْرُ مِنْ خَاصَّةً وَقَوْلُ الْعَامَّةِ ذَهَبْتُ إِلَى عِنْدِهِ لَحْنٌ. وَأَمَّا الْمُضَافُ الَّذِي أَخَلَّ مِنْ عُرَى الْإِضَافَةِ بِعُرْوَةٍ وَاخْتَلَفَ حُكْمُهُ بَيْنَ مَسَاءٍ وَغُدْوَةٍ فَهُوَ لَدُنْ وَلَدُنْ مِنَ الْأَسْمَاءِ الْمُلَازِمَةِ لِلْإِضَافَةِ وَكُلُّ مَا يَأْتِي بَعْدَهَا مَجْرُورٌ بِهِ إِلَّا غُدْوَةً فَإِنَّ الْعَرَبَ نَصَبَتْهَا بِلَدُنْ لِكَثْرَةِ اسْتِعْمَالِهِمْ إِيَّاهَا فِي الْكَلَامِ ثُمَّ نَوَّنَتْهَا أَيْضًا لِيَتَبَيَّنَ بِذٰلِكَ أَنَّهَا مَنْصُوبَةٌ لَا أَنَّهَا مِنْ نَوْعِ الْمَجْرُورَاتِ الَّتِي لَا تَنْصَرِفُ. وَعِنْدَ بَعْضِ النَّحْوِيِّينَ أَنَّ لَدُنْ بِمَعْنَى عِنْدَ وَالصَّحِيحُ أَنَّ بَيْنَهُمَا فَرْقًا لَطِيفًا وَهُوَ أَنَّ عِنْدَ يَشْتَمِلُ مَعْنَاهَا عَلَى مَا هُوَ فِي مَلَكَتِكَ[٤] وَمُكْنَتِكَ مِمَّا دَنَا مِنْكَ وَبَعُدَ عَنْكَ وَلَدُنْ يَخْتَصُّ مَعْنَاهَا بِمَا حَضَرَكَ وَقَرُبَ مِنْكَ. وَأَمَّا الْعَامِلُ الَّذِي يَتَّصِلُ آخِرُهُ بِأَوَّلِهِ وَيَعْمَلُ مَعْكُوسُهُ مِثْلَ عَمَلِهِ فَهُوَ يَا وَمَعْكُوسُهَا أَيْ وَكِلْتَاهُمَا مِنْ حُرُوفِ النِّدَاءِ وَعَمَلُهُمْ فِي الِاسْمِ

---

١ د: مِثْلَ. ٢ «اذا دخلتى»: في س: هي السين التي تدخل؛ وفي ف: هي التي تدخل. ٣ س، و، د، ف: اذ لا. ٤ د: مُلْكَتِكَ، وف: ملكك.

الْمُنَادَى سِيَّانِ وَإِنْ كَانَتْ يَا أَجْوَلَ فِي الْكَلَامِ وَأَكْثَرَ فِي الِاسْتِعْمَالِ وَقَدِ اخْتَارَ بَعْضُهُمْ أَنْ يُنَادَى بِأَيْ الْقَرِيبِ فَقَطْ كَالْهَمْزَةِ.

وَأَمَّا الْعَامِلُ الَّذِي نَائِبُهُ أَرْحَبُ مِنْهُ وَكْرًا وَأَعْظَمُ مَكْرًا وَأَكْثَرُ لِلّٰهِ تَعَالَى ذِكْرًا ١١،٢٤
فَهُوَ بَاءُ الْقَسَمِ وَهٰذِهِ الْبَاءُ هِيَ أَصْلُ حُرُوفِ الْقَسَمِ بِدَلَالَةِ اسْتِعْمَالِهَا مَعَ ظُهُورِ فِعْلِ الْقَسَمِ فِي قَوْلِكَ أُقْسِمُ بِاللهِ وَلِدُخُولِهَا أَيْضًا عَلَى الْمُضْمَرِ كَقَوْلِكَ بِكَ لَأَفْعَلَنَّ وَثُمَّ[1] أُبْدِلَتِ الْوَاوُ مِنْهَا فِي الْقَسَمِ لِأَنَّهُمَا جَمِيعًا مِنْ حُرُوفِ الشَّفَةِ ثُمَّ لِتَنَاسُبِ[2] مَعْنَاهَا[3] لِأَنَّ الْوَاوَ تُفِيدُ الْجَمْعَ وَالْبَاءَ تُفِيدُ الْإِلْصَاقَ وَالْمَعْنَيَانِ مُتَقَارِبَانِ[4] ثُمَّ صَارَتِ الْوَاوُ الْمُبْدَلَةُ مِنَ الْبَاءِ أَدْوَرَ فِي الْكَلَامِ وَأَعْلَقَ بِالْأَقْسَامِ وَلِهٰذَا أَلْغَزَ[5] بِأَنَّهُ أَكْثَرُ لِلهِ تَعَالَى ذِكْرًا ثُمَّ إِنَّ الْوَاوَ أَكْثَرُ مَوْطِنًا مِنَ الْبَاءِ لِأَنَّ الْبَاءَ لَا تَدْخُلُ إِلَّا عَلَى الِاسْمِ وَلَا تَعْمَلُ غَيْرَ الْجَرِّ وَالْوَاوُ تَدْخُلُ عَلَى الِاسْمِ وَالْفِعْلِ وَالْحَرْفِ وَتَجُرُّ تَارَةً بِالْقَسَمِ وَتَارَةً بِإِضْمَارِ رُبَّ وَتَنْتَظِمُ أَيْضًا مَعَ نَوَاصِبِ الْفِعْلِ وَأَدَوَاتِ الْعَطْفِ فَلِهٰذَا وَصَفَهَا بِرُحْبِ الْوَكْرِ وَعُظْمِ الْمَكْرِ. وَأَمَّا الْمَوْطِنُ الَّذِي يَلْبَسُ فِيهِ الذُّكْرَانُ بَرَاقِعَ النِّسْوَانِ وَتَبْرُزُ فِيهِ رَبَّاتُ الْحِجَالِ بِعَمَائِمِ الرِّجَالِ فَهُوَ أَوَّلُ مَرَاتِبِ الْعَدَدِ الْمُضَافِ وَذٰلِكَ مَا بَيْنَ الثَّلَاثَةِ إِلَى الْعَشَرَةِ فَإِنَّهُ يَكُونُ مَعَ الْمُذَكَّرِ بِالْهَاءِ وَمَعَ الْمُؤَنَّثِ بِحَذْفِهَا كَقَوْلِهِ تَعَالَى ﴿سَخَّرَهَا عَلَيْهِمْ سَبْعَ لَيَالٍ وَثَمَانِيَةَ أَيَّامٍ﴾ وَالْهَاءُ فِي هٰذَا الْمَوْطِنِ مِنْ خَصَائِصِ الْمُؤَنَّثِ كَقَوْلِكَ قَائِمٌ وَقَائِمَةٌ وَعَالِمٌ وَعَالِمَةٌ فَقَدْ رَأَيْتَ كَيْفَ انْعَكَسَ فِي هٰذَا الْمَوْطِنِ حُكْمُ الْمُذَكَّرِ وَالْمُؤَنَّثِ حَتَّى انْقَلَبَ كُلٌّ مِنْهُمَا فِي ضِدِّ قَالَبِهِ وَبَرَزَ فِي بِزَّةِ صَاحِبِهِ.

---

١ ف: وإنما. ٢ ف: لتقارب. ٣ س، و: معنيهما (هكذا)، وفي د، ف: معنَيَيْهما. ٤ بعدها في ف: وكلاهما متّفق. ٥ و: أُلغِزَ.

١٢،٢٤ وَأَمَّا الْمَوْضِعُ الَّذِي يَجِبُ فِيهِ حِفْظُ الْمَرَاتِبِ عَلَى الْمَضْرُوبِ وَالضَّارِبِ فَهُوَ حَيْثُ يَشْتَبِهُ الْفَاعِلُ بِالْمَفْعُولِ لِتَعَذُّرِ ظُهُورِ عَلَامَةِ الْإِعْرَابِ فِيهِمَا أَوْ فِي أَحَدِهِمَا وَذٰلِكَ إِذَا كَانَا مَقْصُورَيْنِ مِثْلَ عِيسَى وَمُوسَى أَوْ مِنْ أَسْمَاءِ الْإِشَارَةِ نَحْوَ ذَاكَ وَهٰذَا فَيَجِبُ[١] لِإِزَالَةِ اللَّبْسِ إِقْرَارُ كُلٍّ مِنْهُمَا فِي رُتْبَتِهِ لِيُعْرَفَ الْفَاعِلُ مِنْهُمَا بِتَقَدُّمِهِ وَالْمَفْعُولُ بِتَأَخُّرِهِ. وَأَمَّا الِاسْمُ الَّذِي لَا يُفْهَمُ إِلَّا بِاسْتِضَافَةِ كَلِمَتَيْنِ أَوِ الِاقْتِصَارِ مِنْهُ عَلَى حَرْفَيْنِ فَهُوَ مَهْمَا وَفِيهَا قَوْلَانِ أَحَدُهُمَا أَنَّهَا مُرَكَّبَةٌ مِنْ مَهْ الَّتِي هِيَ بِمَعْنَى اُكْفُفْ وَمِنْ مَا وَالْقَوْلُ الثَّانِي وَهُوَ الصَّحِيحُ إِنَّ الْأَصْلَ مَا فَزِيدَتْ عَلَيْهَا مَا أُخْرَى كَمَا تُزَادُ مَا عَلَى إِنَّ[٢] فَصَارَ لَفْظُهَا مَا مَا فَثَقُلَ عَلَيْهِمْ تَوَالِي كَلِمَتَيْنِ بِلَفْظٍ وَاحِدٍ فَأَبْدَلُوا مِنْ أَلِفِ الْأُولَى هَاءً فَصَارَتَا مَهْمَا وَمَهْمَا مِنْ أَدَوَاتِ الشَّرْطِ وَالْجَزَاءِ وَمَتَى لَفَظْتَ بِهَا لَمْ يَتِمَّ الْكَلَامُ وَلَا عُقِلَ الْمَعْنَى إِلَّا بِإِيرَادِ كَلِمَتَيْنِ بَعْدَهَا كَقَوْلِكَ مَهْمَا تَفْعَلِ ٱفْعَلْ وَتَكُونُ حِينَئِذٍ مُلْتَزِمًا لِلْفِعْلِ وَإِنِ ٱقْتَصَرْتَ مِنْهَا عَلَى حَرْفَيْنِ وَهُمَا مَهْ الَّتِي بِمَعْنَى اُكْفُفْ فُهِمَ الْمَعْنَى وَكُنْتَ مُلْزِمًا مَنْ خَاطَبْتَهُ أَنْ يَكُفَّ. وَأَمَّا الْوَصْفُ الَّذِي إِذَا أُرْدِفَ بِالنُّونِ نَقَصَ صَاحِبُهُ فِي الْعُيُونِ وَقُوِّمَ بِالدُّونِ وَخَرَجَ مِنَ الزَّبُونِ وَتَعَرَّضَ لِلْهُونِ فَهُوَ ضَيْفٌ إِذَا لَحِقَتْهُ النُّونُ ٱسْتَحَالَ إِلَى ضَيْفَنٍ وَهُوَ الَّذِي يَتْبَعُ الضَّيْفَ وَيَتَنَزَّلُ فِي النَّقْدِ مَنْزِلَةَ الزَّيْفِ.

١ بعدها في د، ف: حينئذ. ٢ بالتشديد الظاهر في ف فقط.

الْمَقَامَةُ الْخَامِسَةُ وَالْعِشْرُونَ[1]

١٫٢٥ حَكَى الْحَارِثُ بْنُ هَمَّامٍ قَالَ. شَتَوْتُ بِالْكَرَجِ لِدَيْنٍ أَقْتَضِيهِ. وَأَرَبٍ أَقْضِيهِ. فَبَلَوْتُ مِنْ شِتَائِهَا الْكَالِحِ. وَقُرِّهَا[2] النَّافِخِ. مَا عَرَّفَنِي جَهْدَ الْبَلَاءِ. وَعَكَفَ بِي عَلَى الِاصْطِلَاءِ. فَلَمْ أَكُنْ أُزَايِلُ وِجَارِي. وَمُسْتَوْقَدَ[3] نَارِي. إِلَّا لِضَرُورَةٍ أُدْفَعُ إِلَيْهَا. أَوْ إِقَامَةِ جَمَاعَةٍ أُحَافِظُ عَلَيْهَا. فَاضْطُرِرْتُ فِي يَوْمٍ جَوُّهُ مُزْمَهِرٌّ. وَدَجْنُهُ مُكْفَهِرٌّ. إِلَى أَنْ بَرَزْتُ مِنْ كِنَانِي. لِمُهِمٍّ عَنَانِي. فَإِذَا شَيْخٌ عَارِي الْجِلْدَةِ. بَادِي الْجُرْدَةِ. وَقَدِ اعْتَمَّ بِرَيْطَةٍ. وَاسْتَثْفَرَ بِفُوَيْطَةٍ. وَحَوَالَيْهِ جَمْعٌ كَثِيفُ الْحَوَاشِي. وَهُوَ يُنْشِدُ وَلَا يُحَاشِي.

٢٫٢٥ يَا قَوْمِ لَا يُنْبِئْكُمُ عَنْ فَقْرِي ... أَصْدَقُ مِنْ عُرْيِي أَوَانَ الْقُرِّ
فَاعْتَبِرُوا بِمَا بَدَا مِنْ ضُرِّي ... بَاطِنَ حَالِي وَخَفِيَّ أَمْرِي
وَحَاذِرُوا انْقِلَابَ سِلْمِ الدَّهْرِ ... فَإِنَّنِي كُنْتُ نَبِيهَ الْقَدْرِ
آوِي إِلَى وَفْرٍ وَحَدٍّ يَفْرِي ... تُفِيدُ صُفْرِي وَتُبِيدُ سُمْرِي
وَتَشْتَكِي كُومِي غَدَاةَ أَقْرِي ... فَجَرَّدَ الدَّهْرُ سُيُوفَ الْغَدْرِ
وَشَنَّ غَارَاتِ الرَّزَايَا الْغُبْرِ ... وَلَمْ يَزَلْ يَسْحَتُنِي وَيَبْرِي
حَتَّى عَفَتْ دَارِي وَغَاضَ دَرِّي ... وَبَارَ شِعْرِي[4] فِي الْوَرَى وَسِعْرِي[5]
وَصِرْتُ نِضْوَ فَاقَةٍ وَعُسْرِ ... عَارِيَ الْمَطَا مُجَرَّدًا مِنْ قِشْرِي
كَأَنَّنِي الْمِغْزَلُ فِي التَّعَرِّي ... لَا دِفْءَ لِي فِي الصِّنِّ وَالصِّنَّبْرِ

---

١ في هامش س: تُعْرَف بالكرجيّة، د: الكَرَجية، ف: تعرف بالكَرَجية. ٢ س، و، د، ف: صِرِّها. ٣ ف: ولا مستوقد. ٤ د، ف: سعري. ٥ د، ف: شعري.

غَيْرُ التَّضَحِّي وَٱصْطِلَاءِ الْجَمْرِ   فَهَلْ خِضَمٌّ ذُو رِدَاءٍ غَمْرِ
يَسْتُرُنِي بِمِطْرَفٍ[1] أَوْ طِمْرِ   طِلَابَ وَجْهِ اللّٰهِ لَا لِشُكْرِي

٣،٢٥ ثُمَّ قَالَ يَا أَرْبَابَ الثَّرَاءِ. الرَّافِلِينَ فِي الْفِرَاءِ. مَنْ أُوتِيَ خَيْرًا فَلْيُنْفِقْ. وَمَنِ ٱسْتَطَاعَ أَنْ يُرْفِقَ فَلْيُرْفِقْ. فَإِنَّ الدُّنْيَا غَدُورٌ. وَالدَّهْرَ عَثُورٌ. وَالْمُكْنَةَ زَوْرَةُ طَيْفٍ.[2] وَالْفُرْصَةَ مُزْنَةُ صَيْفٍ. وَإِنِّي وَاللّٰهِ لَطَالَمَا تَلَقَّيْتُ الشِّتَاءَ بِكَافَاتِهِ. وَأَعْدَدْتُ الْأُهَبَ لَهُ قَبْلَ مُوَافَاتِهِ. وَهَا أَنَا الْيَوْمَ يَا سَادَتِي. سَاعِدِي وِسَادَتِي. وَجِلْدَتِي بُرْدَتِي. وَحَفْنَتِي جَفْنَتِي. فَلْيَعْتَبِرِ الْعَاقِلُ بِحَالِي. وَلْيُبَادِرْ صَرْفَ اللَّيَالِي. فَإِنَّ السَّعِيدَ مَنِ ٱتَّعَظَ بِسِوَاهُ. وَٱسْتَعَدَّ لِمَسْرَاهُ. فَقِيلَ لَهُ قَدْ جَلَوْتَ عَلَيْنَا أَدَبَكَ. فَٱجْلُ لَنَا نَسَبَكَ. فَقَالَ تَبًّا لِمُفْتَخِرٍ. بِعَظْمٍ نَخِرٍ. إِنَّمَا الْفَخْرُ بِالتُّقَى. وَالْأَدَبِ الْمُنْتَقَى. ثُمَّ أَنْشَدَ

لَعَمْرُكَ مَا الْإِنْسَانُ إِلَّا ٱبْنُ يَوْمِهِ   عَلَى مَا تَجَلَّى يَوْمُهُ لَا ٱبْنُ أَمْسِهِ
وَمَا الْفَخْرُ بِالْعَظْمِ الرَّمِيمِ وَإِنَّمَا   فَخَارُ الَّذِي يَبْغِي الْفَخَارَ بِنَفْسِهِ

ثُمَّ إِنَّهُ جَلَسَ مُحْقَوْقِفًا. وَٱجْرَنْثَمَ مُقَفْقِفًا. وَقَالَ اللّٰهُمَّ يَا مَنْ غَمَرَ بِنَوَالِهِ. وَأَمَرَ بِسُؤَالِهِ. صَلِّ عَلَى مُحَمَّدٍ وَآلِهِ. وَأَعِنِّي عَلَى الْبَرْدِ وَأَهْوَالِهِ. وَأَتِحْ لِي حُرًّا يُؤْثِرُ مِنْ خَصَاصَةٍ. وَيُؤَاسِي وَلَوْ بِقُصَاصَةٍ.

٤،٢٥ قَالَ الرَّاوِي فَلَمَّا جَلَّى عَنِ النَّفْسِ الْعِصَامِيَّةِ. وَالْمُلَحِ الْأَصْمَعِيَّةِ. جَعَلَتْ[3] عَيْنِي تَعْجُمُهُ. وَمَرَامِي لَحْظِي تَرْجُمُهُ. حَتَّى ٱسْتَبَنْتُ أَنَّهُ أَبُو زَيْدٍ. وَأَنَّ تَعَرِّيَهُ أُحْبُولَةٌ[4] لِصَيْدٍ.[5] وَلَمَحَ هُوَ أَنَّ عِرْفَانِي قَدْ[6] أَدْرَكَهُ. وَلَمْ يَأْمَنْ أَنْ يَهْتِكَهُ. فَقَالَ

---

١ د، ف: مُطرف. ٢ بعدها سقطت ورقتان من نسختي الرقبية من د. ٣ بعدها في هامش س، وفي و، ف: ملامح. ٤ س: حبالة، ف: أحبولة. ٥ ف: صيد. ٦ عندها يستأنف نص د.

أُقْسِمُ بِالسَّمَرِ وَالْقَمَرِ. وَالزُّهْرِ وَالزَّهَرِ. إِنَّهُ لَنْ يَسْتُرَنِي إِلَّا مَنْ طَابَ خِيمُهُ. وَأُشْرِبَ مَاءَ الْمُرُوءَةِ أَدِيمُهُ. فَعَقَلْتُ مَا عَنَاهُ. وَإِنْ لَمْ يَدْرِ الْقَوْمُ مَعْنَاهُ. وَسَاءَنِي مَا يُعَانِيهِ مِنَ الرِّعْدَةِ. وَٱقْشِعْرَارِ الْجِلْدَةِ. فَعَمَدْتُ لِفَرْوَةٍ هِيَ بِالنَّهَارِ رِيَاشِي. وَفِي اللَّيْلِ فِرَاشِي. فَنَضَوْتُهَا عَنِّي. وَقُلْتُ لَهُ ٱقْبَلْهَا مِنِّي. فَمَا كَذَّبَ أَنِ ٱفْتَرَاهَا. وَعَيْنِي تَرَاهَا. ثُمَّ أَنْشَدَ

لِلّٰهِ مَنْ أَلْبَسَنِي فَرْوَةً ... أَضْحَتْ مِنَ الرِّعْدَةِ لِي جُنَّهْ
أَلْبَسَنِيهَا وَاقِيًا مُهْجَتِي ... وُقِّيَ شَرَّ الْإِنْسِ وَالْجِنَّهْ
سَيَكْتَسِي الْيَوْمَ ثَنَائِي وَفِي ... غَدٍ سَيُكْسَى سُنْدُسَ الْجَنَّهْ

٥،٢٥ قَالَ فَلَمَّا فَتَنَ قُلُوبَ الْجَمَاعَةِ. بِٱفْتِنَانِهِ فِي الْبَرَاعَةِ. أَلْقَوْا عَلَيْهِ مِنَ الْفِرَاءِ الْمُغَشَّاةِ. وَالْجِبَابِ الْمُوشَّاةِ. مَا آدَهُ ثِقْلُهُ.[١] وَلَمْ يَكَدْ يُقِلُّهُ. فَٱنْطَلَقَ مُسْتَبْشِرًا بِالْفَرَجِ. مُسْتَنْشِيًا لِلْكَرَجِ. وَتَبِعْتُهُ إِلَى حَيْثُ ٱرْتَفَعَتِ التَّقِيَّةُ. وَبَدَتِ السَّمَاءُ نَقِيَّةً. فَقُلْتُ لَهُ لَشَدَّ مَا قَرَسَكَ[٢] الْبَرْدُ. فَلَا تَتَعَرَّ مِنْ بَعْدُ. فَقَالَ وَيْكَ لَيْسَ مِنَ الْعَدْلِ. سُرْعَةُ الْعَذْلِ. فَلَا تَعْجَلْ بِلَوْمٍ هُوَ ظُلْمٌ. وَلَا تَقْفُ مَا لَيْسَ لَكَ بِهِ عِلْمٌ. فَوَالَّذِي نَوَّرَ الشَّيْبَةَ. وَطَيَّبَ تُرْبَةَ طَيْبَةَ. لَوْلَمْ أَتَعَرَّ لَرُحْتُ بِالْخَيْبَةِ. وَصِفْرِ الْعَيْبَةِ. ثُمَّ نَزَعَ إِلَى الْفِرَارِ. وَتَبَرْقَعَ بِالِٱكْفِهْرَارِ. وَقَالَ أَمَا تَعْلَمُ أَنَّ شِنْشِنَتِي الِٱنْتِقَالُ مِنْ صَيْدٍ إِلَى صَيْدٍ. وَالِٱنْعِطَافُ مِنْ عَمْرٍو إِلَى زَيْدٍ. وَأَرَاكَ قَدْ عُقْتَنِي وَعَقَقْتَنِي. وَأَفَتَّنِي أَضْعَافَ مَا أَفَدْتَنِي. فَأَعْفِنِي عَافَاكَ اللهُ مِنْ لَغْوِكَ. وَٱسْدُدْ دُونِي بَابَ جِدِّكَ وَلَهْوِكَ. فَجَبَذْتُهُ جَبْذَ التِّلْعَابَةِ. وَجَعْجَعْتُ بِهِ لِلدُّعَابَةِ. وَقُلْتُ لَهُ وَاللهِ لَوْ لَمْ أُوَارِكَ. وَأُغَطِّ عَلَى عَوَارِكَ. لَمَا وَصَلْتَ إِلَى صِلَةٍ. وَلَا ٱنْقَلَبْتَ أَكْسَى مِنْ بَصَلَةٍ.

١ د: ثِقَله. ٢ د: قَرَّس.

فَجَازِنِي عَنْ إِحْسَانِي إِلَيْكَ. وَسَتْرِي لَكَ وَعَلَيْكَ. بِأَنْ تَسْمَحَ لِي بِرَدِّ الْفَرْوَةِ. أَوْ تُعَرِّفَنِي كَافَاتِ الشَّتْوَةِ.

٦،٢٥ فَنَظَرَ إِلَيَّ نَظَرَ الْمُتَعَجِّبِ. وَٱزْمَهَرَّ ٱزْمِهْرَارَ الْمُتَغَضِّبِ. ثُمَّ قَالَ أَمَّا رَدُّ الْفَرْوَةِ فَأَبْعَدُ مِنْ رَدِّ أَمْسِ الدَّابِرِ. وَالْمَيْتِ الْغَابِرِ. وَأَمَّا كَافَاتُ الشَّتْوَةِ فَسُبْحَانَ مَنْ طَبَعَ عَلَى ذِهْنِكَ. وَأَوْهَى وِعَاءَ خَزْنِكَ. حَتَّى أُنْسِيتَ مَا أَنْشَدْتُكَ بِالدَّسْكَرَةِ. لِابْنِ سُكَّرَةَ.

جَاءَ الشِّتَاءُ وَعِنْدِي مِنْ حَوَائِجِهِ سَبْعٌ إِذَا الْقَطْرُ عَنْ حَاجَاتِنَا حَبَسَا
كِنٌّ وَكِيسٌ وَكَانُونٌ وَكَاسُ طِلاً بَعْدَ الْكَبَابِ وَكُسٌّ نَاعِمٌ وَكِسَا

ثُمَّ قَالَ لَجَوَابٌ يَشْفِي. خَيْرٌ مِنْ جِلْبَابٍ يُدْفِي. فَٱكْتَفِ بِمَا وَعَيْتَ وَٱنْكَفِي. فَفَارَقْتُهُ وَقَدْ ذَهَبَتْ فَرْوَتِي لِشَقْوَتِي. وَحَصَلْتُ عَلَى الرِّعْدَةِ طُولَ شَتْوَتِي.

الْمَقَامَةُ السَّادِسَةُ وَالْعِشْرُونَ وَتُعْرَفُ بِالرَّقْطَاءِ[1]

١،٢٦ حَدَّثَ الْحَارِثُ بْنُ هَمَّامٍ قَالَ حَلَلْتُ سُوقَ الْأَهْوَازِ. لَابِسًا حُلَّةَ الْإِعْوَازِ. فَلَبِثْتُ فِيهَا مُدَّةً. أُكَابِدُ شِدَّةً. وَأُزَجِّي أَيَّامًا مُسْوَدَّةً. إِلَى أَنْ رَأَيْتُ تَمَادِيَ الْمُقَامِ. مِنْ عَوَادِي الِانْتِقَامِ. فَرَمَقْتُهَا بِعَيْنِ الْقَالِي. وَفَارَقْتُهَا مُفَارَقَةَ الطَّلَلِ الْبَالِي. وَظَعَنْتُ عَنْ وَشَلِهَا. كَمِيشَ الْإِزَارِ. رَاكِضًا إِلَى الْمِيَاهِ الْغِزَارِ. حَتَّى إِذَا سِرْتُ مِنْهَا مَرْحَلَتَيْنِ. وَبَعُدْتُ سُرَى لَيْلَتَيْنِ. تَرَاءَتْ لِي خَيْمَةٌ مَضْرُوبَةٌ. وَنَارٌ مَشْبُوبَةٌ. فَقُلْتُ آتِيهِمَا لَعَلِّي أَنْقَعُ صَدًى. ﴿أَوْ أَجِدُ عَلَى النَّارِ هُدًى﴾.

٢،٢٦ فَلَمَّا انْتَهَيْتُ إِلَى ظِلِّ الْخَيْمَةِ رَأَيْتُ غِلْمَةً رُوقَةً. وَشَارَةً مَرْمُوقَةً. وَشَيْخًا عَلَيْهِ بِزَّةٌ سَنِيَّةٌ. وَلَدَيْهِ فَاكِهَةٌ جَنِيَّةٌ. فَحَيَّيْتُهُ. ثُمَّ تَحَامَيْتُهُ. فَضَحِكَ إِلَيَّ. وَأَحْسَنَ الرَّدَّ عَلَيَّ. وَقَالَ أَلَا تَجْلِسُ إِلَى مَنْ تَرُوقُ فَاكِهَتُهُ. وَتَشُوقُ مُفَاكَهَتُهُ. فَجَلَسْتُ لِاغْتِنَامِ مُحَاضَرَتِهِ. لَا لِالْتِهَامِ مَا بِحَضْرَتِهِ. فَحِينَ سَفَرَ عَنْ آدَابِهِ. وَكَشَرَ عَنْ أَنْيَابِهِ. عَرَفْتُ أَنَّهُ أَبُو زَيْدٍ بِحُسْنِ مُلَحِهِ. وَقُبْحِ قَلَحِهِ. فَتَعَارَفْنَا حِينَئِذٍ. وَحَفَّتْ بِي فَرْحَتَانِ سَاعَتَئِذٍ. وَلَمْ أَدْرِ بِأَيِّهِمَا أَنَا أَصْفَى فَرَحًا. وَأَوْفَى مَرَحًا. أَبِإِسْفَارِهِ. مِنْ دُجُنَّةِ أَسْفَارِهِ. أَمْ بِخِصْبِ رِحَالِهِ. بَعْدَ إِمْحَالِهِ. وَتَاقَتْ نَفْسِي إِلَى أَنْ أَفُضَّ خَتْمَ سِرِّهِ. وَأَبْطُنَ دَاعِيَةَ يُسْرِهِ. فَقُلْتُ لَهُ مِنْ أَيْنَ إِيَابُكَ. وَإِلَى أَيْنَ انْسِيَابُكَ. وَبِمَ امْتَلَأَتْ عِيَابُكَ. فَقَالَ أَمَّا الْمَقْدَمُ فَمِنْ طُوسَ. وَأَمَّا الْمَقْصِدُ[2] فَإِلَى السُّوسِ. وَأَمَّا الْجِدَةُ الَّتِي أَصَبْتُهَا. فَمِنْ رِسَالَةٍ اقْتَضَبْتُهَا. فَسَأَلْتُهُ أَنْ يُفْرِشَنِي[3] دِخْلَتَهُ. وَيَسْرُدَ[4] عَلَيَّ رِسَالَتَهُ. فَقَالَ دُونَ مَرَامِكَ حَرْبُ الْبَسُوسِ. أَوْ تَصْحَبَنِي إِلَى السُّوسِ. فَصَاحَبْتُهُ

---

١ هكذا في متن ق، س؛ وفي د، ف: تعرف بالرقطاء. ٢ و، د، ف: المقصَد. ٣ و: تُفْرِشَني. ٤ و: يَسْرُدُ.

إِلَيْهَا قَهْرًا. وَعَكَفْتُ بِهَا عَلَيْهِ[١] شَهْرًا. وَهْوَ يَعُلُّنِي كَاسَاتِ التَّعْلِيلِ. وَيُجَرِّرُنِي أَعِنَّةَ التَّأْمِيلِ. حَتَّى إِذَا حَرِجَ صَدْرِي. وَعِيلَ صَبْرِي. قُلْتُ لَهُ إِنَّهُ لَمْ يَبْقَ لَكَ عِلَّةٌ. وَلَا لِي[٢] تَعِلَّةٌ. وَفِي غَدٍ أَزْجُرُ غُرَابَ الْبَيْنِ. وَأَرْحَلُ عَنْكَ بِخُفَّيْ حُنَيْنٍ. فَقَالَ حَاشَ لِلهِ أَنْ أُخْلِفَكَ. أَوْ أُخَالِفَكَ. وَمَا أَرْجَأْتُ أَنْ أُحَدِّثَكَ. إِلَّا لِأُلَبِّثَكَ. وَإِذَا كُنْتَ قَدِ ٱسْتَرَبْتَ بِعِدَتِي. وَأَغْرَاكَ ظَنُّ السَّوْءِ بِمُبَاعَدَتِي. فَأَصِخْ لِقَصَصِ سِيرَتِي الْمُمْتَدَّةِ. وَأَضِفْهَا إِلَى أَخْبَارِ الْفَرَجِ بَعْدَ الشِّدَّةِ. فَقُلْتُ لَهُ هَاتِ فَمَا أَطْوَلَ طِيَلَكَ. وَأَهْوَلَ حِيَلَكَ.

٣،٢٦ فَقَالَ اعْلَمْ أَنَّ الدَّهْرَ الْعَبُوسَ. أَلْقَانِي إِلَى طُوسَ. وَأَنَا يَوْمَئِذٍ فَقِيرٌ وَقِيرٌ. لَا فَتِيلَ[٣] لِي وَلَا نَقِيرٌ. فَأَلْجَأَنِي صِفْرُ الْيَدَيْنِ. إِلَى التَّطَوُّقِ بِالدَّيْنِ. فَٱدَّنْتُ لِسُوءِ الِاتِّفَاقِ. مِمَّنْ هُوَ عَسِرُ الْأَخْلَاقِ. وَتَوَهَّمْتُ تَسَنِّيَ النَّفَاقِ. فَتَوَسَّعْتُ فِي الْإِنْفَاقِ. فَمَا أَفَقْتُ حَتَّى بَهَظَنِي دَيْنٌ لَزِمَنِي حَقُّهُ. وَلَازَمَنِي مُسْتَحِقُّهُ. فَحِرْتُ فِي أَمْرِي. وَأَطْلَعْتُ غَرِيمِي عَلَى عُسْرِي. فَلَمْ يُصَدِّقْ إِمْلَاقِي. وَلَا نَزَعَ عَنْ إِرْهَاقِي. بَلْ جَدَّ فِي التَّقَاضِي. وَلَجَّ فِي ٱقْتِيَادِي إِلَى الْقَاضِي. وَكُلَّمَا خَضَعْتُ لَهُ بِالْكَلَامِ. وَٱسْتَنْزَلْتُ مِنْهُ رِفْقَ الْكِرَامِ. وَرَغَّبْتُهُ فِي أَنْ يَنْظُرَ لِي بِمُيَاسَرَةٍ. أَوْ يُنْظِرَنِي إِلَى مَيْسَرَةٍ. قَالَ لَا تَطْمَعْ فِي الْإِنْظَارِ. وَٱحْتِجَانِ النُّضَارِ. فَوَحَقِّكَ مَا تَرَى مَسَالِكَ الْخَلَاصِ. أَوْ تُرِيَنِي سَبَائِكَ الْخِلَاصِ. فَلَمَّا رَأَيْتُ ٱحْتِدَادَ لَدَدِهِ. وَأَنْ لَا مَنَاصَ لِي مِنْ يَدِهِ. شَاغَبْتُهُ. ثُمَّ وَاثَبْتُهُ. لِيُرَافِعَنِي إِلَى وَالِي الْجَرَائِمِ. لَا إِلَى الْحَاكِمِ فِي الْمَظَالِمِ. لِمَا كَانَ بَلَغَنِي مِنْ إِفْضَالِ الْوَالِي وَفَضْلِهِ. وَتَشَدُّدِ الْقَاضِي وَبُخْلِهِ. فَلَمَّا حَضَرْنَا بَابَ أَمِيرِ طُوسَ. آنَسْتُ أَنْ لَا بَأْسَ وَلَا بُوسَ. فَٱسْتَدْعَيْتُ دَوَاةً وَبَيْضَاءَ. وَأَنْشَأْتُ رِسَالَةً رَقْطَاءَ. وَهِيَ

١ ف: عليه بها. ٢ بعدها في ف: في المُقام. ٣ و: قبيل.

٤،٢٦ أَخْلَاقُ سَيِّدِنَا تُحَبُّ. وَبِعَقْوَتِهِ يُلَبُّ. وَقُرْبُهُ تُحَفُ. وَنَأْيُهُ تَلَفُ. وَخُلَّتُهُ نَسَبُ. وَقَطِيعَتُهُ نَصَبُ. وَغَرْبُهُ ذَلِقٌ. وَشُهْبُهُ تَأْتَلِقُ. وَظَلْفُهُ[1] زَانَ. وَقَوِيمُ نَهْجِهِ بَانَ. وَذِهْنُهُ قَلَّبَ وَجَرَّبَ. وَنَعْتُهُ شَرَّقَ وَغَرَّبَ.

سَيِّدٌ قُلَّبٌ سَبُوقٌ مُبِرٌّ   فَطِنٌ مُغْرِبٌ عَزُوفٌ عَيُوفُ
مُخْلِفٌ مُتْلِفٌ[2] أَغَرُّ فَرِيدٌ   نَابِهٌ فَاضِلٌ ذَكِيٌّ أَنُوفُ
مُفْلِقٌ إِنْ أَبَانَ طَبٌّ إِذَا نَا   بَ هِيَاجٌ وَجَلَّ خَطْبٌ مَخُوفُ

٥،٢٦ مَنَاظِمُ شَرَفِهِ تَأْتَلِفُ. وَشُؤْبُوبُ حِبَائِهِ يَكِفُ. وَنَائِلُ يَدَيْهِ فَاضَ. وَشُحُّ قَلْبِهِ غَاضَ. وَخِلْفُ سَخَائِهِ يُحْتَلَبُ. وَذَهَبُ عِيَابِهِ يُحْتَرَبُ. مَنْ لَفَّ لِفَّهُ فَلَجَ[3] وَغَلَبَ. وَتَاجِرُ بَابِهِ جَلَبَ وَخَلَبَ.[4] كَفَّ عَنْ هَضْمِ بَرِيٍّ. وَبَرِئَ مِنْ دَنَسِ غَوِيٍّ. وَقَرَنَ لِيَانَهُ بِعِزٍّ. وَنَكَّبَ عَنْ مَذْهَبِ كَزٍّ. لَيْسَ بِوَثَّابٍ عِنْدَ نَهْزَةِ شَرٍّ. بَلْ يَعِفُّ عِفَّةَ بَرٍّ.

فَلِذَا يُحَبُّ وَيُسْتَحَقُّ عَفَافُهُ   شَغَفًا بِهِ فَلُبَابُهُ خَلَّابُ
أَخْلَاقُهُ غُرٌّ تَرِفُّ وَفُوقُهُ   فُوقٌ إِذَا نَاضَلْتَهُ غَلَّابُ
سُجُحٌ يَهَشُّ[5] وَذُو تَلَافٍ إِنْ هَفَا   خِلٌّ فَلَيْسَ بِحَقِّهِ يُرْتَابُ
لَا بَاخِلٌ بَلْ بَاذِلٌ خِرْقٌ إِذَا   يُعْتَرُّ بَرْزٌ لَا يَلِيهِ بَابُ
إِنْ عَضَّ أَزْلٌ فَلَّ غَرْبَ عِضَاضِهِ   بِمَنَابِهِ فَانْحَتَّ مِنْهُ نَابُ

١ د: ظُلْفُه؛ ف: ظَلْفُه. ٢ «مخلف متلف»: في س، و: متلف مخلف. ٣ و: فلح. ٤ «جلب وخلب»: و: خلب وجلب. ٥ د، ف: تَهِشّ.

٦،٢٦ وَجَدِيرٌ بِمَنْ لَبَّ وَفَطَنَ. وَقَرُبَ وَشَطَنَ. أَنْ أَذْعَنَ لِقَرِيعِ زَمَنٍ. وَجَابِرِ زَمِنٍ. مُذْ رَضِعَ ثَدْيَ لِبَانِهِ. خُصَّ بِإِفَاضَةِ تَهْتَانِهِ. نَعَشَ وَفَرَّجَ. وَضَافَرَ فَأَبْهَجَ. وَنَافَرَ فَأَزْعَجَ. وَفَاءَ بِحَقٍّ أَبْلَجَ. أَتْعَبَ مَنْ سَيَلِي. وَقُرِّظَ إِذْ هُزَّ وَبُلِيَ. وَتَوَّجَ صِفَاتِهِ. بِحُبِّ عُفَاتِهِ.

فَلَا خَلَا ذَا بَهْجَةٍ يَمْتَدُّ ظِلُّ خِصْبِهِ
فَإِنَّهُ بَرٌّ بِمَنْ آنَسَ ضَوْءَ شُهْبِهِ
زَانَ مَزَايَا ظَرْفِهِ بِلُبْسِ خَوْفِ رَبِّهِ

٧،٢٦ فَلْيَهْنِ سَيِّدَنَا فَوْزُهُ بِمَفَاخِرَ تَأَثَّلَتْ وَجَلَّتْ. وَفَوْتُهُ بِصَنَائِعَ تَمَّتْ وَنَمَّتْ. وَيُلَائِمُ قُرْبَ[١] حَضْرَتِهِ. غَوْثُ رِقِّهِ بِحَظٍّ مِنْ حُظْوَتِهِ. فَإِنَّهُ تَلِيدُ نَدْبٍ. وَشَرِيدُ جَدْبٍ. وَجَرِيحُ نُوَبٍ أَثَّرَتْ. وَنَاظِمُ قَلَائِدَ تَسَيَّرَتْ. إِذَا جَاشَ لِخُطْبَةٍ فَلَا يُوجَدُ قَائِلٌ. ثُمَّ قُسٌّ ثُمَّ بَاقِلٌ. فَإِنْ حَبَّرَ قُلْتَ حِبَرٌ نُمْنِمَتْ. وَخِلْتَ رِيَاضًا قَدْ نَمَتْ. هٰذَا ثُمَّ شِرْبُهُ بَرْضٌ. وَقُوتُهُ قَرْضٌ. وَفَلَقُهُ غَسَقٌ. وَجِلْبَابُهُ خَلَقٌ. وَقَدْ قَلِقَ لِتَوَغُّرِ غَرِيمٍ غَاشِمٍ. يَسْتَحِثُّهُ بِحَقٍّ لَازِمٍ. فَإِنْ مَنَّ سَيِّدُنَا بِكَفِّهِ. بِهِبَاتِ كَفِّهِ. تَوَشَّحَ بِمَجْدٍ فَاقَ. وَبَاءَ بِأَجْرِ فَكِّي مِنْ وَثَاقٍ. لَا خَلَتْ سَجَايَا خُلْقِهِ. تَرْفُدُ شَائِمَ بَرْقِهِ. بِمَنِّ رَبٍّ أَزَلِيٍّ. حَيٍّ أَبَدِيٍّ.

٨،٢٦ قَالَ فَلَمَّا ٱسْتَشَفَّ ٱلْأَمِيرُ لَآلِيهَا. وَلَمَحَ السِّرَّ ٱلْمُودَعَ فِيهَا. أَوْعَزَ فِي ٱلْحَالِ بِقَضَاءِ دَيْنِي. وَفَصْلِ مَا بَيْنَ خَصْمِي وَبَيْنِي. ثُمَّ ٱسْتَخْلَصَنِي لِمُكَاثَرَتِهِ. وَٱخْتَصَّنِي بِأَثَرَتِهِ. فَلَبِثْتُ بِضْعَ سِنِينَ أَنْعَمُ فِي ضِيَافَتِهِ. وَأَرْتَعُ فِي رِيفِ رَأْفَتِهِ. حَتَّى إِذَا غَمَرَتْنِي مَوَاهِبُهُ. وَأَطَالَ ذَيْلِي ذَهَبُهُ. تَلَطَّفْتُ فِي ٱلِٱرْتِحَالِ. عَلَى مَا تَرَى مِنْ حُسْنِ

---

١ س، د، ف (في متن الشرح): قُرْب.

الحَالِ. قَالَ فَقُلْتُ لَهُ شُكْرًا لِمَنْ أَتَاحَ لَكَ لُقْيَانَ السَّمْحِ الْكَرِيمِ. وَأَنْقَذَكَ بِهِ مِنْ ضُغْطَةِ الْغَرِيمِ. فَقَالَ الحَمْدُ للهِ عَلَى سَعَادَةِ الْجَدِّ. وَالْخُلُوصِ مِنَ الخَصْمِ الأَلَدِّ. ثُمَّ قَالَ أَيُّمَا أَحَبُّ إِلَيْكَ أَنْ أُحْذِيَكَ مِنَ الْعَطَاءِ. أَمْ أُتْحِفَكَ بِالرِّسَالَةِ الرَّقْطَاءِ. فَقُلْتُ إِمْلَاءُ الرِّسَالَةِ أَحَبُّ إِلَيَّ. فَقَالَ وَهْوَ وَحَقِّكَ أَخَفُّ عَلَيَّ. فَإِنَّ نِحْلَةَ مَا يَلِجُ فِي الآذَانِ. أَهْوَنُ مِنْ نِحْلَةِ مَا يَخْرُجُ مِنَ الأَرْدَانِ. ثُمَّ كَأَنَّهُ أَنِفَ وَاسْتَحْيَا. فَجَمَعَ لِي بَيْنَ الرِّسَالَةِ وَالْحُذْيَا. فَفُزْتُ مِنْهُ بِسَهْمَيْنِ. وَفَصَلْتُ عَنْهُ بِغُنْمَيْنِ. وَأُبْتُ إِلَى وَطَنِي قَرِيرَ الْعَيْنِ. بِمَا حُزْتُ مِنَ الرِّسَالَةِ وَالْعَيْنِ.

الْمَقَامَةُ السَّابِعَةُ وَالْعِشْرُونَ[1]

١،٢٧ حَكَى الْحَارِثُ بْنُ هَمَّامٍ قَالَ مِلْتُ فِي رَيِّقِ زَمَانِي الَّذِي غَبَرَ. إِلَى مُجَاوَرَةِ أَهْلِ الْوَبَرِ. لِآخُذَ إِخْذَ[2] نُفُوسِهِمِ الْأَبِيَّةِ. وَأَلْسِنَتِهِمِ الْعَرَبِيَّةِ. فَشَمَّرْتُ تَشْمِيرَ مَنْ لَا يَأْلُو جُهْدًا. وَجَعَلْتُ أَضْرِبُ فِي الْأَرْضِ غَوْرًا وَنَجْدًا. إِلَى أَنِ ٱقْتَنَيْتُ هَجْمَةً مِنَ الرَّاغِيَةِ. وَثَلَّةً مِنَ الثَّاغِيَةِ. ثُمَّ أَوَيْتُ إِلَى عَرَبٍ أَرْدَافِ أَقْيَالٍ. وَأَبْنَاءِ أَقْوَالٍ. فَأَوْطَنُونِي أَمْنَعَ جَنَابٍ. وَفَلُّوا عَنِّي حَدَّ كُلِّ نَابٍ. فَمَا تَأَوَّبَنِي عِنْدَهُمْ هَمٌّ. وَلَا قَرَعَ صَفَاتِي سَهْمٌ.

٢،٢٧ إِلَى أَنْ أَضْلَلْتُ فِي لَيْلَةٍ مُنِيرَةِ الْبَدْرِ. لَقْحَةً غَزِيرَةَ الدَّرِّ. فَلَمْ أَطِبْ نَفْسًا بِإِلْغَاءِ طَلَبِهَا. وَإِلْقَاءِ حَبْلِهَا عَلَى غَارِبِهَا. فَتَدَثَّرْتُ فَرَسًا مِحْضَارًا. وَٱعْتَقَلْتُ لَدْنًا خَطَّارًا. وَسَرَيْتُ لَيْلَتِي جَمْعَاءَ. أَجُوبُ الْبَيْدَاءَ. وَأَقْتَرِي كُلَّ شَجْرَاءَ وَمَرْدَاءَ. إِلَى أَنْ نَشَرَ الصُّبْحُ رَايَاتِهِ. وَحَيْعَلَ الدَّاعِي إِلَى صَلَاتِهِ. فَنَزَلْتُ عَنْ مَتْنِ الرَّكُوبَةِ. لِأَدَاءِ الْمَكْتُوبَةِ. ثُمَّ حُلْتُ فِي صَهْوَتِهَا. وَفَرَرْتُ عَنْ شَحْوَتِهَا. وَسِرْتُ لَا أَرَى أَثَرًا إِلَّا قَفَوْتُهُ. وَلَا نَشَزًا إِلَّا عَلَوْتُهُ. وَلَا وَادِيًا إِلَّا جَزَعْتُهُ. وَلَا رَاكِبًا إِلَّا ٱسْتَطْلَعْتُهُ. وَجِدِّي مَعَ ذٰلِكَ يَذْهَبُ هَدَرًا. وَلَا يَجِدُ وِرْدُهُ صَدَرًا.

٣،٢٧ إِلَى أَنْ حَانَتْ صَكَّةُ عُمَيٍّ. وَلَفْحُ هَجِيرٍ يُذْهِلُ غَيْلَانَ عَنْ مَيٍّ. وَكَانَ يَوْمًا أَطْوَلَ مِنْ ظِلِّ الْقَنَاةِ. وَأَحَرَّ مِنْ دَمْعِ الْمِقْلَاتِ. فَأَيْقَنْتُ أَنِّي إِنْ لَمْ أَسْتَكِنَّ مِنَ الْوَقْدَةِ. وَأَسْتَجِمَّ بِالرَّقْدَةِ. أَدْنَفَنِي[3] اللُّغُوبُ. وَعَلِقَتْ بِي شَعُوبُ. فَعُجْتُ[4] إِلَى

١ في هامش س: تعرف بالوبرية (؟)؛ وفي د: البدوية؛ وفي ف: الوَبَرِيَّة. ٢ د، و: أخذ. ٣ ف: وأدنفني. ٤ ف: قعجت.

سَرْحَةٍ كَثِيفَةِ ٱلْأَغْصَانِ. وَرِيقَةِ ٱلْأَفْنَانِ. لِأُغَوِّرَ تَحْتَهَا إِلَى ٱلْمُغَيْرِبَانِ. فَوَٱللهِ مَا ٱسْتَرْوَحَ نَفْسِي. وَلَا ٱسْتَرَاحَ فَرَسِي.[1] حَتَّى نَظَرْتُ إِلَى سَانِحٍ. فِي هَيْئَةِ سَائِحٍ. وَهُوَ يَنْتَجِعُ نُجْعَتِي. وَيَشْتَدُّ إِلَى بُقْعَتِي. فَكَرِهْتُ ٱنْعِيَاجَهُ إِلَى مَعَاجِي. فَٱسْتَعَذْتُ بِٱللهِ مِنْ شَرِّ كُلِّ مُفَاجِي. ثُمَّ تَرَجَّيْتُ أَنْ يَتَصَدَّى مُنْشِدًا. أَوْ يَتَبَدَّى مُرْشِدًا. فَلَمَّا ٱقْتَرَبَ مِنْ سَرْحَتِي. وَكَادَ يَحُلُّ[2] بِسَاحَتِي. أَلْفَيْتُهُ شَيْخَنَا ٱلسَّرُوجِيَّ مُتَّشِحًا بِجِرَابِهِ. وَمُضْطَغِنًا أُهْبَةَ تَجْوَابِهِ. فَآنَسَنِي إِذْ وَرَدَ. وَأَنْسَانِي مَا شَرَدَ.

٤،٢٧ ثُمَّ ٱسْتَوْضَحْتُهُ مِنْ أَيْنَ أَثَرُهُ. وَكَيْفَ عُجَرُهُ وَبُجَرُهُ. فَأَنْشَدَ بَدِيهًا. وَلَمْ يَقُلْ إِيهًا.

قُلْ لِمُسْتَطْلِعٍ دَخِيلَةَ أَمْرِي   لَكَ عِنْدِي كَرَامَةٌ وَعَزَازَهْ
أَنَا مَا بَيْنَ جَوْبِ أَرْضٍ فَأَرْضٍ   وَسُرًى فِي مَفَازَةٍ فَمَفَازَهْ
زَادِيَ ٱلصَّيْدُ وَٱلْمَطِيَّةُ نَعْلِي   وَجَهَازِي ٱلْجِرَابُ وَٱلْعُكَّازَهْ
فَإِذَا مَا هَبَطْتُ مِصْرًا فَبَيْتِي   غُرْفَةُ ٱلْخَانِ وَٱلنَّدِيمُ جُزَازَهْ
لَيْسَ لِي مَا أُسَاءُ إِنْ فَاتَ أَوْ أَحْـ   ـزَنُ إِنْ حَاوَلَ ٱلزَّمَانُ ٱبْتِزَازَهْ
غَيْرَ أَنِّي أَبِيتُ خِلْوًا مِنَ ٱلْهَمِّ   وَنَفْسِي عَنِ ٱلْأَسَى مُنْحَازَهْ
أَرْقُدُ ٱللَّيْلَ مِلْءَ جَفْنِي وَقَلْبِي   بَارِدٌ مِنْ حَرَارَةٍ وَحَزَازَهْ
لَا أُبَالِي مِنْ أَيِّ كَأْسٍ تَفَوَّقْـ   ـتُ وَلَا مَا حَلَاوَةٌ مِنْ مَزَازَهْ
لَا وَلَا أَسْتَجِيزُ أَنْ أَجْعَلَ ٱلذُّ   لَّ مَجَازًا إِلَى تَسَنِّي إِجَازَهْ
وَإِذَا مَطْلَبٌ كَسَا حُلَّةَ ٱلْعَا   رِ فَبُعْدًا لِمَنْ يَرُومُ نَجَازَهْ
وَمَتَى ٱهْتَزَّ لِلدَّنَاءَةِ نِكْسٌ   عَافَ طَبْعِي طِبَاعَهُ وَٱهْتِزَازَهْ
فَٱلْمَنَايَا وَلَا ٱلدَّنَايَا وَخَيْرٌ   مِنْ رُكُوبِ ٱلْخَنَا رُكُوبُ ٱلْجِنَازَهْ

١ ف: ما استروح نفسي ولا استراح نَفَسي. ٢ ف: يُحِلّ.

٥،٢٧ ثُمَّ رَفَعَ إِلَيَّ طَرْفَهُ. وَقَالَ لِأَمْرٍ مَا جَدَعَ قَصِيرٌ[١] أَنْفَهُ. فَأَخْبَرْتُهُ خَبَرَ نَاقَتِي السَّارِحَةِ. وَمَا عَانَيْتُهُ فِي يَوْمِي وَالْبَارِحَةِ. فَقَالَ دَعِ ٱلِالْتِفَاتَ. إِلَى مَا فَاتَ. وَالطِّمَاحَ. إِلَى مَا طَاحَ. وَلَا تَأْسَ عَلَى مَا ذَهَبَ. وَلَوْ أَنَّهُ وَادٍ مِنْ ذَهَبٍ. وَلَا تَسْتَمِلْ مَنْ مَالَ عَنْ رِيحِكَ. وَأَضْرِمْ نَارَ تَبَارِيحِكَ. وَلَوْ كَانَ ٱبْنَ بُوحِكَ. أَوْ شَقِيقَ رُوحِكَ.

٦،٢٧ ثُمَّ قَالَ هَلْ لَكَ فِي أَنْ نَقِيلَ. وَنَتَحَامَى[٢] الْقَالَ وَالْقِيلَ. فَإِنَّ الْأَبْدَانَ أَنْضَاءُ تَعَبٍ. وَالْهَاجِرَةَ ذَاتُ لَهَبٍ. وَلَنْ يَصْقُلَ الْخَاطِرَ. وَيُنَشِّطَ الْفَاتِرَ. كَقَائِلَةِ الْهَوَاجِرِ. وَخُصُوصًا فِي شَهْرَيْ نَاجِرٍ. فَقُلْتُ ذَاكَ إِلَيْكَ. وَمَا أُرِيدُ أَنْ أَشُقَّ عَلَيْكَ. فَٱفْتَرَشَ التُّرْبَ وَٱضْطَجَعَ. وَأَظْهَرَ أَنْ قَدْ هَجَعَ. وَٱرْتَفَقْتُ عَلَى أَنْ أَحْرُسَ. وَلَا أَنْعَسَ. فَأَخَذَتْنِي السِّنَةُ. إِذْ زُمَّتِ الْأَلْسِنَةُ. فَلَمْ أُفِقْ إِلَّا وَاللَّيْلُ قَدْ تَوَلَّجَ. وَالنَّجْمُ[٣] قَدْ تَبَلَّجَ. وَلَا السَّرُوجِيَّ وَلَا الْمُسْرَجَ.[٤] فَبِتُّ بِلَيْلَةٍ نَابِغِيَّةٍ. وَأَحْزَانٍ يَعْقُوبِيَّةٍ. أُسَاوِرُ الْوُجُومَ. وَأُسَاهِرُ النُّجُومَ. أُفَكِّرُ تَارَةً فِي رُجْلَتِي. وَأُخْرَى فِي رَجْعَتِي.

٧،٢٧ إِلَى أَنْ وَضَحَ لِي عِنْدَ ٱفْتِرَارِ ثَغْرِ الضَّوِّ.[٥] فِي وَجْهِ الْجَوِّ. رَاكِبٌ يَخِدُ فِي الدَّوِّ. فَأَلْمَعْتُ إِلَيْهِ بِثَوْبِي. وَرَجَوْتُ أَنْ يُعَرِّجَ إِلَى صَوْبِي. فَلَمْ يَعْبَأْ بِإِلْمَاعِي. وَلَا أَوَى لِٱلْتِيَاعِي. بَلْ سَارَ عَلَى هِينَتِهِ. وَأَصْمَانِي بِسَهْمِ إِهَانَتِهِ. فَأَوْفَضْتُ إِلَيْهِ لِأَسْتَرْدِفَهُ. وَأَحْتَمِلَ تَغَطْرُفَهُ. فَلَمَّا أَدْرَكْتُهُ بَعْدَ الْأَيْنِ. وَأَجَلْتُ فِيهِ مَسْرَحَ الْعَيْنِ. وَجَدْتُ نَاقَتِي مَطِيَّتَهُ. وَضَالَّتِي لُقْطَتَهُ. فَمَا كَذَّبْتُ أَنْ أَذْرَيْتُهُ عَنْ سَنَامِهَا. وَجَاذَبْتُهُ طَرَفَ زِمَامِهَا. وَقُلْتُ لَهُ أَنَا صَاحِبُهَا وَمُضِلُّهَا. وَلِي رِسْلُهَا وَنَسْلُهَا.

---

١ د: قُصَيْر. ٢ ف، و: تقيل وتحامى. ٣ ف: والصُّبح. ٤ «ولا السَّرُوجيَّ ولا المُسْرَجَ»: س: لا السروجيُّ ولا المُسْرَج. ٥ س، ق، د، ف: الضوء.

فَلَا تَكُنْ كَأَشْعَبَ. فَتُتْعِبَ وَتَتْعَبَ. فَأَخَذَ يَلْدَغُ وَيَصِئِي.[١] وَيَتَقَحُ وَلَا يَسْتَحِي. وَبَيْنَا هُوَ يَنْزُو وَيَلِينُ. وَيَسْتَأْسِدُ وَيَسْتَكِينُ. إِذْ غَشِيَنَا أَبُو زَيْدٍ لَابِسًا جِلْدَ النَّمِرِ. وَهَاجِمًا هُجُومَ السَّيْلِ الْمُنْهَمِرِ.

٨،٢٧ فَخِفْتُ وَاللهِ أَنْ يَكُونَ يَوْمُهُ كَأَمْسِهِ. وَبَدْرُهُ مِثْلَ شَمْسِهِ. فَأَلْحَقَ بِالْقَارِظَيْنِ. وَأَصِيرَ خَبَرًا بَعْدَ عَيْنٍ. فَلَمْ أَرَ إِلَّا أَنْ أُذَكِّرَهُ الْعُهُودَ الْمَنْسِيَّةَ. وَالْفَعْلَةَ الْإِمْسِيَّةَ.[٢] وَنَاشَدْتُهُ اللهَ أَوَافَى الْيَوْمَ[٣] لِلتَّلَافِي. أَمْ لِمَا فِيهِ إِتْلَافِي. فَقَالَ مَعَاذَ اللهِ أَنْ أُجْهِزَ عَلَى مَكْلُومِي. أَوْ أَصِلَ حَرُورِي بِسَمُومِي. بَلْ وَافَيْتُكَ لِأَخْبُرَ كُنْهَ حَالِكَ. وَأَكُونَ يَمِينًا لِشِمَالِكَ. فَسَكَنَ عِنْدَ ذٰلِكَ جَاشِي. وَٱنْجَابَ ٱسْتِيحَاشِي. وَأَطْلَعْتُهُ طِلْعَ اللِّقْحَةِ. وَتَبَرْقُعَ صَاحِبِي بِالْقِحَةِ. فَنَظَرَ إِلَيْهِ نَظَرَ لَيْثِ الْعِرِّيسَةِ. إِلَى الْفَرِيسَةِ. ثُمَّ أَشْرَعَ قِبَلَهُ الرُّمْحَ. وَأَقْسَمَ لَهُ بِمَنْ أَنَارَ الصُّبْحَ. لَئِنْ لَمْ يَنْجُ مَنْجَى[٤] الذُّبَابِ. وَيَرْضَ مِنَ الْغَنِيمَةِ بِالْإِيَابِ. لَيُورِدَنَّ سِنَانَهُ وَرِيدَهُ. وَلَيَفْجَعَنَّ بِهِ وَلِيدَهُ وَوَدِيدَهُ. فَنَبَذَ زِمَامَ النَّاقَةِ وَحَاصَ. وَأَفْلَتَ وَلَهُ حُصَاصٌ. فَقَالَ لِي أَبُو زَيْدٍ تَسَلَّمْهَا وَتَسَنَّمْهَا. فَإِنَّهَا إِحْدَى الْحُسْنَيَيْنِ. وَوَيْلٌ أَهْوَنُ مِنْ وَيْلَيْنِ.

٩،٢٧ قَالَ الْحَارِثُ بْنُ هَمَّامٍ فَحِرْتُ بَيْنَ لَوْمِ أَبِي زَيْدٍ وَشُكْرِهِ. وَزِنَةِ نَفْعِهِ بِضُرِّهِ. فَكَأَنَّهُ نُوجِيَ بِذَاتِ صَدْرِي. أَوْ تَكَهَّنَ مَا خَامَرَ سِرِّي. فَقَابَلَنِي بِوَجْهٍ طَلِيقٍ. وَأَنْشَدَ بِلِسَانٍ ذَلِيقٍ.

يَا أَخِي الْحَامِلَ ضَيْمِي   دُونَ إِخْوَانِي وَقَوْمِي
إِنْ يَكُنْ سَاءَكَ أَمْسِي   فَلَقَدْ سَرَّكَ يَوْمِي
فَاغْتَفِرْ ذَاكَ لِهٰذَا   وَٱطَّرِحْ شُكْرِي وَلَوْمِي

---

١ ف: يصي. ٢ د: الأَمسية. ٣ ليس في س. ٤ د: منجأ.

ثُمَّ قَالَ أَنَا تَئِقٌ. وَأَنْتَ مَئِقٌ. فَكَيْفَ نَتَّفِقُ. وَوَلَّى[١] يَفْرِي أَدِيمَ ٱلْأَرْضِ. وَيَرْكُضُ طِرْفَهُ أَيَّمَا رَكْضٍ. فَمَا عَدَوْتُ أَنِ ٱقْتَعَدْتُ مَطِيَّتِي. وَعُدْتُ لِطِيَّتِي. حَتَّى وَصَلْتُ إِلَى حِلَّتِي. بَعْدَ ٱللَّتَيَّا وَٱلَّتِي.

تَفْسِيرُ مَا أُودِعَ هٰذِهِ ٱلْمَقَامَةَ مِنَ ٱلْأَلْفَاظِ ٱللُّغَوِيَّةِ وَٱلْأَمْثَالِ ٱلْعَرَبِيَّةِ

١٠،٢٧ قَوْلُهُ رَيْقُ زَمَانِي يَعْنِي أَوَّلَهُ وَرَائِقَهُ وَقَدْ يُشَدَّدُ فَيُقَالُ[٢] رَيِّقٌ.[٣] وَقَوْلُهُ آخُذُ إِخْذَ نُفُوسِهِمْ[٤] يَعْنِي أَقْتَدِي بِهِمْ يُقَالُ مِنْهُ أَخَذَ إِخْذَهُ وَأَخْذَهُ بِكَسْرِ ٱلْهَمْزَةِ وَفَتْحِهَا. وَٱلْهَجْمَةُ نَحْوَ ٱلْمَائَةِ مِنَ ٱلْإِبِلِ وَٱلثَّلَّةُ ٱلْقَطِيعُ مِنَ ٱلْغَنَمِ. وَٱلرَّاغِيَةُ مِنَ[٥] ٱلْإِبِلِ وَٱلنَّاغِيَةُ ٱلشَّاءُ وَمِنْهُ قَوْلُهُمْ مَا لَهُ رَاغِيَةٌ وَلَا نَاغِيَةٌ أَيْ لَا نَاقَةٌ وَلَا شَاةٌ. وَقَوْلُهُ أَرْدَافُ أَقْيَالٍ أَيْ يَخْلُفُونَ ٱلْمُلُوكَ إِذَا غَابُوا. وَقَوْلُهُ أَبْنَاءُ أَقْوَالٍ أَيْ فُصَحَاءُ يُقَالُ لِلْمِنْطِيقِ إِنَّهُ ٱبْنُ أَقْوَالٍ. وَقَوْلُهُ فَتَدَثَّرْتُ فَرَسًا مِحْضَارًا ٱلتَّدَثُّرُ ٱلْوُثُوبُ عَلَى ظَهْرِ ٱلْفَرَسِ وَٱلْمِحْضَارُ وَٱلْمِحْضِيرُ ٱلشَّدِيدُ ٱلْعَدْوِ مَأْخُوذٌ مِنَ ٱلْحُضْرِ.[٦] وَقَوْلُهُ أَقْتَرِي كُلَّ شَجْرَاءَ وَمَرْدَاءَ ٱلِاقْتِرَاءُ تَتَبُّعُ ٱلْأَرْضِ وَٱلشَّجْرَاءُ ذَاتُ ٱلشَّجَرِ وَٱلْمَرْدَاءُ ٱلْخَالِيَةُ مِنَ ٱلنَّبَاتِ وَمِنْهُ ٱشْتِقَاقُ ٱلْأَمْرَدِ لِخُلُوِّ وَجْهِهِ مِنَ ٱلشَّعْرِ.

١١،٢٧ وَقَوْلُهُ حَيْعَلَ ٱلدَّاعِي إِلَى صَلَاتِهِ يَعْنِي بِهِ قَوْلَ ٱلْمُؤَذِّنِ حَيَّ عَلَى ٱلصَّلَاوةِ حَيَّ عَلَى ٱلْفَلَاحِ وَٱلْمَصْدَرُ مِنْهُ ٱلْحَيْعَلَةُ وَمِثْلُهُ مِنَ ٱلْمَصَادِرِ[٧] ٱلْهَيْلَلَةُ وَٱلْحَمْدَلَةُ وَٱلْحَوْقَلَةُ وَٱلْبَسْمَلَةُ وَٱلْحَسْبَلَةُ وَٱلسَّبْحَلَةُ وَٱلْجَعْفَلَةُ فَٱلْهَيْلَلَةُ حِكَايَةُ قَوْلِ لَا إِلٰهَ إِلَّا

١ د: ثم ولى. ٢ عدها في س: الياء. ٣ «وقد يشدد ويقال ريق»: في ف: وقد يخفف فيقال ريْق. ٤ بعدها في د: الأبية. ٥ في ق فقط. ٦ بعده في ف: وهو العدو. ٧ من المصادر: ليس في س.

اللهُ وَالْحَمْدَلَةُ حِكَايَةُ قَوْلِ الْحَمْدُ لِلهِ وَالْحَوْقَلَةُ حِكَايَةُ قَوْلِ لَا حَوْلَ وَلَا قُوَّةَ إِلَّا بِاللهِ وَالْبَسْمَلَةُ حِكَايَةُ قَوْلِ بِسْمِ اللهِ وَالْحَسْبَلَةُ حِكَايَةُ قَوْلِ حَسْبُنَا اللهُ وَالسَّبْحَلَةُ حِكَايَةُ قَوْلِ سُبْحَانَ اللهِ وَالْجَعْفَلَةُ حِكَايَةُ قَوْلِ جُعِلْتُ فِدَاكَ. وَقَوْلُهُ نَزَلْتُ عَنْ مَتْنِ الرَّكُوبَةِ يَعْنِي الْمَرْكُوبَةَ يُقَالُ نَاقَةٌ رَكُوبٌ وَرَكُوبَةٌ وَحَلُوبٌ وَحَلُوبَةٌ وَقَدْ قُرِئَ ﴿فَمِنْهَا رَكُوبَتُهُمْ﴾. وَالصَّهْوَةُ مَقْعَدُ الْفَارِسِ وَالشَّجْوَةُ الْخُطْوَةُ وَالْجِزْعُ قَطْعُ الْوَادِي عَرْضًا. وَقَوْلُهُ صَكَّةَ عُمَيٍّ يَعْنِي بِهِ قَائِمَ الظَّهِيرَةِ وَقَدِ اخْتُلِفَ فِي أَصْلِهِ فَقِيلَ كَانَ عُمَيٌّ رَجُلًا مِغْوَارًا فَغَزَا قَوْمًا عِنْدَ قَائِمِ الظَّهِيرَةِ وَصَكَّهُمْ صَكَّةً شَدِيدَةً فَصَارَ مَثَلًا لِكُلِّ مَنْ جَاءَ ذٰلِكَ الْوَقْتَ وَقِيلَ الْمُرَادُ[١] بِهِ الظَّبْيُ لِأَنَّهُ يَسْدَرُ[٢] فِي الْهَوَاجِرِ فَيَصْطَكُّ بِمَا يَسْتَقْبِلُهُ كَاصْطِكَاكِ الْأَعْمَى ثُمَّ صُغِّرَ الْأَعْمَى تَصْغِيرَ التَّرْخِيمِ فَقِيلَ عُمَيٌّ كَمَا صَغَّرُوا أَسْوَدَ وَأَزْهَرَ فَقَالُوا سُوَيْدٌ وَزُهَيْرٌ. وَقَوْلُهُ كَانَ يَوْمًا أَطْوَلَ مِنْ ظِلِّ الْقَنَاةِ يُوصَفُ الْيَوْمُ الطَّوِيلُ بِظِلِّ الْقَنَاةِ كَمَا يُوصَفُ الْيَوْمُ الْقَصِيرُ بِإِبْهَامِ الْقَطَاةِ وَالْعَرَبُ يَزْعُمُونَ أَنَّ ظِلَّ الرُّمْحِ أَطْوَلُ ظِلٍّ وَمِنْهُ قَوْلُ الشَّاعِرِ[٣] شُبْرُمَةَ بْنِ الطُّفَيْلِ[٤]

وَيَوْمٍ كَظِلِّ الرُّمْحِ قَصَّرَ طُولَهُ ... دَمُ الزِّقِّ عَنَّا وَاصْطِفَاقُ الْمَزَاهِرِ

١٢،٢٧ وَقَوْلُهُ أَحَرُّ مِنْ دَمْعِ الْمِقْلَاتِ الْمِقْلَاتُ الْمَرْأَةُ الَّتِي لَا يَعِيشُ لَهَا وَلَدٌ فَدَمْعُهَا أَبَدًا حَارٌّ لِحُزْنِهَا لِأَنَّهُ يُقَالُ إِنَّ دَمْعَةَ الْحُزْنِ حَارَّةٌ وَدَمْعَةَ السُّرُورِ بَارِدَةٌ وَلِهٰذَا قِيلَ لِلْمَدْعُوِّ لَهُ أَقَرَّ اللهُ عَيْنَهُ مَأْخُوذٌ مِنَ الْقُرِّ وَهُوَ الْبَرْدُ وَقِيلَ لِلْمَدْعُوِّ عَلَيْهِ أَسْخَنَ اللهُ عَيْنَكَ مَأْخُوذٌ مِنَ السُّخْنَةِ وَهِيَ الْحَرَارَةُ وَقِيلَ إِنَّ إِقْرَارَ الْعَيْنِ مَأْخُوذٌ مِنَ الْقَرَارِ فَكَأَنَّهُ دَعَا لَهُ أَنْ يُرْزَقَ مَا يُقِرُّ عَيْنَهُ حَتَّى لَا يَطْمَحُ إِلَى مَا لِغَيْرِهِ وَكَانَتْ

١ و: أُرِيدَ. ٢ د: يسدُر. ٣ ليس في س، ف. ٤ شبرمة بن الطفيل: ليس في د.

الْجَاهِلِيَّةُ تَزْعُمُ أَنَّ الْمِقْلَاتَ إِذَا وَطِئَتْ عَلَى قَتِيلٍ عَاشَ وَلَدُهَا وَإِلَى هٰذَا أَشَارَ بِشْرُ بْنُ أَبِي خَازِمٍ فِي قَوْلِهِ

تَظَلُّ مَقَالِيتُ النِّسَاءِ يَطَأْنَهُ يَقُلْنَ أَلَا يُلْقَى عَلَى الْمَرْءِ مِئْزَرُ

وَقَوْلُهُ عَلِقَتْ بِي شَعُوبُ يَعْنِي الْمَنِيَّةَ وَلَا يَدْخُلُ هٰذَا الاِسْمَ أَدَاةُ التَّعْرِيفِ مِثْلُ دِجْلَةَ وَعَرَفَةَ. وَقَوْلُهُ أُغَوِّرُ تَحْتَهَا إِلَى الْمُغَيْرِبَانِ التَّغْوِيرُ النُّزُولُ لِلْقَائِلَةِ كَمَا أَنَّ التَّعْرِيسَ النُّزُولُ آخِرَ اللَّيْلِ لِلتَّهْوِيمِ أَوِ الاِسْتِرَاحَةِ وَالْمُغَيْرِبَانُ تَصْغِيرُ الْمَغْرِبِ وَكَانَ قِيَاسُ تَصْغِيرِهِ الْمُغَيْرِبُ إِلَّا أَنَّ الْعَرَبَ أَلْحَقَتْ[1] آخِرَهُ أَلِفًا وَنُونًا عَلَى طَرِيقِ الشُّذُوذِ.

١٣،٢٧ وَقَوْلُهُ مُضْطَغِنًا أُهْبَةَ تَجْوَابِهِ الاِضْطِغَانُ أَنْ يَحْمِلَ الشَّيْءَ تَحْتَ حِضْنِهِ وَالاِضْطِبَانُ أَنْ يَجْعَلَهُ تَحْتَ ضِبْنِهِ وَالضِّبْنُ مَا بَيْنَ الْإِبْطِ وَالْكَشْحِ وَكِلَاهُمَا مُتَقَارِبٌ وَيُقَالُ أَنَّ[2] أَوَّلَ مَرَاتِبِ الْحَمْلِ الْإِبْطُ ثُمَّ يَلِيهِ[3] الضِّبْنُ وَهُوَ أَسْفَلُ الْإِبْطِ[4] ثُمَّ[5] الْحِضْنُ وَهُوَ عِنْدَ الْجَنْبِ[6] وَالتَّجْوَابُ مَصْدَرُ جَابَ وَجَمِيعُ الْمَصَادِرِ الَّتِي جَاءَتْ عَلَى تَفْعَالٍ هِيَ بِفَتْحِ التَّاءِ إِلَّا قَوْلُهُمْ تِبْيَانٌ وَتِلْقَاءٌ لَا غَيْرَ[7] وَقَوْلُهُ عُجَرِي وَبُجَرِي يُرِيدُ بِهِ جَمِيعَ أَمْرِي الظَّاهِرَ وَالْبَاطِنَ وَأَصْلُ الْعُجَرِ الْعُقَدُ النَّاتِيَةُ فِي الْعَصَبِ وَالْبُجَرُ الْعُقَدُ النَّاتِيَةُ فِي الْبَطْنِ. وَقَوْلُهُ وَلَمْ يَقُلْ إِيهًا أَيْ لَمْ يَأْمُرْنِي بِالْكَفِّ يُقَالُ لِلْمُسْتَزَادِ إِيهِ وَلِلْمُسْتَكَفِّ إِيهًا وَقَوْلُهُ لِأَمْرٍ مَّا جَدَعَ قَصِيرٌ أَنْفَهُ قَصِيرٌ هٰذَا مَوْلَى جَذِيمَةَ[8] الْأَبْرَشِ وَكَانَ جَدَعَ أَنْفَهُ بِيَدِهِ حِينَ قَتَلَتِ الزَّبَّاءُ مَوْلَاهُ ثُمَّ أَتَاهَا وَأَوْهَمَهَا أَنَّ

١ بعدها فوق السطر في ق: في. ٢ يقال أن: في ق فقط. ٣ ليس في د، وفي ق: تحته. ٤ «وهو أسفل الإبط»: ليس في ق. ٥ بعدها في ق: تحته. ٦ من «وكلاهما متقارب» إلى هاهنا في هامش ق. ٧ بعدها في هامش س: وقيل تنصال؛ وفي و: وزاد بعضهم تنصال؛ وبعدها في د: وقال بعضهم تنضال (هكذا) أيضا؛ وبعدها في ف: وزاد بعضهم تيصال. ٨ من «الأبرش» إلى هاهنا موجود جزئيا في هامش ق، وفي متن باقي النسخ.

عَمْرَو بْنَ عَدِيٍّ ٱبْنَ أُخْتِ جَذِيمَةَ هُوَ ٱلَّذِي جَدَعَ أَنْفَهُ ٱتِّهَامًا لَهُ بِأَنَّهُ غَشَّ خَالَهُ جَذِيمَةَ إِذَا أَشَارَ عَلَيْهِ بِقَصْدِهَا فَحَظِيَ بِهٰذَا ٱلْقَوْلِ عِنْدَهَا حَتَّى جَهَّزَتْهُ مِرَارًا إِلَى ٱلْعِرَاقِ فَكَانَ يَأْتِيهَا بِالطُّرَفِ مِنْهُ إِلَى أَنِ ٱسْتَصْحَبَ فِي آخِرِ نَوْبَةٍ ٱلرِّجَالَ فِي ٱلصَّنَادِيقِ فَتَوَصَّلَ إِلَى قَتْلِهَا وَٱلْأَخْذِ بِثَأْرِ مَوْلَاهُ مِنْهَا وَقِصَّتُهُ مَشْهُورَةٌ.

١٤،٢٧ وَقَوْلُهُ وَلَوْ كَانَ ٱبْنَ بُوحِكَ يَعْنِي وَلَدَ ٱلصُّلْبِ إِشَارَةً إِلَى أَنَّهُ وُلِدَ فِي بَاحَةِ ٱلدَّارِ وَهِيَ عَرْصَتُهَا وَجَمْعُهَا بُوحٌ وَقِيلَ إِنَّ ٱلْبُوحَ مِنْ أَسْمَاءِ ٱلذَّكَرِ. وَقَوْلُهُ شَهْرَا[١] نَاجِرٍ هُمَا شَهْرَا ٱلْحَرِّ وَقِيلَ إِنَّهُمَا حَزِيرَانُ وَتَمُّوزُ وَأَنْكَرَ[٢] ٱبْنُ دُرَيْدٍ هٰذَا ٱلْقَوْلَ وَقَالَ هُمَا طُلُوعُ نَجْمَيْنِ. وَقَوْلُهُ بِتُّ[٣] بِلَيْلَةٍ نَابِغِيَّةٍ أَوْمَأَ بِهِ إِلَى قَوْلِ ٱلنَّابِغَةِ «فَبِتُّ كَأَنِّي سَاوَرَتْنِي ضَئِيلَةٌ»[٤] ٱلْبَيْتَ[٥] وَقَوْلُهُ أَلْمَعْتُ إِلَيْهِ بِثَوْبِي يَعْنِي أَشَرْتُ يُقَالُ مِنْهُ أَلْمَعَ وَلَمَعَ بِمَعْنًى. وَقَوْلُهُ يَلْدَغُ وَيَصِيءُ هٰذَا مَثَلٌ يُضْرَبُ لِمَنْ يَظْلِمُ وَيَشْكُو يُقَالُ صَأَتِ ٱلْعَقْرَبُ تَصِيءُ صَئِيًّا[٦] بِفَتْحِ ٱلصَّادِ وَكَسْرِهَا إِذَا صَوَّتَتْ وَكَذٰلِكَ ٱلْفَرْخُ وَمَا أَحْسَنَ قَوْلَ ٱبْنِ ٱلرُّومِيِّ فِي هٰذَا ٱلْمَعْنَى

تُشْكِي ٱلْمُحِبَّ وَتَشْكُو وَهِيَ ظَالِمَةٌ   كَٱلْقَوْسِ تُصْمِي ٱلرَّمَايَا وَهِيَ مِرْنَانُ

وَقَوْلُهُ يَنْزُو وَيَلِينُ هٰذَا ٱلْمَثَلُ يُضْرَبُ لِمَنْ يَتَعَزَّزُ ثُمَّ يَذِلُّ وَيُقَالُ إِنَّ أَصْلَهُ ٱلْجَدْيُ يَنْزُو وَهُوَ صَغِيرٌ فَإِذَا كَبِرَ لَانَ. وَقَوْلُهُ لَابِسًا جِلْدَ ٱلنَّمِرِ هٰذَا ٱلْمَثَلُ يُضْرَبُ لِلْمُتَقَحِّمِ ٱلْجَرِيءِ لِأَنَّ ٱلنَّمِرَ أَجْرَأُ سَبُعٍ وَأَقَلُّهُ ٱحْتِمَالًا لِلضَّيْمِ وَمِنْ هٰذَا ٱشْتِقَاقُ قَوْلِهِمْ تَنَمَّرَ أَيْ صَارَ مِثْلَ ٱلنَّمِرِ.

---

١ في س، و، د، ف: شهري. ٢ بعدها في س، و، د: أبو بكر. ٣ ليس في و. ٤ في هامش ق: باقي البيت مِنَ الرَّقْشِ في أَنْيابِها السَّمُّ ناقِعُ، وهو في متن سائر النسخ. ٥ في ق فقط. ٦ س، و، د، ف: صَئِيًا وصِئِيًا.

١٥،٢٧ وَقَوْلُهُ فَأَلْحَقَ بِالْقَارِظَيْنِ الْأَصْلُ فِي الْقَارِظِ أَنَّهُ الَّذِي يَجْنِي الْقَرَظَ وَهُوَ النَّبَاتُ الْمَدْبُوغُ بِهِ وَالْقَارِظَانِ الْمُشَارُ إِلَيْهِمَا أَحَدُهُمَا مِنْ عَنَزَةَ وَالْآخَرُ مِنَ النَّمِرِ بْنِ قَاسِطٍ وَكَانَا خَرَجَا يَجْنِيَانِ[1] الْقَرَظَ فَلَمْ يَرْجِعَا وَلَا عُرِفَ لَهُمَا خَبَرٌ فَضُرِبَ بِهِمَا الْمَثَلُ لِكُلِّ غَائِبٍ لَا يُرْجَى إِيَابُهُ وَإِلَيْهِمَا أَشَارَ أَبُو ذُؤَيْبٍ فِي قَوْلِهِ

وَحَتَّى يَؤُوبَ الْقَارِظَانِ كِلَاهُمَا ... وَيُنْشَرَ فِي الْقَتْلَى كُلَيْبٌ لِوَائِلِ

وَقَوْلُهُ[2] حَرُورِي بِسَمُومِي الْحَرُورُ الرِّيحُ الْحَارَّةُ لَيْلًا وَالسَّمُومُ الرِّيحُ الْحَارَّةُ نَهَارًا وَقَدْ تُقَامُ إِحْدَاهُمَا مُقَامَ الْأُخْرَى مَجَازًا وَقَالَ بَعْضُهُمُ الْحَرُورُ يَكُونُ لَيْلًا وَنَهَارًا وَالسَّمُومُ لَا يَكُونُ إِلَّا نَهَارًا.[3] وَقَوْلُهُ لَيْثُ الْعِرِّيسَةِ يَعْنِي مَأْوَى السَّبُعِ يُقَالُ فِيهِ عِرِّيسٌ وَعِرِّيسَةٌ بِإِثْبَاتِ الْهَاءِ وَحَذْفِهَا كَمَا يُقَالُ غَابٌ وَغَابَةٌ وَعَرِينٌ وَعَرِينَةٌ فَأَمَّا الْغِيلُ وَالْخِيسُ فَلَمْ يُلْحِقُوا بِهِمَا الْهَاءَ. وَقَوْلُهُ أَفْلَتَ وَلَهُ حُصَاصٌ هٰذَا الْمَثَلُ يُضْرَبُ لِمَنْ نَجَا مِنْ هَلَكَةٍ أَشْفَى عَلَيْهَا بَعْدَ مَا كَادَ يَهْوِي فِيهَا وَالْحُصَاصُ الْعَدْوُ وَقِيلَ إِنَّهُ الضُّرَاطُ. وَقَوْلُهُ وَيْلٌ أَهْوَنُ مِنْ وَيْلَيْنِ هٰذَا الْمَثَلُ يُضْرَبُ تَسْلِيَةً لِمَنْ نَالَهُ بَعْضُ الْمَكْرُوهِ وَمِثْلُهُ قَوْلُ الشَّاعِرِ[4] «وَبَعْضُ الشَّرِّ أَهْوَنُ مِنْ بَعْضٍ».[5]

١٦،٢٧ وَقَوْلُهُ أَنَا تَئِقٌ وَأَنْتَ مَئِقٌ فَكَيْفَ نَتَّفِقُ هٰذَا الْمَثَلُ يُضْرَبُ لِلْمُتَنَافِيَيْنِ فِي الْخُلُقِ فَإِنَّ التَّئِقَ هُوَ الْمُمْتَلِئُ غَيْظًا مَأْخُوذٌ مِنْ قَوْلِهِمْ أَتْأَقْتُ الْإِنَاءَ إِذَا مَلَأْتَهُ وَالْمَئِقُ هُوَ الْبَاكِي فَكَأَنَّ التَّئِقَ يَنْزَعُ إِلَى الشَّرِّ لِغَيْظِهِ وَالْمَئِقُ يَضِيقُ ذَرْعًا بِاحْتِمَالِهِ.[6] وَقَوْلُهُ

١ و: يجتنيان. ٢ بعدها في د: أصل. ٣ «وقال بعضهم الحرور يكون ليلا ونهارا والسموم لا يكون إلا نهارًا»: في هامش ق، وفي متنَيْ س، ف: وقال بعضهم الحرور يكون ليلا ونهارا والسموم يختص بالنهار؛ وفي متن و: وذُكِرَ أنّ الحرور يكون ليلا ونهارا والسموم يختص بالنهار. ٤ ف: الراجز. ٥ «وبَعْضُ الشَّرِّ أَهْوَنُ من بَعْضٍ»: و: حَنانَيْكَ بعض الشر أهون من بعض؛ وفي د، ف: أبا مُنْذِرٍ أفْنَيْتَ فاسْتَبْقِ بعضَنا / حُنانَيْكَ بعض الشر أهون من بعض. ٦ في هامش س: ومثله قولهم أنا كَلِفٌ وأنت صَلِفٌ فمتى نأتَلِفُ؛ وفي هامش و: ومثله قولهم أنا كَلِفٌ وأنت صَلِفٌ فكيف نأتَلِفُ؛ وفي متن ف: ومثله قول بعضهم أنا كَلِفٌ وأنت صَلِفٌ فكيف نأتَلِفُ.

لِطِيَّتِي يَعْنِي لِقَصْدِي وَوِجْهَتِي وَقَدْ يُقَالُ فِيهَا طِيَةٌ بِالتَّخْفِيفِ. وَقَوْلُهُ بَعْدَ اللَّتَيَّا وَالَّتِي اللَّتَيَّا تَصْغِيرُ الَّتِي وَهُوَ عَلَى غَيْرِ قِيَاسِ التَّصْغِيرِ الْمُطَّرِدِ لِأَنَّ الْقِيَاسَ أَنْ يُضَمَّ أَوَّلُ الاِسْمِ إِذَا صُغِّرَ وَقَدْ أُقِرَّ هٰذَا الاِسْمُ عَلَى فَتْحَتِهِ الْأَصْلِيَّةِ عِنْدَ تَصْغِيرِهِ إِلَّا أَنَّ الْعَرَبَ عَوَّضَتْهُ عَنْ ضَمِّ أَوَّلِهِ بِأَنْ زَادَتْ أَلِفًا فِي آخِرِهِ وَأَجْرَتْ أَسْمَاءَ الْإِشَارَةِ عِنْدَ تَصْغِيرِهَا عَلَى حُكْمِهِ فَقَالَتْ فِي تَصْغِيرِ الَّذِي وَالَّتِي اللَّذَيَّا وَاللَّتَيَّا وَفِي تَصْغِيرِ ذَا وَذَاكَ ذَيَّا وَذَيَّاكَ[1] وَقَدِ ٱخْتُلِفَ فِي مَعْنَى قَوْلِهِمْ بَعْدَ اللَّتَيَّا وَالَّتِي فَقِيلَ هُمَا مِنْ أَسْمَاءِ الدَّاهِيَةِ وَقِيلَ الْمُرَادُ بِهِمَا بَعْدَ[2] صَغِيرِ الْمَكْرُوهِ وَكَبِيرِهِ.

١ ذَيَّا وذَيَّاك: سقطت من ف. ٢ ليس في و.

الْمَقَامَةُ الثَّامِنَةُ وَالْعِشْرُونَ[1]

١،٢٨ أَخْبَرَ الْحَارِثُ بْنُ هَمَّامٍ قَالَ ٱسْتَبْضَعْتُ فِي بَعْضِ أَسْفَارِيَ الْقَنْدَ. وَقَصَدْتُ بِهِ[2] سَمَرْقَنْدَ. وَكُنْتُ يَوْمَئِذٍ قَوِيمَ الشَّطَاطِ. جَمُومَ النَّشَاطِ. أَرْمِي عَنْ قَوْسِ الْمِرَاحِ. إِلَى غَرَضِ الْأَفْرَاحِ. وَأَسْتَعِينُ بِمَاءِ الشَّبَابِ. عَلَى مَلَامِحِ السَّرَابِ. فَوَافَيْتُهَا بُكْرَةَ عَرُوبَةَ. بَعْدَ أَنْ كَابَدْتُ الصُّعُوبَةَ. فَسَعَيْتُ وَمَا وَنَيْتُ. إِلَى أَنْ حَصَلَ الْبَيْتُ. فَلَمَّا نَقَلْتُ إِلَيْهِ قَنْدِي. وَمَلَكْتُ قَوْلَ عِنْدِي. عُجْتُ إِلَى الْحَمَّامِ عَلَى الْأَثَرِ. فَأَمَطْتُ عَنِّي وَعْثَاءَ السَّفَرِ. وَأَخَذْتُ فِي غُسْلِ الْجُمْعَةِ بِالْأَثَرِ. ثُمَّ بَادَرْتُ فِي هَيْئَةِ الْخَاشِعِ. إِلَى مَسْجِدِهَا الْجَامِعِ. لِأَلْحَقَ بِمَنْ يَقْرُبُ مِنَ الْإِمَامِ. وَيُقَرِّبُ أَفْضَلَ الْأَنْعَامِ.

٢،٢٨ فَحَظِيتُ بِأَنْ جَلَّيْتُ فِي الْحَلْبَةِ. وَتَخَيَّرْتُ الْمَرْكَزَ لِاسْتِمَاعِ الْخُطْبَةِ. وَلَمْ يَزَلِ النَّاسُ ﴿يَدْخُلُونَ فِي دِينِ ٱللَّهِ أَفْوَاجًا﴾. وَيَرِدُونَ فُرَادَى وَأَزْوَاجًا. حَتَّى إِذَا ٱكْتَظَّ الْجَامِعُ بِحَفْلِهِ. وَأَظَلَّ تَسَاوِي الشَّخْصِ وَظِلِّهِ. بَرَزَ الْخَطِيبُ فِي أُهْبَتِهِ. مُتَهَادِيًا خَلْفَ عُصْبَتِهِ. فَٱرْتَقَى فِي مِنْبَرِ الدَّعْوَةِ. إِلَى أَنْ مَثَلَ بِالذِّرْوَةِ. فَسَلَّمَ مُشِيرًا بِالْيَمِينِ. ثُمَّ جَلَسَ حَتَّى خُتِمَ نَظْمُ التَّأْذِينِ. ثُمَّ قَامَ وَقَالَ

٣،٢٨ الْحَمْدُ لِلّٰهِ الْمَمْدُوحِ الْأَسْمَاءِ. الْمَحْمُودِ الْآلَاءِ. الْوَاسِعِ الْعَطَاءِ. الْمَدْعُوِّ لِحَسْمِ اللَّأْوَاءِ. مَالِكِ الْأُمَمِ. وَمُصَوِّرِ الرِّمَمِ. وَأَهْلِ[3] السَّمَاحِ وَالْكَرَمِ. وَمُهْلِكِ عَادٍ وَإِرَمَ. أَدْرَكَ كُلَّ سِرٍّ عِلْمُهُ. وَوَسِعَ كُلَّ مُصِرٍّ حِلْمُهُ. وَعَمَّ كُلَّ عَالَمٍ طَوْلُهُ.

١ في هامش س: وتعرف بالسمرقندية؛ د: بالسَّمَرْقَنْدِيَّة؛ ف: وهي بالسمرقندية. ٢ ليس في و. ٣ د: ومُكْرِم أهل.

وَهَدَّ كُلَّ مَارِدٍ حَوْلَهُ. أَحْمَدُهُ حَمْدَ مُوَحِّدٍ مُسْلِمٍ. وَأَدْعُوهُ دُعَاءَ مُؤَمِّلٍ مُسَلِّمٍ. وَهُوَ اللّٰهُ لَا إِلٰهَ إِلَّا هُوَ الْوَاحِدُ الْأَحَدُ. الْعَادِلُ الصَّمَدُ. لَا وَلَدَ لَهُ وَلَا وَالِدَ.[1] وَلَا رِدْءَ مَعَهُ وَلَا مُسَاعِدَ. أَرْسَلَ مُحَمَّدًا لِلْإِسْلَامِ مُمَهِّدًا. وَلِلْمِلَّةِ مُوَطِّدًا. وَلِأَدِلَّةِ الرُّسُلِ مُؤَكِّدًا. وَلِلْأَسْوَدِ وَالْأَحْمَرِ مُسَدِّدًا. وَصَلَ الْأَرْحَامَ. وَعَلَّمَ الْأَحْكَامَ. وَوَسَمَ الْحَلَالَ وَالْحَرَامَ. وَرَسَمَ الْإِحْلَالَ وَالْإِحْرَامَ. كَرَّمَ اللّٰهُ مَحَلَّهُ. وَكَمَّلَ الصَّلَاةَ وَالسَّلَامَ لَهُ. وَرَحِمَ آلَهُ الْكُرَمَاءَ. وَأَهْلَهُ الرُّحَمَاءَ. مَا هَمَرَ رُكَامٌ. وَهَدَرَ حَمَامٌ. وَسَرَحَ سَوَامٌ. وَسَطَا حُسَامٌ.

٤،٢٨ اِعْمَلُوا رَحِمَكُمُ اللّٰهُ عَمَلَ الصُّلَحَاءِ. وَاكْدَحُوا لِمَعَادِكُمْ كَدْحَ الْأَصِحَّاءِ. وَارْدَعُوا أَهْوَاءَكُمْ رَدْعَ الْأَعْدَاءِ. وَأَعِدُّوا لِلرِّحْلَةِ إِعْدَادَ السُّعَدَاءِ. وَادَّرِعُوا حُلَلَ الْوَرَعِ. وَدَاوُوا عِلَلَ الطَّمَعِ. وَسَوُّوا أَوَدَ الْعَمَلِ. وَعَاصُوا وَسَاوِسَ الْأَمَلِ. وَصَوِّرُوا لِأَوْهَامِكُمْ حُؤُولَ الْأَحْوَالِ. وَحُلُولَ الْأَهْوَالِ. وَمُسَاوَرَةَ الْأَعْلَالِ. وَمُصَارَمَةَ الْمَالِ[2] وَالْآلِ. وَادَّكِرُوا الْحِمَامَ وَسَكْرَةَ مَصْرَعِهِ. وَالرَّمْسَ وَهَوْلَ مُطَّلَعِهِ.[3] وَاللَّحْدَ وَوَحْدَةَ مُودَعِهِ. وَالْمَلَكَ وَرَوْعَةَ سُؤَالِهِ وَمَطْلَعِهِ. وَالْمَحُوا الدَّهْرَ وَلُؤْمَ كَرِّهِ. وَسُوءَ مِحَالِهِ وَمَكْرِهِ. كَمْ طَمَسَ مَعْلَمًا. وَأَمَرَّ مَطْعَمًا. وَطَحْطَحَ عَرَمْرَمًا. وَدَمَّرَ مَلِكًا مُكَرَّمًا. هَمُّهُ سَكُّ الْمَسَامِعِ. وَسَحُّ الْمَدَامِعِ. وَإِكْدَاءُ الْمَطَامِعِ. وَإِرْدَاءُ الْمُسْمِعِ وَالسَّامِعِ. عَمَّ حُكْمُهُ الْمُلُوكَ وَالرَّعَاعَ. وَالْمَسُودَ وَالْمُطَاعَ. وَالْمَحْسُودَ وَالْحُسَّادَ. وَالْأَسَاوِدَ وَالْآسَادَ. مَا مَوَّلَ إِلَّا مَالَ. وَعَكَسَ الْآمَالَ. وَلَا[4] وَصَلَ إِلَّا وَصَالَ. وَكَلَمَ الْأَوْصَالَ. وَلَا سَرَّ إِلَّا وَسَاءَ. وَلَؤُمَ وَأَسَاءَ. وَلَا أَصَحَّ إِلَّا وَلَّدَ الدَّاءَ. وَرَوَّعَ الْأَوِدَّاءَ.

١ و:لا ولد له والدُ؛ ف: لا ولدَ له ولا والدٍ. ٢ ف: مآل. ٣ ف: مَطْلَعِهِ. ٤ ف: وما.

٥،٢٨ اللهَ اللهَ. رَعَاكُمُ اللهُ. إِلَامَ مُدَاوَمَةُ اللَّهْوِ. وَمُوَاصَلَةُ السَّهْوِ. وَطُولُ الْإِصْرَارِ. وَحَمْلُ الْآصَارِ. وَاطِّرَاحُ كَلَامِ الْحُكَمَاءِ. وَمُعَاصَاةُ إِلٰهِ السَّمَاءِ. أَمَا الْهَرَمُ حَصَادُكُمْ. وَالْمَدَرُ مِهَادُكُمْ. أَمَا الْحِمَامُ مُدْرِكُكُمْ. وَالصِّرَاطُ مَسْلَكُكُمْ. أَمَا السَّاعَةُ مَوْعِدُكُمْ. وَالسَّاهِرَةُ مَوْرِدُكُمْ. أَمَا أَهْوَالُ الطَّامَّةِ لَكُمْ مُرْصَدَةٌ. أَمَا دَارُ الْعُصَاةِ الْحُطَمَةُ الْمُوصَدَةُ.[1] حَارِسُهُمْ مَالِكٌ. وَرُوَاؤُهُمْ حَالِكٌ. وَطَعَامُهُمُ السُّمُومُ. وَهَوَاؤُهُمُ السَّمُومُ. لَا مَالَ أَسْعَدَهُمْ وَلَا وَلَدَ. وَلَا عَدَدَ حَمَاهُمْ وَلَا عُدَدَ.

٦،٢٨ أَلَا رَحِمَ اللهُ آمْرَأً مَلَكَ هَوَاهُ. وَأَمَّ مَسَالِكَ هُدَاهُ. وَأَحْكَمَ طَاعَةَ مَوْلَاهُ. وَكَدَّ[2] لِرَوْحِ مَأْوَاهُ. وَعَمِلَ مَا دَامَ الْعُمْرُ مُطَاوِعًا. وَالدَّهْرُ مُوَادِعًا. وَالصِّحَّةُ كَامِلَةً. وَالسَّلَامَةُ حَاصِلَةً. وَإِلَّا دَهِمَهُ عَدَمُ الْمَرَامِ. وَحَصَرُ الْكَلَامِ. وَإِلْمَامُ الْآلَامِ. وَحُمُومُ الْحِمَامِ. وَهُدُوءُ[3] الْحَوَاسِّ. وَمِرَاسُ الْأَرْمَاسِ. آهًا[4] لَهَا حَسْرَةً أَلَمُهَا مُؤَكَّدٌ. وَأَمَدُهَا سَرْمَدٌ. وَمُمَارِسُهَا مُكْمَدٌ. مَا لِوَلَهِهِ حَاسِمٌ. وَلَا لِسَدَمِهِ رَاحِمٌ. وَلَا لَهُ مِمَّا عَرَاهُ عَاصِمٌ. أَلْهَمَكُمُ اللهُ أَحْمَدَ الْإِلْهَامِ. وَرَدَّاكُمْ رِدَاءَ الْإِكْرَامِ. وَأَحَلَّكُمْ دَارَ السَّلَامِ. وَأَسْأَلُهُ الرَّحْمَةَ لَكُمْ وَلِأَهْلِ مِلَّةِ الْإِسْلَامِ. وَهُوَ أَسْمَحُ الْكِرَامِ. وَالْمُسَلِّمُ وَالسَّلَامُ.

٧،٢٨ قَالَ الْحَارِثُ بْنُ هَمَّامٍ فَلَمَّا رَأَيْتُ الْخُطْبَةَ نُخْبَةً بِلَا سَقَطٍ. وَعَرُوسًا بِغَيْرِ نُقَطٍ. دَعَانِي الْإِعْجَابُ بِنَمَطِهَا الْعَجِيبِ. إِلَى آسْتِجْلَاءِ وَجْهِ الْخَطِيبِ. فَأَخَذْتُ أَتَوَسَّمُهُ جِدًّا. وَأُقَلِّبُ الطَّرْفَ فِيهِ مُجِدًّا. إِلَى أَنْ وَضَحَ لِي بِصِدْقِ الْعَلَامَاتِ. أَنَّهُ أَبُو زَيْدٍ ذُو[5] الْمَقَامَاتِ. وَلَمْ يَكُنْ بُدٌّ مِنَ الصَّمْتِ. فِي ذٰلِكَ الْوَقْتِ. فَأَمْسَكْتُ حَتَّى تَحَلَّلَ مِنَ[6] الْفَرْضِ. وَحَلَّ الِانْتِشَارُ فِي الْأَرْضِ. ثُمَّ وَاجَهْتُ

١ ف: مؤصدة. ٢ ف: كد وكدح. ٣ د، و، ف: هدوّ. ٤ ف: وآها. ٥ د: شيخنا ذو؛ ف: شيخنا صاحب. ٦ بعدها في د: النّفل.

تِلْقَاءَهُ. وَٱبْتَدَرْتُ لِقَاءَهُ. فَلَمَّا لَحَظَنِي خَفَّ فِي ٱلْقِيَامِ. وَأَحْفَى فِي ٱلْإِكْرَامِ. ثُمَّ ٱسْتَصْحَبَنِي إِلَى دَارِهِ. وَأَوْدَعَنِي خَصَائِصَ أَسْرَارِهِ.

٨،٢٨ وَحِينَ ٱنْتَشَرَ جَنَاحُ ٱلظَّلَامِ. وَحَانَ مِيقَاتُ ٱلْمَنَامِ. أَحْضَرَ أَبَارِيقَ ٱلْمُدَامِ. مَعْكُومَةً بِٱلْفِدَامِ. فَقُلْتُ أَتَحْسُوهَا أَمَامَ ٱلنَّوْمِ. وَأَنْتَ إِمَامُ ٱلْقَوْمِ. فَقَالَ مَهْ أَنَا بِٱلنَّهَارِ خَطِيبٌ. وَبِٱللَّيْلِ أَطِيبُ. فَقُلْتُ وَٱللهِ مَا أَدْرِي أَأَعْجَبُ مِنْ تَسَلِّيكَ عَنْ أُنَاسِكَ. وَمَسْقَطِ رَاسِكَ. أَمْ مِنْ خِطَابَتِكَ مَعَ أَدْنَاسِكَ. وَمَدَارِ كَاسِكَ. فَأَشَاحَ بِوَجْهِهِ عَنِّي. ثُمَّ قَالَ ٱسْمَعْ مِنِّي.

لَا تَبْكِ إِلْفًا نَأَى وَلَا دَارَا ... وَدُرْ مَعَ ٱلدَّهْرِ كَيْفَمَا دَارَا
وَٱتَّخِذِ ٱلنَّاسَ كُلَّهُمْ سَكَنًا ... وَمَثِّلِ ٱلْأَرْضَ كُلَّهَا دَارَا
وَٱصْبِرْ عَلَى خُلْقِ مَنْ تُعَاشِرُهُ ... وَدَارِهِ فَٱللَّبِيبُ مَنْ دَارَا
وَلَا تُضِعْ فُرْصَةَ ٱلسُّرُورِ فَمَا ... تَدْرِي أَيَوْمًا تَعِيشُ أَمْ دَارَا
وَٱعْلَمْ بِأَنَّ ٱلْمَنُونَ جَائِلَةٌ[1] ... وَقَدْ أَدَارَتْ عَلَى ٱلْوَرَى دَارَا
وَأَقْسَمَتْ لَا تَزَالُ قَانِصَةً ... مَا كَرَّ عَصْرَا ٱلْمَحْيَا وَمَا دَارَا
فَكَيْفَ تُرْجَى ٱلنَّجَاةُ مِنْ شَرَكٍ ... لَمْ يَنْجُ مِنْهُ كِسْرَى وَلَا دَارَا

٩،٢٨ قَالَ فَلَمَّا ٱعْتَوَرَتْنَا ٱلْكُؤُوسُ. وَطَرِبَتِ ٱلنُّفُوسُ. جَرَّعَنِي ٱلْيَمِينَ ٱلْغَمُوسَ. عَلَى أَنْ أَحْفَظَ عَلَيْهِ ٱلنَّامُوسَ. فَٱتَّبَعْتُ مَرَامَهُ. وَرَعَيْتُ ذِمَامَهُ. وَنَزَّلْتُهُ بَيْنَ ٱلْمَلَإِ مَنْزِلَةَ ٱلْفُضَيْلِ. وَسَدَلْتُ ٱلذَّيْلَ. عَلَى مَخَازِي ٱللَّيْلِ. وَلَمْ يَزَلْ ذٰلِكَ دَأْبَهُ وَدَابِي. إِلَى أَنْ تَهَيَّأَ إِيَابِي. فَوَدَّعْتُهُ وَهْوَ مُصِرٌّ عَلَى ٱلتَّدْلِيسِ. وَمُسِرٌّ حَسْوَ ٱلْخَنْدَرِيسِ.

---

١ س: حائلة.

الْمَقَامَةُ التَّاسِعَةُ وَالْعِشْرُونَ[1]

١،٢٩ حَكَى الْحَارِثُ بْنُ هَمَّامٍ قَالَ أَلْجَأَنِي حُكْمُ دَهْرٍ قَاسِطٍ. إِلَى أَنْ أَنْتَجِعَ أَرْضَ وَاسِطٍ. فَقَصَدْتُهَا وَأَنَا لَا أَعْرِفُ بِهَا سَكَنًا. وَلَا أَمْلِكُ فِيهَا مَسْكَنًا. وَلَمَّا حَلَلْتُهَا حُلُولَ الْحُوتِ بِالْبَيْدَاءِ. وَالشَّعْرَةِ الْبَيْضَاءِ فِي اللِّمَّةِ السَّوْدَاءِ. قَادَنِي الْحَظُّ النَّاقِصُ. وَالْجَدُّ النَّاكِصُ. إِلَى خَانٍ يَنْزِلُهُ شُذَّاذُ الْآفَاقِ. وَأَخْلَاطُ الرِّفَاقِ. وَهُوَ لِنَظَافَةِ مَكَانِهِ. وَظَرَافَةِ سُكَّانِهِ. يُرْغِبُ[2] الْغَرِيبَ فِي إِيطَانِهِ. وَيُنْسِيهِ هَوَى أَوْطَانِهِ. فَاسْتَفْرَدْتُ مِنْهُ بِحُجْرَةٍ. وَلَمْ أُنَافِسْ فِي أُجْرَةٍ.

٢،٢٩ فَمَا كَانَ إِلَّا كَلَمْحِ طَرْفٍ. أَوْ خَطِّ حَرْفٍ. حَتَّى سَمِعْتُ جَارِي بَيْتَ بَيْتٍ. يَقُولُ لِنَزِيلِهِ فِي الْبَيْتِ. قُمْ يَا بُنَيَّ لَا قَعَدَ جَدُّكَ. وَلَا قَامَ ضِدُّكَ. وَاسْتَصْحِبْ ذَا الْوَجْهِ الْبَدْرِيِّ. وَاللَّوْنِ الدُّرِّيِّ. وَالْأَصْلِ النَّقِيِّ. وَالْجِسْمِ الشَّقِيِّ. الَّذِي قُبِضَ وَنُشِرَ. وَسُجِنَ وَشُهِرَ. وَسُقِيَ وَفُطِمَ. وَأُدْخِلَ النَّارَ بَعْدَمَا لُطِمَ. ثُمَّ ارْكُضْ إِلَى السُّوقِ. رَكْضَ الْمَشُوقِ. فَقَايِضْ بِهِ اللَّاقِحَ الْمُلْقِحَ. الْمُفْسِدَ الْمُصْلِحَ. الْمُكْمِدَ الْمُفْرِحَ.[3] الْمُعَنِّيَ الْمُرَوِّحَ. ذَا الزَّفِيرِ الْمُحْرِقِ. وَالْحَنِينِ الْمُشْرِقِ. وَاللَّفْظِ الْمُقْنِعِ. وَالنَّيْلِ الْمُمْتِعِ. الَّذِي إِذَا طَرَقَ.[4] رَعَدَ وَبَرَقَ. وَبَاحَ بِالْحُرَقِ. وَنَفَثَ فِي الْخِرَقِ.

٣،٢٩ قَالَ فَلَمَّا قَرَّتْ شِقْشِقَةُ الْهَادِرِ. وَلَمْ يَبْقَ إِلَّا صَدَرُ الصَّادِرِ. بَرَزَ فَتًى يَمِيسُ. وَمَا مَعَهُ أَنِيسُ. فَرَأَيْتُهَا عُضْلَةً تَلْعَبُ بِالْعُقُولِ. وَتُغْرِي بِالدُّخُولِ. فِي الْفُضُولِ.

---

١ في هامش س: تُعرَف بالواسِطية؛ وفي د: الواسطية؛ وفي ف: وهي الواسطية. ٢ و،د، ف: يُرَغِّب. ٣ س، و: المُفْرِح. ٤ د، ف: طُرِق.

فَٱنْطَلَقْتُ فِي إِثْرِ ٱلْغُلَامِ. لِأَخْبُرَ فَحْوَى ٱلْكَلَامِ. فَلَمْ يَزَلْ يَسْعَى سَعْيَ ٱلْعَفَارِيتِ. وَيَتَفَقَّدُ نَضَائِدَ ٱلْحَوَانِيتِ. حَتَّى ٱنْتَهَى عِنْدَ ٱلرَّوَاحِ. إِلَى حِجَارَةِ ٱلْقَدَّاحِ. فَنَاوَلَ بَائِعَهَا رُغَيْفًا. وَتَنَاوَلَ مِنْهُ حَجَرًا لَطِيفًا. فَعَجِبْتُ مِنْ فَطَانَةِ ٱلْمُرْسِلِ وَٱلْمُرْسَلِ. وَعَلِمْتُ أَنَّهَا سَرُوجِيَّةٌ وَإِنْ لَمْ أَسْأَلْ. وَمَا كَذَّبْتُ أَنْ بَادَرْتُ إِلَى ٱلْخَانِ. مُنْطَلِقَ ٱلْعِنَانِ. لِأَنْظُرَ كُنْهَ فَهْمِي. وَهَلْ قَرْطَسَ فِي ٱلتَّكَهُّنِ سَهْمِي.

٤،٢٩ فَإِذَا أَنَا فِي ٱلْفِرَاسَةِ فَارِسٌ. وَأَبُو زَيْدٍ بِوَصِيدِ ٱلْخَانِ جَالِسٌ. فَتَهَادَيْنَا بُشْرَى ٱلِٱلْتِقَاءِ. وَتَقَارَضْنَا تَحِيَّةَ ٱلْأَصْدِقَاءِ. ثُمَّ قَالَ مَا ٱلَّذِي نَابَكَ. حَتَّى زَايَلْتَ جَنَابَكَ. فَقُلْتُ دَهْرٌ هَاضَ. وَجَوْرٌ فَاضَ. فَقَالَ وَٱلَّذِي أَنْزَلَ ٱلْمَطَرَ مِنَ ٱلْغَمَامِ. وَأَخْرَجَ ٱلثَّمَرَ مِنَ ٱلْأَكْمَامِ. لَقَدْ فَسَدَ ٱلزَّمَانُ. وَعَمَّ ٱلْعُدْوَانُ. وَعُدِمَ ٱلْمِعْوَانُ. وَٱللهُ ٱلْمُسْتَعَانُ. فَكَيْفَ أَفْلَتَّ. وَعَلَى أَيِّ وَصْفَيْكَ أَجْفَلْتَ. فَقُلْتُ ٱتَّخَذْتُ ٱللَّيْلَ قَمِيصًا. وَأَدْلَجْتُ فِيهِ خَمِيصًا. فَأَطْرَقَ يَنْكُتُ فِي ٱلْأَرْضِ. وَيُفَكِّرُ فِي ٱرْتِيَادِ ٱلْقَرْضِ وَٱلْفَرْضِ. ثُمَّ ٱهْتَزَّ هِزَّةَ مَنْ أَكْثَبَهُ قَنَصٌ. أَوْ بَدَتْ لَهُ فُرَصٌ. وَقَالَ قَدْ عَلِقَ بِقَلْبِي أَنْ تُصَاهِرَ مَنْ يَأْسُو جِرَاحَكَ. وَيَرِيشُ جَنَاحَكَ.

٥،٢٩ فَقُلْتُ وَكَيْفَ أَجْمَعُ بَيْنَ غُلٍّ وَقُلٍّ. وَمَنِ ٱلَّذِي يَرْغَبُ فِي ضُلِّ بْنِ ضُلٍّ. فَقَالَ أَنَا ٱلْمُشِيرُ بِكَ وَإِلَيْكَ. وَٱلْوَكِيلُ لَكَ وَعَلَيْكَ. مَعَ أَنَّ دِينَ ٱلْقَوْمِ جَبْرُ ٱلْكَسِيرِ. وَفَكُّ ٱلْأَسِيرِ. وَٱحْتِرَامُ ٱلْعَشِيرِ. وَٱسْتِنْصَاحُ ٱلْمُشِيرِ. إِلَّا أَنَّهُمْ لَوْ خَطَبَ إِلَيْهِمْ إِبْرَاهِيمُ بْنُ أَدْهَمَ. أَوْ جَبَلَةُ بْنُ ٱلْأَيْهَمِ. لَمَا زَوَّجُوهُ إِلَّا عَلَى خَمْسِ مِائَةِ دِرْهَمٍ. ٱقْتِدَاءً بِمَا مَهَرَ ٱلرَّسُولُ صَلَّى ٱللهُ عَلَيْهِ زَوْجَاتِهِ. وَعَقَدَ بِهِ أَنْكِحَةَ بَنَاتِهِ. عَلَى أَنَّكَ لَنْ تُطَالَبَ بِصَدَاقٍ. وَلَا تُلْجَأَ إِلَى طَلَاقٍ. ثُمَّ إِنِّي سَأَخْطُبُ فِي مَوْقِفِ عَقْدِكَ. وَمَجْمَعِ حَشْدِكَ. خُطْبَةً لَمْ تَفْتُقْ رَتْقَ سَمْعٍ. وَلَا خُطِبَ بِمِثْلِهَا فِي جَمْعٍ.

٦،٢٩ قَالَ الْحَارِثُ بْنُ هَمَّامٍ فَٱزْدَهَانِي بِوَصْفِ الْخُطْبَةِ الْمَتْلُوَّةِ. دُونَ الْخِطْبَةِ الْمَجْلُوَّةِ. حَتَّى قُلْتُ لَهُ قَدْ وَكَلْتُ إِلَيْكَ هٰذَا الْخَطْبَ. فَدَبِّرْهُ تَدْبِيرَ مَنْ طَبَّ لِمَنْ حَبَّ. فَنَهَضَ مُهَرْوِلًا. ثُمَّ عَادَ مُتَهَلِّلًا. وَقَالَ أَبْشِرْ بِإِعْتَابِ الدَّهْرِ. وَٱحْتِلَابِ الدَّرِّ. فَقَدْ وُلِّيتُ الْعَقْدَ. وَأُكْفِلْتُ النَّقْدَ. وَكَأَنْ قَدْ. ثُمَّ أَخَذَ فِي مُوَاعَدَةِ أَهْلِ الْخَانِ. وَإِعْدَادِ حَلْوَاءِ الْخِوَانِ. فَلَمَّا مَدَّ اللَّيْلُ أَطْنَابَهُ. وَأَغْلَقَ كُلُّ ذِي بَابٍ بَابَهُ. أَذَّنَ فِي الْجَمَاعَةِ أَلَا ٱحْضُرُوا فِي هٰذِهِ السَّاعَةِ. فَلَمْ يَبْقَ فِيهِمْ إِلَّا مَنْ لَبَّى صَوْتَهُ. وَحَضَرَ بَيْتَهُ. فَلَمَّا ٱصْطَفُّوا لَدَيْهِ. وَٱجْتَمَعَ الشَّاهِدُ وَالْمَشْهُودُ عَلَيْهِ. جَعَلَ يَرْفَعُ الْأَصْطُرْلَابَ وَيَضَعُهُ. وَيَلْحَظُ التَّقْوِيمَ وَيَدَعُهُ. إِلَى أَنْ نَعَسَ الْقَوْمُ. وَغَشِيَ النَّوْمُ. فَقُلْتُ لَهُ يَا هٰذَا ضَعِ الْفَأْسَ فِي الرَّأْسِ. وَخَلِّصِ النَّاسَ.[1] فَنَظَرَ نَظْرَةً فِي النُّجُومِ. ثُمَّ ٱنْتَشَطَ مِنْ عُقْلَةِ الْوُجُومِ. وَأَقْسَمَ بِالطُّورِ. وَالْكِتَابِ الْمَسْطُورِ. لَيَنْكَشِفَنَّ سِرُّ هٰذَا الْأَمْرِ الْمَسْتُورِ. وَلَيَنْتَشِرَنَّ ذِكْرُهُ إِلَى يَوْمِ النُّشُورِ. ثُمَّ إِنَّهُ جَثَا عَلَى رُكْبَتِهِ. وَٱسْتَرْعَى الْأَسْمَاعَ لِخُطْبَتِهِ.

٧،٢٩ وَقَالَ الْحَمْدُ لِلّٰهِ الْمَلِكِ الْمَحْمُودِ. الْمَالِكِ الْوَدُودِ. مُصَوِّرِ كُلِّ مَوْلُودٍ. وَمَآلِ كُلِّ مَطْرُودٍ. سَاطِحِ الْمِهَادِ. وَمُوَطِّدِ الْأَطْوَادِ. وَمُرْسِلِ الْأَمْطَارِ. وَمُسَهِّلِ الْأَوْطَارِ. عَالِمِ الْأَسْرَارِ وَمُدْرِكِهَا. وَمُدَمِّرِ الْأَمْلَاكِ وَمُهْلِكِهَا. وَمُكَوِّرِ الدُّهُورِ وَمُكَرِّرِهَا. وَمُورِدِ الْأُمُورِ وَمُصْدِرِهَا. عَمَّ سَمَاحُهُ وَكَمَلَ. وَهَطَلَ رُكَامُهُ وَهَمَلَ. وَطَاوَعَ السُّؤْلَ وَالْأَمَلَ. وَأَوْسَعَ الْمُرْمِلَ وَالْأَرْمَلَ. أَحْمَدُهُ حَمْدًا مَمْدُودًا مَدَاهُ. وَأُوَحِّدُهُ كَمَا وَحَّدَهُ الْأَوَّاهُ. وَهُوَ اللّٰهُ لَا إِلٰهَ لِلْأُمَمِ سِوَاهُ. وَلَا صَادِعَ لِمَا عَدَّلَهُ وَسَوَّاهُ. أَرْسَلَ مُحَمَّدًا عَلَمًا لِلْإِسْلَامِ. وَإِمَامًا لِلْحُكَّامِ. وَمُسَدِّدًا لِلرَّعَاعِ. وَمُعَطِّلًا أَحْكَامَ وَدٍّ وَسُوَاعٍ.[2] أَعْلَمَ وَعَلَّمَ.

١ بعدها في ف: من النُّعاس. ٢ في متن ق: سواعَ، مع تصحيح في الهامش، وهي غير مشكّلة في باقي النسخ.

وَحَكَّمَ وَأَحْكَمَ.[١] وَأَصَّلَ الْأُصُولَ وَمَهَّدَ. وَأَكَّدَ الْوُعُودَ وَأَوْعَدَ. وَاصَلَ اللهُ لَهُ الْإِكْرَامَ. وَأَوْدَعَ رُوحَهُ[٢] السَّلَامَ. وَرَحِمَ آلَهُ وَأَهْلَهُ الْكِرَامَ. مَا لَمَعَ آلٌ. وَمَلَعَ رَالٌ. وَطَلَعَ هِلَالٌ. وَسُمِعَ إِهْلَالٌ.

٨،٢٩ اِعْمَلُوا رَعَاكُمُ اللهُ أَصْلَحَ الْأَعْمَالِ. وَاسْلُكُوا مَسَالِكَ الْحَلَالِ. وَاطَّرِحُوا الْحَرَامَ وَدَعُوهُ. وَاسْمَعُوا أَمْرَ اللهِ وَعُوهُ. وَصِلُوا الْأَرْحَامَ وَرَاعُوهَا. وَعَاصُوا الْأَهْوَاءَ وَارْدَعُوهَا. وَصَاهِرُوا لُحَمَ الصَّلَاحِ وَالْوَرَعِ. وَصَارِمُوا رَهْطَ اللَّهْوِ وَالطَّمَعِ. وَمُصَاهِرُكُمْ أَطْهَرُ الْأَحْرَارِ مَوْلِدًا. وَأَسْرَاهُمْ سُؤْدَدًا. وَأَحْلَاهُمْ مَوْرِدًا. وَأَصَحُّهُمْ مَوْعِدًا. وَهَا هُوَ أَمَّكُمْ. وَحَلَّ حَرَمَكُمْ. مُمْلِكًا عَرُوسَكُمُ الْمُكَرَّمَةَ. وَمَاهِرًا لَهَا كَمَا مَهَرَ الرَّسُولُ[٣] أُمَّ سَلَمَةَ. وَهُوَ أَكْرَمُ صِهْرٍ أُودِعَ الْأَوْلَادَ. وَمُلِّكَ مَا أَرَادَ. وَمَا سَهَا مُمْلِكُهُ وَلَا وَهِمَ. وَلَا وَكِسَ مُلَاحِمُهُ وَلَا وُصِمَ. أَسْأَلُ اللهَ لَكُمْ إِحْمَادَ وِصَالِهِ وَدَوَامَ إِسْعَادِهِ. وَأَلْهَمَ كُلًّا إِصْلَاحَ[٤] حَالِهِ وَالْإِعْدَادَ لِمَعَادِهِ. وَلَهُ الْحَمْدُ السَّرْمَدُ. وَالْمَدْحُ لِرَسُولِهِ مُحَمَّدٍ.[٥]

٩،٢٩ فَلَمَّا فَرَغَ مِنْ خُطْبَتِهِ الْبَدِيعَةِ النِّظَامِ. الْعَرِيَّةِ مِنَ الْإِعْجَامِ. عَقَدَ الْعَقْدَ عَلَى الْخَمْسِ الْمِئِينَ. وَقَالَ لِي بِالرِّفَاءِ وَالْبَنِينَ. ثُمَّ أَحْضَرَ الْحَلْوَاءَ الَّتِي كَانَ أَعَدَّهَا. وَأَبْدَى الْآبِدَةَ عِنْدَهَا. فَأَقْبَلْتُ إِقْبَالَ الْجَمَاعَةِ عَلَيْهَا. وَكِدْتُ أُهْوِي بِيَدِي إِلَيْهَا. فَزَجَرَنِي عَنِ الْمُؤَاكَلَةِ. وَأَنْهَضَنِي لِلْمُنَاوَلَةِ. فَوَاللهِ مَا كَانَ بِأَسْرَعَ مِنْ تَصَافُحِ الْأَجْفَانِ. حَتَّى خَرَّ الْقَوْمُ لِلْأَذْقَانِ. فَلَمَّا رَأَيْتُهُمْ كَأَعْجَازِ نَخْلٍ خَاوِيَةٍ. أَوْ صَرْعَى[٦] بِنْتِ خَابِيَةٍ. عَلِمْتُ أَنَّهَا لَإِحْدَى الْكُبَرِ. وَأُمُّ الْعِبَرِ. فَقُلْتُ لَهُ يَا عُدَيَّ نَفْسِهِ. وَعُبَيْدَ فَلْسِهِ. أَأَعْدَدْتَ لِلْقَوْمِ حَلْوَى. أَمْ بَلْوَى. فَقَالَ لَمْ أَعْدُ خَبِيصَ الْبَنْجِ.

---

١ هكذا في س، د، وغير مشكّلة في ق، و. ٢ بعدها في د، ف: دار. ٣ بعدها في ف: صلى الله عليه وسلم.
٤ في س: صلاح. ٥ بعدها في ف: صلى الله عليه وسلم. ٦ ف: كصرعى.

فِي صِحَافِ الْخَلَنْجِ. فَقُلْتُ أُقْسِمُ بِمَنْ أَطْلَعَهَا زُهْرًا. وَهَدَى بِهَا السَّارِينَ طُرًّا. ﴿لَقَدْ جِئْتَ شَيْئًا نُكْرًا﴾. وَأَبْقَيْتَ لَكَ فِي الْمُخْزِيَاتِ ذِكْرًا. ثُمَّ حِرْتُ فِكْرَةً فِي صَيُّورِ أَمْرِهِ. وَخِيفَةً مِنْ عَدْوَى عَرِّهِ. حَتَّى طَارَتْ نَفْسِي شَعَاعًا. وَأُرْعِدَتْ فَرَائِصِي ٱرْتِيَاعًا. فَلَمَّا رَأَى ٱسْتِطَارَةَ فَرَقِي. وَٱسْتِشَاطَةَ قَلَقِي. قَالَ مَا هٰذَا الْفِكْرُ الْمُرْمِضُ. وَالرَّوْعُ الْمُومِضُ. فَإِنْ يَكُنْ فِكْرُكَ فِي أَجْلِي. مِنْ أَجْلِي. فَأَنَا الْآنَ أَرْتَعُ وَأَطْفِرُ. وَأُقْوِي هٰذِهِ الْبُقْعَةَ مِنِّي وَأُقْفِرُ. وَكَمْ مِثْلِهَا فَارَقْتُهَا وَهْيَ تَصْفِرُ. وَإِنْ يَكُنْ نَظَرًا لِنَفْسِكَ. وَحَذَرًا مِنْ حَبْسِكَ. فَتَنَاوَلْ فُضَالَةَ الْخَبِيصِ. وَطِبْ نَفْسًا عَنِ الْقَمِيصِ. حَتَّى تَأْمَنَ الْمُسْتَعْدِيَ وَالْمُعْدِيَ. وَيَتَمَهَّدَ لَكَ الْمُقَامُ بَعْدِي. وَإِلَّا فَالْمَفَرَّ الْمَفَرَّ. قَبْلَ أَنْ تُسْحَبَ وَتُجَرَّ.

١٠،٢٩ ثُمَّ عَمَدَ لِاسْتِخْرَاجِ مَا فِي الْبُيُوتِ. مِنَ الْأَكْيَاسِ وَالتُّخُوتِ. وَجَعَلَ يَسْتَخْلِصُ خَالِصَةَ كُلِّ مَخْزُونٍ. وَنُخْبَةَ كُلِّ مَذْرُوعٍ وَمَوْزُونٍ. حَتَّى غَادَرَ مَا أَلْغَاهُ فَخُّهُ. كَعَظْمٍ ٱسْتُخْرِجَ مُخُّهُ. فَلَمَّا هَمَّنَ مَا ٱصْطَفَاهُ وَرَزَّمَ. وَشَمَّرَ عَنْ ذِرَاعَيْهِ وَتَحَزَّمَ. أَقْبَلَ عَلَيَّ إِقْبَالَ مَنْ لَبِسَ الصَّفَاقَةَ. وَخَلَعَ الصَّدَاقَةَ. وَقَالَ هَلْ لَكَ فِي الْمُصَاحَبَةِ إِلَى الْبَطِيحَةِ. لِأَصِلَكَ[1] بِأُخْرَى مَلِيحَةٍ. فَأَقْسَمْتُ لَهُ بِالَّذِي جَعَلَهُ مُبَارَكًا أَيْنَمَا كَانَ. وَلَمْ يَجْعَلْهُ مِمَّنْ خَانَ فِي خَانٍ. إِنَّهُ لَا قِبَلَ لِي بِنِكَاحِ حُرَّتَيْنِ. وَمُعَاشَرَةِ ضَرَّتَيْنِ. ثُمَّ قُلْتُ لَهُ قَوْلَ الْمُتَطَبِّعِ بِطِبَاعِهِ. الْكَائِلِ لَهُ بِصَاعِهِ قَدْ كَفَتْنِي الْأُولَى فَخْرًا. فَٱطْلُبْ آخَرَ لِلْأُخْرَى. فَتَبَسَّمَ مِنْ كَلَامِي. وَدَلَفَ لِالْتِزَامِي. فَلَوَيْتُ عَنْهُ عِذَارِي. وَأَبْدَيْتُ لَهُ ٱزْوِرَارِي. فَلَمَّا بَصُرَ بِٱنْقِبَاضِي. وَتَجَلَّى لَهُ إِعْرَاضِي. أَنْشَدَ

١ ف: لأزوّجك.

١١،٢٩ يَا صَارِفًا عَنِّي الْمَوَ   دَّةَ وَالزَّمَانُ لَهُ صُرُوفْ
وَمُعَنِّفِي فِي فَضْحِ مَنْ   جَاوَرْتُ تَعْنِيفَ الْعَسُوفْ
لَا تَلْحَنِي فِيمَا أَتَيْـ   ـتُ فَإِنَّنِي بِهِمْ عَرُوفْ
وَلَقَدْ نَزَلْتُ بِهِمْ فَلَمْ   أَرَهُمْ يُرَاعُونَ الضُّيُوفْ
وَبَلَوْتُهُمْ فَوَجَدْتُهُمْ   لَمَّا سَبَكْتُهُمُ زُيُوفْ
مَا فِيهِمِ إِلَّا مُخِيفٌ   إِنْ تَمَكَّنَ أَوْ مَخُوفْ
لَا بِالصَّفِيِّ وَلَا الْوَفِيِّ   وَلَا الْحَفِيِّ وَلَا الْعَطُوفْ
فَوَثَبْتُ فِيهِمْ وَثْبَةَ الذِّ   ئْبِ الضَّرِيِّ عَلَى الْخَرُوفْ
وَتَرَكْتُهُمْ صَرْعَى كَأَنَّـ   ـهُمُ سُقُوا كَأْسَ الْحُتُوفْ
وَتَحَكَّمَتْ فِيمَا اقْتَنَوْ   هُ يَدِي وَهُمْ رُغْمُ الْأُنُوفْ
ثُمَّ انْثَنَيْتُ بِمَغْنَمٍ   حُلْوِ الْمَجَانِي وَالْقُطُوفْ
١٢،٢٩ وَلَطَالَمَا خَلَّفْتُ مَكْـ   ـلُومَ الْحَشَا خَلْفِي يَطُوفْ
وَوَتَرْتُ أَرْبَابَ الْأَرَا   ئِكِ وَالدَّرَانِكِ وَالسُّجُوفْ
وَلَكَمْ بَلَغْتُ بِحِيلَتِي   مَا لَيْسَ يُبْلَغُ بِالسُّيُوفْ
وَوَقَفْتُ فِي هَوْلٍ تُرَا   عُ الْأُسْدُ فِيهِ مِنَ الْوُقُوفْ
وَلَكَمْ سَفَكْتُ وَكَمْ فَتَكْتُ   وَكَمْ هَتَكْتُ حِمَى أُنُوفْ
وَكَمِ ارْتِكَاضٍ مُوبِقٍ   لِي فِي الذُّنُوبِ وَكَمْ خُفُوفْ
لٰكِنَّنِي أَعْدَدْتُ حُسْـ   ـنَ الظَّنِّ بِالْمَوْلَى الرَّؤُوفْ

قَالَ فَلَمَّا انْتَهَى إِلَى هٰذَا الْبَيْتِ لَجَّ فِي الِاسْتِعْبَارِ. وَأَلَظَّ بِالِاسْتِغْفَارِ. حَتَّى اسْتَمَالَ هَوَى قَلْبِيَ الْمُنْحَرِفِ. وَرَجَوْتُ لَهُ مَا يُرْجَى لِلْمُقْتَرِفِ الْمُعْتَرِفِ.

ثُمَّ إِنَّهُ غَيَّضَ دَمْعَهُ ٱلْمُنْهَلَّ. وَتَأَبَّطَ جِرَابَهُ وَٱنْسَلَّ. وَقَالَ لِٱبْنِهِ ٱحْتَمِلِ ٱلْبَاقِي. وَٱللهُ ٱلْوَاقِي.

١٣،٢٩ قَالَ ٱلْمُخْبِرُ بِهٰذِهِ ٱلْحِكَايَةِ فَلَمَّا رَأَيْتُ ٱنْسِيَابَ ٱلْحَيَّةِ وَٱلْحُيَيَّةِ. وَٱنْتِهَاءَ ٱلدَّاءِ إِلَى ٱلْكَيَّةِ. عَلِمْتُ أَنَّ تَرَبُّثِي بِٱلْخَانِ. مَجْلَبَةٌ لِلْهَوَانِ. فَضَمَمْتُ رُحَيْلِي. وَجَمَعْتُ لِلرِّحْلَةِ ذَيْلِي. وَبِتُّ لَيْلَتِي أَسْرِي إِلَى ٱلطِّيبِ. وَأَحْتَسِبُ ٱللهَ عَلَى ٱلْخَطِيبِ.

الْمَقَامَةُ الثَّلَاثُونَ[١]

١،٣٠ حَكَى الْحَارِثُ بْنُ هَمَّامٍ قَالَ ارْتَحَلْتُ مِنْ مَدِينَةِ الْمَنْصُورِ. إِلَى بَلْدَةِ صُورٍ. فَلَمَّا حَصَلْتُ بِهِ ذَا رِفْعَةٍ وَخَفْضٍ. وَمَالِكَ رَفْعٍ وَخَفْضٍ. تُقْتُ إِلَى مِصْرَ تَوَقَانَ السَّقِيمِ إِلَى الْأُسَاةِ. وَالْكَرِيمِ إِلَى الْمُوَاسَاةِ. فَرَفَضْتُ عَلَائِقَ الِاسْتِقَامَةِ. وَنَفَضْتُ عَوَائِقَ الْإِقَامَةِ. وَٱعْرَوْرَيْتُ ظَهْرَ ٱبْنِ النَّعَامَةِ. وَأَجْفَلْتُ نَحْوَهَا إِجْفَالَ النَّعَامَةِ. فَلَمَّا دَخَلْتُهَا بَعْدَ مُعَانَاةِ الْأَيْنِ. وَمُدَانَاةِ الْحَيْنِ. كَلِفْتُ بِهَا كَلَفَ النَّشْوَانِ بِالْاصْطِبَاحِ. وَالْحَيْرَانِ بِتَنَفُّسِ الصَّبَاحِ.

٢،٣٠ فَبَيْنَمَا أَنَا يَوْمًا بِهَا أَطُوفُ. وَتَحْتِي فَرَسٌ قَطُوفٌ. إِذْ رَأَيْتُ عَلَى جُرْدٍ مِنَ الْخَيْلِ. عُصْبَةً كَمَصَابِيحِ اللَّيْلِ. فَسَأَلْتُ لِانْتِجَاعِ النُّزْهَةِ. عَنِ الْعُصْبَةِ[٢] وَالْوِجْهَةِ. فَقِيلَ أَمَّا الْقَوْمُ فَشُهُودٌ. وَأَمَّا الْمَقْصِدُ فَإِمْلَاكٌ مَشْهُودٌ. فَحَدَتْنِي مَيْعَةُ النَّشَاطِ. عَلَى أَنْ سِرْتُ مَعَ الْفُرَّاطِ. لِأَفُوزَ بِحَلَاوَةِ اللُّقَاطِ. وَأَحُوزَ حَلْوَاءَ السِّمَاطِ. فَأَفْضَيْنَا بَعْدَ مُكَابَدَةِ الْعَنَاءِ. إِلَى دَارٍ رَفِيعَةِ الْبِنَاءِ. وَسِيعَةِ الْفِنَاءِ. تَشْهَدُ لِبَانِيهَا بِالثَّرَاءِ وَالسَّنَاءِ. فَلَمَّا نَزَلْنَا عَنْ صَهَوَاتِ الْخُيُولِ. وَقَدَّمْنَا الْأَقْدَامَ لِلدُّخُولِ. رَأَيْتُ دِهْلِيزَهَا مُجَلَّلًا بِأَطْمَارٍ مُخَرَّقَةٍ. وَمُكَلَّلًا بِمَخَارِفَ مُعَلَّقَةٍ. وَهُنَاكَ شَخْصٌ عَلَى قَطِيفَةٍ. فَوْقَ دَكَّةٍ لَطِيفَةٍ. فَرَابَنِي عُنْوَانُ الصَّحِيفَةِ. وَمَرْأَى هٰذِهِ الطَّرِيفَةِ.

٣،٣٠ وَدَعَانِي التَّطَيُّرُ بِتِلْكَ الْمَنَاحِسِ. إِلَى أَنْ عَمَدْتُ لِذٰلِكَ الْجَالِسِ. فَعَزَمْتُ عَلَيْهِ بِمُصَرِّفِ الْأَقْدَارِ. لِيُعَرِّفَنِي[٣] مَنْ رَبُّ هٰذِهِ الدَّارِ. فَقَالَ لَيْسَ لَهَا مَالِكٌ

---

١ في هامش س: تعرف بالمصرية؛ وفي د: الصُّورِيَّة؛ وفي ف: وهي الصورية. ٢ عن العصبة: ساقطة من س.
٣ هكذا في د، وفي ق: لِيُعَرِّفنى؛ وفي س: لَيعرّفنى، وفي و: لتعرّفْني؛ وفي ف: ليعرّفَني.

مُعَيَّنٌ. وَلَا صَاحِبٌ مُبَيَّنٌ. إِنَّمَا هِيَ مَصْطَبَةُ[1] الْمُقَيِّفِينَ وَالْمُدَرْوِزِينَ. وَوَلِيجَةُ الْمُشَقْشِقِينَ[2] وَالْمُجَلْوِزِينَ. فَقُلْتُ فِي نَفْسِي إِنَّا لِلهِ عَلَى ضَلَّةِ الْمَسْعَى. وَإِمْحَالِ الْمَرْعَى. وَهَمَمْتُ فِي الْحَالِ بِالرُّجْعَى. لٰكِنِّي ٱسْتَهْجَنْتُ الْعَوْدَ مِنْ فَوْرِي. وَالْقَهْقَرَةَ دُونَ غَيْرِي. فَوَلَجْتُ الدَّارَ مُتَجَرِّعًا الْغُصَصَ. كَمَا يَلِجُ الْعُصْفُورُ الْقَفَصَ.

٤،٣٠ فَإِذَا فِيهِ أَرَائِكُ مَنْقُوشَةٌ. وَطَنَافِسُ مَفْرُوشَةٌ. وَنَمَارِقُ مَصْفُوفَةٌ. وَسُجُوفٌ مَرْصُوفَةٌ. وَقَدْ أَقْبَلَ الْمُمَلَّكُ يَمِيسُ فِي بُرْدَتِهِ. وَيَتَبَهْنَسُ بَيْنَ حَفَدَتِهِ. فَحِينَ جَلَسَ كَأَنَّهُ ٱبْنُ مَاءِ السَّمَاءِ. نَادَى مُنَادٍ مِنْ قِبَلِ الْأَحْمَاءِ. وَحُرْمَةِ سَاسَانَ أُسْتَاذِ الْأُسْتَاذِينَ. وَقُدْوَةِ الشَّحَّاذِينَ. لَا عَقَدَ هٰذَا الْعَقْدَ الْمُبَجَّلَ. فِي هٰذَا الْيَوْمِ الْأَغَرِّ الْمُحَجَّلِ. إِلَّا الَّذِي جَالَ وَجَابَ. وَشَبَّ فِي الْكُدْيَةِ وَشَابَ. فَأَعْجَبَ رَهْطَ الصِّهْرِ مَا أَشَارُوا إِلَيْهِ. وَأَذِنُوا فِي إِحْضَارِ الْمَنْصُوصِ عَلَيْهِ. فَبَرَزَ حِينَئِذٍ شَيْخٌ قَدْ أَمَالَ الْمَلَوَانِ قَامَتَهُ. وَنَوَّرَ الْفَتَيَانِ ثَغَامَتَهُ. فَتَبَاشَرَتِ الْجَمَاعَةُ بِإِقْبَالِهِ. وَتَبَادَرَتْ إِلَى ٱسْتِقْبَالِهِ. فَلَمَّا جَلَسَ عَلَى زِرْبِيَّتِهِ.[3] وَسَكَنَتِ الضَّوْضَاءُ لِهَيْبَتِهِ. اِزْدَلَفَ إِلَى مَسْنَدِهِ. وَمَسَحَ سَبَلَتَهُ بِيَدِهِ.

٥،٣٠ ثُمَّ قَالَ الْحَمْدُ لِلهِ الْمُبْتَدِئِ بِالْإِفْضَالِ. الْمُبْتَدِعِ لِلنَّوَالِ. الْمُتَقَرَّبِ إِلَيْهِ[4] بِالسُّؤَالِ. الْمُؤَمَّلِ[5] لِتَحْقِيقِ الْآمَالِ. الَّذِي شَرَعَ الزَّكَاةَ فِي الْأَمْوَالِ. وَزَجَرَ عَنْ نَهْرِ السُّؤَّالِ. وَنَدَبَ إِلَى مُوَاسَاةِ الْمُضْطَرِّ. وَأَمَرَ بِإِطْعَامِ الْقَانِعِ وَالْمُعْتَرِّ. وَوَصَفَ عِبَادَهُ الْمُقَرَّبِينَ. فِي كِتَابِهِ الْمُبِينِ. فَقَالَ وَهُوَ أَصْدَقُ الْقَائِلِينَ ﴿وَٱلَّذِينَ فِيٓ أَمْوَٰلِهِمْ حَقٌّ مَّعْلُومٌ. لِّلسَّآئِلِ وَٱلْمَحْرُومِ﴾. أَحْمَدُهُ عَلَى مَا رَزَقَ مِنْ طُعْمَةٍ هَنِيَّةٍ. وَأَعُوذُ بِهِ مِنِ ٱسْتِمَاعِ دَعْوَةٍ بِلَا نِيَّةٍ. وَأَشْهَدُ أَنْ لَا إِلٰهَ إِلَّا اللهُ وَحْدَهُ لَا شَرِيكَ

١ د: مِصْطَبة. ٢ س، و: المسقسقين. ٣ . ف: زُرْبيته. ٤ و: المتفرّد. ٥ س: المؤمّل.

لَهُ إِلٰهُ[1] يَجْزِي الْمُتَصَدِّقِينَ وَالْمُتَصَدِّقَاتِ. وَيَمْحَقُ الرِّبَا وَيُرْبِي[2] الصَّدَقَاتِ. وَأَشْهَدُ أَنَّ مُحَمَّدًا عَبْدُهُ الرَّحِيمُ. وَرَسُولُهُ الْكَرِيمُ. اِبْتَعَثَهُ لِيَنْسَخَ الظُّلْمَةَ بِالضِّيَاءِ. وَيَنْتَصِفَ لِلْفُقَرَاءِ مِنَ الْأَغْنِيَاءِ. فَرَفَقَ صَلَّى اللّٰهُ عَلَيْهِ وَسَلَّمَ بِالْمِسْكِينِ. وَخَفَضَ جَنَاحَهُ لِلْمُسْتَكِينِ. وَفَرَضَ الْحُقُوقَ فِي أَمْوَالِ الْمُثْرِينَ. وَبَيَّنَ مَا يَجِبُ لِلْمُقِلِّينَ عَلَى الْمُكْثِرِينَ. صَلَّى اللّٰهُ عَلَيْهِ صَلَاةً تُحْظِيهِ بِالزُّلْفَةِ. وَعَلَى أَصْفِيَائِهِ أَهْلِ الصُّفَّةِ.

٦،٣٠ أَمَّا بَعْدُ فَإِنَّ اللّٰهَ تَعَالَى شَرَعَ النِّكَاحَ لِتَتَعَفَّفُوا. وَسَنَّ التَّنَاسُلَ لِكَيْ تَتَضَاعَفُوا. فَقَالَ سُبْحَانَهُ لِتَعْرِفُوا[3] ﴿إِنَّا خَلَقْنَاكُمْ مِنْ ذَكَرٍ وَأُنْثَى وَجَعَلْنَاكُمْ شُعُوبًا وَقَبَائِلَ لِتَعَارَفُوا﴾. وَهٰذَا أَبُو الدَّرَّاجِ. وَلَّاجُ بْنُ خَرَّاجٍ. ذُو الْوَجْهِ الْوَقَاحِ. وَالْإِفْكِ الصُّرَاحِ. وَالْهَرِيرِ وَالصِّيَاحِ. وَالْإِبْرَامِ وَالْإِلْحَاحِ. يَخْطُبُ سَلِيطَةَ أَهْلِهَا. وَشَرِيطَةَ بَعْلِهَا. قَنْبَسَ. بِنْتَ أَبِي الْعَنْبَسِ. لِمَا بَلَغَهُ مِنِ الْتِحَافِهَا. بِإِلْحَافِهَا. وَإِسْرَافِهَا. فِي إِسْفَافِهَا. وَانْكِمَاشِهَا. عَلَى مَعَاشِهَا. وَانْتِعَاشِهَا. عِنْدَ هِرَاشِهَا. وَقَدْ بَذَلَ لَهَا مِنَ الصَّدَاقِ شَلَّاقًا وَعُكَّازًا. وَصِقَاعًا وَكَرَّازًا. فَأَنْكِحُوهُ إِنْكَاحَ مِثْلِهِ. وَصِلُوا حَبْلَكُمْ بِحَبْلِهِ. ﴿وَإِنْ خِفْتُمْ عَيْلَةً فَسَوْفَ يُغْنِيكُمُ اللّٰهُ مِنْ فَضْلِهِ﴾. أَقُولُ قَوْلِي هٰذَا وَأَسْتَغْفِرُ اللّٰهَ الْعَظِيمَ لِي وَلَكُمْ. وَأَسْأَلُهُ أَنْ يُكْثِرَ فِي الْمَصَاطِبِ نَسْلَكُمْ. وَيَحْرُسَ مِنَ الْمَعَاطِبِ شَمْلَكُمْ.

٧،٣٠ فَلَمَّا فَرَغَ الشَّيْخُ مِنْ خُطْبَتِهِ. وَأَبْرَمَ لِلْخَتَنِ عَقْدَ خِطْبَتِهِ. تَسَاقَطَ مِنَ النِّثَارِ. مَا اسْتَغْرَقَ حَدَّ الْإِكْثَارِ. وَأَغْرَى الشَّحِيحَ بِالْإِيثَارِ. ثُمَّ نَهَضَ الشَّيْخُ يَسْحَبُ ذَلَاذِلَهُ. وَيَقْدُمُ أَرَاذِلَهُ.

٨،٣٠ قَالَ الْحَارِثُ بْنُ هَمَّامٍ فَتَبِعْتُهُ لِأَنْظُرَ عُرْجَةَ الْقَوْمِ. وَأُكْمِلَ بَهْجَةَ الْيَوْمِ. فَعَاجَ بِهِمْ إِلَى سِمَاطٍ زَيَّنَتْهُ طُهَاتُهُ. وَتَنَاصَفَتْ فِي الْحُسْنِ جِهَاتُهُ. فَحِينَ رَبَعَ كُلُّ

---

١ ف: إِلٰهًا. ٢ و: ويُرَبِّي. ٣ بعدها في هامش ق، وفي د، ف: يا أيها الناس.

شَخْصٍ فِي رُبْضَتِهِ.[١] وَطَفِقَ يَرْتَعُ فِي رَوْضَتِهِ. اِنْسَلَلْتُ مِنَ الصَّفِّ. وَفَرَرْتُ مِنَ الزَّحْفِ. فَحَانَتْ مِنَ الشَّيْخِ لَفْتَةٌ إِلَيَّ. وَنَظْرَةٌ هَجَمَ بِهِ طَرْفُهُ عَلَيَّ. فَقَالَ إِلَى أَيْنَ يَا بُرَمُ. هَلَّا عَاشَرْتَ مُعَاشَرَةَ مَنْ فِيهِ كَرَمُ. فَقُلْتُ وَالَّذِي خَلَقَهَا طِبَاقًا. وَطَبَّقَهَا إِشْرَاقًا. لَا ذُقْتُ لَمَاقًا. وَلَا لُسْتُ رُقَاقًا. أَوْ تُخْبِرَنِي أَيْنَ مَدَبُّ صِبَاكَ. وَمِنْ أَيْنَ مَهَبُّ صَبَاكَ. فَتَنَفَّسَ الصُّعَدَاءَ مِرَارًا. وَأَرْسَلَ الْبُكَاءَ مِدْرَارًا. حَتَّى إِذَا ٱسْتَنْزَفَ الدَّمْعَ. اِسْتَنْصَتَ الْجَمْعَ. وَقَالَ لِي ٱسْمَعْ.[٢]

مَسْقِطُ[٣] الرَّأْسِ سَرُوجُ　　وَبِهَا كُنْتُ أَمُوجُ
بَلْدَةٌ يُوجَدُ فِيهَا　　كُلُّ شَيْءٍ وَيَرُوجُ
وِرْدُهَا مِنْ سَلْسَبِيلٍ　　وَصَحَارِيهَا مُرُوجُ
وَبَنُوهَا وَمَغَانِيهِمْ　　نُجُومٌ وَبُرُوجُ
حَبَّذَا نَفْحَةُ رَيَّا　　هَا وَمَرْآهَا الْبَهِيجُ
وَأَزَاهِيرُ رُبَاهَا　　حِينَ تَنْجَابُ الثُّلُوجُ
مَنْ رَآهَا قَالَ مَرْسَى　　جَنَّةِ الدُّنْيَا سَرُوجُ
وَلِمَنْ يَنْزَاحُ عَنْهَا　　زَفَرَاتٌ وَنَشِيجُ
مِثْلُ مَا لَاقَيْتُ مُذْ زَحْـ　　ـزَحَنِي عَنْهَا الْعُلُوجُ
عَبْرَةٌ تَهْمِي وَشَجْوٌ　　كُلَّمَا قَرَّ يَهِيجُ
وَهُمُومٌ كُلَّ يَوْمٍ　　خَطْبُهَا خَطْبٌ مَرِيجُ
وَمَسَاعٍ[٤] فِي التَّرَجِّي　　قَاصِرَاتُ الْخَطْوِ عُوجُ
لَيْتَ يَوْمِي حُمَّ لَمَّا　　حُمَّ لِي مِنْهَا الْخُرُوجُ

١ د، ف: رِبْضته؛ و: رَبْضته.　٢ ف: أَرْعِنِي السمع.　٣ و،د، ف: مسقَط.　٤ ف: مساحٍ.

قَالَ فَلَمَّا بَيَّنَ بَلَدَهُ. وَوَعَيْتُ مَا أَنْشَدَهُ. أَيْقَنْتُ أَنَّهُ عَلَّامَتُنَا أَبُو زَيْدٍ. وَإِنْ كَانَ الْهَرَمُ قَدْ أَوْثَقَهُ بِقَيْدٍ. فَبَادَرْتُ إِلَى مُصَافَحَتِهِ. وَٱغْتَنَمْتُ مُؤَاكَلَتَهُ مِنْ صَحْفَتِهِ.[1] وَظَلْتُ مُدَّةَ مَقَامِي بِمِصْرَ أَعْشُو إِلَى شُوَاظِهِ. وَأَحْشُو صَدَفَتِيَّ مِنْ دُرَرِ أَلْفَاظِهِ. إِلَى أَنْ نَعَبَ بَيْنَنَا غُرَابُ الْبَيْنِ. فَفَارَقْتُهُ مُفَارَقَةَ الْجَفْنِ لِلْعَيْنِ.

١ و: صحيفته؛ ف: صفحته.

الْمَقَامَةُ الْحَادِيَةُ وَالثَّلَاثُونَ[1]

٣١،١ حَدَّثَ[2] الْحَارِثُ بْنُ هَمَّامٍ قَالَ كُنْتُ فِي عُنْفُوَانِ الشَّبَابِ. وَرَيْعَانِ الْعَيْشِ اللُّبَابِ. أَقْلِي الاِكْتِنَانَ بِالْغَابِ. وَأَهْوَى الاِنْدِلَاقَ مِنَ الْقِرَابِ. لِعِلْمِي أَنَّ السَّفَرَ يَنْفِجُ السُّفَرَ. وَيُنْتِجُ[3] الظَّفَرَ. وَمُعَاقَرَةَ الْوَطَنِ. تَعْقِرُ الْفِطَنَ. وَتُحَقِّرُ مَنْ قَطَنَ. فَأَجَلْتُ قِدَاحَ الاِسْتِشَارَةِ. وَاقْتَدَحْتُ زِنَادَ الاِسْتِخَارَةِ. ثُمَّ اسْتَجَشْتُ جَأْشًا أَثْبَتَ مِنَ الْحِجَارَةِ. وَأَصْعَدْتُ إِلَى سَاحِلِ الشَّأْمِ لِلتِّجَارَةِ.

٣١،٢ فَلَمَّا خَيَّمْتُ بِالرَّمْلَةِ. وَأَلْقَيْتُ بِهَا عَصَا الرِّحْلَةِ. صَادَفْتُ بِهَا رِكَابًا تُعَدُّ لِلسُّرَى. وَرِحَالًا تُشَدُّ إِلَى أُمِّ الْقُرَى. فَعَصَفَتْ بِي رِيحُ الْغَرَامِ. وَاهْتَاجَ لِي شَوْقٌ إِلَى الْبَيْتِ الْحَرَامِ. فَزَمَمْتُ نَاقَتِي. وَنَبَذْتُ عُلَقِي وَعَلَاقَتِي.

وَقُلْتُ لِلَائِمِي أَقْصِرْ فَإِنِّي ... سَأَخْتَارُ الْمَقَامَ عَلَى الْمُقَامِ
وَأُنْفِقُ مَا جَمَعْتُ بِأَرْضِ جَمْعٍ ... وَأَسْلُو بِالْحَطِيمِ عَنِ الْحُطَامِ

٣١،٣ ثُمَّ انْتَظَمْتُ مَعَ رُفْقَةٍ كَنُجُومِ اللَّيْلِ. لَهُمْ فِي السَّيْرِ جِرْيَةُ السَّيْلِ. وَإِلَى الْخَيْرِ جَرْيُ الْخَيْلِ. فَلَمْ نَزَلْ بَيْنَ إِدْلَاجٍ وَتَأْوِيبٍ. وَإِيجَافٍ وَتَقْرِيبٍ. إِلَى أَنْ حَبَتْنَا أَيْدِي الْمَطَايَا بِالتُّحْفَةِ. فِي إِيصَالِنَا إِلَى الْجُحْفَةِ. فَحَلَلْنَاهَا مُتَأَهِّبِينَ لِلْإِحْرَامِ. مُتَبَاشِرِينَ بِإِدْرَاكِ الْمَرَامِ. فَلَمْ يَكُ إِلَّا أَنْ أَنَخْنَا[4] الرَّكَائِبَ. وَحَطَطْنَا الْحَقَائِبَ. حَتَّى طَلَعَ عَلَيْنَا مِنْ بَيْنِ الْهِضَابِ. شَخْصٌ ضَاحِي الْإِهَابِ. وَهُوَ يُنَادِي يَا أَهْلَ

---

١ في هامش س: وتعرف بالمَكّيةِ؛ وفي د: الرَّملية، ف: وهي الرملية. ٢ ف: حكى. ٣ س: يَنْتِجُ. ٤ س، ف: أنخنا بها.

ذَا ٱلنَّادِي. هَلُمَّ إِلَى مَا يُنْجِي يَوْمَ ٱلتَّنَادِي. فَٱنْخَرَطَ إِلَيْهِ ٱلْحَجِيجُ وَٱنْصَلَتُوا. وَٱحْتَفُّوا بِهِ وَأَنْصَتُوا. فَلَمَّا رَأَى تَأَثُّفَهُمْ حَوْلَهُ. وَٱسْتِعْظَامَهُمْ قَوْلَهُ. تَسَنَّمَ إِحْدَى ٱلْإِكَامِ.[1] ثُمَّ تَنَحْنَحَ مُسْتَفْتِحًا لِلْكَلَامِ. وَقَالَ

٤،٣١ يَا مَعْشَرَ ٱلْحُجَّاجِ. ٱلنَّاسِلِينَ مِنَ ٱلْفِجَاجِ. أَتَعْقِلُونَ مَا تُوَاجِهُونَ. وَإِلَى مَنْ تَتَوَجَّهُونَ. أَمْ تَدْرُونَ عَلَى مَنْ تَقْدَمُونَ. وَعَلَامَ تُقْدِمُونَ. أَتَخَالُونَ أَنَّ ٱلْحَجَّ هُوَ ٱخْتِيَارُ ٱلرَّوَاحِلِ. وَقَطْعُ ٱلْمَرَاحِلِ. وَٱتِّخَاذُ ٱلْمَحَامِلِ. وَإِيقَارُ ٱلزَّوَامِلِ. أَمْ تَظُنُّونَ أَنَّ ٱلنُّسُكَ هُوَ نَضْوُ ٱلْأَرْدَانِ. وَإِنْضَاءُ ٱلْأَبْدَانِ. وَمُفَارَقَةُ ٱلْوِلْدَانِ. وَٱلتَّنَائِي عَنِ ٱلْبُلْدَانِ. كَلَّا وَٱللهِ بَلْ هُوَ ٱجْتِنَابُ ٱلْخَطِيَّةِ. قَبْلَ ٱجْتِلَابِ ٱلْمَطِيَّةِ. وَإِخْلَاصُ ٱلنِّيَّةِ. فِي قَصْدِ تِلْكَ ٱلْبَنِيَّةِ. وَإِمْحَاضُ ٱلطَّاعَةِ. عِنْدَ وِجْدَانِ ٱلِٱسْتِطَاعَةِ. وَإِصْلَاحُ ٱلْمُعَامَلَاتِ. أَمَامَ إِعْمَالِ ٱلْيَعْمَلَاتِ.

٥،٣١ فَوَٱلَّذِي شَرَعَ ٱلْمَنَاسِكَ لِلنَّاسِكِ. وَأَرْشَدَ ٱلسَّالِكَ فِي ٱللَّيْلِ ٱلْحَالِكِ. مَا يُنْقِي[2] ٱلِٱغْتِسَالُ بِٱلذَّنُوبِ. مِنَ ٱلِٱنْغِمَاسِ فِي ٱلذُّنُوبِ. وَلَا تَعْدِلُ[3] تَعْرِيَةُ ٱلْأَجْسَامِ. بِتَعْبِيَةِ ٱلْأَجْرَامِ. وَلَا تُغْنِي لِبْسَةُ ٱلْإِحْرَامِ. عَنِ ٱلْمُتَلَبِّسِ بِٱلْحَرَامِ. وَلَا يَنْفَعُ ٱلِٱضْطِبَاعُ بِٱلْإِزَارِ. مَعَ ٱلِٱضْطِلَاعِ بِٱلْأَوْزَارِ. وَلَا يُجْدِي ٱلتَّقَرُّبُ بِٱلْحَلْقِ. مَعَ ٱلتَّقَلُّبِ فِي ظُلْمِ ٱلْخَلْقِ. وَلَا يَرْحَضُ ٱلتَّنَسُّكُ فِي ٱلتَّقْصِيرِ. دَرَنَ[4] ٱلتَّمَسُّكِ بِٱلتَّقْصِيرِ. وَلَا يَسْعَدُ بِعَرَفَةَ. غَيْرُ أَهْلِ ٱلْمَعْرِفَةِ. وَلَا يَزْكُو بِٱلْخَيْفِ. مَنْ يَرْغَبُ فِي ٱلْحَيْفِ. وَلَا يَشْهَدُ ٱلْمَقَامُ.[5] إِلَّا لِمَنِ[6] ٱسْتَقَامَ. وَلَا يَحْظَى بِقَبُولِ ٱلْحِجَّةِ.[7] مَنْ زَاغَ عَنِ ٱلْمَحَجَّةِ. فَرَحِمَ ٱللهُ ٱمْرَأً صَفَا. قَبْلَ مَسْعَاهُ إِلَى ٱلصَّفَا. وَوَرَدَ شَرِيعَةَ ٱلرِّضَا.

١ و: الأُكام؛ د، ف: الآكام. ٢ . د: يُنَقِّي. ٣ س، و: يَعْدل. ٤ و: دون. ٥ ف: المقامَ. ٦ ف: مَنْ.
٧ د: الحَجّة.

قَبْلَ شُرُوعِهِ عَلَى ٱلْأَضَا. وَنَزَعَ عَنْ تَلْبِيسِهِ. قَبْلَ نَزْعِ مَلْبُوسِهِ. وَفَاضَ بِمَعْرُوفِهِ. قَبْلَ ٱلْإِفَاضَةِ مِنْ تَعْرِيفِهِ.

٦،٣١ ثُمَّ رَفَعَ عَقِيرَتَهُ بِصَوْتٍ أَسْمَعَ ٱلصُّمَّ. وَكَادَ يُزَعْزِعُ ٱلْجِبَالَ ٱلشُّمَّ. وَأَنْشَدَ

مَا ٱلْحَجُّ سَيْرُكَ[1] تَأْوِيبًا وَإِدْلَاجَا   وَلَا ٱعْتِيَامُكَ[2] أَجْمَالًا وَأَحْدَاجَا

ٱلْحَجُّ أَنْ تَقْصِدَ ٱلْبَيْتَ ٱلْحَرَامَ عَلَى   تَجْرِيدِكَ ٱلْحَجَّ لَا تَقْضِي بِهِ حَاجَا

وَتَمْتَطِي كَاهِلَ ٱلْإِنْصَافِ مُتَّخِذًا   رَدْعَ ٱلْهَوَى هَادِيًا وَٱلْحَقَّ مِنْهَاجَا

وَأَنْ تُوَاسِيَ[3] مَا أُوتِيتَ مَقْدُرَةً   مَنْ مَدَّ كَفًّا إِلَى جَدْوَاكَ مُحْتَاجَا

فَهٰذِهِ إِنْ حَوَتْهَا حَجَّةٌ كَمُلَتْ   وَإِنْ خَلَا ٱلْحَجُّ مِنْهَا كَانَ إِخْدَاجَا

حَسْبُ ٱلْمُرَائِينَ غَبْنًا أَنَّهُمْ غَرَسُوا   وَمَا جَنَوْا وَلَقُوا كَدًّا وَإِزْعَاجَا

وَأَنَّهُمْ حُرِمُوا أَجْرًا وَمَحْمَدَةً   وَأَلْحَمُوا عِرْضَهُمْ مَنْ عَابَ أَوْ هَاجَا

أُخَيَّ ٱبْغِ[4] بِمَا تُبْدِيهِ مِنْ قُرَبٍ   وَجْهَ ٱلْمُهَيْمِنِ وَلَّاجًا وَخَرَّاجَا

فَلَيْسَ تَخْفَى عَلَى ٱلرَّحْمٰنِ خَافِيَةٌ   إِنْ أَخْلَصَ ٱلْعَبْدُ فِي ٱلطَّاعَاتِ أَوْ دَاجَا

وَبَادِرِ ٱلْمَوْتَ بِٱلْحُسْنَى تُقَدِّمُهَا   فَمَا يُنَهْنِهُ[5] دَاعِي ٱلْمَوْتِ إِنْ فَاجَا

وَٱقْنَ ٱلتَّوَاضُعَ خُلْقًا لَا تُزَايِلُهُ   عَنْكَ ٱللَّيَالِي وَلَوْ أَلْبَسْنَكَ ٱلتَّاجَا

وَلَا تَشِمْ كُلَّ خَالٍ لَاحَ بَارِقُهُ   وَلَوْ تَرَاءَى هَتُونَ ٱلسَّكْبِ ثَجَّاجَا

مَا كُلُّ دَاعٍ بِأَهْلٍ أَنْ يُصَاخَ لَهُ   كَمْ قَدْ أَصَمَّ بِنَعْيٍ بَعْضُ مَنْ نَاجَا

وَمَا ٱللَّبِيبُ سِوَى مَنْ بَاتَ مُقْتَنِعًا   بِبُلْغَةٍ تُدْرِجُ ٱلْأَيَّامَ إِدْرَاجَا

فَكُلُّ كُثْرٍ إِلَى قُلٍّ مَغَبَّتُهُ   وَكُلُّ نَازٍ إِلَى لِينٍ وَإِنْ هَاجَا

---

١ في تعليق على ق وفي س: سيرَك. ٢ في تعليق على ق وفي س: اعتيامَك. ٣ س: تؤاسي. ٤ د، ف: فابْغِ.
٥ س، و: يُنَهْنِه.

٧،٣١ قَالَ الرَّاوِي فَلَمَّا أَلْقَحَ عُقْمَ ٱلْأَفْهَامِ . بِسِحْرِ ٱلْكَلَامِ . ٱسْتَرْوَحْتُ رِيحَ أَبِي زَيْدٍ . وَمَادَ بِيَ الِارْتِيَاحُ إِلَيْهِ أَيَّ مَيْدٍ . فَمَكَثْتُ حَتَّى ٱسْتَوْعَبَ نَثَّ حِكْمَتِهِ . وَٱنْحَدَرَ مِنْ أَكَمَتِهِ . ثُمَّ دَلَفْتُ إِلَيْهِ لِأَتَصَفَّحَ صَفَحَاتِ مُحَيَّاهُ . وَأَسْتَشِفَّ جَوْهَرَ حُلَاهُ .[1] فَإِذَا هُوَ الضَّالَّةُ الَّتِي أَنْشُدُهَا .[2] وَنَاظِمُ ٱلْقَلَائِدِ اللَّاتِي أُنْشِدُهَا . فَعَانَقْتُهُ عِنَاقَ اللَّامِ لِلْأَلِفِ . وَنَزَّلْتُهُ مَنْزِلَةَ ٱلْبُرْءِ عِنْدَ الدَّنِفِ . وَسَأَلْتُهُ أَنْ يُلَازِمَنِي فَأَبَى . أَوْ يُزَامِلَنِي فَنَبَا . وَقَالَ آلَيْتُ فِي حَجَّتِي هٰذِهِ أَنْ لَا أَحْتَقِبَ وَلَا أَعْتَقِبَ . وَلَا أَكْتَسِبَ وَلَا أَنْتَسِبَ . وَلَا أَرْتَفِقَ . وَلَا أُرَافِقَ . وَلَا أُوَافِقَ مَنْ يُنَافِقُ .

٨،٣١ ثُمَّ ذَهَبَ يُهَرْوِلُ . وَغَادَرَنِي أُوَلْوِلُ . فَلَمْ أَزَلْ أُقْرِيهِ نَظَرِي . وَأَوَدُّ لَوْ يَمْشِي عَلَى نَاظِرِي . حَتَّى تَوَقَّلَ أَحَدَ ٱلْأَطْوَادِ . وَوَقَفَ لِلْحَجِيجِ بِٱلْمِرْصَادِ . فَحِينَ[3] شَاهَدَ إِيضَاعَ الرُّكْبَانِ فِي الْكُثْبَانِ . وَقَّعَ بِالْبَنَانِ عَلَى الْبَنَانِ . وَٱنْدَفَعَ يُنْشِدُ

لَيْسَ مَنْ زَارَ رَاكِبًا   مِثْلَ سَاعٍ عَلَى الْقَدَمْ
لَا وَلَا خَادِمٌ أَطَا   عَ كَعَاصٍ مِنَ الْخَدَمْ
كَيْفَ يَا قَوْمِ يَسْتَوِي   سَعْيُ بَانٍ وَمَنْ هَدَمْ
سَيُقِيمُ الْمُفَرِّطُو   نَ غَدًا مَأْتَمَ النَّدَمْ
وَيَقُولُ الَّذِي تَقَرَّ   بَ طُوبَى لِمَنْ خَدَمْ
وَيْكِ يَا نَفْسُ قَدِّمِي   صَالِحًا عِنْدَ ذِي الْقِدَمْ
وَٱزْدَرِي زُخْرُفَ الْحَيَا   ةِ فَوِجْدَانُهُ[4] عَدَمْ
وَٱذْكُرِي مَصْرَعَ الْحِمَا   مِ إِذَا خَطْبُهُ صَدَمْ
وَٱنْدُبِي فِعْلَكِ الْقَبِيـ   ـحَ وَسُحِّي[5] لَهُ بِدَمْ

١ د: حِلاه. ٢ د، و، ف: أَنْشَدَهَا. ٣ ف: فلما. ٤ ف: وُجْدانه. ٥ د: سَحِّي؛ ف: سِحِّي.

وَٱدْبُغِــيهِ بِتَوْبَــةٍ قَبْــلَ أَنْ يَحْلَمَ ٱلْأَدَمْ
فَـعَـسَى ٱللّٰهُ أَنْ يَقِيــكِ ٱلسَّعِيرَ ٱلَّذِي ٱحْتَدَمْ
يَوْمَ لَا عَــثْرَةٌ تُقَــا لُ وَلَا يَنْـفَـعُ ٱلسَّـدَمْ

ثُمَّ إِنَّهُ أَغْمَضَ عَضْبَ لِسَانِهِ. وَٱنْطَلَقَ لِشَانِهِ.

٩،٣١ فَمَا زِلْتُ فِي كُلِّ مَوْرِدٍ نَرِدُهُ. وَمُعَرَّسٍ نَتَوَسَّدُهُ. أَتَفَقَّدُهُ فَأَفْقِدُهُ.[١] وَأَسْتَنْجِدُ بِمَنْ يَنْشُدُهُ فَلَا يَجِدُهُ. حَتَّى خِلْتُ أَنَّ ٱلْجِنَّ ٱخْتَطَفَتْهُ. أَوِ ٱلْأَرْضَ ٱقْتَطَفَتْهُ. فَمَا كَابَدْتُ فِي ٱلْغُرْبَةِ. كَهٰذِهِ ٱلْكُرْبَةِ. وَلَا مُنِيتُ فِي سَفْرَةٍ. بِمِثْلِهَا مِنْ زَفْرَةٍ.

١ هكذا في هامش ق، وفي س، ف؛ وفي متون ق، و، د: أفتقده.

ٱلْمَقَامَةُ ٱلثَّانِيَةُ وَٱلثَّلَاثُونَ[1]

حَكَى ٱلْحَارِثُ بْنُ هَمَّامٍ قَالَ أَجْمَعْتُ حِينَ قَضَيْتُ مَنَاسِكَ ٱلْحَجِّ. وَأَقَمْتُ وَظَائِفَ ١،٣٢
ٱلْعَجِّ وَٱلثَّجِّ. أَنْ أَقْصِدَ طَيْبَةَ. مَعَ رُفْقَةٍ مِنْ بَنِي شَيْبَةَ. لِأَزُورَ قَبْرَ ٱلْمُصْطَفَى. وَأَخْرُجَ مِنْ قَبِيلِ مَنْ حَجَّ وَجَفَا.[2] فَأُرْجِفَ بِأَنَّ ٱلْمَسَالِكَ شَاغِرَةٌ. وَعَرَبَ ٱلْحَرَمَيْنِ مُتَشَاجِرَةٌ. فَحِرْتُ بَيْنَ إِشْفَاقٍ يُثَبِّطُنِي. وَأَشْوَاقٍ تُنَشِّطُنِي. إِلَى أَنْ أُلْقِيَ فِي رُوعِي ٱلِٱسْتِسْلَامُ. وَتَغْلِيبُ زِيَارَةِ قَبْرِهِ عَلَيْهِ ٱلسَّلَامُ. فَٱعْتَمْتُ[3] ٱلْقُعْدَةَ. وَأَعْدَدْتُ ٱلْعُدَّةَ. وَسِرْتُ وَٱلرُّفْقَةَ لَا نَلْوِي عَلَى عُرْجَةٍ. وَلَا نَنِي فِي تَأْوِيبٍ وَلَا دُلْجَةٍ. حَتَّى وَافَيْنَا بَنِي حَرْبٍ. وَقَدْ آبُوا مِنْ حَرْبٍ. فَأَزْمَعْنَا أَنْ نُقَضِّيَ ظِلَّ ٱلْيَوْمِ. فِي حِلَّةِ ٱلْقَوْمِ.

وَبَيْنَمَا نَحْنُ نَتَخَيَّرُ ٱلْمُنَاخَ. وَنَرُودُ ٱلْوِرْدَ ٱلنُّقَاخَ. إِذْ رَأَيْنَاهُمْ يَرْكُضُونَ. ﴿كَأَنَّهُمْ ٢،٣٢
إِلَى نَصْبٍ يُوفِضُونَ﴾[4] فَرَابَنَا ٱنْثِيَالُهُمْ. وَسَأَلْنَا مَا بَالُهُمْ. فَقِيلَ قَدْ حَضَرَ نَادِيَهُمْ فَقِيهُ ٱلْعَرَبِ. فَإِهْرَاعُهُمْ لِهٰذَا ٱلسَّبَبِ. فَقُلْتُ لِرُفْقَتِي أَلَا نَشْهَدُ مَجْمَعَ ٱلْحَيِّ. لِنَتَبَيَّنَ ٱلرُّشْدَ مِنَ ٱلْغَيِّ. فَقَالُوا لَقَدْ أَسْمَعْتَ إِذْ دَعَوْتَ. وَنَصَحْتَ وَمَا أَلَوْتَ. ثُمَّ نَهَضْنَا نَتَّبِعُ ٱلْهَادِي. وَنَؤُمُّ ٱلنَّادِيَ. حَتَّى إِذَا أَظْلَلْنَا عَلَيْهِ. وَٱسْتَشْرَفْنَا ٱلْفَقِيهَ ٱلْمَنْهُودَ إِلَيْهِ. أَلْفَيْتُهُ أَبَا زَيْدٍ ذَا ٱلشُّقَرِ وَٱلْبُقَرِ. وَٱلْفَوَاقِرِ وَٱلْفِقَرِ. وَقَدِ ٱعْتَمَّ ٱلْقَفْدَاءَ. وَٱشْتَمَلَ ٱلصَّمَّاءَ. وَقَعَدَ[5] ٱلْقُرْفُصَاءَ. وَأَعْيَانُ ٱلْحَيِّ بِهِ مُحْتَفُّونَ. وَأَخْلَاطُهُمْ عَلَيْهِ مُلْتَفُّونَ. وَهُوَ يَقُولُ سَلُونِي عَنِ ٱلْمُعْضِلَاتِ. وَٱسْتَوْضِحُوا

١ في هامش س: تعرف بالفقيهية (هكذا)؛ وفي د: الحَربية؛ وفي ف: الطِّيبيَّة. ٢ «وجفا»: سقطت من و.
٣ ف: أَعْتَمْتُ. ٤ «نَصْبٍ»: هكذا في ق، س، د؛ وهي من قراءات الآية؛ والكلمة مطموسة في و، وفي ف: نُصُبٍ، وهي قراءة حفص. ٦ سقطت الورقة التالية من مخطوطة و.

مِنِّي ٱلْمُشْكِلَاتِ. فَوَٱلَّذِي فَطَرَ ٱلسَّمَاءَ. وَعَلَّمَ آدَمَ ٱلْأَسْمَاءَ. إِنِّي لَفَقِيهُ ٱلْعَرَبِ ٱلْعَرْبَاءِ. وَأَعْلَمُ مَنْ تَحْتَ ٱلْجَرْبَاءِ. فَصَمَدَ لَهُ فَتًى فَتِيقُ ٱللِّسَانِ. جَرِيءُ ٱلْجَنَانِ. وَقَالَ إِنِّي حَاضَرْتُ فُقَهَاءَ ٱلدُّنْيَا. حَتَّى ٱنْتَخَلْتُ مِنْهُمْ مِائَةَ فُتْيَا. فَإِنْ كُنْتَ مِمَّنْ يَرْغَبُ عَنْ بَنَاتِ غَيْرٍ. وَيَرْغَبُ مِنَّا فِي مَيْرٍ. فَٱسْتَمِعْ وَأَجِبْ. لِتُقَابَلَ بِمَا يَجِبُ. فَقَالَ ٱللهُ أَكْبَرُ. سَيَبِينُ ٱلْمَخْبَرُ. وَيَنْكَشِفُ ٱلْمُضْمَرُ. ﴿فَٱصْدَعْ بِمَا تُؤْمَرُ﴾.

٣،٣٢ قَالَ مَا تَقُولُ فِي مَنْ تَوَضَّأَ ثُمَّ لَمَسَ ظَهْرَ نَعْلِهِ. قَالَ ٱنْتَقَضَ وُضُوءُهُ بِفِعْلِهِ.

النَّعْلُ الزَّوْجَةُ.[١]

قَالَ فَإِنْ تَوَضَّأَ ثُمَّ أَكْأَهُ ٱلْبَرْدُ. قَالَ يُجَدِّدُ ٱلْوُضُوءَ مِنْ بَعْدُ.

الْبَرْدُ النَّوْمُ.

قَالَ أَيَمْسَحُ ٱلْمُتَوَضِّئُ أُنْثَيَيْهِ. قَالَ قَدْ نُدِبَ إِلَيْهِ. وَلَمْ يُوجَبْ[٢] عَلَيْهِ.

الْأُنْثَيَانِ الْأُذُنَانِ.[٣]

قَالَ أَيَجُوزُ ٱلْوُضُوءُ مِمَّا يَقْذِفُهُ ٱلثُّعْبَانُ. قَالَ وَهَلْ أَنْظَفُ مِنْهُ لِلْعُرْبَانِ.

الثُّعْبَانُ جَمْعُ ثَعْبٍ وَهُوَ مَسِيلُ الْوَادِي.

قَالَ أَيُسْتَبَاحُ مَاءُ ٱلضَّرِيرِ. قَالَ نَعَمْ وَيُجْتَنَبُ مَاءُ ٱلْبَصِيرِ.

الضَّرِيرُ حَرْفُ الْوَادِي وَالْبَصِيرُ الْكَلْبُ.

قَالَ أَيَحِلُّ ٱلطَّوْفُ[٤] فِي ٱلرَّبِيعِ. قَالَ يُكْرَهُ ذَاكَ لِلْحَدَثِ ٱلشَّنِيعِ.

الطَّوْفُ التَّغَوُّطُ وَالرَّبِيعُ النَّهْرُ.[٥]

١ ورد هذا الشرح والذي يليه في هامش ق، ثم وردت الأربعة شروح التالية في غضون النص، ثم جاءت البقية كل منها في سطر على حدة كما جاءت في س أيضا، بينما في و وردت الشروح كلها في عامود قائم بذاته يسار الورقة. ٢ د: يَجِبْ. ٣ استُبدل في س موضع هذه المسألة بموضع التي بعدها. ٤ ف: التطوُّف. ٥ بعدها في د: الصغير.

قَالَ أَيَجِبُ ٱلْغُسْلُ عَلَى مَنْ أَمْنَى. قَالَ لَا وَلَوْ ثَنَّى.

أَمْنَى نَزَلَ مِنًى يُقَالُ مِنْهُ مَنَى وَأَمْنَى وَٱمْتَنَى.

قَالَ فَهَلْ يَجِبُ عَلَى ٱلْجُنُبِ غَسْلُ فَرْوَتِهِ. قَالَ أَجَلْ وَغَسْلُ إِبْرَتِهِ.

ٱلْفَرْوَةُ جِلْدَةُ ٱلرَّأْسِ وَٱلْإِبْرَةُ عَظْمُ ٱلْمِرْفَقِ.[١]

قَالَ فَإِنْ أَخَلَّ بِغَسْلِ فَأْسِهِ. قَالَ هُوَ كَمَا لَوْ أَلْغَى غَسْلَ رَأْسِهِ.

ٱلْفَأْسُ ٱلْعَظْمُ ٱلْمُشْرِفُ عَلَى نُقْرَةِ ٱلْقَفَا.

قَالَ مَا تَقُولُ فِيمَنْ تَيَمَّمَ ثُمَّ رَأَى رَوْضًا. قَالَ بَطَلَ تَيَمُّمُهُ فَلْيَتَوَضَّا.

وَٱلرَّوْضُ هَاهُنَا جَمْعُ رَوْضَةٍ وَهِيَ ٱلصُّبَابَةُ تَبْقَى فِي ٱلْحَوْضِ.

قَالَ أَيَجُوزُ أَنْ يَسْجُدَ ٱلرَّجُلُ فِي ٱلْعَذِرَةِ. قَالَ نَعَمْ وَلْيُجَانِبِ ٱلْقَذِرَةَ. ٤،٣٢

ٱلْعَذِرَةُ فِنَاءُ ٱلدَّارِ.

قَالَ فَهَلْ لَهُ ٱلسُّجُودُ عَلَى ٱلْخِلَافِ. قَالَ لَا وَلَا عَلَى أَحَدِ ٱلْأَطْرَافِ.

ٱلْخِلَافُ ٱلْكُمُّ.

قَالَ فَإِنْ سَجَدَ عَلَى شِمَالِهِ. قَالَ لَا بَأْسَ بِفِعَالِهِ.

ٱلشِّمَالُ جَمْعُ شَمْلَةٍ.

قَالَ[٢] فَهَلْ يَجُوزُ ٱلسُّجُودُ عَلَى ٱلْكُرَاعِ. قَالَ نَعَمْ دُونَ ٱلذِّرَاعِ.

ٱلْكُرَاعُ مَا ٱسْتَطَالَ مِنَ ٱلْحَرَّةِ.[٣]

قَالَ أَيُصَلِّي عَلَى رَأْسِ ٱلْكَلْبِ. قَالَ نَعَمْ كَسَائِرِ ٱلْهَضْبِ.[٤]

رَأْسُ ٱلْكَلْبِ ثَنِيَّةٌ مَعْرُوفَةٌ.[٥]

---

١ بعدها في ف: قال أيجب عليه غَسْلُ صَحِيفته قال نعم كَغَسْلِ شَفَتِه. الصحيفة أَسِرَّة الوجه. قال أيجوزُ الغُسلُ في الجِرابِ. قال هو كالغُسلِ في الجِبابِ. الجِراب جوف البئر. ٢ من هاهنا تستأنف النسخة الرقمية للمخطوطة و. ٣ بعدها في و، ف: وهي أرض ذات حجارة سود. ٤. ق: العَضْب. ٥ بعدها في ف: قال أيجوز للدَّارِس حَمْلُ المَصاحف. قال لا ولا حملُها في المَلاحف. الدارس الحائض.

قَالَ مَا تَقُولُ فِيمَنْ صَلَّى وَعَانَتُهُ بَارِزَةٌ. قَالَ صَلَاتُهُ جَائِزَةٌ.

الْعَانَةُ الْجَمَاعَةُ مِنْ حُمُرِ الْوَحْشِ.

قَالَ فَإِنْ صَلَّى وَعَلَيْهِ صَوْمٌ. قَالَ يُعِيدُ وَلَوْ صَلَّى مَائَةَ يَوْمٍ.

الصَّوْمُ ذَرْقُ النَّعَامِ.

قَالَ فَإِنْ حَمَلَ جِرْوًا وَصَلَّى. قَالَ هُوَ كَمَا لَوْ حَمَلَ بَاقِلَّى.

الْجِرْوُ الصِّغَارُ مِنَ الْقِثَّاءِ وَالرُّمَّانِ.

قَالَ أَتَصِحُّ صَلَاةُ حَامِلِ الْقَرْوَةِ. قَالَ لَا وَلَوْ صَلَّى فَوْقَ[1] الْمَرْوَةِ.

الْقَرْوَةُ مِيلَغَةُ الْكَلْبِ.

قَالَ فَإِنْ قَطَرَ عَلَى ثَوْبِ الْمُصَلِّي نَجْوٌ. قَالَ يَمْضِي فِي صَلَاتِهِ وَلَا غَرْوَ.

النَّجْوُ السَّحَابُ الَّذِي قَدْ هَرَاقَ[2] مَاءَهُ.

٥،٣٢ قَالَ أَيَجُوزُ أَنْ يَؤُمَّ الرِّجَالَ[3] مُقَنَّعٌ. قَالَ نَعَمْ وَيَؤُمُّهُمْ[4] مُدَرَّعٌ.

الْمُقَنَّعُ لَابِسُ الْمِغْفَرِ وَالْمُدَرَّعُ لَابِسُ الدِّرْعِ.

قَالَ فَإِنْ أَمَّهُمْ مَنْ فِي يَدِهِ وَقْفٌ. قَالَ يُعِيدُونَ وَلَوْ أَنَّهُمْ أَلْفٌ.

الْوَقْفُ السِّوَارُ مِنَ الْعَاجِ أَوِ الذَّبْلِ وَأَرَادَ أَنَّهُ لَا يَجُوزُ لِلرِّجَالِ الِائْتِمَامُ بِالنِّسَاءِ.

قَالَ فَإِنْ أَمَّهُمْ مَنْ فَخْذُهُ بَادِيَةٌ. قَالَ صَلَاتُهُ وَصَلَاتُهُمْ مَاضِيَةٌ.

الْفَخْذُ الْعَشِيرَةُ وَبَادِيَةٌ[5] يَسْكُنُونَ الْبَدْوَ وَاخْتَارَ بَعْضُ أَهْلِ اللُّغَةِ تَسْكِينَ الْخَاءِ مِنْ هٰذِهِ الْفَخْذِ[6] لِيَحْصُلَ[7] الْفَرْقُ بَيْنَهَا وَبَيْنَ الْفَخِذِ مِنَ الْأَعْضَاءِ.[8]

١ ق: علي، وفي هامش: فوق خ بخطه (أي علّم الحريري بخطه على كلمة «على» بحرف الخاء بمعنى «خطأ»).
٢ د: هراق، وهو. ٣ زيدت في هامش ق. ٤ زيدت في هامش ق. ٥ بعدها في ف: أي. ٦ ليست في س. ٧ س: ليقع. ٨ «الفخذ من الأعضاء»: في ف: العضو.

قَالَ فَإِنْ أَمَّهُمُ ٱلثَّوْرُ ٱلْأَجَمُّ. قَالَ صَلِّ وَخَلَاكَ ذَمٌّ.

ٱلثَّوْرُ ٱلسَّيِّدُ وَٱلْأَجَمُّ ٱلَّذِي لَا رُمْحَ مَعَهُ.

قَالَ أَيَدْخُلُ ٱلْقَصْرُ فِي صَلَاةِ ٱلشَّاهِدِ. قَالَ لَا وَٱلْغَائِبِ ٱلشَّاهِدِ.

صَلَاةُ ٱلشَّاهِدِ صَلَاةُ ٱلْمَغْرِبِ سُمِّيَتْ بِذٰلِكَ لِإِقَامَتِهَا عِنْدَ طُلُوعِ ٱلنَّجْمِ[1] لِأَنَّ ٱلنَّجْمَ يُسَمَّى ٱلشَّاهِدَ.

قَالَ أَيَجُوزُ لِلْمَعْذُورِ أَنْ يُفْطِرَ فِي شَهْرِ رَمَضَانَ. قَالَ مَا رُخِّصَ فِيهِ إِلَّا لِلصِّبْيَانِ. ٦،٣٢

ٱلْمَعْذُورُ ٱلْمَخْتُونُ وَهُوَ أَيْضًا ٱلْمُعْذَرُ.[2]

قَالَ فَهَلْ لِلْمُعَرِّسِ أَنْ يَأْكُلَ فِيهِ. قَالَ نَعَمْ بِمِلْءِ فِيهِ.

ٱلْمُعَرِّسُ ٱلْمُسَافِرُ ٱلَّذِي يَنْزِلُ فِي آخِرِ[3] لَيْلِهِ لِيَسْتَرِيحَ ثُمَّ يَرْتَحِلُ.

قَالَ فَإِنْ أَفْطَرَ فِيهِ ٱلْعُرَاةُ. قَالَ لَا تُنْكِرُ عَلَيْهِمِ ٱلْوُلَاةُ.

ٱلْعُرَاةُ ٱلَّذِينَ تَأْخُذُهُمُ ٱلْعُرَوَاءُ وَهِيَ ٱلْحُمَّى بِرَعْدَةٍ.

قَالَ فَإِنْ أَكَلَ ٱلصَّائِمُ بَعْدَمَا أَصْبَحَ. قَالَ هُوَ أَحْوَطُ لَهُ وَأَصْلَحُ.

أَصْبَحَ أَيِ ٱسْتَصْبَحَ بِٱلْمِصْبَاحِ.

قَالَ فَإِنْ عَمَدَ لِأَنْ أَكَلَ لَيْلًا. قَالَ لِيُشَمِّرْ لِلْقَضَاءِ ذَيْلًا.

ٱللَّيْلُ وَلَدُ[4] ٱلْحُبَارَى وَقِيلَ هُوَ وَلَدُ ٱلْكَرَوَانِ.

قَالَ فَإِنْ أَكَلَ قَبْلَ أَنْ تَتَوَارَى ٱلْبَيْضَاءُ. قَالَ يَلْزَمُهُ وَٱللّٰهِ[5] ٱلْقَضَاءُ.

ٱلْبَيْضَاءُ مِنْ أَسْمَاءِ ٱلشَّمْسِ.

قَالَ فَإِنِ ٱسْتَثَارَ ٱلصَّائِمُ ٱلْكَيْدَ. قَالَ أَفْطَرَ وَمَنْ أَحَلَّ ٱلصَّيْدَ.

ٱلْكَيْدُ ٱلْقَيْءُ وَٱسْتَثَارَهُ أَيِ ٱسْتَدْعَاهُ.

قَالَ أَلَهُ أَنْ يُفْطِرَ بِإِلْحَاحِ ٱلطَّابِخِ. قَالَ نَعَمْ لَا بِطَاهِي ٱلْمَطَابِخِ.

---

١ «لأن النجم»: سقطت من ق. ٢ ف: المعذّر. ٣ «في آخر»: في ق: آخرَ. ٤ س: فرخ. ٥ س: وأبيه.

الطَّابِخُ الحُمَّى الصَّالِبِ.

قَالَ فَإِنْ ضَحِكَتِ الْمَرْأَةُ فِي صَوْمِهَا. قَالَ بَطَلَ صَوْمُ يَوْمِهَا.

ضَحِكَتْ هَاهُنَا أَيْ حَاضَتْ وَمِنْهُ قَوْلُهُ تَعَالَى ﴿فَضَحِكَتْ فَبَشَّرْنَاهَا بِإِسْحَاقَ﴾.

قَالَ فَإِنْ ظَهَرَ الجُدَرِيُّ عَلَى ضَرَّتِهَا. قَالَ تُفْطِرُ إِنْ آذَنَ بِمَضَرَّتِهَا.

الضَرَّةُ أَصْلُ الإِبْهَامِ وَأَصْلُ الثَّدْيِ أَيْضًا.

٧،٣٢ قَالَ مَا يَجِبُ فِي مَائَةِ مِصْبَاحٍ. قَالَ حِقَّتَانِ يَا صَاحِ.

الْمِصْبَاحُ النَّاقَةُ الَّتِي تُصْبِحُ فِي الْمَبْرَكِ.

قَالَ فَإِنْ مَلَكَ عَشْرَ خَنَاجِرَ. قَالَ يُخْرِجُ شَاتَيْنِ وَلَا يُشَاجِرُ.

الخَنَاجِرُ النُّوقُ الْغِزَارُ وَأَحَدُهَا خَنْجَرٌ وَخُنْجُورٌ.[1]

قَالَ فَإِنْ سَمَحَ[2] لِلسَّاعِي بِجَمِيمَتِهِ. قَالَ يَا بُشْرَى لَهُ يَوْمَ قِيَامَتِهِ.

السَّاعِي جَابِي الصَّدَقَةِ وَالجَمِيمَةُ خِيَارُ الْمَالِ.

قَالَ أَيَسْتَحِقُّ حَمَلَةُ[3] الأَوْزَارِ مِنَ الزَّكَاةِ جُزْءًا.[4] قَالَ نَعَمْ إِذَا كَانُوا غُزًّى.

الأَوْزَارُ السِّلَاحُ وَغُزًّى جَمْعُ غَازٍ.

٨،٣٢ قَالَ أَيَجُوزُ لِلْحَاجِّ أَنْ يَعْتَمِرَ. قَالَ لَا وَلَا أَنْ يَخْتَمِرَ.

الاِعْتِمَارُ لُبْسُ الْعَمَارَةِ[5] وَهِيَ الْعِمَامَةُ[6] وَالاِخْتِمَارُ لُبْسُ الْخِمَارِ.

قَالَ فَهَلْ لَهُ أَنْ يَقْتُلَ الشُّجَاعَ. قَالَ نَعَمْ كَمَا يَقْتُلُ السِّبَاعَ.

الشُّجَاعُ الحَيَّةُ.

قَالَ فَإِنْ قَتَلَ زَمَّارَةً فِي الحَرَمِ. قَالَ عَلَيْهِ بَدَنَةٌ مِنَ النَّعَمِ.

---

١ د: خَنجورٌ. ٢ د: سَمُحَ. ٣ ق: حَمْلة. ٤ ف: جُزًّا. ٥ ف: العِمارة. ٦ د: العَمامة.

الزَّمَّارَةُ النَّعَامَةُ وَٱسْمُ صَوْتِهَا الزِّمَارُ.[١]

قَالَ فَإِنْ رَمَى سَاقَ حُرٍّ فَجَدَّلَهُ. قَالَ يُخْرِجُ شَاةً بَدَلَهُ.

سَاقُ حُرٍّ ذَكَرُ الْقَمَارِيِّ.

قَالَ فَإِنْ قَتَلَ أُمَّ عَوْفٍ بَعْدَ الْإِحْرَامِ. قَالَ يَتَصَدَّقُ بِقَبْضَةٍ مِنْ طَعَامٍ.

أُمُّ عَوْفٍ الْجَرَادَةُ.

قَالَ أَيَجِبُ عَلَى الْحَاجِّ ٱسْتِصْحَابُ الْقَارِبِ. قَالَ نَعَمْ لِيَسُوقَهُمْ إِلَى الْمَشَارِبِ.

الْقَارِبُ طَالِبُ الْمَاءِ بِاللَّيْلِ. الْحَاجُّ ٱسْمٌ لِلْجَمْعِ وَالْوَاحِدِ.[٢]

قَالَ مَا تَقُولُ فِي الْحَرَامِ بَعْدَ السَّبْتِ. قَالَ قَدْ حَلَّ فِي ذٰلِكَ الْوَقْتِ.

الْحَرَامُ الْمُحْرِمُ وَالسَّبْتُ حَلْقُ الرَّأْسِ وَحَلَّ مِنْ تَحْلِيلِ الْحَجِّ.

٩٫٣٢ قَالَ مَا تَقُولُ فِي بَيْعِ الْكُمَيْتِ. قَالَ حَرَامٌ كَبَيْعِ الْمَيْتِ.

الْكُمَيْتُ الْخَمْرُ.

قَالَ أَيَجُوزُ بَيْعُ الْخَلِّ بِلَحْمِ الْحَمَلِ. قَالَ لَا وَلَا بِلَحْمِ الْحَمَلِ.

الْخَلُّ ٱبْنُ الْمَخَاضِ وَلَا يَحِلُّ بَيْعُ اللَّحْمِ بِالْحَيَوَانِ سَوَاءٌ كَانَ مِنْ جِنْسِهِ أَمْ مِنْ غَيْرِ جِنْسِهِ.

قَالَ أَيَحِلُّ بَيْعُ الْهَدِيَّةِ. قَالَ لَا[٣] وَلَا بَيْعُ السَّبِيَّةِ.[٤]

الْهَدِيَّةُ بِالتَّشْدِيدِ مَا يُهْدَى إِلَى الْكَعْبَةِ[٥] وَالسَّبِيَّةُ[٦] الْخَمْرُ.

قَالَ مَا تَقُولُ فِي بَيْعِ الْعَقِيقَةِ. قَالَ مَحْظُورٌ عَلَى الْحَقِيقَةِ.

الْعَقِيقَةُ مَا يُذْبَحُ عَنِ الْمَوْلُودِ فِي الْيَوْمِ السَّابِعِ مِنْ وِلَادَتِهِ.

١ ف: الزَّمَّار. ٢ «الحاج...» الخ: في هامش س؛ وناقصة في ف؛ وفي و: «والحاج...» الخ، وفي د: الحاج اسم للجمع والواحد والقارب طالب ماء بالليل. ٣. ساقطة من ف. ٤ س: السَّبيئة. ٥ بعدها في س، و، د، ف: ويقال الهَدْيَةُ بتسْكين الدال وتخفيف الياء. ٦ س: السَّبيئة.

قَالَ أَيَجُوزُ بَيْعُ الدَّاعِي عَلَى الرَّاعِي. قَالَ لَا وَلَا عَلَى السَّاعِي.

الدَّاعِي بَقِيَّةُ اللَّبَنِ فِي الدَّرْعِ. السَّاعِي جَابِي الصَّدَقَةِ وَقَدْ مَرَّ تَفْسِيرُهُ.[١]

قَالَ أَيُبَاعُ الصَّقْرُ بِالتَّمْرِ. قَالَ لَا وَمَالِكِ الْخَلْقِ وَالْأَمْرِ.

الصَّقْرُ الدِّبْسُ.

قَالَ أَيَشْتَرِي الْمُسْلِمُ سَلَبَ الْمُسْلِمَاتِ. قَالَ نَعَمْ وَيُورَثُ عَنْهُ إِذَا مَاتَ.

السَّلَبُ لِحَاءُ الشَّجَرِ وَهُوَ أَيْضًا خُوصُ الثُّمَامِ.

قَالَ فَهَلْ يَجُوزُ أَنْ يُبْتَاعَ الشَّافِعُ. قَالَ مَا لِجَوَازِهِ مِنْ دَافِعٍ.

الشَّافِعُ الشَّاةُ الَّتِي مَعَهَا سَخْلُهَا.[٢]

قَالَ أَيُبَاعُ الْإِبْرِيقُ عَلَى بَنِي الْأَصْفَرِ. قَالَ يُكْرَهُ كَبَيْعِ الْمِغْفَرِ.

الْإِبْرِيقُ السَّيْفُ الصَّقِيلُ الْكَثِيرُ الْمَاءِ وَبَنُو الْأَصْفَرِ الرُّومُ.

قَالَ أَيَجُوزُ أَنْ يَبِيعَ الرَّجُلُ صَيْفِيَّهُ. قَالَ لَا وَلٰكِنْ لِيَبِعْ صَفِيَّهُ.

الصَّيْفِيُّ الْوَلَدُ عَلَى الْكِبَرِ وَالصَّفِيُّ النَّاقَةُ الْغَزِيرُ الدَّرِّ.

قَالَ فَإِنِ اشْتَرَى عَبْدًا فَبَانَ بِأُمِّهِ جِرَاحٌ. قَالَ مَا فِي رَدِّهِ[٣] جُنَاحٌ.

الْأُمُّ مُجْتَمَعُ الدِّمَاغِ.

قَالَ أَتَثْبُتُ الشُّفْعَةُ لِلشَّرِيكِ فِي الصَّحْرَاءِ. قَالَ لَا وَلَا لِلشَّرِيكِ فِي الصَّفْرَاءِ.

الصَّحْرَاءُ الْأَتَانُ الَّتِي تُمَازِجُ بَيَاضُهَا غُبْرَةٌ.[٤]

١٠،٣٢ قَالَ أَيَحِلُّ أَنْ يُحْمَى مَاءُ الْبِئْرِ وَالْخَلَا. قَالَ إِنْ كَانَا[٥] فِي الْفَلَا فَلَا.

يُحْمَى يُمْنَعُ وَالْخَلَا الْكَلَأُ.

قَالَ مَا تَقُولُ فِي مَيْتَةِ الْكَافِرِ. قَالَ حِلٌّ لِلْمُقِيمِ وَالْمُسَافِرِ.

---

١ «وقد مر تفسيره»: في ق فقط. ٢ «قال فهَلْ يَجوزُ أن يُبْتاعَ الشافِعُ...» الخ: لم ترد هذه المسألة في هذا الموضع من س بل وردت فيما بعد في شكل مغاير. ٣ بعدها في ف: مِنْ. ٤ بعدها في د، ف: والصفراء الناقة، وبعدها في و: والصفراء ناقة أو أتان. ٥ ف: كان.

الْكَافِرُ الْبَحْرُ وَمَيْتَتُهُ السَّمَكُ الطَّافِي فَوْقَ مَائِهِ.[١]

قَالَ أَيَجُوزُ أَنْ يُضَحَّى بِالْحُولِ. قَالَ هُوَ أَجْدَرُ بِالْقَبُولِ.

الْحُولُ جَمْعُ حَائِلٍ.

قَالَ فَهَلْ يُضَحَّى بِالطَّالِقِ. قَالَ نَعَمْ وَيُقْرَى مِنْهَا الطَّارِقُ.

الطَّالِقُ النَّاقَةُ تُرْسَلُ تَرْعَى حَيْثُ شَاءَتْ.

قَالَ فَإِنْ ضَحَّى قَبْلَ ظُهُورِ الْغَزَالَةِ. قَالَ شَاةُ لَحْمٍ بِلَا مَحَالَةٍ.

الْغَزَالَةُ الشَّمْسُ وَقَالَ بَعْضُهُمْ يُقَالُ طَلَعَتِ الْغَزَالَةُ وَلَا يُقَالُ غَرَبَتْ.[٢]

قَالَ أَيَحِلُّ الْكَسْبُ[٣] بِالطَّرْقِ. قَالَ هُوَ كَالْقِمَارِ بِلَا فَرْقٍ.

الطَّرْقُ الضَّرْبُ بِالْحَصَى وَهُوَ مِنْ أَفْعَالِ الْكَهَنَةِ.

قَالَ أَيُسَلِّمُ الْقَائِمُ عَلَى الْقَاعِدِ. قَالَ مَحْظُورٌ فِيمَا بَيْنَ الْأَبَاعِدِ. ١١،٣٢

الْقَاعِدُ الَّتِي قَعَدَتْ عَنِ الْحَيْضِ أَوْ[٤] عَنِ الْأَزْوَاجِ.

قَالَ أَيَنَامُ الْعَاقِلُ تَحْتَ الرَّقِيعِ. قَالَ أَحْبِبْ بِهِ فِي الْبَقِيعِ.

الرَّقِيعُ السَّمَاءُ وَعَنَى بِالْبَقِيعِ بَقِيعَ[٥] الْمَدِينَةِ.

قَالَ أَيُمْنَعُ الذِّمِّيُّ مِنْ قَتْلِ الْعَجُوزِ. قَالَ مُعَارَضَتُهُ فِي الْعَجُوزِ لَا تَجُوزُ.

الْعَجُوزُ الْخَمْرُ وَقَتْلُهَا مِزَاجُهَا.[٦]

قَالَ أَيَجُوزُ أَنْ يَنْتَقِلَ الرَّجُلُ عَنْ عِمَارَةِ أَبِيهِ. قَالَ مَا جُوِّزَ لِخَامِلٍ وَلَا نَبِيهٍ.

الْعِمَارَةُ الْقَبِيلَةُ.[٧]

---

١ و: مائه. ٢ بعدها في س، ف: وضدها الجَوْنةُ تسمَّى عند مغيبها لأنها تسودُّ حين تَغيب منه قول الشاعر تُبادِرُ الجَوْنَةَ أنْ تَغيبا. ٣ ف: التكسُّب. ٤ د: و. ٥ ساقطة من ف. ٦ هكذا في ق، وفي سائر النسخ: مَزْجُها.

٧ وردت هذه المسألة موضعَ التي قبلها في س حيث وردت بعدها: «قال أيجوز ذبح الشافع قال ما لجوازه من دافع. الشافع الشاة التي معها سخلها» وهي رواية مغايرة لمسألة جاءت آنفًا. وفي و وردت المسألتان جميعًا كل واحدة في موضعها.

قَالَ مَا تَقُولُ فِي التَّهَوُّدِ.   قَالَ هُوَ مِفْتَاحُ التَّزَهُّدِ.

التَّهَوُّدُ التَّوْبَةُ وَمِنْهُ قَوْلُهُ تَعَالَى ﴿إِنَّا هُدْنَا إِلَيْكَ﴾.

قَالَ مَا تَقُولُ فِي صَبْرِ الْبَلِيَّةِ.   قَالَ أَعْظِمْ بِهِ مِنْ خَطِيَّةٍ.

الصَّبْرُ الْحَبْسُ وَالْبَلِيَّةُ النَّاقَةُ تُحْبَسُ عِنْدَ قَبْرِ صَاحِبِهَا فَلَا تُسْقَى وَلَا تُعْلَفُ إِلَى أَنْ تَمُوتَ وَكَانَتِ الْجَاهِلِيَّةُ تَزْعُمُ أَنَّ صَاحِبَهَا يُحْشَرُ عَلَيْهَا.[١]

١٢،٣٢ قَالَ أَيَحِلُّ ضَرْبُ السَّفِيرِ.   قَالَ نَعَمْ وَالْحَمْلُ عَلَى الْمُسْتَشِيرِ.

السَّفِيرُ مَا تَسَاقَطَ مِنْ وَرَقِ الشَّجَرِ وَالْمُسْتَشِيرُ الْجَمَلُ السَّمِينُ وَهُوَ أَيْضًا الْجَمَلُ الَّذِي يَعْرِفُ اللَّاقِحَ مِنَ الْحَائِلِ.

قَالَ أَيُعَزِّرُ الرَّجُلُ أَبَاهُ.   قَالَ يَفْعَلُهُ الْبَرُّ وَلَا يَأْبَاهُ.

التَّعْزِيرُ التَّعْظِيمُ وَالنُّصْرَةُ.[٢]

قَالَ مَا تَقُولُ فِيمَنْ أَفْقَرَ أَخَاهُ.   قَالَ حَبَّذَا مَا تَوَخَّاهُ.

أَفْقَرَهُ أَعَارَهُ نَاقَةً يَرْكَبُ فَقَارَهَا.

قَالَ فَإِنْ أَعْرَى وَلَدَهُ.   قَالَ يَا حُسْنَ مَا ٱعْتَمَدَهُ.

أَعْرَاهُ أَعْطَاهُ ثَمَرَةَ نَخْلَةٍ عَامًا.

قَالَ فَإِنْ أَصْلَى مَمْلُوكَهُ النَّارَ.   قَالَ لَا إِثْمَ عَلَيْهِ وَلَا عَارٌ.

الْمَمْلُوكُ الْعَجِينُ الَّذِي قَدْ أُجِيدَ عَجْنُهُ حَتَّى قَوِيَ.

قَالَ أَيَجُوزُ لِلْمَرْأَةِ أَنْ تَصْرِمَ بَعْلَهَا.   قَالَ مَا حَظَرَ أَحَدٌ فِعْلَهَا.

الْبَعْلُ النَّخْلُ الَّذِي يَشْرَبُ بِعُرُوقِهِ مِنَ الْأَرْضِ.

قَالَ فَهَلْ تُؤَدَّبُ الْمَرْأَةُ عَلَى الْخَجَلِ.   قَالَ أَجَلْ.

١ سترد هذه المسألة في موضع لاحق من س. ٢ بعدها في ف: والتوقير.

الْخَجَلُ سُوءُ ٱحْتِمَالِ الْغِنَى.[١]

قَالَ مَا تَقُولُ فِي مَنْ نَحَتَ أَثْلَةَ أَخِيهِ. قَالَ أَثِمَ وَلَوْ أَذِنَ لَهُ فِيهِ.

نَحَتَ أَثْلَتَهُ إِذَا ٱغْتَابَهُ وَقَدَحَ فِي عِرْضِهِ.[٢]

قَالَ أَيَحْجُرُ الْحَاكِمُ عَلَى صَاحِبِ الثَّوْرِ. قَالَ نَعَمْ لِيَأْمَنَ غَائِلَةَ الْجَوْرِ.

الثَّوْرُ الْجُنُونُ.

١٣،٣٢ قَالَ فَهَلْ لَهُ أَنْ يَضْرِبَ عَلَى يَدِ الْيَتِيمِ. قَالَ نَعَمْ إِلَى أَنْ يَسْتَقِيمَ.[٣]

يُقَالُ ضَرَبَ عَلَى يَدِهِ إِذَا حَجَرَ عَلَيْهِ.

قَالَ فَهَلْ يَجُوزُ أَنْ يَتَّخِذَ لَهُ رَبَضًا. قَالَ لَا وَلَوْ كَانَ لَهُ رِضًى.

الرَّبَضُ الزَّوْجَةُ.

قَالَ فَمَتَى يَبِيعُ بَدَنَ السَّفِيهِ. قَالَ حِينَ يَرَى لَهُ الْحَظَّ فِيهِ.

الْبَدَنُ الدِّرْعُ الْقَصِيرَةُ.

قَالَ فَهَلْ يَجُوزُ أَنْ يَبْتَاعَ لَهُ حَشًّا. قَالَ نَعَمْ إِذَا لَمْ يَكُنْ مُغَشًّى.

الْحَشُّ النَّخْلُ الْمُجْتَمِعُ.

١٤،٣٢ قَالَ أَيَجُوزُ أَنْ يَكُونَ الْحَاكِمُ ظَالِمًا. قَالَ نَعَمْ إِذَا كَانَ عَالِمًا.

الظَّالِمُ الَّذِي يَشْرَبُ اللَّبَنَ قَبْلَ أَنْ يَرُوبَ وَيُخْرَجَ زُبْدُهُ.

قَالَ أَيُسْتَقْضَى مَنْ لَيْسَتْ لَهُ بَصِيرَةٌ. قَالَ نَعَمْ إِذَا حَسُنَتْ مِنْهُ السِّيرَةُ.

الْبَصِيرَةُ هَاهُنَا التُّرْسُ.

قَالَ فَإِنْ تَعَرَّى مِنَ الْعَقْلِ. قَالَ ذَاكَ عُنْوَانُ الْفَضْلِ.

الْعَقْلُ ضَرْبٌ مِنَ الْوَشْيِ.

---

١ بعدها في ش: «الدَّقعُ سوء احتمال الفقر ومنه قوله عليه السلام في النساء إنكن اذا شبعتن خجلتن واذا جعتن دقعتن». وفي و، ف: «... اذا جعتن دقعتن واذا شبعتن خجلتن». ٢ بعدها في س: «قال ما تقول في صبر البلية» الواردة في موضع سابق في سائر النسخ. ٣ . في د: يرشُد ويستقيم.

قَالَ فَإِنْ كَانَ لَهُ زَهْوُ جَبَّارٍ. قَالَ لَا إِنْكَارَ[1] وَلَا إِكْبَارَ.

الزَّهْوُ الْبُسْرُ الْمُتَلَوِّنُ وَالْجَبَّارُ النَّخْلُ الَّذِي فَاتَ الْيَدَ وَضِدُّهُ الْقَاعِدُ.

قَالَ أَيَجُوزُ أَنْ يَكُونَ الشَّاهِدُ مُرِيبًا. قَالَ نَعَمْ إِذَا كَانَ أَرِيبًا.

الْمُرِيبُ الَّذِي تَكْثُرُ عِنْدَهُ اللَّبَنُ الرَّائِبُ.

قَالَ فَإِنْ بَانَ أَنَّهُ لَاطَ. قَالَ هُوَ كَمَا لَوْ خَاطَ.

لَاطَ الْحَوْضَ إِذَا طَيَّنَهُ.

قَالَ فَإِنْ عُثِرَ عَلَى أَنَّهُ غَرْبَلَ. قَالَ تُرَدُّ شَهَادَتُهُ وَلَا تُقْبَلُ.

غَرْبَلَ أَيْ قَتَلَ.[2]

قَالَ فَإِنْ وَضَحَ أَنَّهُ مَائِنٌ. قَالَ هُوَ وَصْفٌ لَهُ زَائِنٌ.

الْمَائِنُ الَّذِي يَعُولُ وَيَكْفِي الْمَؤُونَةَ مِنْ مَانَ يَمُونُ.

١٥،٣٢ قَالَ مَا يَجِبُ عَلَى عَابِدِ الْحَقِّ. قَالَ يُحَلَّفُ بِإِلَاهِ الْخَلْقِ.

الْعَابِدُ هَاهُنَا الْجَاحِدُ وَالْحَقُّ هَاهُنَا الدَّيْنُ.

قَالَ مَا تَقُولُ فِي مَنْ فَقَأَ عَيْنَ بُلْبُلٍ عَامِدًا. قَالَ تُفْقَأُ عَيْنُهُ قَوْلًا وَاحِدًا.

الْبُلْبُلُ الرَّجُلُ الْخَفِيفُ.

قَالَ فَإِنْ جَرَحَ قَطَاةَ ٱمْرَأَةٍ فَمَاتَتْ. قَالَ النَّفْسُ بِالنَّفْسِ إِذَا فَاتَتْ.

الْقَطَاةُ مَا بَيْنَ الْوَرِكَيْنِ.

قَالَ فَإِنْ أَلْقَتِ الْحَامِلُ حَشِيشًا مِنْ ضَرْبِهِ. قَالَ لِيُكَفِّرْ بِالْإِعْتَاقِ عَنْ ذَنْبِهِ.

الْحَشِيشُ الْجَنِينُ الْمُلْقَى مَيِّتًا.

قَالَ مَا يَجِبُ عَلَى الْمُخْتَفِي فِي الشَّرْعِ. قَالَ الْقَطْعُ لِإِقَامَةِ الرَّدْعِ.

---

١ بعدها في ف: عليه. ٢ بعدها في س، و، ف: ومنه قول الراجز تَرَى الْمُلوكَ حَوْلَهُ مُغَرْبَلَه.

ٱلْمُخْتَفِي نَبَّاشُ ٱلْقُبُورِ.[١]

قَالَ فَإِنْ سَرَقَ ثَمِينًا مِنْ ذَهَبٍ. قَالَ لَا قَطْعَ كَمَا لَوْ غَصَبَ.

ٱلثَّمِينُ ٱلثُّمْنُ كَمَا يُقَالُ فِي ٱلنِّصْفِ نَصِيفٌ وَفِي ٱلسُّدْسِ سَدِيسٌ.

قَالَ فَإِنْ بَانَ عَلَى ٱلْمَرْأَةِ ٱلسَّرَقُ. قَالَ لَا حَرَجَ عَلَيْهَا وَلَا فَرَقَ.

ٱلسَّرَقُ ٱلْحَرِيرُ ٱلْأَبْيَضُ.

قَالَ أَيَنْعَقِدُ نِكَاحٌ لَمْ يَشْهَدْهُ ٱلْقَوَارِي. قَالَ لَا وَٱلْخَالِقِ ٱلْبَارِي.

ٱلْقَوَارِي ٱلشُّهُودُ لِأَنَّهُمْ يَقْرُونَ ٱلْأَشْيَاءَ أَيْ يَتَتَبَّعُونَهَا.

قَالَ مَا تَقُولُ فِي عَرُوسٍ بَاتَتْ بِلَيْلَةٍ حُرَّةٍ. ثُمَّ رُدَّتْ فِي حَافِرَتِهَا بِسُحْرَةٍ.

قَالَ يَجِبُ لَهَا نِصْفُ ٱلصَّدَاقِ. وَلَا تَلْزَمُهَا عِدَّةُ ٱلطَّلَاقِ.

يُقَالُ بَاتَتِ ٱلْعَرُوسُ بِلَيْلَةٍ حُرَّةٍ إِذَا ٱمْتَنَعَتْ عَلَى زَوْجِهَا[٢] فَإِنِ ٱفْتَضَّهَا قِيلَ بَاتَتْ بِلَيْلَةٍ شَيْبَاءَ وَٱلرَّدُّ فِي ٱلْحَافِرَةِ بِمَعْنَى ٱلرُّجُوعِ فِي ٱلطَّرِيقِ ٱلْأَوَّلِ وَكَنَى بِهِ عَنْ طَلَاقِهَا وَرَدِّهَا[٣] إِلَى أَهْلِهَا.

١٦،٣٢ فَقَالَ لَهُ ٱلسَّائِلُ. لِلّٰهِ دَرُّكَ مِنْ بَحْرٍ لَا يُغَضْغِضُهُ ٱلْمَائِحُ. وَحِبْرٍ لَا يَبْلُغُ مَدْحَهُ ٱلْمَادِحُ. ثُمَّ أَطْرَقَ إِطْرَاقَ ٱلْحَيِيِّ. وَأَرَمَّ إِرْمَامَ ٱلْعَيِيِّ. فَقَالَ لَهُ أَبُو زَيْدٍ إِيهٍ يَا فَتًى. فَإِلَى مَتَى وَإِلَى مَتَى. فَقَالَ إِنَّهُ لَمْ يَبْقَ فِي كِنَانَتِي مِرْمَاةٌ. وَلَا بَعْدَ إِشْرَاقِ صُبْحِكَ مُمَارَاةٌ. فَبِٱللّٰهِ أَيُّ ٱبْنِ أَرْضٍ أَنْتَ. فَمَا أَحْسَنَ مَا أَبَنْتَ. فَأَنْشَدَ بِلِسَانٍ ذَلِقٍ. وَصَوْتٍ صَهْصَلِقٍ.

---

١ بعدها في ف: قال فما يُصنَعُ بمَنْ سرَقَ أساوِدَ الدّارِ. قال يُقطَعُ إنْ ساوَينَ رُبعَ دينارٍ. الأساودُ الآلات المستعملة كالإجانة والقدر الجفنة (هكذا). ٢ بعدها في و قبل استئناف الشرح: ومنه قول النابغة شمسٌ موانعُ كل ليلة حرّةٍ يُخلفن ظن الفاحش المغيار. ٣ ف: قبل وِردها.

أَنَـا فِي الْعَـالَمِ مُـثْلَهْ وَلأَهْـلِ الْعِلْمِ قِبْـلَهْ
غَـيْرَ أَنِّي كُلَّ يَوْمٍ بَيْنَ تَعْـرِيسٍ وَرِحْـلَهْ
وَالْغَرِيبُ الدَّارِ لَوْ حَـلَّ بِطُوبَى لَمْ تَطِبْ لَهْ

ثُمَّ قَالَ اللَّهُمَّ كَمَا جَعَلْتَنَا مِمَّنْ هُدِيَ وَيَهْدِي. فَٱجْعَلْهُمْ مِمَّنْ يَهْتَدِي وَيُهْدِي. فَسَاقَ إِلَيْهِ الْقَوْمُ ذَوْدًا مَعَ قَيْنَةٍ. وَسَأَلُوهُ أَنْ يَزُورَهُمُ الْفَيْنَةَ بَعْدَ الْفَيْنَةِ. فَنَهَضَ يُمَنِّيهِمِ الْعَوْدَ. وَيُزَجِّي الْأَمَةَ وَالذَّوْدَ.

١٧،٣٢ قَالَ الْحَارِثُ بْنُ هَمَّامٍ فَٱعْتَرَضْتُهُ فَقُلْتُ[١] عَهْدِي بِكَ سَفِيهًا. فَمَتَى صِرْتَ فَقِيهًا. فَظَلَّ هُنَيَّةً يَجُولُ. ثُمَّ أَنْشَدَ يَقُولُ.

لَبِسْتُ لِكُلِّ زَمَانٍ لَبُوسًا وَلَابَسْتُ صَرْفَيْهِ نُعْمَى وَبُوسَى
وَعَاشَرْتُ كُلَّ جَلِيسٍ بِمَا يُلَائِمُهُ لِأَرُوقَ الْجَلِيسَا
فَعِنْدَ الرُّوَاةِ أُدِيرُ الْكَلَامَ وَبَيْنَ السُّقَاةِ أُدِيرُ الْكُؤُوسَا
وَطَوْرًا بِوَعْظِي أُسِيلُ الدُّمُوعَ وَطَوْرًا بِلَهْوِي أَسُرُّ النُّفُوسَا
وَأَقْرِي الْمَسَامِعَ إِمَّا نَطَقْتُ بَيَانًا يَقُودُ الْحَرُونَ الشَّمُوسَا
وَإِنْ شِئْتُ أَرْعَفُ كَفِّي الْيَرَاعَ فَسَاقَطَ دُرًّا يُحَلِّي الطُّرُوسَا
وَكَمْ مُشْكِلَاتٍ حَكَيْنَ السُّهَى خَفَاءً فَصِرْنَ بِكَشْفِي شُمُوسَا
وَكَمْ مُلَحٍ لِي خَلَبْنَ الْعُقُولَ وَأَسَأَرْنَ فِي كُلِّ قَلْبٍ رَسِيسَا
وَعَذْرَاءَ فُهْتُ بِهَا فَانْثَنَى عَلَيْهَا الثَّنَاءُ طَلِيقًا حَبِيسَا
عَلَى أَنَّنِي مِنْ زَمَانٍ خُصِصْتُ بِكَيْدٍ وَلَا كَيْدَ فِرْعَوْنَ مُوسَى
يُسَعِّرُ لِي كُلَّ يَوْمٍ وَغًى أَطَا مِنْ لَظَاهَا وَطِيسًا وَطِيسَا

١ بعدها في د، ف: له.

وَيَطْـرُقُـنِي بِـالْخُـطُوبِ الَّتِي   يُذِبْنَ الْقُوَى وَيُشِبْنَ الرُّؤُوسَا
وَيُـدْنِي إِلَيَّ الْبَعِيـدَ الْبَغِيضَ   وَيُبْعِـدُ عَنِّي الْقَـرِيبَ الْأَنِيسَـا
وَلَوْلَا خَسَـاسَـةُ أَخْـلَاقِـهِ   لَمَا كَانَ حَظِّي مِنْهُ خَسِيسَا

١٨،٣٢ فَقُلْتُ لَهُ خَفِّضِ الْأَحْزَانَ. وَلَا تَلُمِ الزَّمَانَ. وَٱشْكُرْ لِمَنْ نَقَلَكَ عَنْ مَذْهَبِ إِبْلِيسَ. إِلَى مَذْهَبِ ٱبْنِ إِدْرِيسَ. فَقَالَ دَعِ الْهِتَارَ. وَلَا تَهْتِكِ الْأَسْتَارَ. وَٱنْهَضْ بِنَا لِنَضْرِبَ. إِلَى مَسْجِدِ يَثْرِبَ. فَعَسَى أَنْ نَرْحَضَ بِالْمَزَارِ. دَرَنَ الْأَوْزَارِ. فَقُلْتُ هَيْهَاتَ أَنْ أَسِيرَ. أَوْ أَفْقَهَ التَّفْسِيرَ. فَقَالَ تَاللهِ لَقَدْ أَوْجَبْتَ ذِمَمًا. وَطَلَبْتَ إِذْ طَلَبْتَ أَمَمًا. فَهَاكَ مَا يَشْفِي النَّفْسَ. وَيَنْفِي اللَّبْسَ. قَالَ فَلَمَّا أَوْضَحَ لِيَ الْمُعَمَّى. وَكَشَفَ عَنِّي الْغُمَّى. شَدَدْنَا الْأَكْوَارَ. وَسِرْتُ وَسَارَ. وَلَمْ أَزَلْ مِنْ مُسَامَرَتِهِ. مُدَّةَ مُسَايَرَتِهِ. فِيمَا أَنْسَانِي طَعْمَ الْمَشَقَّةِ. وَوَدِدْتُ مَعَهُ بُعْدَ الشُّقَّةِ. حَتَّى إِذَا دَخَلْنَا مَدِينَةَ الرَّسُولِ. وَفُزْنَا مِنَ الزِّيَارَةِ بِالسُّولِ. أَشْأَمَ وَأَعْرَقَ. وَغَرَّبَ وَشَرَّقَ.

ٱلْمَقَامَةُ ٱلثَّالِثَةُ وَٱلثَّلَاثُونَ[١]

١٫٣٣ أَخْبَرَ[٢] ٱلْحَارِثُ بْنُ هَمَّامٍ قَالَ عَاهَدْتُ ٱللهَ تَعَالَى مُذْ يَفَعْتُ. أَلَّا أُؤَخِّرَ ٱلصَّلَاةَ مَا ٱسْتَطَعْتُ. فَكُنْتُ مَعَ جَوْبِ ٱلْفَلَوَاتِ. وَلَهْوِ ٱلْخَلَوَاتِ. أُرَاعِي أَوْقَاتَ ٱلصَّلَوَاتِ. وَأُحَاذِرُ مِنْ مَأْثَمِ ٱلْفَوَاتِ. وَإِذَا رَافَقْتُ فِي رِحْلَةٍ. أَوْ حَلَلْتُ بِحِلَّةٍ. مَرْحَبْتُ بِصَوْتِ ٱلدَّاعِي إِلَيْهَا. وَٱقْتَدَيْتُ بِمَنْ يُحَافِظُ عَلَيْهَا. فَٱتَّفَقَ حِينَ دَخَلْتُ تَفْلِيسَ.[٣] أَنْ صَلَّيْتُ مَعَ زُمْرَةٍ[٤] مَفَالِيسَ. فَلَمَّا قَضَيْنَا ٱلصَّلَاةَ. وَأَزْمَعْنَا ٱلِٱنْفِلَاتَ. بَرَزَ شَيْخٌ بَادِي ٱللَّقْوَةِ. بَالِي ٱلْكِسْوَةِ وَٱلْقُوَّةِ. فَقَالَ عَزَمْتُ عَلَى مَنْ خُلِقَ[٥] مِنْ طِينَةِ ٱلْحُرِّيَّةِ. وَتَفَوَّقَ دَرَّ ٱلْعَصَبِيَّةِ. إِلَّا مَا تَكَلَّفَ لِي لُبْثَةً. وَٱسْتَمَعَ مِنِّي نَفْثَةً. ثُمَّ لَهُ ٱلْخِيَارُ مِنْ بَعْدُ. وَبِيَدِهِ ٱلْبَذْلُ وَٱلرَّدُّ. فَعَقَدَ لَهُ ٱلْقَوْمُ ٱلْحُبَى. وَرَسَوْا أَمْثَالَ ٱلرُّبَى.

٢٫٣٣ فَلَمَّا آنَسَ حُسْنَ إِنْصَاتِهِمْ. وَرَزَانَةَ حَصَاتِهِمْ. قَالَ يَا أُولِي ٱلْأَبْصَارِ ٱلرَّامِقَةِ. وَٱلْبَصَائِرِ ٱلرَّائِقَةِ. أَمَا يُغْنِي عَنِ ٱلْخَبَرِ ٱلْعِيَانُ. وَيُنْبِئُ عَنِ ٱلنَّارِ ٱلدُّخَانُ. شَيْبٌ لَائِحٌ. وَوَهْنٌ[٦] فَادِحٌ.[٧] وَدَاءٌ وَاضِحٌ. وَٱلْبَاطِنُ فَفَاضِحٌ.[٨] وَلَقَدْ كُنْتُ وَٱللهِ مِمَّنْ مَلَكَ وَمَالَ.[٩] وَوَلِيَ وَآلَ. وَرَفَدَ وَنَالَ. وَوَصَلَ وَصَالَ. فَلَمْ تَزَلِ ٱلْجَوَائِحُ تُسْحِتُ.[١٠] وَٱلنَّوَائِبُ تَنْحَتُ.[١١] حَتَّى ٱلْوَكْرُ قَفْرٌ. وَٱلْكَفُّ صِفْرٌ. وَٱلشِّعَارُ ضُرٌّ. وَٱلْعَيْشُ مُرٌّ. وَٱلصِّبْيَةُ يَتَضَاغَوْنَ مِنَ ٱلطَّوَى. وَيَتَمَنَّوْنَ مُصَاصَةَ ٱلنَّوَى. وَلَمْ أَقُمْ هٰذَا ٱلْمَقَامَ ٱلشَّائِنَ. وَأَكْشِفْ لَكُمُ ٱلدَّفَائِنَ. إِلَّا بَعْدَمَا شَقِيتُ وَلَقِيتُ.

---

١ في هامش س: تُعْرَف بالتفليسية؛ د: التَّفْليسية؛ وفي ف: وتعرف بالتفليسية. ٢ ف: حكى. ٣ هكذا في جميع النسخ. ٤ مضافة في هامش ق، وفي و: عُصْبة، وساقطة من د. ٥ و: خَلَق. ٦ في هامش س، وفي د: ضعفٌ. ٧ س: بايح. ٨ ف: فاضح. ٩ ف: أنال. ١٠ و: تَسْحِت، ف: تسْحَت. ١١ ف: تَنْحَت.

وَشِبْتُ مِمَّا لَقِيتُ. فَلَيْتَنِي لَمْ أَكُنْ بَقِيتُ. ثُمَّ تَأَوَّهَ تَأَوُّهَ الْأَسِيفِ. وَأَنْشَدَ بِصَوْتٍ ضَعِيفٍ.

٣،٣٣ أَشْكُو إِلَى الرَّحْمٰنِ سُبْحَانَهُ تَقَلُّبَ الدَّهْرِ وَعُدْوَانَهُ
وَحَادِثَاتٍ قَرَعَتْ مَرْوَتِي وَقَوَّضَتْ مَجْدِي وَبُنْيَانَهُ
وَٱهْتَصَرَتْ عُودِي وَيَا وَيْلَ مَنْ تَهْتَصِرُ الْأَحْدَاثُ أَغْصَانَهُ
وَأَمْحَلَتْ رَبْعِي حَتَّى جَلَتْ مِنْ رَبْعِيَ الْمُمْحِلِ جِرْذَانَهُ
وَغَادَرَتْنِي حَائِرًا بَائِرًا أُكَابِدُ الْفَقْرَ وَأَشْجَانَهُ
مِنْ بَعْدِ مَا كُنْتُ أَخَا ثَرْوَةٍ يَسْحَبُ فِي النِّعْمَةِ أَرْدَانَهُ
يَخْتَبِطُ الْعَافُونَ أَوْرَاقَهُ وَيَحْمَدُ السَّارُونَ نِيرَانَهُ
فَأَصْبَحَ الْيَوْمَ كَأَنْ لَمْ يَكُنْ أَعَانَهُ الدَّهْرُ الَّذِي عَانَهُ
وَٱزْوَرَّ مَنْ كَانَ لَهُ زَائِرًا وَعَافَ عَافِي الْعُرْفِ عِرْفَانَهُ
فَهَلْ فَتًى يَحْزُنُهُ مَا يَرَى مِنْ ضُرِّ شَيْخٍ دَهْرُهُ خَانَهُ
فَيَفْرُجَ الْهَمَّ الَّذِي هَمَّهُ وَيُصْلِحَ الشَّأْنَ الَّذِي شَانَهُ

٤،٣٣ قَالَ الرَّاوِي فَصَبَتِ الْجَمَاعَةُ إِلَى أَنْ تَسْتَثْبِتَهُ. لِتَسْتَنْجِشَ خُبْأَتَهُ. وَتَسْتَنْفِضَ حَقِيبَتَهُ. فَقَالَتْ لَهُ قَدْ عَرَفْنَا قَدْرَ زِنَتِكَ.[١] وَرَأَيْنَا دَرَّ مُزْنَتِكَ. فَعَرِّفْنَا دَوْحَةَ شُعْبَتِكَ.[٢] وَٱحْسِرِ اللِّثَامَ عَنْ نِسْبَتِكَ.[٣] فَأَعْرَضَ إِعْرَاضَ مَنْ مُنِيَ بِالْإِعْنَاتِ. أَوْ بُشِّرَ بِالْبَنَاتِ. وَجَعَلَ يَلْعَنُ الضَّرُورَاتِ. وَيَتَأَفَّفُ مِنْ تَغَيُّضِ الْمُرُوءَاتِ. ثُمَّ أَنْشَدَ بِلَفْظٍ صَادِعٍ. وَجَرْسٍ خَادِعٍ.

١ ف: رُتْبَتِك. ٢ س: شِعْبَتِك. ٣ س: نُسْبَتِك.

لَعَمْرُكَ مَا كُلُّ فَرْعٍ يَدُلُّ   جَنَاهُ اللَّذِيذُ عَلَى أَصْلِهِ
فَكُلْ مَا حَلَا حِينَ تُؤْتَى بِهِ   وَلَا تَسْأَلِ الشُّهْدَ عَنْ نَحْلِهِ
وَمَيِّزْ إِذَا مَا ٱعْتَصَرْتَ الْكُرُومَ   سُلَافَةَ عَصْرِكَ مِنْ خَلِّهِ
لِتُغْلِيَ وَتُرْخِصَ عَنْ خِبْرَةٍ   وَتَشْرِيَ كُلًّا شِرَى مِثْلِهِ
فَعَارٌ عَلَى الْفَطِنِ اللَّوْذَعِيِّ   دُخُولُ الْغَمِيزَةِ فِي عَقْلِهِ

٥،٣٣ قَالَ فَٱزْدَهَى الْقَوْمُ بِذَكَائِهِ وَدَهَائِهِ. وَٱخْتَلَبَهُمْ بِحُسْنِ أَدَائِهِ مَعَ دَائِهِ. حَتَّى جَمَعُوا لَهُ خَبَايَا الْخُبَنِ.[١] وَخَفَايَا الثُّبَنِ. وَقَالُوا لَهُ يَا هٰذَا إِنَّكَ حُمْتَ عَلَى رَكِيَّةٍ بَكِيَّةٍ. وَتَعَرَّضْتَ لِحَلِيَّةٍ خَلِيَّةٍ. فَخُذْ هٰذِهِ الصُّبَابَةَ. وَهَبْهَا لَا خَطَأً وَلَا إِصَابَةً. فَنَزَّلَ قُلَّهُمْ مَنْزِلَةَ الْكُثْرِ. وَوَصَلَ قَبُولَهُ بِالشُّكْرِ. ثُمَّ تَوَلَّى يَجُرُّ شِقَّهُ. وَيَنْهَبُ بِالْخَبْطِ طُرُقَهُ.

٦،٣٣ قَالَ الْمُخْبِرُ بِهٰذِهِ الْحِكَايَةِ. فَصُوِّرَ لِي أَنَّهُ مُحِيلٌ[٢] لِحِلْيَتِهِ. مُتَصَنِّعٌ فِي مِشْيَتِهِ. فَنَهَضْتُ أَنْهَجُ مِنْهَاجَهُ. وَأَقْفُو أَدْرَاجَهُ. وَهُوَ يَلْحَظُنِي شَزْرًا. وَيُوسِعُنِي هَجْرًا.[٣] حَتَّى إِذَا خَلَا الطَّرِيقُ. وَأَمْكَنَ التَّحْقِيقُ. نَظَرَ إِلَيَّ نَظَرَ مَنْ هَشَّ وَبَشَّ. وَمَاحَضَ بَعْدَمَا غَشَّ. وَقَالَ إِنِّي لَإِخَالُكَ أَخَا غُرْبَةٍ. وَرَائِدَ صُحْبَةٍ. فَهَلْ لَكَ فِي رَفِيقٍ يَرْفُقُ بِكَ وَيُرْفِقُ. وَيَنْفُقُ عَلَيْكَ وَيُنْفِقُ. فَقُلْتُ لَهُ لَوْ أَتَانِي هٰذَا الرَّفِيقُ. لَوَاتَانِي التَّوْفِيقُ. فَقَالَ لِي قَدْ وَجَدْتَ فَٱغْتَبِطْ. وَٱسْتَكْرَمْتَ فَٱرْتَبِطْ. ثُمَّ ضَحِكَ مَلِيًّا. وَتَمَثَّلَ لِي بَشَرًا سَوِيًّا. فَإِذَا هُوَ شَيْخُنَا السَّرُوجِيُّ لَا قَلَبَةَ بِجِسْمِهِ. وَلَا شُبْهَةَ فِي وَسْمِهِ. فَفَرِحْتُ بِلُقْيَتِهِ. وَكَذِبِ لَقْوَتِهِ. وَهَمَمْتُ بِمَلَامَتِهِ. عَلَى سُوءِ مَقَامَتِهِ. فَشَحَا فَاهُ. وَأَنْشَدَ قَبْلَ أَنْ أَلْحَاهُ.

---

١ ق: الخُبُن. ٢ د: مخيل. ٣ س: هُجّرا.

ظَهَرْتُ بِرَثٍّ لِكَيْمَا يُقَالَ فَقِيرٌ يُزَجِّي الزَّمَانَ الْمُزَجَّى
وَأَظْهَرْتُ لِلنَّاسِ أَنْ قَدْ فُلِجْتُ فَكَمْ نَالَ قَلْبِي بِهِ مَا تَرَجَّى
وَلَوْلَا الرَّثَاثَةُ لَمْ يُرْثَ لِي وَلَوْلَا التَّفَالُجُ لَمْ أَلْقَ فُلْجَا

ثُمَّ قَالَ إِنَّهُ لَمْ يَبْقَ[١] بِهٰذِهِ الْأَرْضِ مَرْتَعٌ. وَلَا فِي أَهْلِهَا مَطْمَعٌ. فَإِنْ كُنْتَ الرَّفِيقَ. فَالطَّرِيقَ الطَّرِيقَ. فَسِرْنَا مِنْهَا مُتَجَرِّدَيْنِ. وَرَافَقْتُهُ عَامَيْنِ أَجْرَدَيْنِ. وَكُنْتُ عَلَى أَنْ أَصْحَبَهُ مَا عِشْتُ. فَأَبَى الدَّهْرُ الْمُشِتُّ.

١ بعدها في ف: لي.

ٱلْمَقَامَةُ ٱلرَّابِعَةُ وَٱلثَّلَاثُونَ[١]

١،٣٤ حَكَى[٢] ٱلْحَارِثُ بْنُ هَمَّامٍ قَالَ لَمَّا جُبْتُ ٱلْبِيدَ. إِلَى زَبِيدَ. صَحِبَنِي غُلَامٌ قَدْ كُنْتُ رَبَّيْتُهُ إِلَى أَنْ بَلَغَ أَشُدَّهُ. وَثَقَّفْتُهُ حَتَّى أَكْمَلَ رُشْدَهُ. وَكَانَ قَدْ أَنِسَ بِأَخْلَاقِي. وَخَبَرَ مَجَالِبَ وِفَاقِي. فَلَمْ يَكُنْ يَتَخَطَّى مَرَامِي. وَلَا يُخْطِئُ فِي ٱلْمَرَامِي. لَا جَرَمَ أَنَّ قُرْبَهُ ٱلتَاطَتْ بِصَفَرِي. وَأَخْلَصْتُهُ لِحَضَرِي وَسَفَرِي. فَأَلْوَى بِهِ ٱلدَّهْرُ ٱلْمُبِيدُ. حِينَ ضَمَّتْنَا زَبِيدُ. فَلَمَّا شَالَتْ نَعَامَتُهُ. وَسَكَنَتْ نَأْمَتُهُ. بَقِيتُ عَامًا. لَا أُسِيغُ طَعَامًا. وَلَا أُرِيغُ غُلَامًا. حَتَّى أَلْجَأَتْنِي شَوَائِبُ ٱلْوَحْدَةِ. وَمَتَاعِبُ ٱلْقَوْمَةِ وَٱلْقَعْدَةِ. إِلَى أَنْ أَعْتَاضَ عَنِ ٱلدُرِّ ٱلْخَرَزَ. وَأَرْتَادَ مَنْ هُوَ سِدَادٌ مِنْ عَوَزٍ. فَقَصَدْتُ مَنْ يَبِيعُ ٱلْعَبِيدَ. بِسُوقِ زَبِيدَ. فَقُلْتُ أُرِيدُ غُلَامًا يُعْجِبُ إِذَا قُلِّبَ. وَيُحْمَدُ إِذَا جُرِّبَ. وَلْيَكُنْ مِمَّنْ خَرَّجَهُ ٱلْأَكْيَاسُ. وَأَخْرَجَهُ إِلَى ٱلسُّوقِ ٱلْإِفْلَاسُ. فَٱهْتَزَّ كُلٌّ مِنْهُمْ لِمَطْلَبِي وَوَثَبَ. وَبَذَلَ تَحْصِيلَهُ عَنْ كَثَبٍ. ثُمَّ دَارَتِ ٱلْأَهِلَّةُ دَوْرَهَا. وَتَقَلَّبَتْ كَوْرَهَا وَحَوْرَهَا. وَمَا نَجَزَ مِنْ وُعُودِهِمْ وَعْدٌ. وَلَا سَحَّ لَهَا رَعْدٌ.

٢،٣٤ فَلَمَّا رَأَيْتُ ٱلنَّخَّاسِينَ. نَاسِينَ أَوْ مُتَنَاسِينَ. عَلِمْتُ أَنْ لَيْسَ كُلُّ مَنْ خَلَقَ يَفْرِي. وَأَنْ لَنْ يَحُكَّ جِلْدِي مِثْلُ ظُفْرِي. فَرَفَضْتُ مَذْهَبَ ٱلتَّفْوِيضِ. وَبَرَزْتُ إِلَى ٱلسُّوقِ بِٱلصُّفْرِ وَٱلْبِيضِ. فَإِنِّي لَأَسْتَعْرِضُ ٱلْغِلْمَانَ. وَأَسْتَعْرِفُ ٱلْأَثْمَانَ. إِذْ عَارَضَنِي رَجُلٌ قَدِ ٱخْتَطَمَ بِلِثَامٍ. وَقَبَضَ عَلَى زَنْدِ غُلَامٍ. وَقَالَ

---

١ في س: تُعْرَفُ بِالزَّبِيدِيَّةِ؛ وفي د: الزَّبِيدِيَّةُ؛ وفي ف: وَتُعْرَفُ بِالزَّبِيدِيَّةِ. ٢ في د: أَخْبَرَ.

مَنْ يَشْتَرِي مِنِّي غُلَامًا صَنَعَا فِي خَلْقِهِ وَخُلْقِهِ قَدْ بَرَعَا
بِكُلِّ مَا نُطْتَ بِهِ مُضْطَلِعًا يَشْفِيكَ إِنْ قَالَ وَإِنْ قُلْتَ وَعَى
وَإِنْ تُصِبْكَ عَثْرَةٌ يَقُلْ لَعَا وَإِنْ تَسُمْهُ السَّعْيَ فِي النَّارِ سَعَى
وَإِنْ تُصَاحِبْهُ وَلَوْ يَوْمًا رَعَى وَإِنْ تُقَنِّعْهُ بِظِلْفٍ قَنِعَا
وَهْوَ عَلَى الْكَيْسِ الَّذِي قَدْ جَمَعَا مَا فَاهَ قَطُّ كَاذِبًا وَلَا ٱدَّعَى
وَلَا أَجَابَ مَطْمَعًا حِينَ دَعَا وَلَا ٱسْتَجَازَ نَثَّ سِرٍّ أُودِعَا
وَطَالَمَا أَبْدَعَ فِي مَا صَنَعَا وَفَاقَ فِي النَّثْرِ وَفِي النَّظْمِ مَعَا
وَاللهِ لَوْلَا ضَنْكُ عَيْشٍ صَدَعَا وَصِبْيَةٌ أَضْحَوْا عُرَاةً جُوَّعَا
مَا بِعْتُهُ بِمُلْكِ كِسْرَى أَجْمَعَا

٣،٣٤ قَالَ فَلَمَّا تَأَمَّلْتُ خَلْقَهُ الْقَوِيمَ. وَحُسْنَهُ الصَّمِيمَ. خِلْتُهُ مِنْ وِلْدَانِ جَنَّةِ النَّعِيمِ. وَقُلْتُ ﴿مَا هٰذَا بَشَرًا إِنْ هٰذَا إِلَّا مَلَكٌ كَرِيمٌ﴾. ثُمَّ ٱسْتَنْطَقْتُهُ عَنِ ٱسْمِهِ. لَا لِرَغْبَةٍ فِي عِلْمِهِ. بَلْ لِأَنْظُرَ أَيْنَ فَصَاحَتُهُ مِنْ صَبَاحَتِهِ. وَكَيْفَ لَهْجَتُهُ مِنْ بَهْجَتِهِ. فَلَمْ يَنْطِقْ بِحُلْوَةٍ وَلَا مُرَّةٍ. وَلَا فَاهَ فَوْهَةَ ٱبْنِ أَمَةٍ وَلَا حُرَّةٍ. فَضَرَبْتُ عَنْهُ صَفْحًا. وَقُلْتُ قُبْحًا لِعِيِّكَ وَشُقْحًا. فَغَارَ فِي الضَّحِكِ[1] وَأَنْجَدَ. ثُمَّ أَنْغَضَ رَأْسَهُ إِلَيَّ وَأَنْشَدَ

يَا مَنْ تَلَهَّبَ غَيْظُهُ إِذْ لَمْ أَبُحْ بِٱسْمِي لَهُ مَا هٰكَذَا مَنْ يُنْصِفُ
إِنْ كَانَ لَا يُرْضِيكَ إِلَّا كَشْفُهُ فَأَصِخْ لَهُ أَنَا يُوسُفٌ أَنَا يُوسُفُ
وَلَقَدْ كَشَفْتُ لَكَ الْغِطَاءَ فَإِنْ تَكُنْ فَطِنًا عَرَفْتَ وَمَا إِخَالُكَ تَعْرِفُ

١ د، ف: الضِّحْك.

٤٫٣٤ قَالَ فَسَرَى[1] عَتْبِي بِشِعْرِهِ. وَٱسْتَبَى لُبِّي بِسِحْرِهِ. حَتَّى شُدِهْتُ عَنِ التَّحْقِيقِ. وَأُنْسِيتُ قِصَّةَ يُوسُفَ الصِّدِّيقِ. وَلَمْ يَكُنْ لِي هَمٌّ إِلَّا مُسَاوَمَةَ مَوْلَاهُ فِيهِ. وَٱسْتِطْلَاعَ طِلْعِ الثَّمَنِ لِأُوَفِّيَهُ. وَكُنْتُ أَحْسِبُ أَنَّهُ سَيَنْظُرُ شَزْرًا إِلَيَّ. وَيُغْلِي السِّيمَةَ عَلَيَّ. فَمَا حَلَّقَ إِلَى حَيْثُ حَلَّقْتُ. وَلَا ٱعْتَلَقَ بِمَا بِهِ ٱعْتَلَقْتُ. بَلْ قَالَ إِنَّ الْعَبْدَ[2] إِذَا نَزُرَ ثَمَنُهُ. وَخَفَّتْ مُؤْنَتُهُ. تَبَرَّكَ بِهِ مَوْلَاهُ. وَٱلْتَحَفَ عَلَيْهِ هَوَاهُ. وَإِنِّي لَأُوثِرُ تَحْبِيبَ هٰذَا الْغُلَامِ إِلَيْكَ. بِأَنْ أُخَفِّفَ ثَمَنَهُ عَلَيْكَ. فَزِنْ مِائَتَيْ دِرْهَمٍ إِنْ شِيتَ. وَٱشْكُرْ لِي مَا حَيِيتَ. فَنَقَدْتُهُ الْمَبْلَغَ فِي الْحَالِ. كَمَا يُنْقَدُ فِي الرَّخِيصِ الْحَلَالُ. وَلَمْ يَخْطُرْ لِي بِبَالٍ. أَنَّ كُلَّ مُرْخَصٍ غَالٍ. فَلَمَّا تَحَقَّقَتِ الصَّفْقَةُ. وَحَقَّتِ الْفُرْقَةُ. هَمَلَتْ عَيْنَا الْغُلَامِ. وَلَا هُمُولَ دَمْعِ الْغَمَامِ. ثُمَّ أَقْبَلَ عَلَى صَاحِبِهِ وَقَالَ

٥٫٣٤ لَحَاكَ اللهُ هَلْ مِثْلِي يُبَاعُ   لِكَيْمَا تَشْبَعَ الْكَرِشُ الْجِيَاعُ
وَهَلْ فِي شِرْعَةِ الْإِنْصَافِ أَنِّي   أُكَلَّفُ خُطَّةً لَا تُسْتَطَاعُ
وَأَنْ أُبْلَى بِرَوْعٍ بَعْدَ رَوْعٍ   وَمِثْلِي حِينَ يُبْلَى لَا يُرَاعُ
أَمَا جَرَّبْتَنِي فَخَبَرْتَ مِنِّي   نَصَائِحَ لَمْ يُمَازِجْهَا خِدَاعُ
وَكَمْ أَرْصَدْتَنِي شَرَكًا لِصَيْدٍ   فَعُدْتُ وَفِي حَبَائِلِيَ السِّبَاعُ
وَنُطْتَ بِيَ الْمَصَاعِبَ فَٱسْتَقَادَتْ   مُطَاوِعَةً وَكَانَ بِهَا ٱمْتِنَاعُ
وَأَيُّ كَرِيهَةٍ لَمْ أُبْلِ فِيهَا   وَغُنْمٍ لَمْ يَكُنْ لِي فِيهِ بَاعُ
وَمَا أَبْدَتْ لِيَ الْأَيَّامُ جُرْمًا   فَيُكْشَفَ فِي مُصَارَمَتِي الْقِنَاعُ
وَلَمْ تَعْثُرْ بِحَمْدِ اللهِ مِنِّي   عَلَى عَيْبٍ يُكَتَّمُ أَوْ يُذَاعُ

١ و، ف: فسرَّى. ٢ ف: الغُلَامَ.

فَأَنَّى سَاغَ عِنْدَكَ نَبْذُ عَهْدِي كَمَا نَبَذَتْ بُرَايَتَهَا الصَّنَاعُ
وَلِمْ سَمَحَتْ قَرُونُكَ بِٱمْتِهَانِي وَأَنْ أُشْرَى كَمَا يُشْرَى الْمَتَاعُ[1]
وَهَلَّا صُنْتَ عِرْضِي عَنْهُ صَوْنِي حَدِيثَكَ يَوْمَ جَدَّ بِنَا الْوَدَاعُ
وَقُلْتَ لِمَنْ يُسَاوِمُ فِيَّ هٰذَا سَكَابِ فَمَا يُعَارُ وَلَا يُبَاعُ
فَمَا أَنَا دُونَ ذَاكَ الطِّرْفِ لٰكِنْ طِبَاعُكَ فَوْقَهَا تِلْكَ الطِّبَاعُ
عَلَى أَنِّي سَأُنْشِدُ عِنْدَ بَيْعِي أَضَاعُونِي وَأَيَّ فَتًى أَضَاعُوا

قَالَ فَلَمَّا وَعَى الشَّيْخُ أَبْيَاتَهُ. وَعَقَلَ مُنَاغَاتَهُ. تَنَفَّسَ الصُّعَدَاءَ. وَبَكَى حَتَّى ٦،٣٤
أَبْكَى الْبُعَدَاءَ. ثُمَّ قَالَ لِي إِنِّي أُحِلُّ هٰذَا الْغُلَامَ مَحَلَّ وَلَدِي. وَلَا أُمَيِّزُهُ عَنْ أَفْلَاذِ
كَبِدِي. وَلَوْلَا خُلُوُّ مُرَاحِي. وَخُبُوُّ مِصْبَاحِي. لَمَا دَرَجَ عَنْ عُشِّي. إِلَى أَنْ يُشَيِّعَ
نَعْشِي. وَقَدْ رَأَيْتَ مَا نَزَلَ بِهِ مِنْ لَوْعَةِ الْبَيْنِ. وَالْمُؤْمِنُ هَيْنٌ لَيْنٌ. فَهَلْ لَكَ فِي
تَسْلِيَةِ قَلْبِهِ. وَتَسْرِيَةِ كَرْبِهِ. بِأَنْ تُعَاهِدَنِي عَلَى الْإِقَالَةِ فِيهِ مَتَى ٱسْتَقَلْتُ. وَأَنْ لَا
تَسْتَثْقِلَنِي إِذَا ثَقَّلْتُ. فَفِي الْآثَارِ الْمُنْتَقَاةِ. الْمُدَوَّنَةِ عَنِ الثِّقَاتِ.[2] مَنْ أَقَالَ نَادِمًا
بَيْعَتَهُ. أَقَالَهُ اللهُ عَثْرَتَهُ.

قَالَ الْحَارِثُ بْنُ هَمَّامٍ فَوَعَدْتُهُ وَعْدًا أَبْرَزَهُ الْحَيَاءُ. وَفِي الْقَلْبِ أَشْيَاءُ. ٧،٣٤
فَٱسْتَدْنَى حِينَئِذٍ الْغُلَامَ إِلَيْهِ. وَقَبَّلَ مَا بَيْنَ عَيْنَيْهِ. وَأَنْشَدَ وَالدَّمْعُ يَرْفَضُّ مِنْ
جَفْنَيْهِ.

خَفِّضْ فَدَتْكَ النَّفْسُ مَا تُلَاقِي مِنْ بُرَحَاءِ الْوَجْدِ وَالْإِشْفَاقِ
فَمَا تَطُولُ مُدَّةُ الْفِرَاقِ وَلَا تَنِي رَكَائِبُ التَّلَاقِي
بِحُسْنِ عَوْنِ الْقَادِرِ الْخَلَّاقِ

١ ق: المُباعُ. ٢ ف: المَرْوِيَّةِ عَنِ الثِّقاةِ.

ثُمَّ قَالَ لَهُ أَسْتَوْدِعُكَ مَنْ هُوَ نِعْمَ الْمَوْلَى. وَشَمَّرَ ذَيْلَهُ وَوَلَّى. فَلَبِثَ الْغُلَامُ فِي زَفِيرٍ وَعَوِيلٍ. رَيْثَمَا يُقْطَعُ مَدَى مِيلٍ. فَلَمَّا ٱسْتَفَاقَ. وَكَفْكَفَ دَمْعَهُ الْمُهْرَاقَ. قَالَ أَتَدْرِي لِمَ أَعْوَلْتُ. وَعَلَامَ عَوَّلْتُ. فَقُلْتُ أَظُنُّ فِرَاقَ مَوْلَاكَ. هُوَ الَّذِي أَبْكَاكَ. فَقَالَ إِنَّكَ لَفِي وَادٍ وَأَنَا فِي وَادٍ. وَلَكَمْ بَيْنَ مُرِيدٍ وَمُرَادٍ. ثُمَّ أَنْشَدَ

لَمْ أَبْكِ وَاللهِ عَلَى إِلْفٍ نَـزَحْ وَلَا عَـلَى فَوْتِ نَعِيـمٍ وَفَـرَحْ
وَإِنَّمَا مَدْمَعُ أَجْفَـانِي سَـفَحْ عَلَى غَبِيٍّ لَحْـظُهُ حِينَ طَـمَحْ
وَرَّطَـهُ حَتَّى تَعَنَّى وَٱفْـتَضَحْ وَضَيَّعَ الْمَنْقُوشَةَ الْبِيضَ الْوَضَحْ
وَيْكَ أَمَا نَاجَتْكَ هَاتِيكَ الْمُلَحْ بِـأَنَّنِي حُـرٌّ وَبَيْـعِي لَمْ يَحِحْ
إِذْ كَانَ فِي يُوسُفَ مَعْنًى قَدْ وَضَحْ

٨،٣٤ قَالَ فَتَمَثَّلَتْ مَقَالُهُ فِي مِرْآةِ الْمُدَاعِبِ. وَمَعْرِضِ الْمُلَاعِبِ. فَتَصَلَّبَ تَصَلُّبَ الْمُحِقِّ. وَتَبَرَّأَ مِنْ طِينَةِ الرِّقِّ. فَجُلْنَا فِي مُخَاصَمَةٍ. اِتَّصَلَتْ بِمُلَاكَمَةٍ. وَأَفْضَتْ إِلَى مُحَاكَمَةٍ. فَلَمَّا أَوْضَحْنَا لِلْقَاضِي الصُّورَةَ. وَتَلَوْنَا عَلَيْهِ السُّورَةَ. قَالَ أَلَا إِنَّ مَنْ أَنْذَرَ فَقَدْ أَعْذَرَ. وَمَنْ حَذَّرَ كَمَنْ بَشَّرَ. وَمَنْ بَصَّرَ فَمَا قَصَّرَ. وَإِنَّ فِيمَا شَرَحْتُمَاهُ لَدَلِيلًا عَلَى أَنَّ هٰذَا الْغُلَامَ قَدْ نَبَّهَكَ فَمَا ٱرْعَوَيْتَ. وَنَصَحَ لَكَ فَمَا وَعَيْتَ. فَٱسْتُرْ دَاءَ بَلَهِكَ وَٱكْتُمْهُ. وَلُمْ نَفْسَكَ وَلَا تَلُمْهُ. وَحَذَارِ مِنِ ٱعْتِلَاقِهِ. وَالطَّمَعَ فِي ٱسْتِرْقَاقِهِ. فَإِنَّهُ حُرُّ الْأَدِيمِ. غَيْرُ مُعَرَّضٍ لِلتَّقْوِيمِ. وَقَدْ كَانَ أَبُوهُ أَحْضَرَهُ أَمْسِ. قُبَيْلَ أُفُولِ الشَّمْسِ. وَٱعْتَرَفَ بِأَنَّهُ فَرْعُهُ الَّذِي أَنْشَاهُ. وَأَنْ لَا وَارِثَ لَهُ سِوَاهُ. فَقُلْتُ لِلْقَاضِي أَوَتَعْرِفُ أَبَاهُ. أَخْزَاهُ اللهُ. فَقَالَ وَهَلْ يُجْهَلُ أَبُو زَيْدٍ الَّذِي جُرْحُهُ جُبَارٌ. وَعِنْدَ كُلِّ قَاضٍ لَهُ أَخْبَارٌ وَإِخْبَارٌ. فَتَحَرَّقْتُ حِينَئِذٍ وَحَوْلَقْتُ. وَأَفَقْتُ وَلٰكِنْ حِينَ فَاتَ الْوَقْتُ. وَأَيْقَنْتُ أَنَّ لِثَامَهُ كَانَ شَرَكَ مَكِيدَتِهِ. وَبَيْتَ

قَصِيدَتِهِ. فَنَكَّسَ طَرْفِي مَا لَقِيتُ. وَآلَيْتُ أَنْ لَا أُعَامِلَ مُتَلَثِّمًا[1] مَا بَقِيتُ. وَلَمْ أَزَلْ أَتَأَوَّهُ لِخُسْرِ صَفْقَتِي. وَالِافْتِضَاحِ بَيْنَ رُفْقَتِي. فَقَالَ لِيَ ٱلْقَاضِي. حِينَ رَأَى ٱمْتِعَاضِي. وَحَرُّ[2] ٱرْتِمَاضِي. يَا هٰذَا مَا ذَهَبَ مِنْ مَالِكَ مَا وَعَظَكَ. وَلَا أَجْرَمَ إِلَيْكَ مَنْ أَيْقَظَكَ. فَٱتَّعِظْ بِمَا نَابَكَ. وَكَاتِمْ أَصْحَابَكَ مَا أَصَابَكَ. وَتَذَكَّرْ أَبَدًا مَا دَهِمَكَ. لِتَقِيَ ٱلذِّكْرَى دَرَاهِمَكَ. وَتَخَلَّقْ بِخُلُقِ مَنِ ٱبْتُلِيَ فَصَبَرَ. وَتَجَلَّتْ لَهُ ٱلْعِبَرُ فَٱعْتَبَرَ.

٩،٣٤ فَوَدَّعْتُهُ[3] لَابِسًا ثَوْبَ ٱلْخَجَلِ وَالْحَزَنِ. سَاحِبًا ذَيْلَ[4] ٱلْغَبْنِ وَالْغَبَنِ. وَنَوَيْتُ مُكَاشَفَةَ أَبِي زَيْدٍ بِالْهَجْرِ. وَمُصَارَمَتَهُ يَدَ ٱلدَّهْرِ. فَجَعَلْتُ أَتَنَكَّبُ عَنْ ذَرَاهُ. وَأَتَجَنَّبُ أَنْ أَرَاهُ. إِلَى أَنْ غَشِيَنِي فِي طَرِيقٍ ضَيِّقٍ. فَحَيَّانِي تَحِيَّةَ شَيِّقٍ. فَمَا زِدْتُ عَلَى أَنْ عَبَسْتُ. وَمَا نَبَسْتُ. فَقَالَ مَا بَالُكَ شَمَخْتَ[5] بِأَنْفِكَ. عَلَى إِلْفِكَ. فَقُلْتُ أَأُنْسِيتَ أَنَّكَ ٱحْتَلْتَ وَخَتَلْتَ. وَفَعَلْتَ فَعْلَتَكَ ٱلَّتِي فَعَلْتَ. فَأَضْرَطَ بِي مُتَهَازِيًا. ثُمَّ أَنْشَدَ مُتَلَافِيًا.

يَا مَنْ بَدَا مِنْهُ صُدُو   دٌ مُوحِشٌ وَتَجَهُّمُ

وَغَدَا يَرِيشُ مَلَاوِمًا   مِنْ دُونِهِنَّ ٱلْأَسْهُمُ

وَيَقُولُ هَلْ حُرٌّ يُبَا   عُ كَمَا يُبَاعُ ٱلْأَدْهَمُ

أَقْصِرْ فَمَا أَنَا فِيهِ بِدْ   عًا مِثْلَ مَا تَتَوَهَّمُ

قَدْ بَاعَتِ ٱلْأَسْبَاطُ قَبْـ   ـلِي يُوسُفًا وَهُمُ هُمُ

هٰذَا وَأُقْسِمُ بِالَّتِي   يَسْرِي إِلَيْهَا ٱلْمُتْهِمُ

وَالطَّائِفِينَ بِهَا وَهُمْ   شُعْثُ ٱلنَّوَاصِي سُهَّمُ

---

[1] ف: مُلَثَّمًا. [2] قبلها في ف: وتَبَيَّنَ. [3] قبلها في ف: قال الحارث بن همام. [4] س، ف: ذَيْلَيْ. [5] د: شامخًا.

مَا قُمْتُ ذَاكَ الْمَوْقِفَ الْـــمُخْزِي وَعِنْدِي دِرْهَمُ
فَٱعْذِرْ أَخَاكَ وَكُفَّ عَنْـــهُ مَلَامَ مَنْ لَا يَفْـهَمُ

ثُمَّ قَالَ أَمَّا مَعْذِرَتِي فَقَدْ لَاحَتْ. وَأَمَّا دَرَاهِمُكَ فَقَدْ طَاحَتْ. فَإِنْ كَانَ ٱقْشِعْرَارُكَ مِنِّي. وَٱزْوِرَارُكَ عَنِّي. لِفَرْطِ شَفَقَتِكَ. عَلَى غُبَّرِ نَفَقَتِكَ. فَلَسْتُ مِمَّنْ يَلْسَعُ مَرَّتَيْنِ. وَيُوطِئُ عَلَى جَمْرَتَيْنِ. وَإِنْ كُنْتَ طَوَيْتَ كَشْحَكَ. وَأَطَعْتَ شُحَّكَ. لِتَسْتَنْقِذَ مَا عَلِقَ بِأَشْرَاكِي. فَلْتَبْكِ عَلَى عَقْلِكَ الْبَوَاكِي. قَالَ الْحَارِثُ بْنُ هَمَّامٍ فَٱضْطَرَّنِي بِلَفْظِهِ الْخَالِبِ. وَسِحْرِهِ الْغَالِبِ. إِلَى أَنْ عُدْتُ لَهُ صَفِيًّا. وَبِهِ حَفِيًّا. وَنَبَذْتُ فَعْلَتَهُ ظِهْرِيًّا. وَإِنْ كَانَتْ شَيْئًا فَرِيًّا.

ٱلْمَقَامَةُ ٱلْخَامِسَةُ وَٱلثَّلَاثُونَ[١]

١،٣٥ رَوَى[٢] ٱلْحَارِثُ بْنُ هَمَّامٍ قَالَ مَرَرْتُ فِي تَطْوَافِي بِشِيرَازَ. عَلَى نَادٍ يَسْتَوْقِفُ ٱلْمُجْتَازَ. وَلَوْ كَانَ عَلَى أَوْفَازٍ. فَلَمْ أَسْتَطِعْ تَعَدِّيَهِ. وَلَا خَطَتْ قَدَمِي فِي تَخَطِّيهِ. فَعُجْتُ إِلَيْهِ لِأَسْبُكَ سِرَّ جَوْهَرِهِ. وَأَنْظُرَ كَيْفَ ثَمَرُهُ مِنْ زَهَرِهِ. فَإِذَا أَهْلُهُ أَفْرَادٌ. وَٱلْعَائِجُ إِلَيْهِمْ مُفَادٌ. وَبَيْنَمَا نَحْنُ فِي فُكَاهَةٍ أَطْرَبَ مِنَ ٱلْأَغَارِيدِ. وَأَطْيَبَ مِنْ حَلَبِ ٱلْعَنَاقِيدِ. إِذِ ٱحْتَفَّ بِنَا ذُو طِمْرَيْنِ. قَدْ كَادَ يُنَاهِزُ ٱلْعُمْرَيْنِ. فَحَيَّا بِلِسَانٍ طَلِيقٍ. وَأَبَانَ إِبَانَةَ مِنْطِيقٍ. ثُمَّ ٱحْتَبَى حُبْوَةَ ٱلْمُنْتَدِينَ. وَقَالَ ٱجْعَلْنَا ٱللّٰهُمَّ[٣] مِنَ ٱلْمُهْتَدِينَ.

٢،٣٥ فَٱزْدَرَاهُ ٱلْقَوْمُ لِطِمْرَيْهِ. وَنَسُوا أَنَّ ٱلْمَرْءَ بِأَصْغَرَيْهِ. وَأَخَذُوا يَتَدَاعَوْنَ فَصْلَ ٱلْخِطَابِ. وَيَعْتَدُّونَ عُودَهُ مِنَ ٱلْأَحْطَابِ. وَهُوَ لَا يُفِيضُ بِكَلِمَةٍ. وَلَا يُبِينُ عَنْ سِمَةٍ. إِلَى أَنْ سَبَرَ قَرَائِحَهُمْ. وَخَبَرَ شَائِلَهُمْ وَرَاجِحَهُمْ. فَحِينَ ٱسْتَخْرَجَ دَفَائِنَهُمْ. وَٱسْتَنْثَلَ كَنَائِنَهُمْ. قَالَ يَا قَوْمِ لَوْ عَلِمْتُمْ أَنَّ وَرَاءَ ٱلْفِدَامِ. صَفْوَ ٱلْمُدَامِ. لَمَا ٱحْتَقَرْتُمْ ذَا أَخْلَاقٍ. وَقُلْتُمْ مَا لَهُ مِنْ خَلَاقٍ. ثُمَّ فَجَّرَ مِنْ يَنَابِيعِ ٱلْأَدَبِ. وَٱلنُّكَتِ ٱلنُّخَبِ. مَا جَلَبَ[٤] بَدَائِعَ ٱلْعَجَبِ. وَٱسْتَوْجَبَ أَنْ يُكْتَبَ بِذَوْبِ ٱلذَّهَبِ. فَلَمَّا خَلَبَ كُلَّ خِلْبٍ. وَقَلَبَ إِلَيْهِ كُلَّ قَلْبٍ. تَحَلْحَلَ لِيَرْحَلَ. وَتَأَهَّبَ لِيَذْهَبَ. فَعَلِقَتِ ٱلْجَمَاعَةُ بِذَيْلِهِ. وَعَاقَتْ مَسْرَبَ سَيْلِهِ. وَقَالَتْ لَهُ قَدْ أَرَيْتَنَا وَسْمَ قِدْحِكَ. فَخَبِّرْنَا عَنْ قَيْضِكَ وَمُحِّكَ. فَصَمَتَ صُمُوتَ مَنْ أُفْحِمَ. ثُمَّ أَعْوَلَ حَتَّى رُحِمَ.

---

١ في هامش س: تعرف بالشيرازية؛ وفي د: الشيرازية. المقامة ناقصة من نسختي الرقية من ف. ٢ في هامش س: حكى صح، وفي و: حكى. ٣ ف: اللهم اجعلنا. ٤ د: جلب به.

٣،٣٥ قَالَ الرَّاوِي فَلَمَّا رَأَيْتُ شَوْبَ أَبِي زَيْدٍ وَرَوْبَهُ. وَأُسْلُوبَهُ الْمَأْلُوفَ وَصَوْبَهُ. تَأَمَّلْتُ الشَّيْخَ عَلَى سُهُومَةِ مُحَيَّاهُ. وَسُهُوكَةِ رَيَّاهُ. فَإِذَا هُوَ إِيَّاهُ. فَكَتَمْتُ سِرَّهُ كَمَا يُكْتَمُ الدَّاءُ الدَّخِيلُ. وَسَتَرْتُ مَكْرَهُ وَإِنْ لَمْ يَكُنْ يُحِيلُ. حَتَّى إِذَا نَزَعَ عَنْ إِعْوَالِهِ. وَقَدْ عَرَفَ عُثُورِي عَلَى حَالِهِ. رَمَقَنِي بِعَيْنٍ مِضْحَاكٍ. ثُمَّ طَفِقَ يُنْشِدُ بِلِسَانٍ مُتَبَاكٍ.

أَسْتَغْفِرُ اللهَ وَأَعْنُو لَهُ   مِنْ فَرَطَاتٍ أَثْقَلَتْ ظَهْرِيَهْ
يَا قَوْمِ كَمْ مِنْ عَاتِقٍ عَانِسٍ   مَمْدُوحَةِ الْأَوْصَافِ فِي الْأَنْدِيَهْ
قَتَلْتُهَا لَا أَتَّقِي وَارِثًا   يَطْلُبُ مِنِّي قَوَدًا أَوْ دِيَهْ
وَكُلَّمَا ٱسْتُذْنِبْتُ فِي قَتْلِهَا   أَحَلْتُ بِالذَّنْبِ عَلَى الْأَقْضِيَهْ
وَلَمْ تَزَلْ نَفْسِي فِي غَيِّهَا   وَقَتْلِهَا الْأَبْكَارَ مُسْتَشْرِيَهْ
حَتَّى نَهَانِي الشَّيْبُ لَمَّا بَدَا   فِي مَفْرِقِي عَنْ تِلْكُمُ الْمَعْصِيَهْ
فَلَمْ أُرِقْ مُذْ شَابَ فَوْدِي دَمًا   مِنْ عَاتِقٍ يَوْمًا وَلَا مُصْبِيَهْ
وَهَا أَنَا الْآنَ عَلَى مَا يُرَى   مِنِّي وَمِنْ حِرْفَتِي الْمُكْدِيَهْ
أَرُبُّ بِكْرًا طَالَ[1] تَعْنِيسُهَا   وَحَجْبُهَا حَتَّى عَنِ الْأَهْوِيَهْ
وَهْيَ عَلَى التَّعْنِيسِ مَخْطُوبَةٌ   كَخِطْبَةِ الْغَانِيَةِ الْمُغْنِيَهْ
وَلَيْسَ يَكْفِينِي لِتَجْهِيزِهَا   عَلَى[2] الرِّضَى بِالدُّونِ إِلَّا مِيَهْ
وَالْيَدُ لَا تُوكِي عَلَى دِرْهَمٍ   وَالْأَرْضُ قَفْرٌ وَالسَّمَا مُصْحِيَهْ
فَهَلْ مُعِينٌ لِي عَلَى نَقْلِهَا   مَصْحُوبَةً بِالْقَيْنَةِ الْمُلْهِيَهْ
فَيَغْسِلَ ٱلْهَمَّ بِصَابُونِهِ   وَالْقَلْبَ مِنْ أَفْكَارِهِ الْمُضْنِيَهْ
وَيَقْتَنِي مِنِّي الثَّنَاءَ الَّذِي   تَضُوعُ رَيَّاهُ مَعَ الْأَدْعِيَهْ

١ في متن ق: طفلاً، مشطوبة، وفي الهامش ما أثبتناه. ٢ في هامش س: مع.

٤،٣٥ قَالَ فَلَمْ يَبْقَ فِي الْجَمَاعَةِ إِلَّا مَنْ نَدِيَتْ لَهُ كَفُّهُ. وَٱنْبَاعَ إِلَيْهِ[١] عُرْفُهُ. فَلَمَّا نَجَحَتْ بِغْيَتُهُ. وَكَمَلَتْ مِائَتُهُ. أَخَذَ يُثْنِي عَلَيْهِمْ بِصَالِحٍ. وَيُشَمِّرُ عَنْ سَاقٍ سَارِحٍ. فَتَبِعْتُهُ لِأَسْتَعْرِفَ رَبِيبَةَ خِدْرِهِ. وَمَنْ قَتَلَ فِي حِدْثَانِ أَمْرِهِ. فَكَأَنَّ وَشْكَ قِيَامِي. مَثَّلَ لَهُ مَرَامِي. فَٱزْدَلَفَ مِنِّي. وَقَالَ ٱفْقَهْ عَنِّي.

قَتْلُ مِثْلِي يَا صَاحِ مَزْجُ الْمُدَامِ ... لَيْسَ قَتْلِي بِلَهْذَمٍ أَوْ حُسَامِ
وَالَّتِي عُنِّسَتْ هِيَ الْبِكْرُ بِنْتُ الْـ ... ـكَرْمِ لَا الْبِكْرُ مِنْ بَنَاتِ الْكِرَامِ
وَلِتَجْهِيزِهَا إِلَى الْكَاسِ وَالطَّا ... سِ قِيَامِي الَّذِي تَرَى وَمَقَامِي[٢]
فَتَفَهَّمْ مَا قُلْتُهُ وَتَحَكَّمْ ... فِي التَّغَاضِي إِنْ شِئْتَ أَوْ فِي الْمَلَامِ

ثُمَّ قَالَ أَنَا عِرْبِيدٌ. وَأَنْتَ رِعْدِيدٌ. وَبَيْنَنَا بَوْنٌ بَعِيدٌ. ثُمَّ وَدَّعَنِي وَٱنْطَلَقَ. وَزَوَّدَنِي نَظْرَةً مِنْ ذِي عَلَقٍ.

---

١ ق: له. ٢ د: مُقامي.

الْمَقَامَةُ السَّادِسَةُ وَالثَّلَاثُونَ تُعْرَفُ بِالْمَلَطِيَّةِ[1]

١،٣٦ أَخْبَرَ الْحَارِثُ بْنُ هَمَّامٍ قَالَ أَنَخْتُ بِمَلَطْيَةَ[2] مَطِيَّةَ الْبَيْنِ. وَحَقِيبَتِي مَلْأَى مِنَ الْعَيْنِ. فَجَعَلْتُ هِجِّيرَايَ. مُذْ أَلْقَيْتُ بِهَا عَصَايَ. أَنْ أَتَوَرَّدَ مَوَارِدَ الْمَرَحِ. وَأَتَصَيَّدَ شَوَارِدَ الْمُلَحِ. فَلَمْ يَفُتْنِي بِهَا مَنْظَرٌ وَلَا مَسْمَعٌ. وَلَا خَلَا مِنِّي مَلْعَبٌ وَلَا مَرْتَعٌ. حَتَّى إِذَا لَمْ يَبْقَ لِي فِيهَا مَأْرَبٌ. وَلَا فِي الثَّوَاءِ بِهَا مَرْغَبٌ. عَمَدْتُ لِإِنْفَاقِ الذَّهَبِ. فِي ٱبْتِيَاعِ الْأُهَبِ. فَلَمَّا أَكْمَلْتُ ٱلْإِعْدَادَ. وَتَهَيَّأَ الظَّعْنُ مِنْهَا أَوْ كَادَ. رَأَيْتُ تِسْعَةَ رَهْطٍ قَدْ سَبَأُوا قَهْوَةً. وَٱرْتَبَأُوا رُبْوَةً. وَدَمَاثَتُهُمْ قَيْدُ الْأَلْحَاظِ. وَفُكَاهَتُهُمْ حُلْوَةُ الْأَلْفَاظِ. فَنَحَوْتُهُمْ طَلَبًا لِمُنَادَمَتِهِمْ لَا لِمُدَامَتِهِمْ. وَشَعَفًا بِمُمَازَجَتِهِمْ لَا بِزُجَاجَتِهِمْ.

٢،٣٦ فَلَمَّا ٱنْتَظَمْتُ عَاشِرَهُمْ. وَأَضْحَيْتُ مُعَاشِرَهُمْ. أَلْفَيْتُهُمْ أَبْنَاءَ عَلَّاتٍ. وَقَذَائِفَ فَلَوَاتٍ. إِلَّا أَنَّ لُحْمَةَ الْأَدَبِ. قَدْ أَلَّفَتْ شَمْلَهُمْ أُلْفَةَ النَّسَبِ. وَسَاوَتْ بَيْنَهُمْ فِي الرُّتَبِ. حَتَّى لَاحُوا مِثْلَ كَوَاكِبِ الْجَوْزَاءِ. وَكَالْجُمْلَةِ[3] الْمُتَنَاسِبَةِ الْأَجْزَاءِ. فَأَبْهَجَنِي ٱلِاهْتِدَاءُ إِلَيْهِمْ. وَأَحْمَدْتُ الطَّالِعَ الَّذِي أَطْلَعَنِي عَلَيْهِمْ. وَطَفِقْتُ أُفِيضُ بِقِدْحِي مَعَ قِدَاحِهِمْ. وَأَسْتَشْفِي بِرِيَاحِهِمْ لَا بِرَاحِهِمْ. حَتَّى أَدَّتْنَا شُجُونُ الْمُفَاوَضَةِ. إِلَى التَّحَاجِي بِالْمُقَايَضَةِ. كَقَوْلِكَ إِذَا عَنَيْتَ بِهِ الْكَرَامَاتِ. مَا مِثْلُ النَّوْمِ فَاتَ.

---

١ في هامش س: تعرف بالملطية؛ وفي د: المَلْطِيَّة؛ وفي ف: المَلَطية. ٢ د: بِمَلْطِيَةَ؛ س، ف، و: بِمَلَطِيَّةَ. ٣ د، ف: وبدَوا كالجملة.

٣،٣٦ فَأَنْشَأْنَا نَجْلُو السُّهَى وَالْقَمَرَ. وَنَجْنِي الشَّوْكَ وَالثَّمَرَ. وَبَيْنَا نَحْنُ نَنْشُرُ الْقَشِيبَ وَالرَّثَّ. وَنَنْشُلُ السَّمِينَ وَالْغَثَّ. طَلَعَ[1] عَلَيْنَا شَيْخٌ قَدْ ذَهَبَ حِبْرُهُ وَسِبْرُهُ. وَبَقِيَ خُبْرُهُ وَسَبْرُهُ. فَمَثَلَ مُثُولَ مَنْ يَسْمَعُ وَيَنْظُرُ. وَيَلْتَقِطُ مَا نَنْثُرُ. إِلَى أَنْ نُفِضَتِ الْأَكْيَاسُ. وَحَصْحَصَ الْيَاسُ. فَلَمَّا رَأَى إِجْبَالَ الْقَرَائِحِ. وَإِكْدَاءَ الْمَاتِحِ وَالْمَائِحِ. جَمَعَ أَذْيَالَهُ. وَوَلَّانَا قَذَالَهُ. وَقَالَ مَا كُلُّ سَوْدَاءَ تَمْرَةٌ. وَلَا كُلُّ صَهْبَاءَ خَمْرَةٌ.

٤،٣٦ فَاعْتَلَقْنَا بِهِ اعْتِلَاقَ الْحِرْبَاءِ بِالْأَعْوَادِ. وَضَرَبْنَا دُونَ وِجْهَتِهِ بِالْأَسْدَادِ. وَقُلْنَا لَهُ إِنَّ دَوَاءَ الشَّقِّ أَنْ يُحَاصَ. وَإِلَّا فَالْقِصَاصَ الْقِصَاصَ. فَلَا تَطْمَعْ فِي أَنْ تَجْرَحَ.[2] وَتُنْهِرَ الْفَتْقَ وَتَسْرَحَ. فَلَوَى عِنَانَهُ رَاجِعًا. ثُمَّ جَثَمَ بِمَكَانِهِ رَاصِعًا. وَقَالَ أَمَّا إِذَا اسْتَثَرْتُمُونِي بِالْبَحْثِ. فَسَأَحْكُمُ[3] حُكْمَ سُلَيْمَانَ فِي الْحَرْثِ.

٥،٣٦ اِعْلَمُوا يَا ذَوِي الشَّمَائِلِ الْأَدَبِيَّةِ. وَالشَّمُولِ الذَّهَبِيَّةِ. أَنَّ وَضْعَ الْأُحْجِيَّةِ. لِامْتِحَانِ الْأَلْمَعِيَّةِ. وَاسْتِخْرَاجِ الْخَبِيَّةِ الْخَفِيَّةِ. وَشَرْطُهَا أَنْ تَكُونَ ذَاتَ مُمَاثَلَةٍ حَقِيقِيَّةٍ. وَأَلْفَاظٍ مَعْنَوِيَّةٍ. وَلَطِيفَةٍ أَدَبِيَّةٍ. فَمَتَى نَافَتْ هٰذَا النَّمَطَ. ضَاهَتِ السَّقَطَ. وَلَمْ تَدْخُلِ السَّفَطَ. وَلَمْ أَرَكُمْ حَافَظْتُمْ عَلَى هٰذِهِ الْحُدُودِ. وَلَا مِزْتُمْ بَيْنَ الْمَقْبُولِ وَالْمَرْدُودِ. فَقُلْنَا لَهُ صَدَقْتَ.[4] فَكِلْ لَنَا مِنْ لُبَابِكَ. وَأَفِضْ عَلَيْنَا مِنْ عُبَابِكَ. فَقَالَ أَفْعَلُ لِئَلَّا يَرْتَابَ الْمُبْطِلُونَ. وَيَظُنُّوا بِيَ الظُّنُونَ.

٦،٣٦ ثُمَّ قَابَلَ نَاظُورَةَ الْقَوْمِ وَقَالَ

يَا مَنْ سَمَا بِذَكَاءٍ فِي الْفَضْلِ وَارِي الزِّنَادِ
مَاذَا يُمَاثِلُ قَوْلِي جُوعٌ أُمِدَّ بِزَادِ

١ ف: وغل. ٢ بعدها في ف: وتطرح. ٣ ف: فَلَأَحْكُمُ. ٤ ف: صدقت وبالحق نطقت.

ثُمَّ ضَحِكَ إِلَى الثَّانِي وَأَنْشَدَ

يَا ذَا ٱلَّذِي فَاقَ فَضْلاً وَلَمْ يُدَنِّسْهُ شَيْنُ
مَا مِثْلُ قَوْلِ الْمُحَاجِي ظَهْرٌ أَصَابَتْهُ عَيْنُ

ثُمَّ لَحَظَ الثَّالِثَ وَأَنْشَأَ يَقُولُ

يَا مَنْ نَتَائِجُ فِكْرِهِ مِثْلُ النُّقُودِ الْجَائِزَهْ
مَا مِثْلُ قولِكَ لِلَّذِي حَاجَيْتَ صَادَفَ جَائِزَهْ

ثُمَّ أَتْلَعَ إِلَى الرَّابِعِ وَقَالَ

أَيَا مُسْتَنْبِطَ الْغَامِضِ مِنْ لُغْزٍ وَإِضْمَارِ
أَلَا ٱكْشِفْ لِيَ مَا مِثْلُ تَنَاوَلْ أَلْفَ دِينَارِ

ثُمَّ رَمَى الْخَامِسَ بِبَصَرِهِ وَأَنْشَدَ[1]

يَا أَيُّهَذَا الْأَلْمَعِيُّ أَخُو الذَّكَاءِ الْمُنْجَلِي
مَا مِثْلُ أَهْمَلَ حِلْيَةً بَيِّنْ هُدِيتَ وَعَجِّلِ

٧،٣٦ ثُمَّ ٱلْتَفَتَ لِفْتَ السَّادِسِ وَقَالَ

يَا مَنْ تُقَصِّرُ عَنْ مَدَاهُ خُطَى مُجَارِيهِ وَتَضْعُفْ
مَا مِثْلُ قَوْلِكَ لِلَّذِي أَضْحَى يُحَاجِيكَ ٱكْفُفِ ٱكْفُفْ

١ ف: وقال.

ثُمَّ خَلَجَ السَّابِعَ بِحَاجِبِهِ وَقَالَ[1]

يَا مَنْ لَهُ فِطْنَةٌ تَجَلَّتْ   وَرُتْبَةٌ فِي الذَّكَاءِ جَلَّتْ
بَيِّنْ فَمَا زِلْتَ ذَا بَيَانٍ   مَا مِثْلُ قَوْلِي الشَّقِيقُ أَفْلَتْ

ثُمَّ ٱسْتَنْصَتَ الثَّامِنَ وَأَنْشَدَهُ[2]

يَا مَنْ حَدَائِقُ فَضْلِهِ   مَطْلُولَةُ الْأَزْهَارِ غَضَّهْ
مَا مِثْلُ قَوْلِكَ لِلْمُحَا   جِي ذِي الْحِجَى مَا ٱخْتَارَ فِضَّهْ

ثُمَّ حَدَجَ التَّاسِعَ بِبَصَرِهِ وَقَالَ

يَا مَنْ يُشَارُ إِلَيْهِ فِي الْـ   ـقَلْبِ الذَّكِيِّ وَفِي الْبَرَاعَهْ
أَوْضِحْ لَنَا مَا مِثْلُ قَوْ   لِكَ لِلْمُحَاجِي دُسْ جَمَاعَهْ

قَالَ الرَّاوِي فَلَمَّا انْتَهَى إِلَيَّ. هَزَّ مَنْكِبَيَّ. وَقَالَ

يَا مَنْ لَهُ النُّكَتُ الَّتِي   يُشْجِي الْخُصُومَ بِهَا وَيَنْكُتْ
أَنْتَ الْمُبِينُ فَقُلْ لَنَا   مَا مِثْلُ قَوْلِي خَالِيَ ٱسْكُتْ

ثُمَّ قَالَ قَدْ أَنْهَلْتُكُمْ وَأَمْهَلْتُكُمْ. وَإِنْ شِئْتُمْ أَنْ أُعَلَّكُمْ عَلَّلْتُكُمْ.
٨،٣٦ قَالَ فَأَلْجَأَنَا لَهَبُ الْغُلَلِ. إِلَى ٱسْتِسْقَاءِ الْعَلَلِ. فَقَالَ لَسْتُ كَمَنْ يَسْتَأْثِرُ عَلَى
نَدِيمِهِ. وَلَا مِمَّنْ سَمْنُهُ فِي أَدِيمِهِ. ثُمَّ كَرَّ عَلَى الْأَوَّلِ وَأَنْشَدَ[3]

١ د: وأنشد. ٢ س، د، ف، و: وأنشد. ٣ ف: وقال.

يَا مَنْ إِذَا أَشْكَلَ الْمُعَمَّى   جَلَتْهُ[١] أَفْكَارُهُ الدَّقِيقَهْ
إِنْ قَالَ يَوْمًا لَكَ الْمُحَاجِي   خُذْ تِلْكَ مَا مِثْلُهُ حَقِيقَهْ

ثُمَّ ثَنَى جِيدَهُ إِلَى الثَّانِي وَقَالَ

يَا مَنْ بَدَا بَيَانُهُ   عَنْ فَضْلِهِ مُبَيِّنَا[٢]
مَاذَا مِثَالُ قَوْلِهِمْ   حِمَارُ وَحْشٍ[٣] زُيِّنَا[٤]

ثُمَّ أَوْحَى إِلَى الثَّالِثِ بِلَحْظِهِ وَأَنْشَدَ[٥]

يَا مَنْ غَدَا فِي فَضْلِهِ   وَذَكَائِهِ كَالْأَصْمَعِي
مَا مِثْلُ قَوْلِكَ لِلَّذِي   حَاجَاكَ[٦] أَنْفِقْ تَقْمَعِ

ثُمَّ حَمْلَقَ إِلَى الرَّابِعِ وَقَالَ[٧]

يَا مَنْ إِذَا مَا عَوِيصٌ   دَجَا أَنَارَ ظَلَامَهْ
مَاذَا يُمَاثِلُ قَوْلِي   اِسْتَنْشِ رِيحَ مُدَامَهْ

ثُمَّ أَوْمَضَ إِلَى الْخَامِسِ وَقَالَ[٨]

يَا مَنْ تَنَزَّهَ فَهْمُهُ   عَنْ أَنْ يُرَوِّيَ أَوْ يَشُكَّا
مَا مِثْلُ قَوْلِكَ لِلَّذِي   أَضْحَى يُحَاجِي غَطِّ هَلْكَى

١ د: جَلَّتْه. ٢ س و: مُجَلِّيا. ٣ . ف: الوحش. ٤ س، و: حُلِّيا. ٥ س، و، د، ف: وقال. ٦ س، د: حاجيتَ. ٧ ف: وأنشد. ٨ س: وأنشأ يقول.

ثُمَّ أَقْبَلَ قِبَلَ السَّادِسِ وَأَنْشَدَ[١] ٩،٣٦

يَا أَخَا الْفِطْنَةِ الَّتِي   بَانَ فِيهَا كَمَالُهُ
سَارَ بِاللَّيْلِ مُدَّةً   أَيُّ شَيْءٍ مِثَالُهُ

ثُمَّ نَحَا بَصَرَهُ إِلَى السَّابِعِ وَقَالَ

يَا مَنْ تَحَلَّى بِفَهْمٍ   أَقَامَ فِي النَّاسِ سُوقَهْ
لَكَ الْبَيَانُ فَبَيِّنْ   مَا مِثْلُ أَحْبِبْ فَرُوقَهْ

ثُمَّ قَصَدَ قَصْدَ الثَّامِنِ وَأَنْشَدَ

يَا مَنْ تَبَوَّأَ ذِرْوَةً   فِي الْفَضْلِ[٢] فَاقَتْ كُلَّ ذِرْوَهْ
مَا مِثْلُ قَوْلِكَ أَعْطِ إِبْـ   ـرِيقًا يَلُوحُ بِغَيْرِ عُرْوَهْ

ثُمَّ ٱبْتَسَمَ إِلَى التَّاسِعِ وَقَالَ

يَا مَنْ حَوَى حُسْنَ الدِّرَا   يَةِ وَالْبَيَانِ بِغَيْرِ شَكِّ
مَا مِثْلُ قَوْلِكَ لِلْمُحَا   جِي ذِي الذَّكَاءِ الثَّوْرُ مِلْكِي

ثُمَّ قَبَضَ بِجُمْعِهِ عَلَى رُدْنِي وَقَالَ

يَا مَنْ سَمَا بِثُقُوبِ فِطْنَتِهِ   فِي الْمُشْكِلَاتِ وَنُورِ كَوْكَبِهِ
مَاذَا مِثَالُ صَفِيرُ جَحْفَلَةٍ   بَيِّنْهُ تِبْيَانًا يُنَمُّ بِهِ

١ وأنشأ يقول. ٢ ف: المجد.

٣٦،١٠ قَالَ الْحَارِثُ بْنُ هَمَّامٍ فَلَمَّا أَطْرَبَنَا بِمَا سَمِعْنَاهُ. وَطَالَبْنَا بِكَشْفِ[١] مَعْنَاهُ. قُلْنَا لَهُ لَسْنَا مِنْ خَيْلِ هٰذَا الْمَيْدَانِ. وَلَا لَنَا بِحَلِّ هٰذِهِ الْعُقَدِ يَدَانِ. فَإِنْ أَبَنْتَ. مَنَنْتَ. وَإِنْ كَتَمْتَ. غَمَمْتَ. فَظَلَّ يُشَاوِرُ نَفْسَهُ. وَيُقَلِّبُ قِدْحَيْهِ. حَتَّى هَانَ بَذْلُ الْمَاعُونِ عَلَيْهِ. فَأَقْبَلَ حِينَئِذٍ عَلَى الْجَمَاعَةِ. وَقَالَ[٢] سَأُعَلِّمُكُمْ مَا لَمْ تَكُونُوا تَعْلَمُونَ. وَلَا ظَنَنْتُمْ أَنَّكُمْ تُعَلَّمُونَ. فَأَوْكُوا عَلَيْهِ الْأَوْعِيَةَ. وَرَوِّضُوا بِهِ الْأَنْدِيَةَ. ثُمَّ أَخَذَ فِي تَفْسِيرٍ صَقَلَ بِهِ الْأَذْهَانَ. وَاسْتَفْرَغَ مَعَهُ الْأَرْدَانَ. حَتَّى آضَتِ الْأَفْهَامُ أَنْوَرَ مِنَ الشَّمْسِ. وَالْأَكْمَامُ كَأَنْ لَمْ تَغْنَ[٣] بِالْأَمْسِ.

٣٦،١١ وَلَمَّا هَمَّ بِالْمَفَرِّ. سُئِلَ عَنِ الْمَقَرِّ. فَتَنَفَّسَ كَمَا تَتَنَفَّسُ الثَّكُولُ. وَأَنْشَأَ يَقُولُ.

كُلُّ شِعْبٍ لِيَ شِعْبُ ... وَبِهِ رَبْعِيَ رَحْبُ
غَيْرَ أَنِّي بِسَرُوجٍ ... مُسْتَهَامُ الْقَلْبِ صَبُّ
هِيَ أَرْضِي الْبِكْرُ وَالْجَوُّ الَّذِي مِنْهُ الْمَهَبُّ
وَإِلَى رَوْضَتِهَا الْغَنَّاءِ دُونَ الرَّوْضِ أَصْبُو
مَا حَلَا لِي بَعْدَهَا حُلْوٌ وَلَا اعْذَوْذَبَ عَذْبُ

قَالَ الرَّاوِي فَقُلْتُ لِأَصْحَابِي هٰذَا أَبُو زَيْدٍ السَّرُوجِيُّ. الَّذِي أَدْنَى مُلَحِهِ الْأَحَاجِيُّ. وَأَخَذْتُ أَصِفُ لَهُمْ حُسْنَ تَوْشِيَتِهِ. وَانْقِيَادَ الْكَلَامِ لِمَشِيَّتِهِ.[٤] ثُمَّ الْتَفَتُّ فَإِذَا بِهِ قَدْ طَمَرَ. وَنَاءَ بِمَا قَمَرَ. فَعَجِبْنَا مِمَّا صَنَعَ.[٥] وَلَمْ نَدْرِ أَيْنَ سَكَعَ وَصَقَعَ.

١ ف: مُكَاشَفَةً. ٢ ف: وقال يا أهل البلاغة والبراعة. ٣ د: تُغْنَى. ٤ . «وانقياد الكلام لمشيته»: سقطت من ف. ٥ ف: صنع إذ وقع.

تَفْسِيرُ الْأَحَاجِيِّ الْمُودَعَةِ هٰذِهِ الْمَقَامَةَ

١٢،٣٦ أَمَّا جُوعٌ أُمِدَّ بِزَادٍ فَمِثْلُهُ طَوَامِيرُ. وَأَمَّا ظَهْرٌ أَصَابَتْهُ عَيْنٌ فَمِثْلُهُ مَطَاعِينُ. وَأَمَّا صَادَفَ جَائِزَةً فَمِثْلُهُ[١] الْفَاصِلَةُ. وَأَمَّا تَنَاوَلَ أَلْفَ دِينَارٍ فَمِثْلُهُ هَادِيَةٌ. وَأَمَّا أَهْمَلَ حِلْيَةً فَمِثْلُهُ الْغَاشِيَةُ. وَأَمَّا ٱكْفُفِ ٱكْفُفْ فَمِثْلُهُ مَهْمَهْ. وَأَمَّا الشَّقِيقُ أَفْلَتَ فَمِثْلُهُ الْأَخْطَارُ. وَأَمَّا مَا ٱخْتَارَ فِضَّةً فَمِثْلُهُ أَبَارِقَةٌ لِأَنَّ الرِّقَةَ مِنْ أَسْمَاءِ الْفِضَّةِ وَقَدْ نَطَقَ بِهَا النَّبِيُّ صَلَّى اللّٰهُ عَلَيْهِ وَسَلَّمَ فَقَالَ «فِي الرِّقَةِ رُبْعُ الْعُشْرِ». وَأَمَّا دُسْ جَمَاعَةً فَمِثْلُهُ طَافِيَةٌ. وَأَمَّا خَالِي ٱسْكُتْ فَمِثْلُهُ خَالِصَهْ لِأَنَّكَ إِذَا نَادَيْتَ مُضَافًا إِلَى نَفْسِكَ جَازَ لَكَ حَذْفُ الْيَاءِ وَإِثْبَاتُهَا سَاكِنَةً وَمُتَحَرِّكَةً وَقَدْ حَذَفَ هَاهُنَا حَرْفَ النِّدَاءِ كَمَا حَذَفَهُ فِي أَصْلِ الْأُحْجِيَّةِ وَصَهْ بِمَعْنَى اسْكُتْ. وَأَمَّا خُذْ تِلْكَ فَمِثْلُهُ هَاتِيكَ. وَأَمَّا حِمَارُ وَحْشٍ زُيِّنَا[٢] فَمِثْلُهُ فَرَازِينُ لِأَنَّ الْفَرَا حِمَارُ الْوَحْشِ وَمِنْهُ الْخَبَرُ «كُلُّ الصَّيْدِ فِي جَوْفِ الْفَرَا». وَأَمَّا قَوْلُهُ أَنْفِقْ تَقْمَعْ فَمِثْلُهُ مُنْتَقِمٌ لِأَنَّ الْأَمْرَ مِنْ مَانَ يَمُونُ مُنْ وَمُضَارِعَ وَقَمَتْ تَقِمُ.

١٣،٣٦ أَمَّا ٱسْتَنْشِ رِيحَ مُدَامَةٍ فَمِثْلُهُ رَحْرَاحٌ لِأَنَّ الْأَمْرَ مِنِ ٱسْتِدْعَاءِ الرَّائِحَةِ رَحْ. وَأَمَّا غَطِّ هَلْكَى فَمِثْلُهُ صُنْبُورٌ لِأَنَّ الْبُورَ هُمُ الْهَلْكَى وَفِي الْقُرْآنِ ﴿وَكُنْتُمْ قَوْمًا بُورًا﴾. وَأَمَّا سَارَ بِاللَّيْلِ مُدَّةً فَمِثْلُهُ سَرَاحِينُ. وَأَمَّا أَجِبْ فُرُوقَهُ فَمِثْلُهُ مِقْلَاعٌ لِأَنَّ الْأَمْرَ مِنْ وَمَقَ يَمِقُ مِقْ وَاللَّاعُ الْجَبَانُ يُقَالُ فُلَانٌ هَاعٌ لَاعٌ إِذَا كَانَ جَبَانًا جَزُوعًا. وَأَمَّا أَعْطِ إِبْرِيقًا يَلُوحُ بِغَيْرِ عُرْوَةٍ فَمِثْلُهُ أُسْكُوبٌ لِأَنَّ الْأَوْسَ الْعَطَاءُ وَالْأَمْرُ مِنْهُ أُسْ[٣] وَالْكُوبُ الْإِبْرِيقُ بِغَيْرِ عُرْوَةٍ. وَأَمَّا الثَّوْرُ مِلْكِي فَمِثْلُهُ اللَّآلِي لِأَنَّ اللَّأَى عَلَى وَزْنِ الْقَنَا هُوَ ثَوْرُ الْوَحْشِ. أَمَّا صَفِيرُ جَحْفَلَةٍ فَمِثْلُهُ مُكَاشَفَةٌ لِأَنَّ الْمُكَاءَ الصَّفِيرُ

١ س: مثاله. ٢ س: حُلِّيا. ٣ و: بعدها في و: ومنه اشتقاق المواساة.

قَالَ اللّٰهُ تَعَالَى ﴿وَمَا كَانَ صَلَاتُهُمْ عِنْدَ الْبَيْتِ إِلَّا مُكَاءً وَتَصْدِيَةً﴾ وَالْأَصْلُ فِي الْمُكَاءِ الْمَدُّ وَلٰكِنَّهُ قَصَرَهُ فِي هٰذِهِ الْأُحْجِيَّةِ كَمَا حَذَفَ هَمْزَةَ الْفَرَا فِي أُحْجِيَّتِهِ وَكِلَا الْأَمْرَيْنِ مِنْ قَصْرِ الْمَمْدُودِ وَحَذْفِ الْمَهْمُوزِ[1] جَائِزٌ.

١ س: همز المهموز، وفي و، د، ف: همزة المهموز.

الْمَقَامَةُ السَّابِعَةُ وَالثَّلَاثُونَ[1]

١،٣٧ حَكَى الْحَارِثُ بْنُ هَمَّامٍ قَالَ أَصْعَدْتُ إِلَى صَعْدَةَ. وَأَنَا ذُو شَطَاطٍ يَحْكِي الصَّعْدَةَ. وَٱشْتِدَادٍ يَبْدُرُ بَنَاتِ صَعْدَةَ. فَلَمَّا رَأَيْتُ نَضْرَتَهَا. وَرَعَيْتُ خُضْرَتَهَا. سَأَلْتُ نَحَارِيرَ الرُّوَاةِ. عَمَّنْ تَحْوِيهِ مِنَ السَّرَاةِ. وَمَعَادِنِ الْخَيْرَاتِ. لِأَتَّخِذَهُ جِذْوَةً فِي الظُّلُمَاتِ. وَنَجْدَةً فِي الظُّلَامَاتِ. فَنُعِتَ لِي قَاضٍ بِهَا رَحِيبُ الْبَاعِ. خَصِيبُ الرِّبَاعِ. تَمِيمِيُّ النَّسَبِ وَالطِّبَاعِ. فَلَمْ أَزَلْ أَتَقَرَّبُ إِلَيْهِ بِالْإِلْمَامِ. وَأَتَنَفَّقُ عَلَيْهِ بِالْإِجْمَامِ. حَتَّى صِرْتُ صَدَى صَوْتِهِ. وَسَلْمَانَ بَيْتِهِ. وَكُنْتُ مَعَ ٱشْتِيَارِ شُهْدِهِ. وَٱنْتِشَاقِ رَنْدِهِ. أَشْهَدُ مَشَاجِرَ الْخُصُومِ. وَأَسْفِرُ بَيْنَ الْمَعْصُومِ مِنْهُمْ وَالْمَوْصُومِ.

٢،٣٧ فَبَيْنَمَا الْقَاضِي جَالِسٌ لِلْإِسْجَالِ. فِي يَوْمِ الْمَحْفِلِ وَالِاحْتِفَالِ. إِذْ دَخَلَ شَيْخٌ بَالِي الرِّيَاشِ. بَادِي الِارْتِعَاشِ. فَتَبَصَّرَ الْحَفْلَ تَبَصُّرَ نَقَّادٍ. ثُمَّ زَعَمَ أَنَّ لَهُ خَصْمًا غَيْرَ مُنْقَادٍ. فَلَمْ يَكُنْ إِلَّا كَضَوْءِ شَرَارَةٍ. أَوْ وَحْيِ إِشَارَةٍ. حَتَّى أُحْضِرَ غُلَامٌ. كَأَنَّهُ ضِرْغَامٌ. فَقَالَ الشَّيْخُ أَيَّدَ اللهُ الْقَاضِيَ. وَعَصَمَهُ مِنَ التَّغَاضِي. إِنَّ ٱبْنِي هٰذَا كَالْقَلَمِ الرَّدِيِّ.[2] وَالسَّيْفِ الصَّدِيِّ.[3] يَجْهَلُ أَوْصَافَ الْإِنْصَافِ. وَيَرْضَعُ أَخْلَافَ الْخِلَافِ. إِنْ أَقْدَمْتُ أَحْجَمَ. وَإِذَا أَعْرَبْتُ أَعْجَمَ. وَإِنْ أَذْكَيْتُ أَخْمَدَ. وَمَتَى شَوَيْتُ رَمَّدَ. مَعَ أَنِّي كَفَلْتُهُ مُذْ دَبَّ. إِلَى أَنْ شَبَّ. وَكُنْتُ[4] لَهُ أَلْطَفَ مِنْ رَبِّي وَرَبَّ. فَأَكْبَرَ الْقَاضِي مَا شَكَا إِلَيْهِ. وَأَطْرَفَ بِهِ مَنْ حَوَالَيْهِ. ثُمَّ قَالَ أَشْهَدُ أَنَّ الْعُقُوقَ أَحَدُ الثُّكْلَيْنِ. وَلَرُبَّ عُقْمٍ أَقَرُّ لِلْعَيْنِ.

١ في هامش س: تعرف بالصعيدية؛ وفي د: الصَّعْدِيَّة؛ وفي ف: الصعيدية. ٢ ق: الرديء. ٣ ق: الصديء.
٤ ق: فكنت.

٣٫٣٧ فَقَالَ ٱلْغُلَامُ. وَقَدْ أَمْعَضَهُ هٰذَا ٱلْكَلَامُ وَٱلَّذِي نَصَبَ ٱلْقُضَاةَ لِلْعَدْلِ. وَمَلَّكَهُمْ أَعِنَّةَ ٱلْفَضْلِ وَٱلْفَصْلِ. إِنَّهُ مَا دَعَا قَطُّ إِلَّا أَمَّنْتُ. وَلَا ٱدَّعَى إِلَّا آمَنْتُ. وَلَا لَبَّى إِلَّا أَحْرَمْتُ. وَلَا أَوْرَى إِلَّا أَضْرَمْتُ. بَيْدَ أَنَّهُ كَمَنْ يَبْغِي بَيْضَ ٱلْأَنُوقِ. وَيَطْلُبُ ٱلطَّيَرَانَ مِنَ ٱلنُّوقِ. فَقَالَ لَهُ ٱلْقَاضِي وَبِمَ أَعْنَتَكَ. وَٱمْتَحَنَ طَاعَتَكَ. قَالَ إِنَّهُ مُذْ صَفِرَ مِنَ ٱلْمَالِ. وَمُنِيَ بِٱلْإِمْحَالِ. يَسُومُنِي أَنْ أَتَلَمَّظَ بِٱلسُّؤَالِ. وَأَسْتَمْطِرَ سُحْبَ[1] ٱلنَّوَالِ. لِيَفِيضَ شِرْبُهُ ٱلَّذِي غَاضَ. وَيَنْجَبِرَ مِنْ حَالِهِ مَا ٱنْهَاضَ. وَقَدْ كَانَ حِينَ أَخَذَنِي بِٱلدَّرْسِ. وَعَلَّمَنِي أَدَبَ ٱلنَّفْسِ. أَشْرَبَ قَلْبِي أَنَّ ٱلْحِرْصَ مَتْعَبَةٌ. وَٱلطَّمَعَ مَعْيَبَةٌ.[2] وَٱلشَّرَهَ مَتْخَمَةٌ. وَٱلْمَسْأَلَةَ مَلْأَمَةٌ. ثُمَّ أَنْشَدَنِي مِنْ فَلْقِ[3] فِيهِ. وَنَحْتِ قَوَافِيهِ.

٤٫٣٧
ٱرْضَ بِأَدْنَى ٱلْعَيْشِ وَٱشْكُرْ عَلَيْهْ شُكْرَ مَنِ ٱلْقُلُّ كَثِيرٌ لَدَيْهْ
وَجَانِبِ ٱلْحِرْصَ ٱلَّذِي لَمْ يَزَلْ يَحُطُّ قَدْرَ ٱلْمُتَرَاقِي إِلَيْهْ
وَحَامِ عَنْ عِرْضِكَ وَٱسْتَبْقِهِ كَمَا يُحَامِي ٱللَّيْثُ عَنْ لِبْدَتَيْهْ
وَٱصْبِرْ عَلَى مَا نَابَ مِنْ فَاقَةٍ صَبْرَ أُولِي ٱلْعَزْمِ وَأَغْمِضْ عَلَيْهْ
وَلَا تُرِقْ مَاءَ ٱلْمُحَيَّا وَلَوْ خَوَّلَكَ ٱلْمَسْؤُولُ مَا فِي يَدَيْهْ
فَٱلْحُرُّ مَنْ إِنْ قَذِيَتْ عَيْنُهُ أَخْفَى قَذَى جَفْنَيْهِ عَنْ نَاظِرَيْهْ
وَمَنْ إِذَا أَخْلَقَ دِيبَاجُهُ لَمْ يَرَ أَنْ يُخْلِقَ دِيبَاجَتَيْهْ

٥٫٣٧ قَالَ فَعَبَسَ ٱلشَّيْخُ وَٱكْفَهَرَّ. وَٱنْدَرَأَ عَلَى ٱبْنِهِ وَهَرَّ. وَقَالَ لَهُ صَهْ يَا عُقَقُ. يَا مَنْ هُوَ ٱلشَّجَى وَٱلشَّرَقُ. وَيْكَ أَتُعَلِّمُ أُمَّكَ ٱلْبِضَاعَ. وَظِئْرَكَ ٱلْإِرْضَاعَ. لَقَدْ

---

١ س: سُحُبْ، وفوقها «معا»؛ وفي د، و: سُحُب. ٢ ق: مَعْتَبَة، وعليها علامة تصحيح، على أنَّ الصحيح مطموس، فأثبتناه من س، د، و؛ وفي ف: معتبة. ٣ د: فِلْق.

تَحَكَّكَتِ ٱلْعَقْرَبُ بِٱلْأَفْعَى. وَٱسْتَنَّتِ ٱلْفِصَالُ حَتَّى ٱلْقَرْعَى. ثُمَّ كَأَنَّهُ نَدِمَ عَلَى مَا فَرَطَ مِنْ فِيهِ. وَحَدَتْهُ ٱلْمِقَةُ[1] عَلَى تَلَافِيهِ. فَرَنَا إِلَيْهِ بِعَيْنِ عَاطِفٍ. وَخَفَضَ لَهُ جَنَاحَ مُلَاطِفٍ. وَقَالَ[2] وَيْكَ يَا بُنَيَّ إِنَّ مَنْ أُمِرَ بِٱلْقَنَاعَةِ. وَزُجِرَ عَنِ ٱلضَّرَاعَةِ. هُمْ أَرْبَابُ ٱلْبِضَاعَةِ. وَأُولُو ٱلْمَكْسَبَةِ بِٱلصِّنَاعَةِ. فَأَمَّا ذَوُو ٱلضَّرُورَاتِ. فَقَدِ ٱسْتُثْنِيَ بِهِمْ فِي ٱلْمَحْظُورَاتِ. وَهَبْكَ جَهِلْتَ هٰذَا ٱلتَّأْوِيلَ. وَلَمْ يَبْلُغْكَ مَا قِيلَ. أَلَسْتَ ٱلَّذِي عَارَضَ أَبَاهُ. إِذْ[3] قَالَ وَمَا حَابَاهُ.

٦٫٣٧ لَا تَقْعُدَنَّ عَلَى ضُرٍّ وَمَسْغَبَةٍ   لِكَيْ يُقَالَ عَزِيزُ ٱلنَّفْسِ مُصْطَبِرُ
وَٱنْظُرْ بِعَيْنِكَ هَلْ أَرْضٌ مُعَطَّلَةٌ   مِنَ ٱلنَّبَاتِ كَأَرْضٍ حَفَّهَا ٱلشَّجَرُ
فَعَدِّ عَمَّا تُشِيرُ ٱلْأَغْبِيَاءُ بِهِ   فَأَيُّ فَضْلٍ لِعُودٍ مَا لَهُ ثَمَرُ
وَٱرْحَلْ رِكَابَكَ عَنْ رَبْعٍ ظَمِئْتَ بِهِ   إِلَى ٱلْجَنَابِ ٱلَّذِي يَهْمِي بِهِ ٱلْمَطَرُ
وَٱسْتَنْزِلِ ٱلرِّيَّ مِنْ دَرِّ ٱلسَّحَابِ فَإِنْ   بُلَّتْ يَدَاكَ بِهِ فَلْيَهْنِكَ ٱلظَّفَرُ
وَإِنْ رُدِدْتَ فَمَا فِي ٱلرَّدِّ مَنْقَصَةٌ   عَلَيْكَ قَدْ رُدَّ مُوسَى قَبْلُ وَٱلْخَضِرُ

٧٫٣٧ قَالَ فَلَمَّا رَأَى ٱلْقَاضِي تَنَافِيَ قَوْلِ ٱلْفَتَى وَفِعْلِهِ. وَتَحَلِّيَهُ بِمَا لَيْسَ مِنْ أَهْلِهِ. نَظَرَ إِلَيْهِ بِعَيْنِ غَضْبَى. وَقَالَ أَتَمِيمِيًّا مَرَّةً وَقَيْسِيًّا أُخْرَى. أُفٍّ لِمَنْ يَنْقُضُ مَا يَقُولُ. وَيَتَلَوَّنُ كَمَا تَتَلَوَّنُ ٱلْغُولُ. فَقَالَ ٱلْغُلَامُ وَٱلَّذِي جَعَلَكَ مِفْتَاحًا لِلْحَقِّ. وَفَتَّاحًا بَيْنَ ٱلْخَلْقِ. لَقَدْ أُنْسِيتُ مُذْ أَسِيتُ. وَصَدِئَ ذِهْنِي مُذْ صَدِيتُ. عَلَى أَنَّهُ أَيْنَ ٱلْبَابُ ٱلْفُتُحُ. وَٱلْعَطَاءُ ٱلسُّرُحُ. وَهَلْ بَقِيَ مَنْ يَتَبَرَّعُ بِٱللُّهَى. وَإِذَا ٱسْتُطْعِمَ يَقُولُ هَا. فَقَالَ لَهُ ٱلْقَاضِي مَهْ. فَمَعَ ٱلْخَوَاطِئِ سَهْمٌ صَائِبٌ. وَمَا كُلُّ بَرْقٍ خَالِبٌ. فَمَيِّزِ ٱلْبُرُوقَ إِذَا شِمْتَ. وَلَا تَشْهَدْ إِلَّا بِمَا عَلِمْتَ. فَلَمَّا تَبَيَّنَ لِلشَّيْخِ أَنَّ ٱلْقَاضِيَ

١ س: الأُلفة. ٢ بعدها في ف: له. ٣ س، ف: فيما.

قَدْ غَضِبَ لِلْكِرَامِ. وَأَعْظَمَ تَخْيِيلَ جَمِيعِ ٱلْأَنَامِ. عَلِمَ أَنَّهُ سَيَنْصُرُ كَلِمَتَهُ. وَيُظْهِرُ أُكْرُومَتَهُ. فَمَا كَذَّبَ أَنْ نَصَبَ شَبَكَتَهُ. وَشَوَى فِي ٱلْحَرِيقِ سَمَكَتَهُ. وَأَنْشَأَ يَقُولُ

٨،٣٧ يَا أَيُّهَا ٱلْقَاضِي ٱلَّذِي عِلْمُهُ وَحِلْمُهُ أَرْسَخُ مِنْ رَضْوَى
قَدِ ٱدَّعَى هٰذَا عَلَى جَهْلِهِ أَنْ لَيْسَ فِي ٱلدُّنْيَا أَخُو جَدْوَى
وَمَا دَرَى أَنَّكَ مِنْ مَعْشَرٍ عَطَاؤُهُمْ كَٱلْمَنِّ وَٱلسَّلْوَى
فَجُدْ بِمَ يَثْنِيهِ مُسْتَخْزِيًا مِمَّا ٱفْتَرَى مِنْ كَذِبِ ٱلدَّعْوَى
وَأَثْنِي جَذْلَانَ أُثْنِي بِمَا أَوْلَيْتَ مِنْ جَدْوَى وَمِنْ عَدْوَى

قَالَ فَهَشَّ ٱلْقَاضِي لِقَوْلِهِ. وَأَجْزَلَ لَهُ مِنْ طَوْلِهِ. ثُمَّ لَفَتَ وَجْهَهُ إِلَى ٱلْغُلَامِ. وَقَدْ نَصَلَ لَهُ أَسْهُمَ ٱلْمَلَامِ. وَقَالَ لَهُ أَرَأَيْتَ بُطْلَ زُعْمِكَ. وَخَطَأَ وَهْمِكَ. فَلَا تَعْجَلْ بَعْدَهَا بِذَمٍّ. وَلَا تَنْحَتْ عُودًا قَبْلَ عَجْمٍ. وَإِيَّاكَ وَتَأَبِّيكَ. عَنْ مُطَاوَعَةِ أَبِيكَ. فَإِنَّكَ إِنْ عُدْتَ تَعُقُّهُ. حَاقَ بِكَ مِنِّي مَا تَسْتَحِقُّهُ. فَسُقِطَ ٱلْفَتَى فِي يَدِهِ. وَلَاذَ بِحَقْوِ وَالِدِهِ. ثُمَّ نَهَضَ يَحْفِدُ. وَتَبِعَهُ ٱلشَّيْخُ يُنْشِدُ.

مَنْ ضَامَهُ أَوْ ضَارَهُ دَهْرُهُ فَلْيَقْصِدِ ٱلْقَاضِيَ فِي صَعْدَهْ
سَمَاحُهُ أَزْرَى بِمَنْ قَبْلَهُ وَعَدْلُهُ أَتْعَبَ مَنْ بَعْدَهْ

٩،٣٧ قَالَ ٱلرَّاوِي فَحِرْتُ بَيْنَ تَعْرِيفِ ٱلشَّيْخِ وَتَنْكِيرِهِ. إِلَى أَنِ ٱحْرَوْرَفَ لِمَسِيرِهِ. فَنَاجَيْتُ ٱلنَّفْسَ بِٱتِّبَاعِهِ. وَلَوْ إِلَى رِبَاعِهِ. لَعَلِّي أَظْهَرُ عَلَى أَسْرَارِهِ. وَأَعْرِفُ شَجَرَةَ نَارِهِ. فَنَبَذْتُ ٱلْعُلَقَ. وَٱنْطَلَقْتُ حِينَ ٱنْطَلَقَ. وَلَمْ يَزَلْ يَخْطُو وَأَعْتَقِبُ. وَيَبْعُدُ وَأَقْتَرِبُ. إِلَى أَنْ تَرَاءَى ٱلشَّخْصَانِ. وَحَقَّ ٱلتَّعَارُفُ عَلَى ٱلْخُلْصَانِ. فَأَبْدَى ٱلْإِهْتِشَاشَ. وَرَفَعَ ٱلْإِرْتِعَاشَ. وَقَالَ مَنْ كَاذَبَ أَخَاهُ فَلَا عَاشَ. فَعَرَفْتُ عِنْدَ

ذٰلِكَ أَنَّهُ ٱلسَّرُوجِيُّ بِلَا مَحَالَةٍ. وَلَا حُؤُولِ حَالَةٍ. وَأَسْرَعْتُ[1] إِلَيْهِ لِأُصَافِحَهُ. وَأَسْتَعْرِفَ سَانِحَهُ وَبَارِحَهُ. فَقَالَ دُونَكَ ٱبْنَ أَخِيكَ ٱلْبَرَّ. وَتَرَكَنِي وَمَرَّ. فَلَمْ يَعْدُ ٱلْفَتَى أَنِ ٱفْتَرَّ. ثُمَّ فَرَّ كَمَا فَرَّ. فَعُدْتُ وَقَدِ ٱسْتَبَنْتُ عَيْنَهُمَا. وَلٰكِنْ أَيْنَ هُمَا.

١ د: وبادرت.

الْمَقَامَةُ الثَّامِنَةُ وَالثَّلاثُونَ[١]

١،٣٨ حَكَى الْحَارِثُ بْنُ هَمَّامٍ قَالَ حُبِّبَ إِلَيَّ مُذْ سَعَتْ قَدَمِي. وَنَفَثَ قَلَمِي. أَنْ أَتَّخِذَ الْأَدَبَ شِرْعَةً. وَالِاقْتِبَاسَ مِنْهُ نُجْعَةً. فَكُنْتُ أُنَقِّبُ عَنْ أَحْبَارِهِ.[٢] وَخَزَنَةِ أَسْرَارِهِ. فَإِذَا أَلْفَيْتُ مِنْهُمْ بُغْيَةَ الْمُلْتَمِسِ. وَجِذْوَةَ الْمُقْتَبِسِ. شَدَدْتُ[٣] يَدِي[٤] بِغَرْزِهِ. وَٱسْتَنْزَلْتُ مِنْهُ زَكَاةَ كَنْزِهِ. عَلَى أَنِّي لَمْ أَلْقَ كَالسَّرُوجِيِّ فِي غَزَارَةِ السُّحْبِ.[٥] وَوَضْعِ الْهِنَاءِ مَوَاضِعَ النُّقْبِ. إِلَّا أَنَّهُ كَانَ أَسْيَرَ مِنَ الْمَثَلِ. وَأَسْرَعَ مِنَ الْقَمَرِ فِي النُّقَلِ. وَكُنْتُ لِهَوَى مُلَاقَاتِهِ. وَٱسْتِحْسَانِ مَقَامَاتِهِ. أَرْغَبُ فِي الِاغْتِرَابِ. وَأَسْتَعْذِبُ السَّفَرَ الَّذِي هُوَ قِطْعَةٌ مِنَ الْعَذَابِ.

٢،٣٨ فَلَمَّا تَطَوَّحْتُ إِلَى مَرْوَ. وَلَا غَرْوَ. بَشَّرَنِي بِمَلْقَاهُ زَجْرُ الطَّيْرِ. وَالْفَأْلُ الَّذِي هُوَ بَرِيدُ الْخَيْرِ. فَلَمْ أَزَلْ أَنْشُدُهُ فِي الْمَحَافِلِ. وَعِنْدَ تَلَقِّي الْقَوَافِلِ. فَلَا أَجِدُ عَنْهُ مُخْبِرًا. وَلَا أَرَى لَهُ أَثَرًا وَلَا عِثْيَرًا. حَتَّى غَلَبَ الْيَأْسُ الطَّمَعَ. وَٱنْزَوَى التَّأْمِيلُ وَٱنْقَمَعَ. فَإِنِّي لَذَاتَ يَوْمٍ بِحَضْرَةِ وَالِي مَرْوَ. وَكَانَ مِمَّنْ جَمَعَ الْفَضْلَ وَالسَّرْوَ. إِذْ طَلَعَ أَبُو زَيْدٍ فِي خَلَقٍ[٦] مِمْلَاقٍ. وَخُلُقٍ مَلَّاقٍ. فَحَيَّا الْوَالِيَ تَحِيَّةَ الْمُحْتَاجِ. إِذَا لَقِيَ رَبَّ التَّاجِ.

٣،٣٨ ثُمَّ قَالَ لَهُ اِعْلَمْ وُقِيتَ الذَّمَّ. وَكُفِيتَ الْهَمَّ. أَنَّ مَنْ عُذِقَتْ بِهِ الْأَعْمَالُ. أُعْلِقَتْ بِهِ الْآمَالُ. وَمَنْ رُفِعَتْ لَهُ الدَّرَجَاتُ. رُفِعَتْ إِلَيْهِ الْحَاجَاتُ. وَأَنَّ السَّعِيدَ مَنْ إِذَا قَدَرَ. وَوَاتَاهُ الْقَدَرُ.[٧] أَدَّى زَكَاةَ النِّعَمِ. كَمَا يُؤَدِّي زَكَاةَ النَّعَمِ. وَٱلْتَزَمَ

١ في هامش س: تعرف بالمروية؛ وفي د: المَرْوِيَّة؛ وفي ف: وهي المروية. ٢ و، ف: أخباره. ٣ ف: سددت.
٤ د: يديَّ، و: رحلي. ٥ ق: السُّحُب. ٦ د: خُلُقٍ. ٧ سقطت الورقة التي تليها في و.

لِأَهْلِ الْحُرَمِ.[١] كَمَا[٢] يَلْتَزِمُ[٣] لِلْأَهْلِ وَالْحَرَمِ.[٤] وَقَدْ أَصْبَحْتَ بِحَمْدِ اللهِ عَمِيدَ مِصْرِكَ. وَعِمَادَ عَصْرِكَ. تُزْجَى الرَّكَائِبُ إِلَى حَرَمِكَ. وَتُرْجَى الرَّغَائِبُ مِنْ كَرَمِكَ. وَتُنْزَلُ الْمَطَالِبُ بِسَاحَتِكَ. وَتُسْتَنْزَلُ الرَّاحَةُ مِنْ رَاحَتِكَ. ﴿وَكَانَ فَضْلُ اللهِ عَلَيْكَ عَظِيمًا﴾. وَإِحْسَانُهُ لَدَيْكَ عَمِيمًا. ثُمَّ إِنِّي شَيْخٌ تَرِبَ بَعْدَ الْإِتْرَابِ. وَعَدِمَ الْإِعْشَابَ حِينَ شَابَ. قَصَدْتُكَ مِنْ مَحَلَّةٍ نَازِحَةٍ. وَحَالَةٍ رَازِحَةٍ. آمُلُ مِنْ بَحْرِكَ دُفْعَةً. وَمِنْ جَاهِكَ رِفْعَةً. وَالتَّأْمِيلُ أَفْضَلُ وَسَائِلِ السَّائِلِ. وَنَائِلِ النَّائِلِ. فَأَوْجِبْ لِي مَا يَجِبُ عَلَيْكَ. وَأَحْسِنْ كَمَا أَحْسَنَ اللهُ إِلَيْكَ. وَإِيَّاكَ أَنْ تَلْوِيَ عِذَارَكَ. عَمَّنِ ٱزْدَارَكَ. وَأَمَّ دَارَكَ. أَوْ تَقْبِضَ رَاحَكَ. عَمَّنِ ٱمْتَاحَكَ. وَٱمْتَارَ سَمَاحَكَ. فَوَاللهِ مَا مَجُدَ مَنْ جَمَدَ. وَلَا رَشَدَ مَنْ حَشَدَ. بَلِ اللَّبِيبُ مَنْ إِذَا وَجَدَ جَادَ. وَإِنْ بَدَأَ بِعَائِدَةٍ عَادَ. وَالْكَرِيمُ مَنْ إِذَا ٱسْتُوهِبَ الذَّهَبَ. لَمْ يَهَبْ أَنْ يَهَبَ.

٤،٣٨ ثُمَّ أَمْسَكَ يَرْقُبُ أُكُلَ غَرْسِهِ. وَيَرْصُدُ مَطِيَّةَ[٥] نَفْسِهِ. وَأَحَبَّ الْوَالِي أَنْ يَعْلَمَ هَلْ نُطْفَتُهُ ثَمْدٌ. أَمْ لِقَرِيحَتِهِ مَدَدٌ. فَأَطْرَقَ يُرَوِّي فِي ٱسْتِيرَاءِ زَنْدِهِ. وَٱسْتِشْفَافِ فِرِنْدِهِ. وَٱلْتَبَسَ عَلَى أَبِي زَيْدٍ سِرُّ صَمْتَتِهِ. وَإِرْجَاءُ[٦] صِلَتِهِ. فَتَوَغَّرَ غَضَبًا. وَأَنْشَدَ مُقْتَضِبًا.

لَا تَحْقِرَنَّ أُبَيْتَ اللَّعْنَ ذَا أَدَبٍ   لِأَنْ بَدَا خَلَقَ السِّرْبَالِ سُبْرُوتَا
وَلَا تُضِعْ لِأَخِي التَّأْمِيلِ حُرْمَتَهُ   أَكَانَ ذَا لَسَنٍ أَمْ كَانَ سِكِّيتَا
وَٱنْفَحْ بِعُرْفِكَ مَنْ وَافَاكَ مُخْتَبِطًا   وَٱنْعَشْ بِغَوْثِكَ مَنْ أَلْفَيْتَ مَنْكُوتَا
فَخَيْرُ مَالِ الْفَتَى مَالٌ أَشَادَ لَهُ   ذِكْرًا تَنَاقَلَهُ الرُّكْبَانُ أَوْ صِيتَا

---

١ . ف: الحَرَم. ٢ ف: ما. ٣ ف: يُلْتَزَم. ٤ د، ف: الحَرَم. ٥ د: مَطِيبة. ٦ في هامش س، وفي و، د: سَبَبُ إرْجاءِ؛ وفي ف: إرجاءِ.

وَمَا عَلَى ٱلْمُشْتَرِي حَمْدًا بِمَوْهِبَةٍ   غَبْنٌ وَلَوْ كَانَ مَا أَعْطَاهُ يَاقُوتَا
لَوْلَا ٱلْمُرُوءَةُ ضَاقَ ٱلْعُذْرُ عَنْ فَطِنٍ   إِذَا ٱشْرَأَبَّ إِلَى مَا جَاوَزَ ٱلْقُوتَا
لٰكِنَّهُ لِٱبْتِنَاءِ ٱلْمَجْدِ جَدَّ وَمَنْ   حُبِّ ٱلسَّمَاحِ ثَنَى نَحْوَ ٱلْغِنَى[1] لِيتَا
وَمَا تَنَشَّقَ نَشْرَ ٱلشُّكْرِ ذُو كَرَمٍ   إِلَّا وَأَزْرَى بِنَشْرِ ٱلْمِسْكِ مَفْتُوتَا
وَٱلْحَمْدُ وَٱلْبُخْلُ لَمْ يُقْضَ ٱجْتِمَاعُهُمَا   حَتَّى لَقَدْ خِيلَ ذَا ضَبًّا وَذَا حُوتَا
وَٱلسَّمْحُ فِي ٱلنَّاسِ مَحْبُوبٌ خَلَائِقُهُ   وَٱلْجَامِدُ ٱلْكَفِّ مَا يَنْفَكُّ مَمْقُوتَا
وَلِلشَّحِيحِ عَلَى أَمْوَالِهِ عِلَلٌ   يُوسِعْنَهُ أَبَدًا ذَمًّا وَتَبْكِيتَا
فَجُدْ بِمَا جَمَعَتْ كَفَّاكَ مِنْ نَشَبٍ   حَتَّى يُرَى مُجْتَدِي جَدْوَاكَ مَبْهُوتَا
وَخُذْ نَصِيبَكَ مِنْهُ قَبْلَ رَائِعَةٍ   مِنَ ٱلزَّمَانِ تُرِيكَ ٱلْعُودَ مَنْحُوتَا
فَٱلدَّهْرُ أَنْكَدُ مِنْ أَنْ تَسْتَمِرَّ بِهِ   حَالٌ تَكَرَّهْتَ تِلْكَ ٱلْحَالَ أَمْ شِيتَا

٥،٣٨ فَقَالَ لَهُ ٱلْوَالِي تَاللّٰهِ لَقَدْ أَحْسَنْتَ. فَأَيُّ وَلَدِ ٱلرَّجُلِ أَنْتَ. فَنَظَرَ إِلَيْهِ عَنْ عُرُضٍ. وَأَنْشَدَ وَهُوَ مُغْضٍ.

لَا تَسْأَلِ ٱلْمَرْءَ مَنْ أَبُوهُ وَرُزْ   خِلَالَهُ ثُمَّ صِلْهُ أَوْ فَٱصْرِمِ
فَمَا يَشِينُ ٱلسُّلَافَ حِينَ حَلَا   مَذَاقُهَا كَوْنُهَا ٱبْنَةَ ٱلْحِصْرِمِ

قَالَ فَقَرَّبَهُ ٱلْوَالِي لِبَيَانِهِ ٱلْفَاتِنِ. حَتَّى أَحَلَّهُ مَقْعَدَ ٱلْخَاتِنِ. ثُمَّ فَرَضَ لَهُ مِنْ سُيُوبِ نَيْلِهِ. مَا آذَنَ بِطُولِ ذَيْلِهِ. وَقِصَرِ لَيْلِهِ. فَنَهَضَ عَنْهُ بِرُدْنٍ مَلْآنَ. وَقَلْبٍ جَذْلَانَ.

١ ف: العُلا.

وَتَبِعْتُهُ حَاذِيًا حَذْوَهُ. وَقَافِيًا خَطْوَهُ. حَتَّى إِذَا خَرَجَ مِنْ بَابِهِ. وَفَصَلَ عَنْ غَابِهِ. ٦،٣٨
قُلْتُ لَهُ هُنِّيتَ بِمَا[١] أُوتِيتَ. وَمُلِّيتَ مَا[٢] أُولِيتَ. فَأَسْفَرَ وَجْهُهُ وَتَلَأْلَا. وَوَالَى شُكْرًا لِلّٰهِ تَعَالَى. ثُمَّ خَطَرَ ٱخْتِيَالًا. وَأَنْشَدَ ٱرْتِجَالًا.

مَنْ يَكُنْ نَالَ بِالْحَمَاقَةِ حَظًّا   أَوْ سَمَا قَدْرُهُ لِطِيبِ الْأُصُولِ
فَبِفَضْلِي ٱنْتَفَعْتُ لَا بِفُضُولِي   وَبِقَوْلِي ٱرْتَفَعْتُ لَا بِقُيُولِي

ثُمَّ قَالَ تَعْسًا لِمَنْ جَدَبَ[٣] الْأَدَبَ. وَطُوبَى لِمَنْ جَدَّ فِيهِ وَدَأَبَ. ثُمَّ وَدَّعَنِي وَذَهَبَ. وَأَوْدَعَنِي اللَّهَبَ.

---

١ س: ما.   ٢ د، و، ف: بما.   ٣ و: جذب.

الْمَقَامَةُ التَّاسِعَةُ وَالثَّلَاثُونَ[1]

١،٣٩ حَدَّثَ الْحَارِثُ بْنُ هَمَّامٍ قَالَ لَهِجْتُ مُذِ اخْضَرَّ إِزَارِي. وَبَقَلَ عِذَارِي. بِأَنْ أَجُوبَ الْبَرَارِي. عَلَى ظُهُورِ الْمَهَارِي. أُنْجِدُ طَوْرًا. وَأَسْلُكُ[2] غَوْرًا. حَتَّى فَلَيْتُ الْمَعَالِمَ وَالْمَجَاهِلَ. وَبَلَوْتُ الْمَنَازِلَ وَالْمَنَاهِلَ. وَأَدْمَيْتُ السَّنَابِكَ وَالْمَنَاسِمَ. وَأَنْضَيْتُ السَّوَابِقَ وَالرَّوَاسِمَ. فَلَمَّا مَلِلْتُ الْإِصْحَارَ. وَقَدْ سَنَحَ لِي أَرَبٌ بِصُحَارَ. مِلْتُ إِلَى اخْتِبَارِ[3] التَّيَّارِ. وَاخْتِيَارِ الْفُلْكِ السَّيَّارِ. فَنَقَلْتُ إِلَيْهِ أَسَاوِدِي. وَاسْتَصْحَبْتُ زَادِي وَمَزَاوِدِي. ثُمَّ رَكِبْتُ فِيهِ رُكُوبَ حَاذِرٍ نَاذِرٍ. عَاذِلٍ لِنَفْسِهِ وَعَاذِرٍ.

٢،٣٩ فَلَمَّا شَرَعْنَا فِي الْقُلْعَةِ. وَرَفَعْنَا الشُّرُعَ لِلسُّرْعَةِ.[4] سَمِعْنَا مِنْ شَاطِئِ الْمَرْسَى. حِينَ دَجَا اللَّيْلُ وَأَغْسَى.[5] هَاتِفًا يَقُولُ يَا أَهْلَ ذَا الْفُلْكِ الْقَوِيمِ. الْمُزْجَى[6] فِي الْبَحْرِ الْعَظِيمِ. بِتَقْدِيرِ الْعَزِيزِ الْعَلِيمِ. هَلْ أَدُلُّكُمْ عَلَى تِجَارَةٍ تُنْجِيكُمْ[7] مِنْ عَذَابٍ أَلِيمٍ. فَقُلْنَا لَهُ أَقْبِسْنَا نَارَكَ أَيُّهَا الدَّلِيلُ. وَأَرْشِدْنَا كَمَا يُرْشِدُ الْخَلِيلَ الْخَلِيلُ. فَقَالَ أَتَسْتَصْحِبُونَ ابْنَ سَبِيلٍ. زَادُهُ فِي زَبِيلٍ. وَظِلُّهُ غَيْرُ ثَقِيلٍ. وَمَا يَبْغِي سِوَى مَقِيلٍ. فَأَجْمَعْنَا عَلَى الْجُنُوحِ إِلَيْهِ. وَأَنْ لَا نَبْخَلَ بِالْمَاعُونِ عَلَيْهِ.

٣،٣٩ فَلَمَّا اسْتَوَى عَلَى الْفُلْكِ. قَالَ أَعُوذُ بِمَالِكِ الْمُلْكِ. مِنْ مَسَالِكِ الْهُلْكِ. ثُمَّ قَالَ إِنَّا رُوِينَا فِي الْأَخْبَارِ. الْمَنْقُولَةِ عَنِ الْأَحْبَارِ. أَنَّ[8] اللهَ تَعَالَى مَا أَخَذَ عَلَى الْجُهَّالِ أَنْ يَتَعَلَّمُوا. حَتَّى أَخَذَ عَلَى الْعُلَمَاءِ أَنْ يُعَلِّمُوا. وَإِنَّ مَعِي لَعُوذَةً. عَنِ الْأَنْبِيَاءِ مَأْخُوذَةً. وَعِنْدِي لَكُمْ نَصِيحَةٌ. بَرَاهِينُهَا صَحِيحَةٌ. وَمَا وَسِعَنِي الْكِتْمَانُ. وَلَا مِنْ

١ في هامش س: تعرف بالبحرية؛ وفي د: العُمانيّة؛ وفي ف: وهي العمانية. ٢ بعدها في س، د، ف: تارةً.
٣ ف: اجتياز. ٤ د: للشِّرْعة. ٥ و: أرسا. ٦ د، ف: المُزَجَّى. ٧ س، د، ف: تُنْجِيكم، وهي مطموسة في و.
٨ س: إنَّ.

خِيمِي الْحِرْمَانُ. فَتَدَبَّرُوا الْقَوْلَ وَتَفَهَّمُوا. وَٱعْمَلُوا بِمَا تُعَلَّمُونَ وَعَلِّمُوا. ثُمَّ صَاحَ صَيْحَةَ الْمُبَاهِي. وَقَالَ أَتَدْرُونَ مَا هِيَ. هِيَ وَاللهِ حِرْزُ السَّفْرِ. عِنْدَ مَسِيرِهِمْ فِي الْبَحْرِ. وَالْجُنَّةُ مِنَ الْغَمِّ. إِذَا جَاشَ مَوْجُ الْيَمِّ. وَبِهَا ٱسْتَعْصَمَ نُوحٌ يَوْمَ[١] الطُّوفَانِ. وَنَجَا وَمَنْ مَعَهُ مِنَ الْحَيَوَانِ. عَلَى مَا صَدَعَتْ بِهِ آيُ الْقُرْآنِ. ثُمَّ قَرَأَ بَعْدَ أَسَاطِيرَ تَلَاهَا. وَزَخَارِفَ جَلَاهَا.[٢] ﴿وَقَالَ ارْكَبُوا فِيهَا بِسْمِ اللهِ مَجْرَاهَا وَمُرْسَاهَا.﴾ ثُمَّ تَنَفَّسَ تَنَفُّسَ الْمُغْرَمِينَ. أَوْ عِبَادِ اللهِ الْمُكْرَمِينَ.[٣] وَقَالَ أَمَّا أَنَا فَقَدْ قُمْتُ فِيكُمْ مَقَامَ الْمُبَلِّغِينَ. وَنَصَحْتُ لَكُمْ نُصْحَ الْمُبَالِغِينَ. وَسَلَكْتُ بِكُمْ مَحَجَّةَ الرَّاشِدِينَ. فَٱشْهَدِ ٱللّٰهُمَّ وَأَنْتَ خَيْرُ الشَّاهِدِينَ.

٤،٣٩ قَالَ الْحَارِثُ بْنُ هَمَّامٍ فَأَعْجَبَنَا بَيَانُهُ الْبَادِي الطُّلَاوَةِ. وَعَجَّتْ لَهُ أَصْوَاتُنَا بِالتِّلَاوَةِ. وَآنَسَ قَلْبِي مِنْ جَرْسِهِ. مَعْرِفَةَ عَيْنِ شَمْسِهِ. فَقُلْتُ لَهُ بِالَّذِي سَخَّرَ الْبَحْرَ اللُّجِّيَّ. أَلَسْتَ السَّرُوجِيَّ. فَقَالَ لِي بَلَى. وَهَلْ يَخْفَى ٱبْنُ جَلَا. فَأَحْمَدْتُ حِينَئِذٍ السَّفَرَ. وَسَفَرْتُ عَنْ نَفْسِي إِذْ سَفَرَ. وَلَمْ نَزَلْ نَسِيرُ وَالْبَحْرُ رَهْوٌ. وَالْجَوُّ صَحْوٌ. وَالْعَيْشُ صَفْوٌ. وَالزَّمَانُ لَهْوٌ. وَأَنَا أَجِدُ لِلُقْيَانِهِ. وَجْدَ الْمُثْرِي بِعِقْيَانِهِ. وَأَفْرَحُ[٤] بِمُنَاجَاتِهِ. فَرَحَ[٥] الْغَرِيقِ بِمَنْجَاتِهِ. إِلَى أَنْ عَصَفَتِ الْجَنُوبُ. وَعَسَفَتِ[٦] الْخُبُوبُ.[٧] وَنَسِيَ السَّفْرُ مَا كَانَ. وَجَاءَهُمُ الْمَوْجُ مِنْ كُلِّ مَكَانٍ. فَمِلْنَا لِهٰذَا الْحَدَثِ الثَّائِرِ.[٨] إِلَى إِحْدَى الْجَزَائِرِ. لِنُرِيحَ وَنَسْتَرِيحَ. رَيْثَمَا تُؤَاتِي الرِّيحُ. فَتَمَادَى ٱعْتِيَاصُ الْمَسِيرِ. حَتَّى نَفِدَ الزَّادُ غَيْرَ الْيَسِيرِ. فَقَالَ لِي أَبُو زَيْدٍ إِنَّهُ لَنْ يُحْرَزَ جَنَى الْعُودِ بِالْقُعُودِ. فَهَلْ لَكَ فِي ٱسْتِثَارَةِ السُّعُودِ بِالصُّعُودِ. فَقُلْتُ لَهُ إِنِّي لَكَ لَأَتْبَعُ[٩] مِنْ ظِلِّكَ. وَأَطْوَعُ مِنْ نَعْلِكَ.

١ ف: مِن. ٢ و: جلّاها. ٣ س: المُكرِّمين. ٤ ق: أبتهج. ٥ ق: ابتهاج. ٦ ق: عَسَّفَتْ. ٧ و،د: الجُنوب. ٨ ف: السائر، وهو خطأ. ٩ ف: لأتبع لك.

٣٩.٥ فَنَهَدْنَا[1] إِلَى الْجَزِيرَةِ. عَلَى ضَعْفِ[2] الْمَرِيرَةِ.[3] لِنَرْكُضَ فِي ٱمْتِرَاءِ الْمِيرَةِ. وَكِلَانَا لَا يَمْلِكُ فَتِيلًا. وَلَا يَهْتَدِي فِيهَا سَبِيلًا.[4] فَأَقْبَلْنَا نَجُوسُ خِلَالَهَا. وَنَتَفَيَّأُ ظِلَالَهَا. حَتَّى أَفْضَيْنَا إِلَى قَصْرٍ مَشِيدٍ. لَهُ بَابٌ مِنْ حَدِيدٍ. وَدُونَهُ زُمْرَةٌ مِنْ عَبِيدٍ. فَنَاسَمْنَاهُمْ لِنَتَّخِذَهُمْ سُلَّمًا إِلَى الِارْتِقَاءِ. وَأَرْشِيَةً لِلِاسْتِقَاءِ. فَأَلْفَيْنَا كُلًّا مِنْهُمْ فِي مَسْكٍ كَسِيرٍ. وَكَرْبٍ أَسِيرٍ.[5] فَقُلْنَا أَيَّتُهَا الْغِلْمَةُ. لِمَ[6] هٰذِهِ[7] الْغُمَّةُ. فَلَمْ يُجِيبُوا النِّدَاءَ. وَلَا فَاهُوا بِبَيْضَاءَ وَلَا سَوْدَاءَ. فَلَمَّا رَأَيْنَا نَارَهُمْ نَارَ الْحُبَاحِبِ. وَخُبْرَهُمْ كَسَرَابِ السَّبَاسِبِ. قُلْنَا شَاهَتِ الْوُجُوهُ. وَقُبِحَ اللُّكَعُ وَمَنْ يَرْجُوهُ. فَابْتَدَرَ خَادِمٌ قَدْ عَلَتْهُ كِبْرَةٌ. وَعَرَتْهُ عَبْرَةٌ. وَقَالَ يَا قَوْمِ لَا تُوسِعُونَا سَبًّا. وَلَا تُوجِعُونَا عَتْبًا. فَإِنَّا لَفِي حُزْنٍ شَامِلٍ. وَشُغْلٍ عَنِ الْحَدِيثِ شَاغِلٍ. فَقَالَ[8] لَهُ أَبُو زَيْدٍ نَفِّسْ خِنَاقَ الْبَثِّ. وَٱنْفُثْ إِنْ قَدَرْتَ عَلَى النَّفْثِ. فَإِنَّكَ سَتَجِدُ مِنِّي عَرَّافًا كَافِيًا. وَوَصَّافًا شَافِيًا. فَقَالَ ٱعْلَمْ أَنَّ رَبَّ هٰذَا الْقَصْرِ هُوَ قُطْبُ هٰذِهِ الْبُقْعَةِ. وَشَاهُ هٰذِهِ الرُّقْعَةِ. إِلَّا أَنَّهُ لَمْ يَخْلُ مِنْ كَمَدٍ. لِخُلُوِّهِ مِنْ وَلَدٍ. وَلَمْ يَزَلْ يَسْتَكْرِمُ الْمَغَارِسَ. وَيَتَخَيَّرُ مِنَ الْمَفَارِشِ النَّفَائِسَ. إِلَى أَنْ بُشِّرَ بِحَمْلِ عَقِيلَةٍ. وَآذَنَتْ رَقْلَتُهُ بِفَسِيلَةٍ. فَنُذِرَتْ لَهُ[9] النُّذُورُ. وَأُحْصِيَتِ الْأَيَّامُ وَالشُّهُورُ. وَلَمَّا حَانَ النِّتَاجُ. وَصِيغَ الطَّوْقُ وَالتَّاجُ. عَسُرَ مَخَاضُ الْوَضْعِ. حَتَّى خِيفَ عَلَى الْأَصْلِ وَالْفَرْعِ. فَمَا فِينَا مَنْ يَعْرِفُ قَرَارًا. وَلَا يَطْعَمُ النَّوْمَ إِلَّا غِرَارًا. ثُمَّ أَجْهَشَ بِالْبُكَاءِ وَأَعْوَلَ. وَرَدَّدَ الِاسْتِرْجَاعَ وَطَوَّلَ.

٣٩.٦ فَقَالَ لَهُ أَبُو زَيْدٍ ٱسْكُنْ يَا هٰذَا وَٱسْتَبْشِرْ. وَٱبْشِرْ بِالْفَرَجِ وَبَشِّرْ. فَعِنْدِي عَزِيمَةُ الطَّلْقِ. الَّتِي ٱنْتَشَرَ سَمْعُهَا فِي الْخَلْقِ. فَتَبَادَرَتِ الْغِلْمَةُ إِلَى مَوْلَاهُمْ.

١ د: نهضنا. ٢ د، ف: ضُعْفِ. ٣ و، ف: على ضعف من المريرة. ٤ بعدها سقطت ورقة من نسختي الرقية من س. ٥ «فِي مَسْكٍ كَسِيرٍ. وَكَرْبٍ أَسِيرٍ»: في ف: كَئِيبًا حَسِيرًا حَتَّى خِلْنَاهُ كَسِيرًا أَوْ أَسِيرًا. ٦ ف: ما. ٧ د: هٰذي. ٨ بعدها في ف: لَه. ٩ ليس في د.

وَتَسَارَعَتْ[1] مُتَبَاشِرِينَ بِٱنْكِشَافِ بَلْوَاهُمْ. فَلَمْ يَكُنْ إِلَّا كَلَا وَلَا حَتَّى بَرَزَ مَنْ هَلْمَمَ بِنَا إِلَيْهِ. فَلَمَّا دَخَلْنَا عَلَيْهِ. وَمَثَلْنَا بَيْنَ يَدَيْهِ. قَالَ لِأَبِي زَيْدٍ لِيَهْنِكَ مَنَالُكَ. إِنْ صَدَقَ مَقَالُكَ. وَلَمْ يَفِلْ فَالُكَ. فَٱسْتَحْضَرَ قَلَمًا مُبْرِيًّا. وَزَبَدًا بَحْرِيًّا. وَزَعْفَرَانًا قَدْ دِيفَ. فِي مَاءِ وَرْدٍ نَظِيفٍ. فَمَا إِنْ رَجَعَ النَّفَسُ. حَتَّى أُحْضِرَ مَا ٱلْتُمِسَ. فَسَجَدَ أَبُو زَيْدٍ وَعَفَّرَ. وَسَبَّحَ وَٱسْتَغْفَرَ.[2] ثُمَّ أَخَذَ الْقَلَمَ وَٱسْحَنْفَرَ. وَكَتَبَ عَلَى الزَّبَدِ بِٱلْمُزَعْفَرِ.

أَيُّهٰذَا الْجَنِينُ إِنِّي نَصِيحٌ لَكَ وَالنُّصْحُ مِنْ شُرُوطِ الدِّينِ
أَنْتَ مُسْتَعْصِمٌ بِكِنٍّ كَنِينٍ وَقَرَارٍ مِنَ السُّكُونِ مَكِينِ
مَا تَرَى فِيهِ مَا يَرُوعُكَ مِنْ إِلْفٍ مُدَاجٍ وَلَا عَدُوٍّ مُبِينِ
فَمَتَى مَا بَرَزْتَ مِنْهُ تَحَوَّلْتَ إِلَى مَنْزِلِ الْأَذَى وَالْهُونِ[3]
وَتَرَاءَى لَكَ الشَّقَاءُ الَّذِي تَلْقَى فَتَبْكِي لَهُ بِدَمْعٍ هَتُونِ
فَٱسْتَدِمْ عَيْشَكَ الرَّغِيدَ وَحَاذِرْ أَنْ تَبِيعَ الْمَحْقُوقَ بِٱلْمَظْنُونِ
وَٱحْتَرِسْ مِنْ مُخَادِعٍ لَكَ يَرْقِيكَ لِيُلْقِيكَ فِي الْعَذَابِ الْمُهِينِ
وَلَعَمْرِي لَقَدْ نَصَحْتُ وَلٰكِنْ كَمْ نَصِيحٍ مُشَبَّهٍ بِظَنِينِ

ثُمَّ إِنَّهُ طَمَسَ الْمَكْتُوبَ عَلَى غَفْلَةٍ. وَتَفَلَ عَلَيْهِ مِائَةَ تَفْلَةٍ. وَشَدَّ الزَّبَدَ فِي خِرْقَةِ ٧،٣٩
حَرِيرٍ. بَعْدَمَا ضَمَّخَهَا بِعَبِيرٍ. وَأَمَرَ بِتَعْلِيقِهَا عَلَى فَخْذِ الْمَاخِضِ. وَأَنْ لَا تَعْلَقَ بِهَا يَدُ حَائِضٍ. فَلَمْ يَكُنْ إِلَّا كَذَوَاقِ شَارِبٍ. أَوْ فُوَاقِ حَالِبٍ.[4] حَتَّى ٱنْدَلَقَ شَخْصُ الْوَلَدِ. لِخِصِّيصَى الزَّبَدِ. بِقُدْرَةِ الْوَاحِدِ الصَّمَدِ. فَٱمْتَلَأَ الْقَصْرُ حُبُورًا. وَٱسْتُطِيرَ

١ في ق فقط. ٢ بعدها في ف: وأبعَدَ الحاضِرينَ ونفَّر. ٣ بعدها تستأنف نسختي من س. ٤ ق: كفواق حالب أو ذواق شارب.

عَمِيدُهُ وَعَبِيدُهُ سُرُورًا. وَأَحَاطَتِ ٱلْجَمَاعَةُ بِأَبِي زَيْدٍ تُثْنِي عَلَيْهِ. وَتُقَبِّلُ يَدَيْهِ. وَتَتَبَرَّكُ بِمَسَاسِ طِمْرَيْهِ. حَتَّى خُيِّلَ إِلَيَّ أَنَّهُ ٱلْقَرَنِيُّ أُوَيْسٌ. أَوِ ٱلْأَسَدِيُّ دُبَيْسٌ. ثُمَّ ٱنْثَالَ عَلَيْهِ مِنْ جَوَائِزِ ٱلْمُجَازَاةِ. وَوَصَائِلِ ٱلصِّلَاتِ. مَا قَيَّضَ لَهُ ٱلْغِنَى. وَبَيَّضَ وَجْهَ ٱلْمُنَى. وَلَمْ يَخَلْ[1] يَنْتَابُهُ ٱلدَّخَلُ. مُذْ نُتِجَ ٱلسَّخَلُ. إِلَى أَنْ أُعْطِيَ ٱلْبَحْرُ ٱلْأَمَانَ. وَتَسَنَّى ٱلْإِتْمَامُ إِلَى عُمَانَ. فَٱكْتَفَى أَبُو زَيْدٍ بِٱلنِّحْلَةِ. وَتَأَهَّبَ لِلرِّحْلَةِ. فَلَمْ يَسْمَحِ ٱلْوَالِي بِحَرَكَتِهِ.[2] بَعْدَ تَجْرِبَةِ بَرَكَتِهِ. بَلْ أَوْعَزَ بِضَمِّهِ إِلَى حُزَانَتِهِ. وَأَنْ تُطْلَقَ يَدُهُ فِي خِزَانَتِهِ.

٨،٣٩ قَالَ ٱلْحَارِثُ بْنُ هَمَّامٍ فَلَمَّا رَأَيْتُهُ قَدْ مَالَ. إِلَى حَيْثُ يُكْتَسَبُ ٱلْمَالُ. أَنْحَيْتُ عَلَيْهِ بِٱلتَّعْنِيفِ. وَهَجَّنْتُ لَهُ مُفَارَقَةَ[3] ٱلْمَأْلَفِ وَٱلْأَلِيفِ. فَقَالَ إِلَيْكَ عَنِّي. وَٱسْمَعْ مِنِّي.

لَا تَصْبُوَنَّ إِلَى وَطَنْ   فِيهِ تُضَامُ وَتُمْتَهَنْ
وَٱرْحَلْ عَنِ ٱلدَّارِ ٱلَّتِي   تُعْلِي ٱلْوِهَادَ عَلَى ٱلْقُنَنْ
وَٱهْرُبْ إِلَى كِنٍّ يَقِي   وَلَوْ أَنَّهُ حِضْنَا حَضَنْ
وَٱرْبَأْ بِنَفْسِكَ أَنْ تُقِيمَ   بِحَيْثُ يَغْشَاكَ ٱلدَّرَنْ
وَجُبِ ٱلْبِلَادَ فَأَيُّهَا   أَرْضَاكَ فَٱخْتَرْهُ وَطَنْ
وَدَعِ ٱلتَّذَكُّرَ لِلْمَعَا   هِدِ وَٱلْحَنِينَ إِلَى ٱلسَّكَنْ
وَٱعْلَمْ بِأَنَّ ٱلْحُرَّ فِي   أَوْطَانِهِ يَلْقَى ٱلْغَبَنْ
كَٱلدُّرِّ فِي ٱلْأَصْدَافِ يُسْتَزْ   رَى وَيُبْخَسُ فِي ٱلثَّمَنْ

١ و، ف: يَزَلْ. ٢ ق: لم يفسح الوالي في حركته. ٣ «هجنت له مفارقة»: في ق: لمفارقته.

ثُمَّ قَالَ حَسْبُكَ مَا ٱسْتَمَعْتَ. وَحَبَّذَا أَنْتَ لَوِ ٱتَّبَعْتَ. فَأَوْضَحْتُ لَهُ مَعَاذِيرِي. وَقُلْتُ لَهُ كُنْ عَذِيرِي. فَعَذَرَ وَٱعْتَذَرَ. وَزَوَّدَ حَتَّى لَمْ يَذَرْ. ثُمَّ شَيَّعَنِي تَشْيِيعَ الْأَقَارِبِ. إِلَى أَنْ رَكِبْتُ فِي الْقَارِبِ. فَوَدَّعْتُهُ وَأَنَا أَشْكُو الْفِرَاقَ وَأَذُمُّهُ. وَأَوَدُّ لَوْ كَانَ هَلَكَ الْجَنِينُ وَأُمُّهُ.

الْمَقَامَةُ الْأَرْبَعُونَ[١]

١،٤٠ أَخْبَرَ الْحَارِثُ بْنُ هَمَّامٍ قَالَ أَزْمَعْتُ التَّبْرِيزَ مِنْ تَبْرِيزَ. حِينَ نَبَتْ بِالذَّلِيلِ وَالْعَزِيزِ. وَخَلَتْ مِنَ الْمُجِيرِ وَالْمُجِيزِ. فَبَيْنَا أَنَا فِي إِعْدَادِ الْأُهْبَةِ. وَٱرْتِيَادِ الصُّحْبَةِ. لَقِيتُ[٢] أَبَا زَيْدٍ السَّرُوجِيَّ مُلْتَفًّا بِكِسَاءٍ. وَمُحْتَفًّا بِنِسَاءٍ. فَسَأَلْتُهُ عَنْ خَطْبِهِ. وَإِلَى أَيْنَ يَسْرُبُ مَعَ سِرْبِهِ. فَأَوْمَأَ إِلَى ٱمْرَأَةٍ مِنْهُنَّ بَاهِرَةِ السُّفُورِ. ظَاهِرَةِ النُّفُورِ. وَقَالَ تَزَوَّجْتُ هٰذِهِ لِتُؤْنِسَنِي فِي الْغُرْبَةِ. وَتَرْحَضَ عَنِّي قَشَفَ الْعُزْبَةِ. فَلَقِيتُ مِنْهَا عَرَقَ الْقِرْبَةِ. تَمْطُلُنِي بِحَقِّي. وَتُكَلِّفُنِي فَوْقَ طَوْقِي. فَأَنَا مِنْهَا نِضْوُ وَجًى. وَحِلْفُ شَجْوٍ وَشَجًى. وَهَا نَحْنُ قَدْ تَسَاعَيْنَا إِلَى الْحَاكِمِ. لِيَضْرِبَ عَلَى يَدِ الظَّالِمِ. فَإِنِ ٱنْتَظَمَ بَيْنَنَا الْوِفَاقُ. وَإِلَّا فَالطَّلَاقُ وَالِانْطِلَاقُ. قَالَ فَمِلْتُ إِلَى أَنْ أَخْبُرَ لِمَنِ الْغَلَبُ. وَكَيْفَ يَكُونُ الْمُنْقَلَبُ. فَجَعَلْتُ شُغْلِي دَبْرَ أُذُنِي. وَصَحِبْتُهُمَا وَإِنْ كُنْتُ لَا أُغْنِي.

٢،٤٠ فَلَمَّا حَضَرَا الْقَاضِيَ وَكَانَ مِمَّنْ يَرَى فَضْلَ الْإِمْسَاكِ. وَيَضِنُّ بِنُفَاثَةِ السِّوَاكِ. جَثَا أَبُو زَيْدٍ بَيْنَ يَدَيْهِ. وَقَالَ أَيَّدَ اللّٰهُ الْقَاضِيَ وَأَحْسَنَ إِلَيْهِ. إِنَّ مَطِيَّتِي هٰذِهِ أَبِيَّةُ الْقِيَادِ. كَثِيرَةُ الشِّرَادِ. مَعَ أَنِّي أَطْوَعُ لَهَا مِنْ بَنَانِهَا. وَأَحْنَى عَلَيْهَا مِنْ جَنَانِهَا. فَقَالَ لَهَا الْقَاضِي وَيْحَكِ أَمَا عَلِمْتِ أَنَّ النُّشُوزَ يُغْضِبُ الرَّبَّ. وَيُوجِبُ الضَّرْبَ. فَقَالَتْ إِنَّهُ مِمَّنْ يَدُورُ خَلْفَ الدَّارِ. وَيَأْخُذُ الْجَارَ بِالْجَارِ.[٣] فَقَالَ لَهُ الْقَاضِي تَبًّا لَكَ أَتَبْذُرُ فِي السِّبَاخِ. وَتَسْتَفْرِخُ حَيْثُ لَا إِفْرَاخَ. أُغْرُبْ[٤] عَنِّي لَا نَعِمَ عَوْفُكَ. وَلَا أَمِنَ خَوْفُكَ. فَقَالَ أَبُو زَيْدٍ إِنَّهَا وَمُرْسِلِ الرِّيَاحِ. لَأَكْذَبُ[٥]

١ في هامش س: تُعْرَفُ بِالتَّبْرِيزِيَّةِ؛ وفي د: التَّبْرِيزِيَّةُ؛ في ف: وَهْيَ التبريزية. ٢ ف: أَلْفَيْتُ بِهَا. ٣ بعدها في د: وليسَ لي على ذلك اصطبار. ٤ د، ف: أُعْزُبْ. ٥ ف: لَأُكْذَبُ.

مِنْ سَجَاحِ. فَقَالَتْ بَلْ هُوَ وَمَنْ طَوَّقَ الْحَمَامَةَ. وَجَنَّحَ النَّعَامَةَ. أَكْذَبُ مِنْ أَبِي ثُمَامَةَ. حِينَ مَخْرَقَ بِالْيَمَامَةِ. فَزَفَرَ أَبُو زَيْدٍ زَفِيرَ الشُّوَاظِ. وَٱسْتَشَاطَ ٱسْتِشَاطَةَ الْمُغْتَاظِ. وَقَالَ لَهَا وَيْلَكِ يَا دَفَارِ يَا فَجَارِ. يَا غُصَّةَ الْبَعْلِ وَالْجَارِ. أَتَعْمِدِينَ فِي الْخَلْوَةِ لِتَعْذِيبِي. وَتُبْدِينَ فِي الْحَفْلَةِ تَكْذِيبِي. وَقَدْ عَلِمْتِ أَنِّي حِينَ بَنَيْتُ عَلَيْكِ. وَرَنَوْتُ إِلَيْكِ. أَلْفَيْتُكِ أَقْبَحَ مِنْ قِرْدَةٍ. وَأَيْبَسَ مِنْ قِدَّةٍ. وَأَخْشَنَ مِنْ لِيفَةٍ. وَأَنْتَنَ مِنْ جِيفَةٍ. وَأَثْقَلَ مِنْ هَيْضَةٍ. وَأَقْذَرَ مِنْ حَيْضَةٍ. وَأَبْرَزَ مِنْ قِشْرَةٍ. وَأَبْرَدَ مِنْ قِرَّةٍ. وَأَحْمَقَ مِنْ رِجْلَةٍ. وَأَوْسَعَ مِنْ دِجْلَةَ. فَسَتَرْتُ عُوَارَكِ. وَلَمْ أُبْدِ عَارَكِ. عَلَى أَنَّهُ لَوْ حَبَتْكِ شِيرِينُ بِجَمَالِهَا. وَزُبَيْدَةُ بِمَالِهَا. وَبِلْقِيسُ بِعَرْشِهَا. وَبُورَانُ بِفَرْشِهَا. وَالزَّبَّاءُ بِمُلْكِهَا. وَرَابِعَةُ بِنُسْكِهَا. وَخِنْدِفُ بِفَخْرِهَا. وَالْخَنْسَاءُ بِشِعْرِهَا فِي صَخْرِهَا. لَأَنِفْتُ أَنْ تَكُونِي قَعِيدَةَ رَحْلِي. وَطَرُوقَةَ فَحْلِي.

٣،٤٠ قَالَ فَتَذَمَّرَتِ الْمَرْأَةُ وَتَنَمَّرَتْ. وَحَسَرَتْ عَنْ سَاعِدِهَا وَشَمَّرَتْ. وَقَالَتْ لَهُ يَا أَلْأَمَ مِنْ مَادِرٍ. وَأَشْأَمَ مِنْ قَاشِرٍ. وَأَجْبَنَ مِنْ صَافِرٍ. وَأَطْيَشَ مِنْ طَامِرٍ. أَتَرْمِينِي بِشَنَارِكَ. وَتَفْرِي عِرْضِي بِشِفَارِكَ. وَأَنْتَ تَعْلَمُ أَنَّكَ أَحْقَرُ مِنْ قُلَامَةٍ. وَأَعْيَبُ مِنْ بَغْلَةِ أَبِي دُلَامَةَ. وَأَفْضَحُ مِنْ حَبْقَةٍ. فِي حَلْقَةٍ. وَأَحْيَرُ مِنْ بَقَّةٍ. فِي حُقَّةٍ. وَهَبْكَ الْحَسَنَ فِي لَفْظِهِ وَوَعْظِهِ.[1] وَالشَّعْبِيَّ فِي عِلْمِهِ وَحِفْظِهِ. وَالْخَلِيلَ فِي عَرُوضِهِ وَنَحْوِهِ. وَجَرِيرًا فِي غَزَلِهِ وَهَجْوِهِ. وَقُسًّا فِي فَصَاحَتِهِ وَخِطَابَتِهِ. وَعَبْدَ الْحَمِيدِ فِي بَلَاغَتِهِ وَكِتَابَتِهِ. وَأَبَا عَمْرٍو فِي قِرَاءَتِهِ وَإِعْرَابِهِ. وَٱبْنَ قُرَيْبٍ فِي رِوَايَتِهِ عَنْ أَعْرَابِهِ. أَتَظُنُّنِي أَرْضَاكَ إِمَامًا لِمِحْرَابِي. وَحُسَامًا لِقِرَابِي. لَا وَاللهِ وَلَا بَوَّابًا لِبَابِي. وَلَا عَصًا لِجِرَابِي. فَقَالَ لَهُمَا الْقَاضِي أَرَاكُمَا شَنًّا وَطَبَقَةً. وَحِدَأَةً وَبُنْدُقَةً. فَٱتْرُكْ أَيُّهَا الرَّجُلُ اللَّدَدَ. وَٱسْلُكْ فِي سَيْرِكَ الْجَدَدَ. وَأَمَّا أَنْتِ فَكُفِّي عَنْ سِبَابِهِ.

---

١ ف: وَعْظِهِ وَلَفْظِهِ.

وَقَرِّي إِذَا أَتَى الْبَيْتَ مِنْ بَابِهِ. فَقَالَتِ الْمَرْأَةُ وَاللهِ مَا أَسْجُنُ عَنْهُ لِسَانِي. إِلَّا إِذَا كَسَانِي. وَلَا أَرْفَعُ لَهُ شِرَاعِي. دُونَ إِشْبَاعِي. فَحَلَفَ أَبُو زَيْدٍ بِالْمُحَرِّجَاتِ الثَّلَاثِ. أَنَّهُ لَا يَمْلِكُ سِوَى أَطْمَارِهِ الرِّثَاثِ. فَنَظَرَ الْقَاضِي فِي قَصَصِهِمَا نَظَرَ الْأَلْمَعِيِّ. وَأَفْكَرَ فِكْرَةَ اللَّوْذَعِيِّ. ثُمَّ أَقْبَلَ عَلَيْهِمَا بِوَجْهٍ قَدْ قَطَّبَهُ. وَمِجَنٍّ قَدْ قَلَبَهُ.[1] وَقَالَ أَلَمْ يَكْفِكُمَا التَّسَافُهُ فِي مَجْلِسِ الْحُكْمِ. وَالْإِقْدَامُ عَلَى هٰذَا الْجُرْمِ. حَتَّى تَرَاقَيْتُمَا مِنْ فُحْشِ الْمُقَاذَعَةِ. إِلَى خُبْثِ الْمُخَادَعَةِ. وَأَيْمُ اللهِ لَقَدْ أَخْطَأَتِ ٱسْتُكُمَا الْحُفْرَةَ. وَلَمْ يُصِبْ سَهْمُكُمَا الثُّغْرَةَ. فَإِنَّ أَمِيرَ الْمُؤْمِنِينَ. أَعَزَّ اللهُ بِبَقَائِهِ الدِّينَ. نَصَبَنِي لِأَقْضِيَ بَيْنَ الْخُصَمَاءِ. لَا لِأَقْضِيَ دَيْنَ الْغُرَمَاءِ. وَحَقِّ نِعْمَتِهِ الَّتِي أَحَلَّتْنِي هٰذَا الْمَحَلَّ. وَمَلَّكَتْنِي الْعَقْدَ وَالْحَلَّ. لَئِنْ لَمْ تُوضِحَا لِي جَلِيَّةَ خَطْبِكُمَا. وَخَبِيئَةَ خِبِّكُمَا. لَأُنَدِّدَنَّ بِكُمَا فِي الْأَمْصَارِ. وَلَأَجْعَلَنَّكُمَا عِبْرَةً لِأُولِي الْأَبْصَارِ. فَأَطْرَقَ أَبُو زَيْدٍ إِطْرَاقَ الشُّجَاعِ. ثُمَّ قَالَ لَهُ سَمَاعِ سَمَاعِ.

٤،٤٠ أَنَا السَّرُوجِيُّ وَهٰذِي عِرْسِي ... وَلَيْسَ كُفْؤُ الْبَدْرِ غَيْرَ الشَّمْسِ
وَمَا تَنَافَى أُنْسُهَا وَأُنْسِي ... وَلَا تَنَاءَى دَيْرُهَا عَنْ قَسِّي[2]
وَلَا عَدَتْ سُقْيَايَ أَرْضَ غَرْسِي ... لٰكِنَّنَا[3] مُنْذُ لَيَالٍ خَمْسِ
نُصْبِحُ فِي ثَوْبِ الطَّوَى وَنُمْسِي ... لَا نَعْرِفُ الْمَضْغَ وَلَا التَّحَسِّي
حَتَّى كَأَنَّا لِخُفُوتِ النَّفْسِ ... أَشْبَاحُ مَوْتَى نُشِرُوا مِنْ رَمْسِ
فَحِينَ عَزَّ الصَّبْرُ وَالتَّأَسِّي ... وَشَفَّنَا الضُّرُّ الْأَلِيمُ الْمَسِّ
قُمْنَا لِسَعْدِ الْجَدِّ أَوْ لِلنَّحْسِ ... هٰذَا الْمَقَامَ لِاجْتِلَابِ فَلْسِ
وَالْفَقْرُ يُلْجِي الْحُرَّ حِينَ يُرْسِي ... إِلَى التَّجَلِّي[4] فِي لِبَاسِ اللَّبْسِ

١ د: قَلَّبَه. ٢ ف: قُسِّي. ٣ ف: لكِنَّا. ٤ د: التحلِّي.

فَهٰذِهِ حَالِي وَهٰذَا دَرْسِي   فَٱنْظُرْ إِلَى يَوْمِي وَسَلْ عَنْ أَمْسِي
وَأْمُرْ بِجَبْرِي إِنْ تَشَا أَوْ حَبْسِي   فَفِي يَدَيْكَ صِحَّتِي وَنُكْسِي

٥،٤٠ فَقَالَ لَهُ ٱلْقَاضِي لِيَثُبْ أُنْسُكَ. وَلْتَطِبْ نَفْسُكَ. فَقَدْ حَقَّ لَكَ أَنْ تُغْفَرَ خَطِيَّتُكَ. وَتُوَفَّرَ عَطِيَّتُكَ. فَثَارَتِ ٱلزَّوْجَةُ عِنْدَ ذٰلِكَ وَٱسْتَطَالَتْ. وَأَشَارَتْ إِلَى ٱلْحَاضِرِينَ وَقَالَتْ.

يَا أَهْلَ تَبْرِيزَ لَكُمْ حَاكِمٌ   أَوْفَى عَلَى ٱلْحُكَّامِ تَبْرِيزَا
مَا فِيهِ مِنْ عَيْبٍ سِوَى أَنَّهُ   يَوْمَ ٱلنَّدَى قِسْمَتُهُ ضِيزَى
قَصَدْتُهُ وَٱلشَّيْخُ نَبْغِي جَنَى   عُودٍ لَهُ مَا زَالَ مَهْزُوزَا
فَسَرَّحَ ٱلشَّيْخَ[1] وَقَدْ نَالَ مِنْ   جَدْوَاهُ تَخْصِيصًا وَتَمْيِيزَا
وَرَدَّنِي أَخْيَبَ مِنْ شَائِمٍ   بَرْقًا خَفَا فِي شَهْرِ تَمُّوزَا
كَأَنَّهُ لَمْ يَدْرِ أَنِّي ٱلَّتِي   لَقَّنْتِ ٱلشَّيْخَ[2] ٱلْأَرَاجِيزَا
وَأَنَّنِي إِنْ شِئْتُ غَادَرْتُهُ   أُضْحُوكَةً فِي أَهْلِ تَبْرِيزَا

٦،٤٠ قَالَ فَلَمَّا رَأَى ٱلْقَاضِي ٱجْتِرَاءَ جَنَانِهِمَا. وَٱنْصِلَاتَ لِسَانِهِمَا. عَلِمَ أَنَّهُ قَدْ مُنِيَ مِنْهُمَا بِٱلدَّاءِ ٱلْعَيَاءِ. وَٱلدَّاهِيَةِ ٱلدَّهْيَاءِ. وَأَنَّهُ مَتَى مَنَحَ أَحَدَ ٱلزَّوْجَيْنِ. وَصَرَفَ ٱلْآخَرَ صِفْرَ ٱلْيَدَيْنِ. كَانَ كَمَنْ قَضَى ٱلدَّيْنَ بِٱلدَّيْنِ. أَوْ صَلَّى ٱلْمَغْرِبَ رَكْعَتَيْنِ. فَطَلْسَمَ وَطَرْسَمَ. وَٱخْرَنْطَمَ وَبَرْطَمَ. وَهَمْهَمَ وَغَمْغَمَ. ثُمَّ ٱلْتَفَتَ يَمْنَةً وَشَامَةً. وَتَمَلْمَلَ كَآبَةً وَنَدَامَةً. وَأَخَذَ يَذُمُّ ٱلْقَضَاءَ وَمَتَاعِبَهُ. وَيُعَدِّدُ شَوَائِبَهُ وَنَوَائِبَهُ. وَيُفَنِّدُ طَالِبَهُ وَخَاطِبَهُ. ثُمَّ تَنَفَّسَ كَمَا يَتَنَفَّسُ ٱلْحَرِيبُ. وَٱنْتَحَبَ حَتَّى كَادَ يَفْضَحُهُ

١ هكذا في ق، و، ف (المتن)؛ وفي س وف (الشرح): والشيخَ؛ والصفحة والتي تليها ناقصتان في د. ٢ د، ف: لَقَّنْتُ ذا الشيخ.

النَّجِيبُ. وَقَالَ إِنَّ هٰذَا لَشَيْءٌ عَجِيبٌ. أَأَرْشُقُ فِي مَوْقِفٍ بِسَهْمَيْنِ. أَأُلْزَمُ فِي قَضِيَّةٍ مَغْرَمَيْنِ.[1] أَأُطِيقُ أَنْ أُرْضِيَ الْخَصْمَيْنِ. وَمِنْ أَيْنَ وَمِنْ أَيْنَ. ثُمَّ عَطَفَ إِلَى حَاجِبِهِ. الْمُنَفِّذِ[2] لِمَآرِبِهِ. وَقَالَ مَا هٰذَا يَوْمُ حُكْمٍ وَقَضَاءٍ. وَفَصْلٍ وَإِمْضَاءٍ. هٰذَا يَوْمُ الِاغْتِمَامِ. هٰذَا يَوْمُ الِاغْتِرَامِ. هٰذَا يَوْمُ الْبُحْرَانِ. هٰذَا يَوْمُ الْخُسْرَانِ. هٰذَا يَوْمٌ عَصِيبٌ. هٰذَا يَوْمٌ نُصَابُ فِيهِ وَلَا نُصِيبُ. فَأَرِحْنِي مِنْ هٰذَيْنِ الْمِهْذَارَيْنِ. وَٱقْطَعْ لِسَانَهُمَا بِدِينَارَيْنِ. ثُمَّ فَرِّقِ الْأَصْحَابَ. وَأَغْلِقِ الْبَابَ. وَأَشِعْ أَنَّهُ يَوْمٌ مَذْمُومٌ. وَأَنَّ الْقَاضِيَ فِيهِ مَهْمُومٌ. لِئَلَّا يَحْضُرَنِي خُصُومٌ. قَالَ فَأَمَّنَ الْحَاجِبُ عَلَى دُعَائِهِ. وَتَبَاكَى لِبُكَائِهِ. ثُمَّ نَقَدَ أَبَا زَيْدٍ وَعِرْسَهُ الْمِثْقَالَيْنِ. وَقَالَ أَشْهَدُ أَنَّكُمَا لَأَحْيَلُ الثَّقَلَيْنِ. لٰكِنِ ٱحْتَرِمَا مَجَالِسَ الْحُكَّامِ. وَٱجْتَنِبَا فِيهَا فُحْشَ الْكَلَامِ. فَمَا كُلُّ قَاضٍ قَاضِيَ تَبْرِيزَ. وَلَا كُلَّ وَقْتٍ تُسْمَعُ الْأَرَاجِيزُ. فَقَالَا لَهُ مِثْلُكَ مَنْ حَجَبَ. وَشُكْرُكَ قَدْ وَجَبَ. وَنَهَضَا وَقَدْ حَظِيَا[3] بِدِينَارَيْنِ. وَأَصْلَيَا قَلْبَ الْقَاضِي نَارَيْنِ.

تَفْسِيرُ مَا تَضَمَّنَ هٰذِهِ الْمَقَامَةُ مِنَ الْأَلْفَاظِ اللُّغَوِيَّةِ وَالْأَمْثَالِ الْعَرَبِيَّةِ

٧،٤٠ قَوْلُهُ لَقِيتُ مِنْهَا عَرَقَ الْقِرْبَةِ هٰذَا مَثَلٌ يُضْرَبُ لِمَنْ يَلْقَى شِدَّةً فِي الْأَمْرِ الَّذِي يُزَاوِلُهُ كَمَا أَنَّ حَامِلَ الْقِرْبَةِ يَلْقَى جَهْدًا حَتَّى يَعْرَقَ. وَقَوْلُهُ جَعَلْتُهُ دَبْرَ أُذُنِي يَعْنِي ٱطَّرَحْتُهُ وَهُوَ كَقَوْلِهِ تَعَالَى ﴿فَنَبَذُوهُ وَرَاءَ ظُهُورِهِمْ﴾. وَقَوْلُهُ أَكْذَبُ مِنْ سَجَاحِ يَعْنِي الَّتِي تَنَبَّأَتْ فِي عَهْدِ مُسَيْلِمَةَ الْكَذَّابِ وَسَارَتْ إِلَيْهِ لِتُنَاظِرَهُ وَتَخْتَبِرَهُ ثُمَّ آمَنَتْ بِهِ وَوَهَبَتْ نَفْسَهَا لَهُ وَهٰذَا الِاسْمُ مَبْنِيٌّ عَلَى الْكَسْرِ مِثْلَ حَذَامِ وَقَطَامِ لِكَوْنِهِ

١ . ف: بِمَغْرَمَين؛ والصفحة ناقصة في د، و. ٢ . ف: المُنفِذ. ٣ د: حُظِيا.

مِنَ ٱلْأَسْمَاءِ ٱلْمَعْدُولَةِ وَٱشْتِقَاقُهُ مِنَ ٱلسَّجَاحَةِ وَهِيَ ٱلسُّهُولَةُ وَمِنْهُ قَوْلُهُمْ مَلَكْتَ فَأَسْجِحْ. وَقَوْلُهُمْ أَكْذَبُ مِنْ أَبِي ثُمَامَةَ هٰذِهِ كُنْيَةُ مُسَيْلِمَةَ ٱلْكَذَّابِ وَكَانَ تَنَبَّأَ بِٱلْيَمَامَةِ وَمَخْرَقَ بِهَا إِلَى أَنْ سَارَ إِلَيْهِ خَالِدُ بْنُ ٱلْوَلِيدِ وَقَتَلَهُ. وَقَوْلُهُ لَا نَعِمَ عَوْفُكَ ٱلْعَوْفُ ٱلْحَالُ وَهُوَ أَيْضًا ٱلذَّكَرُ وَيُدْعَى لِلْبَانِي عَلَى أَهْلِهِ فَيُقَالُ لَهُ نَعِمَ عَوْفُكَ. وَقَوْلُهُ يَا دَفَارِ وَيَا فَجَارِ هٰذَانِ ٱلِٱسْمَانِ مَعْدُولَانِ عَنْ دَفِرَةٍ وَفَاجِرَةٍ وَٱلدَّفْرُ ٱلنَّتْنُ وَبِهِ سُمِّيَتِ ٱلدُّنْيَا أُمَّ دَفْرٍ وَكُلُّ مَا سُمِّيَ بِصِفَةٍ غَالِبَةٍ ثُمَّ عُدِلَ بِهَا إِلَى فَعَالِ بُنِيَ عَلَى ٱلْكَسْرِ عِنْدَ ٱلنِّدَاءِ كَقَوْلِكَ يَا لَكَاعِ يَا خَبَاثِ يَا دَفَارِ يَا فَجَارِ وَلَا يَجُوزُ ٱسْتِعْمَالُ ذٰلِكَ فِي غَيْرِ ٱلنِّدَاءِ إِلَّا فِي ضَرُورَةِ ٱلشِّعْرِ كَقَوْلِ ٱلشَّاعِرِ

أُطَوِّفُ مَا أُطَوِّفُ ثُمَّ آوِي   إِلَى بَيْتٍ قَعِيدَتُهُ لَكَاعِ

٨،٤٠ وَأَمَّا قَوْلُهُ أَحْمَقُ مِنْ رِجْلَةٍ فَهِيَ ضَرْبٌ مِنَ ٱلْحَمْضِ تَنْبُتُ فِي مَجَارِي ٱلسَّيْلِ فَيَجْتَرِفُهَا. وَأَمَّا قَوْلُهَا أَلْأَمُ مِنْ مَادِرٍ فَهُوَ رَجُلٌ مِنْ بَنِي هِلَالِ بْنِ عَامِرٍ كَانَ ٱتَّخَذَ حَوْضًا لِسَقْيِ إِبْلِهِ فَلَمَّا رَوِيَتْ سَلَحَ فِيهِ وَمَدَرَهُ بِسَلْحِهِ لِئَلَّا يُنْتَفَعَ بِهِ مِنْ بَعْدِهِ. وَأَمَّا قَوْلُهَا أَشْأَمُ مِنْ قَاشِرٍ فَإِنَّهُ فَحْلٌ كَانَ فِي بَعْضِ قَبَائِلِ سَعْدِ بْنِ زَيْدِ مَنَاةٍ مَا طَرَقَ إِبْلًا إِلَّا مَاتَتْ وَقِيلَ ٱلْمُرَادُ بِهِ ٱلْعَامُ ٱلْمُجْدِبُ وَسُمِّيَ قَاشِرًا لِقَشْرِهِ وَجْهَ ٱلْأَرْضِ مِنَ ٱلنَّبَاتِ. وَأَمَّا قَوْلُهَا أَجْبَنُ مِنْ صَافِرٍ فَقَدِ ٱخْتُلِفَ فِي تَفْسِيرِهِ قَالَ بَعْضُهُمْ عُنِيَ بِهِ كُلُّ مَا يَصْفِرُ مِنَ ٱلطَّيْرِ وَخُصَّ بِٱلْجُبْنِ لِكَثْرَةِ مَا يَتَّقِيهِ مِنْ جَوَارِحِ ٱلْجَوِّ وَمَصَائِدِ ٱلْأَرْضِ وَقِيلَ إِنَّهُ طَائِرٌ بِعَيْنِهِ إِذَا جَنَّهُ ٱللَّيْلُ تَعَلَّقَ بِبَعْضِ ٱلْأَغْصَانِ وَلَمْ يَزَلْ يَصْفِرُ طُولَ لَيْلَتِهِ خَوْفًا مِنْ أَنْ يَنَامَ فَيُؤْخَذَ وَقِيلَ إِنَّهُ ٱلَّذِي يَصْفِرُ بِٱلْمَرْأَةِ لِرِيبَةٍ فَهُوَ يَجْبُنُ وَقْتَ صَفِيرِهِ مَخَافَةَ أَنْ يُظْهَرَ عَلَى

أَمْرِهِ وَقِيلَ إِنَّ ٱلْمُرَادَ بِهِ فِي ٱلْمَثَلِ ٱلْمَصْفُورُ بِهِ وَهُوَ ٱلَّذِي يُنْذَرُ بِالصَّفِيرِ[١] فَعَلَى هٰذَا ٱلْقَوْلِ فَاعِلٌ هَاهُنَا بِمَعْنَى مَفْعُولٍ كَقَوْلِهِ تَعَالَى ﴿مِنْ مَاءٍ دَافِقٍ﴾ أَيْ مَدْفُوقٍ وَكَقَوْلِهِمْ رَاحِلَةٌ بِمَعْنَى مَرْحُولَةٍ وَهُوَ كَثِيرٌ فِي كَلَامِهِمْ وَقَدْ جَاءَ مَفْعُولٌ بِمَعْنَى فَاعِلٍ كَقَوْلِهِ تَعَالَى ﴿حِجَابًا مَسْتُورًا﴾ أَيْ سَاتِرًا.[٢] وَأَمَّا قَوْلُهَا أَطْيَشُ مِنْ طَامِرٍ فَالْمُرَادُ بِهِ ٱلْبُرْغُوثُ وَيُسَمَّى طَامِرَ بْنَ طَامِرٍ لِكَثْرَةِ وُثُوبِهِ.

٩،٤٠ وَأَمَّا قَوْلُ ٱلْقَاضِي أَرَاكُمَا شَنًّا وَطَبَقَةَ وَحِدَأَةَ وَبُنْدُقَةَ فَإِنَّهُ أَرَادَ بِهِ أَنَّ كُلًّا مِنْكُمَا كُفْءٌ لِصَاحِبِهِ وَمُقَاوِمٌ لَهُ وَلِكُلٍّ مِنَ ٱلْمَثَلَيْنِ تَفْسِيرٌ مُخْتَلَفٌ فِيهِ. أَمَّا شَنٌّ وَطَبَقَةُ فَإِنَّ ٱلْعُلَمَاءَ مُخْتَلِفُونَ فِي مَعْنَى قَوْلِهِمْ وَافَقَ شَنٌّ طَبَقَةَ فَقَالَ ٱلْأَكْثَرُونَ إِنَّهُمَا قَبِيلَتَانِ فَشَنٌّ هُوَ ٱبْنُ أَفْصَى[٣] ٱبْنِ دُعْمِيِّ بْنِ جَدِيلَةَ بْنِ أَسَدِ بْنِ رَبِيعَةَ بْنِ نِزَارٍ. وَطَبَقَةُ حَيٌّ مِنْ إِيَادٍ وَكَانَتْ طَبَقَةُ لَا تُطَاقُ فَأَوْقَعَتْ بِهَا شَنٌّ فَٱنْتَصَفَتْ مِنْهَا وَقَالَ بَعْضُهُمْ كَانَ شَنٌّ رَجُلًا مِنْ دُهَاةِ ٱلْعَرَبِ وَكَانَ أَلْزَمَ نَفْسَهُ أَلَّا يَتَزَوَّجَ إِلَّا بِٱمْرَأَةٍ تُلَائِمُهُ فَكَانَ يَجُوبُ ٱلْبِلَادَ فِي ٱرْتِيَادِ طِلْبَتِهِ فَصَاحَبَهُ رَجُلٌ فِي بَعْضِ أَسْفَارِهِ فَلَمَّا أَخَذَ مِنْهُمَا ٱلسَّيْرُ قَالَ لَهُ شَنٌّ أَتَحْمِلُنِي أَمْ أَحْمِلُكَ فَقَالَ لَهُ ٱلرَّجُلُ يَا جَاهِلُ هَلْ يَحْمِلُ ٱلرَّاكِبُ ٱلرَّاكِبَ فَأَمْسَكَ وَسَارَا حَتَّى أَتَيَا عَلَى زَرْعٍ فَقَالَ لَهُ شَنٌّ أَتُرَى هٰذَا ٱلزَّرْعَ أُكِلَ أَمْ لَا فَقَالَ لَهُ يَا جَاهِلُ أَمَا تَرَاهُ فِي سُنْبُلِهِ فَأَمْسَكَ إِلَى أَنِ ٱسْتَقْبَلَتْهُمَا جَنَازَةٌ فَقَالَ لَهُ شَنٌّ أَتُرَى صَاحِبَهَا حَيًّا[٤] فَقَالَ لَهُ مَا رَأَيْتُ أَجْهَلَ مِنْكَ أَتُرَاهُمْ حَمَلُوا إِلَى ٱلْقَبْرِ حَيًّا ثُمَّ إِنَّهُمَا وَصَلَا إِلَى قَرْيَةِ ٱلرَّجُلِ فَصَارَ بِهِ إِلَى مَنْزِلِهِ وَكَانَتْ لَهُ بِنْتٌ تُسَمَّى طَبَقَةَ فَأَخَذَ يُطْرِفُهَا بِحَدِيثِ رَفِيقِهِ فَقَالَتْ لَهُ مَا نَطَقَ إِلَّا بِالصَّوَابِ وَلَا ٱسْتَفْهَمَكَ إِلَّا عَمَّا يُسْتَفْهَمُ عَنْ مِثْلِهِ أَمَّا قَوْلُهُ أَتَحْمِلُنِي أَمْ أَحْمِلُكَ فَإِنَّهُ أَرَادَ

١ بعدها في و: أي إذا صُفِرَ به هرب هذا قول ابن الأعرابي؛ وبعدها في د، ف: لِيَهْرُبَ. ٢ «وهو كثير في كلامهم...» إلى هاهنا وارد في هامش ق وفي متن باقي الأصول. ٣ د: أقصى، ف: أفضى. ٤ بعدها في د: أم لا.

أَتُحَدِّثُنِي أَمْ أُحَدِّثُكَ حَتَّى نَقْطَعَ الطَّرِيقَ بِالْحَدِيثِ وَأَمَّا قَوْلُهُ أَتَرَى هٰذَا الزَّرْعَ قَدْ أُكِلَ فَإِنَّهُ أَرَادَ هَلِ ٱسْتَسْلَفَ أَهْلُهُ ثَمَنَهُ[1] وَأَمَّا ٱسْتِفْهَامُهُ عَنْ حَيٰوةِ صَاحِبِ الْجَنَازَةِ فَإِنَّهُ أَرَادَ بِهِ أَخَلَّفَ عَقِبًا يُحْيَا ذِكْرُهُ بِهِ أَمْ لَا فَلَمَّا خَرَجَ إِلَى الرَّجُلِ حَدَّثَهُ بِتَأْوِيلِ ٱبْنَتِهِ كَلَامَهُ فَخَطَبَهَا إِلَيْهِ فَزَوَّجَهُ إِيَّاهَا فَلَمَّا سَارَ بِهَا إِلَى قَوْمِهِ وَخَبَرُوا مَا فِيهَا مِنَ الدَّهَاءِ وَالْفِطْنَةِ قَالُوا وَافَقَ شَنٌّ طَبَقَةَ فَسَارَتْ مَثَلًا وَحُكِيَ أَنَّ الْأَصْمَعِيَّ سُئِلَ عَنْ تَفْسِيرِ هٰذَا الْمَثَلِ فَقَالَ أَظُنُّ الشَّنَّ وِعَاءً مِنْ أَدَمٍ كَانَ قَدِ ٱسْتَشَنَّ فَلَمَّا ٱتُّخِذَ لَهُ غِطَاءٌ وَافَقَهُ ضُرِبَ فِيهِ هٰذَا الْمَثَلُ.

١٠،٤٠ وَأَمَّا حِدَأَةٌ وَبُنْدُقَةٌ فَأَنَّهُ يُقَالُ فِي الْمَثَلِ الْمَضْرُوبِ لِمَنْ يُفَزَّعُ بِعَدُوِّهِ أَوْ يُبْلَى بِنَظِيرِهِ حِدَأً حِدَأً وَرَاءَكِ بُنْدُقَةٌ وَكَانَ الْأَصْلُ حِدَأَةٌ بِإِثْبَاتِ الْهَاءِ فَرُخِّمَ فِي النِّدَاءِ وَقَدِ ٱخْتُلِفَ فِي الْمُرَادِ بِهِمَا فَقِيلَ هُمَا الطَّائِرُ الْمَعْرُوفُ وَبُنْدُقَةُ الرَّامِي وَقِيلَ إِنَّهُمَا قَبِيلَتَانِ مِنْ سَعْدِ الْعَشِيرَةِ فَأَغَارَتْ حِدَأَةٌ وَكَانَتْ تَنْزِلُ بِالْكُوفَةِ عَلَى بُنْدُقَةَ وَكَانَتْ تَنْزِلُ بِالْيَمَنِ فَنَالَتْ مِنْهُمْ ثُمَّ كَرَّتْ بُنْدُقَةُ عَلَى حِدَأَةَ فَأَنْحَتْ عَلَيْهِمْ وَرَوَى بَعْضُهُمْ هٰذَا الْمَثَلَ حَدًا حَدًا غَيْرَ مَهْمُوزٍ عَلَى مِثَالِ عَصًا وَقَفًا وَزَعَمَ أَنَّهُ ٱسْمُ الْقَبِيلَةِ. وَأَمَّا قَوْلُهُ أَخْطَأَتِ ٱسْتُكَ الْحُفْرَةَ فَإِنَّهُ مَثَلٌ يُضْرَبُ لِمَنْ يُخْطِئُ فِي مَقْصِدِهِ وَيَضَعُ الشَّيْءَ فِي غَيْرِ مَوْضِعِهِ. وَأَمَّا قَوْلُهُ طَلْسَمَ وَطَرْسَمَ فَمَعْنَى طَلْسَمَ كَرَّهَ وَجْهَهُ وَمَعْنَى طَرْسَمَ أَطْرَقَ. وَقَوْلُهُ إِخْرَنْطَمَ وَبَرْطَمَ أَيْ غَضِبَ وَقَطَّبَ وَقِيلَ مَعْنَى ٱخْرَنْطَمَ أَيْ غَضِبَ مَعَ تَكَبُّرٍ وَمَعْنَى بَرْطَمَ أَيْ غَضِبَ مَعَ تَعَبُّسٍ. وَقَوْلُهُ هَمْهَمَ وَغَمْغَمَ أَيْ لَمْ يُبَيِّنِ الْكَلَامَ.

١ بعدها في س، د: أم لا.

الْمَقَامَةُ الْحَادِيَةُ وَالْأَرْبَعُونَ[1]

١،٤١ حَدَّثَ الْحَارِثُ بْنُ هَمَّامٍ قَالَ أَطَعْتُ دَوَاعِيَ التَّصَابِي. فِي غُلَوَاءِ شَبَابِي. فَلَمْ أَزَلْ زِيرًا لِلْغِيدِ. وَأُذُنًا لِلْأَغَارِيدِ. إِلَى أَنْ وَافَى النَّذِيرُ. وَوَلَّى الْعَيْشُ النَّضِيرُ. فَقَرِمْتُ إِلَى رُشْدِ ٱلِٱنْتِبَاهِ. وَنَدِمْتُ عَلَى مَا فَرَّطْتُ فِي جَنْبِ اللهِ. ثُمَّ أَخَذْتُ فِي كَسْعِ[2] الْهَنَاتِ بِالْحَسَنَاتِ. وَتَلَافِي الْهَفَوَاتِ قَبْلَ الْفَوَاتِ. فَمِلْتُ عَنْ مُغَادَاةِ الْغَادَاتِ. إِلَى مُلَاقَاةِ التُّقَاةِ. وَعَنْ مُقَانَاةِ الْقَيْنَاتِ. إِلَى مُدَانَاةِ أَهْلِ الدِّيَانَاتِ. وَآلَيْتُ أَلَّا أَصْحَبَ إِلَّا مَنْ نَزَعَ عَنِ الْغَيِّ. وَفَاءَ مَنْشَرُهُ إِلَى الطَّيِّ. وَإِنْ أَلْفَيْتُ مَنْ هُوَ خَلِيعُ الرَّسَنِ. مَدِيدُ الْوَسَنِ. أَنْأَيْتُ دَارِي عَنْ دَارِهِ. وَفَرَرْتُ عَنْ عَرِّهِ وَعَارِهِ.

٢،٤١ فَلَمَّا أَلْقَتْنِي الْغُرْبَةُ بِتِنِّيسَ. وَأَحَلَّتْنِي مَسْجِدَهَا الْأَنِيسَ. رَأَيْتُ بِهِ[3] ذَا حَلْقَةٍ مُلْتَحِمَةٍ. وَنَظَّارَةٍ مُزْدَحِمَةٍ. وَهُوَ يَقُولُ بِجَأْشٍ مَتِينٍ.[4] وَلِسَانٍ مُبِينٍ. مِسْكِينٌ ٱبْنُ آدَمَ وَأَيُّ مِسْكِينٍ. رَكَنَ مِنَ الدُّنْيَا إِلَى غَيْرِ رَكِينٍ. وَٱسْتَعْصَمَ مِنْهَا بِغَيْرِ مَكِينٍ. وَذُبِحَ مِنْ حُبِّهَا بِغَيْرِ سِكِّينٍ. يَكْلَفُ بِهَا لِغَبَاوَتِهِ. وَيَكْلَبُ عَلَيْهَا لِشَقَاوَتِهِ. وَيَعْتَدُّ فِيهَا لِمُفَاخَرَتِهِ. وَلَا يَتَزَوَّدُ مِنْهَا لِآخِرَتِهِ. أُقْسِمُ بِمَنْ مَرَجَ الْبَحْرَيْنِ. وَنَوَّرَ الْقَمَرَيْنِ. وَرَفَعَ قَدْرَ الْحَجَرَيْنِ. لَوْ عَقَلَ ٱبْنُ آدَمَ. لَمَا نَادَمَ. وَلَوْ أَفْكَرَ[5] فِيمَا قَدَّمَ. لَبَكَى الدَّمَ. وَلَوْ ذَكَرَ الْمُكَافَاةَ. لَاسْتَدْرَكَ مَا فَاتَ. وَلَوْ نَظَرَ فِي الْمَآلِ. لَحَسَّنَ قُبْحَ الْأَعْمَالِ. يَا عَجَبًا كُلَّ الْعَجَبِ. لِمَنْ يَقْتَحِمُ ذَاتَ اللَّهَبِ. فِي ٱكْتِنَازِ الذَّهَبِ.

١ في هامش س: تُعْرَفُ بالتِّنِّيسِيَّة؛ وفي د: التنيسية؛ وفي ف: وهي التنيسية. ٢ ف: كسع. ٣ هكذا في ق، س، وفي و: بها، وفي ف: ناقصة. ٤ ف: مَكين. ٥ ف: فكّر.

وَخَزْنِ ٱلنَّشَبِ.[١] لِذَوِي ٱلنَّسَبِ. ثُمَّ مِنَ ٱلْبِدْعِ ٱلْعَجِيبِ. أَنْ يَعِظَكَ وَخْطُ ٱلْمَشِيبِ. وَتُؤْذِنُ شَمْسُكَ بِٱلْمَغِيبِ. وَلَسْتَ تَرَى أَنْ تُنِيبَ. وَتُهَذِّبَ ٱلْمَعِيبَ. ثُمَّ ٱنْدَفَعَ يُنْشِدُ. إِنْشَادَ مَنْ يُرْشِدُ.

٣،٤١ يَا وَيْحَ مَنْ أَنْذَرَهُ شَيْبُهُ   وَهْوَ عَلَى غَيِّ ٱلصِّبَا مُنْكَمِشْ
يَعْشُو إِلَى نَارِ ٱلْهَوَى بَعْدَمَا   أَصْبَحَ مِنْ ضُعْفِ ٱلْقُوَى يَرْتَعِشْ
وَيَمْتَطِي ٱللَّهْوَ وَيَعْتَدُّهُ   أَوْطَأَ مَا يَفْتَرِشُ ٱلْمُفْتَرِشْ
لَمْ يَهَبِ ٱلشَّيْبَ ٱلَّذِي مَا رَأَى   نُجُومَهُ ذُو ٱللُّبِّ إِلَّا دُهِشْ
وَلَا ٱنْتَهَى عَمَّا نَهَاهُ ٱلنُّهَى   عَنْهُ وَلَا بَالَى بِعِرْضٍ خُدِشْ
فَذَاكَ إِنْ مَاتَ فَسُحْقًا لَهُ   وَإِنْ يَعِشْ فَهْوَ كَمَنْ[٢] لَمْ يَعِشْ
لَا خَيْرَ فِي مَحْيَا ٱمْرِئٍ نَشْرُهُ   كَنَشْرِ مَيْتٍ بَعْدَ عَشْرٍ نُبِشْ
وَحَبَّذَا مَنْ عِرْضُهُ طَيِّبٌ   يَرُوقُ حُسْنًا مِثْلَ بُرْدٍ رُقِشْ
فَقُلْ لِمَنْ قَدْ شَاكَهُ ذَنْبُهُ   هَلَكْتَ يَا مِسْكِينُ أَوْ تَنْتَقِشْ
فَأَخْلِصِ ٱلتَّوْبَةَ تَطْمِسْ بِهَا   مِنَ ٱلْخَطَايَا ٱلسُّودِ مَا قَدْ نُقِشْ
وَعَاشِرِ ٱلنَّاسَ بِخُلْقٍ رِضًى   وَدَارِ مَنْ طَاشَ وَمَنْ لَمْ يَطِشْ
وَرِشْ جَنَاحَ ٱلْحُرِّ إِنْ حَصَّهُ   زَمَانُهُ لَا كَانَ مَنْ لَمْ يَرِشْ
وَأَنْجِدِ ٱلْمَوْتُورَ ظُلْمًا فَإِنْ   عَجَزْتَ عَنْ إِنْجَادِهِ فَٱسْتَجِشْ
وَٱنْعَشْ إِذَا نَادَاكَ ذُو كَبْوَةٍ   عَسَاكَ فِي ٱلْحَشْرِ بِهِ تَنْتَعِشْ
وَهَاكَ كَأْسَ ٱلنُّصْحِ فَٱشْرَبْ وَجُدْ   بِفَضْلَةِ ٱلْكَأْسِ عَلَى مَنْ عَطِشْ

١ «وخزن النشب»: في متن ق: والحزن؛ وفي هامش ما أثبتنا، وهو الموجود في باقي الأصول. ٢ «فهوكمن»: في و: عُدَّ كَمَنْ، وفي ف: عُدَّ كَأَنْ.

٤٫٤١ قَالَ فَلَمَّا فَرَغَ مِنْ مُبْكِيَاتِهِ. وَقَضَى إِنْشَادَ أَبْيَاتِهِ. نَهَضَ صَبِيٌّ قَدْ شَدَنَ. وَأَعْرَى الْبَدَنَ. وَقَالَ يَا ذَوِي الْحَصَاةِ. وَالْإِنْصَاتِ إِلَى الْوَصَاةِ. قَدْ وَعَيْتُمُ الْإِنْشَادَ. وَفَقِهْتُمُ الْإِرْشَادَ. فَمَنْ نَوَى مِنْكُمْ أَنْ يَقْبَلَ. وَيُصْلِحَ الْمُسْتَقْبَلَ. فَلْيُبِنْ بِبِرِّي عَنْ نِيَّتِهِ. وَلَا يَعْدِلْ عَنِّي بِعَطِيَّتِهِ. فَوَالَّذِي يَعْلَمُ الْأَسْرَارَ. وَيَغْفِرُ الْإِصْرَارَ. إِنَّ سِرِّي لَكَمَا تَرَوْنَ. وَإِنَّ وَجْهِي لَيَسْتَوْجِبُ الصَّوْنَ. فَأَعِينُونِي رُزِقْتُمُ الْعَوْنَ. قَالَ وَأَخَذَ الشَّيْخُ فِيمَا يَعْطِفُ عَلَيْهِ الْقُلُوبَ. وَيُسَنِّي لَهُ الْمَطْلُوبَ. حَتَّى أَنْبَطَ حَفْرُهُ. وَٱعْشَوْشَبَ قَفْرُهُ. فَلَمَّا أَنْ تَرِعَ الْكِيسُ. ٱنْصَلَتَ يَمِيسُ. وَيَحْمَدُ تِنِّيسَ. وَلَمْ يَحُلْ لِلشَّيْخِ الْمُقَامُ. بَعْدَمَا ٱنْصَاعَ الْغُلَامُ. فَٱسْتَرْفَعَ الْأَيْدِيَ بِالدُّعَاءِ. ثُمَّ نَحَا نَحْوَ الِانْكِفَاءِ.

٥٫٤١ قَالَ الرَّاوِي فَٱرْتَحْتُ إِلَى أَنْ أَعْجُمَهُ. وَأُحِلَّ مُتَرْجَمَهُ. فَتَبِعْتُهُ وَهُوَ يَشْتَدُّ فِي سَمْتِهِ. وَلَا يَفْتُقُ رَتْقَ صَمْتِهِ. فَلَمَّا أَمِنَ الْمُفَاجِي. وَأَمْكَنَ التَّنَاجِي. لَفَتَ جِيدَهُ إِلَيَّ. وَسَلَّمَ تَسْلِيمَ الْبَشَاشَةِ عَلَيَّ. ثُمَّ قَالَ أَرَاقَكَ ذَكَاءُ ذَاكَ الشُّوَيْدِنِ. فَقُلْتُ إِي وَالْمُؤْمِنِ الْمُهَيْمِنِ. قَالَ إِنَّهُ فَتَى السَّرُوجِيِّ. وَمَخْرَجُ[1] الدُّرِّ مِنَ اللُّجِّيِّ. فَقُلْتُ أَشْهَدُ إِنَّكَ لَشَجَرَةُ ثَمَرَتِهِ. وَشُوَاظُ شَرَرَتِهِ. فَصَدَّقَ كِهَانَتِي. وَٱسْتَحْسَنَ إِبَانَتِي.

٦٫٤١ ثُمَّ قَالَ هَلْ لَكَ فِي ٱبْتِدَارِ الْبَيْتِ. لِنَتَنَازَعَ كَأْسَ الْكُمَيْتِ. فَقُلْتُ لَهُ وَيْحَكَ ﴿أَتَأْمُرُونَ النَّاسَ بِالْبِرِّ وَتَنْسَوْنَ أَنْفُسَكُمْ﴾. فَٱفْتَرَّ ٱفْتِرَارَ مُتَضَاحِكٍ. وَمَرَّ غَيْرَ مُمَاحِكٍ. ثُمَّ بَدَا لَهُ أَنْ تَرَاجَعَ إِلَيَّ. وَقَالَ ٱحْفَظْهَا عَنِّي وَعَلَيَّ.

ٱصْرِفْ بِصِرْفِ الرَّاحِ عَنْكَ الْأَسَى   وَرَوِّحِ الْقَلْبَ وَلَا تَكْتَئِبْ
وَقُلْ لِمَنْ لَامَكَ فِيمَا بِهِ   تَدْفَعُ عَنْكَ الْهَمَّ قَدْكَ ٱتَّئِبْ

١ د، ف: وَمُخْرِجٍ؛ و: وَمُخْرِجُ.

ثُمَّ قَالَ أَمَّا أَنَا فَسَأَنْطَلِقُ. إِلَى حَيْثُ أَصْطَبِحُ وَأَغْتَبِقُ. وَإِذَا كُنْتَ لَا تَصْحَبُ. وَتُلَائِمُ[١] مَنْ يَطْرَبُ. فَلَسْتَ لِي بِرَفِيقٍ. وَلَا طَرِيقُكَ لِي بِطَرِيقٍ. فَخَلِّ سَبِيلِي وَنَكِّبْ. وَلَا تُنَقِّرْ عَنِّي وَلَا تُنَقِّبْ. ثُمَّ وَلَّى مُدْبِرًا وَلَمْ يُعَقِّبْ.

قَالَ الْحَارِثُ بْنُ هَمَّامٍ فَالْتَهَبْتُ وَجْدًا عِنْدَ انْطِلَاقِهِ. وَوَدِدْتُ لَوْ لَمْ أُلَاقِهِ.

١ ف: ولا تلائم.

الْمَقَامَةُ الثَّانِيَةُ وَالْأَرْبَعُونَ[1]

١،٤٢ حَكَى الْحَارِثُ بْنُ هَمَّامٍ قَالَ تَرَامَتْ بِي مَرَامِي النَّوَى. وَمَسَارِي الْهَوَى. إِلَى أَنْ صِرْتُ ٱبْنَ كُلِّ تُرْبَةٍ. وَأَخَا كُلِّ غُرْبَةٍ. إِلَّا أَنِّي لَمْ أَكُنْ أَقْطَعُ وَادِيًا. وَلَا أَشْهَدُ نَادِيًا. إِلَّا لِاقْتِبَاسِ الْأَدَبِ الْمُسْلِي عَنِ الْأَشْجَانِ. الْمُغْلِي قِيمَةَ الْإِنْسَانِ. حَتَّى عُرِفَتْ لِي هٰذِهِ الشِّنْشِنَةُ. وَتَنَاقَلَتْهَا عَنِّي الْأَلْسِنَةُ. وَصَارَتْ أَعْلَقَ بِي مِنَ الْهَوَى بِبَنِي عُذْرَةَ. وَالشَّجَاعَةِ بِآلِ أَبِي صُفْرَةَ. فَلَمَّا أَلْقَيْتُ الْجِرَانَ بِنَجْرَانَ. وَٱصْطَفَيْتُ بِهَا الْخُلَّانَ وَالْجِيرَانَ. تَخِذْتُ أَنْدِيَتَهَا مُعْتَمَرِي. وَمَوْسِمَ فُكَاهَتِي وَسَمَرِي. فَكُنْتُ أَتَعَهَّدُهَا صَبَاحَ مَسَاءَ. وَأَظْهَرُ فِيهَا عَلَى مَا سَرَّ وَسَاءَ.

٢،٤٢ فَبَيْنَمَا أَنَا فِي نَادٍ مَحْشُودٍ. وَمَحْفِلٍ مَشْهُودٍ. إِذْ جَثَمَ لَدَيْنَا هِمٌّ. عَلَيْهِ هِدْمٌ. فَحَيَّا تَحِيَّةَ مَلِقٍ. بِلِسَانٍ ذَلِقٍ. ثُمَّ قَالَ يَا بُدُورَ الْمَحَافِلِ. وَبُحُورَ النَّوَافِلِ. قَدْ بَيَّنَ الصُّبْحُ لِذِي عَيْنَيْنِ. وَنَابَ الْعِيَانُ مَنَابَ عَدْلَيْنِ. فَمَاذَا تَرَوْنَ. فِيمَا تَرَوْنَ. أَتُحْسِنُونَ الْعَوْنَ. أَمْ تَنْأَوْنَ. إِذْ تُدْعَوْنَ. فَقَالُوا لَهُ تَاللهِ لَقَدْ غِظْتَ. وَرُمْتَ أَنْ تُنْبِطَ فَغِضْتَ. فَنَاشَدَهُمُ اللهَ عَمَّاذَا صَدَّهُمْ. حَتَّى ٱسْتَوْجَبَ رَدَّهُمْ. فَقَالُوا كُنَّا نَتَنَاضَلُ بِالْأَلْغَازِ. كَمَا يُتَنَاضَلُ يَوْمَ الْبِرَازِ. فَمَا تَمَالَكَ أَنْ شَعَّثَ مِنَ الْمَنْضُولِ. وَأَلْحَقَ هٰذَا الْفَضْلَ بِنَمَطِ الْفُضُولِ. فَلَسَنَهُ[2] لُسُنُ[3] الْقَوْمِ. وَوَخَزُوهُ بِأَسِنَّةِ اللَّوْمِ. وَأَخَذَ هُوَ يَتَنَصَّلُ مِنْ هَفْوَتِهِ. وَيَتَنَدَّمُ عَلَى فَوْهَتِهِ. وَهُمْ مُضِبُّونَ عَلَى مُؤَاخَذَتِهِ. وَمُلَبُّونَ دَاعِيَ مُنَابَذَتِهِ. إِلَى أَنْ قَالَ لَهُمْ يَا قَوْمِ إِنَّ ٱلِاحْتِمَالَ مِنْ كَرَمِ الطَّبْعِ. فَعَدُّوا عَنِ

١ في هامش ش: تُعرف بالنجرانية؛ وفي د: النَّجْرانية؛ وفي ف: وهي النجرانية. ٢ ف: لَسَنَتْه. ٣ و: لسَن؛ ف: لُسُن.

اللَّذْعِ وَالقَذْعِ. ثُمَّ هَلُمَّ إِلَى أَنْ نُلْغِزَ. وَنُحَكِّمَ الْمُبَرِّزَ. فَسَكَنَ عِنْدَ ذٰلِكَ تَوَقُّدُهُمْ. وَٱنْحَلَّتْ عُقَدُهُمْ. وَرَضُوا بِمَا شَرَطَ عَلَيْهِمْ وَلَهُمْ. وَٱقْتَرَحُوا أَنْ يَكُونَ أَوَّلَهُمْ. فَأَمْسَكَ رَيْثَمَا يُعْقَدُ شِسْعٌ. أَوْ يُشَدُّ نِسْعٌ.

٣،٤٢ ثُمَّ قَالَ اِسْمَعُوا وُقِيتُمُ الطَّيْشَ. وَمُلِّيتُمُ[١] العَيْشَ. وَأَنْشَدَ مُلْغِزًا فِي مِرْوَحَةِ الْخَيْشِ.

وَجَارِيَةٍ فِي سَيْرِهَا مُشْمَعِلَّةٍ وَلٰكِنْ عَلَى إِثْرِ الْمَسِيرِ قُفُولُهَا
لَهَا سَائِقٌ مِنْ جِنْسِهَا يَسْتَحِثُّهَا عَلَى أَنَّهُ فِي الاِحْتِثَاثِ رَسِيلُهَا
تُرَى فِي أَوَانِ الْقَيْظِ تَنْطُفُ بِالنَّدَى وَيَبْدُو إِذَا وَلَّى الْمَصِيفُ قُحُولُهَا

٤،٤٢ ثُمَّ قَالَ وَهَاكُمْ يَا أُولِي الْفَضْلِ. وَمَرَاكِزَ العَقْلِ. وَأَنْشَدَ مُلْغِزًا فِي حَابُولِ النَّخْلِ.

وَمُنْتَسِبٍ إِلَى أُمٍّ تَنَشَّأَ أَصْلُهُ مِنْهَا
يُعَانِقُهَا وَقَدْ كَانَتْ نَفَتْهُ بُرْهَةً عَنْهَا
بِهِ يَتَوَصَّلُ الْجَانِي وَلَا يُلْحَى وَلَا يُنْهَى

٥،٤٢ ثُمَّ قَالَ وَدُونَكُمُ الْخَفِيَّةَ الْعَلَمِ. الْمُعْتَكِرَةَ الظُّلَمِ. وَأَنْشَدَ مُلْغِزًا فِي الْقَلَمِ.

وَمَأْمُومٍ بِهِ عُرِفَ الْإِمَامُ كَمَا بَاهَتْ بِصُحْبَتِهِ الْكِرَامُ
لَهُ إِذْ يَرْتَوِي طَيْشَانُ صَادٍ وَيَسْكُنُ حِينَ يَعْرُوهُ الْأُوَامُ
وَيُذْرِي حِينَ يُسْتَسْعَى دُمُوعًا يَرُقْنَ كَمَا يَرُوقُ الاِبْتِسَامُ

١ في متن ق: هُنِّيتم؛ وفي الهامش: مُلِّيتم.

٦،٤٢ ثُمَّ قَالَ وَعَلَيْكُمْ بِالْوَاضِحَةِ الدَّلِيلِ. الْفَاضِحَةِ مَا قِيلَ. وَأَنْشَدَ مُلْغِزًا فِي الْمِيلِ.

وَمَا نَاكِحٌ أُخْتَيْنِ جَهْرًا وَخُفْيَةً   وَلَيْسَ عَلَيْهِ فِي النِّكَاحِ سَبِيلُ
مَتَى يَغْشَ هٰذِي يَغْشَ فِي الْحَالِ هٰذِهِ   وَإِنْ مَالَ بَعْلٌ لَمْ تَجِدْهُ يَمِيلُ
يَزِيدُهُمَا عِنْدَ الْمَشِيبِ تَعَهُّدًا   وَبِرًّا وَهٰذَا فِي الْبُعُولِ قَلِيلُ

٧،٤٢ ثُمَّ قَالَ وَهٰذِهِ يَا أُولِي الْأَلْبَابِ. مِعْيَارُ الْآدَابِ. وَأَنْشَدَ مُلْغِزًا فِي الدُّولَابِ.

وَجَافٍ وَهْوَ مَوْصُولٌ   وُصُولٌ لَيْسَ بِالْجَافِي[1]
غَرِيقٌ بَارِزٌ فَٱعْجَبْ   لَهُ مِنْ رَاسِبٍ طَافِ
يَسُحُّ دُمُوعَ مَهْضُومٍ   وَيَهْضِمُ هَضْمَ مِتْلَافِ
وَتُخْشَى مِنْهُ حِدَّتُهُ   وَلٰكِنْ قَلْبُهُ صَافِ

٨،٤٢ قَالَ فَلَمَّا رَشَقَ. بِالْخَمْسِ الَّتِي نَسَقَ. قَالَ يَا قَوْمِ تَدَبَّرُوا هٰذِهِ الْخَمْسَ. وَٱعْقِدُوا عَلَيْهَا الْخَمْسَ. ثُمَّ رَأْيَكُمْ وَضَمَّ الذَّيْلِ. أَوِ الِازْدِيَادَ مِنْ هٰذَا الْكَيْلِ. قَالَ فَٱسْتَفَزَّتِ الْقَوْمَ شَهْوَةُ الزِّيَادَةِ. عَلَى مَا أُشْرِبُوا مِنَ الْبَلَادَةِ. فَقَالُوا لَهُ إِنَّ وُقُوفَنَا دُونَ حَدِّكَ. لَيُفْحِمُنَا عَنِ ٱسْتِيرَاءِ زَنْدِكَ.[2] فَإِنْ أَتْمَمْتَ عَشْرًا فَمِنْ عِنْدِكَ. فَٱهْتَزَّ ٱهْتِزَازَ مَنْ فَلَجَ سَهْمُهُ. وَٱنْخَزَلَ خَصْمُهُ. ثُمَّ ٱفْتَتَحَ النُّطْقَ بِالْبَسْمَلَةِ. وَأَنْشَدَ مُلْغِزًا فِي الْمُزَمَّلَةِ.

وَمَسْرُورَةٍ مَغْمُومَةٍ طُولَ دَهْرِهَا   وَمَا هِيَ تَدْرِي مَا السُّرُورُ وَلَا الْغَمُّ
تُقَرَّبُ أَحْيَانًا لِأَجْلِ جَنِينِهَا   وَكَمْ وَلَدٍ لَوْلَاهُ طُلِّقَتِ الْأُمُّ

١ «وصول ليس بالجافي»: في س: وما ذو الوَصْلِ كالجافي. ٢ بعدها في ف: واستشفاف فرندك.

وَتُبْعِدُ أَحْيَانًا وَمَا حَالَ عَهْدُهَا وَإِبْعَادُ مَنْ لَمْ يَسْتَحِلْ عَهْدَهُ ظُلْمُ
إِذَا قَصُرَ اللَّيْلُ ٱسْتُلِذَّ وِصَالُهَا وَإِنْ طَالَ فَالْإِعْرَاضُ عَنْ وَصْلِهَا نُعْمُ
لَهَا مَلْبَسٌ بَادٍ أَنِيقٌ مُبَطَّنٌ بِمَا يُزْدَرَى لٰكِنْ لِمَا يُزْدَرَى الْحُكْمُ

٩،٤٢ ثُمَّ كَشَرَ عَنْ أَنْيَابِهِ الصُّفْرِ. وَأَنْشَدَ مُلْغِزًا فِي الظُّفْرِ.

وَمَرْهُوبِ الشَّبَا نَامٍ وَمَا يَرْعَى وَلَا يَشْرَبْ
يُرَى فِي الْعَشْرِ دُونَ النَّحْرِ فَٱسْمَعْ وَصْفَهُ وَٱعْجَبْ

١٠،٤٢ ثُمَّ تَخَازَرَ تَخَازُرَ الْعِفْرِيتِ. وَأَنْشَدَ مُلْغِزًا فِي طَاقَةِ الْكِبْرِيتِ.

وَمَا مَحْقُورَةٌ تُدْنَى وَتُقْصَى وَمَا مِنْهَا إِذَا فَكَّرْتَ بُدُّ
لَهَا رَأْسَانِ مُشْتَبِهَانِ جِدًّا وَكُلٌّ مِنْهُمَا لِأَخِيهِ ضِدُّ
تُعَذَّبُ إِنْ هُمَا خُضِبَا وَتُلْغَى إِذَا عَدِمَا الْخِضَابَ وَلَا تُعَدُّ

١١،٤٢ ثُمَّ تَخَمَّطَ تَخَمُّطَ الْقَرْمِ. وَأَنْشَدَ فِي حَلَبِ الْكَرْمِ.

وَمَا شَيْءٌ إِذَا فَسَدَا تَحَوَّلَ غَيُّهُ رَشَدَا
وَإِنْ هُوَ رَاقَ أَوْصَافًا أَثَارَ الشَّرَّ حَيْثُ بَدَا
زَكِيُّ الْعِرْقِ وَالِدُهُ وَلٰكِنْ بِئْسَ مَا وَلَدَا

١٢،٤٢ ثُمَّ ٱعْتَضَدَ عَصَا ٱلتَّسْيَارِ. وَأَنْشَدَ مُلْغِزًا فِي ٱلطَّيَّارِ.

وَذِي طَيْشَةٍ شِقُّهُ مَائِلُ   وَمَا عَابَهُ بِهِمَا عَاقِلُ
يُرَى أَبَدًا فَوْقَ عُلِّيَّةٍ[1]   كَمَا يَعْتَلِي ٱلْمَلِكُ ٱلْعَادِلُ
تَسَاوَى لَدَيْهِ ٱلْحَصَا وَٱلنُّضَارُ   وَمَا يَسْتَوِي ٱلْحَقُّ وَٱلْبَاطِلُ
وَأَعْجَبُ أَوْصَافِهِ إِنْ نَظَرْتَ   كَمَا يَنْظُرُ ٱلْكَيِّسُ ٱلْفَاضِلُ
تَرَاضِي ٱلْخُصُومِ بِهِ حَاكِمًا   وَقَدْ عَرَفُوا أَنَّهُ مَائِلُ

١٣،٤٢ قَالَ فَظَلَّتِ ٱلْأَفْكَارُ تَهِيمُ فِي أَوْدِيَةِ ٱلْأَوْهَامِ. وَتَجُولُ جَوَلَانَ ٱلْمُسْتَهَامِ. إِلَى أَنْ طَالَ ٱلْأَمَدُ. وَحَصْحَصَ ٱلْكَمَدُ. فَلَمَّا رَآهُمْ يَزْنِدُونَ وَلَا سَنَا. وَيُقَضُّونَ ٱلنَّهَارَ بِٱلْمُنَى. قَالَ يَا قَوْمِ إِلَامَ تَنْظُرُونَ. وَحَتَّامَ تُنْظَرُونَ. أَلَمْ يَأْنِ لَكُمُ ٱسْتِخْرَاجُ ٱلْخَبِيِّ. أَوِ ٱسْتِسْلَامُ ٱلْغَبِيِّ. فَقَالُوا تَاللهِ لَقَدْ أَعْوَصْتَ. وَنَصَبْتَ ٱلشَّرَكَ فَقَنَصْتَ.[2] فَتَحَكَّمْ كَيْفَ شِيتَ. وَحُزِ ٱلْغُنْمَ وَٱلصِّيتَ. فَفَرَضَ عَنْ كُلِّ مُعَمًّى فَرْضًا. وَٱسْتَخْلَصَهُ مِنْهُمْ نَضًّا. ثُمَّ فَتَحَ ٱلْأَقْفَالَ. وَوَسَمَ ٱلْأَغْفَالَ. وَحَاوَلَ ٱلْإِجْفَالَ. فَٱعْتَلَقَ بِهِ مِدْرَهُ ٱلْقَوْمِ. وَقَالَ لَهُ لَا لُبْسَةَ بَعْدَ ٱلْيَوْمِ. فَٱسْتَنْسِبْ قَبْلَ ٱلِٱنْطِلَاقِ. وَهَبْهَا مُتْعَةَ ٱلطَّلَاقِ.

١٤،٤٢ فَأَطْرَقَ حَتَّى قُلْنَا مُرِيبٌ. ثُمَّ أَنْشَدَ وَٱلدَّمْعُ مُجِيبٌ.[3]

سَرُوجُ مَطْلِعُ شَمْسِي وَرَبْعُ لَهْوِي وَأُنْسِي[4]
لٰكِنْ حُرِمْتُ نَعِيمِي بِهَا وَلَذَّةَ نَفْسِي
وَٱعْتَضْتُ عَنْهَا ٱغْتِرَابًا أَمَرَّ يَوْمِي وَأَمْسِي

١ و، د، ف: عِلِّيَة.   ٢ ق: اقتنصت.   ٣ س: يُجِيب.   ٤ ما بعدها إلى كلمة «بجادة» (٤٣،٢) في المقامة التالية ساقط من النسخة الرقمية من و.

مَا لِي مَـقَـرٌّ بِـأَرْضٍ وَلَا قَـرَارٌ لِعَـنْسِيْ
يَوْمًا بِنَجْـدٍ وَيَوْمًا بِالشَّـامِ[١] أُضْحِي وَأُمْـسِي
أُزْجِي الزَّمَانَ بِقُوتٍ مُنَغَّصٍ مُسْتَخَـسِّ
لَا أَبِيتُ وَعِـنْدِي فَـلْسٌ وَمَنْ لِي بِفَـلْسِ
وَمَنْ يَعِـشْ مِثْلَ عَيْشِي بَاعَ الْحَيَاةَ بِبَخْـسِ

ثُمَّ إِنَّهُ ٱخْتَبَنَ خُلَاصَةَ النَّضِّ. وَنَدَرَ[٢] ضَارِبًا فِي الْأَرْضِ. فَنَاشَدْنَاهُ أَنْ يَعُودَ. وَأَسْنَيْنَا لَهُ الْوُعُودَ. فَلَا وَأَبِيكَ مَا رَجَعَ. وَلَا التَّرْغِيبُ لَهُ نَجَعَ.

١ س: بالشأم. ٢ د: بدر.

ٱلْمَقَامَةُ ٱلثَّالِثَةُ وَٱلْأَرْبَعُونَ[١]

١،٤٣ أَخْبَرَ[٢] ٱلْحَارِثُ بْنُ هَمَّامٍ قَالَ هَفَا بِي ٱلْبَيْنُ ٱلْمُطَوِّحُ. وَٱلسَّيْرُ ٱلْمُبَرِّحُ. إِلَى أَرْضٍ يَضِلُّ بِهَا ٱلْخِرِّيتُ. وَتَفْرَقُ فِيهَا ٱلْمَصَالِيتُ. فَوَجَدْتُ مَا يَجِدُ ٱلْحَائِرُ ٱلْوَحِيدُ. وَرَأَيْتُ مَا كُنْتُ مِنْهُ أَحِيدُ. إِلَّا أَنِّي شَجَّعْتُ قَلْبِي ٱلْمَزْؤُودَ. وَنَسَأْتُ نِضْوِي ٱلْمَجْهُودَ. وَسِرْتُ سَيْرَ ٱلضَّارِبِ بِقِدْحَيْنِ. ٱلْمُسْتَسْلِمِ لِلْحَيْنِ. وَلَمْ أَزَلْ بَيْنَ وَخْدٍ وَذَمِيلٍ. وَإِجَازَةِ مِيلٍ بَعْدَ مِيلٍ. إِلَى أَنْ كَادَتِ ٱلشَّمْسُ تَجِبُ. وَٱلضِّيَاءُ يَحْتَجِبُ. فَٱرْتَعْتُ لِإِظْلَالِ ٱلظَّلَامِ. وَٱقْتِحَامِ جَيْشٍ حَامٍ. وَلَمْ أَدْرِ أَأَكُفُّ ٱلذَّيْلَ وَأَرْتَبِطُ. أَمْ أَعْتَمِدُ ٱللَّيْلَ وَأَخْتَبِطُ.

٢،٤٣ وَبَيْنَا أَنَا أُقَلِّبُ ٱلْعَزْمَ. وَأَمْتَخِضُ ٱلْحَزْمَ. تَرَاءَى لِي شَبَحُ جَمَلٍ. مُسْتَذْرٍ بِجَبَلٍ. فَتَرَجَّيْتُهُ قُعْدَةَ مُرِيحٍ. وَقَصَدْتُهُ قَصْدَ مُشِيحٍ. فَإِذَا ٱلظَّنُّ كَهَانَةٌ. وَٱلرَّكُوبُ[٣] عَيْرَانَةٌ. وَٱلْمُرِيحُ قَدِ ٱزْدَمَلَ[٤] بِجَادِهِ. وَٱكْتَحَلَ بِرُقَادِهِ.[٥] فَجَلَسْتُ عِنْدَ رَأْسِهِ. حَتَّى هَبَّ مِنْ نُعَاسِهِ. فَلَمَّا ٱزْدَهَرَ سِرَاجَاهُ. وَأَحَسَّ بِمَنْ فَاجَاهُ. نَفَرَ كَمَا يَنْفِرُ ٱلْمُرِيبُ. وَقَالَ أَخُوكَ أَمِ ٱلذِّيبُ. فَقُلْتُ بَلْ خَابِطُ لَيْلٍ ضَلَّ ٱلْمَسْلَكَ. فَأَضِئْ لِي أَقْدَحْ لَكَ. فَقَالَ لِيَسْرُ عَنْكَ هَمُّكَ. فَرُبَّ أَخٍ[٦] لَمْ تَلِدْهُ أُمُّكَ. فَٱنْسَرَى عِنْدَ ذٰلِكَ إِشْفَاقِي. وَسَرَى ٱلْوَسَنُ إِلَى آمَاقِي. فَقَالَ عِنْدَ ٱلصَّبَاحِ يَحْمَدُ ٱلْقَوْمُ ٱلسُّرَى. فَهَلْ تَرَى كَمَا أَرَى. فَقُلْتُ إِنِّي لَكَ لَأَطْوَعُ مِنْ حِذَائِكَ. وَأَوْفَقُ مِنْ غِذَائِكَ.

١ د: البَدَوِيَّة المعروفة بالبِكْر والثَّيِّب؛ ف: وهي البِكْرِيَّة. ٢ ف: حكى. ٣ في هامش ق، وفي س، ف: القُعدَةُ؛ وفي د: الرَّكُوبة. ٤ من كلمة «أنسي» (٤٢،١٣) في المقامة السابقة إلى هاهنا ساقط من النسخة الرقمية من و. ٥ بعدها في س: قال. ٦ بعدها في ف: لك.

٣،٤٣ فَصَدَعَ بِمَحَبَّتِي. وَبَخْبَخَ بِصُحْبَتِي. ثُمَّ ٱحْتَمَلْنَا مُجِدِّينَ. وَٱرْتَحَلْنَا مُدْلِجِينَ. وَلَمْ نَزَلْ نُعَانِي السُّرَى. وَنُعَاصِي الْكَرَى. إِلَى أَنْ بَلَغَ اللَّيْلُ غَايَتَهُ. وَرَفَعَ الْفَجْرُ رَايَتَهُ. فَلَمَّا أَسْفَرَ الْفَاضِحُ. وَلَمْ يَبْقَ إِلَّا وَاضِحٌ. تَوَسَّمْتُ رَفِيقَ رِحْلَتِي. وَسَمِيرَ لَيْلَتِي. فَإِذَا هُوَ أَبُو زَيْدٍ مَطْلَبُ النَّاشِدِ. وَمَعْلَمُ الرَّاشِدِ. فَتَهَادَيْنَا تَحِيَّةَ الْمُحِبَّيْنِ. إِذَا ٱلْتَقَيَا بَعْدَ الْبَيْنِ. ثُمَّ تَبَاثَثْنَا الْأَسْرَارَ. وَتَنَاثَثْنَا الْأَخْبَارَ. وَبَعِيرِي يَنْحِطُ مِنَ الْكَلَالِ. وَرَاحِلَتُهُ تَزِفُّ زَفِيفَ الرَّالِ. فَأَعْجَبَنِي ٱشْتِدَادُ أَسْرِهَا. وَٱمْتِدَادُ صَبْرِهَا. فَأَخَذْتُ أَسْتَشِفُّ جَوْهَرَهَا. وَأَسْأَلُهُ مِنْ أَيْنَ تَخَيَّرَهَا. فَقَالَ إِنَّ لِهٰذِهِ النَّاقَةِ. خَبَرًا حُلْوَ الْمَذَاقَةِ. مَلِيحَ السِّيَاقَةِ. فَإِنْ أَحْبَبْتَ ٱسْتِمَاعَهُ فَأَنِخْ. وَإِنْ لَمْ تَشَأْ فَلَا تُصِخْ. فَأَنَخْتُ لِقَوْلِهِ نِضْوِي. وَأَهْدَفْتُ السَّمْعَ لِمَا يَرْوِي.

٤،٤٣ فَقَالَ ٱعْلَمْ أَنِّي ٱسْتَعْرَضْتُهَا بِحَضْرَمَوْتَ. وَكَابَدْتُ فِي تَحْصِيلِهَا الْمَوْتَ. وَمَا زِلْتُ أَجُوبُ عَلَيْهَا الْبُلْدَانَ. وَأَطِسُ بِهَا[1] الظِّرَّانَ. إِلَى أَنْ وَجَدْتُهَا عُبْرَ أَسْفَارٍ. وَعُدَّةَ فِرَارٍ.[2] لَا يَلْحَقُهَا الْعَنَاءُ.[3] وَلَا تُوَاهِقُهَا وَجْنَاءُ. وَلَا تَدْرِي مَا الْهِنَاءُ. فَأَرْصَدْتُهَا لِلْخَيْرِ وَالشَّرِّ. وَأَحْلَلْتُهَا مَحَلَّ الْبَرِّ السَّرِّ. فَٱتَّفَقَ أَنْ نَدَّتْ مُذْ مُدَّةٍ.[4] وَمَا لِي سِوَاهَا مِنْ قُعْدَةٍ.[5] فَٱسْتَشْعَرْتُ الْأَسَفَ. وَٱسْتَشْرَفْتُ التَّلَفَ. وَنَسِيتُ كُلَّ رُزْءٍ سَلَفَ. وَمَكَثْتُ ثَلَاثًا لَا أَسْتَطِيعُ ٱنْبِعَاثًا. وَلَا أَطْعَمُ النَّوْمَ إِلَّا حِثَاثًا. ثُمَّ أَخَذْتُ فِي ٱسْتِقْرَاءِ الْمَسَالِكِ. وَتَفَقُّدِ الْمَسَارِحِ وَالْمَبَارِكِ. وَأَنَا لَا أَسْتَنْشِي مِنْهَا رِيحًا. وَلَا أَسْتَغْشِي يَأْسًا مُرِيحًا. وَكُلَّمَا ٱدَّكَرْتُ مَضَاءَهَا فِي السَّيْرِ. وَٱنْبِرَاءَهَا لِمُبَارَاةِ الطَّيْرِ. لَاعَنِي الِادِّكَارُ. وَٱسْتَهْوَتْنِي الْأَفْكَارُ.

---

١ ف: بأخْفافِها. ٢ هكذا في س، و، د؛ وهي غير معجمة في ق؛ وفي ف: قرار. ٣ هكذا في جميع النسخ إلا أنها وردت في ق بنقطة باهتة فوق السنّة ونقطتين باهتتين تحت السنة فلعلها «العياء». ٤ س، د: مذ مدَّةٌ.
٥ من قعدة: في ق فقط؛ وفي باقي النسخ: قعدةٌ.

٥،٤٣ فَبَيْنَمَا أَنَا فِي حِوَاءِ بَعْضِ ٱلْأَحْيَاءِ إِذْ سَمِعْتُ مِنْ شَخْصٍ مُبْتَعِدٍ.[١] وَصَوْتٍ مُنْجَرِدٍ.[٢] مَنْ ضَلَّتْ لَهُ مَطِيَّةٌ. حَضْرَمِيَّةٌ وَطِيَّةٌ. جِلْدُهَا قَدْ وُسِمَ. وَعُرُّهَا قَدْ حُسِمَ. وَزِمَامُهَا قَدْ ضُفِرَ. وَظَهْرُهَا كَأَنْ قَدْ كُسِرَ ثُمَّ جُبِرَ. تَزِينُ ٱلْمَاشِيَةَ. وَتُعِينُ ٱلنَّاشِيَةَ. وَتَقْطَعُ ٱلْمَسَافَةَ ٱلنَّائِيَةَ. وَتَظَلُّ أَبَدًا لَكَ مُدَانِيَةً. لَا يَعْتَوِرُهَا ٱلْوَنَى. وَلَا يَعْتَرِضُهَا ٱلْوَجَى. وَلَا تُحْوِجُ إِلَى ٱلْعَصَا. وَلَا تَعْصِي فِيمَنْ عَصَى. قَالَ أَبُو زَيْدٍ فَجَذَبَنِي ٱلصَّوْتُ إِلَى ٱلصَّائِتِ. وَبَشَّرَنِي بِدَرْكِ ٱلْفَائِتِ. فَلَمَّا أَفْضَيْتُ[٣] إِلَيْهِ. وَسَلَّمْتُ عَلَيْهِ. قُلْتُ لَهُ سَلِّمِ ٱلْمَطِيَّةَ. وَتَسَلَّمِ ٱلْعَطِيَّةَ. فَقَالَ وَمَا مَطِيَّتُكَ. غُفِرَتْ خَطِيَّتُكَ. قُلْتُ نَاقَةٌ جُثَّتُهَا كَٱلْهَضْبَةِ. وَذِرْوَتُهَا كَٱلْقُبَّةِ. وَحَلَبُهَا مِلْءُ[٤] ٱلْعُلْبَةِ. وَكُنْتُ أُعْطِيتُ بِهَا عِشْرِينَ. إِذْ حَلَّتْ بِيَبْرِينَ. فَٱسْتَزَدْتُ ٱلَّذِي أَعْطَى. وَدَرَيْتُ أَنَّهُ أَخْطَا. قَالَ فَأَعْرَضَ عَنِّي حِينَ سَمِعَ صِفَتِي. وَقَالَ لَسْتَ بِصَاحِبِ لُقَطَتِي. فَأَخَذْتُ بِتَلَابِيبِهِ. وَأَصْرَرْتُ عَلَى تَكْذِيبِهِ. وَهَمَمْتُ بِتَمْزِيقِ جَلَابِيبِهِ. وَهُوَ يَقُولُ يَا هٰذَا مَا مَطِيَّتِي بِطِلْبَتِكَ. فَٱكْفُفْ مِنْ غَرْبِكَ. وَعَدِّ عَنْ سَبِّكَ. وَإِلَّا فَقَاضِنِي إِلَى حَكَمِ هٰذَا ٱلْحَيِّ. ٱلْبَرِيءِ مِنَ ٱلْغَيِّ. فَإِنْ أَوْجَبَهَا لَكَ فَتَسَلَّمْ. وَإِنْ زَوَاهَا عَنْكَ فَلَا تَتَكَلَّمْ. فَلَمْ أَرَ دَوَاءَ قِصَّتِي. وَلَا مَسَاغَ غُصَّتِي. إِلَّا أَنْ آتِيَ ٱلْحَكَمَ. وَلَوْ لَكَمْ.

٦،٤٣ فَٱنْخَرَطْنَا إِلَى شَيْخٍ رَكِينِ ٱلنِّصْبَةِ. أَنِيقِ ٱلْعِصْبَةِ. يُؤْنَسُ مِنْهُ سُكُونُ ٱلطَّائِرِ. وَأَنْ لَيْسَ بِٱلْجَائِرِ. فَٱنْدَرَأْتُ أَتَظَلَّمُ وَأَتَأَلَّمُ. وَصَاحِبِي مُرِمٌّ لَا يَتَرَمْرَمُ. حَتَّى إِذَا تَثَلَّتْ[٥] كِنَانَتِي. وَقَضَيْتُ مِنَ ٱلْقَصَصِ لُبَانَتِي. أَبْرَزَ نَعْلًا رَزِينَةَ ٱلْوَزْنِ. مَحْذُوَّةً لِمَسْلَكِ ٱلْحَزْنِ. وَقَالَ هٰذِهِ ٱلَّتِي عَرَّفْتُ. وَإِيَّاهَا وَصَفْتُ. فَإِنْ كَانَتْ هِيَ ٱلَّتِي أُعْطِيَ بِهَا عِشْرِينَ. وَهَا هُوَ مِنَ ٱلْمُبْصِرِينَ. فَقَدْ كَذَبَ فِي دَعْوَاهُ. وَكَبُرَ مَا ٱفْتَرَاهُ. ٱللّٰهُمَّ إِلَّا أَنْ يَمُدَّ قَذَالَهُ. وَيُبَيِّنْ مِصْدَاقَ مَا قَالَهُ. فَقَالَ ٱلْحَكَمُ ٱللّٰهُمَّ غَفْرًا. وَجَعَلَ

---

١ ف: متبعِّد. ٢ ف: متجرد. ٣ و: أفضْتُ. ٤ س: مِلْءَ. ٥ د: أنثلت.

يُقَلِّبُ ٱلنَّعْلَ بَطْنًا وَظَهْرًا. ثُمَّ قَالَ أَمَّا هٰذِهِ ٱلنَّعْلُ فَنَعْلِي. وَأَمَّا مَطِيَّتُكَ فَفِي رَحْلِي. فَٱنْهَضْ لِتَسَلُّمِ نَاقَتِكَ. وَٱفْعَلِ ٱلْخَيْرَ بِحَسَبِ طَاقَتِكَ.

٧.٤٣ فَقُمْتُ وَقُلْتُ

أُقْسِمُ بِٱلْبَيْتِ ٱلْعَتِيقِ ذِي ٱلْحُرَمْ   وَٱلطَّائِفِينَ ٱلْعَاكِفِينَ فِي ٱلْحَرَمْ
إِنَّكَ نِعْمَ مَنْ إِلَيْهِ يُحْتَكَمْ[1]   وَخَيْرُ قَاضٍ فِي ٱلْأَعَارِيبِ حَكَمْ
فَٱسْلَمْ وَدُمْ دَوْمَ ٱلنَّعَامِ وَٱلنَّعَمْ

فَأَجَابَ مِنْ غَيْرِ رَوِيَّةٍ. وَلَا عَقْدِ نِيَّةٍ. وَقَالَ

جُزِيتَ عَنْ شُكْرِكَ خَيْرًا يَا ٱبْنَ عَمّْ   إِذْ لَسْتُ أَسْتَوْجِبُ شُكْرًا يُلْتَزَمْ
شَرُّ ٱلْأَنَامِ مَنْ إِذَا ٱسْتُقْضِيَ ظَلَمْ   ثُمَّ مَنِ ٱسْتُرْعِيَ فَلَمْ يَرْعَ ٱلْحُرَمْ
فَذَانِ وَٱلْكَلْبُ سَوَاءٌ فِي ٱلْقِيَمْ

ثُمَّ إِنَّهُ نَفَّذَ بَيْنَ يَدَيَّ. مَنْ سَلَّمَ ٱلنَّاقَةَ إِلَيَّ. وَلَمْ يَمْتَنَّ[2] عَلَيَّ. فَرُحْتُ[3] أَجُرُّ ذَيْلَ ٱلطَّرَبِ. وَأَقُولُ يَا لِلْعَجَبِ.

٨.٤٣ قَالَ ٱلْحَارِثُ بْنُ هَمَّامٍ فَقُلْتُ لَهُ تَٱللهِ لَقَدْ أَطْرَفْتَ. وَهَرَفْتَ بِمَا عَرَفْتَ. فَنَاشَدْتُكَ ٱللهَ هَلْ لَقِيتَ[4] أَسْحَرَ مِنْكَ بَلَاغَةً. وَأَحْسَنَ لِلَّفْظِ صِيَاغَةً. فَقَالَ ٱللّٰهُمَّ نَعَمْ. فَٱسْمَعْ[5] وَٱنْعَمْ. كُنْتُ عَزَمْتُ. حِينَ أَتْهَمْتُ. عَلَى أَنْ أَتَّخِذَ ظَعِينَةً. لِتَكُونَ لِي مُعِينَةً. فَحِينَ تَعَيَّنَ ٱلْخِطْبُ.[6] وَكَادَ ٱلْأَمْرُ يَسْتَتِبُّ. أَفْكَرْتُ فِكْرَ ٱلْمُتَحَرِّزِ مِنَ ٱلْوَهْمِ. ٱلْمُتَأَمِّلِ كَيْفَ مَسْقَطُ ٱلسَّهْمِ. وَبِتُّ لَيْلَتِي أُنَاجِي ٱلْقَلْبَ ٱلْمُعَذَّبَ. وَأُقَلِّبُ

١ س: أنك ما بين الورى نِعمَ الحَكَمْ. ٢ ق: يَمْتَنْ، و: يَمْتُنْ. ٣ بعدها في ف: نَجِيحَ الأَرَبِ. ٤ ف: ألفيت.
٥ ف: فاستمع. ٦ و: الخَطْبُ، وبعدها في ف: المُلبّ.

الْعَزْمَ الْمُذَبْذَبَ. إِلَى أَنْ أَجْمَعْتُ عَلَى أَنْ أُسْحِرَ. وَأُشَاوِرَ أَوَّلَ مَنْ أُبْصِرُ. فَلَمَّا قَوَّضَتِ الظُّلْمَةُ أَطْنَابَهَا. وَوَلَّتِ الشُّهُبُ[1] أَذْنَابَهَا. غَدَوْتُ غُدُوَّ الْمُتَعَرِّفِ. وَٱبْتَكَرْتُ ٱبْتِكَارَ الْمُتَعَيِّفِ. فَٱنْبَرَى لِي يَافِعٌ. فِي وَجْهِهِ شَافِعٌ. فَتَيَمَّنْتُ بِمَنْظَرِهِ الْبَهِيجِ. وَٱسْتَقْدَحْتُ رَأْيَهُ فِي التَّزْوِيجِ. فَقَالَ أَوَتَبْغِيهَا عَوَانًا. أَمْ بِكْرًا تُعَانَى. فَقُلْتُ اِخْتَرْ لِي مَا تَرَى. فَقَدْ أَلْقَيْتُ إِلَيْكَ الْعُرَى. فَقَالَ إِلَيَّ التَّبْيِينُ. وَعَلَيْكَ التَّعْيِينُ. فَٱسْمَعْ أَنَا أَفْدِيكَ. بَعْدَ دَفْنِ أَعَادِيكَ.

٩،٤٣ أَمَّا الْبِكْرُ فَالدُّرَّةُ الْمَخْزُونَةُ. وَالْبَيْضَةُ الْمَكْنُونَةُ. وَالثَّمَرَةُ الْبَاكُورَةُ.[2] وَالسُّلَافَةُ الْمَذْخُورَةُ.[3] وَالرَّوْضَةُ الْأُنُفُ. وَالطَّوْقُ الَّذِي ثَمُنَ وَشَرُفَ. لَمْ يُدَنِّسْهَا لَامِسٌ. وَلَا ٱسْتَغْشَاهَا لَابِسٌ. وَلَا مَارَسَهَا عَابِثٌ. وَلَا أَوْكَسَهَا[4] طَامِثٌ. وَلَهَا الْوَجْهُ الْحَيِيُّ. وَالطَّرْفُ الْخَفِيُّ. وَاللِّسَانُ الْعَيِيُّ. وَالْقَلْبُ النَّقِيُّ.[5] ثُمَّ هِيَ الدُّمْيَةُ الْمُلَاعَبَةُ. وَاللُّعْبَةُ الْمُدَاعَبَةُ. وَالْغَزَالَةُ الْمُغَازَلَةُ. وَالْمُلْحَةُ الْكَامِلَةُ. وَالْوِشَاحُ الطَّاهِرُ الْقَشِيبُ. وَالضَّجِيعُ الَّذِي يُشِبُّ وَلَا يُشِيبُ.

١٠،٤٣ وَأَمَّا الثَّيِّبُ فَالْمَطِيَّةُ الْمُذَلَّلَةُ. وَاللُّهْنَةُ الْمُعَجَّلَةُ. وَالْبُغْيَةُ الْمُسَهَّلَةُ. وَالطَّبَّةُ الْمُعَلِّلَةُ. وَالْقَرِينَةُ الْمُتَحَبِّبَةُ. وَالْحَلِيلَةُ[6] الْمُتَقَرِّبَةُ. وَالصَّنَاعُ الْمُدَبِّرَةُ. وَالْفَطِنَةُ الْمُخْتَبِرَةُ. ثُمَّ إِنَّهَا عُجَالَةُ الرَّاكِبِ. وَأُنْشُوطَةُ الْخَاطِبِ. وَقُعْدَةُ الْعَاجِزِ. وَنُهْزَةُ الْمُبَارِزِ. عَرِيكَتُهَا لَيِّنَةٌ. وَعُقْلَتُهَا هَيِّنَةٌ. وَدِخْلَتُهَا مُتَبَيِّنَةٌ. وَخِدْمَتُهَا مُزَيِّنَةٌ. وَأُقْسِمُ لَقَدْ صَدَقْتَ[7] فِي النَّعْتَيْنِ. وَأَجْلَيْتَ[8] الْمَهَاتَيْنِ. فَبِأَيَّتِهِمَا هَامَ قَلْبُكَ. وَعَلَى أَيَّتِهِمَا قَامَ زُبُّكَ.

---

١ س: الشُّهْبُ. ٢ الثمرة الباكورة»: س، و، ف: الباكورة الجَنِّية. ٣ السلَافة المذخورة: س، و: السلافة الشهية؛ ف: السلافة الهنية. ٤ د، ف: وكسها. ٥ و: التقي النقي. ٦ ف: والخليلة. ٧ و،د، ف: صَدَقْتُ.
٨ و،د، ف: جلوتُ.

١١،٤٣ قَالَ أَبُو زَيْدٍ فَرَأَيْتُهُ جَنْدَلَةً يَتَّقِيهَا ٱلْمَرَاجِمُ. وَتَدْمَى[١] مِنْهَا ٱلْمَحَاجِمُ. إِلَّا أَنِّي قُلْتُ لَهُ كُنْتُ سَمِعْتُ أَنَّ ٱلْبِكْرَ أَشَدُّ حُبًّا. وَأَقَلُّ خِبًّا. فَقَالَ لَعَمْرِي قَدْ قِيلَ هٰذَا. وَلٰكِنْ كَمْ قَوْلٍ آذَى. وَيْحَكَ أَمَا هِيَ ٱلْمُهْرَةُ ٱلْأَبِيَّةُ ٱلْعِنَانِ. وَٱلْمَطِيَّةُ ٱلْبَطِيَّةُ ٱلْإِذْعَانِ. وَٱلزَّنْدَةُ ٱلْمُتَعَسِّرَةُ ٱلِاقْتِدَاحِ. وَٱلْقَلْعَةُ ٱلْمُسْتَصْعَبَةُ ٱلِافْتِتَاحِ. ثُمَّ إِنَّ مَؤُونَتَهَا كَثِيرَةٌ. وَمَعُونَتَهَا يَسِيرَةٌ. وَعِشْرَتَهَا صَلِفَةٌ. وَدَالَّتَهَا مُكَلِّفَةٌ. وَيَدَهَا خَرْقَاءُ. وَفِتْنَتَهَا صَمَّاءُ. وَعَرِيكَتَهَا خَشْنَاءُ. وَلَيْلَتَهَا لَيْلَاءُ. وَفِي رِيَاضَتِهَا عَنَاءٌ. وَعَلَى خِبْرَتِهَا[٢] غِشَاءٌ. وَطَالَمَا أَخْزَتِ ٱلْمُنَازِلَ. وَفَرَكَتِ ٱلْمُغَازِلَ. وَأَحْنَقَتِ ٱلْهَازِلَ. وَأَضْرَعَتِ ٱلْفَنِيقَ ٱلْبَازِلَ. ثُمَّ إِنَّهَا ٱلَّتِي تَقُولُ أَنَا أَلْبَسُ وَأَجْلِسُ. فَٱطْلُبْ[٣] مَنْ يُطَلِّقُ وَيَحْبِسُ.[٤]

١٢،٤٣ فَقُلْتُ لَهُ فَمَا تَرَى فِي ٱلثَّيِّبِ. يَا أَبَا ٱلطَّيِّبِ. فَقَالَ وَيْحَكَ أَتَرْغَبُ فِي فُضَالَةِ ٱلْمَآكِلِ.[٥] وَخُثَارَةِ[٦] ٱلْمَنْهَلِ.[٧] وَٱللِّبَاسِ ٱلْمُسْتَبْذَلِ. وَٱلْوِعَاءِ ٱلْمُسْتَعْمَلِ. وَٱلذَّوَّاقَةِ ٱلْمُتَطَرِّفَةِ. وَٱلْخَرَّاجَةِ ٱلْمُتَصَرِّفَةِ. وَٱلْوَقَاحِ ٱلْمُتَسَلِّطَةِ. وَٱلْمُحْتَكِرَةِ ٱلْمُتَسَخِّطَةِ. ثُمَّ كَلِمَتُهَا كُنْتُ وَصِرْتُ. وَطَالَمَا بُغِيَ عَلَيَّ فَنُصِرْتُ. وَشَتَّانَ بَيْنَ ٱلْيَوْمِ وَأَمْسِ. وَأَيْنَ ٱلْقَمَرُ مِنَ ٱلشَّمْسِ. وَإِنْ كَانَتِ ٱلْحَنَّانَةَ ٱلْبَرُوكَ.[٨] أَوِ[٩] ٱلطَّمَّاحَةَ ٱلْهَلُوكَ.[١٠] فَهِيَ ٱلْغُلُّ ٱلْقَمِلُ. وَٱلْجُرْحُ ٱلَّذِي لَا يَنْدَمِلُ.

١٣،٤٣ فَقُلْتُ لَهُ فَهَلْ تَرَى أَنْ أَتَرَهَّبَ. وَأَسْلُكَ هٰذَا ٱلْمَذْهَبَ. فَٱنْتَهَرَنِي ٱنْتِهَارَ ٱلْمُؤَدِّبِ. عِنْدَ زَلَّةِ ٱلْمُتَأَدِّبِ. ثُمَّ قَالَ وَيْلَكَ أَتَقْتَدِي بِٱلرُّهْبَانِ. وَٱلْحَقُّ قَدِ ٱسْتَبَانَ. أُفٍّ لَكَ. وَلِوَهْنِ رَأْيِكَ. وَتَبًّا لَكَ وَلِأُولٰئِكَ. أَتُرَاكَ مَا سَمِعْتَ بِأَنْ لَا

١ د، ف: تُدْمَى. ٢ ف: خمرتها. ٣ هكذا في س، د؛ وهي غير مشكلة في ق، وفي و: أَطْلُبُ. ٤ هكذا على ما يبدو في ق، وفي و، د، ف، وهي غير معجمة في س. ٥ . ف: المآكل. ٦ س، و، د: وثُمالة. ٧ ف: المناهل.
٨ و: البرول. ٩ و، ف: و. ١٠ و: الهلول.

رُهْبَانِيَّةَ فِي ٱلْإِسْلَامِ. وَلَا حُدِّثْتَ بِمَنَاكِحِ[1] نَبِيِّكَ عَلَيْهِ[2] ٱلسَّلَامُ. ثُمَّ أَمَا تَعْلَمُ أَنَّ ٱلسَّكَنَ[3] ٱلصَّالِحَةَ تَرُبُّ بَيْتَكَ. وَتُلَبِّي صَوْتَكَ. وَتَغُضُّ طَرْفَكَ. وَتُطَيِّبُ عَرْفَكَ. وَبِهَا تَرَى قُرَّةَ عَيْنِكَ. وَرَيْحَانَةَ أَنْفِكَ. وَفَرْحَةَ قَلْبِكَ. وَخُلْدَ ذِكْرِكَ.[4] وَتِعِلَّةَ يَوْمِكَ وَغَدِكَ.[5] فَكَيْفَ رَغِبْتَ عَنْ سُنَّةِ ٱلْمُرْسَلِينَ. وَمُتْعَةِ ٱلْمُتَأَهِّلِينَ. وَشِرْعَةِ ٱلْمُحْصَنِينَ. وَمَجْلَبَةِ ٱلْمَالِ وَٱلْبَنِينَ. وَٱللّٰهِ لَقَدْ سَاءَنِي فِيكَ. مَا سَمِعْتُ مِنْ فِيكَ. ثُمَّ أَعْرَضَ إِعْرَاضَ ٱلْمُغْضَبِ. وَنَزَا نَزَوَانَ ٱلْعُنْظُبِ. فَقُلْتُ لَهُ قَاتَلَكَ ٱللّٰهُ أَتَنْطَلِقُ مُتَبَخْتِرًا. وَتَدَعُنِي مُتَحَيِّرًا.[6] فَقَالَ أَظُنُّكَ تَدَّعِي ٱلْحَيْرَةَ. لِتَجْلِدَ عُمَيْرَةَ. وَتَسْتَغْنِيَ عَنِ ٱلْمُهَيْرَةِ. فَقُلْتُ لَهُ قَبَّحَ ٱللّٰهُ ظَنَّكَ. وَلَا أَشَبَّ قَرْنَكَ. ثُمَّ رُحْتُ عَنْهُ مَرَاحَ ٱلْخَزْيَانِ. وَتُبْتُ مِنْ مُشَاوَرَةِ ٱلصِّبْيَانِ.

١٤،٤٣ قَالَ ٱلْحَارِثُ بْنُ هَمَّامٍ فَقُلْتُ لَهُ أُقْسِمُ بِمَنْ أَنْبَتَ ٱلْأَيْكَ. إِنَّ ٱلْجَدَلَ مِنْكَ وَإِلَيْكَ. فَأَغْرَبَ فِي ٱلضَّحِكِ وَطَرِبَ طَرَبَةَ ٱلْمُنْهَتِكِ.[7] ثُمَّ قَالَ ٱلْعَقِ ٱلْعَسَلَ. وَلَا تَسَلْ. فَأَخَذْتُ أُسْهِبُ فِي مَدْحِ ٱلْأَدَبِ. وَأُفَضِّلُ رَبَّهُ عَلَى ذِي ٱلنَّشَبِ. وَهُوَ يَنْظُرُ إِلَيَّ نَظَرَ ٱلْمُسْتَجْهِلِ. وَيُغْضِي عَنِّي إِغْضَاءَ ٱلْمُمْهِلِ.[8] فَلَمَّا أَسْرَفْتُ[9] فِي ٱلْعَصَبِيَّةِ. لِلْعِصَابَةِ[10] ٱلْأَدَبِيَّةِ. قَالَ لِي صَهْ. وَٱسْمَعْ مِنِّي وَٱفْقَهْ.

يَقُولُونَ إِنَّ جَمَالَ ٱلْفَتَى وَزِينَتَهُ أَدَبٌ رَاسِخُ
وَمَا إِنْ يَزِينُ سِوَى ٱلْمُكْثِرِينَ وَمَنْ طَوْدُ سُودَدِهِ شَامِخُ

---

١ في متن ق، وفي د: بما نكح، والصحيح في هامش ق، وفي س، و، ف. ٢ بعدها في س، ف: أزكى. ٣ بعدها في ق: القرينة (مشطوبة)؛ وفي ف: القرينة. ٤ وخلد ذكرك: ساقطة من د. ٥ «وخُلْدَ ذِكْرِكَ. وتَعِلَّةِ يَوْمِكَ وغَدِكَ»: هكذا في ق، ف؛ وفي س: وذخيرة يومك وغدك؛ وفي و: وخلد ذكرك وذخيرة يومك وغدك؛ وفي د: وتعلة يومك وغدك ٦ س: مُحَيَّرًا، وفي الهامش: وتدعني متحيرا. ٧ ف: المنهمك. ٨ ف: المتمهل. ٩ في هامش ق، وفي س، و، ف: أفرطت. ١٠ س، د، ف: للعُصْبة.

فَـأَمَّــا الْفَــقِــيرُ فَخَــيْرٌ لَهُ مِنَ الْأَدَبِ الْقُــرْصُ وَالْكَامِخُ
وَأَيُّ جَـمَـالٍ لَهُ أَنْ يُقَــالَ أَدِيبٌ يُعَــلِّمُ أَوْ نَــاسِخُ

١٥،٤٣ ثُمَّ قَالَ سَيَضِحُ[١] لَكَ صِدْقُ لَهْجَتِي. وَٱسْتِنَارَةُ حُجَّتِي. وَسِرْنَا لَا نَأْلُو جُهْدًا. وَلَا نَسْتَفِيقُ جَهْدًا. حَتَّى أَدَّانَا السَّيْرُ. إِلَى قَرْيَةٍ عَزَبَ عَنْهَا الْخَيْرُ. فَدَخَلْنَاهَا لِلِٱرْتِيَادِ. وَكِلَانَا مُنْفِضٌ مِنَ الزَّادِ. فَمَا إِنْ بَلَغْنَا الْمَحَطَّ. وَالْمَنَاخَ الْمُخْتَطَّ. أَوْ لَقِينَا غُلَامٌ لَمْ يَبْلُغِ الْحِنْثَ. وَعَلَى عَاتِقِهِ ضِغْثٌ. فَحَيَّاهُ أَبُو زَيْدٍ تَحِيَّةَ الْمُسْلِمِ. وَسَأَلَهُ وَقْفَةَ الْمُفْهِمِ. فَقَالَ وَعَمَّ تَسْأَلُ وَفَّقَكَ اللّٰهُ. قَالَ أَيُبَاعُ هَاهُنَا الرُّطَبُ. بِالْخُطَبِ. قَالَ لَا وَاللّٰهِ. قَالَ وَلَا الْبَلَحُ. بِالْمُلَحِ. قَالَ كَلَّا وَاللّٰهِ. قَالَ وَلَا الثَّمَرُ. بِالسَّمَرِ. قَالَ هَيْهَاتَ وَاللّٰهِ. قَالَ وَلَا الْعَصِيدَةُ. بِالْقَصِيدَةِ.[٢] قَالَ ٱسْكُتْ عَافَاكَ اللّٰهُ. قَالَ وَلَا الثَّرَائِدُ. بِالْفَرَائِدِ. قَالَ أَيْنَ يُذْهَبُ بِكَ أَرْشَدَكَ اللّٰهُ. قَالَ وَلَا الدَّقِيقُ. بِالْمَعْنَى الدَّقِيقِ. قَالَ عَدِّ عَنْ هٰذَا أَصْلَحَكَ اللّٰهُ.

١٦،٤٣ وَٱسْتَحْلَى أَبُو زَيْدٍ تَرَاجُعَ السُّؤَالِ وَالْجَوَابِ. وَالتَّكَايُلَ مِنْ هٰذَا الْجِرَابِ. وَلَمَحَ الْغُلَامُ أَنَّ الشَّوْطَ بَطِينٌ. وَالشَّيْخَ شُوَيْطِينٌ.[٣] فَقَالَ لَهُ حَسْبُكَ يَا شَيْخُ فَقَدْ عَرَفْتُ فَنَّكَ. وَٱسْتَبَنْتُ أَنَّكَ. فَخُذِ الْجَوَابَ صُبْرَةً. وَٱكْتَفِ بِهِ خِبْرَةً. أَمَّا بِهٰذَا الْمَكَانِ فَلَا يُشْتَرَى الشِّعْرُ بِشَعِيرَةٍ. وَلَا النَّثْرُ بِنُثَارَةٍ. وَلَا الْقِصَصُ بِقُصَاصَةٍ. وَلَا الرِّسَالَةُ بِغُسَالَةٍ. وَلَا حِكَمُ[٤] لُقْمَانَ بِلُقْمَةٍ. وَلَا أَخْبَارُ الْمَلَاحِمِ بِلَحْمَةٍ. وَأَمَّا جِيلُ هٰذَا الزَّمَانِ فَمَا مِنْهُمْ مَنْ يَمِيحُ. إِذَا صِيغَ لَهُ الْمَدِيحُ. وَلَا مَنْ يُجِيزُ. إِذَا أُنْشِدَ[٥] لَهُ الْأَرَاجِيزُ. وَلَا مَنْ يُغِيثُ. إِذَا أَطْرَبَهُ[٦] الْحَدِيثُ. وَلَا مَنْ يَمِيرُ. وَلَوْ أَنَّهُ أَمِيرٌ. وَعِنْدَهُمْ أَنَّ مَثَلَ الْأَدِيبِ. كَالرَّبْعِ الْجَدِيبِ. إِنْ لَمْ تَجِدِ

١ و: سيصحّ. ٢ «العصيدة بالقصيدة»: س، ف، و: العَصائِدُ بِالقَصائِدِ. ٣ س: شُيَيْطِين. ٤ د: حُكْمُ.
٥ س، و: نُظِمَت. ٦ س، و: حين يطربه.

الرَّبْعَ دِيمَةٌ. لَمْ تَكُنْ لَهُ قِيمَةٌ. وَلَا دَانَتْهُ بَهِيمَةٌ. وَكَذَا الْأَدَبُ. إِنْ لَمْ يَعْضُدْهُ نَشَبٌ. فَدَرْسُهُ نَصَبٌ. وَحِزْبُهُ[١] حَصَبٌ. ثُمَّ انْسَدَرَ يَعْدُو. وَوَلَّى يَحْدُو. فَقَالَ لِي أَبُو زَيْدٍ أَعَلِمْتَ أَنَّ الْأَدَبَ قَدْ بَارَ. وَوَلَّتْ أَنْصَارُهُ الْأَدْبَارَ. فَبُؤْتُ لَهُ بِحُسْنِ الْبَصِيرَةِ. وَسَلَّمْتُ بِحُكْمِ الضَّرُورَةِ.

١٧،٤٣ فَقَالَ دَعْنَا الْآنَ مِنَ الْمِصَاعِ. وَخُضْ فِي حَدِيثِ الْقِصَاعِ. وَاعْلَمْ أَنَّ الْأَسْجَاعَ. لَا تُشْبِعُ مَنْ جَاعَ. فَمَا التَّدْبِيرُ فِيمَا يُمْسِكُ الرَّمَقَ. وَيُطْفِئُ الْحُرَقَ.[٢] فَقُلْتُ الْأَمْرُ إِلَيْكَ. وَالزِّمَامُ بِيَدَيْكَ. فَقَالَ أَرَى أَنْ تَرْهَنَ سَيْفَكَ. لِتُشْبِعَ جَوْفَكَ وَضَيْفَكَ. فَنَاوِلْنِيهِ وَأَقِمْ. لِأَنْقَلِبَ إِلَيْكَ بِمَا نَلْتَقِمْ.[٣] فَأَحْسَنْتُ بِهِ الظَّنَّ. وَقَلَّدْتُهُ السَّيْفَ وَالرَّهْنَ. فَمَا لَبِثَ أَنْ رَكِبَ النَّاقَةَ. وَرَفَضَ الصِّدْقَ وَالصَّدَاقَةَ. فَمَكَثْتُ مَلِيًّا أَتَرَقَّبُهُ. ثُمَّ نَهَضْتُ أَتَعَقَّبُهُ. فَكُنْتُ كَمَنْ ضَيَّعَ اللَّبَنَ فِي الصَّيْفِ. وَلَمْ أَلْقَهُ وَلَا السَّيْفَ.

١ ف: وخَزْنُهُ. ٢ د، ف: الحَرَق. ٣ و، د، ف: تلتقم.

الْمَقَامَةُ الرَّابِعَةُ وَالْأَرْبَعُونَ[1]

١،٤٤ حَكَى الْحَارِثُ بْنُ هَمَّامٍ قَالَ عَشَوْتُ فِي لَيْلَةٍ دَاجِيَةِ الظُّلَمِ. فَاحِمَةِ اللِّمَمِ. إِلَى نَارٍ تُضْرَمُ عَلَى عَلَمٍ. وَتُخْبِرُ عَنْ كَرَمٍ. وَكَانَتْ لَيْلَةً جَوُّهَا مَقْرُورٌ. وَجَيْبُهَا مَزْرُورٌ. وَنَجْمُهَا مَغْمُومٌ. وَغَيْمُهَا مَرْكُومٌ. وَأَنَا فِيهَا أَصْرَدُ مِنْ عَيْنِ الْحِرْبَاءِ. وَالْعَنْزِ الْجَرْبَاءِ. فَلَمْ أَزَلْ أَنُصُّ عَنْسِي. وَأَقُولُ طُوبَى لَكِ وَلِنَفْسِي. إِلَى أَنْ تَبَصَّرَ الْمُوقِدُ آلِي. وَتَبَيَّنَ إِرْقَالِي. فَانْحَدَرَ يَعْدُو الْجَمَزَى. وَيُنْشِدُ مُرْتَجِزًا.

٢،٤٤ حُيِّيتَ مِنْ خَابِطِ لَيْلٍ سَارِي   هَدَاهُ بَلْ أَهْدَاهُ ضَوْءُ النَّارِ
إِلَى رَحِيبِ الْبَاعِ رَحْبِ الدَّارِ   مُرَحِّبٍ بِالطَّارِقِ الْمُمْتَارِ
تَرْحَابَ جَعْدِ الْكَفِّ بِالدِّينَارِ   لَيْسَ بِمُزْوَرٍّ عَنِ الزُّوَّارِ
وَلَا بِمِعْتَامِ الْقِرَى مِنْخَارِ   إِذَا اقْشَعَرَّتْ تُرَبُ الْأَقْطَارِ
وَضَنَّتِ الْأَنْوَاءُ بِالْأَمْطَارِ   فَهْوَ عَلَى بُؤْسِ الزَّمَانِ الضَّارِي
جَمُّ الرَّمَادِ مُرْهَفُ الشِّفَارِ   لَمْ يَخْلُ فِي لَيْلٍ وَلَا نَهَارِ
مِنْ نَحْرِ وَارٍ وَاقْتِدَاحِ وَارِي

٣،٤٤ ثُمَّ تَلَقَّانِي بِمُحَيًّا حَيِيٍّ. وَصَافَحَنِي بِرَاحَةِ أَرْيَحِيٍّ. وَاقْتَادَنِي إِلَى بَيْتٍ عِشَارُهُ تَخُورُ. وَأَعْشَارُهُ تَفُورُ. وَوَلَائِدُهُ تَمُورُ. وَمَوَائِدُهُ تَدُورُ. وَبِأَكْسَارِهِ أَضْيَافٌ قَدْ جَلَبَهُمْ جَالِبِي. وَقَلَبُوا[2] فِي قَالَبِي. وَهُمْ يَجْتَنُونَ فَاكِهَةَ الشِّتَاءِ. وَيَمْرَحُونَ مَرَحَ ذَوِي الْفَتَاءِ. فَأَخَذْتُ مَأْخَذَهُمْ فِي الِاصْطِلَاءِ. وَوَجَدْتُ بِهِمْ وَجْدَ الثَّمِلِ

١ في د: الشَّتَوِيَّةُ وَتُعْرَفُ بِاللُّغْزِيَّةِ؛ وفي ف: وَتُعْرَفُ بِالشَّتَوِيَّةِ. ٢ ف: قُلِّبوا.

بِالطِّلَاءِ. وَلَمَّا أَنْ سَرَى الْحَصَرُ. وَٱنْسَرَى الْخَصَرُ. أُتِينَا بِمَوَائِدَ كَالْهَالَاتِ دَوْرًا. وَالرَّوْضَاتِ نَوْرًا. وَقَدْ شُحِنَّ بِأَطْعِمَةِ الْوَلَائِمِ. وَحُمِينَ مِنَ الْعَائِبِ وَاللَّائِمِ. فَرَفَضْنَا مَا قِيلَ فِي الْبِطْنَةِ. وَرَأَيْنَا الْإِمْعَانَ فِيهَا مِنَ الْفِطْنَةِ.

٤،٤٤ حَتَّى إِذَا ٱكْتَلْنَا بِصَاعِ الْحُطَمِ. وَأَشْفَيْنَا عَلَى خَطَرِ التُّخَمِ. تَعَاوَرْنَا مَشُوشَ الْغَمَرِ. ثُمَّ تَبَوَّأْنَا مَقَاعِدَ السَّمَرِ. وَأَخَذَ كُلٌّ[١] مِنَّا يَشُولُ بِلِسَانِهِ. وَيَنْشُرُ مَا فِي صِوَانِهِ. مَا عَدَا شَيْخًا مُشْتَهِبًا فَوْدَاهُ. مُخْلَوْلِقًا بُرْدَاهُ. فَإِنَّهُ رَبَضَ حَجْرَةً. وَأَوْسَعَنَا هُجْرَةً. فَغَاظَنَا تَجَنُّبُهُ. الْمُلْتَبِسُ مُوجِبُهُ. الْمَعْذُورُ فِيهِ مُؤَنِّبُهُ. إِلَّا أَنَّا أَلَنَّا لَهُ الْقَوْلَ. وَخَشِينَا فِي الْمَسْأَلَةِ الْعَوَلَ. وَكُلَّمَا رُمْنَا أَنْ يَفِيضَ كَمَا فِضْنَا. أَوْ يُفِيضَ فِي مَا أَفَضْنَا. أَعْرَضَ إِعْرَاضَ الْعِلْيَةِ عَنِ الْأَرْذَلِينَ. وَتَلَا ﴿إِنْ هٰذَا إِلَّا أَسَاطِيرُ الْأَوَّلِينَ﴾. ثُمَّ كَأَنَّ الْحَمِيَّةَ هَاجَتْهُ. وَالنَّفْسَ الْأَبِيَّةَ نَاجَتْهُ. فَدَلَفَ وَٱزْدَلَفَ. وَخَلَعَ الصَّلَفَ. وَبَذَلَ أَنْ يَتَلَافَى مَا سَلَفَ. ثُمَّ ٱسْتَرْعَى سَمْعَ السَّامِرِ. وَٱنْدَفَعَ كَالسَّيْلِ الْهَامِرِ. وَقَالَ

٥،٤٤ عِنْدِي أَعَاجِيبُ أَرْوِيهَا بِلَا كَذِبِ عَنِ الْعِيَانِ فَكَنُّونِي أَبَا الْعَجَبِ
رَأَيْتُ يَا قَوْمِ أَقْوَامًا غِذَاؤُهُمُ بَوْلُ الْعَجُوزِ وَمَا أَعْنِي ٱبْنَةَ الْعِنَبِ

بَوْلُ الْعَجُوزِ لَبَنُ الْبَقَرَةِ وَالْعَجُوزُ أَيْضًا مِنْ أَسْمَاءِ الْخَمْرِ.

وَمُسْنِتِينَ مِنَ الْأَعْرَابِ قُوتُهُمُ أَنْ يَشْتَوُوا خِرْقَةً تُغْنِي مِنَ السَّغَبِ

الْخِرْقَةُ الْقِطْعَةُ مِنَ الْجَرَادِ.

---

١ بعدها في ف: واحد.

وَقَـادِرِينَ مَتَى مَـا سَـاءَ صَـنْعُهُـمُ   أَوْ قَصَّرُوا فِيهِ قَالُوا الذَّنْبُ لِلْحَطَبِ

الْقَادِرُ الطَّابِخُ وَالْقَدِيرُ الْمَطْبُوخُ فِي الْقِدْرِ[١]

وَكَاتِبِـينَ وَمَـا خَطَّـتْ أَنَامِـلُهُـمُ   حَرْفًا وَلَا قَرَؤُوا مَا خُطَّ فِي الْكُتُبِ

الْكَاتِبُونَ الْخَرَّازُونَ يُقَالُ كَتَبَ السِّقَاءَ وَالْمَزَادَةَ إِذَا خَرَزَهُمَا وَكَتَبَ الْبَغْلَةَ وَالنَّاقَةَ إِذَا جَمَعَ بَيْنَ شُفْرَيْهَا[٢] وَخَاطَهُمَا[٣]

وَتَـابِعِينَ عُـقَـابًا فِي مَـسِيرِهِمُ   عَلَى تَكَمِّيهِمُ فِي الْبَيْضِ وَالْيَلَبِ

الْعُقَابُ الرَّايَةُ وَكَانَتْ رَايَةُ النَّبِيِّ صَلَّى اللهُ عَلَيْهِ وَسَلَّمَ تُسَمَّى الْعُقَابَ.

وَمُنْتَدِينَ ذَوِي نُبْلٍ بَدَتْ لَهُمُ   نَبِيلَةٌ فَـانْثَنَوْا مِنْهَا إِلَى الْهَرَبِ ٦،٤٤

النَّبِيلَةُ الْجِيفَةُ وَمِنْهُ تَنَبَّلَ الْبَعِيرُ[٤] إِذَا مَاتَ وَأَرْوَحَ.[٥]

وَعُصْبَةٌ لَمْ تَـرَ الْبَيْتَ الْعَتِيقَ وَقَدْ   حَجَّـتْ جُثِيًّا بِلَا شَكٍّ عَلَى الرُّكَبِ

وَمَعْنَى حَجَّتْ جُثِيًّا أَيْ غَلَبَتْ بِالْحُجَّةِ مُجَادِلِينَ جَاثِينَ عَلَى الرُّكَبِ وَجُثِيٌّ جَمْعُ جَاثٍ.

وَنِسْوَةٌ بَيْنَمَا[٦] أَدْلَجْنَ مِنْ حَـلَبٍ   صَبَّحْنَ كَاظِـمَةً مِنْ غَيْرِ مَا تَعَبِ

---

١ وردت هذه البيت وشرحها في هامش ق مع علامة تدل على وجوب إدخالها بعد كلمة «الجراد» ثم جاءت مشطوبة في الورقة التالية بعد كلمة «اللبن» وهي موضعها في س، و؛ وفي د جاءت بعد «خاطهما»، وفي ف وردت في موضعها الصحيح على ما أثبتنا هاهنا. وفي س، و، د، وشرح ف: القادر الطابخ في القدر والقدير المطبوخ فيها. ٢ في د: شفرتيها. ٣ «وَكَتَبَ البَغْلَةَ والنَّاقَةَ إِذَا جَمَعَ بَيْنَ شُفْرِيها وَخَاطَهُمَا»: في هامش ق، وناقص في س، و. ٤ في ف: الأمير. ٥ الشرح ناقص في د، وبعدها في ف: يعني نتن. ٦ في ف: بَعْدَمَا.

كَاظِمَةُ فِي هٰذَا الْمَوْضِعِ مِنْ كَظْمِ الْغَيْظِ.

وَمُدْلِجِينَ سَرَوْا مِنْ أَرْضِ كَاظِمَةٍ   وَأَصْبَحُوا[1] حِينَ لَاحَ الصُّبْحُ فِي حَلَبِ

أَيْ أَصْبَحُوا يَحْلِبُونَ اللَّبَنَ.

وَيَافِعًا لَمْ يُلَامِسْ قَطُّ غَانِيَةً   شَاهَدْتُهُ وَلَهُ نَسْلٌ مِنَ الْعَقِبِ[2]

النَّسْلُ هَاهُنَا الْعَدْوُ وَمِنْهُ قَوْلُهُ تَعَالَى ﴿مِنْ كُلِّ حَدَبٍ يَنْسِلُونَ﴾ وَالعَقِبُ مُؤَخَّرُ الْقَدَمِ.

٧،٤٤ وَشَائِبًا غَيْرَ مُخْفٍ لِلْمَشِيبِ بَدَا   فِي الْبَدْوِ وَهْوَ فَتِيُّ السِّنِّ لَمْ يَشِبِ

الشَّائِبُ هَاهُنَا مَازِجُ اللَّبَنِ وَالْمَشِيبُ اللَّبَنُ الْمَمْزُوجُ يُقَالُ فِيهِ مَشُوبٌ وَمَشِيبٌ.

وَمُرْضَعًا بِلِبَانٍ لَمْ يَفُهْ فَمُهُ   رَأَيْتُهُ فِي شِجَارٍ بَيْنَ السَّبَبِ

الشِّجَارُ الْمِحَفَّةُ مَا لَمْ تَكُنْ مُظَلَّلَةً فَإِنْ ظُلِّلَتْ فَهُوَ الْهَوْدَجُ. وَالسَّبَبُ هَاهُنَا الْحَبْلُ وَمِنْهُ قَوْلُهُ تَعَالَى ﴿فَلْيَمْدُدْ بِسَبَبٍ إِلَى السَّمَاءِ﴾

وَزَارِعًا ذُرَّةً حَتَّى إِذَا حُصِدَتْ   صَارَتْ غُبَيْرَاءَ يَهْوَاهَا أَخُو الطَّرَبِ

الْغُبَيْرَاءُ الْمُسْكِرُ[3] الْمُتَّخَذُ مِنَ الذُّرَّةِ وَفِي الْحَدِيثِ «إِيَّاكُمْ وَالْغُبَيْرَاءَ فَإِنَّهَا خَمْرُ الْعَالَمِ» وَتُسَمَّى السُّكُرْكَةَ أَيْضًا.

---

١ في ف: فَأَصْبَحُوا. ٢ بعدها في د: اليَافِعُ الَّذِي قَدْ تَرَعْرَعَ وَنَاهَزَ البُلُوغَ وَ. ٣ س، د: السَّكَر.

وَرَاكِضًا[1] وَهْوَ مَغْلُولٌ عَلَى فَرَسٍ   قَدْ غُلَّ أَيْضًا وَمَا يَنْفَكُّ عَنْ خَبَبِ

الْمَغْلُولُ هَاهُنَا الْعَطْشَانُ وَغُلَّ أَيْ عَطِشَ.

وَذَا يَدٍ طُلُقٍ يَقْتَادُ رَاحِلَةً   مُسْتَعْجِلًا وَهْوَ مَأْسُورٌ أَخُو كُرَبِ

الْمَأْسُورُ الَّذِي يَجِدُ الْأُسْرَ[2] وَهْوَ ٱحْتِبَاسُ الْبَوْلِ

وَجَالِسًا مَاشِيًا تَهْوِي مَطِيَّتُهُ   بِهِ وَمَا فِي الَّذِي أَوْرَدْتُ مِنْ رِيَبِ ٨،٤٤

الْجَالِسُ الْآتِي نَجْدًا وَالْمَاشِي الَّذِي كَثُرَتْ مَاشِيَتُهُ وَعَلَيْهِ فَسَّرَ بَعْضُهُمْ قَوْلَ اللّٰهِ تَعَالَى ﴿أَنِ ٱمْشُوا﴾ كَأَنَّهُ دُعَاءٌ لَهُمْ بِالنَّمَاءِ وَكَثْرَةِ الْمَاشِيَةِ.

وَحَائِكًا أَجْذَمَ الْكَفَّيْنِ ذَا خَرَسٍ   فَإِنْ عَجِبْتُمْ فَكَمْ فِي الْخَلْقِ مِنْ عَجَبِ

الْحَائِكُ هَاهُنَا الَّذِي إِذَا مَشَى حَرَّكَ مَنْكِبَيْهِ وَفَحَّجَ بَيْنَ رُكْبَتَيْهِ.[3]

وَذَا شَطَاطٍ كَصَدْرِ الرُّمْحِ قَامَتُهُ   صَادَفْتُهُ بِمِنًى يَشْكُو مِنَ الْحَدَبِ

الْحَدَبُ مَا ٱرْتَفَعَ مِنَ الْأَرْضِ.

وَسَاعِيًا فِي مَسَرَّاتِ الْأَنَامِ يَرَى   إِفْرَاحَهُمْ مَأْثَمًا كَالظُّلْمِ وَالْكَذِبِ

إِفْرَاحُهُمْ إِثْقَالُهُمْ بِالدَّيْنِ وَمِنْهُ قَوْلُهُ عَلَيْهِ السَّلَامُ «لَا يُتْرَكُ فِي الْإِسْلَامِ مُفْرَحٌ».[4]

---

١ ف: وراكِبًا. ٢ د: الأَسر. ٣ . بعدها في س، د: وَصَادِعًا بِالقَنَا مِنْ غَيْرِ أَنْ عَلِقَت كَفَّاهُ يَوْمًا بِرُمْحٍ لَا وَلَمْ يَثِبِ. القَنَا ٱرْتِفَاعُ الأَنْفِ وَتَحَدُّبُ وَسَطِهِ وَصَدَعَ بِهِ أَيْ كَشَفَهُ، وهي سوف ترد لاحقا في ق، و، ف. ٤ بعدها في د: أي مُثْقَل؛ وفي ف: أي مُثْقَل من الدين أو يُقْضَى عنه دينه.

وَمُغْرَمًا بِمُنَاجَاةِ الرِّجَالِ لَهُ   وَمَا لَهُ فِي حَدِيثِ الْخَلْقِ مِنْ أَرَبِ

الْخَلْقُ هَاهُنَا الْكِذْبُ وَمِنْهُ قَوْلُهُ تَعَالَى ﴿إِنْ هٰذَا إِلَّا خَلْقُ الْأَوَّلِينَ﴾ .

٩،٤٤ وَذَا ذِمَامٍ وَفَتْ بِالْعَهْدِ ذِمَّتُهُ   وَلَا ذِمَامَ لَهُ فِي مَذْهَبِ الْعَرَبِ

الذِّمَامُ[١] الثَّانِي جَمْعُ ذِمَّةٍ وَهِيَ الْبِئْرُ الْقَلِيلَةُ الْمَاءِ وَعَنَى بِالْمَذْهَبِ الْمَسْلَكَ أَيْ مَا لَهُ آبَارٌ قَلِيلَةُ الْمَاءِ بِالْبَدْوِ.[٢]

وَذَا قُوًى مَا ٱسْتَبَانَتْ قَطُّ لِينَتُهُ   وَلِينُهُ مُسْتَبِينٌ غَيْرُ مُحْتَجِبِ

اللِّينُ النَّخْلُ الدَّقَلُ وَمِنْهُ قَوْلُهُ تَعَالَى ﴿مَا قَطَعْتُمْ مِّنْ لِينَةٍ﴾ .

وَسَاجِدًا فَوْقَ فَحْلٍ غَيْرَ مُكْتَرِثٍ   بِمَا أَتَى بَلْ يَرَاهُ أَفْضَلَ الْقُرَبِ

الْفَحْلُ الْحَصِيرُ الْمُتَّخَذُ مِنْ فُحَّالِ النَّخْلِ.

وَعَاذِرًا مُؤْلِمًا مَنْ ظَلَّ يَعْذِرُهُ   مَعَ التَّلَطُّفِ وَالْمَعْذُورُ فِي صَخَبِ

الْعَاذِرُ الْخَاتِنُ وَالْمَعْذُورُ الْمَخْتُونُ.

وَبَلْدَةً مَا بِهَا مَاءٌ لِمُغْتَرِفٍ   وَالْمَاءُ يَجْرِي عَلَيْهَا جَرْيَ مُنْسَرِبِ

الْبَلْدَةُ الْفُرْجَةُ بَيْنَ الْحَاجِبَيْنِ وَتُسَمَّى أَيْضًا الْبُلْجَةَ.

١٠،٤٤ وَقَرْيَةً دُونَ أُفْحُوصِ الْقَطَا شُحِنَتْ   بِدَيْلَمٍ عَيْشُهُمْ مِنْ خُلْسَةِ السَّلَبِ

---

١ بعدها في د: الأَوَّلُ العَهْدُ و. ٢ مَا لَهُ آبَارٌ قَلِيلَةُ المَاءِ بِالبَدْوِ»: في د: مَا لَهُ فِي البَدْوِ آبَارٌ قَلِيلَةُ المَاءِ.

الْقَرْيَةُ بَيْتُ النَّمْلِ وَالدَّيْلَمُ النَّمْلُ الْكَثِيرُ.

وَكَوْكَبًا يَتَوَارَى عِنْدَ رُؤْيَتِهِ الْـإِنْسَانُ حَتَّى يُرَى فِي أَمْنَعِ الْحُجُبِ

الْكَوْكَبُ النُّكْتَةُ مِنَ الْبَيَاضِ الَّتِي تَحْدُثُ فِي الْعَيْنِ وَالْإِنْسَانُ هَاهُنَا إِنْسَانُ الْعَيْنِ.

وَرَوْثَةً قُوِّمَتْ مَالاً لَهُ خَطَرٌ وَنَفْسُ صَاحِبِهَا بِالْمَالِ لَمْ تَطِبِ

الرَّوْثَةُ مُقَدَّمُ الْأَنْفِ.

وَصَحْفَةً مِنْ نُضَارٍ خَالِصٍ شُرِيَتْ بَعْدَ الْمِكَاسِ بِقِيرَاطٍ مِنَ الذَّهَبِ

النُّضَارُ هَاهُنَا شَجَرُ النَّبْعِ وَقَوْلُ بَعْضِ التَّابِعِينَ لَا بَأْسَ بِأَنْ يُشْرَبَ فِي قَدَحِ النُّضَارِ عَنَى بِهِ هٰذَا.[١]

وَمُسْتَجِيشًا بِخَشْخَاشٍ لِيَدْفَعَ مَا أَظَلَّهُ مِنْ أَعَادِيهِ فَلَمْ يَخِبِ

الْخَشْخَاشُ الْجَمَاعَةُ عَلَيْهِمْ دُرُوعٌ وَأَسْلِحَةٌ.

وَطَالَمَا مَرَّ بِي كَلْبٌ وَفِي فَمِهِ ثَوْرٌ وَلٰكِنَّهُ ثَوْرٌ بِلَا ذَنَبِ[٢] ١١،٤٤

الثَّوْرُ الْقِطْعَةُ مِنَ الْأَقِطِ.

وَكَمْ رَأَى نَاظِرِي فِيلاً عَلَى جَمَلٍ وَقَدْ تَوَرَّكَ فَوْقَ الرَّحْلِ وَالْقَتَبِ

---

١ «وَقَوْلُ بَعْضِ التَّابِعِينَ لَا بَأْسَ بِأَنْ يُشْرَبَ فِي قَدَحِ النُّضَارِ عَنَى بِهِ هٰذا»: في س: وفي حديث إِبْرَاهِيمَ النَّخَعِيِّ لا بَأْسَ بِأَنْ يُشْرَبَ فِي قَدَحِ النُّضَارِ؛ وفي و، ف: ومنه قول إِبْرَاهِيمَ النَّخَعِيِّ لا بَأْس بِأَنْ يُشْرَبَ فِي قَدَحِ النُّضَارِ عَنَى بِهِ هٰذا؛ وفي د: وَإِيَّاهُ عَنَى إِبْرَاهِيمَ النَّخَعِيِّ بقوله لَا بَأْسَ بِأَنْ يُشْرَبَ فِي قَدَحِ النُّضَارِ. ٢ في س، و، د: غَنَبِ.

الْفِيلُ الرَّجُلُ الْفَائِلُ الرَّأْيِ.

وَعَايَنَتْ[١] مُقْلَتِي عَيْنَيْنِ مَاؤُهُمَا   يَجْرِي مِنَ الْغَرْبِ وَالْعَيْنَانِ فِي حَلَبِ

الْغَرْبُ مَجْرَى الدَّمْعِ وَالْعَيْنَانِ هَاهُنَا الْمُقْلَتَانِ.[٢]

وَكَمْ لَقِيتُ بِعُرْضِ الْبِيدِ مُشْتَكِيًا   وَمَا ٱشْتَكَى قَطُّ فِي جِدٍّ وَلَا لَعِبِ

الْمُشْتَكِي الْمُتَّخِذُ شَكْوَةً وَهِيَ الْقِرْبَةُ الصَّغِيرَةُ.

وَكُنْتُ أَبْصَرْتُ كَرَّازًا لِرَاعِيَةٍ   بِالدَّوِّ يَنْظُرُ مِنْ عَيْنَيْنِ كَالشُّهُبِ

الْكَرَّازُ الْكَبْشُ الَّذِي يَحْمِلُ عَلَيْهِ الرَّاعِي أَدَاتَهُ.

١٢،٤٤ وَصَادِعًا بِالْقَنَا مِنْ غَيْرِ أَنْ عَلِقَتْ   كَفَّاهُ يَوْمًا بِرُمْحٍ لَا وَلَمْ يَثِبِ

الْقَنَا ٱرْتِفَاعُ الْأَنْفِ وَتَحَدُّبُ وَسَطِهِ وَصَدَعَ بِهِ أَيْ كَشَفَهُ.[٣]

وَكَمْ نَزَلْتُ بِأَرْضٍ لَا نَخِيلَ بِهَا   وَبَعْدَ يَوْمٍ رَأَيْتُ الْبُسْرَ فِي الْقُلُبِ

الْبُسْرُ جَمْعُ بُسْرَةٍ وَهِيَ الْمَاءُ الْحَدِيثُ الْعَهْدِ بِالْمَطَرِ وَالْقُلُبُ جَمْعُ قَلِيبٍ.

وَكَمْ رَأَيْتُ بِأَقْطَارِ الْفَلَا طَبَقًا   يَطِيرُ فِي الْجَوِّ مُنْصَبًّا إِلَى صَبَبِ

الطَّبَقُ الْقِطْعَةُ مِنَ الْجَرَادِ.

١ في هامش ق، وفي د، ف: وَكَمْ رَأَتْ مُقْلَتِي؛ وفي و، ف استبدل مكانها بالبيت التي تليها بيتَيْن. ٢ بعدها ف و،د: وَحَلَبُ البَلْدَةُ المَعْرُوفَةُ. ٣ وردت البيت وشرحها آنفا في س،د.

وَكَمْ مَشَايِخَ فِي الدُّنْيَا رَأَيْتُهُمُ   مُخَلَّدِينَ وَمَنْ يَنْجُو مِنَ الْعَطَبِ

الْمُخَلَّدُ الَّذِي أَبْطَأَ شَيْبُهُ.

وَكَمْ بَدَا لِي وَحْشٌ يَشْتَكِي سَغَبًا   بِمَنْطِقٍ ذَلِقٍ أَمْضَى مِنَ الْقُضُبِ

الْوَحْشُ الرَّجُلُ الْجَائِعُ.

١٣،٤٤ وَكَمْ دَعَانِي مُسْتَنْجٍ فَحَادَثَنِي   وَمَا أَخَلَّ وَلَا أَخْلَلْتُ بِالْأَدَبِ

الْمُسْتَنْجِي الْجَالِسُ عَلَى نَجْوَةٍ وَهِيَ الْمَكَانُ الْمُرْتَفِعُ.

وَكَمْ أَنَخْتُ قَلُوصِي تَحْتَ جُنْبُذَةٍ   تُظِلُّ مَا شِئْتَ مِنْ عُرُبٍ[1] وَمِنْ عُرُبِ

الْجُنْبُذَةُ الْقُبَّةُ وَالْعُرُبُ جَمْعُ عَرُوبٍ وَهِيَ[2] الْمُتَحَبِّبَةُ إِلَى زَوْجِهَا.[3]

وَكَمْ نَظَرْتُ إِلَى مَنْ سُرَّ سَاعَتَهُ   وَدَمْعُهُ مُسْتَهِلُّ الْقَطْرِ كَالسُّحُبِ

سُرَّ أَيْ قُطِعَ سِرَرُهُ وَسُرُّهُ[4] وَيُسَمَّى مَا يَبْقَى بَعْدَ الْقَطْعِ السُّرَّةَ

وَكَمْ رَأَيْتُ قَمِيصًا ضَرَّ صَاحِبَهُ   حَتَّى ٱنْثَنَى وَاهِيَ الْأَعْضَاءِ وَالْعَصَبِ

الْقَمِيصُ الدَّابَّةُ الْكَثِيرَةُ الْقِمَاصِ.[5]

وَكَمْ إِزَارٍ لَوَ أَنَّ الدَّهْرَ أَتْلَفَهُ   لَجَفَّ لِبْدُ حَثِيثِ السَّيْرِ مُضْطَرِبِ

١ ف: عُجْمِ. ٢ بعدها في هامش س وفي د: المرأة. ٣ جاءت بعدها مشطوبة في هامش س: ومن ذلك قوله تعالى ﴿عُرُبًا أَتْرَابًا﴾، وفي ف: من قوله تعالى ﴿عُرُبًا أَتْرَابًا﴾. ٤ وسُرُّه: سقطت من د، ف. ٥ بعدها في ف: وهو الوثوب والقفز.

الْإِزَارُ الْمَرْأَةُ وَمِنْهُ قَوْلُ الشَّاعِرِ فِدًى لَكَ مِنْ أَخِي ثِقَةٍ إِزَارِي.[1]

هٰـذَا وَكَمْ مِنْ أَفَـانِينٍ مُـعَجِّبَـةٍ عِنْدِي وَمِنْ مُلَحٍ تُلْهِي وَمِنْ نُخَبِ
فَإِنْ فَطِنْتُمْ لِلَحْنِ الْقَوْلِ بَـانَ لَكُمْ صِـدْقِي وَدَلَّكُمُ طَـلْعِي عَلَى رُطَبِي
وَإِنْ شُـدِهْتُمْ فَإِنَّ الْعَـارَ فِيهِ عَلَى مَنْ لَا يُمَيِّـزُ بَيْنَ الْعُودِ وَالْخَشَبِ

١٤،٤٤ قَالَ الْحَارِثُ بْنُ هَمَّامٍ فَطَفِقْنَا نَخْبُطُ فِي تَقْلِيبِ قَرِيضِهِ. وَتَأْوِيلِ مَعَارِيضِهِ. وَهُوَ يَلْهُو بِنَا لَهْوَ الْخَلِيِّ بِالشَّجِي. وَيَقُولُ لَيْسَ بِعُشِّكِ فَادْرُجِي. إِلَى أَنْ تَعَسَّرَ النِّتَاجُ. وَاسْتَحْكَمَ الِارْتِتَاجُ. فَأَلْقَيْنَا إِلَيْهِ الْمَقَادَةَ. وَخَطَبْنَا مِنْهُ الْإِفَادَةَ. فَوَقَفَنَا بَيْنَ الطَّمَعِ وَالْيَأْسِ. وَقَالَ الْإِينَاسُ قَبْلَ الْإِبْسَاسِ. فَعَلِمْنَا أَنَّهُ مِمَّنْ يَرْغَبُ فِي الشُّكْمِ. وَيَرْتَشِي فِي الْحُكْمِ. وَسَاءَ أَبَا مَثْوَانَا أَنْ نُعَرَّضَ لِلْغُرْمِ. أَوْ نُخَيَّبَ بِالرَّغْمِ. فَأَحْضَرَ نَاقَةً عِيدِيَّةً. وَحُلَّةً سَعِيدِيَّةً. وَقَالَ لَهُ خُذْهُمَا حَلَالًا. وَلَا تَرْزَأْ أَضْيَافِي زِبَالًا. فَقَالَ أَشْهَدُ أَنَّهَا شِنْشِنَةٌ أَخْزَمِيَّةٌ. وَأَرْيَحِيَّةٌ حَاتِمِيَّةٌ. ثُمَّ قَابَلَنَا بِوَجْهٍ بِشْرُهُ يَشِفُّ. وَنَضْرَتُهُ تَرِفُّ. وَقَالَ يَا قَوْمِ إِنَّ اللَّيْلَ قَدِ اجْلَوَّذَ. وَالنُّعَاسَ قَدِ اسْتَحْوَذَ. فَافْزَعُوا إِلَى الْمَرَاقِدِ. وَاغْتَنِمُوا رَاحَةَ الرَّاقِدِ. لِتَشْرَبُوا نَشَاطًا. وَتُبْعَثُوا نِشَاطًا. فَتَعُوا مَا أُفَسِّرُ. وَيَتَسَهَّلَ لَكُمُ الْمُتَعَسِّرُ. فَاسْتَصْوَبَ كُلٌّ مَا رَآهُ. وَتَوَسَّدَ وِسَادَةَ كَرَاهُ.

١٥،٤٤ فَلَمَّا وَسِنَتِ الْأَجْفَانُ. وَأَغْفَتِ الضِّيفَانُ. وَثَبَ إِلَى النَّاقَةِ فَرَحَلَهَا. ثُمَّ ارْتَحَلَهَا وَرَحَّلَهَا. وَقَالَ مُخَاطِبًا لَهَا.

سَـرُوجَ يَـا نَـاقُ فَـسِيرِي وَخِدِي وَأَدْلِجِي وَأَوِّبِي وَأَسْئِدِي
حَتَّى تَطَا خُفَّاكِ مَرْعَاهَا النَّدِي فَتَـنْعَمِي حِينَئِذٍ وَتَسْـعَدِي

[1] بعدها في س: وقيل عنى نفسه؛ وفي و: وقيل عنى الشاعر نفسه.

إِيهٍ فَدَتْكِ النُّوقُ جِدِّي وَٱجْهَدِي وَتَـأْمَنِي أَنْ تُتْهِـمِي أَوْ تُنْجِـدِي
وَٱقْـتَنِعِي بِالتَّشَحِ عِنْـدَ الْمَوْرِدِ وَٱفْرِي أَدِيمَ فَدْفَـدٍ فَفَـدْفَـدِ
فَقَدْ حَلَفْتُ حَلْفَةَ الْمُجْتَهِدِ وَلَا تَحُطِّي دُونَ ذَاكَ الْمَقْصِدِ
إِنَّكِ إِنْ أَحْلَلْتِنِي فِي بَلَدِي بِحُرْمَةِ الْبَيْتِ الرَّفِيعِ الْعَمَدِ[1]
حَلَلْتِ مِنِّي بِمَحَلِّ الْوَلَدِ

قَالَ فَعَلِمْتُ أَنَّهُ السَّرُوجِيُّ الَّذِي إِذَا بَاعَ ٱنْبَاعَ. وَإِذَا مَلَأَ الصَّاعَ ٱنْصَاعَ. وَلَمَّا ٱنْبَلَجَ صَبَاحُ الْيَوْمِ. وَهَبَّ النُّوَّامُ مِنَ النَّوْمِ. أَعْلَمْتُهُمْ أَنَّ الشَّيْخَ حِينَ أَغْشَاهُمُ السُّبَاتَ. طَلَّقَهُمُ الْبَتَاتَ. وَرَكِبَ النَّاقَةَ وَفَاتَ. فَأَخَذَهُمْ مَا قَدُمَ وَمَا حَدُثَ. وَنَسُوا مَا طَابَ مِنْهُ بِمَا خَبُثَ. ثُمَّ ٱنْشَعَبْنَا فِي كُلِّ مَشْعَبٍ. وَذَهَبْنَا تَحْتَ كُلِّ كَوْكَبٍ.

١٦،٤٤ قَالَ الْقَاسِمُ[2] بْنُ عَلِيٍّ[3] قَدْ فَسَّرْتُ سِرَّ كُلِّ لُغْزٍ تَحْتَهُ وَلَمْ أُبْعِدْ عَلَى مَنْ يَقْرَأُهُ كَشْفَهُ وَقَدْ بَقِيَتْ أَلْفَاظٌ اشْتَمَلَتْ عَلَيْهَا[4] هٰذِهِ الْمَقَامَةُ رُبَّمَا الْتَبَسَ تَفْسِيرُهَا عَلَى بَعْضِ مَنْ تَقَعُ إِلَيْهِ[5] فَأَحْبَبْتُ إِيضَاحَهَا[6] لَهُ لِيُكْفَى حَيْرَةَ الشُّبْهَةِ وَكُلْفَةَ الْفِكْرَةِ وَوَصْمَةَ الْبَحْثِ وَالْمَسْأَلَةِ وَبِاللهِ تَعَالَى الِاسْتِعَانَةُ وَالْقُوَّةُ. قَوْلُهُ عَشَوْتُ إِلَى نَارٍ يَعْنِي تَنَوَّرْتُهَا فَقَصَدْتُهَا فَإِنْ لَمْ تَقْصِدْهَا قُلْتَ عَشَوْتُ عَنْهَا كَقَوْلِهِ تَعَالَى ﴿وَمَنْ يَعْشُ عَنْ ذِكْرِ الرَّحْمٰنِ نُقَيِّضْ لَهُ شَيْطَانًا﴾ أَيْ مَنْ يُعْرِضْ وَقَوْلُهُ وَكُنْتُ[7]

١ ف: العُمُدِ. ٢ . و: الشيخ الإمام أبو القاسم، وفي د: الشيخ الرئيس أبو محمد القاسم. ٣ بعدها في و: الحريري رحمه الله تعالى، وفي د: رضي الله عنه، وفي ف: رحمه الله تعالى. ٤ اشتملت عليها: في و: احتضنتها. ٥ و: يقع إليه. ٦ في متن ق: تفسيرها، وفوقها «إيضاحها»، وهو المثبت في سائر الأصول. ٧ هكذا في ق، س، و، على حلاف نص المقامة، وفي د: وأنا فيها؛ وفي ف: وأنا.

أَصْرَدَ مِنْ عَيْنِ الْحِرْبَاءِ وَالْعَنْزِ الْجَرْبَاءِ هٰذَانِ مَثَلَانِ يُضْرَبَانِ لِمَنْ يَبْلُغُ مِنْهُ الْبَرْدُ وَذٰلِكَ لِأَنَّ الْحِرْبَاءَ تَدُورُ أَبَدًا مَعَ الشَّمْسِ وَتَسْتَقْبِلُهَا بِعَيْنِهَا[1] وَالْعَنْزُ الْجَرْبَاءُ لَا تَدْفَأُ فِي الشِّتَاءِ لِقِلَّةِ شَعْرِهَا وَذَكَرَ بَعْضُهُمْ أَنَّ الْعَنْزَ الْجَرْبَاءَ تَصْحِيفُ الْمَثَلِ الْأَوَّلِ وَقَوْلُهُ نَحْرُ وَارٍ يَعْنِي[2] الْجَمَلَ الْمُكْتَنِزَ شَحْمًا الْكَثِيرَ[3] مُخًّا

١٧،٤٤ وَقَوْلُهُ عِشَارُهُ تَخُورُ وَأَعْشَارُهُ تَفُورُ الْعِشَارُ النُّوقُ الْحَوَامِلُ[4] وَالْأَعْشَارُ الْبُرْمَةُ الْعَظِيمَةُ كَأَنَّهَا شُعِّبَتْ لِعِظَمِهَا يُقَالُ بُرْمَةٌ أَعْشَارٌ وَجَفْنَةٌ أَكْسَارٌ وَثَوْبٌ أَسْمَالٌ وَبُرْدٌ أَخْلَاقٌ وَحَبْلٌ أَرْمَامٌ وَوَصْفُ الْجَمَاعَةِ مِنْهَا كَوَصْفِ الْوَاحِدِ وَقَوْلُهُ فَاكِهَةُ الشِّتَاءِ كَنَى بِهَا عَنِ النَّارِ وَمِنْهُ قَوْلُ بَعْضِ الْمُحْدَثِينَ

النَّارُ فَاكِهَةُ الشِّتَاءِ فَمَنْ يُرِدْ أَكْلَ الْفَوَاكِهِ شَاتِيًا فَلْيَصْطَلِ
إِنَّ الْفَوَاكِهَ فِي الشِّتَاءِ شَهِيَّةٌ وَالنَّارُ لِلْمَقْرُورِ أَفْضَلُ مَأْكَلِ

قَوْلُهُ مَوَائِدَ كَالْهَالَاتِ يَعْنِي دَارَاتِ الْقَمَرِ[5] وَدَارَةُ الشَّمْسِ تُسَمَّى الطُّفَاوَةَ وَقَوْلُهُ مَشُوشُ الْغَمَرِ يَعْنِي الْمِنْدِيلَ يُقَالُ مَشَّ يَدَهُ بِالْمِنْدِيلِ أَيْ مَسَحَهَا وَمِنْهُ قَوْلُ ٱمْرِئِ الْقَيْسِ

نَمُشُّ بِأَعْرَافِ الْجِيَادِ أَكُفَّنَا إِذَا نَحْنُ قُمْنَا عَنْ شِوَاءٍ مُضَهَّبِ[6]

١ «تَدورُ أَبَدًا مَعَ الشَّمْسِ وتَسْتَقْبِلُها بِعَيْنِها»: في و، د: يدور أبدا مع الشمس ويستقبلها بعينه؛ وبعدها في هامش س، وفي و، د، ف: ولذلك شبَّه ابن الرومي الرقيب بالحرباء في قوله: / ما بالُها قد حُسِّنَتْ ورَقيبُها / أبدًا قبيحٌ قُبِّحَ الرُّقَبَاءُ // ما ذاك إلّا انها شَمْسُ الضُّحَى / أبدًا يكونُ رَقيبَها الحِرْباءُ //. ٢ بعدها في س: بالواري. ٣ شحما الكثير: ساقط من و. ٤ بعدها في س، و، د: واحدتها عُشَرَاءُ وهي التي أتى عليها في الحَمْلِ عَشَرَةُ أَشْهُرٍ ثم لا يزال ذلك اسمَها حتى تَضَعَ وبعد ما تضع («وبعد ما تضع» ساقطة من د). ٥ بعدها في س، و: واحدتها هالة؛ وفي د: واحدها هالة. ٦ بعدها في و: وقيل المش المسح بالشيء الخشن.

وَقَوْلُهُ مُشْتَبِهًا فَوْدَاهُ أَيْ صَارَا مِنَ الشَّيْبِ فِي لَوْنِ الْأَشْهَبِ وَمِنْهُ قَوْلُ امْرِئِ الْقَيْسِ أَيْضًا

قَالَتِ الْخَنْسَاءُ لَمَّا جِئْتُهَا   شَابَ بَعْدِي رَأْسُ هٰذَا وَاشْتَهَبْ[١]

١٨،٤٤ وَقَوْلُهُ رَبَضَ حَجْرَةً يَعْنِي نَاحِيَةً وَيُقَالُ فِي الْمَثَلِ لِمَنْ يُشَارِكُ فِي الرَّجَاءِ وَيُجَانِبُ عِنْدَ الْبَلَاءِ يَرْتَعُ وَسَطًا وَيَرْبِضُ حَجْرَةً وَقَوْلُهُ فَاسْتَرْعَى سَمْعَ السَّامِرِ يَعْنِي السُّمَّارَ لِأَنَّ السَّامِرَ اسْمٌ لِلْجَمْعِ كَالْحَاضِرِ اسْمٌ لِلْحَيِّ النَّازِلِينَ عَلَى الْمَاءِ وَكَالْبَاقِرِ اسْمٌ لِجَمَاعَةِ الْبَقَرِ وَقَالَ بَعْضُ أَهْلِ اللُّغَةِ هُوَ اسْمٌ لِلْبَقَرِ مَعَ رُعَاتِهَا وَاشْتِقَاقُ السَّامِرِ مِنَ السَّمَرِ وَهُوَ ظِلُّ الْقَمَرِ مَأْخُوذٌ مِنَ السُّمْرَةِ فَلَمَّا كَانَ غَالِبُ أَحْوَالِ السُّمَّارِ أَنَّهُمْ يَتَحَدَّثُونَ فِي ظِلِّ الْقَمَرِ اشْتُقَّ لَهُمُ اسْمٌ مِنْهُ وَإِلَى هٰذَا يَرْجِعُ قَوْلُهُمْ لَا أُكَلِّمُهُ الْقَمَرَ وَالسَّمَرَ[٢] وَقَوْلُهُ لَيْسَ بِعُشِّكِ فَادْرُجِي هٰذَا مَثَلٌ يُضْرَبُ لِمَنْ يَتَعَاطَى مَا لَا يَنْبَغِي لَهُ وَالْعُشُّ مَا يَكُونُ فِي شَجَرَةٍ فَإِنْ كَانَ فِي حَائِطٍ أَوْ كَهْفِ جَبَلٍ فَهُوَ وَكْرٌ وَقَوْلُهُ الْإِينَاسُ قَبْلَ الْإِبْسَاسِ هٰذَا مَثَلٌ أَيْضًا وَمَعْنَاهُ أَنَّهُ يَنْبَغِي أَنْ يُؤْنَسَ الْإِنْسَانُ ثُمَّ يُكَلَّفُ[٣] وَأَصْلُهُ أَنَّ حَالِبَ النَّاقَةِ يُؤَنِّسُهَا حِينَ يَرُومُ حَلَبَهَا ثُمَّ يُبِسُّ بِهَا لِلْحَلَبِ وَالْإِبْسَاسُ أَنْ يَقُولَ لَهَا بُسْ بُسْ لِتَسْكُنَ وَتَدُرَّ[٤] وَإِذَا كَانَتِ النَّاقَةُ تَدُرُّ عَلَى الْإِبْسَاسِ سُمِّيَتِ الْبَسُوسَ[٥] وَقَوْلُهُ يَرْغَبُ فِي الشُّكْمِ وَالشُّكْمُ مَا أَعْطَيْتَهُ عَلَى سَبِيلِ الْمُجَازَاةِ فَإِنْ أَعْطَيْتَ[٦] مُبْتَدِئًا فَهُوَ الشُّكْدُ[٧]

---

١ في متن ق: أشهب، وهي مصححة في الهامش، وفي سائر الأصول ما أثبتناه. ٢ «القمر والسمر»: في و: السمر والقمر. ٣ د: يكلَّف. ٤ و: وتَدُرُّ. ٥ «وإذا كانَتْ . . . البَسوسَ»: في س، و، د، ف: وتُسَمَّى الناقةُ التي تَدُرُّ على الإبْساسِ البَسوسَ. ٦ و: تبرَّعتَ بالعَطاء. ٧ بعدها في هامش س: ومنه قول الراجز // شُكْمي عَتيدٌ وكذاكَ شُكْدي / للخَيْرِ والشَّرِّ بقاءٌ عِنْدي // فانظر اذا لمْ . . ؟ . . / فالأَرْضُ مَهْما استُودِعَتْ تُؤَدِّي؛ وفي و: ومنه قول الراجز / شُكْمي عَتيدٌ وكَذاكَ شُكْدي / للخَيْرِ والشَّرَّ بَقاءٌ عِنْدي / كَالأَرْضِ مَهْما استُودِعَتْ تُؤَدِّي.

١٩،٤٤ وَقَوْلُهُ سَاءَ أَبَا مَثْوَانَا يَعْنِي الْمُضِيفَ الَّذِي آوَوْا إِلَيْهِ وَثَوَوْا عِنْدَهُ وَقَوْلُهُ نَاقَةٌ عِيدِيَّةٌ قِيلَ إِنَّهَا مَنْسُوبَةٌ إِلَى فَحْلٍ مُنْجِبٍ ٱسْمُهُ عِيدٌ وَقِيلَ هِيَ مَنْسُوبَةٌ إِلَى فَخْذٍ مِنْ مَهْرَةَ اسْمُهُ عِيدٌ[1] وَكَانَتْ مَهْرَةُ وَعِيدٌ يَتَّخِذَانِ نَجَائِبَ الْإِبِلِ فَنُسِبَتْ إِلَيْهِمَا وَقَوْلُهُ حُلَّةً سَعِيدِيَّةً هِيَ مَنْسُوبَةٌ إِلَى سَعِيدِ بْنِ الْعَاصِ وَكَانَ رَسُولُ اللهِ صَلَّى اللهُ عَلَيْهِ وَسَلَّمَ كَسَاهُ وَهُوَ غُلَامٌ حُلَّةً فَنُسِبَ جِنْسُهَا إِلَيْهِ وَقَوْلُهُ لَا تَرْزَأُ أَضْيَافِي زِبَالًا أَيْ لَا تَرْزَأُهُمْ شَيْئًا وَإِنْ قَلَّ وَالْأَصْلُ فِي الزِّبَالِ مَا تَحْمِلُهُ النَّمْلَةُ بِفِيهَا وَقَوْلُهُ شِنْشِنَةٌ أَخْزَمِيَّةٌ أَشَارَ بِهِ إِلَى الْمَثَلِ الَّذِي ضَرَبَهُ جَدُّ حَاتِمِ بْنِ عَبْدِ اللهِ بْنِ سَعْدِ بْنِ الْحَشْرَجِ بْنِ أَخْزَمَ الطَّائِيِّ حِينَ نَشَأَ حَاتِمٌ وَتَقَيَّلَ أَخْلَاقَ جَدِّهِ أَخْزَمَ فِي الْجُودِ فَقَالَ شِنْشِنَةٌ أَعْرِفُهَا مِنْ أَخْزَمَ وَتَمَثَّلَ عَقِيلُ بْنُ عُلَّفَةَ بِهِ حِينَ قَالَ

إِنَّ بَنِيَّ ضَرَّجُونِي بِالدَّمِ ... مَنْ يَلْقَ آسَادَ الرِّجَالِ يُكْلَمِ
شِنْشِنَةٌ أَعْرِفُهَا مِنْ أَخْزَمِ

وَمَنِ ادَّعَى أَنَّ الْمَثَلَ لَهُ فَقَدْ سَهَا فِيهِ

٢٠،٤٤ وَقَوْلُهُ اِجْلَوَّذَ أَيْ أَسْرَعَ فِي الذَّهَابِ وَمِثْلُهُ اخْرَوَّطَ وَقَوْلُهُ وَثَبَ إِلَى النَّاقَةِ فَرَحَلَهَا يَعْنِي شَدَّ عَلَيْهَا الرَّحْلَ وَبِهِ سُمِّيَتِ الرَّاحِلَةُ لِأَنَّهَا فَاعِلَةٌ بِمَعْنَى مَفْعُولَةٍ كَقَوْلِهِ تَعَالَى ﴿مِنْ مَاءٍ دَافِقٍ﴾ أَيْ مَدْفُوقٍ[2] وَالرَّاحِلَةُ تَقَعُ عَلَى النَّاقَةِ وَالْجَمَلِ وَدُخُولُ الْهَاءِ فِيهَا لِلْمُبَالَغَةِ مِثْلَ دَاهِيَةٍ وَرَاوِيَةٍ وَقَوْلُهُ ارْتَحَلَهَا أَيْ رَكِبَهَا وَفِي الْحَدِيثِ إِنَّ النَّبِيَّ صَلَّى اللهُ عَلَيْهِ وَسَلَّمَ سَجَدَ فَرَكِبَهُ الْحَسَنُ عَلَيْهِ السَّلَامُ فَأَبْطَأَ فِي

---

١ بعدها في هامش س، وفي و: يقالُ لهم بنو عيد بن الآمري على وزن العامري بن مهرة. ٢ . في هامش ق: ﴿فِي عِيشَةٍ راضِيَةٍ﴾ مرضية، وفي هامش س: كقوله تعالى ﴿فِي عِيشَةٍ راضِيَةٍ﴾ أي مرضية، وفي و، ف: كقوله تعالى ﴿فِي عِيشَةٍ راضِيَةٍ﴾ أي مرضية وقوله سبحانه ﴿مِنْ مَاءٍ دافِقٍ﴾ أي مدفوق، وفي د: كقوله تعالى ﴿فِي عِيشَةٍ راضِيَةٍ﴾ أي مرضية و﴿مِنْ مَاءٍ دافِقٍ﴾ أي مدفوق.

سُجُودِهِ فَلَمَّا قَضَى صَلَاتَهُ قَالَ إِنَّ ابْنِي ٱرْتَحَلَنِي فَكَرِهْتُ أَنْ أُعْجِلَهُ وَقَوْلُهُ وَرَحَّلَهَا أَيْ أَزْعَجَهَا وَأَشْخَصَهَا وَأَجَدَّ بِهَا فِي الرَّحِيلِ وَمِنْهُ الْخَبَرُ تَخْرُجُ عِنْدَ اقْتِرَابِ السَّاعَةِ نَارٌ مِنْ قَعْرِ عَدَنَ تُرَحِّلُ النَّاسَ.

وَقَوْلُهُ فَأَدْلِجِي وَأَوِّبِي وَأَسْئِدِي الْإِدْلَاجُ أَنْ تَسِيرَ اللَّيْلَ كُلَّهُ وَالِاسْمُ مِنْهُ الدَّلْجَةُ ٢١،٤٤
بِفَتْحِ الدَّالِ وَالِادِّلَاجُ بِالتَّشْدِيدِ أَنْ تَسِيرَ مِنْ آخِرِهِ وَالِاسْمُ مِنْهُ الدُّلْجَةُ بِضَمِّ الدَّالِ وَقِيلَ إِنَّ الدُّلْجَةَ بِفَتْحِ الدَّالِ وَضَمِّهَا بِمَعْنًى[١] وَالتَّأْوِيبُ سَيْرُ النَّهَارِ وَحْدَهُ وَالْإِسَادُ أَنْ تَسِيرَ لَيْلًا وَنَهَارًا وَالنَّشْحُ أَنْ تَشْرَبَ دُونَ الرِّيِّ وَقَوْلُهُ فَأَخَذَهُمْ مَا قَدُمَ وَمَا حَدُثَ يُقَالُ ذٰلِكَ لِمَنْ يَسْتَوْلِي عَلَيْهِ الْهَمُّ[٢] وَالدَّالُ مِنْ حدث تُضَمُّ فِي هٰذَا الْمَوْضِعِ وَحْدَهُ لِتُوَافِقَ لَفْظَ قَدُمَ فَإِنْ أُفْرِدَ حدث عَنْ قَدُمَ وَجَبَ فَتْحُ الدَّالِ مِنْ حدث وَمِثْلُهُ قَوْلُهُمْ[٣] هَنَأَنِي[٤] وَمَرَأَنِي بِحَذْفِ الْأَلِفِ مِنْ مَرَأَنِي إِذَا ذُكِرَ مَعَ هَنَأَنِي فَإِنْ أَفْرَدْتَهُ وَجَبَ أَنْ تَقُولَ أَمْرَأَنِي الشَّيْءُ[٥] وَقَوْلُهُ ذَهَبْنَا تَحْتَ كُلِّ كَوْكَبٍ هٰذَا الْمَثَلُ يُضْرَبُ لِمَنْ تَخْتَلِفُ فِي السَّفَرِ طُرُقُهُمْ وَتَتَبَايَنُ سُبُلُهُمْ.

١ . بعدها في د: واحدٍ. ٢ «يستولي عليه الهم»: في د: تَستولي الهُموم عليه وتَتلاعَب. ٣ ق: قوله.
٤ بعدها في س، و: الشَّيْءُ. ٥ بعدها في س، و، د: وكذلك يقولون رِجْسٌ نِجْسٌ فيَكْسِرونَ النُّونَ مِنْ نَجَسٍ ويُسْكِنونَ الجيمَ لِيُزاوِجَ لَفْظَةَ رِجْسٍ فإنْ أُفْرِدَ قيلَ نَجَسٌ بِفَتْحِ النُّونِ والجيمِ كما قال الله تعالى ﴿إِنَّمَا الْمُشْرِكُونَ نَجَسٌ﴾ .

الْمَقَامَةُ الْخَامِسَةُ وَالْأَرْبَعُونَ[1]

١،٤٥ حَكَى الْحَارِثُ بْنُ هَمَّامٍ قَالَ كُنْتُ أَخَذْتُ عَنْ أُولِي التَّجَارِيبِ. أَنَّ السَّفَرَ مِرْآةُ الْأَعَاجِيبِ. فَلَمْ أَزَلْ أَجُوبُ كُلَّ تَنُوفَةٍ. وَأَقْتَحِمُ كُلَّ مَخُوفَةٍ. حَتَّى ٱجْتَلَيْتُ[2] كُلَّ أُطْرُوفَةٍ. فَمِنْ أَحْسَنِ مَا لَمَحْتُهُ. وَأَغْرَبِ مَا ٱسْتَمْلَحْتُهُ. أَنِّي[3] حَضَرْتُ قَاضِيَ الرَّمْلَةِ. وَكَانَ مِنْ أَرْبَابِ الدَّوْلَةِ وَالصَّوْلَةِ. وَقَدْ تَرَافَعَ إِلَيْهِ بَالٍ فِي بَالٍ. وَذَاتُ جَمَالٍ فِي أَسْمَالٍ. فَهَمَّ الشَّيْخُ بِالْكَلَامِ. وَتِبْيَانِ الْمَرَامِ. فَمَنَعَتْهُ الْفَتَاةُ مِنَ الْإِفْصَاحِ. وَخَسَأَتْهُ عَنِ النُّبَاحِ. ثُمَّ نَضَتْ عَنْهَا فَضْلَةَ الْوِشَاحِ. وَأَنْشَدَتْ بِلِسَانِ السَّلِيطَةِ الْوَقَاحِ.

٢،٤٥ يَا قَاضِيَ الرَّمْلَةِ يَا ذَا الَّذِي ... فِي يَدِهِ التَّمْرَةُ وَالْجَمْرَهْ
إِلَيْكَ أَشْكُو جَوْرَ بَعْلِي ٱلَّذِي ... لَمْ يَحْجُجِ الْبَيْتَ سِوَى مَرَّهْ
وَلَيْتَهُ لَمَّا قَضَى نُسْكَهُ ... وَخَفَّ ظَهْرًا إِذْ رَمَى الْجَمْرَهْ
كَانَ عَلَى رَأْيِ أَبِي يُوسُفٍ ... فِي صِلَةِ الْحَجَّةِ بِالْعُمْرَهْ
هٰذَا عَلَى أَنِّيَ مُذْ ضَمَّنِي ... إِلَيْهِ لَمْ أَعْصِ لَهُ أَمْرَهْ
فَمُرْهُ إِمَّا أُلْفَةً حُلْوَةً ... تُرْضِي وَإِمَّا فُرْقَةً مُرَّهْ
مِنْ قَبْلِ أَنْ أَخْلَعَ ثَوْبَ الْحَيَا ... فِي طَاعَةِ الشَّيْخِ أَبِي مُرَّهْ

٣،٤٥ فَقَالَ لَهُ الْقَاضِي قَدْ سَمِعْتَ بِمَا عَزَتْكَ إِلَيْهِ. وَتَوَعَّدَتْكَ عَلَيْهِ. فَجَانِبْ مَا عَرَّكَ. وَحَاذِرْ أَنْ تُفْرِكَ وَتُعْرَكَ. فَجَثَا الشَّيْخُ عَلَى ثَفِنَاتِهِ. وَفَجَّرَ يَنْبُوعَ نَفَثَاتِهِ. وَقَالَ

١ في هامش س: تُعْرَفُ بِالرَّمْلِيَّةِ؛ وفي د: الرَّمْلِيَّةُ؛ وفي ف: وَهِيَ الرَّمْلِيَّةُ. ٢ ف: اجتلبت. ٣ ف: أَنْ.

اِسْمَعْ عَدَاكَ الذَّمُّ قَوْلَ ٱمْرِئٍ يُوضِحُ فِيمَا رَابَهَا عُذْرَهْ
وَاللهِ مَا أَعْرَضْتُ عَنْهَا قِلًى وَلَا هَوَى قَلْبِي قَضَى نَذْرَهْ
وَإِنَّمَا الدَّهْرُ عَدَا صَرْفُهُ فَٱبْتَزَّنَا الدُّرَّةَ وَالذَّرَّهْ
فَمَنْزِلِي قَفْرٌ كَمَا جِيدُهَا عُطْلٌ مِنَ الْجَزْعَةِ وَالشَّذْرَهْ
وَكُنْتُ مِنْ قَبْلُ أَرَى فِي الْهَوَى وَدِينِهِ رَأْيَ بَنِي عُذْرَهْ
فَمُذْ نَبَا الدَّهْرُ هَجَرْتُ الدُّمَى هِجْرَانَ عَفٍّ آخِذٍ حِذْرَهْ
وَمِلْتُ عَنْ حَرْثِيَ لَا رَغْبَةً عَنْهُ وَلٰكِنْ أَتَّقِي بَذْرَهْ
فَلَا تَلُمْ مَنْ هٰذِهِ حَالُهُ وَٱعْطِفْ عَلَيْهِ وَٱحْتَمِلْ هَذْرَهْ

٤،٤٥ قَالَ فَٱلْتَظَتِ الْمَرْأَةُ مِنْ مَقَالِهِ. وَأَنْتَضَتِ الْحُجَجَ لِجِدَالِهِ. وَقَالَتْ لَهُ وَيْلَكَ يَا مَرْقَعَانُ. يَا مَنْ هُوَ لَا طَعَامٌ وَلَا طِعَانٌ. أَتَضِيقُ بِالْوَلَدِ ذَرْعًا. وَلِكُلِّ أَكُولَةٍ مَرْعًى. لَقَدْ ضَلَّ فَهْمُكَ. وَأَخْطَأَ سَهْمُكَ. وَسَفِهَتْ نَفْسُكَ. وَشَقِيَتْ بِكِ عِرْسُكَ. فَقَالَ لَهَا الْقَاضِي أَمَّا أَنْتِ فَلَوْ جَادَلْتِ الْخَنْسَاءَ. لَانْثَنَتْ عَنْكِ خَرْسَاءَ. وَأَمَّا هُوَ فَإِنْ كَانَ صَدَقَ فِي زَعْمِهِ. وَدَعْوَى عُدْمِهِ. فَلَهُ فِي هَمٍّ قَبْقَبِهِ. مَا يَشْغَلُهُ عَنْ ذَبْذَبِهِ. فَأَطْرَقَتْ تَنْظُرُ ٱزْوِرَارًا. وَلَا تُرْجِعُ حِوَارًا. حَتَّى قُلْنَا قَدْ رَاجَعَهَا الْخَفَرُ. أَوْ حَاقَ بِهَا الظَّفَرُ. فَقَالَ لَهَا الشَّيْخُ تَعْسًا لَكِ إِنْ زَخْرَفْتِ. أَوْ كَتَمْتِ مَا عَرَفْتِ. فَقَالَتْ وَيْحَكَ وَهَلْ بَعْدَ الْمُنَافَرَةِ كَتْمٌ. أَوْ بَقِيَ لَنَا عَلَى سِرٍّ خَتْمٌ. وَمَا فِينَا إِلَّا مَنْ صَدَقَ. وَهَتَكَ صَوْنَهُ إِذْ نَطَقَ. فَلَيْتَنَا لَاقَيْنَا الْبَكَمَ. وَلَمْ نَلْقَ الْحَكَمَ. ثُمَّ ٱلْتَفَعَتْ بِوِشَاحِهَا. وَتَبَاكَتْ لِٱفْتِضَاحِهَا. وَجَعَلَ الْقَاضِي يَعْجَبُ مِنْ خَطْبِهِمَا وَيُعَجِّبُ. وَيَلُومُ لَهُمَا[١] الدَّهْرَ وَيُؤَنِّبُ. ثُمَّ أَحْضَرَ مِنَ الْوَرِقِ[٢] أَلْفَيْنِ. وَقَالَ أَرْضِيَا بِهِمَا

١ د: وَيَلُومُ الدَّهْرَ لَهُمَا. ٢ هكذا في و؛ وفي د: الوَرْق.

الْأَجْوَفَيْنِ. وَعَاصِيَا النَّازِغَ بَيْنَ الْإِلْفَيْنِ. فَشَكَرَاهُ عَلَى حُسْنِ السَّرَاحِ. وَٱنْطَلَقَا وَهُمَا كَالْمَاءِ وَالرَّاحِ.

٥،٤٥ وَطَفِقَ الْقَاضِي بَعْدَ مَسْرَحِهِمَا. وَتَنَائِي شَبَحِهِمَا يُثْنِي عَلَى أَدَبِهِمَا. وَيَقُولُ هَلْ مِنْ عَارِفٍ بِهِمَا. فَقَالَ لَهُ عَيْنُ أَعْوَانِهِ. وَخَالِصَةُ خُلْصَانِهِ. أَمَّا الشَّيْخُ فَالسَّرُوجِيُّ الْمَشْهُودُ بِفَضْلِهِ. وَأَمَّا الْمَرْأَةُ فَقَعِيدَةُ رَحْلِهِ. وَأَمَّا تَحَاكُمُهُمَا فَمَكِيدَةٌ مِنْ فِعْلِهِ. وَأُحْبُولَةٌ مِنْ حَبَائِلِ خَتْلِهِ. فَأَحْفَظَ الْقَاضِيَ مَا سَمِعَ. وَتَلَهَّبَ كَيْفَ خُدِعَ. ثُمَّ قَالَ لِلْوَاشِي بِهِمَا. قُمْ فَرُدَّهُمَا. ثُمَّ ٱقْصِدْهُمَا وَصِدْهُمَا. فَنَهَضَ يَنْفُضُ مِذْرَوَيْهِ. ثُمَّ عَادَ يَضْرِبُ أَصْدَرَيْهِ. فَقَالَ لَهُ الْقَاضِي. أَظْهِرْنَا عَلَى مَا نَبَثْتَ. وَلَا تُخْفِ عَنَّا مَا ٱسْتَخْبَثْتَ. فَقَالَ مَا زِلْتُ أَسْتَقْرِي الطُّرُقَ. وَأَسْتَفْتِحُ الْغُلُقَ. إِلَى أَنْ أَدْرَكْتُهُمَا مُصْحِرَيْنِ. وَقَدْ زَمَّا مَطِيَّ الْبَيْنِ. فَرَغَّبْتُهُمَا فِي الْعَلَلِ. وَكَفَلْتُ لَهُمَا بِنَيْلِ الْأَمَلِ. فَأُشْرِبَ قَلْبُ الشَّيْخِ أَنْ يَيْأَسَ. وَقَالَ الْفِرَارُ بِقُرَابٍ[1] أَكْيَسُ. وَقَالَتْ هِيَ بَلِ الْعَوْدُ أَحْمَدُ. وَالْفَرُوقَةُ يَكْمَدُ.

٦،٤٥ فَلَمَّا تَبَيَّنَ الشَّيْخُ سَفَهَ رَأْيِهَا. وَغَرَرَ ٱجْتِرَائِهَا. أَمْسَكَ ذَلَاذِلَهَا. ثُمَّ أَنْشَأَ يَقُولُ لَهَا.

دُونَكِ نُصْحِي فَٱقْتَفِي سُبُلَهْ ... وَٱغْنَيْ[2] عَنِ التَّفْصِيلِ بِالْجُمْلَهْ
طِيرِي مَتَى نَقَّرْتِ عَنْ نَخْلَةٍ ... وَطَلِّقِيهَا بَتَّةً بَتْلَهْ
وَحَاذِرِي الْعَوْدَ إِلَيْهَا وَلَوْ ... سَبَّلَهَا نَاطُورُهَا الْأَبْلَهْ
فَخَيْرُ مَا لِلِّصِّ أَنْ لَا يُرَى ... بِبُقْعَةٍ فِيهَا لَهُ عَمْلَهْ

١ د: قِرَابٍ. ٢ غير مشكلة في س، وفي د: واغني.

٧٫٤٥ ثُمَّ قَالَ لِي لَقَدْ عَنَّيْتَ. فِيمَا[١] وُلِّيتَ. فَٱرْجِعْ مِنْ حَيْثُ جِئْتَ. وَقُلْ لِمُرْسِلِكَ إِنْ شِئْتَ.

رُوَيْدَكَ لَا تُعْقِبْ جَمِيلَكَ بِٱلْأَذَى فَتُضْحِي وَشَمْلُ ٱلْمَالِ وَٱلْحَمْدِ مُنْصَدِعْ[٢]
وَلَا تَتَغَضَّبْ مِنْ تَزَيُّدِ سَائِلٍ فَمَا هُوَ فِي صَوْغِ ٱللِّسَانِ بِمُبْتَدِعْ
وَإِنْ تَكُ قَدْ سَاءَتْكَ مِنِّي خَدِيعَةٌ فَقَبْلَكَ شَيْخُ ٱلْأَشْعَرِيِّينَ قَدْ خُدِعْ

٨٫٤٥ فَقَالَ[٣] ٱلْقَاضِي قَاتَلَهُ ٱللّٰهُ فَمَا أَحْسَنَ شُجُونَهُ. وَأَمْلَحَ فُنُونَهُ. ثُمَّ إِنَّهُ أَصْحَبَ رَائِدَهُ بُرْدَيْنِ. وَصُرَّةً مِنَ ٱلْعَيْنِ. وَقَالَ لَهُ. سِرْ سَيْرَ مَنْ لَا يَرَى ٱلِٱلْتِفَاتَ. إِلَى أَنْ تَرَى ٱلشَّيْخَ وَٱلْفَتَاةَ. فَتُبَلَّ يَدَهُمَا[٤] بِهٰذَا ٱلْحِبَاءِ. وَبَيِّنْ لَهُمَا ٱنْخِدَاعِي لِلْأُدَبَاءِ. قَالَ ٱلرَّاوِي. فَلَمْ أَرَ فِي ٱلِٱغْتِرَابِ كَهٰذَا ٱلْعُجَابِ. وَلَا سَمِعْتُ بِمِثْلِهِ مِمَّنْ جَالَ وَجَابَ.

١ د: بِمَا. ٢ د: فَتَضْحِي. ٣ بعدها في ف: له. ٤ س: فَحِينئذ بُلَّ يَدَهما؛ وفي و: فَبُلَّ يَدَهما؛ وفي ف: قَبِّلْ (هكذا) يديْهما.

الْمَقَامَةُ السَّادِسَةُ وَالْأَرْبَعُونَ[1]

١،٤٦ حَدَّثَ[2] الْحَارِثُ بْنُ هَمَّامٍ قَالَ نَزَعَ بِي إِلَى حَلَبَ. شَوْقٌ غَلَبَ. وَطَلَبٌ يَا لَهُ مِنْ طَلَبٍ. وَكُنْتُ يَوْمَئِذٍ خَفِيفَ الْحَاذِ. حَثِيثَ النَّفَاذِ. فَأَخَذْتُ أُهْبَةَ السَّيْرِ. وَخَفَفْتُ نَحْوَهَا خُفُوفَ الطَّيْرِ. وَلَمْ أَزَلْ مُذْ حَلَلْتُ رُبُوعَهَا. وَٱرْتَبَعْتُ رَبِيعَهَا. أُفَانِي الْأَيَّامَ. فِيمَا يَشْفِي الْغَرَامَ. وَيُرْوِي الْأُوَامَ. إِلَى أَنْ أَقْصَرَ الْقَلْبُ عَنْ وُلُوعِهِ. وَٱسْتَطَارَ غُرَابُ الْبَيْنِ بَعْدَ وُقُوعِهِ. فَأَغْرَانِي الْبَالُ الْخِلْوُ. وَالْمَرَحُ الْحُلْوُ. بِأَنْ أَقْصِدَ حِمْصَ. لِأَصْطَافَ بِبُقْعَتِهَا. وَأَسْبُرَ رَقَاعَةَ أَهْلِ رُقْعَتِهَا. فَأَسْرَعْتُ إِلَيْهَا إِسْرَاعَ النَّجْمِ. إِذَا ٱنْقَضَّ لِلرَّجْمِ. فَحِينَ خَيَّمْتُ بِرُسُومِهَا. وَوَجَدْتُ رَوْحَ نَسِيمِهَا. لَمَحَ طَرْفِي شَيْخًا قَدْ أَقْبَلَ هَرِيرُهُ. وَأَدْبَرَ غَرِيرُهُ. وَعِنْدَهُ عَشَرَةُ صِبْيَانٍ. صِنْوَانٌ وَغَيْرُ صِنْوَانٍ. فَطَاوَعْتُ فِي قَصْدِهِ الْحِرْصَ. لِأَخْبُرَ بِهِ أُدَبَاءَ حِمْصَ. فَبَشَّ بِي حِينَ وَافَيْتُهُ. وَحَيَّا بِأَحْسَنَ مِمَّا حَيَّيْتُهُ. فَجَلَسْتُ إِلَيْهِ لِأَبْلُوَ جَنَى نُطْقِهِ. وَأَكْتَنِهَ كُنْهَ حُمْقِهِ.

٢،٤٦ فَمَا لَبِثَ أَنْ أَشَارَ بِعُصَيَّتِهِ. إِلَى كُبْرِ أُصَيْبِيَتِهِ. وَقَالَ لَهُ أَنْشِدِ الْأَبْيَاتَ الْعَوَاطِلَ. وَٱحْذَرْ أَنْ تُمَاطِلَ. فَجَثَا جِثْوَةَ لَيْثٍ. وَأَنْشَدَ مِنْ غَيْرِ رَيْثٍ.

أَعْدِدْ لِحُسَّادِكَ حَدَّ السِّلَاحْ　　وَأَوْرِدِ الْآمِلَ وِرْدَ السَّمَاحْ
وَصَارِمِ اللَّهْوَ وَوَصْلَ الْمَهَا　　وَأَعْمِلِ الْكُومَ وَسُمْرَ الرِّمَاحْ
وَٱسْعَ لِإِدْرَاكِ مَحَلٍّ سَمَا　　عِمَادُهُ لَا لِٱدِّرَاعِ الْمِرَاحْ

[1] في هامش س: تُعْرَفُ بِالحَلَبِيَّةِ وَالحِمْصِيَّةِ؛ وفي ف: وَهْيَ الحَلَبِيَّةُ؛ وفي د: الحَلَبِيَّةُ. [2] في ف: رَوَى.

وَاللهِ مَا السُّؤْدَدُ حَسْوُ الطِّلَا وَلَا مَرَادُ[1] الْحَمْدِ رُودٌ رَدَاحْ
وَاهًا لِحُرٍّ صَدْرُهُ وَاسِعٌ[2] وَهَمُّهُ مَا سَرَّ أَهْلَ الصَّلَاحْ
مَوْرِدُهُ حُلْوٌ لِسُؤَّالِهِ وَمَالُهُ مَا سَأَلُوهُ مُطَاحْ
مَا أَسْمَعَ الْآمِلَ رَدًّا وَلَا مَاطَلَهُ وَالْمَطْلُ لُؤْمٌ صُرَاحْ
وَلَا أَطَاعَ اللَّهْوَ لَمَّا دَعَا وَلَا كَسَا رَاحًا لَهُ كَأْسَ رَاحْ
سَوَّدَهُ إِصْلَاحُهُ سِرَّهُ وَرَدْعُهُ أَهْوَاءَهُ وَالطِّمَاحْ
وَحَصَّلَ الْمَدْحَ لَهُ عِلْمُهُ مَا مُهِرَ الْعُورُ مُهُورَ الصِّحَاحْ

فَقَالَ لَهُ أَحْسَنْتَ يَا بُدَيْرُ. يَا رَأْسَ الدَّيْرِ.

٣،٤٦ ثُمَّ قَالَ لِتِلْوِهِ. الْمُشْتَبِهِ بِصِنْوِهِ. أُدْنُ يَا نُوَيْرَةُ. يَا قَمَرَ الدُّوَيْرَةِ. فَدَنَا وَلَمْ يَتَبَاطَا. حَتَّى حَلَّ مِنْهُ مَقْعَدَ الْمُعَاطَى. فَقَالَ لَهُ أَجِلِ الْأَبْيَاتَ الْعَرَائِسَ. وَإِنْ لَمْ يَكُنَّ نَفَائِسَ. فَبَرَى الْقَلَمَ وَقَطَّ. ثُمَّ احْتَجَرَ اللَّوْحَ وَخَطَّ.

فَتَنَتْنِي فَجَنَّتْنِي تَجَنِّي بِتَجَنٍّ يَفْتَنُّ غِبَّ تَجَنِّي
شَغَفَتْنِي بِجَفْنِ ظَبْيٍ غَضِيضٍ غَنِجٍ يَقْتَضِي تَغَيُّضَ جَفْنِي
غَشِيَتْنِي بِزِينَتَيْنِ فَشَقَّتْنِي بِزِيٍّ يَشِفُّ بَيْنَ تَثَنِّي
فَتَظَنَّيْتُ تَجْتَبِينِي فَتَجْزِينِي بِنَفْثٍ يَشْفِي تَخَيُّبَ ظَنِّي
ثَبَّتَتْ فِيَّ غِشَّ جَيْبٍ بِتَزْيِينِ خَبِيثٍ يَبْغِي تَشَفِّيَ ضِغْنِ[3]
فَنَزَتْ فِي تَجَنُّبِي فَثَنَتْنِي بِنَشِيجٍ يُشْجِي بِفَنٍّ فَفَنِّ

١ هكذا في ق، و، ف؛ وفي س، د: مُراد. ٢ «صَدْرُهُ وَاسِعٌ»: في ف: وَاسِعٍ صَدْرُهُ. ٣ في د: ضِغْنِي.

فَلَمَّا نَظَرَ الشَّيْخُ إِلَى مَا حَبَّرَهُ. وَتَصَفَّحَ مَا زَبَرَهُ.[١] قَالَ لَهُ بُورِكَ فِيكَ مِنْ طَلَا. كَمَا بُورِكَ فِي لَا وَلَا.

٤،٤٦ ثُمَّ هَتَفَ أُقْرُبْ. يَا قُطْرُبُ. فَٱقْتَرَبَ مِنْهُ فَتًى يَحْكِي نَجْمَ دُجْيَةٍ. أَوْ تِمْثَالَ دُمْيَةٍ. فَقَالَ لَهُ أُرْقُمِ الْأَبْيَاتَ الْأَخْيَافَ. وَتَجَنَّبِ الْخِلَافَ. فَأَخَذَ الْقَلَمَ وَرَقَمَ.

اِسْمَحْ فَبَثُّ السَّمَاحِ زَيْنٌ   وَلَا تُخِبْ آمِلاً تَضَيَّفْ
وَلَا تُجِزْ رَدَّ ذِي سُؤَالٍ   فَتَنٌ أَمْ فِي السُّؤَالِ خَفَّفْ
وَلَا تَظُنَّ الدُّهُورَ تُبْقِي   مَالَ ضَنِينٍ وَلَوْ تَقَشَّفْ
وَٱحْلُمْ فَجَفْنُ الْكِرَامِ يُغْضِي   وَصَدْرُهُمْ فِي الْعَطَاءِ نَفْنَفْ
وَلَا تَخُنْ عَهْدَ ذِي وِدَادٍ   ثَبْتٍ وَلَا تَبْغِ مَا تَزَيَّفْ

فَقَالَ لَهُ لَا شَلَّتْ[٢] يَدَاكَ. وَلَا كَلَّتْ[٣] مُدَاكَ.

٥،٤٦ ثُمَّ نَادَى يَا غَشَمْشَمُ. يَا عِطْرَ مَنْشَمٍ. فَلَبَّاهُ غُلَامٌ كَدُرَّةِ غَوَّاصٍ. أَوْ جُؤْذَرِ قَنَّاصٍ. فَقَالَ لَهُ أُكْتُبِ الْأَبْيَاتَ الْمَتَائِمَ. وَلَا تَكُنْ مِنَ الْمَشَائِيمِ. فَتَنَاوَلَ الْقَلَمَ الْمُثَقَّفَ. وَكَتَبَ وَلَمْ يَتَوَقَّفْ.

زُيِّنَتْ زَيْنَبُ بِقَدٍّ يَقُدُّ   وَتَلَاهُ وَيْلَاهُ نَهْدٌ يَهُدُّ
جُنْدُهَا جِيدُهَا وَظَرْفٌ وَطَرْفٌ   نَاعِسٌ تَاعِسٌ بِحَدٍّ يَحُدُّ
قَدْرُهَا قَدْ زَهَا وَتَاهَتْ وَبَاهَتْ   وَٱعْتَدَتْ وَٱغْتَدَتْ بِخَدٍّ يَخُدُّ
فَارَقَتْنِي فَأَرَّقَتْنِي وَشَطَّتْ   وَسَطَتْ ثُمَّ نَمَّ وَجْدٌ وَجَدُّ
فَدَنَتْ فُدِّيَتْ وَحَنَّتْ وَحَيَّتْ   مُغْضَبًا مُغْضِيًا يَوَدُّ يُودُّ

١ د: زَبَّره. ٢ و: شُلَّتْ. ٣ د: كُلَّتْ.

فَطَفِقَ الشَّيْخُ يَتَأَمَّلُ مَا سَطَرَهُ. وَيُقَلِّبُ فِيهِ نَظَرَهُ. فَلَمَّا ٱسْتَحْسَنَ خَطَّهُ. وَٱسْتَصَحَّ ضَبْطَهُ. قَالَ لَهُ لَا شَلَّ عَشْرُكَ. وَلَا ٱسْتُخْبِثَ نَشْرُكَ.

٦،٤٦ ثُمَّ أَهَابَ بِفَتًى فَتَّانٍ. يَسْفِرُ عَنْ أَزْهَارِ بُسْتَانٍ. فَقَالَ لَهُ أَنْشِدِ ٱلْبَيْتَيْنِ ٱلْمُطْرِفَيْنِ. ٱلْمُشْتَبِهَيِ ٱلطَّرَفَيْنِ. ٱللَّذَيْنِ أَسْكَتَا كُلَّ نَافِثٍ. وَأَمِنَا أَنْ يُعَزَّزَا بِثَالِثٍ. فَقَالَ لَهُ ٱسْمَعْ لَا وُقِرَ سَمْعُكَ. وَلَا هُزِمَ جَمْعُكَ. وَأَنْشَدَ مِنْ غَيْرِ تَلَبُّثٍ. وَلَا تَرَبُّثٍ.[1]

سِمْ سِمَةً تَحْسُنُ آثَارُهَا ‏ ‏ وَٱشْكُرْ لِمَنْ أَعْطَى وَلَوْ سِمْسِمَهْ
وَٱلْمَكْرُ مَهْمَا ٱسْتَطَعْتَ لَا تَأْتِهِ ‏ ‏ لِتَقْتَنِي ٱلسُّؤْدَدَ وَٱلْمَكْرُمَهْ

فَقَالَ لَهُ أَجَدْتَ يَا زُغْلُولُ. يَا أَبَا ٱلْغُلُولِ.

٧،٤٦ ثُمَّ نَادَى أَوْضِحْ يَا يَاسِينُ. مَا يُشْكِلُ مِنْ ذَوَاتِ ٱلسِّينِ. فَنَهَضَ وَلَمْ يَتَأَنَّ. وَأَنْشَدَ بِصَوْتٍ أَغَنَّ

نِقْسُ ٱلدَّوَاةِ وَرُسْغُ ٱلْكَفِّ مُثْبَتَةٌ ‏ ‏ سِينَاهُمَا إِنْ هُمَا خُطَّا وَإِنْ دُرِسَا
وَهٰكَذَا ٱلسِّينُ فِي قَسْبٍ وَبَاسِقَةٍ ‏ ‏ وَٱلسَّفْحِ وَٱلْبَخْسِ وَٱقْسِرْ وَٱقْتَبِسْ قَبَسَا
وَفِي تَقَسَّسْتُ بِٱللَّيْلِ ٱلْكَلَامَ وَفِي ‏ ‏ مُسَيْطِرٍ وَشَمُوسٍ وَٱتَّخِذْ جَرَسَا
وَفِي قَرِيسٍ وَبَرْدٍ قَارِسٍ فَخُذِ ٱلصْـ ‏ ‏ ـصَوَابَ مِنِّي وَكُنْ لِلْعِلْمِ مُقْتَبِسَا

فَقَالَ لَهُ أَحْسَنْتَ يَا نُغَيْشُ. يَا صَنَّاجَةَ ٱلْجَيْشِ.

٨،٤٦ ثُمَّ قَالَ ثِبْ يَا عَنْبَسَةُ. وَبَيِّنِ ٱلصَّادَاتِ ٱلْمُلْتَبِسَةَ. فَوَثَبَ وَثْبَةَ شِبْلٍ مُثَارٍ. ثُمَّ أَنْشَدَ مِنْ غَيْرِ عِثَارٍ.

---

[1] ف: تَرَيُّثٍ.

بِالصَّادِ يُكْتَبُ قَدْ قَبَصْتُ دَرَاهِمًا   بِأَنَامِلِي وَأَصِخْ لِتَسْتَمِعَ الْخَبَرْ
وَبَصَقْتُ أَبْصُقُ وَالصِّمَاخُ وَصَنْجَةٌ   وَالْقَصُّ وَهْوَ الصَّدْرُ وَاقْتَصَّ الْأَثَرْ
وَبَخَصْتُ مُقْلَتَهُ وَهٰذِي فُرْصَةٌ   قَدْ أُرْعِدَتْ مِنْهُ الْفَرِيصَةُ لِلْخَوَرْ
وَقَصَرْتُ هِنْدًا أَيْ حَبَسْتُ وَقَدْ دَنَا   فِصْحُ النَّصَارَى وَهْوَ عِيدٌ مُنْتَظَرْ
وَقَرَصْتُهُ وَالْخَمْرُ قَارِصَةٌ إِذَا   حَذَتِ اللِّسَانَ وَكُلُّ هٰذَا مُسْتَطَرْ

فَقَالَ لَهُ رَعْيًا لَكَ يَا بُنَيَّ. فَلَقَدْ أَقْرَرْتَ عَيْنَيَّ.

٩،٤٦ ثُمَّ اسْتَنْهَضَ ذَا جُثَّةٍ كَالْبَيْذَقِ. وَنَعْشَةٍ كَالسَّوْذَقِ. وَأَمَرَهُ بِأَنْ يَقِفَ بِالْمِرْصَادِ. وَيَسْرُدَ مَا يَجْرِي عَلَى السِّينِ وَالصَّادِ. فَنَهَضَ يَسْحَبُ بُرْدَيْهِ. ثُمَّ أَنْشَدَ مُشِيرًا بِيَدَيْهِ.

إِنْ شِئْتَ بِالسِّينِ فَاكْتُبْ مَا أُبَيِّنُهُ   وَإِنْ تَشَأْ فَهْوَ بِالصَّادَاتِ يُكْتَتَبُ
مَغْسٌ وَفَقْسٌ وَمُسْطَارٌ وَمُمَّلِسٌ   وَسَالِغٌ وَسِرَاطُ الْحَقِّ وَالسَّقَبُ

الْمَغْسُ الْوَجَعُ الْمُعْتَرِضُ فِي الْجَوْفِ وَهْوَ مُسَكَّنُ الْغَيْنِ وَالْفَقْسُ فَقْسُ الْبَيْضَةِ وَالْمُسْطَارُ الْخَمْرَةُ الْمُزَّةُ وَيُقَالُ لَهَا الْمُسْطَارَةُ أَيْضًا وَالْمُمَّلِسُ الَّذِي يَسْقُطُ مِنْ يَدِكَ وَلَا تَشْعُرُ بِهِ وَالسَّالِغُ آخِرُ أَسْنَانِ ذَوَاتِ الظِّلْفِ وَالسَّقَبُ الْقُرْبُ.[١]

وَالسَّامِغَانِ وَصَقْرٌ[٢] وَالسَّوِيقُ وَمِسْلَاقٌ وَعَنْ كُلِّ هٰذَا تُفْصِحُ الْكُتُبُ

السَّامِغَانِ جَانِبَا الْفَمِ وَالْمِسْلَاقُ الشَّدِيدُ الصَّوْتِ وَمِنْهُ قَوْلُهُ تَعَالَى ﴿سَلَقُوكُمْ بِأَلْسِنَةٍ حِدَادٍ﴾.[٣]

---

١ وردت هذه السطور من الشرح في هذا الموضع من ق، د، و؛ بينما وردت بعد الأبيات في س، ونقصت من ف. ٢ د، ف: السَّقْر. ٣ «السَّامِغَانِ . . . حِدَادٍ»: ناقص في ف.

فَقَالَ لَهُ أَحْسَنْتَ يَا حِبِقَّةُ[1]. يَا عَيْنَ بَقَّةٍ.

ثُمَّ نَادَى يَا دَغْفَلُ. يَا أَبَا زَنْفَلٍ. فَلَبَّاهُ فَتًى أَحْسَنُ مِنْ بَيْضَةٍ. فِي رَوْضَةٍ. ١٠،٤٦
فَقَالَ لَهُ مَا عَقْدُ هِجَاءِ ٱلْأَفْعَالِ. ٱلَّتِي آخِرُهَا حَرْفُ ٱعْتِلَالٍ.[2] فَقَالَ ٱسْمَعْ لَا صَمَّ[3] صَدَاكَ. وَلَا سَمِعْتَ عِدَاكَ. ثُمَّ أَنْشَدَ. وَمَا ٱسْتَرْشَدَ.

إِذَا ٱلْفِعْلُ يَوْمًا غُمَّ عَنْكَ هِجَاؤُهُ   فَأَلْحِقْ بِهِ تَاءَ ٱلْخِطَابِ وَلَا تَقِفْ
فَإِنْ تَرَ قَبْلَ ٱلتَّاءِ يَاءً فَكَتْبُهُ   بِيَاءٍ وَإِلَّا فَهْوَ يُكْتَبُ بِٱلْأَلِفْ
وَلَا تَحْسَبِ ٱلْفِعْلَ ٱلثُّلَاثِيَّ وَٱلَّذِي   تَعَدَّاهُ وَٱلْمَهْمُوزُ فِي ذَاكَ يَخْتَلِفْ

فَطَرِبَ ٱلشَّيْخُ لِمَا أَدَّاهُ. ثُمَّ عَوَّذَهُ وَفَدَّاهُ.

ثُمَّ قَالَ هَلُمَّ يَا قَعْقَاعُ. يَا بَاقِعَةَ ٱلْبِقَاعِ. فَأَقْبَلَ فَتًى أَحْسَنُ مِنْ نَارِ ٱلْقِرَى. ١١،٤٦
فِي عَيْنِ ٱبْنِ ٱلسُّرَى. فَقَالَ لَهُ ٱصْدَعْ بِتَمْيِيزِ ٱلظَّاءِ مِنَ ٱلضَّادِ. لِتَصْدَعَ بِهِ أَكْبَادَ ٱلْأَضْدَادِ. فَٱهْتَزَّ لِقَوْلِهِ وَٱهْتَشَّ. ثُمَّ أَنْشَدَ بِصَوْتٍ أَجَشَّ.

أَيُّهَا ٱلسَّائِلِي عَنِ ٱلضَّادِ وَٱلظَّا   ءِ[4] لِكَيْلَا تُضِلَّهُ ٱلْأَلْفَاظُ
إِنَّ حِفْظَ ٱلظَّاءَاتِ يُغْنِيكَ فَٱسْمَعْـ   ـهَا ٱسْتِمَاعَ ٱمْرِئٍ لَهُ ٱسْتِيقَاظُ
هِيَ ظَمْيَاءُ وَٱلْمَظَالِمُ وَٱلْإِظْـ   ـلَامُ وَٱلظَّلْمُ وَٱلظُّبَى وَٱللِّحَاظُ
وَٱلْعَظَا وَٱلظَّلِيمُ وَٱلظَّبْيُ وَٱلشَّيْـ   ـظَمُ وَٱلظِّلُّ وَٱللَّظَى وَٱلشُّوَاظُ
وَٱلتَّظَنِّي وَٱللَّفْظُ وَٱلنَّظْمُ وَٱلتَّقْـ   ـرِيظُ وَٱلْقَيْظُ وَٱلظَّمَا وَٱللَّمَاظُ
وَٱلْحِظَى وَٱلنَّظِيرُ وَٱلظِّئْرُ وَٱلْجَا   حِظُ وَٱلنَّاظِرُونَ وَٱلْأَيْقَاظُ
وَٱلتَّشَظِّي وَٱلظِّلْفُ وَٱلْعَظْمُ وَٱلظُّنْـ   ـبُوبُ وَٱلظَّهْرُ وَٱلشَّظَا وَٱلشِّظَاظُ

١ ف: حِبَقَّةُ؛ وفي هامش ق: تقول العرب لمن يصغّر إليه نفسه خبقة بخاء معجمة بواحدة من فوق وغير معجمة. ٢ د: الاِعْتِلَالِ. ٣ ف: صُمَّ. ٤ الضَّادِ وَالظَّاءِ في د: الظَّاءِ وَالضَّادِ.

وَالْأَظَافِيرُ وَالْمُظَفَّرُ وَالْمَحْظُورُ وَالْحَافِظُونَ وَالْإِحْفَاظُ
وَالْحَظِيرَاتُ وَالْمَظِنَّةُ وَالظِّنَّةُ وَالْكَاظِمُونَ وَالْمُغْتَاظُ
وَالْوَظِيفَاتُ وَالْمُوَاظِبُ وَالْكِظَّةُ وَالِانْتِظَارُ وَالْإِلْظَاظُ
وَوَظِيفٌ وَظَالِعٌ وَعَظِيمٌ وَظَهِيرٌ وَالفَظُّ وَالْإِغْلَاظُ
وَنَظِيفٌ وَالظَّرْفُ وَالظِّلْفُ الظَّا هِرُ ثُمَّ الْفَظِيعُ وَالْوُعَّاظُ
وَعُكَاظٌ وَالظَّعْنُ وَالْمَظُّ وَالْحَنْظَلُ وَالْقَارِظَانِ وَالْأَوْشَاظُ

١٢،٤٦ الْمَظُّ رُمَّانُ الْبَرِّ وَالْقَارِظُ جَانِي الْقَرَظِ وَهْوَ النَّبَاتُ الْمَدْبُوغُ بِهِ وَالْأَوْشَاظُ الْأَخْلَاطُ وَالْجَمَاعَاتُ.[1]

وَظِرَابُ الظِّرَانِ وَالشَّظَفُ الْبَا هِظُ وَالْجَعْظَرِيُّ وَالْجَوَّاظُ

الظِّرَابُ الرُّبَا الصِّغَارُ وَاحِدُهَا ظَرِبٌ وَالظِّرَّانُ الْحِجَارَةُ الْمُحَدَّدَةُ وَاحِدُهَا ظَرَرٌ[2] وَالْجَعْظَرِيُّ الْمُتَنَفِّخُ بِمَا لَيْسَ عِنْدَهُ وَالْجَوَّاظُ الْفَاخِرُ وَقِيلَ الْأَكُولُ الْمُخْتَالُ.[3]

وَالظَّرَابِينُ وَالْحَنَاظِبُ وَالْعُنْظُبُ ثُمَّ الظَّيَّانُ وَالْأَرْعَاظُ

الظَّرَابِينُ جَمْعُ ظَرِبَانٍ وَهِيَ دَابَّةٌ لَا يُطَاقُ فَسْوُهَا وَتُجْمَعُ أَيْضًا عَلَى ظَرَابِيَّ بِحَذْفِ النُّونِ[4] وَالْحَنَاظِبُ ذُكُورُ الْخَنَافِسِ وَالْعُنْظُبُ ذَكَرُ الْجَرَادِ وَالظَّيَّانُ يَاسَمِينُ الْبَرِّ وَالْأَرْعَاظُ جَمْعُ رُعْظٍ وَهْوَ مَدْخَلُ النَّصْلِ فِي السَّهْمِ.[5]

١ «المَظُّ . . . الجَمَاعَاتُ»: ناقص في ف. ٢ بعدها في د: وَالشَّظَفُ البُؤْسُ وَسُوءُ العَيْنِ وَالبَاهِظُ المُثْقِلُ.
٣ «الظِّرَابُ الرُّبَا . . . المُخْتَالُ»: ناقص في ف. ٤ . بعدها في س، ووَعَلَى ظِرْبَى وَهْوَ جَمْعٌ شَاذٌّ؛ وفي د: وَعَلَى ظِرْبَى وَهْوَ جَمْعٌ شَاذٌّ وَلَمْ يَجِئْ عَلَى فِعْلَى إِلَّا هٰذَا وَحِجْلَى جَمْعُ حَجَلٍ. ٥ . «الظَّرَابِينُ . . . السَّهْمِ»: ناقص في ف.

وَالشَّنَاظِي وَالدَّلَنْظ وَالظَّأْبُ وَالظَّبْــظَابُ وَالْعُـنْظُوَانُ وَالْجِنْعَاظُ

١٣،٤٦ الشَّنَاظِي نَوَاحِي الْجَبَلِ وَالدَّلَنْظُ الدَّفْعُ وَالظَّأْبُ الصَّخَبُ وَقَدْ تُبْدَلُ الْبَاءُ مِنْهُ مِيمًا وَقِيلَ إِنَّ الظَّأْبَ وَالظَّأْمَ ٱسْمَانِ لِسَلَفِ الرَّجُلِ وَالْعُنْظُوَانُ نَبْتٌ وَالظَّبْظَابُ الدَّاءُ يُقَالُ مَا بِهِ ظَبْظَابٌ كَمَا يُقَالُ مَا بِهِ قَلَبَةٌ وَالْجِنْعَاظُ الْأَحْمَقُ وَقِيلَ إِنَّهُ الْمُتَسَخِّطُ عِنْدَ الطَّعَامِ.[1]

وَالشَّنَاظِيرُ وَالتَّعَاظُلُ وَالْعِظْـلِمُ وَالْبَظْـرُ بَعْـدُ وَالْإِنْعَـاظ

الشَّنَاظِيرُ جَمْعُ شِنْظِيرٍ وَهُوَ السَّيِّئُ الْخُلُقِ[2] وَالتَّعَاظُلُ تَلَازُمُ الْجَرَادِ وَالْكِلَابِ عِنْدَ السِّفَادِ وَالْعِظْلِمُ الْخِطْمِيُّ.[3]

هِيَ هٰذِي سِوَى النَّوَادِرِ فَٱحْفَظْــهَا لِتَـقْـفُوَ آثَـارَكَ الْحُـفَّـاظُ
وَٱقْضِ فِي مَا صَرَفْتَ مِنْهَا كَمَا تَقْــضِيهِ فِي أَصْلِهِ كَقَيْظٍ وَقَاظُوا

فَقَالَ لَهُ الشَّيْخُ أَحْسَنْتَ لَا فُضَّ فُوكَ. وَلَا بُرَّ مَنْ يَجْفُوكَ. فَوَاللهِ إِنَّكَ مَعَ الصِّبَا الْغَضِّ. لَأَحْفَظُ مِنَ الْأَرْضِ. وَأَجْمَعُ مِنْ يَوْمِ الْعَرْضِ. وَلَقَدْ أَوْرَدْتُكَ وَرُفْقَتَكَ زُلَالِي. وَثَقَّفْتُكُمْ تَثْقِيفَ الْعَوَالِي.[4] ﴿فَٱذْكُرُونِي أَذْكُرْكُمْ وَٱشْكُرُوا لِي وَلَا تَكْفُرُونِ﴾.

١٤،٤٦ قَالَ الْحَارِثُ بْنُ هَمَّامٍ فَعَجِبْتُ لِمَا أَبْدَى مِنْ بَرَاعَةٍ. مَعْجُونَةٍ بِرَقَاعَةٍ. وَأَظْهَرَ مِنْ حَذَاقَةٍ. مَمْزُوجَةٍ بِحَمَاقَةٍ. وَلَمْ يَزَلْ بَصَرِي يُصَعِّدُ فِيهِ وَيُصَوِّبُ. وَيُنَقِّرُ

١ «الشَّنَاظِي ... الطَّعَامِ»: ناقص في ف. ٢ و، د: الخُلْق. ٣ د: الخَطْمِيّ؛ «الشَّنَاظِيرُ ... الخِطْمِيُّ»: ناقص في ف. ٤ بعدها في د: وَأَلْحَقْتُكُمْ جَنَاحَ تَكْرِمَتِي. وَسَقَفْتُكُمْ سُلَافَةَ كَرْمَتِي. حَتَّى لَحِقْتُمْ بِالعَلْيَةِ. وَتَحَضَلَّيْتُمْ مِّنَ الأَدَبِ بِأَحْسَنِ الحِلْيَةِ.

عَنْهُ وَيُنَقِّبُ. وَكُنْتُ كَمَنْ يَنْظُرُ فِي ظَلْمَاءَ. أَوْ يَسْرِي فِي يَهْمَاءِ.[١] فَلَمَّا ٱسْتَرَاثَ تَنَبُّهِي. وَٱسْتَبَانَ تَدَلُّهِي. حَمْلَقَ إِلَيَّ وَتَبَسَّمَ. وَقَالَ لَمْ يَبْقَ مَنْ يَتَوَسَّمُ. فَبُهِتُّ لِفَحْوَى كَلَامِهِ. وَوَجَدْتُهُ أَبَا زَيْدٍ عِنْدَ ٱبْتِسَامِهِ. وَأَخَذْتُ أَلُومُهُ عَلَى تَدَيُّرِ بُقْعَةِ النَّوْكَى. وَتَخَيُّرِ حِرْفَةِ الْحَمْقَى. فَكَأَنَّ وَجْهَهُ أُسِفَّ رَمَادًا. أَوْ أُشْرِبَ سَوَادًا. إِلَّا أَنَّهُ أَنْشَدَ وَمَا تَمَادَى.

تَخَيَّرْتُ حِمْصَ وَهٰذِي الصِّنَاعَهْ لِأُرْزَقَ حُظْوَةَ أَهْلِ الرَّقَاعَهْ
فَمَا يَصْطَفِي الدَّهْرُ غَيْرَ الرَّقِيعِ وَلَا يُوطِنُ الْمَالَ إِلَّا بِقَاعَهْ
وَلَا لِأَخِي اللُّبِّ مِنْ دَهْرِهِ سِوَى مَا لِعَيْرٍ رَبِيطٍ بِقَاعَهْ

١٥،٤٦ ثُمَّ قَالَ أَمَا إِنَّ التَّعْلِيمَ أَشْرَفُ صِنَاعَةٍ. وَأَرْبَحُ بِضَاعَةٍ. وَأَنْجَحُ شَفَاعَةٍ. وَأَفْضَلُ بَرَاعَةٍ. وَرَبُّهُ ذُو إِمْرَةٍ مُطَاعَةٍ. وَهَيْبَةٍ مُشَاعَةٍ. وَرَعِيَّةٍ مِطْوَاعَةٍ. يَتَسَيْطَرُ تَسَيْطُرَ أَمِيرٍ. وَيُرَتِّبُ تَرْتِيبَ وَزِيرٍ. وَيَتَحَكَّمُ تَحَكُّمَ قَدِيرٍ. وَيَتَشَبَّهُ بِذِي مُلْكٍ كَبِيرٍ. لَوْلَا[٢] أَنَّهُ يَخْرَفُ فِي أَمَدٍ يَسِيرٍ. وَيَتَّسِمُ بِحُمْقٍ شَهِيرٍ. وَيَتَقَلَّبُ بِعَقْلٍ صَغِيرٍ. وَلَا يُنَبِّئُكَ مِثْلُ خَبِيرٍ. فَقُلْتُ لَهُ تَاللهِ إِنَّكَ لَٱبْنُ الْأَيَّامِ. وَعَلَمُ الْأَعْلَامِ. وَالسَّاحِرُ اللَّاعِبُ بِالْأَفْهَامِ. الْمُذَلَّلُ لَهُ سُبُلُ الْكَلَامِ. ثُمَّ لَمْ أَزَلْ مُعْتَكِفًا بِنَادِيهِ. وَمُغْتَرِفًا مِنْ سَيْلِ وَادِيهِ. إِلَى أَنْ غَابَتِ الْأَيَّامُ الْغُرُّ. وَنَابَتِ الْأَحْدَاثُ الْغُبْرُ. فَفَارَقْتُهُ وَلِعَيْنِي الْعِبَرُ.

١ و، ف: بَهماء. ٢ «لولا»: ف: إلَّا.

الْمَقَامَةُ السَّابِعَةُ وَالْأَرْبَعُونَ[1]

١،٤٧ حَكَى الْحَارِثُ بْنُ هَمَّامٍ قَالَ اِحْتَجْتُ إِلَى الْحِجَامَةِ. وَأَنَا بِحَجْرِ الْيَمَامَةِ. فَأُرْشِدْتُ إِلَى شَيْخٍ يَحْجُمُ بِلَطَافَةٍ. وَيَسْفِرُ عَنْ نَظَافَةٍ. فَبَعَثْتُ غُلَامِي لِإِحْضَارِهِ. وَأَرْصَدْتُ نَفْسِي لِاِنْتِظَارِهِ. فَأَبْطَأَ بَعْدَمَا ٱنْطَلَقَ. حَتَّى خِلْتُهُ قَدْ أَبَقَ. أَوْ رَكِبَ ﴿طَبَقًا عَنْ طَبَقٍ﴾. ثُمَّ عَادَ عَوْدَ الْمُخْفِقِ مَسْعَاهُ. الْكَلِّ عَلَى مَوْلَاهُ. فَقُلْتُ لَهُ وَيْلَكَ أَبْطَءَ فِنْدٍ. وَصُلُودَ زَنْدٍ. فَزَعَمَ أَنَّ الشَّيْخَ أَشْغَلُ مِنْ ذَاتِ النِّحْيَيْنِ. وَفِي حَرْبٍ كَحَرْبِ حُنَيْنٍ. فَعِفْتُ الْمَمْشَى إِلَى حَجَّامٍ. وَحِرْتُ بَيْنَ إِقْدَامٍ وَإِحْجَامٍ. ثُمَّ رَأَيْتُ أَنْ لَا[2] تَعْنِيفَ. عَلَى مَنْ يَأْتِي الْكَنِيفَ.

٢،٤٧ فَلَمَّا شَهِدْتُ مَوْسِمَهُ. وَشَاهَدْتُ مِيسَمَهُ. رَأَيْتُ شَيْخًا هَيْئَتُهُ نَظِيفَةٌ. وَحَرَكَتُهُ خَفِيفَةٌ. وَعَلَيْهِ مِنَ النَّظَّارَةِ أَطْوَاقٌ. وَمِنَ الزِّحَامِ طِبَاقٌ. وَبَيْنَ يَدَيْهِ فَتًى كَالصَّمْصَامَةِ. مُسْتَهْدِفٌ لِلْحِجَامَةِ. وَالشَّيْخُ يَقُولُ لَهُ أَرَاكَ قَدْ أَبْرَزْتَ رَاسَكَ. قَبْلَ أَنْ تُبْرِزَ قِرْطَاسَكَ. وَوَلَّيْتَنِي قَذَالَكَ. وَلَمْ تَقُلْ لِي ذَا لَكَ. وَلَسْتُ مِمَّنْ يَبِيعُ نَقْدًا بِدَيْنٍ. وَلَا يَطْلُبُ أَثَرًا بَعْدَ عَيْنٍ. فَإِنْ أَنْتَ رَضَخْتَ بِالْعَيْنِ. حُجِمْتَ فِي الْأَخْدَعَيْنِ. وَإِنْ كُنْتَ تَرَى الشُّحَّ أَوْلَى. وَخَزْنَ الْفَلْسِ فِي النَّفْسِ أَحْلَى. فَٱقْرَأْ ﴿عَبَسَ وَتَوَلَّى﴾. وَٱغْرُبْ عَنِّي وَإِلَّا. فَقَالَ الْفَتَى وَالَّذِي حَرَّمَ صَوْغَ الْمَيْنِ. كَمَا حَرَّمَ صَيْدَ الْحَرَمَيْنِ. إِنِّي لَأَفْلَسُ مِنِ ٱبْنِ يَوْمَيْنِ. فَثِقْ بِسَيْلِ تَلْعَتِي. وَأَنْظِرْنِي إِلَى سَعَتِي. فَقَالَ لَهُ الشَّيْخُ وَيْحَكَ إِنَّ مَثَلَ الْوُعُودِ. كَغَرْسِ الْعُودِ. هُوَ بَيْنَ أَنْ يُدْرِكَهُ الْعَطَبُ. أَوْ يُدْرَكَ مِنْهُ الرُّطَبُ. فَمَا يُدْرِينِي أَيَحْصُلُ مِنْ عُودِكَ

---

١ في هامش س: تُعْرَفُ بِالْحَجَّامِ؛ وفي ف: وَهِيَ الْحَجْرِيَّةُ؛ وفي د: الْحَجْرِيَّةُ. ٢ في د وف: أَلَّا.

جَنًى. أَمْ أَحْصُلُ مِنْهُ عَلَى ضَنًى. ثُمَّ مَا ٱلثِّقَةُ بِأَنَّكَ حِينَ تَبْتَعِدُ. سَتَفِي بِمَا تَعِدُ. وَقَدْ صَارَ ٱلْغَدْرُ كَٱلتَّحْجِيلِ. فِي حِلْيَةِ هٰذَا ٱلْجِيلِ. فَأَرِحْنِي بِٱللهِ مِنَ ٱلتَّعْذِيبِ. وَٱرْحَلْ إِلَى حَيْثُ يَعْوِي ٱلذِّيبُ.

٣،٤٧ فَٱسْتَوَى ٱلْغُلَامُ إِلَيْهِ. وَقَدِ ٱسْتَوْلَى ٱلْخَجَلُ عَلَيْهِ. وَقَالَ وَٱللهِ مَا يَخِيسُ بِٱلْعَهْدِ. غَيْرُ ٱلْخَسِيسِ ٱلْوَغْدِ. وَلَا يَرِدُ غَدِيرَ ٱلْغَدْرِ. إِلَّا ٱلْوَضِيعُ ٱلْقَدْرِ. وَلَوْ عَرَفْتَ مَنْ أَنَا. لَمَا أَسْمَعْتَنِي ٱلْخَنَا. لٰكِنَّكَ جَهِلْتَ فَقُلْتَ. وَحَيْثُ وَجَبَ أَنْ تَسْجُدَ بُلْتَ. وَمَا أَقْبَحَ ٱلْغُرْبَةَ وَٱلْإِقْلَالَ. وَأَحْسَنَ قَوْلَ مَنْ قَالَ.

إِنَّ ٱلْغَرِيبَ ٱلطَّوِيلَ ٱلذَّيْلِ مُمْتَهَنٌ   فَكَيْفَ حَالُ غَرِيبٍ مَا لَهُ قُوتُ
لٰكِنَّهُ مَا تَشِينُ ٱلْحُرَّ مُوجِعَةٌ   فَٱلْمِسْكُ يُسْحَقُ وَٱلْكَافُورُ مَفْتُوتُ
وَطَالَمَا أُصْلِيَ ٱلْيَاقُوتُ جَمْرَ غَضًى   ثُمَّ ٱنْطَفَى ٱلْجَمْرُ وَٱلْيَاقُوتُ يَاقُوتُ

٤،٤٧ فَقَالَ لَهُ ٱلشَّيْخُ يَا وَيْلَةَ أَبِيكَ. وَعَوْلَةَ أَهْلِيكَ. أَأَنْتَ فِي مَوْقِفِ فَخْرٍ يُظْهَرُ. وَحَسَبٍ يُشْهَرُ. أَمْ مَوْقِفِ جِلْدٍ يُكْشَطُ. وَقَفًا يُشْرَطُ. وَهَبْ أَنَّ لَكَ ٱلْبَيْتَ. كَمَا ٱدَّعَيْتَ. أَيَحْصُلُ بِذٰلِكَ. حَجْمُ قَذَالِكَ. لَا وَٱللهِ وَلَوْ أَنَّ أَبَاكَ أَنَافَ. عَلَى عَبْدِ مَنَافٍ. أَوْ لِخَالِكَ دَانَ. عَبْدُ ٱلْمَدَانِ. فَلَا تَضْرِبْ فِي حَدِيدٍ بَارِدٍ. وَلَا تَطْلُبْ مَا لَسْتَ لَهُ بِوَاجِدٍ. وَبَاهِ إِذَا بَاهَيْتَ بِمَوْجُودِكَ. لَا بِجُدُودِكَ. وَبِمَحْصُولِكَ. لَا بِأُصُولِكَ. وَبِصِفَاتِكَ. لَا بِرُفَاتِكَ. وَبِأَعْلَاقِكَ. لَا بِأَعْرَاقِكَ. وَلَا تُطِعِ ٱلطَّمَعَ فَيُذِلَّكَ. وَلَا تَتَّبِعِ ٱلْهَوَى فَيُضِلَّكَ. وَلِلّٰهِ ٱلْقَائِلُ لِٱبْنِهِ

بُنَيَّ ٱسْتَقِمْ فَٱلْعُودُ تَنْمِي عُرُوقُهُ   قَوِيمًا وَيَغْشَاهُ إِذَا مَا ٱلْتَوَى ٱلتَّوَى
وَلَا تُطِعِ ٱلْحِرْصَ ٱلْمُذِلَّ وَكُنْ فَتًى   إِذَا ٱلْتَهَبَتْ أَحْشَاؤُهُ بِٱلطَّوَى طَوَى

وَعَاصِ ٱلْهَوَى ٱلْمُرْدِي فَكَمْ مِنْ مُحَلِّقٍ إِلَى ٱلنَّجْمِ لَمَّا أَنْ أَطَاعَ ٱلْهَوَى هَوَى
وَأَسْعِفْ ذَوِي ٱلْقُرْبَى فَيَقْبُحُ أَنْ يُرَى عَلَى مَنْ إِلَى ٱلْحُرِّ ٱللُّبَابِ ٱنْضَوَى ضَوَى
وَحَافِظْ عَلَى مَنْ لَا يَخُونُ إِذَا نَبَا زَمَانٌ وَمَنْ يَرْعَى إِذَا مَا ٱلنَّوَى نَوَى
وَإِنْ تَقْتَدِرْ فَٱصْفَحْ فَلَا خَيْرَ فِي ٱمْرِئٍ إِذَا ٱعْتَلَقَتْ أَظْفَارُهُ بِٱلشَّوَى شَوَى
وَإِيَّاكَ وَٱلشَّكْوَى فَلَمْ تَرَ ذَا نُهًى شَكَا بَلْ أَخُو ٱلْجَهْلِ ٱلَّذِي مَا ٱرْعَوَى عَوَى

٥،٤٧ فَقَالَ ٱلْغُلَامُ لِلنَّظَّارَةِ يَا لَلْعَجِيبَةِ. وَٱلطُّرْفَةِ ٱلْغَرِيبَةِ. أَنْفٌ فِي ٱلسَّمَاءِ. وَٱسْتٌ فِي ٱلْمَاءِ. وَلَفْظٌ كَٱلصَّهْبَاءِ. وَفِعْلٌ كَٱلْحَصْبَاءِ. ثُمَّ أَقْبَلَ عَلَى ٱلشَّيْخِ بِلِسَانٍ سَلِيطٍ. وَغَيْظٍ مُسْتَشِيطٍ. وَقَالَ أُفٍّ لَكَ مِنْ صَوَّاغٍ بِٱللِّسَانِ. رَوَّاغٍ عَنِ ٱلْإِحْسَانِ. تَأْمُرُ بِٱلْبِرِّ. وَتَعُقُّ عُقُوقَ ٱلْهِرِّ. فَإِنْ يَكُنْ سَبَبُ تَعَنُّتِكَ. نَفَاقَ صَنْعَتِكَ. فَرَمَاهَا ٱللهُ بِٱلْكَسَادِ. وَإِفْسَادِ ٱلْحُسَّادِ. حَتَّى تُرَى أَفْرَغَ مِنْ حَجَّامِ سَابَاطَ. وَأَضْيَقَ رِزْقًا مِنْ سَمِّ ٱلْخِيَاطِ. فَقَالَ لَهُ ٱلشَّيْخُ بَلْ سَلَّطَ ٱللهُ عَلَيْكَ بَثْرَ ٱلْفَمِ. وَتَبَيُّغَ ٱلدَّمِ. حَتَّى تُلْجَأَ إِلَى حَجَّامٍ عَظِيمِ ٱلِاشْتِطَاطِ. ثَقِيلِ ٱلِاشْتِرَاطِ. كَلِيلِ ٱلْمِشْرَاطِ. كَثِيرِ ٱلْمُخَاطِ وَٱلضُّرَاطِ. قَالَ فَلَمَّا تَبَيَّنَ ٱلْفَتَى أَنَّهُ يَشْكُو إِلَى غَيْرِ مُصْمِتٍ. وَيُرَاوِدُ ٱسْتِفْتَاحَ بَابٍ مُصْمَتٍ. أَضْرَبَ عَنْ رَجْعِ ٱلْكَلَامِ. وَٱحْتَفَزَ لِلْقِيَامِ.

٦،٤٧ وَعَلِمَ ٱلشَّيْخُ أَنَّهُ قَدْ أَلَامَ. بِمَا أَسْمَعَ ٱلْغُلَامَ. فَجَنَحَ إِلَى سِلْمِهِ. وَبَذَلَ أَنْ يُذْعِنَ لِحُكْمِهِ. وَلَا يَبْغِيَ أَجْرًا عَلَى حَجْمِهِ. وَأَبَى ٱلْغُلَامُ إِلَّا ٱلْمَشْيَ بِدَائِهِ. وَٱلْهَرَبَ مِنْ لِقَائِهِ. وَمَا زَالَا فِي حِجَاجٍ وَسِبَابٍ. وَلِزَازٍ وَجِذَابٍ. إِلَى أَنْ ضَجَّ ٱلْفَتَى مِنَ ٱلشِّقَاقِ. وَتَلَا رُدْنُهُ سُورَةَ ٱلِانْشِقَاقِ. فَأَعْوَلَ حِينَئِذٍ لِوَفَارَةِ خُسْرِهِ. وَٱنْعِطَاطِ عِرْضِهِ وَطِمْرِهِ. وَأَخَذَ ٱلشَّيْخُ يَعْتَذِرُ مِنْ فَرَطَاتِهِ. وَيُغَيِّضُ مِنْ عَبَرَاتِهِ. وَهُوَ لَا يُصْغِي إِلَى ٱعْتِذَارِهِ. وَلَا يُقْصِرُ عَنِ ٱسْتِعْبَارِهِ. إِلَى أَنْ قَالَ لَهُ فَدَاكَ عَمُّكَ.

وَعَدَاكَ مَا يَغُمُّكَ. أَمَا تَسْأَمُ الْإِعْوَالَ. أَمَا تَعْرِفُ الِاحْتِمَالَ. أَمَا تَسْمَعُ[١] بِمَنْ أَقَالَ. وَأَخَذَ بِقَوْلِ مَنْ قَالَ

أَخْمِدْ بِحِلْمِكَ مَا يُذْكِيهِ ذُو سَفَهٍ   مِنْ نَارِ غَيْظِكَ وَٱصْفَحْ إِنْ جَنَى جَانِ[٢]
فَالْحِلْمُ أَفْضَلُ مَا ٱزْدَانَ اللَّبِيبُ بِهِ   وَالْأَخْذُ بِالْعَفْوِ أَحْلَى مَا جَنَى جَانِ[٣]

٧،٤٧ فَقَالَ لَهُ الْغُلَامُ أَمَا إِنَّكَ لَوْ ظَهَرْتَ عَلَى عَيْشِي الْمُنْكَدِرِ. لَعَذَرْتَ فِي دَمْعِي الْمُنْهَمِرِ. وَلٰكِنْ هَانَ عَلَى الْأَمْلَسِ مَا لَاقَى الدَّبِرُ. ثُمَّ كَأَنَّهُ نَزَعَ إِلَى الِاسْتِحْيَاءِ. فَأَقْلَعَ عَنِ الْبُكَاءِ. وَفَاءَ إِلَى الِارْعِوَاءِ. وَقَالَ لِلشَّيْخِ قَدْ صِرْتُ إِلَى مَا ٱشْتَهَيْتَ. فَٱرْقَعْ مَا أَوْهَيْتَ. فَقَالَ هَيْهَاتَ شَغَلَتْ شِعَابِي جَدْوَايَ. فَشِمْ بَارِقَ سِوَايَ. ثُمَّ إِنَّهُ نَهَضَ يَسْتَقْرِي الصُّفُوفَ. وَيَسْتَجْدِي الْوُقُوفَ. وَيُنْشِدُ فِي ضِمْنِ مَا هُوَ يَطُوفُ.

أُقْسِمُ بِالْبَيْتِ الْحَرَامِ الَّذِي   تَهْوِي إِلَيْهِ الزُّمَرُ الْمُحْرِمَهْ
لَوْ أَنَّ عِنْدِي قُوتَ يَوْمٍ لَمَا   مَسَّتْ يَدِي الْمِشْرَاطَ وَالْمِحْجَمَهْ
وَلَا ٱرْتَضَتْ نَفْسِي الَّتِي لَمْ تَزَلْ   تَسْمُو إِلَى الْمَجْدِ بِهٰذِي السِّمَهْ
وَلَا ٱشْتَكَى هٰذَا الْفَتَى غِلْظَةً   مِنِّي وَلَا شَاكَتْهُ مِنِّي حُمَهْ
لٰكِنْ صُرُوفُ الدَّهْرِ غَادَرْنَنِي   كَخَابِطٍ فِي اللَّيْلَةِ الْمُظْلِمَهْ
وَٱضْطَرَّنِي الْفَقْرُ إِلَى مَوْقِفٍ   مِنْ دُونِهِ خَوْضُ اللَّظَى الْمُضْرَمَهْ
فَهَلْ فَتًى تُدْرِكُهُ رِقَّةٌ   عَلَيَّ أَوْ تَعْطِفُهُ مَرْحَمَهْ

١ س، و، د: أَلَمْ تسمع؛ ف: أَمَا سمعت. ٢ و، ف، د: جَانِي. ٣ و، ف، د: جَانِي.

٨،٤٧ قَالَ الْحَارِثُ بْنُ هَمَّامٍ فَكُنْتُ أَوَّلَ مَنْ أَوَى لِبَلْوَاهُ. وَرَقَّ لِشَكْوَاهُ. فَنَفَحْتُهُ بِدِرْهَمَيْنِ. وَقُلْتُ لَا كَانَا وَلَوْ كَانَ ذَا مَيْنٍ. فَابْتَهَجَ بِبَاكُورَةِ جَنَاهُ. وَتَفَاءَلَ بِهِمَا لِغِنَاهُ. وَلَمْ تَزَلِ الدَّرَاهِمُ تَنْهَالُ عَلَيْهِ. وَتَنْثَالُ لَدَيْهِ. حَتَّى آلَ ذَا عِيشَةٍ خَضْرَاءَ. وَحَقِيبَةٍ بَجْرَاءَ. فَازْدَهَاهُ الْفَرَحُ عِنْدَ ذٰلِكَ. وَهَنَّأَ نَفْسَهُ بِمَا هُنَالِكَ. وَقَالَ لِلْغُلَامِ هٰذَا رَيْعٌ أَنْتَ بَذْرُهُ. وَحَلَبٌ لَكَ شَطْرُهُ. فَهَلُمَّ لِنَقْتَسِمَ. وَلَا نَحْتَشِمَ. فَتَقَاسَمَاهُ بَيْنَهُمَا شَقَّ[1] الْأَبْلُمَةِ. وَنَهَضَا مُتَّفِقَيِ الْكَلِمَةِ. وَلَمَّا انْتَظَمَ[2] عَقْدُ الِاصْطِلَاحِ. وَهَمَّ الشَّيْخُ بِالرَّوَاحِ. قُلْتُ لَهُ قَدْ تَبَوَّغَ دَمِي. وَنَقَلْتُ إِلَيْكَ قَدَمِي. فَهَلْ لَكَ أَنْ تَحْجُمَنِي. وَتُكَفْكِفَ مَا دَهَمَنِي. فَصَوَّبَ طَرْفَهُ وَصَعَّدَ. ثُمَّ ازْدَلَفَ إِلَيَّ وَأَنْشَدَ.

٩،٤٧ كَيْفَ رَأَيْتَ خُدْعَتِي وَخَتْلِي ... وَمَا جَرَى بَيْنِي وَبَيْنَ سَخْلِي
حَتَّى انْثَنَيْتُ فَائِزًا بِالْخَصْلِ ... أَرْعَى رِيَاضَ الْخِصْبِ بَعْدَ الْمَحْلِ[3]
بِاللهِ يَا مُهْجَةَ قَلْبِي قُلْ لِي ... هَلْ أَبْصَرَتْ عَيْنَاكَ قَطُّ مِثْلِي
يَفْتَحُ بِالرُّقْيَةِ كُلَّ قُفْلِ ... وَيَسْتَبِي بِالسِّحْرِ كُلَّ عَقْلِ
وَيَعْجِنُ الْجِدَّ بِمَاءِ الْهَزْلِ ... إِنْ يَكُنِ الْإِسْكَنْدَرِيُّ قَبْلِي
فَالطَّلُّ قَدْ يَبْدُو أَمَامَ الْوَبْلِ ... وَالْفَضْلُ لِلْوَابِلِ لَا لِلطَّلِّ

قَالَ فَنَبَّهَتْنِي أُرْجُوزَتُهُ عَلَيْهِ. وَأَرَتْنِي أَنَّهُ شَيْخُنَا الْمُشَارُ إِلَيْهِ. فَقَرَّعْتُهُ عَلَى الِابْتِذَالِ. وَالِالْتِحَاقِ بِالْأَرْذَالِ. فَأَعْرَضَ عَمَّا سَمِعَ. وَلَمْ يُبَلْ بِمَا قُرِّعَ. وَقَالَ كُلُّ الْحِذَاءِ يَحْتَذِي الْحَافِي الْوَقِعُ. ثُمَّ قَاصَانِي مُقَاصَاةَ الْمُهَانِ. وَانْطَلَقَ هُوَ وَابْنُهُ كَفَرَسَيْ رِهَانٍ.

١ و،د، ف: شِقّ.   ٢ بعدها في ف: بينهما.   ٣ ما بعدها إلى كلمة «مثل» في ١٠،٤٧ ساقط من و.

١٠،٤٧ قَالَ ٱلْقَاسِمُ بْنُ عَلِيٍّ قَدْ أَوْدَعْتُ هٰذِهِ ٱلْمَقَامَةَ بِضْعَةَ عَشَرَ مَثَلًا مِنْ أَمْثَالِ ٱلْعَرَبِ فَسَّرْتُ[١] مِنْهَا مَا خِلْتُهُ يَلْتَبِسُ عَلَى مَنْ يَقْتَبِسُ أَمَّا قَوْلُهُ بُطْءَ فِنْدٍ فَهُوَ مَوْلَى عَائِشَةَ بِنْتِ سَعْدِ بْنِ أَبِي وَقَّاصٍ وَكَانَتْ بَعَثَتْهُ فِي ٱلْمَدِينَةِ لِيَقْتَبِسَ لَهَا نَارًا فَقَصَدَ مِصْرَ وَأَقَامَ بِهَا سَنَةً ثُمَّ جَاءَهَا بَعْدَ ٱلسَّنَةِ يَشْتَدُّ[٢] وَمَعَهُ جَمْرٌ فَتَبَدَّدَ مِنْهُ فَقَالَ تَعِسَتِ ٱلْعَجَلَةُ. وَأَمَّا ذَاتُ ٱلنِّحْيَيْنِ فَهِيَ ٱمْرَأَةٌ مِنْ تَيْمِ ٱللّٰهِ بْنِ ثَعْلَبَةَ حَضَرَتْ سُوقَ عُكَاظَ وَمَعَهَا نِحْيَا سَمْنٍ فَاسْتَخْلَى بِهَا خَوَّاتُ بْنُ جُبَيْرٍ ٱلْأَنْصَارِيُّ لِيَبْتَاعَهُمَا مِنْهَا فَفَتَحَ أَحَدَهُمَا وَذَاقَهُ وَدَفَعَهُ إِلَيْهَا فَأَخَذَتْهُ بِإِحْدَى يَدَيْهَا ثُمَّ فَتَحَ ٱلْآخَرَ وَذَاقَهُ وَدَفَعَهُ إِلَيْهَا فَأَمْسَكَتْهُ بِيَدِهَا ٱلْأُخْرَى ثُمَّ غَشِيَهَا وَهِيَ لَا تَقْدِرُ عَلَى ٱلدَّفْعِ عَنْ نَفْسِهَا لِحِفْظِهَا فَمَ ٱلنِّحْيَيْنِ وَشُحِّهَا عَلَى ٱلسَّمْنِ فَلَمَّا قَامَ عَنْهَا قَالَتْ لَا هَنَأَكَ فَضُرِبَ بِهَا ٱلْمَثَلُ فِيمَنْ شُغِلَ وَهِيَ فِي هٰذَا ٱلْمَثَلِ مَفْعُولَةٌ لِأَنَّهَا شُغِلَتْ وَأَكْثَرُ ٱلْأَمْثَالِ ٱلَّتِي عَلَى أَفْعَلَ تَأْتِي مِنْ فِعْلِ ٱلْفَاعِلِ.

١١،٤٧ وَأَمَّا قَوْلُهُ أَنْفٌ فِي ٱلسَّمَاءِ وَٱسْتٌ فِي ٱلْمَاءِ يُضْرَبُ هٰذَا ٱلْمَثَلُ لِمَنْ يَتَكَبَّرُ قَوْلًا وَيَصْغُرُ فَعَالًا. وَأَمَّا قَوْلُهُ أَفْرَغُ مِنْ حَجَّامِ سَابَاطٍ فَذُكِرَ أَنَّهُ كَانَ حَجَّامًا مُلَازِمًا سَابَاطَ ٱلْمَدَائِنِ يَحْجُمُ ٱلْجُنْدِيَّ بِدَانِقٍ نَسِيئَةً وَرُبَّمَا مَرَّتْ عَلَيْهِ بُرْهَةٌ لَا يَقْرُبُهُ فِيهَا أَحَدٌ فَكَانَ يَجْرَحُ[٣] أُمَّهُ عِنْدَ تَمَادِي عُطْلَتِهِ فَيَحْجُمُهَا لِكَيْلَا يُقْرَعَ بِٱلْبَطَالَةِ فَمَا زَالَ يَحْجُمُهَا حَتَّى نَزَفَ دَمُهَا وَمَاتَتْ. وَأَمَّا قَوْلُهُ تَشْكُو إِلَى غَيْرِ مُصْمِتٍ فَهُوَ مَثَلٌ[٤] يُضْرَبُ لِمَنْ لَا يَكْتَرِثُ بِشَأْنِ صَاحِبِهِ وَلَا يُبَالِي بِٱسْتِمْرَارِ شِكَايَتِهِ لِأَنَّهُ لَوْ أَشْكَاهُ لَصَمَّتَ[٥] وَأَمْسَكَ عَنِ ٱلْكَلَامِ وَمِنْهُ قَوْلُ ٱلرَّاجِزِ يُخَاطِبُ جَمَلًا لَهُ

إِنَّكَ لَا تَشْكُو إِلَى مُصَمِّتٍ   فَٱصْبِرْ عَلَى ٱلْحِمْلِ ٱلثَّقِيلِ أَوْ مُتِ

١ بعدها في د، ف: وها أنا أفسر. ٢ ليس في س. ٣ س، د، ف: يُبْرِزُ. ٤ إلى ههنا ساقط من و. ٥ و: صَمَتَ.

وَنَحْوَ هٰذَا الْمَثَلِ هَانَ عَلَى الْأَمْلَسِ مَا لَاقَى الدَّبِرُ. وَأَمَّا قَوْلُهُ شَغَلَتْ شِعَابِي جَدْوَايَ فَالْمُرَادُ بِهِ أَنَّهُ لَيْسَ يَفْضُلُ عَنِّي مَا أَصْرِفُهُ إِلَى غَيْرِي وَالشِّعَابُ النَّوَاحِي وَاحِدُهَا شِعْبٌ. وَقَوْلُهُ كُلَّ الْحِذَاءِ يَحْتَذِي الْحَافِي الْوَقِعُ مَعْنَاهُ أَنَّ الْمَجْهُودَ يَقْنَعُ بِمَا يَجِدُ وَالْوَقَعُ أَنْ يُصِيبَ الْحِجَارَةُ الْقَدَمَ فَتُوهِنَهَا. فَأَمَّا الْبَعِيرُ الْمُوَقَّعُ فَهُوَ الَّذِي تَكْثُرُ آثَارُ الدَّبَرِ بِظَهْرِهِ.

الْمَقَامَةُ الثَّامِنَةُ وَالْأَرْبَعُونَ وَتُعْرَفُ بِالْحَرَامِيَّةِ[1]

١،٤٨ رَوَى الْحَارِثُ بْنُ هَمَّامٍ عَنْ أَبِي زَيْدٍ السَّرُوجِيِّ قَالَ مَا زِلْتُ مُذْ رَحَلْتُ عَنْسِي. وَٱرْتَحَلْتُ عَنْ عِرْسِي وَغَرْسِي. أَحِنُّ إِلَى عِيَانِ الْبَصْرَةِ. حَنِينَ[2] الْمَظْلُومِ إِلَى النُّصْرَةِ. لِمَا أَجْمَعَ عَلَيْهِ أَرْبَابُ الدِّرَايَةِ. وَأَصْحَابُ الرِّوَايَةِ. مِنْ خَصَائِصِ مَعَالِمِهَا وَعُلَمَائِهَا. وَمَآثِرِ مَشَاهِدِهَا وَشُهَدَائِهَا. وَأَسْأَلُ اللهَ أَنْ يُوطِئَنِي ثَرَاهَا. لِأَفُوزَ بِمَرْآهَا. وَأَنْ يُمْطِيَنِي قَرَاهَا. لِأَقْتَرِيَ قُرَاهَا. فَلَمَّا أَحَلَّنِيهَا الْحَظُّ. وَسَرَحَ لِي فِيهَا اللَّحْظُ.

رَأَيْتُ بِهَا مَا يَمْلَأُ الْعَيْنَ قُرَّةً   وَيُسْلِي عَنِ الْأَوْطَانِ كُلَّ غَرِيبِ

٢،٤٨ فَغَلَّسْتُ فِي بَعْضِ الْأَيَّامِ. حِينَ نَصَلَ خِضَابُ الظَّلَامِ. وَهَتَفَ أَبُو الْمُنْذِرِ بِالنُّوَّامِ. لِأَخْطُوَ فِي خِطَطِهَا. وَأَقْضِيَ الْوَطَرَ مِنْ تَوَسُّطِهَا. فَأَدَّانِي الِاخْتِرَاقُ فِي مَسَالِكِهَا. وَالِانْصِلَاتُ فِي سِكَكِهَا. إِلَى مَحَلَّةٍ مَوْسُومَةٍ بِالِاحْتِرَامِ. مَنْسُوبَةٍ إِلَى بَنِي حَرَامٍ. ذَاتِ مَسَاجِدَ مَشْهُودَةٍ. وَحِيَاضٍ مَوْرُودَةٍ. وَمَبَانٍ وَثِيقَةٍ. وَمَغَانٍ أَنِيقَةٍ. وَخَصَائِصَ أَثِيرَةٍ. وَمَزَايَا كَثِيرَةٍ.

بِهَا مَا شِئْتَ مِنْ دِينٍ وَدُنْيَا   وَجِيرَانٍ تَنَافَوْا فِي الْمَعَانِي
فَمَشْغُوفٌ بِآيَاتِ الْمَثَانِي   وَمَفْتُونٌ بِرَنَّاتِ الْمَثَانِي
وَمُضْطَلِعٌ بِتَلْخِيصِ الْمَعَانِي   وَمُطَّلِعٌ إِلَى تَخْلِيصِ عَانِ

---

١ في س وفي هامش د: وتعرف بالحرامية؛ وفي ف: الحرامية. ٢ س: ولا حنين.

وَكَمْ مِنْ قَـارِئٍ فِيهَا وَقَـارٍ   أَضَـرَّا بِالْجُـفُونِ وَبِالْجِفَـانِ
وَكَمْ مِنْ مَـعْـلَمٍ لِلْعِـلْمِ فِيهَـا   وَنَـادٍ لِلنَّدَى حُـلْوِ الْمَجَـانِي
وَمَـغْـنًى لَا تَـزَالُ تُغِنُّ فِيهِ   أَغَـارِيدُ الْغَوَانِي وَالْأَغَـانِي
فَصِلْ إِنْ شِئْتَ فِيهَا مَنْ يُصَلِّي   وَإِمَّا شِئْتَ فَادْنُ مِنَ الدِّنَـانِ
وَدُونَكَ صُحْـبَةَ الْأَكْيَاسِ فِيهَا   أَوِ الْكَاسَاتِ مُنْطَلِقَ الْعِنَانِ

٣،٤٨ قَالَ فَبَيْنَمَا أَنَا أَنْفُضُ طُرُقَهَا. وَأَسْتَشِفُّ رَوْنَقَهَا. إِذْ لَمَحْتُ عِنْدَ دُلُوكِ بَرَاحِ. وَإِظْلَالِ الرَّوَاحِ. مَسْجِدًا مُشْتَهِرًا بِطَرَائِفِهِ. مُزْدَهِرًا بِطَوَائِفِهِ. وَقَدْ أَجْرَى أَهْلُهُ ذِكْرَ حُرُوفِ الْبَدَلِ. وَجَرَوْا فِي حَلْبَةِ الْجَدَلِ. فَعُجْتُ نَحْوَهُمْ. لِأَسْتَمْطِرَ نَوْءَهُمْ. لَا لِأَقْتَبِسَ نَحْوَهُمْ. فَلَمْ يَكُ إِلَّا كَقَبْسَةِ الْعَجْلَانِ. حَتَّى ٱرْتَفَعَتِ الْأَصْوَاتُ بِالْأَذَانِ. ثُمَّ رَدِفَ التَّأْذِينَ بُرُوزُ الْإِمَامِ. فَأُغْمِدَتْ ظُبَى الْكَلَامِ. وَحُلَّتِ الْحُبَى لِلْقِيَامِ. وَشُغِلْنَا بِالْقُنُوتِ. عَنِ ٱسْتِمْدَادِ الْقُوتِ. وَبِالسُّجُودِ. عَنِ ٱسْتِنْزَالِ الْجُودِ. وَلَمَّا قُضِيَ الْفَرْضُ. وَكَادَ الْجَمْعُ يَنْفَضُّ. ٱنْبَرَى مِنَ الْجَمَاعَةِ. كَهْلٌ حُلْوُ الْبَرَاعَةِ. لَهُ مَعَ السَّمْتِ الْحَسَنِ. ذَلَاقَةُ اللَّسَنِ. وَفَصَاحَةُ الْحَسَنِ. وَقَالَ يَا جِيرَتِي الَّذِينَ ٱصْطَفَيْتُهُمْ عَلَى أَغْصَانِ شَجَرَتِي. وَجَعَلْتُ خِطَّتَهُمْ دَارَ هِجْرَتِي. وَٱتَّخَذْتُهُمْ كَرِشِي وَعَيْبَتِي. وَأَعْدَدْتُهُمْ لِمَحْضَرِي وَغَيْبَتِي. أَمَا تَعْلَمُونَ أَنَّ لَبُوسَ الصِّدْقِ أَبْهَى الْمَلَابِسِ الْفَاخِرَةِ. وَأَنَّ فُضُوحَ الدُّنْيَا أَهْوَنُ مِنْ فُضُوحِ الْآخِرَةِ. وَأَنَّ الدِّينَ إِمْحَاضُ النَّصِيحَةِ. وَالْإِرْشَادَ عُنْوَانُ الْعَقِيدَةِ الصَّحِيحَةِ. وَأَنَّ الْمُسْتَشَارَ مُؤْتَمَنٌ. وَالْمُسْتَرْشِدَ بِالنُّصْحِ قَمِنٌ.[١] وَأَنَّ أَخَاكَ هُوَ الَّذِي عَذَلَكَ. لَا الَّذِي عَذَرَكَ. وَصَدِيقَكَ مَنْ صَدَقَكَ. لَا مَنْ صَدَّقَكَ. فَقَالَ لَهُ الْحَاضِرُونَ

١ س: قَمَن.

أَيُّهَا الْخِلُّ الْوَدُودُ. وَالْخِدْنُ الْمَوْدُودُ. مَا سِرُّ كَلَامِكَ الْمُلْغِزِ. وَمَا شَرْحُ خِطَابِكَ الْمُوجَزِ. وَمَا الَّذِي تَبْغِيهِ مِنَّا لِيُنْجَزَ.[1] فَوَالَّذِي حَبَانَا بِمَحَبَّتِكَ. وَجَعَلَنَا مِنْ صَفْوَةِ أَحِبَّتِكَ. مَا نَأْلُوكَ نَصْحًا.[2] وَلَا نَدَّخِرُ عَنْكَ نُصْحًا.[3]

٤،٤٨ فَقَالَ جُزِيتُمْ خَيْرًا. وَوُقِيتُمْ ضَيْرًا. فَإِنَّكُمْ مِمَّنْ لَا يَشْقَى بِهِمْ جَلِيسٌ. وَلَا يَصْدُرُ عَنْهُمْ تَلْبِيسٌ. وَلَا يُخَيَّبُ[4] فِيهِمْ مَظْنُونٌ. وَلَا يُطْوَى دُونَهُمْ مَكْنُونٌ. وَسَأُبِثُّكُمْ مَا حَكَّ[5] فِي صَدْرِي. وَأَسْتَفْتِيكُمْ فِيمَا عِيلَ لَهُ[6] صَبْرِي. اِعْلَمُوا أَنِّي كُنْتُ عِنْدَ صُلُودِ الزَّنْدِ. وَصُدُودِ الْجَدِّ. أَخْلَصْتُ مَعَ اللهِ نِيَّةَ الْعَقْدِ. وَأَعْطَيْتُهُ صَفْقَةَ الْعَهْدِ. عَلَى أَلَّا أَسْبَأَ مُدَامًا. وَلَا أُعَاقِرَ نَدَامَى. وَلَا أَحْتَسِيَ قَهْوَةً. وَلَا أَكْتَسِيَ نَشْوَةً. فَسَوَّلَتْ لِيَ النَّفْسُ الْمُضِلَّةُ. وَالشَّهْوَةُ[7] الْمُزِلَّةُ. أَنْ نَادَمْتُ الْأَبْطَالَ. وَعَاطَيْتُ الْأَرْطَالَ. وَأَضَعْتُ الْوَقَارَ. وَارْتَضَعْتُ الْعُقَارَ. وَامْتَطَيْتُ مَطَا الْكُمَيْتِ. وَتَنَاسَيْتُ التَّوْبَةَ كَالْمَيْتِ.[8] ثُمَّ لَمْ أَقْنَعْ بِهَاتِيكُمُ الْمَرَّةِ. فِي طَاعَةِ أَبِي مُرَّةَ. حَتَّى عَكَفْتُ عَلَى الْخَنْدَرِيسِ. فِي يَوْمِ الْخَمِيسِ. وَبِتُّ صَرِيعَ الصَّهْبَاءِ. فِي اللَّيْلَةِ الْغَرَّاءِ. وَهَا أَنَا بَادِي الْكَآبَةِ. لِرَفْضِ الْإِنَابَةِ. نَامِي النَّدَامَةِ. لِوَصْلِ الْمُدَامَةِ. شَدِيدُ الْإِشْفَاقِ. مِنْ نَقْضِ الْمِيثَاقِ. مُعْتَرِفٌ بِالْإِسْرَافِ. فِي عَبِّ السُّلَافِ.

فَيَا قَوْمِ هَلْ كَفَّارَةٌ تَعْرِفُونَهَا   تُبَاعِدُ مِنْ ذَنْبِي وَتُدْنِي إِلَى رَبِّي

٥،٤٨ قَالَ أَبُو زَيْدٍ فَلَمَّا حَلَّ أُنْشُوطَةَ نَفْثِهِ. وَقَضَى الْوَطَرَ مِنِ اشْتِكَاءِ بَثِّهِ. نَاجَتْنِي نَفْسِي يَا أَبَا زَيْدٍ. هٰذِهِ نُهْزَةُ صَيْدٍ. فَشَمِّرْ عَنْ يَدٍ وَأَيْدٍ. فَانْتَهَضْتُ مِنْ مَجْثِمِي انْتِهَاضَ الشَّهْمِ. وَانْخَرَطْتُ مِنَ الصَّفِّ انْخِرَاطَ السَّهْمِ. وَقُلْتُ

١ . بعدها في س،د،و: ولوأعجز. ٢ د،ف: نصحا. ٣ د،ف: نضحا؛ وفي و: نَضْحا. ٤ س،د:يَخيب. ٥ ف: حاك. ٦ ف: فيه. ٧ بعدها في ف: المُذِلَّة. ٨ ف: تَناسيَ المَيْت.

أَيُّهَا ٱلْأَرْوَعُ ٱلَّذِي فَاقَ مَجْدًا وَسُؤْدَدَا
وَٱلَّذِي يَبْتَغِي ٱلرَّشَادَ لِيَنْجُوَ بِهِ غَدَا
إِنَّ عِنْدِي عِلَاجَ مَا بِتُّ مِنْهُ مُسَهَّدَا
فَٱسْتَمِعْهَا عُجَيِّبَةً غَادَرَتْنِي مُلَدَّدَا
أَنَا مِنْ سَاكِنِي سَرُوجَ ذَوِي ٱلدِّينِ وَٱلْهُدَى
كُنْتُ ذَا ثَرْوَةٍ بِهَا وَمُطَاعًا مُسَوَّدَا
مَرْبَعِي مَأْلَفُ ٱلضُّيُوفِ وَمَالِي لَهُمْ سُدَى
أَشْتَرِي ٱلْحَمْدَ بِٱللُّهَى وَأَقِي ٱلْعِرْضَ بِٱلْجَدَا
لَا أُبَالِي بِمُنْفِسٍ طَاحَ فِي ٱلْبَذْلِ وَٱلنَّدَى
أُوقِدُ ٱلنَّارَ بِٱلْيَفَاعِ إِذَا ٱلنِّكْسُ أَخْمَدَا
وَيَرَانِي ٱلْمُؤَمِّلُونَ مَلَاذًا وَمَقْصِدَا
لَمْ يَشِمْ بَارِقِي صَدٍ فَٱنْثَنَى يَشْتَكِي ٱلصَّدَى
لَا وَلَا رَامَ قَابِسٌ قَدْحَ زَنْدِي فَأَصْلَدَا
٦،٤٨ طَالَمَا سَاعَدَ ٱلزَّمَانُ فَأَصْبَحْتُ مُسْعِدَا
فَقَضَى ٱللّٰهُ أَنْ يُغَيِّرَ مَا كَانَ عَوَّدَا
بَوَّأَ ٱلرُّومَ أَرْضَنَا بَعْدَ ضِغْنٍ تَوَلَّدَا
فَٱسْتَبَاحُوا حَرِيمَ مَنْ صَادَفُوهُ مُوَحِّدَا
وَحَوَوْا كُلَّ مَا ٱسْتَتَرَّ بِهَا لِي وَمَا بَدَا
فَتَطَوَّحْتُ فِي ٱلْبِلَادِ طَرِيدًا مُشَرَّدَا
أَجْتَدِي ٱلنَّاسَ بَعْدَمَا كُنْتُ مِنْ قَبْلُ مُجْتَدَى
وَتُرَى بِي خَصَاصَةٌ أَتَمَنَّى لَهَا ٱلرَّدَى

وَالْبَلَاءُ الَّذِي بِهِ شَمْلُ أُنْسِي تَبَدَّدَا
إِسْتِبَاءُ ابْنَتِي الَّتِي أَسَرُوهَا لِتُفْتَدَى
٧،٤٨ فَٱسْتَبِنْ مِحْنَتِي وَمُدَّ إِلَى نُصْرَتِي يَدَا
وَأَجِرْنِي مِنَ الزَّمَانِ فَقَدْ جَارَ وَٱعْتَدَى
وَأَعِنِّي عَلَى فَكَاكِ ٱبْنَتِي مِنْ يَدِ الْعِدَى
فَبِذَا تَنْمَحِي الْمَآثِمُ عَمَّنْ تَمَرَّدَا
وَبِهِ تُقْبَلُ الْإِنَابَةُ مِمَّنْ تَزَهَّدَا
وَهْوَ كَفَّارَةٌ لِمَنْ زَاغَ مِنْ بَعْدِ مَا ٱهْتَدَى
وَلَئِنْ قُمْتُ مُنْشِدًا فَلَقَدْ فُهْتُ مُرْشِدَا
فَٱقْبَلِ النُّصْحَ وَالْهِدَايَةَ وَٱشْكُرْ لِمَنْ هَدَى
وَٱسْمَحِ الْآنَ بِالَّذِي يَتَسَنَّى لِتُحْمَدَا

٨،٤٨ قَالَ أَبُو زَيْدٍ فَلَمَّا أَتْمَمْتُ هَذْرَمَتِي. وَأَوْهَمَ الْمَسْؤُولُ صِدْقَ كَلِمَتِي. أَغْرَاهُ الْقَرَمُ إِلَى الْكَرَمِ بِمُؤَاسَاتِي. وَرَغَّبَهُ الْكَلَفُ بِحَمْلِ الْكُلَفِ فِي مُقَاسَاتِي. فَرَضَخَ لِي عَلَى الْحَافِرَةِ. وَنَضَحَ لِي بِالْعِدَةِ الْوَافِرَةِ. فَٱنْقَلَبْتُ إِلَى وَكْرِي. فَرِحًا بِنُجْحِ مَكْرِي. وَقَدْ حَصَلْتُ مِنْ صَوْغِ الْمَكِيدَةِ. عَلَى سَوْغِ الثَّرِيدَةِ. وَوَصَلْتُ مِنْ حَوْكِ الْقَصِيدَةِ. إِلَى لَوْكِ الْعَصِيدَةِ.

٩،٤٨ قَالَ الْحَارِثُ بْنُ هَمَّامٍ فَقُلْتُ لَهُ سُبْحَانَ مَنْ أَبْدَعَكَ.[١] فَمَا أَعْظَمَ خُدَعَكَ. فَٱسْتَغْرَبَ فِي الضَّحِكِ. ثُمَّ أَنْشَدَ غَيْرَ مُرْتَبِكٍ

١ بعدها في ف: وأَخْبَثَ بِدَعَك.

عِشْ بِالْخِدَاعِ فَأَنْتَ فِي   دَهْرٍ بَنُوهُ كَأُسْدِ بِيشَهْ
وَأَدِرْ قَنَاةَ الْمَكْرِ حَتَّى   تَسْتَدِيرَ رَحَى الْمَعِيشَهْ
وَصِدِ النُّسُورَ فَإِنْ تَعَذَّ   رَ صَيْدُهَا فَٱقْنَعْ بِرِيشَهْ
وَٱجْنِ الثِّمَارَ فَإِنْ تَفُتْكَ   فَرَضِّ نَفْسَكَ بِالْحَشِيشَهْ
وَأَرِحْ فُؤَادَكَ إِنْ نَبَا   دَهْرٌ مِنَ الْفِكَرِ الْمُطِيشَهْ
فَتَغَايُرُ الْأَحْدَاثِ يُؤْ   ذِنُ بِٱسْتِحَالَةِ كُلِّ عِيشَهْ

الْمَقَامَةُ التَّاسِعَةُ وَالْأَرْبَعُونَ[1]

١،٤٩ حَكَى الْحَارِثُ بْنُ هَمَّامٍ قَالَ بَلَغَنِي أَنَّ أَبَا زَيْدٍ حِينَ نَاهَزَ الْقَبْضَةَ. وَٱبْتَزَّهُ قَيْدُ الْهَرَمِ النَّهْضَةَ. أَحْضَرَ ٱبْنَهُ. بَعْدَ مَا ٱسْتَجَاشَ ذِهْنَهُ. وَقَالَ لَهُ يَا بُنَيَّ إِنَّهُ قَدْ دَنَا ٱرْتِحَالِي مِنَ الْفِنَاءِ. وَٱكْتِحَالِي بِمِرْوَدِ الْفَنَاءِ. وَأَنْتَ بِحَمْدِ اللهِ وَلِيُّ عَهْدِي. وَكَبْشُ الْكَتِيبَةِ السَّاسَانِيَّةِ مِنْ بَعْدِي. وَمِثْلُكَ لَا تُقْرَعُ لَهُ الْعَصَا. وَلَا يُنَبَّهُ بِطَرْقِ الْحَصَى. وَلٰكِنْ قَدْ نُدِبَ إِلَى الْإِذْكَارِ. وَجُعِلَ صَيْقَلًا لِلْأَفْكَارِ. وَإِنِّي أُوصِيكَ بِمَا لَمْ يُوصِ بِهِ شِيثُ الْأَنْبَاطَ. وَلَا يَعْقُوبُ الْأَسْبَاطَ. فَٱحْفَظْ وَصِيَّتِي. وَجَانِبْ مَعْصِيَتِي. وَٱحْذُ مِثَالِي. وَٱفْقَهْ أَمْثَالِي. فَإِنَّكَ إِنِ ٱسْتَرْشَدْتَ بِنُصْحِي.[2] وَٱسْتَصْبَحْتَ بِصُبْحِي. أَمْرَعَ خَانُكَ. وَٱرْتَفَعَ دُخَانُكَ. وَإِنْ تَنَاسَيْتَ سُورَتِي. وَنَبَذْتَ مَشُورَتِي. قَلَّ رَمَادُ أَثَافِيكَ. وَزَهِدَ أَهْلُكَ وَرَهْطُكَ فِيكَ.

٢،٤٩ يَا بُنَيَّ إِنِّي جَرَّبْتُ حَقَائِقَ الْأُمُورِ. وَبَلَوْتُ تَصَارِيفَ الدُّهُورِ. فَرَأَيْتُ الْمَرْءَ بِنَشَبِهِ. لَا بِنَسَبِهِ. وَالْفَحْصَ عَنْ مَكْسَبِهِ. لَا عَنْ حَسَبِهِ. وَكُنْتُ سَمِعْتُ أَنَّ الْمَعَايِشَ إِمَارَةٌ. وَتِجَارَةٌ. وَزِرَاعَةٌ. وَصِنَاعَةٌ. فَمَارَسْتُ هٰذِهِ الْأَرْبَعَ. لِأَنْظُرَ أَيُّهَا أَوْفَقُ وَأَنْفَعُ. فَمَا أَحْمَدْتُ مِنْهَا مَعِيشَةً. وَلَا ٱسْتَرْغَدْتُ فِيهَا عِيشَةً. أَمَّا فُرَصُ الْوِلَايَاتِ. وَخُلَسُ الْإِمَارَاتِ. فَكَأَضْغَاثِ الْأَحْلَامِ. وَالْفَيْءِ الْمُنْتَسِخِ بِالظَّلَامِ. وَنَاهِيكَ غُصَّةً بِمَرَارَةِ الْفِطَامِ. وَأَمَّا بَضَائِعُ التِّجَارَاتِ. فَعُرْضَةٌ لِلْمُخَاطَرَاتِ. وَطُعْمَةٌ لِلْغَارَاتِ. وَمَا أَشْبَهَهَا بِالطُّيُورِ الطَّيَّارَاتِ. وَأَمَّا ٱتِّخَاذُ الضِّيَاعِ. وَالتَّصَدِّي لِلِازْدِرَاعِ. فَمَنْهَكَةٌ لِلْأَعْرَاضِ. وَقُيُودٌ عَائِقَةٌ عَنِ الِارْتِكَاضِ. وَقَلَّمَا

١ . في هامش س: تُعرف بالساسانية؛ د: الساسانية؛ ف: وهي الساسانية. ٢ س، و، د: اسْتَنْصَحْتَ نُصْحِي

خَلَا رَبُّهَا عَنْ إِذْلَالٍ. أَوْ رُزِقَ رَوْحَ بَالٍ. وَأَمَّا حِرَفُ أُولِي الصِّنَاعَاتِ. فَغَيْرُ فَاضِلَةٍ عَنِ الْأَقْوَاتِ. وَلَا نَافِقَةٍ فِي جَمِيعِ الْأَوْقَاتِ. وَمُعْظَمُهَا مَعْصُوبٌ بِشَبِيبَةِ الْحَيَاةِ.

٣،٤٩ وَلَمْ أَرَ مَا هُوَ بَارِدُ الْمَغْنَمِ. لَذِيذُ الْمَطْعَمِ. وَافِي الْمَكْسَبِ. صَافِي الْمَشْرَبِ. إِلَّا الْحِرْفَةَ الَّتِي وَضَعَ سَاسَانُ أَسَاسَهَا. وَنَوَّعَ أَجْنَاسَهَا. وَأَضْرَمَ فِي الْخَافِقَيْنِ نَارَهَا. وَأَوْضَحَ لِبَنِي غَبْرَاءَ مَنَارَهَا. فَشَهِدْتُ وَقَائِعَهَا مُعْلِمًا. وَٱخْتَرْتُ سِيمَاهَا لِي مِيسَمًا. إِذْ كَانَتِ الْمَتْجَرَ ٱلَّذِي لَا يَبُورُ. وَالْمَنْهَلَ الَّذِي لَا يَغُورُ. وَالْمِصْبَاحَ الَّذِي يَعْشُو إِلَيْهِ الْجُمْهُورُ. وَيَسْتَصْبِحُ بِهِ الْعُمْيُ وَالْعُورُ. وَكَانَ أَهْلُهَا أَعَزَّ قَبِيلٍ. وَأَسْعَدَ جِيلٍ. لَا يَرْهَقُهُمْ مَسُّ حَيْفٍ. وَلَا يُقْلِقُهُمْ سَلُّ سَيْفٍ. وَلَا يَخْشَوْنَ حُمَةَ لَاسِعٍ. وَلَا يَدِينُونَ لِدَانٍ وَلَا شَاسِعٍ. وَلَا يَرْهَبُونَ مِمَّنْ بَرَقَ وَرَعَدَ. وَلَا يَحْفِلُونَ بِمَنْ قَامَ وَقَعَدَ. أَنْدِيَتُهُمْ مُنَزَّهَةٌ. وَقُلُوبُهُمْ مُرَفَّهَةٌ. وَطُعَمُهُمْ مُعَجَّلَةٌ. وَأَوْقَاتُهُمْ غُرٌّ مُحَجَّلَةٌ. أَيْنَمَا سَقَطُوا. لَقَطُوا. وَحَيْثُمَا ٱنْخَرَطُوا. خَرَطُوا. لَا يَتَّخِذُونَ أَوْطَانًا. وَلَا يَتَّقُونَ سُلْطَانًا. وَلَا يَمْتَازُونَ عَمَّا تَغْدُو خِمَاصًا. وَتَرُوحُ بِطَانًا.

٤،٤٩ فَقَالَ لَهُ ٱبْنُهُ يَا أَبَتِ لَقَدْ صَدَقْتَ. فِيمَا نَطَقْتَ. وَلٰكِنَّكَ رَتَقْتَ. وَمَا فَتَقْتَ. فَبَيِّنْ لِي كَيْفَ أَقْتَطِفُ. وَمِنْ أَيْنَ تُؤْكَلُ الْكَتِفُ. فَقَالَ يَا بُنَيَّ إِنَّ الِارْتِكَاضَ بَابُهَا. وَالنَّشَاطَ جِلْبَابُهَا. وَالْفِطْنَةَ مِصْبَاحُهَا. وَالْقِحَةَ سِلَاحُهَا. فَكُنْ أَجْوَلَ مِنْ قُطْرُبٍ. وَأَسْرَى مِنْ جُنْدُبٍ. وَأَنْشَطَ مِنْ ظَبْيٍ مُقْمِرٍ. وَأَسْلَطَ مِنْ ذِئْبٍ مُتَنَمِّرٍ. وَٱقْدَحْ زَنْدَ جَدِّكَ بِجِدِّكَ. وَٱقْرَعْ بَابَ رَعْيِكَ. بِسَعْيِكَ. وَجُبْ كُلَّ فَجٍّ. وَخُضْ[١] كُلَّ لُجٍّ. وَٱنْتَجِعْ كُلَّ رَوْضٍ. وَأَلْقِ دَلْوَكَ إِلَى كُلِّ حَوْضٍ. وَلَا تَسْأَمِ الطَّلَبَ. وَلَا تَمَلَّ الدَّأَبَ. فَقَدْ كَانَ مَكْتُوبًا عَلَى عَصَا شَيْخِنَا سَاسَانَ

١ ف: لِجٍّ.

مَنْ طَلَبَ جَلَبَ. وَمَنْ جَالَ نَالَ. وَإِيَّاكَ وَالْكَسَلَ فَإِنَّهُ عُنْوَانُ النُّحُوسِ. وَلَبُوسُ ذَوِي الْبُوسِ. وَمِفْتَاحُ الْمَتْرَبَةِ. وَلِقَاحُ الْمَتْعَبَةِ. وَشِيمَةُ الْعَجَزَةِ الْجَهَلَةِ. وَشِنْشِنَةُ الْوُكَلَةِ التُّكَلَةِ. وَمَا ٱشْتَارَ الْعَسَلَ. مَنِ ٱخْتَارَ الْكَسَلَ. وَلَا مَلَأَ الرَّاحَةَ. مَنِ ٱسْتَوْطَأَ الرَّاحَةَ. وَعَلَيْكَ بِالْإِقْدَامِ. وَلَوْ عَلَى الضِّرْغَامِ. فَإِنَّ جُرْأَةَ[١] الْجَنَانِ. تُنْطِقُ اللِّسَانَ. وَتُطْلِقُ الْعِنَانَ. وَبِهَا تُدْرَكُ الْحُظْوَةُ. وَتُمْلَكُ الثَّرْوَةُ. كَمَا أَنَّ الْخَوَرَ صِنْوُ الْكَسَلِ. وَسَبَبُ الْفَشَلِ. وَمَبْطَأَةٌ لِلْعَمَلِ. وَمَخْيَبَةٌ لِلْأَمَلِ. وَلِهٰذَا قِيلَ فِي الْمَثَلِ مَنْ جَسَرَ أَيْسَرَ. وَمَنْ هَابَ خَابَ.

٥،٤٩ ثُمَّ ٱبْرُزْ يَا بُنَيَّ فِي بُكُورِ أَبِي زَاجِرٍ. وَجُرْأَةِ[٢] أَبِي الْحَارِثِ. وَحَزَامَةِ أَبِي قُرَّةَ. وَخَتْلِ أَبِي جَعْدَةَ. وَحِرْصِ أَبِي عُقْبَةَ. وَنَشَاطِ أَبِي وَثَّابٍ. وَمَكْرِ أَبِي الْحُصَيْنِ. وَصَبْرِ أَبِي أَيُّوبَ. وَتَلَطُّفِ أَبِي غَزْوَانَ. وَتَلَوُّنِ أَبِي بَرَاقِشَ.[٣] وَٱخْلُبْ بِصَوْغِ اللِّسَانِ. وَٱخْدَعْ بِسِحْرِ الْبَيَانِ. وَٱرْتَدِ السُّوقَ قَبْلَ الْجَلَبِ. وَٱمْتَرِ الضَّرْعَ قَبْلَ الْحَلَبِ. وَسَائِلِ الرُّكْبَانَ قَبْلَ الْمُنْتَجَعِ. وَدَمِّثْ لِجَنْبِكَ قَبْلَ الْمُضْطَجَعِ. وَٱشْحَذْ بَصِيرَتَكَ لِلْعِيَافَةِ. وَأَنْعِمْ نَظَرَكَ لِلْقِيَافَةِ. فَإِنَّ مَنْ صَدَقَ تَوَسُّمُهُ. طَالَ تَبَسُّمُهُ. وَمَنْ أَخْطَأَتْ فِرَاسَتُهُ. أَبْطَأَتْ فَرِيسَتُهُ. وَكُنْ يَا بُنَيَّ خَفِيفَ الْكَلِّ. قَلِيلَ الدَّلِّ. رَاغِبًا عَنِ الْعَلِّ. قَانِعًا مِنَ الْوَبْلِ بِالطَّلِّ. وَعَظِّمْ وَقْعَ الْحَقِيرِ. وَٱشْكُرْ عَلَى النَّقِيرِ. وَلَا تَقْنَطْ عِنْدَ الرَّدِّ. وَلَا تَسْتَبْعِدْ رَشْحَ الصَّلْدِ. وَلَا تَيْأَسْ مِنْ رَوْحِ اللهِ ﴿إِنَّهُ لَا يَيْأَسُ مِنْ رَوْحِ اللهِ إِلَّا الْقَوْمُ الْكَافِرُونَ﴾. وَإِذَا خُيِّرْتَ بَيْنَ ذُرَّةٍ مَنْقُودَةٍ. وَدُرَّةٍ مَوْعُودَةٍ. فَمِلْ إِلَى النَّقْدِ. وَفَضِّلِ الْيَوْمَ عَلَى الْغَدِ. فَإِنَّ لِلتَّأْخِيرِ آفَاتٍ. وَلِلْعَزَائِمِ بَدَوَاتٍ. وَلِلْعِدَاتِ مُعَقِّبَاتٍ. وَبَيْنَهَا وَبَيْنَ النُّجْزِ[٤] عَقَبَاتٌ.[٥] وَعَلَيْكَ بِصَبْرِ أُولِي

١ ف: جراءة. ٢ . ف: جراءة. ٣ بعدها في ف: وحِيلةِ قَصِير ودَهاءِ عَمْرو ولُطْفِ الشَّعْبِيِّ واحْتِمالِ الأَحْنَفِ وفِطْنَةِ إياسٍ ومَجانَة أَبِي نَواسٍ وطَمَعِ أَشْعَبَ وعارِضَةِ أَبِي العَيْناءِ. ٤ ف: النجاز. ٥ بعدها في هامش ق، وفي س، و، ف: وأيّ عَقَباتٍ.

ٱلْعَزْمِ. وَرِفْقِ ذَوِي ٱلْحَزْمِ. وَجَانِبْ خُرُقَ ٱلْمُشْتَطِّ. وَتَخَلَّقْ بِٱلْخُلُقِ ٱلسَّبْطِ. وَقَيِّدِ ٱلدِّرْهَمَ بِٱلرَّبْطِ. وَشُبِ ٱلْبَذْلَ بِٱلضَّبْطِ. وَلَا تَجْعَلْ يَدَكَ مَغْلُولَةً إِلَى عُنُقِكَ وَلَا تَبْسُطْهَا كُلَّ ٱلْبَسْطِ. وَمَتَى نَبَا بِكَ بَلَدٌ. أَوْ نَابَكَ فِيهِ كَمَدٌ. فَبُتَّ مِنْهُ أَمَلَكَ. وَٱسْرَحْ مِنْهُ جَمَلَكَ. فَخَيْرُ ٱلْبِلَادِ مَا حَمَلَكَ.[1] وَلَا تَسْتَثْقِلَنَّ ٱلرِّحْلَةَ. وَلَا تَكْرَهَنَّ ٱلنُّقْلَةَ. فَإِنَّ أَعْلَامَ شَرِيعَتِنَا. وَأَشْيَاخَ عَشِيرَتِنَا. أَجْمَعُوا عَلَى أَنَّ ٱلْحَرَكَةَ بَرَكَةٌ. وَٱلطَّرَاوَةَ سُفْتَجَةٌ. وَزَرَوْا عَلَى مَنْ زَعَمَ أَنَّ ٱلْغُرْبَةَ كُرْبَةٌ. وَٱلنُّقْلَةَ مُثْلَةٌ. وَقَالُوا هِيَ تَعِلَّةُ مَنِ ٱقْتَنَعَ بِٱلرَّذِيلَةِ. وَرَضِيَ بِٱلْحَشَفِ وَسُوءِ ٱلْكِيلَةِ. وَإِذَا أَزْمَعْتَ عَلَى ٱلِٱغْتِرَابِ. وَأَعْدَدْتَ لَهُ ٱلْعَصَا وَٱلْجِرَابَ. فَتَخَيَّرِ ٱلرَّفِيقَ ٱلْمُسْعِدَ. مِنْ قَبْلِ أَنْ تُصْعِدَ. فَإِنَّ ٱلْجَارَ قَبْلَ ٱلدَّارِ. وَٱلرَّفِيقَ قَبْلَ ٱلطَّرِيقِ.

٦،٤٩ خُـذْهَـا إِلَيْكَ وَصِـيَّةً   لَمْ يُوصِـهَا قَبْـلِي أَحَـدْ
غَـرَّاءَ حَـاوِيَـةً خُـلَا   صَاتِ ٱلْمَعَـانِي وَٱلزُّبَـدْ
نَقَّحْـتُهَـا تَنْـقِـيحَ مَنْ   مَحَضَ ٱلنَّصِيحَةَ وَٱجْتَهَدْ
فَـٱعْـمَلْ بِمَا مَـثَّلْتُـهُ   عَمَلَ ٱللَّبِيبِ أَخِي ٱلرَّشَدْ
حَـتَّى يَقُولَ ٱلنَّـاسُ هٰـذَا ٱلشِّبْلُ مِنْ ذَاكَ ٱلْأَسَدْ

٧،٤٩ ثُمَّ قَالَ يَا بُنَيَّ قَدْ أَوْصَيْتُ. وَٱسْتَقْصَيْتُ. فَإِنِ ٱقْتَدَيْتَ فَوَاهًا لَكَ. وَإِنِ ٱعْتَدَيْتَ فَآهًا مِنْكَ. وَٱللّٰهُ خَلِيفَتِي عَلَيْكَ. وَأَرْجُو أَنْ لَا تُخْلِفَ ظَنِّي فِيكَ. فَقَالَ لَهُ ٱبْنُهُ يَا أَبَتِ لَا وُضِعَ عَرْشُكَ. وَلَا رُفِعَ نَعْشُكَ. فَلَقَدْ قُلْتَ سَدَدًا. وَعَلَّمْتَ رَشَدًا. وَنَحَلْتَ مَا لَمْ يَنْحَلْ وَالِدٌ وَلَدًا. وَلَئِنْ أُمْهِلْتُ بَعْدَكَ. لَا ذُقْتُ فَقْدَكَ. فَلَأَتَأَدَّبَنَّ بِآدَابِكَ ٱلصَّالِحَةِ. وَلَأَقْتَدِيَنَّ بِآثَارِكَ ٱلْوَاضِحَةِ. حَتَّى يُقَالَ مَا أَشْبَهَ ٱللَّيْلَةَ

---

١ جَمَّلَكَ.

بِالْبَارِحَةِ. وَالْغَادِيَةَ بِالرَّائِحَةِ. فَٱهْتَزَّ أَبُو زَيْدٍ لِجَوَابِهِ وَٱبْتَسَمَ. وَقَالَ مَنْ أَشْبَهَ أَبَاهُ فَمَا ظَلَمَ. قَالَ الْحَارِثُ بْنُ هَمَّامٍ فَأُخْبِرْتُ أَنَّ بَنِي سَاسَانَ. حِينَ سَمِعُوا هٰذِهِ الْوَصَايَا الْحِسَانَ. فَضَّلُوهَا عَلَى وَصَايَا لُقْمَانَ. وَحَفِظُوهَا كَمَا تُحْفَظُ أُمُّ الْقُرْآنِ. حَتَّى إِنَّهُمْ لَيَرَوْنَهَا إِلَى الآنَ. أَوْلَى مَا لَقَّنُوهُ الصِّبْيَانَ. وَأَنْفَعَ لَهُمْ مِنْ نِحْلَةِ الْعِقْيَانِ.

الْمَقَامَةُ الْخَمْسُونَ[1]

١،٥٠ حَكَى الْحَارِثُ بْنُ هَمَّامٍ قَالَ أُشْعِرْتُ فِي بَعْضِ الْأَيَّامِ هَمًّا بَرَّحَ بِي ٱسْتِعَارُهُ. وَلَاحَ عَلَيَّ شِعَارُهُ. وَكُنْتُ سَمِعْتُ أَنَّ غِشْيَانَ مَجَالِسِ الذِّكْرِ. يَسْرُو غَوَاشِيَ الْفِكْرِ. فَلَمْ أَرَ لِإِطْفَاءِ مَا بِي مِنَ الْجَمْرَةِ. إِلَّا قَصْدَ الْجَامِعِ بِالْبَصْرَةِ. وَكَانَ إِذْ ذَاكَ مَأْهُولَ الْمَسَانِدِ. مَشْفُوهَ الْمَوَارِدِ. يُجْتَنَى مِنْ رِيَاضِهِ أَزَاهِيرُ الْكَلَامِ. وَيُسْمَعُ فِي أَرْجَائِهِ صَرِيرُ الْأَقْلَامِ. فَٱنْطَلَقْتُ إِلَيْهِ غَيْرَ وَانٍ. وَلَا لَاوٍ عَلَى شَانٍ. فَلَمَّا وَطِئْتُ حَصَاهُ. وَٱسْتَشْرَفْتُ أَقْصَاهُ. تَرَاءَى لِي ذُو أَطْمَارٍ بَالِيَةٍ. فَوْقَ صَخْرَةٍ عَالِيَةٍ. وَقَدْ عَصَبَتْ بِهِ عُصَبٌ لَا يُحْصَى عَدِيدُهُمْ. وَلَا يُنَادَى وَلِيدُهُمْ. فَٱبْتَدَرْتُ قَصْدَهُ. وَتَوَرَّدْتُ وِرْدَهُ. وَرَجَوْتُ أَنْ أَجِدَ شِفَائِي عِنْدَهُ. وَلَمْ أَزَلْ أَنْتَقِلُ[2] فِي الْمَرَاكِزِ. وَأُغْضِي لِلْآكِزِ وَالْوَاكِزِ. إِلَى أَنْ جَلَسْتُ تُجَاهَهُ. وَبِحَيْثُ[3] أَمِنْتُ ٱشْتِبَاهَهُ. فَإِذَا هُوَ شَيْخُنَا السَّرُوجِيُّ ﴿لَا رَيْبَ فِيهِ﴾. وَلَا لَبْسَ يُخْفِيهِ. فَتَسَرَّى[4] بِمَرْآهُ هَمِّي. وَٱرْفَضَّتْ كَتِيبَةُ غَمِّي.

٢،٥٠ وَحِينَ رَآنِي. وَبَصُرَ بِمَكَانِي. قَالَ يَا أَهْلَ الْبَصْرَةِ رَعَاكُمُ اللهُ وَوَقَاكُمْ. وَقَوَّى تُقَاكُمْ. فَمَا أَضْوَعَ رَيَّاكُمْ. وَأَفْضَلَ مَزَايَاكُمْ. بَلَدُكُمْ أَوْفَى الْبِلَادِ طُهْرَةً. وَأَزْكَاهَا فِطْرَةً. وَأَفْسَحُهُ رُقْعَةً. وَأَمْرَعُهَا نُجْعَةً. وَأَقْوَمُهَا قِبْلَةً. وَأَوْسَعُهَا دِجْلَةً. وَأَكْثَرُهَا نَهَرًا وَنَخْلَةً. وَأَحْسَنُهَا تَفْصِيلًا وَجُمْلَةً. دِهْلِيزُ الْبَلَدِ الْحَرَامِ. وَقُبَالَةُ الْبَابِ وَالْمَقَامِ. وَأَحَدُ جَنَاحَيِ الدُّنْيَا. وَالْمِصْرُ الْمُؤَسَّسُ عَلَى التَّقْوَى. لَمْ يَتَدَنَّسْ بِبُيُوتِ النِّيرَانِ.

١ في هامش س: تُعْرَفُ بِالْبَصْرِيَّةِ؛ وفي د: الْبَصْرِيَّةُ؛ وفي ف: وَهِيَ الْبَصْرِيَّةُ. ٢ س، ف: أَتَنَقَّلُ. ٣ ف: بِحَيْثُ.
٤ ف: فَٱنْسَرَى.

وَلَا طِيفَ فِيهِ بِالْأَوْثَانِ. وَلَا سُجِدَ عَلَى أَدِيمِهِ لِغَيْرِ الرَّحْمٰنِ. ذُو الْمَشَاهِدِ الْمَشْهُودَةِ. وَالْمَسَاجِدِ الْمَقْصُودَةِ. وَالْمَعَالِمِ الْمَشْهُورَةِ. وَالْمَقَابِرِ الْمَزُورَةِ. وَالْآثَارِ الْمَحْمُودَةِ. وَالْخِطَطِ الْمَحْدُودَةِ. بِهِ تَلْتَقِي الْفُلْكُ وَالرِّكَابُ. وَالْحِيتَانُ وَالضِّبَابُ. وَالْحَادِي وَالْمَلَّاحُ. وَالْقَانِصُ وَالْفَلَّاحُ. وَالنَّاشِبُ وَالرَّامِحُ. وَالسَّارِحُ وَالسَّابِحُ. وَلَهُ آيَةُ الْمَدِّ الْفَائِضِ. وَالْجَزْرِ الْغَائِضِ.

٣.٥٠ وَأَمَّا أَنْتُمْ فَمَنْ لَا يَخْتَلِفُ فِي خَصَائِصِهِمُ ٱثْنَانِ. وَلَا يُنْكِرُهَا ذُو شَنَآنٍ. دَهْمَاؤُكُمْ أَطْوَعُ رَعِيَّةٍ لِسُلْطَانٍ. وَأَشْكَرُهُمْ لِإِحْسَانٍ. وَزَاهِدُكُمْ أَوْرَعُ الْخَلِيقَةِ. وَأَحْسَنُهُمْ طَرِيقَةً عَلَى الْحَقِيقَةِ. وَعَالِمُكُمْ عَلَّامَةُ كُلِّ زَمَانٍ. وَالْحُجَّةُ[١] فِي كُلِّ أَوَانٍ. وَمِنْكُمْ مَنِ ٱسْتَنْبَطَ عِلْمَ النَّحْوِ وَوَضَعَهُ. وَالَّذِي ٱبْتَدَعَ مِيزَانَ الشِّعْرِ وَٱخْتَرَعَهُ. وَمَا مِنْ فَخْرٍ إِلَّا وَلَكُمْ فِيهِ الْيَدُ الطُّولَى.[٢] وَإِنْ شِئْتُمْ[٣] فَأَنْتُمْ[٤] بِهِ أَحَقُّ وَأَوْلَى. ثُمَّ إِنَّكُمْ أَكْثَرُ أَهْلِ مِصْرٍ مُؤَذِّنِينَ. وَأَحْسَنُهُمْ فِي النُّسُكِ قَوَانِينَ. وَبِكُمُ ٱقْتُدِيَ فِي التَّعْرِيفِ. وَعُرِفَ التَّسْحِيرُ فِي الشَّهْرِ الشَّرِيفِ. وَلَكُمْ إِذَا قَرَّتِ الْمَضَاجِعُ. وَهَجَعَ الْهَاجِعُ. تَذْكَارٌ يُوقِظُ النَّائِمَ. وَيُؤْنِسُ الْقَائِمَ. وَمَا ٱبْتَسَمَ ثَغْرُ فَجْرٍ. وَلَا بَزَغَ نُورُهُ فِي بَرْدٍ وَلَا حَرٍّ. إِلَّا وَلِتَأْذِينِكُمْ بِالْأَسْحَارِ. دَوِيٌّ كَدَوِيِّ الرِّيحِ فِي الْبِحَارِ. وَبِهٰذَا عَنْكُمْ صَدَعَ النَّقْلُ. وَأَخْبَرَ النَّبِيُّ عَلَيْهِ السَّلَامُ مِنْ قَبْلُ. وَبَيَّنَ أَنَّ دَوِيَّكُمْ بِالْأَسْحَارِ. كَدَوِيِّ النَّحْلِ فِي الْقِفَارِ. فَشَرَفًا لَكُمْ بِبِشَارَةِ الْمُصْطَفَى. وَوَاهًا لِمِصْرِكُمْ وَإِنْ كَانَ قَدْ عَفَا. وَلَمْ يَبْقَ مِنْهُ إِلَّا شَفَا.

٤.٥٠ ثُمَّ إِنَّهُ خَزَنَ لِسَانَهُ. وَخَطَمَ بَيَانَهُ. حَتَّى حُدِجَ بِالْأَبْصَارِ. وَقُرِفَ بِالْإِقْصَارِ.[٥] فَتَنَفَّسَ تَنَفُّسَ مَنْ قِيدَ لِقَوَدٍ. أَوْ ضَبَثَتْ بِهِ بَرَاثِنُ أَسَدٍ. ثُمَّ قَالَ أَمَا أَنْتُمْ يَا

---

١ بعدها في ف: البالغة. ٢ بعدها في و، د، ف: والقِدْحُ المُعَلَّى؛ وبعدها في ف: ولا صِيتَ إِلَّا. ٣ ليس في د، ف. ٤ د، ف: وَأَنْتُمْ. ٥ بعدها في ف: ووُسِمَ بِالاِسْتِقْصار.

أَهْلَ الْبَصْرَةِ فَمَا مِنْكُمْ إِلَّا الْعَلَمُ الْمَعْرُوفُ. وَمَنْ لَهُ الْمَعْرِفَةُ وَالْمَعْرُوفُ. وَأَمَّا أَنَا فَمَنْ عَرَفَنِي فَأَنَا ذَاكَ. وَشَرُّ الْمَعَارِفِ مَنْ آذَاكَ. وَمَنْ لَمْ يُثْبِتْ عِرْفَتِي فَسَأَصْدُقُهُ صِفَتِي. أَنَا الَّذِي أَنْجَدَ وَأَتْهَمَ. وَأَيْمَنَ وَأَشْأَمَ. وَأَصْحَرَ وَأَبْحَرَ. وَأَدْلَجَ وَأَسْحَرَ. نَشَأْتُ بِسَرُوجَ. وَرُبِّيتُ عَلَى السُّرُوجِ. ثُمَّ وَلَجْتُ الْمَضَايِقَ. وَفَتَحْتُ الْمَغَالِقَ. وَشَهِدْتُ الْمَعَارِكَ. وَأَلَنْتُ الْعَرَائِكَ. وَٱقْتَدْتُ الشَّوَامِسَ. وَأَرْغَمْتُ الْمَعَاطِسَ. وَأَذَبْتُ الْجَوَامِدَ. وَأَمَعْتُ الْجَلَامِدَ. سَلُوا عَنِّي الْمَشَارِقَ وَالْمَغَارِبَ. وَالْمَنَاسِمَ وَالْغَوَارِبَ. وَالْمَحَافِلَ وَالْجَحَافِلَ. وَالْقَبَائِلَ وَالْقَنَابِلَ. وَٱسْتَوْضِحُونِي مِنْ نَقَلَةِ الْأَخْبَارِ. وَرُوَاةِ الْأَسْمَارِ. وَحُدَاةِ الرُّكْبَانِ. وَحُذَّاقِ الْكُهَّانِ. لِتَعْلَمُوا كَمْ فَجٍّ سَلَكْتُ. وَحِجَابٍ هَتَكْتُ. وَمَهْلَكَةٍ ٱقْتَحَمْتُ. وَمَلْحَمَةٍ أَلْحَمْتُ. وَكَمْ أَلْبَابٍ خَدَعْتُ. وَبِدَعٍ ٱبْتَدَعْتُ. وَفُرَصٍ ٱخْتَلَسْتُ. وَأُسُدٍ ٱفْتَرَسْتُ. وَكَمْ مُحَلِّقٍ غَادَرْتُهُ لَقًى. وَكَامِنٍ ٱسْتَخْرَجْتُهُ بِالرُّقَى. وَحَجَرٍ سَحَرْتُهُ[1] حَتَّى ٱنْصَدَعَ. وَٱسْتَنْبَطْتُ زُلَالَهُ بِالْخُدَعِ.

٥٫٥٠ وَلَكِنْ فَرَطَ مَا فَرَطَ وَالْغُصْنُ رَطِيبٌ. وَالْفَوْدُ غِرْبِيبٌ. وَبُرْدُ الشَّبَابِ قَشِيبٌ. فَأَمَّا الْآنَ وَقَدِ ٱسْتَشَنَّ الْأَدِيمُ. وَتَأَوَّدَ الْقَوِيمُ. وَٱسْتَنَارَ اللَّيْلُ الْبَهِيمُ. فَلَيْسَ إِلَّا النَّدَمُ إِنْ نَفَعَ. وَتَرْقِيعُ الْخَرْقِ الَّذِي قَدِ ٱتَّسَعَ. وَكُنْتُ رُوِيتُ فِي الْأَخْبَارِ الْمُسْنَدَةِ. وَالْآثَارِ الْمُعْتَمَدَةِ. أَنَّ لَكُمْ مِنَ اللهِ تَعَالَى فِي كُلِّ يَوْمٍ نَظْرَةً. وَأَنَّ سِلَاحَ النَّاسِ كُلِّهِمُ الْحَدِيدُ. وَسِلَاحُكُمُ الْأَدْعِيَةُ.[2] فَقَصَدْتُكُمْ أُنْضِي الرَّوَاحِلَ. وَأَطْوِي الْمَرَاحِلَ. حَتَّى قُمْتُ هٰذَا الْمَقَامَ فِيكُمْ.[3] وَلَا مَنَّ لِي عَلَيْكُمْ. إِذْ مَا سَعَيْتُ إِلَّا فِي حَاجَتِي. وَلَا تَعِبْتُ إِلَّا لِرَاحَتِي. وَلَسْتُ أَبْغِي أُعْطِيَتَكُمْ. بَلْ أَسْتَدْعِي أَدْعِيَتَكُمْ. وَلَا أَسْأَلُكُمْ أَمْوَالَكُمْ. بَلْ أَسْتَنْزِلُ سُؤَالَكُمْ. فَٱدْعُوا اللهَ تَعَالَى

١ في ف: شَحَذْتُهُ. ٢ بعدها في ف: وَالتَّوْحِيدُ. ٣ ف: لَدَيْكُمْ.

بِتَوْفِيقِي لِلْمَتَابِ. وَالْإِعْدَادِ لِلْمَآبِ. فَإِنَّهُ رَفِيعُ الدَّرَجَاتِ. مُجِيبُ الدَّعَوَاتِ. وَهُوَ الَّذِي يَقْبَلُ التَّوْبَةَ عَنْ عِبَادِهِ وَيَعْفُو عَنِ السَّيِّئَاتِ. ثُمَّ أَنْشَدَ

٦،٥٠ أَسْتَغْفِرُ اللهَ مِنْ ذُنُوبٍ أَفْرَطْتُ فِيهِنَّ وَٱعْتَدَيْتُ
كَمْ خُضْتُ بَحْرَ الضَّلَالِ جَهْلًا وَرُحْتُ فِي الْغَيِّ وَٱغْتَدَيْتُ
وَكَمْ أَطَعْتُ الْهَوَى ٱغْتِرَارًا وَٱخْتَلْتُ وَٱغْتَلْتُ وَٱفْتَرَيْتُ
وَكَمْ خَلَعْتُ الْعِذَارَ رَكْضًا إِلَى الْمَعَاصِي وَمَا وَنَيْتُ
وَكَمْ تَنَاهَيْتُ فِي التَّخَطِّي إِلَى الْخَطَايَا وَمَا ٱنْتَهَيْتُ
فَلَيْتَنِي كُنْتُ قَبْلَ هٰذَا نَسْيًا وَلَمْ أَجْنِ مَا جَنَيْتُ
فَالْمَوْتُ لِلْمُجْرِمِينَ خَيْرٌ مِنَ الْمَسَاعِي الَّتِي سَعَيْتُ
يَا رَبِّ عَفْوًا فَأَنْتَ أَهْلٌ لِلْعَفْوِ عَنِّي وَإِنْ عَصَيْتُ

٧،٥٠ قَالَ الرَّاوِي فَطَفِقَتِ الْجَمَاعَةُ تُمِدُّهُ بِالدُّعَاءِ. وَهُوَ يُقَلِّبُ وَجْهَهُ فِي السَّمَاءِ. إِلَى أَنْ دَمَعَتْ أَجْفَانُهُ. وَبَدَا رَجَفَانُهُ. فَصَاحَ اللهُ أَكْبَرُ بَانَتْ أَمَارَةُ الِاسْتِجَابَةِ. وَٱنْجَابَتْ غِشَاوَةُ الِاسْتِرَابَةِ. فَجُزِيتُمْ يَا أَهْلَ الْبُصَيْرَةِ. جَزَاءَ مَنْ هَدَى مِنَ الْحَيْرَةِ. فَلَمْ يَبْقَ فِي الْقَوْمِ إِلَّا مَنْ سُرَّ لِسُرُورِهِ. وَرَضَخَ لَهُ بِمَيْسُورِهِ. فَقَبِلَ عَفْوَ بِرِّهِمْ. وَأَقْبَلَ يَهْرِفُ[١] فِي شُكْرِهِمْ. ثُمَّ ٱنْحَدَرَ مِنَ الصَّخْرَةِ. يَؤُمُّ شَاطِئَ الْبَصْرَةِ. وَٱعْتَقَبْتُهُ إِلَى حَيْثُ تَخَالَيْنَا. وَأَمِنَّا التَّجَسُّسَ وَالتَّحَسُّسَ عَلَيْنَا. فَقُلْتُ لَهُ لَقَدْ أَغْرَبْتَ فِي هٰذِهِ النَّوْبَةِ. فَمَا رَأْيُكَ فِي التَّوْبَةِ. فَقَالَ أُقْسِمُ بِعَلَّامِ الْخَفِيَّاتِ. وَغَفَّارِ الْخَطِيَّاتِ. إِنَّ شَأْنِي لَعُجَابٌ. وَإِنَّ دُعَاءَ قَوْمِكَ لَمُجَابٌ. فَقُلْتُ زِدْنِي إِفْصَاحًا. زَادَكَ اللهُ صَلَاحًا. فَقَالَ وَأَبِيكَ لَقَدْ قُمْتُ فِيهِمْ مَقَامَ الْمُرِيبِ الْخَادِعِ. ثُمَّ ٱنْقَلَبْتُ مِنْهُمْ

١ و، ف: يُغْرِقُ.

بِقَلْبِ الْمُنِيبِ الْخَاشِعِ. فَطُوبَى لِمَنْ صَغَتْ قُلُوبُهُمْ إِلَيْهِ. وَوَيْلٌ لِمَنْ بَاتُوا يَدْعُونَ عَلَيْهِ. ثُمَّ وَدَّعَنِي وَٱنْطَلَقَ. وَأَوْدَعَنِي الْقَلَقَ.

٨٫٥٠ فَلَمْ أَزَلْ أُعَانِي لِأَجْلِهِ الْفِكَرَ. وَأَتَشَوَّفُ إِلَى خِبْرَةِ مَا ذَكَرَ. وَكُلَّمَا ٱسْتَنْشَيْتُ خَبَرَهُ مِنَ الرُّكْبَانِ. وَجَوَّابَةِ الْبُلْدَانِ. كُنْتُ كَمَنْ حَاوَرَ عَجْمَاءَ. أَوْ نَادَى صَخْرَةً صَمَّاءَ. إِلَى أَنْ لَقِيتُ بَعْدَ تَرَاخِي الْأَمَدِ. وَتَرَاقِي الْكَمَدِ. رَكْبًا قَافِلِينَ مِنْ سَفَرٍ. فَقُلْتُ هَلْ مِنْ مُغَرِّبَةِ خَبَرٍ. فَقَالُوا إِنَّ عِنْدَنَا لَخَبَرًا أَغْرَبَ مِنَ الْعَنْقَاءِ. وَأَعْجَبَ مِنْ نَظَرِ الزَّرْقَاءِ. فَسَأَلْتُهُمْ إِيضَاحَ مَا قَالُوا. وَأَنْ يَكِيلُوا لِي مَا[1] ٱكْتَالُوا. فَحَكَوْا أَنَّهُمْ أَلَمُّوا بِسَرُوجَ. بَعْدَ أَنْ فَارَقَهَا الْعُلُوجُ. فَرَأَوْا أَبَا زَيْدِهَا الْمَعْرُوفَ. قَدْ لَبِسَ الصُّوفَ. وَأَمَّ الصُّفُوفَ. وَصَارَ بِهَا الزَّاهِدَ الْمَوْصُوفَ. فَقُلْتُ أَتَعْنُونَ ذَا الْمَقَامَاتِ. فَقَالُوا إِنَّهُ الْآنَ ذُو الْكَرَامَاتِ.

٩٫٥٠ فَحَفَزَنِي إِلَيْهِ النِّزَاعُ. وَرَأَيْتُهَا فُرْصَةً لَا تُضَاعُ. فَٱرْتَحَلْتُ رِحْلَةَ الْمُعِدِّ. وَسِرْتُ نَحْوَهُ سَيْرَ الْمُجِدِّ. حَتَّى حَلَلْتُ بِمَسْجِدِهِ. وَقَرَارَةِ مُتَعَبَّدِهِ. فَإِذَا هُوَ قَدْ نَبَذَ صُحْبَةَ أَصْحَابِهِ. وَٱنْتَصَبَ فِي مِحْرَابِهِ. وَهُوَ ذُو عَبَاءَةٍ مَخْلُولَةٍ. وَشَمْلَةٍ مَوْصُولَةٍ. فَهِبْتُهُ مَهَابَةَ مَنْ وَلَجَ عَلَى الْأُسُودِ. وَأَلْفَيْتُهُ مِمَّنْ سِيمَاهُمْ فِي وُجُوهِهِمْ مِنْ أَثَرِ السُّجُودِ. وَلَمَّا فَرَغَ مِنْ سُبْحَتِهِ. حَيَّانِي بِمُسَبِّحَتِهِ. مِنْ غَيْرِ أَنْ نَغَمَ بِحَدِيثٍ. وَلَا ٱسْتَخْبَرَ عَنْ قَدِيمٍ وَلَا حَدِيثٍ. ثُمَّ أَقْبَلَ عَلَى أَوْرَادِهِ. وَتَرَكَنِي أَعْجَبُ مِنِ ٱجْتِهَادِهِ. وَأَغْبِطُ مَنْ يَهْدِي اللهُ مِنْ عِبَادِهِ. وَلَمْ يَزَلْ فِي قُنُوتٍ وَخُشُوعٍ. وَسُجُودٍ وَرُكُوعٍ. وَإِخْبَاتٍ وَخُضُوعٍ. إِلَى أَنْ أَكْمَلَ إِقَامَةَ الْخَمْسِ. وَصَارَ الْيَوْمُ أَمْسِ. فَحِينَئِذٍ ٱنْكَفَأَ بِي إِلَى بَيْتِهِ. وَأَسْهَمَنِي فِي قُرْصِهِ وَزَيْتِهِ. ثُمَّ نَهَضَ إِلَى مُصَلَّاهُ. وَتَخَلَّى بِمُنَاجَاةِ مَوْلَاهُ. حَتَّى إِذَا ٱلْتَمَعَ الْفَجْرُ. وَحَقَّ[2] لِلْمُتَهَجِّدِ الْأَجْرُ.

١ د: مِمَّا؛ و، ف: بِما. ٢ س، و،د: حَقَّ.

عَقَّبَ تَهَجُّدَهُ بِالتَّسْبِيحِ. ثُمَّ ٱضْطَجَعَ ضِجْعَةَ ٱلْمُسْتَرِيحِ. وَجَعَلَ يُرَجِّعُ بِصَوْتٍ فَصِيحٍ.

١٠،٥٠ خَلِّ ٱدِّكَارَ ٱلْأَرْبُعِ وَٱلْمَعْهَدِ ٱلْمُرْتَبَعِ وَٱلظَّاعِنِ ٱلْمُوَدِّعِ
وَعَدِّ عَنْهُ وَدَعِ
وَٱنْدُبْ زَمَانًا سَلَفَا سَوَّدْتَ فِيهِ ٱلصُّحُفَا وَلَمْ تَزَلْ مُعْتَكِفَا
عَلَى ٱلْقَبِيحِ ٱلشَّنِعِ
كَمْ لَيْلَةٍ أَوْدَعْتَهَا مَآثِمًا أَبْدَعْتَهَا لِشَهْوَةٍ أَطَعْتَهَا
فِي مَرْقَدٍ وَمَضْجَعِ
وَكَمْ خُطًى حَثَثْتَهَا فِي خِزْيَةٍ أَحْدَثْتَهَا وَتَوْبَةٍ نَكَثْتَهَا
لِمَلْعَبٍ وَمَرْتَعِ
وَكَمْ تَجَرَّأْتَ عَلَى رَبِّ ٱلسَّمٰوَاتِ ٱلْعُلَى وَلَمْ تُرَاقِبْهُ وَلَا
صَدَقْتَ فِي مَا تَدَّعِي
وَكَمْ غَمَطْتَ[1] بِرَّهُ وَكَمْ أَمِنْتَ مَكْرَهُ وَكَمْ نَبَذْتَ أَمْرَهُ
نَبْذَ ٱلْحِذَا ٱلْمُرَقَّعِ
وَكَمْ رَكَضْتَ فِي ٱللَّعِبْ وَفُهْتَ عَمْدًا بِٱلْكَذِبْ وَلَمْ تُرَاعِ مَا يَجِبْ
مِنْ عَهْدِهِ ٱلْمُتَّبَعِ
فَٱلْبَسْ شِعَارَ ٱلنَّدَمِ وَٱسْكُبْ شَآبِيبَ ٱلدَّمِ قَبْلَ زَوَالِ ٱلْقَدَمِ
وَقَبْلَ سُوءِ ٱلْمَصْرَعِ
وَٱخْضَعْ خُضُوعَ ٱلْمُعْتَرِفْ وَلُذْ مَلَاذَ ٱلْمُقْتَرِفْ وَٱعْصِ هَوَاكَ وَٱنْحَرِفْ

١ ف: غمضت.

عَنْهُ ٱنْحِرَافُ ٱلْمُقْلِعِ

إِلَامَ تَسْهُو وَتَنِي   وَمُعْظَمُ ٱلْعُمْرِ فَنِي   فِي مَا يَضُرُّ ٱلْمُقْتَنِي
وَلَسْتَ بِٱلْمُرْتَدِعِ

أَمَا تَرَى ٱلشَّيْبَ وَخَطْ   وَخَطَّ فِي ٱلرَّأْسِ خُطَطْ   وَمَنْ يَلُحْ وَخْطُ ٱلشَّمَطْ
بِفَوْدِهِ فَقَدْ نُعِي

وَيْحَكِ يَا نَفْسِ ٱحْرِصِي   عَلَى ٱرْتِيَادِ ٱلْمَخْلَصِ   وَطَاوِعِي وَأَخْلِصِي
وَٱسْتَمِعِي ٱلنُّصْحَ وَعِي

وَٱعْتَبِرِي بِمَنْ مَضَى   مِنَ ٱلْقُرُونِ وَٱنْقَضَى   وَٱخْشَيْ مُفَاجَاةَ ٱلْقَضَا
وَحَاذِرِي أَنْ تُخْدَعِي

وَٱنْتَهِجِي سُبْلَ ٱلْهُدَى   وَٱدَّكِرِي وَشْكَ ٱلرَّدَى   فَإِنَّ مَثْوَاكِ غَدَا
فِي قَعْرِ لَحْدٍ بَلْقَعِ

آهًا لَهُ بَيْتِ ٱلْبِلَى   وَٱلْمَنْزِلِ ٱلْقَفْرِ ٱلْخَلَا   وَمَوْرِدِ ٱلسَّفْرِ ٱلْأُلَى
وَٱللَّاحِقِ ٱلْمُتَّبِعِ

بَيْتٌ يُرَى مَنْ أُودِعَهْ   قَدْ ضَمَّهُ وَٱسْتُودِعَهْ   بَعْدَ ٱلْفَضَاءِ وَٱلسَّعَهْ
قِيدَ ثَلَاثِ أَذْرُعِ

لَا فَرْقَ أَنْ يَحُلَّهُ   دَاهِيَةٌ أَوْ أَبْلَهُ   أَوْ مُعْسِرٌ أَوْ مَنْ لَهُ
مُلْكٌ كَمُلْكِ تُبَّعِ

وَبَعْدَهُ ٱلْعَرْضُ ٱلَّذِي   يَحْوِي ٱلْحَيِيَّ وَٱلْبَذِي   وَٱلْمُبْتَدِي وَٱلْمُحْتَذِي
وَمَنْ رَعَى وَمَنْ رُعِي

فَيَا مَفَازَ ٱلْمُتَّقِي   وَرِبْحَ عَبْدٍ قَدْ وُقِي   سُوءَ ٱلْحِسَابِ ٱلْمُوبِقِ
وَهَوْلَ يَوْمِ ٱلْفَزَعِ

وَيَــا خَسَــارَ مَنْ بَغَى　　وَمَنْ تَعَــدَّى وَطَــغَى　　وَشَــبَّ نِيــرَانَ الْوَغَى
لِمَطْعَمٍ أَوْ مَطْمَعِ

يَا مَنْ عَلَيْهِ الْمُتَّكَلْ　　قَدْ زَادَ مَا بِي مِنْ وَجَلْ　　لِمَا ٱجْتَرَحْتُ مِنْ زَلَلْ
فِي عُمْرِيَ الْمُضَيَّعِ

فَٱغْفِرْ لِعَبْدٍ مُجْتَرِمْ　　وَٱرْحَمْ بُكَاهُ الْمُنْسَجِمْ　　فَأَنْتَ أَوْلَى مَنْ رَحِمْ
وَخَيْرُ مَدْعُوٍّ دُعِي

١١،٥٠ قَالَ الْحَارِثُ بْنُ هَمَّامٍ فَلَمْ يَزَلْ يُرَدِّدُهَا بِصَوْتٍ رَقِيقٍ. وَيَصِلُهَا بِزَفِيرٍ وَشَهِيقٍ. حَتَّى بَكَيْتُ لِبُكَاءِ عَيْنَيْهِ. كَمَا كُنْتُ مِنْ قَبْلُ أَبْكِي عَلَيْهِ. ثُمَّ بَرَزَ إِلَى مَسْجِدِهِ. بِوُضُوءِ تَهَجُّدِهِ. فَٱنْطَلَقْتُ رِدْفَهُ. وَصَلَّيْتُ مَعَ مَنْ صَلَّى خَلْفَهُ. وَلَمَّا ٱنْفَضَّ مَنْ حَضَرَ. وَتَفَرَّقُوا شَغَرَ بَغَرَ. أَخَذَ يُهَيْنِمُ بِدَرْسِهِ. وَيَسْبُكُ يَوْمَهُ فِي قَالَبِ أَمْسِهِ. وَفِي ضِمْنِ ذٰلِكَ يُرِنُّ إِرْنَانَ الرَّقُوبِ. وَيَبْكِي وَلَا بُكَاءَ يَعْقُوبَ. حَتَّى ٱسْتَبَنْتُ أَنَّهُ قَدِ أُلْحِقَ[١] بِالْأَفْرَادِ. وَأُشْرِبَ قَلْبُهُ هَوَى الِانْفِرَادِ. فَأَخْطَرْتُ بِقَلْبِي عَزْمَةَ الِارْتِحَالِ. وَتَخْلِيَتَهُ وَالتَّخَلِّي بِتِلْكَ الْحَالِ. فَكَأَنَّهُ تَفَرَّسَ مَا نَوَيْتُ. أَوْ كُوشِفَ بِمَا أَخْفَيْتُ. فَزَفَرَ زَفْرَةَ الْأَوَّاهِ. ثُمَّ قَرَأَ ﴿فَإِذَا عَزَمْتَ فَتَوَكَّلْ عَلَى اللهِ﴾. فَأَسْجَلْتُ عِنْدَ ذٰلِكَ بِصِدْقِ الْمُحَدِّثِينَ. وَأَيْقَنْتُ أَنَّ فِي الْأُمَّةِ مُحَدَّثِينَ. ثُمَّ دَنَوْتُ إِلَيْهِ كَمَا يَدْنُو الْمُصَافِحُ. وَقُلْتُ أَوْصِنِي أَيُّهَا الْعَبْدُ الصَّالِحُ. فَقَالَ ٱجْعَلِ الْمَوْتَ نَصْبَ عَيْنِكَ. وَ﴿هٰذَا فِرَاقُ بَيْنِي وَبَيْنِكَ﴾. فَوَدَّعْتُهُ وَعَبَرَاتِي يَتَحَدَّرْنَ مِنَ الْمَآقِي. وَزَفَرَاتِي يَتَصَعَّدْنَ مِنَ التَّرَاقِي. وَكَانَتْ هٰذِهِ خَاتِمَةَ التَّلَاقِي.

١ د: لَحِقَ، ف: التحق.

قَالَ الشَّيْخُ[١] أَبُو مُحَمَّدٍ[٢] الْقَاسِمُ بْنُ عَلِيٍّ[٣] هٰذَا آخِرُ الْمَقَامَاتِ الَّتِي أَنْشَأْتُهَا ٥١،١
بِالاِغْتِرَارِ. وَأَمْلَيْتُهَا بِلِسَانِ الاِضْطِرَارِ. وَقَدْ أُلْجِئْتُ إِلَى أَنْ رَصَدْتُهَا لِلاِسْتِعْرَاضِ. وَنَادَيْتُ عَلَيْهَا فِي سُوقِ الاِعْتِرَاضِ. هٰذَا مَعَ مَعْرِفَتِي بِأَنَّهَا مِنْ سَقَطِ الْمَتَاعِ. وَمِمَّا يَسْتَوْجِبُ أَنْ يُبَاعَ. وَلَا يُبْتَاعَ. وَلَوْ غَشِيَنِي نُورُ التَّوْفِيقِ. وَنَظَرْتُ لِنَفْسِي نَظَرَ الشَّفِيقِ. لَسَتَرْتُ عَوَارِي الَّذِي لَمْ يَزَلْ مَسْتُورًا. وَلٰكِنْ كَانَ ذٰلِكَ فِي الْكِتَابِ مَسْطُورًا. وَأَنَا أَسْتَغْفِرُ اللّٰهَ تَعَالَى مِمَّا أَوْدَعْتُهَا مِنْ أَبَاطِيلِ اللَّغْوِ. وَأَضَالِيلِ اللَّهْوِ. وَأَسْتَرْشِدُهُ إِلَى مَا يَعْصِمُ مِنَ السَّهْوِ. وَيُحْظِي بِالْعَفْوِ. إِنَّهُ هُوَ أَهْلُ التَّقْوَى وَأَهْلُ الْمَغْفِرَةِ وَوَلِيُّ الْخَيْرَاتِ فِي الدُّنْيَا وَالآخِرَةِ. آخِرُ الْكِتَابِ وَالْحَمْدُ لِلّٰهِ رَبِّ الْعَالَمِينَ وَصَلَوَاتُهُ عَلَى سَيِّدِنَا مُحَمَّدٍ النَّبِيِّ وَآلِهِ وَسَلَّمَ تَسْلِيمًا.

١ بعدها في و: الامام؛ وفي ف: الرئيس. ٢ «الشيخ أبو محمد»: ليس في س، د. ٣ بعدها في ف: برّد الله مضجعه.

١٠٥٢ ق: كَتَبَهُ الْمُبَارَكُ أَحْمَدُ بْنُ عَبْدِ الْعَزِيزِ بْنِ الْمُعَمَّرِ الْأَنْصَارِيِّ مِنْ خَطِّ مُصَنِّفِهَا بَعْدَ الْفَرَاغِ مِنْ نَسْخِهَا.

و: فَرَغَ مِنْ نَسْخِهَا الْعَبْدُ الْفَقِيرُ إِلَى رَحْمَةِ رَبِّهِ وَغُفْرَانِهِ وَعَفْوِهِ يَحْيَى بْنُ مَحْمُودِ بْنِ يَحْيَى بْنِ أَبِي الْحُسَيْنِ بْنِ كُوَّرِيهَا الْوَاسِطِيُّ بِخَطِّهِ وَصُوَرِهِ آخِرَ نَهَارِ يَوْمِ السَّبْتِ سَادِسِ شَهْرِ رَمَضَانَ سَنَةَ أَرْبَعَ وَثَلَاثِينَ وَسِتِّمَائَةٍ حَامِدًا لِلَّهِ تَعَالَى عَلَى نِعَمِهِ وَمُصَلِّيًا عَلَى خَيْرِ خَلْقِهِ سَيِّدِنَا مُحَمَّدٍ النَّبِيِّ وَآلِهِ وَصَحْبِهِ الْأَخْيَارِ الْأَبْرَارِ الْأَطْهَارِ وَشَرَّفَ وَكَرَّمَ وَسَلَّمَ.

Bibliography

Beaumont, Daniel. "A Mighty and Never Ending Affair: Comic Anecdote and Story in Medieval Arabic Literature." *Journal of Arabic Literature* 24 (1993): 139–59.

———. "The Trickster and Rhetoric in the Maqāmāt." *Edebiyât* 5 (1994): 1–14.

England, Samuel. *Medieval Empires and the Culture of Competition: Literary Duels at Christian and Islamic Courts*. Edinburgh: Edinburgh University Press, 2017.

[Al-Hamadhānī]. *The Maqámát of Badí' al-Zamán al-Hamadhání*. Translated by W. J. Prendergast. London: Luzac, 1915.

Hämeen-Anttila, Jaako. *Maqama: A History of a Genre*. Wiesbaden: Harrassowitz, 2002.

Al-Ḥarīrī. *Maqāmāt Abī Zayd al-Sarūjī*. Dar al-Kutub al-Qawmiyyah (Cairo, Egypt), Adab 105.

[———]. *Maqāmāt Abī Zayd al-Sarūjī*. İstanbul Üniversitesi (Istanbul University, Istanbul, Turkey), A 4566.

[———]. *Maqāmāt Abī Zayd al-Sarūjī*. Minasian Collection of Near Eastern Manuscripts (Collection 1147), A286. UCLA Library Special Collections, Charles E. Young Research Library, University of California, Los Angeles.

[———]. *Les Makamat de Hariri; exemplaire orné de peintures exécutées par Yahya ibn Mahmoud ibn Yahya ibn Aboul-Hasan ibn Kouvarriha al-Wasiti*. Bibliothèque nationale de France. Département des manuscrits. Arabe 5847. Online digital edition at Gallica.bnf.fr.

[———]. *Maqāmāt al-Ḥarīrī*. Beirut: al-Ma'ārif, 1873.

[———]. *Les séances de Hariri, publiées en Arabe, avec un commentaire choisi*. Edited by Silvestre de Sacy. Paris: Imprimerie Royale, 1822.

[———]. *Maqāmāt al-Ḥarīrī. Bi-ṣawt Abī 'Āṣim Yaḥyā Fatḥī*. https://www.youtube.com/playlist?list=PL5u9gQWZkoGydsvto65ktF8162dhAdnx1

[———]. *The Assemblies of al-Ḥarîrî*. Translated by Thomas Chenery. London: Williams and Norgate, 1867.

[———]. *The Assemblies of al-Ḥarîrî*. Translated by F. Steingass. London: The Royal Asiatic Society, 1898.

[———]. *Makamy: arabskie srednevekovye plutovskie novelly*. Moscow: Nauka, 1987.

[———]. *Le Livre des Malins: Séances d'un vagabond de génie*. Translated by René R. Khawam. Paris: Phébus, 1992.

[———]. *Maqāmas*. Translated by Luisa Maria Arvide. Granada: Grupo Editorial Universitario, 2009.

[———]. *Mài kǎ mǔ cíhuà* (麦卡姆词话). Translated by Wángdéxīn. Beijing: Huawen Publishing House, 2010–17.

Ibn Khallikān. *Wafayāt al-aʿyān*. Edited by Iḥsān ʿAbbās. Beirut: Dār Ṣādir, 1972; also in Hariri, *Séances*, 1:6–10.

Keegan, Matthew. "Commentarial Acts and Hermeneutical Dramas: The Ethics of Reading al-Ḥarīrī's *Maqāmāt*." PhD diss., New York University, 2017.

Kennedy, Philip F. *Recognition in the Arabic Literary Tradition: Discovery, Deliverance, and Delusion*. Edinburgh: Edinburgh University Press, 2016.

Kilito, Abdelfattah. *Les Séances: Récits et codes culturels chez Hamadhânî et Harîrî*. Paris: Sindbad, 1983.

Lumbard, Joseph. "The Quran in Translation." In *The Study Quran*, edited by Seyyed Hossein Nasr et al., 1601–6. New York: HarperCollins, 2015.

MacKay, Pierre A. "Certificates of Transmission on a Manuscript of the Maqāmāt of Ḥarīrī (MS. Cairo, Adab 105)." *Transactions of the American Philosophical Society* 61, no. 4 (1971): 1–81.

Margoliouth, D. S., and Charles Pellat. "Al-Ḥarīrī." In *Encyclopaedia of Islam, Second Edition*. Leiden: Brill, 1960–2007.

Malti-Douglas, Fedwa. "*Maqāmāt* and *Adab*: 'Al-Maqāmah al-Maḍīriyya' of al-Hamadhānī." *Journal of the American Oriental Society* 105, no. 2 (1985): 247–58.

Neuwirth, Angelika. "Adab Standing Trial—Whose Norms Should Rule Society? The Case of al-Ḥarīrī's al-Maqāmah al-Ramliyah." In *Myths, Historical Archetypes, and Symbolic Figures in Arabic Literature: Towards a New Hermeneutic Approach*, edited by Angelika Neuwirth et al., 205–24. Beirut: Steiner, 1999.

Orfali, Bilal W., and Maurice A. Pomerantz. "Assembling an Author: On the Making of al-Hamadhānī's *Maqāmāt*." In *Concepts of Authorship in Premodern Arabic Texts*, edited by Lale Behzadi and Jaakko Hämeen-Anttila, 107–29. Bamberg: University of Bamberg Press, 2017.

Perec, Georges. *La disparition*. Paris: Denoël, 1969.

Pollock, Sheldon. *Language of the Gods: Sanskrit, Culture and Power in Premodern India*. Berkeley: University of California Press, 2006.

Pomerantz, Maurice A., and Bilal Orfali. "Three Maqāmāt Attributed to Badīʿ al-Zamān al-Hamadhānī." *Journal of Abbasid Studies* 2 (2015): 38–60.

Prendergast, W. J. *The Maqámát of Badí' al-Zamán al-Hamadhání*. London: Luzac, 1915.

[Proclus]. *Procli Archiepiscopi Constantinopolitani Opera omnia*. Edited by J. P. Migne. Paris: Migne, 1864.

Renan, Ernest. "Les Séances de Hariri." In *Essais de morale et de critique*, 287–302. Paris: Michel Lévy, 1859.

Ritter, Helmut. "Autographs in Turkish Libraries." *Oriens* 6 (1953): 63–90.

Rowson, Everett K. "Religion and Politics in the Career of Badīʿ al-Zamān al-Hamadhānī." *Journal of the American Oriental Society* 107 (1987): 653–73.

Rückert, Friedrich. *Die Verwandlungen des Abu Seid von Serug, oder die Makamen des Hariri*. 4th ed. Stuttgart: Cottaschen, 1864.

[Shakespeare, William]. *The Norton Shakespeare*. Edited by Stephen Greenblatt et al. New York: Norton, 2016.

Al-Sharīshī, Abū l-ʿAbbās Aḥmad ibn ʿAbd al-Muʾmin al-Qaysī. *Sharḥ Maqāmāt al-Ḥarīrī*. Edited by Muḥammad Abū l-Faḍl Ibrāhīm. Beirut: Al-ʿAṣriyyah, 1992.

Stewart, Devin J. "The *Maqāma*." In *Arabic Literature in the Post-Classical Period*, edited by Roger Allen and D. S. Richards, 145–58. Cambridge: Cambridge University Press, 2008.

———. "Classical Arabic *Maqāmāt* and the Picaresque Novel." In *Classical Narratives*, edited by Salma Jayyusi. Forthcoming.

Ward, Benedicta. *The Sayings of the Desert Fathers*. Rev. ed. Kalamazoo: Cistercian Publications, 1984.

Yāqūt al-Ḥamawī. *Muʿjam al-udabāʾ*. Edited by Iḥsān ʿAbbās. Beirut: Dār al-Gharb al-Islāmī, 1993.

Zakharia, Katia. *Abū Zayd al-Sarūğī, imposteur et mystique: Relire les Maqāmāt d'al-Ḥarīrī*. Damascus: Institut français d'études arabes de Damas, 2000.

———. "Norme et fiction dans la genèse des Maqāmāt d'al-Ḥarīrī." *Bulletin d'études orientales* 46 (1994): 217–31.

ABOUT THE NYU ABU DHABI INSTITUTE

The Library of Arabic Literature is supported by a grant from the NYU Abu Dhabi Institute, a major hub of intellectual and creative activity and advanced research. The Institute hosts academic conferences, workshops, lectures, film series, performances, and other public programs directed both to audiences within the UAE and to the worldwide academic and research community. It is a center of the scholarly community for Abu Dhabi, bringing together faculty and researchers from institutions of higher learning throughout the region.

NYU Abu Dhabi, through the NYU Abu Dhabi Institute, is a world-class center of cutting-edge research, scholarship, and cultural activity. The Institute creates singular opportunities for leading researchers from across the arts, humanities, social sciences, sciences, engineering, and the professions to carry out creative scholarship and conduct research on issues of major disciplinary, multi-disciplinary, and global significance.

About the Typefaces

The Arabic text is set in DecoType Emiri, drawn by Mirjam Somers, based on the metal typeface in the *naskh* style that was cut for the 1924 Cairo edition of the Qur'an.

This Arabic typeface is controlled by a dedicated font layout engine. ACE, the Arabic Calligraphic Engine, invented by Peter Somers, Thomas Milo, and Mirjam Somers of DecoType, first operational in 1985, pioneered the principle followed by later smart font layout technologies such as OpenType, which is used for all other typefaces in this series.

The Arabic text was set with WinSoft Tasmeem, a sophisticated user interface for DecoType ACE inside Adobe InDesign. Tasmeem was conceived and created by Thomas Milo (DecoType) and Pascal Rubini (WinSoft) in 2005.

The English text is set in Adobe Text, a new and versatile text typeface family designed by Robert Slimbach for Western (Latin, Greek, Cyrillic) typesetting. Its workhorse qualities make it perfect for a wide variety of applications, especially for longer passages of text where legibility and economy are important. Adobe Text bridges the gap between calligraphic Renaissance types of the fifteenth and sixteenth centuries and high-contrast Modern styles of the eighteenth century, taking many of its design cues from early post-Renaissance Baroque transitional types cut by designers such as Christoffel van Dijck, Nicolaus Kis, and William Caslon. While grounded in classical form, Adobe Text is also a statement of contemporary utilitarian design, well suited to a wide variety of print and on-screen applications.

Titles Published by the Library of Arabic Literature

For more details on individual titles, visit www.libraryofarabicliterature.org

Classical Arabic Literature: A Library of Arabic Literature Anthology
Selected and translated by Geert Jan van Gelder (2012)

A Treasury of Virtues: Sayings, Sermons, and Teachings of ʿAlī, by al-Qāḍī al-Quḍāʿī, with the **One Hundred Proverbs** attributed to al-Jāḥiẓ
Edited and translated by Tahera Qutbuddin (2013)

The Epistle on Legal Theory, by al-Shāfiʿī
Edited and translated by Joseph E. Lowry (2013)

Leg over Leg, by Aḥmad Fāris al-Shidyāq
Edited and translated by Humphrey Davies (**4 volumes; 2013–14**)

Virtues of the Imām Aḥmad ibn Ḥanbal, by Ibn al-Jawzī
Edited and translated by Michael Cooperson (**2 volumes; 2013–15**)

The Epistle of Forgiveness, by Abū l-ʿAlāʾ al-Maʿarrī
Edited and translated by Geert Jan van Gelder and Gregor Schoeler (**2 volumes; 2013–14**)

The Principles of Sufism, by ʿĀʾishah al-Bāʿūniyyah
Edited and translated by Th. Emil Homerin (2014)

The Expeditions: An Early Biography of Muḥammad, by Maʿmar ibn Rāshid
Edited and translated by Sean W. Anthony (2014)

Two Arabic Travel Books
Accounts of China and India, by Abū Zayd al-Sīrāfī
Edited and translated by Tim Mackintosh-Smith (2014)
Mission to the Volga, by Aḥmad ibn Faḍlān
Edited and translated by James Montgomery (2014)

Disagreements of the Jurists: A Manual of Islamic Legal Theory, by al-Qāḍī al-Nuʿmān
Edited and translated by Devin J. Stewart (2015)

Consorts of the Caliphs: Women and the Court of Baghdad, by Ibn al-Sāʿī
Edited by Shawkat M. Toorawa and translated by the Editors of the Library of Arabic Literature (2015)

What ʿĪsā ibn Hishām Told Us, by Muḥammad al-Muwayliḥī
Edited and translated by Roger Allen (**2 volumes; 2015**)

The Life and Times of Abū Tammām, by Abū Bakr Muḥammad ibn Yaḥyā al-Ṣūlī
Edited and translated by Beatrice Gruendler (2015)

The Sword of Ambition: Bureaucratic Rivalry in Medieval Egypt, by ʿUthmān ibn Ibrāhīm al-Nābulusī
Edited and translated by Luke Yarbrough (2016)

Brains Confounded by the Ode of Abū Shādūf Expounded, by Yūsuf al-Shirbīnī
Edited and translated by Humphrey Davies (**2 volumes; 2016**)

Light in the Heavens: Sayings of the Prophet Muḥammad, by al-Qāḍī al-Quḍāʿī
Edited and translated by Tahera Qutbuddin (2016)

Risible Rhymes, by Muḥammad ibn Maḥfūẓ al-Sanhūrī
Edited and translated by Humphrey Davies (2016)

A Hundred and One Nights
Edited and translated by Bruce Fudge (2016)

The Excellence of the Arabs, by Ibn Qutaybah
Edited by James E. Montgomery and Peter Webb
Translated by Sarah Bowen Savant and Peter Webb (2017)

Scents and Flavors: A Syrian Cookbook
Edited and translated by Charles Perry (2017)

Arabian Satire: Poetry from 18th-Century Najd, by Ḥmēdān al-Shwēʿir
Edited and translated by Marcel Kurpershoek (2017)

In Darfur: An Account of the Sultanate and its People, by Muḥammad ibn ʿUmar al-Tūnisī
Edited and translated by Humphrey Davies (**2 volumes; 2018**)

War Songs, by ʿAntarah ibn Shaddād
Edited by James E. Montgomery
Translated by James E. Montgomery with Richard Sieburth (**2018**)

Arabian Romantic: Poems on Bedouin Life and Love, by ʿAbdallah ibn Sbayyil
Edited and translated by Marcel Kurpershoek (**2018**)

Dīwān ʿAntarah ibn Shaddād: A Literary-Historical Study
By James E. Montgomery (**2018**)

Stories of Piety and Prayer: Deliverance Follows Adversity, by Muḥassin ibn ʿAlī al-Tanūkhī
Edited and translated by Julia Bray (**2019**)

Tajrīd sayf al-himmah li-stikhrāj mā fī dhimmat al-dhimmah: A Scholarly Edition of ʿUthmān ibn Ibrāhīm al-Nābulusī's Text
By Luke Yarbrough (**2019**)

The Philosopher Responds: An Intellectual Correspondence from the Tenth Century, by Abū Ḥayyān al-Tawḥīdī and Abū ʿAlī Miskawayh
Edited by Bilal Orfali and Maurice A. Pomerantz
Translated by Sophia Vasalou and James E. Montgomery (**2 volumes; 2019**)

The Discourses: Reflections on History, Sufism, Theology, and Literature—Volume One, by al-Ḥasan al-Yūsī
Edited and translated by Justin Stearns (**2020**)

Impostures, by al-Ḥarīrī
Translated by Michael Cooperson
Foreword by Abdelfattah Kilito (**2020**)

Maqāmāt Abī Zayd al-Sarūjī, by al-Ḥarīrī
Edited by Michael Cooperson
Foreword by Abdelfattah Kilito (**2020**)

English-only Paperbacks

About the Editor

Michael Cooperson (PhD Harvard 1994) is professor of Arabic at the University of California, Los Angeles, where he teaches Arabic literature from pre-Islam to the nineteenth century as well as courses on translation from Arabic to English. He has published two monographs on early Abbasid cultural history: *Classical Arabic Biography* (2000) and *Al-Ma'mūn* (2005). He supervises the UCLA Subtitle Project, which trains students to produce English captions for culturally significant Arabic-language videos. He is a consulting member of the Editorial Board of the Library of Arabic Literature, and the editor and translator of Ibn al-Jawzī's *Virtues of the Imam Aḥmad ibn Ḥanbal* (2013). This work received the Sheikh Hamad Prize for Translation and International Understanding, and the English has been reissued as *The Life of Ibn Ḥanbal* (2017). He is also the translator of al-Ḥarīrī's *Impostures*, also published by the Library of Arabic Literature. His other research interests include Maltese language and culture. His study of Arabic sources for medieval Maltese history received the 2016 Malta Historical Society Publication Award for Established Authors.

www.ingramcontent.com/pod-product-compliance
Lightning Source LLC
Chambersburg PA
CBHW030624310726
48979CB00003B/876

* 9 7 8 1 4 7 9 8 0 0 8 9 6 *